Services Marketing

Integrating Customer Focus Across
the Firm

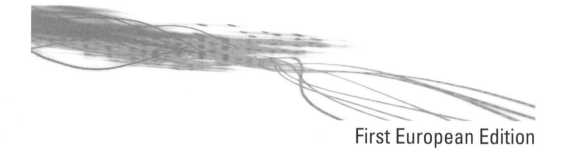

First European Edition

Services Marketing

Integrating Customer Focus Across the Firm

First European Edition

Alan Wilson
University of Strathclyde

Valarie A. Zeithaml
University of North Carolina

Mary Jo Bitner
Arizona State University

Dwayne D. Gremler
Bowling Green State University

The **McGraw·Hill** Companies

London   Boston   Burr Ridge, IL   Dubuque, IA   Madison, WI   New York   San Francisco
St. Louis   Bangkok   Bogotá   Caracas   Kuala Lumpur   Lisbon   Madrid   Mexico City
Milan   Montreal   New Delhi   Santiago   Seoul   Singapore   Sydney   Taipei   Toronto

Services Marketing: Integrating customer focus across the firm
Alan Wilson, Valarie A. Zeithaml, Mary Jo Bitner, and Dwayne D. Gremler
ISBN-13 9780077107956
ISBN-10 0077107950

McGraw-Hill
Higher Education

Published by McGraw-Hill Education
Shoppenhangers Road
Maidenhead
Berkshire
SL6 2QL
Telephone: 44 (0) 1628 502 500
Fax: 44 (0) 1628 770 224
Website: www.mcgraw-hill.co.uk

British Library Cataloguing in Publication Data
A catalogue record for this book is available from the British Library

Library of Congress Cataloguing in Publication Data
The Library of Congress data for this book has been applied for from the Library of Congress

Commissioning Editor: Melanie Havelock
Head of Development: Caroline Prodger
Marketing Manager: Alice Duijser
Head of Production: Bev Shields

Text Design by Hard Lines
Cover design by Fielding Design
Printed and bound in the UK by Ashford Colour Press Ltd., Gosport, Hampshire

ISBN-13 9780077107956
ISBN-10 0077107950

Dedication

To my family – wife, Sandra and son, Duncan and daughter, Kirsty –
who make life so worthwhile.
A.M.W.

To Hugo, my lifelong friend.
V.A.Z.

To my family – husband, Rich, and daughters Andrea and Christa –
for their unfailing love and support.
M.J.B.

To my mother, Pat, for her years of support, and in memory of my father, David.
D.D.G.

Brief Table of Contents

Detailed Table of Contents

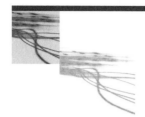

Preface

This European edition of this highly successful *Services Marketing* text is for students and business people who recognize the vital role that services play in the economy and its future. European economies are now dominated by services, and virtually all companies view service as critical to retaining their customers today and in the future. Even manufacturing companies that, in the past, have depended on physical products for their livelihood now recognize that service provides one of their few sustainable competitive advantages.

This new European edition takes the theories, concepts and frameworks that exist in the original American version of the text and applies them to the European context. European examples, cases and readings are used to provide a true European flavour to the material. The material has also been updated and restructured to reflect the latest services marketing thinking.

The foundation of the text is the recognition that services present special challenges that must be identified and addressed. Issues commonly encountered in service organizations – the inability to inventory, the difficulty in synchronizing demand and supply, and challenges in controlling the performance quality of human interactions – need to be articulated and tackled by managers. Many of the strategies include information and approaches that are new to marketing. This text aims to help students and managers understand and address these special challenges of services marketing.

The development of strong customer relationships through quality service (and services) are at the heart of the book's content. The topics covered are equally applicable to organizations whose core product is service (such as banks, transportation companies, hotels, hospitals, educational institutions, professional services, telecommunication) and to organizations that depend on service excellence for competitive advantage (high-technology manufacturers, automotive and industrial products, and so on).

The book's content focuses on the knowledge needed to implement service strategies for competitive advantage across industries. Included are frameworks for customer-focused management, and strategies for increasing customer satisfaction and retention through service. In addition to standard marketing topics (such as pricing), this text introduces students to topics that include management and measurement of service quality, service recovery, the linking of customer measurement to performance measurement, service blueprinting, customer co-production, and cross-functional treatment of issues through integration of marketing with disciplines such as operations and human resources. Each of these topics represents pivotal content for tomorrow's businesses as they structure around process rather than task, engage in one-to-one marketing, mass customize their offerings, and attempt to build strong relationships with their customers.

Distinguishing Content Features

The distinguishing features of the text and the new features in this European edition include the following:

1. **Cross-functional treatment** of issues through integration of marketing with other disciplines such as operations and human resources management.

2. A focus on understanding **the foundations of services marketing** and the customer

before introducing the conceptual framework of the remainder of the book based on the **gaps model**.

3. Greater emphasis on the topic of **service quality** than existing marketing and service marketing texts.

4. Increased focus on **customer expectations and perceptions** and what they imply for marketers.

5. Increased **technology and Internet coverage** throughout the text.

6. A chapter on **service recovery** that includes a conceptual framework for understanding the topic.

7. An improved chapter on **listening to customers through research**.

8. A chapter on **customer-defined service standards**.

9. Consumer-based pricing and **value pricing strategies**.

10. A chapter on **integrated services marketing communications**.

11. Increased focus on **customer relationships and relationship marketing strategies**.

12. An entire chapter that recognizes **human resource challenges and human resource strategies** for delivering customer-focused services.

13. Coverage of new service development processes and a detailed and complete introduction to **service blueprinting** – a tool for describing, designing and positioning services.

14. Coverage of the customer's role in service delivery and strategies for **co-production**.

15. A chapter on the role of **physical evidence**, particularly the physical environment or 'servicescape'.

16. A chapter on the **financial impact** of service quality

To support these topics, there are:

1. **European cases and vignettes**.

2. **'Service Spotlights'** in each chapter providing short **European examples** to illustrate services marketing in action.

3. **Discussion questions** and **exercises** appropriate to the **European context** in each chapter.

4. **Suggestions for further reading** (particularly **European reading**) in each chapter.

5. Short revision lists of **Key concepts** provided at the end of each chapter.

The framework of the book continues to be managerially focused, with every chapter presenting company examples and strategies for addressing key issues. There are integrating frameworks in most chapters. For example, there are frameworks for understanding service recovery strategies, service pricing, integrated marketing communications, customer relationships, customer roles and internal marketing.

Unique Structure

The text features a structure completely different from the standard 4P (marketing mix) structure of introductory marketing texts. The text starts by introducing the reader to the key foundations for service marketing by introducing services (Chapter 1) and understanding the customer, in terms of behaviour (Chapter 2), expectations (Chapter 3) and perceptions (Chapter 4). The remainder of the text is organized around the gaps model of service quality, which is described fully in Chapter 5. Beginning with Chapter 6, the text is organized into parts around the provider gaps in the gaps model. For example, Chapters 6 and 7 deal with understanding customer requirements; Chapters 8, 9 and 10 with aligning service design and standards; Chapters 11 through to 15 with delivering and performing services; and chapters 16 and 17 with managing service promises. Chapter 18 then focuses on the total picture of service and the bottom line. This structure is shown below.

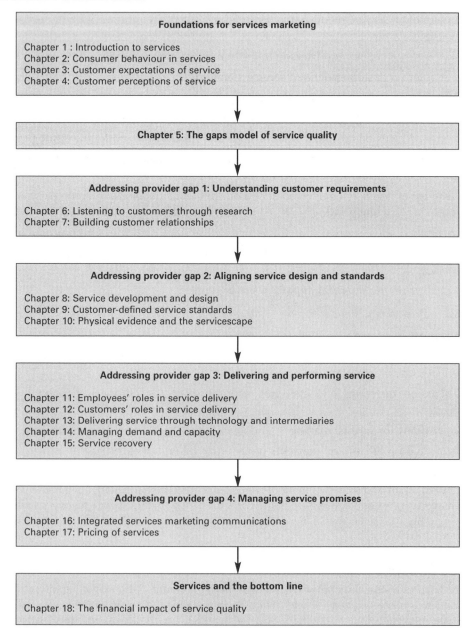

What Courses and Which Students Should Use This Text?

Students need to have completed only a basic marketing course as a prerequisite prior to using this text. The primary target audience for the text is services marketing classes at the undergraduate, postgraduate (both masters and doctoral courses), and executive education levels. Other target audiences are (1) service management classes at both the undergraduate and postgraduate levels and (2) marketing management classes at the postgraduate level in which a lecturer wishes to provide more comprehensive teaching of services than is possible with a standard marketing management text. A subset of chapters would also provide a more concise text for use in a specialized mini-semester course. A further reduced set of chapters may be used to supplement undergraduate and graduate basic marketing courses to enhance the treatment of services.

Online Learning Centre

The Online Learning Centre supporting this textbook contains support material to help lecturers to deliver their module. This includes teaching notes for each of the cases included in the text, answers to end-of-chapter discussion questions and exercises, PowerPoint presentations and figures and tables from the text. There are also supporting resources to help students to grasp the key topics in the services marketing module. For more information, go to 'Technology to Enhance Teaching and Learning' which can be found on page xviii.

Guided Tour

Learning objectives

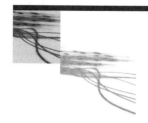

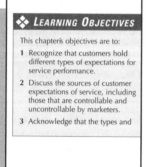

Each chapter opens with a set of learning objectives, summarising what knowledge, skills or understanding readers should acquire from each chapter.

Opening example

Each chapter opens with an example of service marketing in action that helps you to understand how the theory explored in the chapter is relevant to real marketing practice. Examples include Tesco, Virgin, ISS, Starbucks, British Airways, McDonald's, and the London Underground.

Service spotlights

Each chapter is interspersed with numerous short service spotlights that tie the theory to practice and show how European companies bring services to their customers. Examples come from a variety of consumer and business-to-business services and cover industries as diverse as banking, airlines, hotels and tourism. Featured brands include ING, Travelocity, TNT, Scandinavian Airlines, Asda Walmart, Accor Hotels, Expedia and many more.

Key concepts

These are highlighted throughout the chapter in bold, with page number references at the end of each chapter so they can be found quickly and easily. An ideal tool for last minute revision or to check service marketing definitions as you read.

Chapter summary

This briefly reviews and reinforces the main topics you will have covered in each chapter to ensure you have acquired a solid understanding of the key topics. Use it in conjunction with the learning objectives as a quick reference to check you have understood the service marketing ideas explored in the chapter.

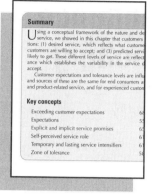

Further reading

Each chapter ends with a list of suggested further reading, listing international research and sources – journals, papers and books – in service marketing. Use this list as a starting point for your reading for assignments or class preparation.

Discussion questions and exercises

Discussion questions encourage you to review and apply the knowledge you have acquired from each chapter. They are a useful revision tool and can also be used by your lecturer as assignments or practice examination questions. The exercises require a little more time and thought, and can be used as assignments or exam practice.

Case studies

The book includes a case study section designed to test how well you can apply the main ideas learned throughout the book to real company examples. The cases integrate a number of service ideas into a fuller example that needs deeper analysis and understanding. Each case study has its own set of questions. Cases include Tesco, Telecom Italia, Jyske Bank, Call Centre Europe and Disneyland Paris.

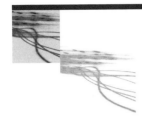

Technology to enhance learning and teaching

 *Visit **www.mcgraw-hill.co.uk/textbooks/wilson** today*

Online Learning Centre (OLC)

After completing each chapter, log on to the supporting Online Learning Centre website. Take advantage of the study tools offered to reinforce the material you have read in the text, and to develop your knowledge in a fun and effective way.

Free resources for students include:

- *Chapter-by-chapter self-test questions online with automated marking for quick revision and to test understanding of key topics*
- *A Glossary of the key terms in the book, useful to test that you understand the important concepts and technical terms of services marketing*
- *Learning Objectives by chapter to remind you of the key points you should have retained after reading each chapter*

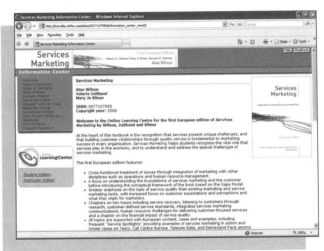

Resources to assist lecturers in delivering their module include:

- *A suite of editable PowerPoint presentations of approximately 30 slides per chapter that cover the key learning outcomes and feature figures from the textbook. Useful for presentation in lectures or as class handouts.*
- *Instructor's manual- a brief summary of the key concepts covered in each chapter, with tips and suggestions for teaching the material in classroom settings.*
- *Case notes for each of the longer end of book case studies.*

 EZTest, a new online testbank format from McGraw-Hill, is available with this title. EZTest enables you to upload testbanks, modify questions and add your own questions, thus creating a testbank that's totally unique to your course! Find out more at: **http://mcgraw-hill.co.uk/he/eztest/**

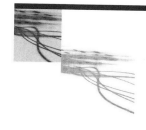

Custom Publishing Solutions: Let us help make our content your solution

At McGraw-Hill Education our aim is to help the lecturer find the most suitable content for their needs and the most appropriate way to deliver the content to their students. Our **custom publishing solutions** offer the ideal combination of content delivered in the way which suits lecturer and students the best.

The idea behind our custom publishing programme is that via a database of over two million pages called Primis, www.primisonline.com, the lecturer can select just the material they wish to deliver to their students:

Lecturers can select chapters from:

- textbooks
- professional books
- case books – Harvard Articles, Insead, Ivey, Darden, Thunderbird and BusinessWeek
- Taking Sides – debate materials

Across the following imprints:

- McGraw-Hill Education
- Open University Press
- Harvard Business School Press
- US and European material

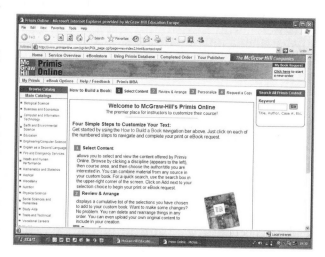

There is also the option to include material authored by lecturers in the custom product – this does not necessarily have to be in English.

We will take care of everything from start to finish in the process of developing and delivering a custom product to ensure that lecturers and students receive exactly the material needed in the most suitable way.

With a **Custom Publishing Solution**, students enjoy the best selection of material deemed to be the most suitable for learning everything they need for their courses – something of real value to support their learning. Teachers are able to use exactly the material they want, in the way they want, to support their teaching on the course.

Please contact your local McGraw-Hill representative with any questions or alternatively contact Warren Eels, e: warren_eels@mcgraw-hill.com.

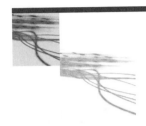

Make the grade!

STUDENT-FRIENDLY GUIDES

Write great essays!

Peter Levin

Open UP Study Skills

The Complete Guide to Referencing and Avoiding Plagiarism

Colin Neville

Open UP Study Skills

'An indispensable study aid' – BBC Radio One

The Student's Guide to

Exam Success

Second Edition

'A lively and friendly introduction to exams and assessments' – New Scientist

Eileen Tracy

30% off any Study Skills book!

Our Study Skills books are packed with practical advice and tips that are easy to put into practice and will really improve the way you study. Topics include:

- Techniques to help you pass exams
- Advice to improve your essay writing
- Help in putting together the perfect seminar presentation
- Tips on how to balance studying and your personal life

www.openup.co.uk/studyskills

Special offer! As a valued customer, buy online and receive 30% off any of our Study Skills books by entering the promo code **getahead**

Visit our website to read helpful hints about essays, exams, dissertations and much more.

Acknowledgements

We would like to acknowledge the suggestions for improvements made by the reviewers of the book. Their feedback on the book and on the stages of the draft manuscript has helped us to improve the European edition for academics' teaching and for their students' learning. Thanks to:

Richard Bentley, Southampton Institute
Gary Bernie, Institute Of Technology Blanchardstown, Ireland
Christo Boshoff, Stellenbosch University, South Africa
Ko De Ruyter, University of Maastricht
Tim Frogett, Anglia Ruskin University
Johan Jonsson, Umea School of Business, Sweden
Lena Larsson-Mossbergh, University of Gothenburg
Line Lervvik Olsen, BI, Norwegian School of Management, Norway
F. McLean, University of Stirling
Mohammed Mirza, University of Huddersfield
Tony Pyne, University of Luton
Sue Vaux Halliday, University of Gloucestershire

We would also like to thank the following case contributors and those who gave permission for material to be reproduced within the textbook:

Accor Hotels (Novotel)
Freefoto.com Ltd
ICFAI Business School Case Development Centre, India
ING Direct
International Institute of Management Development (IMD), Lausanne, Switzerland
ISS, Denmark
Istock.com
Moto Hospitality Ltd
Mohan Lal Agrawal, Jamshedpur, India, Per Vagn Freytag, Southern Denmark University and Bent Thestrup, Call Center Europe, for their case study on Call Center Europe

Every effort has been made to trace and acknowledge ownership of copyright and to clear permission for material reproduced in this book. The publishers will be pleased to make suitable arrangements to clear permission with any copyright holders whom it has not been possible to contact.

We would also like to acknowledge the professional efforts of the McGraw-Hill staff. Our sincere thanks to Melanie Havelock, Caroline Prodger, Bev Shields and Alice Duijser.

Alan Wilson

Valarie A. Zeithaml

Mary Jo Bitner

Dwayne D. Gremler

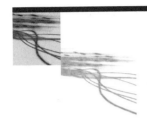

About the Authors

Alan Wilson is Professor of Marketing and Head of the Marketing Department within the University of Strathclyde Business School. Before joining the university, he was a senior consultant and executive trainer within the services division of a London-based marketing consultancy practice and prior to that an Associate Director of a leading London-based marketing research agency. He specializes in the marketing of services, has a PhD in the subject, and was previously the Chief Examiner in Marketing for the Chartered Institute of Bankers in Scotland. He is currently a member of the Governing Council of the Market Research Society and chairs the Society's Professional Development Advisory Board. His book, *Marketing Research: An Integrated Approach*, is in its second edition and he has published in a wide range of marketing and service management journals, for which he has won a number of awards and prizes. Professor Wilson has delivered high-level executive training to a wide range of service organizations in the banking, hospitality, professional service and business-to-business service sectors and has been invited to deliver lectures and seminars on both services marketing and marketing research in a variety of countries throughout the world. He also regularly acts as a marketing and marketing research adviser to a number of Scottish and UK-based service organizations.

Valarie A. Zeithaml is the David S. Van Pelt Distinguished Professor of Marketing at the Kenan-Flagler Business School of the University of North Carolina at Chapel Hill. Since receiving her MBA and PhD in marketing from the Robert H. Smith School of Business at the University of Maryland in 1980, Professor Zeithaml has devoted her career to researching and teaching the topics of service quality and services management. She is the co-author of *Delivering Quality Service: Balancing Customer Perceptions and Expectations* (Free Press, 1990), now in its thirteenth printing; and *Driving Customer Equity: How Customer Lifetime Value Is Reshaping Corporate Strategy* (with Roland Rust and Katherine Lemon, Free Press, 2000). In 2002, *Driving Customer Equity* won the first Berry–American Marketing Association Book Prize for the best marketing book of the past three years.

In 2004, Professor Zeithaml received both the Innovative Contributor to Marketing Award given by the Marketing Management Association and the Outstanding Marketing Educator Award given by the Academy of Marketing Science. In 2001, she received the American Marketing Association's Career Contributions to the Services Discipline Award. She is also the recipient of numerous research awards, including the Robert Ferber Consumer Research Award from the *Journal of Consumer Research*, the Harold H. Maynard Award from the *Journal of Marketing*, the MSI Paul Root Award from the *Journal of Marketing*, the Jagdish Sheth Award from the *Journal of the Academy of Marketing Science* and the William F. O'Dell Award from the *Journal of Marketing Research*. She has consulted with more than 50 service and product companies.

Professor Zeithaml served on the Board of Directors of the American Marketing Association from 2000 to 2003 and is currently an Academic Trustee of the Marketing Science Institute.

Mary Jo Bitner is the PETsMART Chair in Services Leadership in the Marketing Department at the W.P. Carey School of Business, Arizona State University (ASU). She also serves as Academic Director for the Center for Services Leadership at ASU. Dr Bitner was a founding faculty member of the Center for Services Leadership and has been a leader in its emergence as a premier university-based center for the study of services marketing and management. In the mid-1990s she led the development of the W.P. Carey MBA Services Marketing and Management specialization. Alumni of this programme now work in companies across the United States, leading the implementation of services and customer-focused strategies. Dr Bitner has published more than 50 articles and has received a number of awards for her research in leading journals, including the *Journal of Marketing, Journal of the Academy of Marketing Science, Journal of Business Research, Journal of Retailing, International Journal of Service Industry Management* and *Academy of Management Executive*. She has consulted with and presented seminars and workshops for numerous businesses, including Yellow Roadway Corporation, Ford Motor Company, Caremark, IBM Global Services, and RR Donnelley. In 2003, Dr Bitner was honoured with the Career Contributions to the Services Discipline Award by the American Marketing Association's Services Marketing Special Interest Group.

Dwayne D. Gremler is Associate Professor of Marketing at Bowling Green State University (BGSU). He received his MBA and PhD degrees from the W.P. Carey School of Business at Arizona State University. Throughout his academic career, Dr Gremler has been a passionate advocate for the research and instruction of services marketing issues. He has served as Chair of the American Marketing Association's Services Marketing Special Interest Group and has helped organize services marketing conferences in Australia, The Netherlands, France, and the United States. Dr Gremler has been invited to conduct seminars and present research on services marketing issues in several countries. Dr Gremler's research addresses customer loyalty in service businesses, customer–employee interactions in service delivery, service guarantees, and word-of-mouth communication. He has published articles in the *Journal of Service Research, International Journal of Service Industry Management, Journal of the Academy of Marketing Science* and *Journal of Marketing Education*. He has also been the recipient of several research awards at BGSU, including the College of Business Administration Outstanding Scholar Award and the Robert A. Patton Scholarly Achievement Award. While a professor at the University of Idaho, Dr Gremler received the First Interstate Bank Student Excellence in Award for teaching, an award determined by students in the College of Business and Economics.

PART 1
Foundations for Services Marketing

This first part of the text provides you with the foundations needed to begin your study of services marketing. The first chapter identifies up-to-date trends, issues, and opportunities in services as a backdrop for the strategies addressed in remaining chapters. Knowing what customers want and how they assess what they receive is the foundation for designing effective services. Therefore Chapter 2 focuses on what is known about customer behaviour for services, Chapter 3 looks at customer expectations and Chapter 4 considers customer perceptions. Chapter 5 introduces the gaps model of service quality, the framework that provides the structure for the rest of the text. The remaining parts of the book will include information and strategies to address the specific gaps identified by this model, giving you the tools and knowledge to become a services marketing leader.

CHAPTER 01

Introduction to Services

❖ LEARNING OBJECTIVES

This chapter's objectives are to:

1 Explain what services are and identify important trends in services.

2 Explain the need for special services marketing concepts and practices and why the need has developed and is accelerating.

3 Explore the profound impact of technology on service.

4 Outline the basic differences between goods and services and the resulting challenges and opportunities for service businesses.

5 Introduce the expanded marketing mix for services and the philosophy of customer focus, as powerful frameworks and themes that are fundamental to the rest of the text.

6 Introduce the servuction system model and the concept of the services triangle.

CASE STUDY: EUROPE'S POSITION AS A GLOBAL SERVICES PROVIDER

Each year, the US magazine *Forbes* produces a comprehensive list of the world's biggest and most powerful companies as measured by a composite ranking for sales, profits, assets and market value. In 2006, the following 36 European service companies were ranked (in order) within the world's top 100 organizations. Although these organizations only represent the tip of the iceberg of the European service sector, they clearly demonstrate Europe's position as a key global player in the provision of services.

Name	Location of headquarters	Sector
HSBC Group	United Kingdom	Banking
UBS	Switzerland	Financial Services
ING Group	Netherlands	Financial Services
Royal Bank of Scotland	United Kingdom	Banking
BNP Paribas	France	Banking
Banco Santander	Spain	Banking
Barclays	United Kingdom	Banking
HBOS	United Kingdom	Banking
AXA Group	France	Insurance
Allianz Worldwide	Germany	Insurance
Crédit Suisse Group	Switzerland	Financial Services
E.ON	Germany	Utilities
Fortis	Netherlands	Financial Services
Deutsche Telekom	Germany	Telecommunications Services
ABN-Amro Holding	Netherlands	Banking
Société Générale Group	France	Banking
Crédit Agricole	France	Banking
Lloyds TSB Group	United Kingdom	Banking
France Telecom	France	Telecommunications Services
Deutsche Bank Group	Germany	Financial Services
BBVA-Banco Bilbao Vizcaya	Spain	Banking
Siemens Group	Germany	Conglomerates
Electricité de France	France	Utilities
Generali Group	Italy	Insurance
Zurich Financial Services	Switzerland	Insurance
RWE Group	Germany	Utilities
Telefónica	Spain	Telecommunications Services
Aviva	United Kingdom	Insurance
ENEL	Italy	Utilities
Munich Re	Germany	Insurance
Telecom Italia	Italy	Telecommunications Services
UniCredit	Italy	Banking
Unilever	Netherlands/United Kingdom	Food, Drink and Tobacco
Deutsche Post	Germany	Transportation
Suez Group	France	Utilities
Aegon	Netherlands	Insurance

Source: extracted from www.forbes.com[1]

What are services?

Put in the most simple terms, *services are deeds, processes and performances.* Our opening vignette illustrates what is meant by this definition. The services offered by HSBC, AXA Group and France Telecom are not tangible things that can be touched, seen and felt, but rather are intangible deeds and performances. This may be obvious for banking, insurance and telecommunication organizations, but even a product-based organization such as IBM has a range of service offerings including repair and maintenance service for its equipment, consulting services for information technology (IT) and e-commerce applications, training services, Web design and

DISTRIBUTION **Motor trade** **Wholesale trade** **Retail trade**
HOTELS AND RESTAURANTS
TRANSPORT AND COMMUNICATION **Land transport** **Water transport** **Air transport** **Other transport services** **Communication**
BUSINESS AND FINANCE **Banking** **Insurance and pensions** **Other financial services** **Real estate** **Renting of goods** **Computer services** **Research and development** **Other business services**
GOVERNMENT AND OTHER SERVICES **Public administration** **Education** **Health and social work** **Sanitation** **Membership organizations** **Recreation** **Other services** **Domestic services**

FIGURE 1.1 UK Index of Services – classification of services

Source: Office for National Statistics (2006) Methodology of the Experimental Monthly Index of Services, UK.

hosting, and other services. These services may include a final, tangible report, a website, or in the case of training, tangible instructional materials. But for the most part, the entire service is represented to the client through problem analysis activities, meetings with the client, follow-up calls and reporting – a series of deeds, processes and performances.

Although we will rely on the simple, broad definition of *services,* you should be aware that over time *services* and the *service sector of the economy* have been defined in subtly different ways. The variety of definitions can often explain the confusion or disagreements people have when discussing services and when describing industries that comprise the service sector of the economy. Compatible with our simple, broad definition is one that defines services to include 'all economic activities whose output is not a physical product or construction, is generally consumed at the time it is produced, and provides added value in forms (such as convenience, amusement, timeliness, comfort, or health) that are essentially intangible concerns of its first purchaser'.[2] The breadth of industries making up the service sector is evident from the composition of the UK government's Index of Services (see Figure 1.1). The growth in services, to a level where service industries account for around 76 per cent (CIA, 2006 *The World Factbook 2006*) of UK gross domestic product, has led the statistical office of the UK government to develop a monthly index of services from January 2006 to provide an indicator of the growth in the output of service industries.

Services industries, services as products, customer service and derived service

As we begin our discussion of services marketing and management, it is important to draw distinctions between *service industries and companies, services as products, customer service* and ***derived service****.* Sometimes when people think of service, they think only of customer service, but service can be divided into four distinct categories. The tools and strategies you will learn in this text can be applied to any of these categories.

1 *Service industries and companies* include those industries and companies typically classified within the service sector whose core product is a service. All of the following companies can be considered pure service companies: Accor (hotels such as Novotel and Ibis), Lufthansa (transportation) and HSBC (banking). The total services sector comprises a wide range of service organizations, as suggested by Figure 1.1. Organizations in these sectors provide or sell services as their core offering.

2 *Services as products* represent a wide range of intangible product offerings that customers value and pay for in the marketplace. Service products are sold by service companies and by non-service companies such as manufacturers and technology companies. For example, IBM and Hewlett-Packard offer information technology consulting services to the marketplace, competing with firms such as Accenture and PA Consulting, which are traditional pure services firms. Other industry examples include retailers, like Tesco, that sell services such as insurance and photograph processing.

3 *Customer service* is also a critical aspect of what we mean by 'service'. Customer service is the service provided in support of a company's core products. Companies typically do not charge for customer service. Customer service can occur on-site (as when a retail employee helps a customer find a desired item or answers a question), or it can occur over the telephone or via the Internet. Many companies operate customer service call centres or helplines, often staffed around the clock. Quality customer

service is essential to building customer relationships. It should not, however, be confused with the services provided for sale by the company.

4 *Derived service* is yet another way to look at what service means. In an article in the *Journal of Marketing*, Steve Vargo and Bob Lusch argue for a new dominant logic for marketing that suggests that all products and physical goods are valued for the services they provide.[3] Drawing on the work of respected economists, marketers and philosophers, the two authors suggest that the value derived from physical goods is really the service provided by the good, not the good itself. For example, they suggest that a pharmaceutical provides medical services, a razor provides barbering services, and computers provide information and data manipulation services. Although this view is somewhat abstract, it suggests that in the future we may think even more broadly about services than we currently do.

Tangibility spectrum

The broad definition of services implies that **intangibility** is a key determinant of whether an offering is a service. Although this is true, it is also true that very few products are purely intangible or totally tangible. Instead, services tend to be *more intangible* than manufactured products, and manufactured products tend to be *more tangible* than services. For example, the fast-food industry, while classified as a service, also has many tangible components such as the food, the packaging, and so on. Cars, while classified within the manufacturing sector, also supply many intangibles, such as transportation. The **tangibility spectrum** shown in Figure 1.2 captures this idea. Throughout this text, when we refer to services we will be assuming the broad definition of services and acknowledging that there are very few 'pure services' or 'pure goods'. The issues and approaches we discuss are directed toward those offerings that lie on the right-hand side, the intangible side, of the spectrum shown in Figure 1.2.

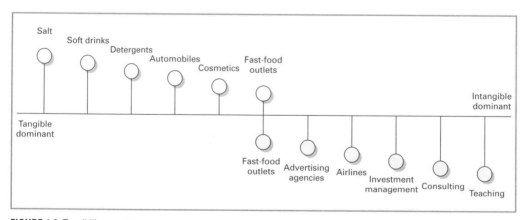

FIGURE 1.2 Tangibility spectrum

Source: G. Lynn Shostack, 'Breaking free from product marketing', *Journal of Marketing* 41 (April 1977), pp. 73–80. Reprinted with permission of the American Marketing Association

Why services marketing?

Why is it important to learn about services marketing, service quality and service management? What are the differences in services versus manufactured-goods marketing that have led to the demand for books and courses on services? Many forces have led to the growth of services marketing, and many industries, companies and individuals have defined the scope of the concepts, frameworks and strategies that define the field. The field of services marketing and management has evolved as a result of these combined forces.

Service-based economies

First, services marketing concepts and strategies have developed in response to the tremendous growth of service industries, resulting in their increased importance to the world economy. The service sector is estimated to represent 71 per cent (CIA, 2006) of the gross domestic product (GDP) of the European Union (Table 1.1). Almost all the absolute growth in numbers of jobs and the fastest growth rates in job formation are in service industries.

There is a growing market for services and increasing dominance of services in economies worldwide, not just in Europe. The tremendous growth and economic contributions of the service sector have drawn increasing attention to the issues and challenges of service sector industries worldwide.

Service as a business imperative in manufacturing and IT

Early in the development of the field of services marketing and management, most of the impetus came from service industries such as banking, transportation and retailing. As these traditional

Country	Attributed to services
Iceland	77
United Kingdom	76
France	76
Belgium	75
Denmark	74
Netherlands	74
Greece	73
Sweden	71
Germany	70
Italy	69
Austria	68
Finland	68
Portugal	67
Spain	66
Switzerland	65
Poland	64
Norway	56
Ireland	49

Source: The World Factbook 2006, published by the Central Intelligence Agency (CIA), www.odci.gov/cia/publications/factbook

TABLE 1.1 Percentage of GDP attributable to services, 2006

service industries evolve and become more competitive, the need for effective services management and marketing strategies continues. Now, however, manufacturing and technology industries such as cars, computers and software are also recognizing the need to provide quality service and revenue-producing services in order to compete worldwide.

From Ericsson and Apple to Hewlett-Packard, and Siemens, companies are recognizing the opportunity to grow and profit through services.[4] Why? Because the quick pace of developing technologies and increasing competition make it difficult to gain strategic competitive advantage through physical products alone. Plus, customers are more demanding. Not only do they expect excellent, high-quality goods and technology, they also expect high levels of customer service and total service solutions along with them.

Service spotlight

At Siemens, the Business Services division was established in 1995 as an international full-service provider of information and communication technology solutions and services. In outsourcing and IT maintenance, it is one of the world's top 10 suppliers with worldwide sales of 5.4 billion euros (2005). The portfolio of services is aimed at supporting technology (including non-Seimens technology) in the following areas:

- Strategic IT consulting
- Business process optimization
- Planning and implementation of innovative business solutions
- Integration of new IT processes into the existing system environment
- Infrastructure services, including maintenance and repair, user support and hotline operation
- Operational services and application management
- Operating the entire IT as part of an outsourcing solution
- Business process outsourcing for financial services and human resources.

(www.siemens.com/sbs)

As manufacturers such as Siemens and IT companies such as IBM transition to become services organizations, the need for special concepts and approaches for managing and marketing services is increasingly apparent.[5]

Deregulated industries and professional service needs

Specific demand for services marketing concepts has come from the deregulated industries and professional services as both these groups have gone through rapid changes in the ways they do business. In the past several decades many very large service industries, including airlines, banking, telecommunications and energy supply, have been deregulated by European governments. As a result, marketing decisions that used to be tightly controlled by the government are now partially, and in some cases totally, within the control of individual firms.[6]

Service spotlight

For example, until the end of 1998, all UK electricity supply pricing was determined and monitored by the government. A householder could only buy electricity from the one designated local supplier. Since that time electricity companies have been free to set their own pricing structures and bundle the purchase of electricity with the supply of other utilities such as gas and telephone. Needless to say, deregulation initially created turmoil in the electricity generation and supply industry, accelerating the need for more sophisticated, customer-based and competition-sensitive marketing.

Providers of professional services (such as dentists, lawyers, accountants, engineers and architects) have also demanded new concepts and approaches for their businesses as these industries have become increasingly competitive and as professional standards have been modified to allow advertising. Whereas traditionally the professions avoided even using the word *marketing,* they are now seeking better ways to understand and segment their customers, to ensure the delivery of quality services, and to strengthen their position amid a growing number of competitors.

Services marketing is different

As the forces described above coincided and evolved, business people realized that marketing and managing services presented issues and challenges not faced in manufacturing and packaged goods companies. As service businesses began to turn to marketing and decided to employ marketing people, they naturally recruited from the best marketers in the world – Procter & Gamble, General Foods and Kodak. People who moved from marketing in packaged goods industries to marketing in airlines, banking and other service industries found that their skills and experiences were not directly transferable. They faced issues and dilemmas in marketing services that their experiences in packaged goods and manufacturing had not prepared them for. These people realized the need for new concepts and approaches for marketing and managing service businesses.

Service marketers responded to these forces and began to work across disciplines and with academics and business practitioners from around the world to develop and document marketing practices for services. As the field evolved, it expanded to address the concerns and needs of *any* business in which service is an integral part of the offering. Frameworks, concepts and strategies developed to address the fact that 'services marketing is different'. As the field continues to evolve in the twenty-first century, new trends will shape the field and accelerate the need for services marketing concepts and tools.

Service equals profits

Through the 1980s and early 1990s many firms jumped on the service bandwagon, investing in service initiatives and promoting service quality as ways to differentiate themselves and create competitive advantage. Many of these investments were based on faith and intuition by managers who believed in serving customers well and who believed in their hearts that quality service made good business sense. Indeed, a dedication to quality service has been the foundation for success for many firms, across industries. In his book *Discovering the Soul of Service*, Leonard Berry describes in detail 14 such companies.[7] The companies featured in his book had been in business an average of 31 years in 1999 when the book was written. These companies had been profitable in all but five of their combined 407 years of existence. Dr Berry discovered through his research that these successful businesses share devotion to nine common service themes, among them values-driven leadership, commitment to investment in employee success, and trust-based relationships with customers and other partners at the foundation of the organization.

Since the mid-1990s firms have demanded hard evidence of the bottom-line effectiveness of service strategies. And researchers are building a convincing case that service strategies, implemented appropriately, can be very profitable. Work sponsored by the Marketing Science Institute suggests that corporate strategies focused on customer satisfaction, revenue generation, and service quality may actually be more profitable than strategies focused on cost-cutting or strategies that attempt to do both simultaneously.[8] Research from the Harvard Business School builds a case for the 'service–profit chain', linking internal service and employee satisfaction to customer value and ultimately to profits.[9] And considerable research shows linkages from customer satisfaction (often driven by service outcomes) to profits.[10]

An important key to these successes is that the right strategies are chosen and that these strategies are implemented appropriately and well. Much of what you learn from this text will guide you in making such correct choices and in providing superior implementation. Throughout the text we will point out the profit implications and tradeoffs to be made with service strategies.

Service and technology

The preceding sections examined the roots of services marketing and the reasons why the field exists. Another major trend – technology, specifically information technology – is currently shaping the field and profoundly influencing the practice of services marketing. In this section we explore trends in technology (positive *and* negative) to set the stage for topics that will be discussed throughout this text. Together with globalization, the influence of technology is the most profound trend affecting services marketing today.

Potential for new service offerings

Looking to the recent past, it is apparent how technology has been the basic force behind service innovations now taken for granted. Automated voice mail, interactive voice response systems, fax machines, mobile phones, automated teller machines (ATMs) and other common services were possible only because of new technologies. Just think how dramatically different your world would be without these basic technology services.

More recently, people have seen the explosion of the Internet, resulting in a host of new services. Internet-based companies like Amazon and eBay offer services previously unheard of. And established companies find that the Internet provides a way to offer new services as well.[11] For example, the *Financial Times* offers an interactive edition that allows customers to organize the newspaper's content to suit their individual preferences and needs.

Many new technology services are on the horizon. For example, some researchers project that the 'connected car' will allow people to access all kinds of existing and new services while on the road. Already many cars are equipped with satellite navigation systems that direct drivers to specific locations. In the future, in-car systems may provide recommendations for shopping by informing drivers when they are in close proximity to their preferred retailer. On a road trip, the system may provide weather forecasts and warnings, and when it is time to stop for the night; the car's system could book a room at a nearby hotel, recommend a restaurant and make dinner reservations.[12]

New ways to deliver service

In addition to providing opportunities for new service offerings, technology is providing vehicles for delivering existing services in more accessible, convenient, productive ways. Technology facilitates basic customer service functions (bill-paying, questions, cheque account records, tracking orders), transactions (both retail and business to business) and learning or information seeking. Companies have moved from face-to-face service to telephone-based service to widespread use of interactive voice response systems to Internet-based customer service and now to wireless service. Interestingly, many companies are coming full circle and now offer human contact as the ultimate form of customer service!

Technology also facilitates transactions by offering a direct vehicle for making purchases. Technology giant Dell offers virtually all its customer service and ordering functions to its business customers via technology. Over 90 per cent of its transactions with customers are completed online. On the consumer side, online shopping and transactions have already revolutionized the music and book businesses. Predictions suggest that online ordering will also rewrite the rules for purchasing jewellery, real estate, hotel rooms and software. Even cars are sold online through organizations such as Jamjar.com.

Service spotlight

Jamjar.com, owned by the Royal Bank of Scotland Group, sells new cars online. You can search almost 2,000 models on a combination of 10 criteria and the car will be delivered to your door. The website is pitched at car buyers who know what they want.

Finally, technology, specifically the Internet, provides an easy way for customers to learn and research. Access to information has never been easier. For example, health-related websites are now among the most frequently accessed sites on the Internet with current estimates indicating that there are now over 100 000 sites offering health-related information.[13] There can be dangers with this, as the public is often unsure as to which sites are providing accurate information and which are providing spurious cures for serious health conditions.

Service spotlight

In the UK, NHS Direct Online, http://www.nhsdirect.nhs.uk/, established in 1999, provides health information online and access to a 24-hour nurse helpline via telephone. Six million people accessed the NHS Direct Online website in the first two years. There were half a million visitors in January 2003. The website gives information on over 70 000 physical National Health Service (NHS) sites providing health services to the public. NHS Direct call centres direct people to these physical offices. NHS Direct has also put 200 touchscreen kiosks in popular locations, equipped with printers and accessible to wheelchair users. Locations include NHS centres, chemists, libraries and supermarkets. Around 300 people use each kiosk every month, which adds up to around 60 000 users a year.[14]

Source: Commission of the European Communities (2004) 'e-Health – making healthcare better for European citizens: an action plan for a European e-Health Area'

Enabling both customers and employees

Technology enables both customers and employees to be more effective in getting and providing service.[15] Through **self-service technologies**, customers can serve themselves more effectively. Via online banking, customers can access their accounts, check balances, apply for loans, shift money between accounts and take care of just about any banking need they might have – all without the assistance of the bank's employees. These online banking services are just one example of the types of self-service technologies that are proliferating across industries.

For employees, technology can provide tremendous support in making them more effective and efficient in delivering service. Customer relationship management and sales support software are broad categories of technology that can aid frontline employees in providing better service. By having immediate access to information about their product and service offerings as well as about particular customers, employees are better able to serve them. This type of information allows employees to customize services to fit the customer's needs. They can also be much more efficient and timely than in the old days when most customer and product information was in paper files or in the heads of sales and customer service representatives.

Extending the global reach of services

Technology infusion results in the potential for reaching out to customers around the globe in ways not possible before. The Internet itself knows no boundaries, and therefore information, customer service and transactions can move across countries and across continents, reaching any customer who has access to the Web.

Service spotlight

Customers of DHL (part of Deutsche Post) using the DHL website can track the location and progress of their packages in real time as they are shipped throughout the world.

Technology also allows employees of international companies to stay in touch easily – to share information, to ask questions, to serve on virtual teams together. All this technology facilitates the global reach as well as the effectiveness of service businesses.

The Internet *is* a service

An interesting way to look at the influence of technology is to realize that the Internet is just 'one big service'. All businesses and organizations that operate on the Internet are essentially providing services – whether they are giving information, performing basic customer service functions or facilitating transactions. Thus all the tools, concepts and strategies you learn in studying services marketing and management have direct application in an Internet or e-business world. Although technology and the Internet are profoundly changing how people do business and what offerings are possible, it is clear that customers still want basic service. They want what they have always wanted: dependable outcomes, easy access, responsive systems, flexibility, apologies and compensation when things go wrong. But now they expect these same outcomes from technology-based businesses and from e-commerce solutions.[16] With hindsight it is obvious that many dot-com start-ups suffered and even failed because of lack of basic customer knowledge and failure of implementation, logistics, and service follow-up.[17]

Paradox	Description
Control/chaos	Technology can facilitate regulation or order, and technology can lead to upheaval or disorder
Freedom/enslavement	Technology can facilitate independence or fewer restrictions, and technology can lead to dependence or more restrictions
New/obsolete	New technologies provide the user with the most recently developed benefits of scientific knowledge, and new technologies are already or soon to be outmoded as they reach the marketplace
Competence/incompetence	Technology can facilitate feelings of intelligence or efficacy, and technology can lead to feelings of ignorance or ineptitude
Efficiency/inefficiency	Technology can facilitate less effort or time spent in certain activities, and technology can lead to more effort or time in certain activities
Fulfils/creates needs	Technology can facilitate the fulfilment of needs or desires, and technology can lead to the development or awareness of needs or desires previously unrealized
Assimilation/isolation	Technology can facilitate human togetherness, and technology can lead to human separation
Engaging/disengaging	Technology can facilitate involvement, flow or activity, and technology can lead to disconnection, disruption or passivity

Source: D.G. Mick and S. Fournier, 'Paradoxes of technology: consumer cognizance, emotions, and coping strategies', *Journal of Consumer Research* 25 (September 1998), pp. 123–47. Copyright © 1998 University of Chicago Press. Reprinted by permission

TABLE 1.2 Eight central paradoxes of technological products

The paradoxes and dark side of technology and service

Although there is clearly great potential for technology to support and enhance services, there are potential negative outcomes as well. Mick and Fournier, well-regarded consumer researchers, have pointed out the many paradoxes of technology products and services for consumers, as shown in Table 1.2.[18] This section highlights some of the general concerns.

Customer concerns about privacy and confidentiality raise major issues for firms as they seek to learn about and interact directly with customers through the Internet. These types of concerns are what have stymied and precluded many efforts to advance technology applications in the health-care industry, for example. Nor are all customers equally interested in using technology as a means of interacting with companies. Research exploring 'customer technology readiness' suggests that some customers are simply not interested or ready to use technology.[19] Employees can also be reluctant to accept and integrate technology into their work lives – especially when they perceive, rightly or wrongly, that the technology will substitute for human labour and perhaps eliminate their jobs.

With technology infusion comes a loss of human contact, which many people believe is detrimental purely from a quality of life and human relationships perspective. Parents may lament that their children spend hours in front of computer screens, interacting with games, seeking information and relating to their friends only through instant messaging without any face-to-face human contact. And workers in organizations become more and more reliant on communicating through technology – even communicating via email with the person in the next office!

Finally, the payback in technology investments is often uncertain. It may take a long time for an investment to result in productivity or customer satisfaction gains. Airlines such as British Airways and KLM have had to use ticket discounting to get passengers to migrate to Internet booking services.

Characteristics of services compared with goods

There is general agreement that differences between goods and services exist and that the distinctive characteristics discussed in this section result in challenges (as well as advantages) for managers of services.[20] It is also important to realize that each of these characteristics could be arranged on a continuum similar to the tangibility spectrum show in Figure 1.2. That is, services tend to be more heterogeneous, more intangible and more difficult to evaluate than goods, but the differences between goods and services are not black and white by any means.[21]

Table 1.3 summarizes the differences between goods and services and the implications of these characteristics. Many of the strategies, tools and frameworks in this text were developed to address these characteristics, which, until the 1980s, had been largely ignored by marketers. It has been suggested that these distinctive characteristics should not be viewed as unique to services but that they are also relevant to goods, that 'all products are services' and that 'economic exchange is fundamentally about service provision'.[22] This is complicated by the fact there is still a growing diversity of activities within the service sector, many of which involve a combination of goods and services within the offering. However, the continuing importance of understanding these differences can be explained as follows:[23]

1 The identification of these characteristics provided the impetus and legitimacy necessary to launch the new field of services marketing and the related academic research.

2 The characteristics identified enabled service researchers to recognize that achieving quality in manufacturing required a different approach to that required for a service quality improvement.

3 Each of the characteristics taken separately or in combination continues to inform research and management in specific service industries, categories and situations.

Goods	Services	Resulting implications
Tangible	Intangible	Services cannot be inventoried Services cannot be easily patented Services cannot be readily displayed or communicated Pricing is difficult
Standardized	Heterogeneous	Service delivery and customer satisfaction depend on employee and customer actions Service quality depends on many uncontrollable factors There is no sure knowledge that the service delivered matches what was planned and promoted
Production separate from consumption	**Inseparability** – simultaneous production and consumption	Customers participate in and affect the transaction Customers affect each other Employees affect the service outcome Decentralization may be essential Mass production is difficult
Non-perishable	Perishable	It is difficult to synchronize supply and demand with services Services cannot be returned or resold

Source: A. Parasuraman, V.A. Zeithaml and L.L. Berry, 'A conceptual model of service quality and its implications for future research', *Journal of Marketing* 49 (Fall 1985) pp. 41–50. Reprinted by permission of the American Marketing Association

TABLE 1.3 Goods versus services

Intangibility

The most basic distinguishing characteristic of services is intangibility. Because services are performances or actions rather than objects, they cannot be seen, felt, tasted or touched in the same manner that you can sense tangible goods. For example, health-care services are actions (such as surgery, diagnosis, examination and treatment) performed by providers and directed towards patients and their families. These services cannot actually be seen or touched by the patient, although the patient may be able to see and touch certain tangible components of the service (like the equipment or hospital room). In fact, many services such as health care are difficult for the consumer to grasp even mentally. Even after a diagnosis or surgery has been completed the patient may not fully comprehend the service performed, although tangible evidence of the service (e.g. incision, bandaging, pain) may be quite apparent.

Resulting marketing implications

Intangibility presents several marketing challenges. Services cannot be patented easily, and new service concepts can therefore easily be copied by competitors. Services cannot be readily displayed or easily communicated to customers, so quality may be difficult for consumers to assess. Decisions about what to include in advertising and other promotional materials are challenging, as is pricing. The actual costs of a 'unit of service' are hard to determine, and the price–quality relationship is complex.

Heterogeneity

Because services are performances, frequently produced by humans, no two services will be precisely alike. The employees delivering the service frequently are the service in the customer's eyes, and people may differ in their performance from day to day or even hour to hour. **Heterogeneity** also results because no two customers are precisely alike; each will have unique demands or experience the service in a unique way. Thus the heterogeneity connected with services is largely the result of human interaction (between and among employees and customers) and all of the vagaries that accompany it. For example, a tax accountant may provide a different service experience to two different customers on the same day, depending on their individual needs and personalities and on whether the accountant is interviewing them when he or she is fresh in the morning or tired at the end of a long day of meetings.

Resulting marketing implications

Because services are heterogeneous across time, organizations and people, ensuring consistent service quality is challenging. Quality actually depends on many factors that cannot be fully controlled by the service supplier, such as the ability of the consumer to articulate his or her needs, the ability and willingness of personnel to satisfy those needs, the presence (or absence) of other customers and the level of demand for the service. Because of these complicating factors, the service manager cannot always know for sure that the service is being delivered in a manner consistent with what was originally planned and promoted. Sometimes services may be provided by a third party, further increasing the potential heterogeneity of the offering. Alternatively, replacement of human inputs by automation and rigorous control of quality improvement procedures can reduce variability in some service sectors.

Simultaneous production and consumption

Whereas most goods are produced first, then sold and consumed, most services are sold first and then produced and consumed simultaneously. For example, a car can be manufactured in Japan, shipped to Paris, sold four months later and consumed over a period of years. But restaurant services cannot be provided until they have been sold, and the dining experience is essentially produced and consumed at the same time. Frequently this situation also means that the customer is present while the service is being produced, and thus views and may even take part in the production process. Simultaneity also means that customers will frequently interact with each other during the service production process and thus may affect each others' experiences. For example, strangers seated next to each other in an aeroplane may well affect the nature of the service experience for each other. That passengers understand this fact is clearly apparent in the way business travellers will often go to great lengths to be sure they are not seated next to families with small children. Another outcome of simultaneous production and consumption is that service producers find themselves playing a role as part of the product itself and as an essential ingredient in the service experience for the consumer.

Resulting marketing implications

Because services are often produced and consumed at the same time, mass production is difficult. The quality of service and customer satisfaction will be highly dependent on what happens in 'real time', including actions of employees and the interactions between employees and customers. Clearly the real-time nature of services also results in advantages in terms of opportunities to customize offerings for individual consumers. Simultaneous production and consumption also means that it is not usually possible to gain significant economies of scale through centralization. Often, operations need to be relatively decentralized so that the service can be delivered directly to the consumer in a convenient location, although the growth of technology-delivered services is changing this requirement for many services. Also because of simultaneous production and consumption, the customer is involved in and observes the production process and thus may affect (positively or negatively) the outcome of the service transaction. However, advances in the Internet and telecommunications have made it possible in some information-based sectors to separate customers in both time and space from production.

Perishability

Perishability refers to the fact that services cannot be saved, stored, resold or returned. A seat on a flight or in a restaurant, an hour of a lawyer's time or telephone line capacity not used cannot be reclaimed and used or resold at a later time. Perishability is in contrast to goods that can be stored in inventory or resold another day, or even returned if the consumer is unhappy. Would it not be nice if a bad haircut could be returned or resold to another consumer? Perishability makes this action an unlikely possibility for most services, although it should be noted that there are services such as education and entertainment where performances can be captured and replayed or rebroadcast time and time again.

Resulting marketing implications

A primary issue that marketers face in relation to service perishability is the inability to hold stock. Demand forecasting and creative planning for capacity utilization are therefore important and challenging decision areas. For example, there is tremendous demand for resort accommodation in the French Alps for skiing in February, but much less demand in July. Yet hotel and chalet owners have the same number of rooms to sell all year round. The fact that services cannot typically be returned or resold also implies a need for strong recovery strategies when things do go wrong. For example, although a bad haircut cannot be returned, the hairdresser can and should have strategies for recovering the customer's goodwill if and when such a problem occurs.

Challenges and questions for service marketers

Because of the basic characteristics of services, marketers of services face some very real and quite distinctive challenges. Answers to questions such as those listed here still elude managers of services:

- *How can service quality be defined and improved* when the product is intangible and nonstandardized?
- *How can new services be designed and tested effectively* when the service is essentially an intangible process?
- *How can the firm be certain it is communicating a consistent and relevant image* when so many elements of the marketing mix communicate to customers and some of these elements are the service providers themselves?
- *How does the firm accommodate fluctuating demand* when capacity is fixed and the service itself is perishable?
- *How can the firm best motivate and select service employees* who, because the service is delivered in real time, become a critical part of the product itself?
- *How should prices be set* when it is difficult to determine actual costs of production and price may be inextricably intertwined with perceptions of quality?
- *How should the firm be organized so that good strategic and tactical decisions* are made when a decision in any of the functional areas of marketing, operations and human resources may have significant impact on the other two areas?
- *How can the balance between standardization and personalization* be determined to maximize both the efficiency of the organization and the satisfaction of its customers?
- *How can the organization protect new service concepts from competitors* when service processes cannot be readily patented?
- *How does the firm communicate quality and value to consumers* when the offering is intangible and cannot be readily tried or displayed?
- *How can the organization ensure the delivery of consistent quality service* when both the organization's employees and the customers themselves can affect the service outcome?

The services triangle

To answer some of these questions, it is important to understand that services marketing is about promises – promises made and promises kept to customers. A strategic framework known as the **services triangle** (illustrated in Figure 1.3) shows the three interlinked groups that work together to develop, promote and deliver these service promises. These key players are labelled on the points of the triangle: the *company* (or strategic business unit (SBU) or department or 'management'), the *customers* and the *employees/technology*. This last group can be the firm's employees and subcontractors that deliver the company's services or it can be the technology such as automated teller machines that supply the service. Between these three points on the triangle, three types of marketing must be successfully carried out for a service to succeed: external marketing, interactive marketing, and internal marketing.

On the right-hand side of the triangle are the *external marketing* efforts that the firm engages in to set up its customers' expectations and make promises to customers regarding what is to be

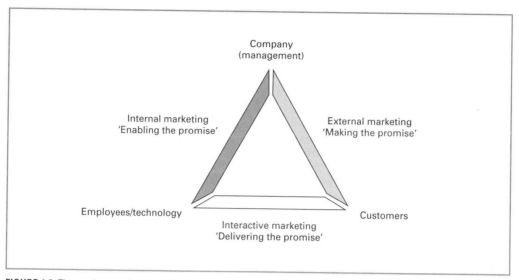

FIGURE 1.3 The services marketing triangle

Source: adapted from M.J. Bitner, 'Building service relationships: it's all about promises', *Journal of the Academy of Marketing Science* 23, no. 4 (1995), pp. 246–51; C. Gronroos, *Service Management and Marketing* (Lexington, MA: Lexington Books, 1990); and P. Kotler, *Marketing Management: Analysis, Planning, Implementation, and Control*, 8th edn (Englewood Cliffs, NJ: Prentice Hall, 1994), p. 470

delivered. Anything or anyone that communicates to the customer before service delivery can be viewed as part of this external marketing function. But external marketing is just the beginning for services marketers: promises made must be kept. On the bottom of the triangle is what has been termed *interactive marketing* or *real-time marketing*. Here is where promises are kept or broken by the firm's employees, technology, subcontractors or agents. If promises are not kept, customers become dissatisfied and eventually leave. The left-hand side of the triangle suggests the critical role played by *internal marketing*. Management engages in these activities to aid the providers in their ability to deliver on the service promise: recruiting, training, motivating, rewarding, and providing equipment and technology. Unless service employees are able and willing to deliver on the promises made, the firm will not be successful, and the services triangle will collapse.

All three sides of the triangle are essential to complete the whole, and the sides of the triangle should be aligned. That is, what is promised through external marketing should be the same as what is delivered; and the enabling activities inside the organization should be aligned with what is expected of service providers and employees.

Services marketing mix

The preceding questions are some of the many raised by managers and marketers of services that will be addressed throughout the text using a variety of tools and strategies. Sometimes these tools are adaptations of traditional marketing tools, as with the **services marketing mix** presented here. Other times they are radically new, as in the case of service blueprinting presented in Chapter 8.

Product	Place	Promotion	Price
Physical good features	Channel type	Promotion blend	Flexibility
Quality level	Exposure	Salespeople	Price level
Accessories	Intermediaries	Selection	Terms
Packaging	Outlet locations	Training	Differentiation
Warranties	Transportation	Incentives	Discounts
Product lines	Storage	Advertising	Allowances
Branding	Managing channels	Media types	
		Types of ads	
		Sales promotion	
		Publicity	
		Internet/Web strategy	

People	Physical Evidence	Process
Employees	Facility design	Flow of activities
Recruiting	Equipment	Standardized
Training	Signage	Customized
Motivation	Employee dress	Number of steps
Rewards	Other tangibles	Simple
Teamwork	Reports	Complex
Customers	Business cards	Customer involvement
Education	Statements	
Training	Guarantees	

TABLE 1.4 Expanded marketing mix for services

Traditional marketing mix

One of the most basic concepts in marketing is the marketing mix, defined as the elements an organization controls that can be used to satisfy or communicate with customers. The traditional marketing mix is composed of the four Ps: *product, price, place* (distribution) and *promotion*.[24] These elements appear as core decision variables in any marketing text or marketing plan. The notion of a mix implies that all the variables are interrelated and depend on each other to some extent. Further, the marketing mix philosophy implies an optimal mix of the four factors for a given market segment at a given point in time.

Key strategy decision areas for each of the four Ps are captured in the first four columns in Table 1.4. Careful management of product, place, promotion and price will clearly also be essential to the successful marketing of services. However, the strategies for the four Ps require some modifications when applied to services. For example, traditionally promotion is thought of as involving decisions related to sales, advertising, sales promotions and publicity. In services these factors are also important, but because services are produced and consumed simultaneously, service delivery people (such as checkout operators, ticket collectors, nurses and telephone personnel) are involved in real-time promotion of the service even if their jobs are typically defined in terms of the operational function they perform.

Expanded mix for services

Because services are usually produced and consumed simultaneously, customers are often present in the firm's factory, interact directly with the firm's personnel and are actually part of the service production process. Also, because services are intangible, customers will often be looking for any tangible cue to help them understand the nature of the service experience. For example, in the hotel industry the design and decor of the hotel as well as the appearance and attitudes of its employees will influence customer perceptions and experiences.

Acknowledgment of the importance of these additional variables has led services marketers to adopt the concept of an expanded marketing mix for services shown in the three remaining columns in Table 1.4.[25] In addition to the traditional four Ps, the services marketing mix includes *people, physical evidence* and *process.*

People All human actors who play a part in service delivery and thus influence the buyer's perceptions: namely, the firm's personnel, the customer, and other customers in the service environment.

All the human actors participating in the delivery of a service provide cues to the customer regarding the nature of the service itself. How these people are dressed, their personal appearance, and their attitudes and behaviours all influence the customer's perceptions of the service. The service provider or contact person can be very important. In fact, for some services, such as consulting, counselling, teaching and other professional relationship-based services, the provider *is* the service. In other cases the contact person may play what appears to be a relatively small part in service delivery – for instance, a telephone installer, an airline baggage handler or an equipment delivery dispatcher. Yet research suggests that even these providers may be the focal point of service encounters that can prove critical for the organization.

In many service situations, customers themselves can also influence service delivery, thus affecting service quality and their own satisfaction. For example, a client of a consulting company can influence the quality of service received by providing needed and timely information and by implementing recommendations provided by the consultant. Similarly, health-care patients greatly affect the quality of service they receive when they either comply or do not comply with health regimes prescribed by the provider.

Customers not only influence their own service outcomes, but they can influence other customers as well. In a theatre, at a football match or in a classroom, customers can influence the quality of service received by others – either enhancing or detracting from other customers' experiences.

Physical evidence The environment in which the service is delivered and where the firm and customer interact, and any tangible components that facilitate performance or communication of the service.

The physical evidence of service includes all the tangible representations of the service such as brochures, letterhead, business cards, report formats, signage and equipment. In some cases it includes the physical facility where the service is offered – the 'servicescape' – for example, the retail bank branch facility. In other cases, such as telecommunication services, the physical facility may be irrelevant. In this case other tangibles such as billing statements and appearance of the telephone engineer's van may be important indicators of quality. Especially when consumers have little on which to judge the actual quality of service, they will rely on these cues, just as they rely on the cues provided by the people and the service process. Physical evidence cues provide excellent opportunities for the firm to send consistent and strong messages regarding the organization's purpose, the intended market segments and the nature of the service.

Process The actual procedures, mechanisms, and flow of activities by which the service is delivered – the service delivery and operating systems.

FIGURE 1.4 easyJet: aligning people, processes and physical evidence[26]
Source: www.easyjet.com

The actual delivery steps that the customer experiences, or the operational flow of the service, also give customers evidence on which to judge the service. Some services are very complex, requiring the customer to follow a complicated and extensive series of actions to complete the process. Highly bureaucratized services frequently follow this pattern, and the logic of the steps involved often escapes the customer. Another distinguishing characteristic of the process that can provide evidence to the customer is whether the service follows a production-line/standardized approach or whether the process is an empowered/customized one. None of these characteristics of the service is inherently better or worse than another. Rather, the point is that these process characteristics are another form of evidence used by the consumer to judge service. For example, two successful airline companies, easyJet and Singapore Airlines, follow extremely different process models. easyJet is a no-frills (no food, no assigned seats), low-priced airline that offers frequent, relatively short flights within Europe. All the evidence it provides is consistent with its vision and market position, as illustrated in Figure 1.4. Singapore Airlines, on the other hand, focuses on the business traveller and is concerned with meeting individual traveller needs. Thus, its process is highly customized to the individual, and employees are empowered to provide nonstandard service when needed. Both airlines have been very successful.

The three new marketing mix elements (people, physical evidence, and process) are included in the marketing mix as separate elements because they are within the control of the firm *and* because any or all of them may influence the customer's initial decision to purchase a service as well as the customer's level of satisfaction and repurchase decisions. Their impact is evident in the **'servuction' system** model (Figure 1.5), developed by two French academics.[27] This model breaks the service delivery process that a customer receives into two parts: that which is visible

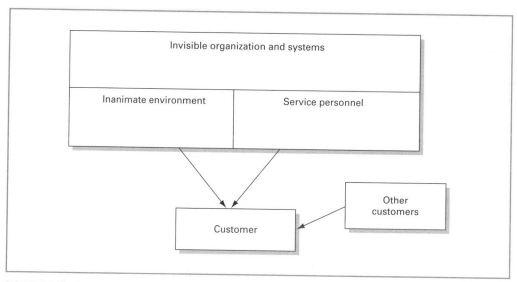

FIGURE 1.5 The 'servuction' system model[28]

to the customer and that which is not. The invisible part is the process element from the extended marketing mix consisting of systems, backroom procedures and the technology or equipment needed to produce the service. In a restaurant this would involve the ordering of ingredients, the cooking facilities and the procedures involved in preparing the food.

The visible part is broken into the inanimate environment (physical evidence) and the service providers or the individuals (people) who interact with the customer during the service experience. The inanimate environment consists of the physical design elements that the customer comes into contact with. This could include aspects such as the lighting, place settings, colour schemes, staff uniforms and the final bill. The model also suggests that customers interact with each other. Their behaviour and characteristics impact on each other's experience. Therefore the benefits derived by customer A come from the interaction with the physical environment and the people (service providers and other customers). Each of these elements is supported and influenced by the process, much of which may be invisible to the customer.

These new marketing mix elements as well as the traditional elements are explored in depth in future chapters.

Staying focused on the customer

A critical theme running throughout the text is *customer focus*. In fact, the subtitle of the book is 'Integrating customer focus across the firm'. From the firm's point of view, all strategies are developed with an eye on the customer, and all implementations are carried out with an understanding of their impact on the customer. From a practical perspective, decisions regarding new services and communication plans will integrate the customer's point of view; operations and human resource decisions will be considered in terms of their impact on customers. All the tools, strategies and frameworks included in this text have customers at their foundation. The services marketing mix just described is clearly an important tool that addresses the uniqueness of services, keeping the customer at the centre.

In this text, we also view customers as assets to be valued, developed and retained. The strategies and tools we offer thus focus on customer relationship-building and loyalty as opposed to a more transactional focus in which customers are viewed as onetime revenue producers. This text looks at customer relationship management not as a software program but as an entire architecture or business philosophy. Every chapter in the text can be considered a component needed to build a complete customer relationship management approach.

Summary

This chapter has set the stage for further learning about services marketing by presenting information on changes in the world economy and business practice that have driven the focus on service: the fact that services dominate the modern economies of the world; the focus on service as a competitive business imperative; specific needs of the deregulated and professional service industries; the role of new service concepts growing from technological advances; and the realization that the characteristics of services result in unique challenges and opportunities. The chapter presented a broad definition of services as deeds, processes and performances, and it drew distinctions among pure services, value-added services, customer service and derived service.

Building on this fundamental understanding of the service economy, the chapter went on to present the key characteristics of services that underlie the need for distinct strategies and concepts for managing service businesses. These basic characteristics are that services are intangible, heterogeneous, produced and consumed simultaneously, and perishable. Because of these characteristics, service managers face a number of challenges in marketing, including the complex problem of how to deliver quality services consistently.

The chapter described two themes that provide the foundation for future chapters: the expanded marketing mix for services; and customer focus as a unifying theme. It also introduced the concept of the services triangle and the 'servuction system'. The remainder of the text focuses on exploring the unique opportunities and challenges faced by organizations that sell and deliver services, and on developing solutions that will help you become an effective services champion and manager.

Key concepts

Derived service	6	Self-service technologies	13
Heterogeneity	16	Services marketing mix	19
Inseparability	15	Services triangle	18
Intangibility	7	Servuction system	22
Perishability	17	Tangibility spectrum	7

Further reading

Berry, L.L. and Parasuraman, A. (1993) 'Building a new academic field: the case of services marketing', *Journal of Retailing*, 69(1), 13–60.

Edgett, S. and Parkinson, S. (1993) 'Marketing for service industries – a review', *Service Industries Journal*, 13(2), 19–39.

Fisk, R.P., Brown, S.W. and Bitner, M.J. (1993) 'Tracking the evolution of the services marketing literature', *Journal of Retailing*, 69(1), 61–91.

Gronroos, C. (2006) 'Adopting a service logic for marketing', *Marketing Theory*, 3(3), 313–37.

Grove, S.J., Fisk, R.P. and John, J. (2003) 'The future of services marketing: forecasts from ten services experts', *Journal of Services Marketing*, 17, 106–19.

Lovelock, C. and Gummesson, E. (2004) 'Whither services marketing? In search of a new paradigm and fresh perspectives', *Journal of Service Research*, 7(1), 20–41.

Martin, C.L. (1999) 'The history, evolution and principles of services marketing: poised for the new millennium', *Marketing Intelligence and Planning*, 17(7), 324–8.

Shostack, G.L. (1977) 'Breaking free from product marketing', *Journal of Marketing*, 41 (April), 73–80.

Vargo, S.L. and Lusch, R.F. (2004) 'The four service marketing myths: remnants of a goods-based, manufacturing model', *Journal of Service Research*, 6(4), 324–35.

Discussion questions

1 What distinguishes service offerings from customer service? Provide specific examples.

2 How is technology changing the nature of service?

3 What are the basic characteristics of services v. goods? What are the implications of these characteristics for Accenture or for easyJet?

4 One of the underlying frameworks for the text is the services marketing mix. Discuss why each of the three new mix elements (process, people and physical evidence) is included. How might each of these communicate with or help to satisfy an organization's customers?

5 Think of a service job you have had or currently have. How effective, in your opinion, was or is the organization in managing the elements of the services marketing mix?

6 Again, think of a service job you have had or currently have. How did or does the organization handle relevant challenges listed in Table 1.2?

7 How can quality service be used in a manufacturing context for competitive advantage? Think of your answer to this question in the context of cars or computers or some other manufactured product you have actually purchased.

Exercises

1 Roughly calculate your budget for an average month. What percentage of your budget goes for services versus goods? Do the services you purchase have value? In what sense? If you had to cut back on your expenses, what would you cut out?

2 Visit two local retail service providers that you believe are positioned very differently (such as IKEA and a local family-owned furniture store, or Burger King and a fine restaurant). From your own observations, compare their strategies on the elements of the services marketing mix.

3 Try a service you have never tried before on the Internet. Analyse the benefits of this service. Was enough information provided to make the service easy to use? How would you compare this service to other methods of obtaining the same benefits?

Notes

[1] Source: www.forbes.com – *The Forbes Global 2000* (published on 30 March 2006).

[2] J.B. Quinn, J.J. Baruch and P.C. Paquette, 'Technology in services', *Scientific American* 257, no. 6 (December 1987), pp. 50–8.

[3] S.L. Vargo and R.F. Lusch, 'Evolving to a new dominant logic for marketing', *Journal of Marketing* 68 (January 2004), pp. 1–17.

[4] M. Sawhney, S. Balasubramanian and V.V. Krishnan, 'Creating growth with services', *Sloan Management Review* (Winter 2004), pp. 34–43.

[5] J.A. Alexander and M.W. Hordes, *S-Business: Reinventing the Services Organization* (New York: SelectBooks, 2003); R. Oliva and R. Kallenberg, 'Managing the transition from products to services', *International Journal of Service Industry Management* 14, no. 2 (2003), pp. 160–72.

[6] R.H.K. Vietor, *Contrived Competition* (Cambridge, MA: Harvard University Press, 1994).

[7] L. Berry, *Discovering the Soul of Service* (New York: Free Press, 1999).

[8] R.T. Rust, C. Moorman, and P.R. Dickson, 'Getting return on quality: revenue expansion, cost reduction, or both?' *Journal of Marketing* 66 (October 2002), pp. 7–24.

[9] J.L. Heskett, T.O. Jones, G.W. Loveman, W.E. Sasser Jr and L.A. Schlesinger, 'Putting the service–profit chain to work', *Harvard Business Review* (March–April 1994), pp. 164–74.

[10] E.W. Anderson and V. Mittal, 'Strengthening the satisfaction–profit chain', *Journal of Service Research* 3, no. 2 (November 2000), pp. 107–20.

[11] L.P. Willcocks and R. Plant, 'Getting from bricks to clicks', *Sloan Management Review* (Spring 2001), pp. 50–9.

[12] 'Revolution digital tomorrow report: technologies that will change marketing', *Revolution* (February 2001), pp. 51–65.

[13] G. Eysenbach, E.R. Sa and T.L. Diepgen, 'Shopping around the Internet today and tomorrow: towards the millennium of cybermedicine', *British Medical Journal* 319 (1999), p. 1294.

[14] Source: Commission of the European Communities (2004) 'e-Health – making healthcare better for European citizens: an action plan for a European e-Health Area'.

15 M.J. Bitner, S.W. Brown and M.L. Meuter, 'Technology infusion in service encounters', *Journal of the Academy of Marketing Science* 28 (Winter 2000), pp. 138–49.

16 M.J. Bitner, 'Self-service technologies: what do customers expect?', *Marketing Management* (Spring 2001), pp. 10–11.

17 R. Hallowell, 'Service in e-commerce: findings from exploratory research', Harvard Business School, Module Note, N9-800-418, 31 May 2000.

18 D.G. Mick and S. Fournier, 'Paradoxes of technology: consumer cognizance, emotions, and coping strategies', *Journal of Consumer Research* 25 (September 1998), pp. 123–47.

19 A. Parasuraman and C.L. Colby, *Techno-Ready Marketing: How and Why Your Customers Adopt Technology* (New York: Free Press, 2001).

20 Discussion of these issues is found in many services marketing publications. The discussion here is based on V.A. Zeithaml, A. Parasuraman and L.L. Berry, 'Problems and strategies in services marketing', *Journal of Marketing* 49 (Spring 1985), pp. 33–46.

21 For research supporting the idea of goods–services continua, see D. Iacobucci, 'An empirical examination of some basic tenets in services: goods–services continua', in *Advances in Services Marketing and Management,* eds T.A. Swartz, D.E. Bowen and S.W. Brown (Greenwich, CT: JAI Press, 1992), vol. 1, pp. 23–52.

22 S.L. Vargo and R.F. Lusch, 'The four service marketing myths', *Journal of Service Research* 6 (May 2004), pp. 324–35.

23 C. Lovelock and E. Gummesson, 'Whither services marketing? In search of a new paradigm and fresh perspectives', *Journal of Services Research* 7 (August 2004), pp. 20–41.

24 E.J. McCarthy and W.D. Perrault Jr, *Basic Marketing: A Global Managerial Approach* (Burr Ridge, IL: Richard D. Irwin, 1993).

25 B.H. Booms and M.J. Bitner, 'Marketing strategies and organizational structures for service firms', in *Marketing of Services,* eds J.H. Donnelly and W.R. George (Chicago: American Marketing Association, 1981), pp. 47–51.

26 Source: www.easyjet.com

27 E. Langeard, J. Bateson, C. Lovelock and P. Eiglier, *Marketing of Services: New Insights from Consumers and Managers* (Cambridge, USA: Marketing Sciences Institute, 1981).

28 Ibid.

CHAPTER 02

Consumer behaviour in services

The chapter's objectives are to:

1 Enhance understanding of how consumers choose and evaluate services, through focusing on factors that are particularly relevant for services.

2 Describe how consumers judge goods versus services in terms of search, experience and credence criteria.

3 Develop the elements of consumer behaviour that a services marketer must understand: choice behaviour, consumer experiences and post-experience evaluation.

4 Examine attitudes towards the use of self service technologies.

5 Explore how differences among consumers (cultural differences, group decision-making) affect consumer behaviour and influence services marketing strategies.

CASE STUDY: CONSUMER PROBLEM: TIME DEFICIENCY

Today's dual-career couples, single-parent families and two-job families are realizing a burning consumer need: more time. Individuals in these and other non-traditional family configurations are overstressed with their work and home obligations and find that dealing with many of life's everyday tasks is overwhelming. For many customers, all types of shopping have become 'drudgery or worse'.[1] Faced with this dilemma, consumers have choices: They can continue to do all these tasks for themselves, or they can decide to employ the services of professionals or friends and relatives to help them out.

The antidote to this **time deficiency** is found in many new services and service features that recover time for consumers. Innovative new services – dog walking, garden maintenance, wedding planning, personal shopping, even passport application preparation – are emerging to deal with tasks that used to be performed by the household but now can be purchased by the time-buying consumer. Conventional services such as retailing, banking and restaurants are also adding peripheral services to make shopping easier, increasing their hours to suit customer schedules, reducing transaction time, improving delivery and providing merchandise or services at home or work. Increased use of the Internet is also saving time for customers. With the Web and home delivery, many shopping tasks can be carried out by customers without even leaving the house and at any time of the day or night.

And there is an increasingly popular parallel phenomenon in business today known as *outsourcing*, which means purchasing whole service functions (such as billing, payroll, secretarial support, maintenance, call-centre operations, network operations, and marketing) from other firms rather than executing them in-house. The motivation for corporations is not so much saving time as it is saving money, better use of limited resources, and focusing on core competencies. Companies that use outsourcing effectively have discovered that in many cases purchasing services outright from another company can be far more economical than the payroll and capital costs of performing them inside. Another benefit, particularly for smaller businesses, is that outsourcing allows the company to focus on its core competencies without the distraction of less central tasks.

The primary objectives of services producers and marketers are identical to those of all marketers: to develop and provide offerings that satisfy consumer needs and expectations, thereby ensuring their own economic survival. To achieve these objectives, service providers need to understand how consumers choose, experience and evaluate their service offerings. However, most of what is known about consumer evaluation processes pertains specifically to goods. The assumption appears to be that services, if not identical to goods, are at least similar enough in the consumer's mind that they are chosen, experienced and evaluated in the same manner.

This chapter challenges that assumption and shows that services' characteristics result in some differences in consumer evaluation processes compared with those used in assessing goods. Recognizing these differences and thoroughly understanding consumer evaluation processes are critical for the customer focus on which effective services marketing is based. Because the premise of this text is that the customer is the heart of effective services marketing, we begin with the customer and maintain this focus throughout the text.

Consumers have a more difficult time evaluating and choosing most services partly because services are intangible and non-standardized and partly because consumption is so closely intertwined with production. These characteristics lead to differences in consumer evaluation processes for goods and services in all stages of the buying and consumption process.

Search, experience and credence properties

One framework for isolating differences in evaluation processes between goods and services is a classification of properties of offerings proposed by economists.[2] Economists first distinguished between two categories of properties of consumer products: **search qualities,** attributes that a consumer can determine before purchasing a product; and **experience qualities,** attributes that can be discerned only after purchase or during consumption. Search qualities include colour, style, price, fit, feel, hardness and smell; experience qualities include taste and wearability. Products such as cars, clothing, furniture, and jewellery are high in search qualities because their attributes can be almost completely determined and evaluated before purchase. Products such as vacations and restaurant meals are high in experience qualities because their attributes cannot be fully known or assessed until they have been purchased and are being consumed. A third category, **credence qualities,** includes characteristics that the consumer may find impossible to evaluate even after purchase and consumption.[3] Examples of offerings high in credence qualities are insurance and brake replacement on cars. Few consumers possess a knowledge of risk or mechanical skills sufficient to evaluate whether these services are necessary or are performed properly, even after they have been prescribed and produced by the seller.

Figure 2.1 arrays products high in search, experience, or credence qualities along a continuum of evaluation ranging from easy to evaluate to difficult to evaluate. Products high in search qualities are the easiest to evaluate (left-hand end of the continuum). Products high in experience qualities are more difficult to evaluate because they must be purchased and con-

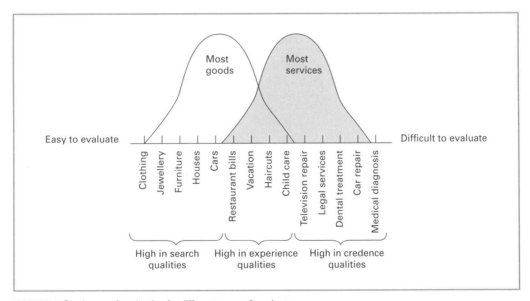

FIGURE 2.1 Continuum of evaluation for different types of products

sumed before assessment is possible (centre of continuum). Products high in credence qualities are the most difficult to evaluate because the consumer may be unaware of or may lack sufficient knowledge to appraise whether the offerings satisfy given wants or needs even after consumption (right-hand end of the continuum). The major premise of this chapter is that most goods fall to the left of the continuum, whereas most services fall to the right because of the distinguishing characteristics described in Chapter 1. These characteristics make services more difficult to evaluate than goods, particularly in advance of purchase. Difficulty in evaluation, in turn, forces consumers to rely on different cues and processes when assessing services.

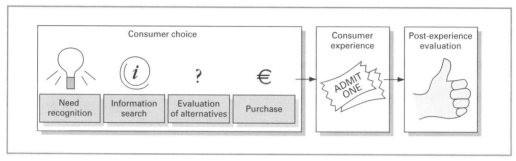

FIGURE 2.2 Stages in consumer decision-making and evaluation of services

The following sections of this chapter build from these basic differences to explore the stages of consumer decision-making and evaluation for services. This discussion is organized around three broad stages of consumer behaviour, as shown in Figure 2.2: consumer choice (linking in to the stages of the buying behaviour process: need recognition, information search, evaluation of alternatives and purchase), the consumer experience of the service while it is being delivered, and post-experience evaluation. Within each of these stages, you will see similarities and differences between goods and services.

Consumer choice

The first important area of consumer behaviour that marketers are concerned with is how customers choose and make decisions and the steps that lead to the purchase of a particular service. This process is similar to that used for goods in some ways and different in others. Customers follow a logical sequence, including **need recognition**, **information search**, evaluation of alternatives, and purchase. The following sections discuss this sequence, particularly focusing on the ways in which services decision-making is different from goods decision-making.

Need recognition

The process of buying a service begins with the recognition that a need or want exists. Although there are many different ways to characterize needs, the most widely known is Maslow's hierarchy, which specifies five need categories arranged in a sequence from basic lower-level needs to higher-level needs. Services can fill all these needs, and they become increasingly important for higher-level social, ego and self-actualization needs.

1 *Physiological needs* are *biological needs such as food, water and sleep.* The recognition of these basic needs is fairly straightforward. Recall the last time you were on

vacation, perhaps sightseeing in a new place. At some point around lunch time, you recognized that you were thirsty and hungry and needed to stop and have lunch. Restaurants, coffee shops, bistros and other service establishments that provided food and water were more likely to became noticeable at this point.

2 *Safety and security needs* include *shelter, protection and security.* Immediately following the terrorist attacks on London, consumers began to recognize their vulnerability and sought ways to increase their safety and security. Instead of travelling on the Underground transport network, consumers switched service purchases to taxis, bicycles and using the Internet for home-based working to satisfy their needs for safety and security.

3 *Social needs* are for *affection, friendship and acceptance.* Social needs are critical to all cultures but are particularly important in the East. In countries like Japan and China, consumers place a great deal of value on social and belonging needs. They spend more time with their families and work colleagues than do those in the West and therefore consume more services that can be shared. The Japanese spend more annually per capita in restaurants, for example, than any other country – 1,300 euros per year compared to 728 euros in the United States, 596 euros in Britain and a mere 362 euros in France.[4] Consumers in all cultures use many types of services to address social needs, including health and dance clubs, dating services and vacations (like Club Med) in which socializing is encouraged.

4 *Ego needs* are for *prestige, success, accomplishment and self-esteem.* Food, safety and belonging are not enough for many consumers, especially those from Western cultures. Individuals also seek to look good to others and to feel good about themselves because of what they have accomplished. Needs to improve oneself and achieve success are responsible for the growth of education, training and other services that increase the skills and prestige of consumers. Personal services such as spa services, plastic surgery, teeth-whitening and gym membership also satisfy these needs

5 *Self-actualization* involves *self-fulfilment and enriching experiences.* Consumers desire to live up to their full potential and enjoy themselves. Some consumers purchase experiences such as skydiving, jungle safaris and bungee-jumping for the pure thrill of the experience, a need quite different from the others in Maslow's hierarchy. Other people self-actualize through classes in oil painting or poetry-writing, thereby expressing feelings and meanings that are unrelated to the basic needs of day-to-day living.

The hierarchical nature of Maslow's need categorization has been disputed, and evidence exists that people with unfilled basic needs can be motivated to self-actualize. We are not concerned with the hierarchical nature in this section; we use it only as a way to discuss different drivers that lead customers to the next stages of consumer behaviour in services.

Information search

Once they recognize a need, consumers obtain information about goods and services that might satisfy this need. Seeking information may be an extensive, formalized process if the service or good is important to the consumer or it represents a major investment (for example, an Australian vacation package or a professional landscape service). In other cases, the information search may be quick and relatively automatic (for example, a restaurant for a quick lunch or a service station for fuel). Consumers use both personal sources (such as friends or experts) and non-personal sources (such as mass or selective media and websites) to gain information about goods and services. Seeking information is a way of reducing risk, helping consumers feel more confident about their choices.

Personal and non-personal sources

When purchasing goods, consumers make use of both personal and non-personal sources because both effectively convey information about search qualities. When purchasing services, on the other hand, consumers seek and rely to a greater extent on personal sources for several reasons.

First, mass and selective media can convey information about search qualities but can communicate far less about experience qualities. By asking friends or experts about services, however, the consumer can obtain information vicariously about experience qualities.

A second reason for greater use of personal sources of information for services is that many types of non-personal sources of information are not as readily available for services. Many service providers are local, independent merchants with neither the experience nor the funds to advertise. Furthermore, cooperative advertising (advertising funded jointly by the retailer and the manufacturer) is used infrequently with services because most local providers are both producer and retailer of the service. And, because professional associations representing lawyers, architects etc. banned advertising for so long, both professionals and consumers tend to resist its use even though it is now permitted.

Finally, because consumers can assess few attributes before purchase of a service, they may feel greater risk in selecting a little-known alternative. Personal influence becomes pivotal as product complexity increases and when objective standards by which to evaluate a product decrease (that is, when experience qualities are high).[5] Managers in service industries clearly recognize the strong influence of word-of-mouth communication .

Interestingly, consumers are now able through the Internet to seek more non-personal information about services in the form of visuals, photographs and even virtual tours.[6] In addition to these tangible representations of the service experience, consumers can also seek the personal opinions of others via the Web through chat rooms, online ratings and consumer complaint web-

FIGURE 2.3 Consumers seek and rely on personal sources in purchasing experience goods and services

sites. Some consumer complaint websites even target a specific firm's current and prospective customers, offering unsolicited information.[7]

Perceived risk

Although some degree of **perceived risk** probably accompanies all purchase transactions, more risk appears to be involved in the purchase of services than in the purchase of goods because services are typically more intangible, variable and perishable. Risk can come in the form of financial risk, time risk, performance risk, social risk or psychological risk, any of which may be greater for services.

The intangible nature of services and their high level of experience qualities imply that services generally must be selected on the basis of less pre-purchase information than is the case for goods. There is clear evidence that greater intangibility (whether for goods or services) increases perceptions of risk.[8] And because services are non-standardized, the consumer will feel some uncertainty about the outcome and consequences each time a service is purchased. In addition, services purchases may involve more perceived risk than other purchases because, with some exceptions, services are not accompanied by warranties or guarantees. Dissatisfied customers can rarely 'return' a service; they have already consumed it by the time they realize their dissatisfaction. Finally, many services are so technical or specialized that consumers possess neither the knowledge nor the experience to evaluate whether they are satisfied, even after they have consumed the service.

The increase in perceived risk in purchasing services suggests the use of strategies to reduce risk. Risk reduction can be accomplished through tactics that reduce risk directly (e.g. guarantees) or by addressing the factors that contribute to the perception of risk (e.g. making the service more tangible).[9] For example, DHL provides tracking numbers for customers so they can follow their shipments online and know exactly where a package is. This system helps reduce the risk for consumers. Offering a free or reduced-cost trial period for a service would be another means to reduce risk. For example, gyms and health clubs often encourage a free trial day for prospective clients to reduce the sense of risk in this important decision. To the extent that it is possible, service providers should emphasize employee training and other procedures to standardize their offerings so that consumers learn to expect a given level of quality, again reducing perceived risk.

Evaluation of service alternatives

The evoked set of alternatives – that group of products that a consumer considers acceptable options in a given product category – is likely to be smaller with services than with goods. One reason involves differences in retailing between goods and services. To purchase goods, consumers generally shop in retail stores that display competing products in close proximity, clearly demonstrating the possible alternatives. To purchase services, on the other hand, the consumer visits an establishment (such as a bank, a dry cleaner or a hair salon) that almost always offers only a single 'brand' for sale. A second reason for the smaller evoked set is that consumers are unlikely to find more than one or two businesses providing the same services in a given geographic area, whereas they may find numerous retail stores carrying the identical manufacturer's product. A third reason for a smaller evoked set is the difficulty of obtaining adequate pre-purchase information about services.

Faced with the task of collecting and evaluating experience qualities, consumers may simply select the first acceptable alternative rather than searching many alternatives. The Internet has the potential to widen the set of alternatives and already has done so in some industries. This trend is most notable in airlines and hotels where comparable information is available through providers such as Travelocity and Expedia.

For non-professional services, consumers' decisions often entail the choice between performing the services for themselves or hiring someone to perform them.[10] Working people may choose between cleaning their own homes or hiring housekeepers, between altering their families' clothes or taking them to a tailor, even between staying home to take care of their children or engaging a day care centre to provide child care. Consumers may consider themselves as sources of supply for many services, including lawn care, tax preparation and preparing meals. Thus, the customer's evoked set frequently includes self-provision of the service. Self-service via technology is also a viable alternative for many services.

CASE STUDY: HOW MUCH DO CUSTOMERS LIKE PROVIDING THEIR OWN SERVICES?

One of the major recent changes in consumer behaviour is the growing tendency for consumers to interact with technology to create services instead of interacting with a live service firm employee. *Self-service technologies* (SSTs) are technological interfaces that allow customers to produce services independent of direct service employee involvement. Examples that you are probably very familiar with are automated teller machines, pay-at-the-pump terminals at service stations and automated airline check-in. All forms of services over the Internet are also self-service technologies, many of which are very innovative. In the UK, for example, users can complete their tax return online rather than use the usual paper forms. Electronic self-ordering is being developed at fast-food chains, and self-scanning at grocery stores is available in Tesco stores.

Interface / Purpose	Categories and examples of SSTs in use			
	Telephone/interactive voice response	**Online/Internet**	**Interactive**	**Video/CD**
Customer service	■ Telephone banking ■ Flight information ■ Order status	■ Package tracking ■ Account information	■ ATMs ■ Hotel checkout	
Transactions	■ Telephone banking ■ Prescription refills	■ Retail purchasing ■ Financial transactions	■ Pay at the pump ■ Hotel checkout ■ Car rental	
Self-help	■ Information telephone lines	■ Internet information search ■ Distance learning	■ Blood pressure machines ■ Tourist information	■ Tax preparation software ■ Television/CD-based training

The chart in this box shows a comprehensive set of categories and examples of self-service technologies in use today. The columns of the matrix represent the types of technologies that companies are using to interface with customers in self-service encounters, and the rows show purposes of the technologies from the customer perspective. As you can see, customers use the technologies to provide customer service (deal with questions about accounts, bill-paying and delivery-tracking), to conduct transactions (order, buy and exchange resources with companies without direct interaction), and to provide self-help (learn, receive information, train themselves and provide their own services).

A study asked customers across a wide range of industries and applications what they think of such technology and found that customers have very strong feelings about them. They both love and hate them, depending on a few key conditions. Customers love them when:

- *They bail them out of difficult situations.* A single parent with a sleeping child in the car needs to get fuel and a fast meal. Using a pay-at-the-pump service station and drive-up fast-food restaurant allows the parent to accomplish these tasks without leaving the sleeping child.

- *They are better than the interpersonal alternative.* Self-service technology has the potential to save customers time, money and psychological costs. The Internet, in particular, allows customers to shop at any time and complete transactions more quickly than they could in person. Internet loans and finance also allow customers to avoid the anxiety of meeting a banker in person and feeling judged.

- *They work as they are supposed to.* When self-service technologies work as they are supposed to, customers are impressed. Many of you have had the experience of using one-click ordering at Amazon. When these transactions work smoothly, as they usually do after the proper setup, the transactions are satisfying.

On the other hand, customers hate self-service technology when the following problems occur:

- *They fail to work.* The researchers found that 60 per cent of the negative stories they heard stemmed from service failures. Broken machines, failed PIN numbers, websites that were down and items not shipped as promised all frustrate consumers.

- *They are poorly designed.* Poorly designed technologies that are difficult to use or understand create hassles for customers, making them feel as though the technology is not worth using. Websites that are difficult to navigate are particularly troublesome. If customers cannot reach information they need within a few clicks (some researchers say that two clicks are all that customers will tolerate), then customers shun the website.

- *The customer messes up.* Customers dislike using technologies that they feel they cannot perform adequately. Even though they feel partially responsible, they will avoid using them in the future. A common frustration is having various user names and passwords for different websites. When confronted with a screen requiring this information – and not recalling it accurately – many customers will give up and go elsewhere.

- *There is no service recovery.* When the process or technology fails, self-service technologies rarely provide ways to recover on the spot. In these cases customers must then call or visit the company, precisely what they were trying to avoid by using the self-service technology.

It is increasingly evident that these technological innovations will be a critical component of customer–firm interactions. If these technologies are to succeed, the researchers contend, they must become more reliable, be better than the interpersonal alternatives and have recovery systems in place when they fail.

Sources: M.L. Meuter, A.L. Ostom, R.I. Roundtree and M.J. Bitner, 'Self-service technologies: understanding customer satisfaction with technology-based service encounters', *Journal of Marketing* 64 (July 2000), pp. 50–64; M.J. Bitner, 'Self-service technologies: what do customers expect?', *Marketing Management* (Spring 2001), pp. 10–11.

Service purchase

Following consideration of alternatives (whether an extensive process or more automatic), consumers make the decision to purchase a particular service or to do it themselves. One of the most interesting differences between goods and services is that most goods are fully produced (at the factory) prior to being purchased by consumers. Thus, consumers, prior to making their final purchase decision, can see and frequently try the exact object that they will buy. For services, much is still unknown at the point of purchase. In many cases, the service is purchased and produced almost simultaneously – as with a restaurant meal or live entertainment. In other cases, consumers pay all or part of the purchase price up front for a service they will not fully experience until it is produced for them much later. This situation arises with services such as packaged holidays or kitchen design, or ongoing services such as health club memberships or university education. In business-to-business situations, long-term contracts for services (such as payroll, network integration or landscaping) may be signed prior to anything being produced at all.

Because of the inherent risk in the purchase decision for services, some providers offer 'free' (or 'deeply discounted') initial trials or extensive tours of their facilities (for example, prospective student and parent tours at universities) in order to reduce risk in the final purchase decision. In business-to-business situations, trust in the provider is paramount when customers sign long-term service contracts, and frequently the contracts themselves spell out in detail the service level agreements and penalties for non-performance.

Consumer experience

Because the choice process for services is inherently risky with many unknowns, the experience itself often dominates the evaluation process. As noted, services are high in experience and credence qualities relative to goods; thus, how consumers evaluate the actual experience of the service is critical in their evaluation process and their decision to repurchase later. In fact, noted customer experience experts have stated that 'the experience is the marketing'.[11]

Much has been written recently about customer experiences and their important role in influencing consumer behaviour. Goods and services companies alike are being admonished to create 'memorable experiences for their customers'.[12]

In this section we describe elements of consumer behaviour that are relevant to understanding service experiences and how customers evaluate them. We do not limit our discussion to fun, exciting or memorable experiences only. Instead, we use the term *customer experience* to encompass service processes that span the mundane to the spectacular. Customers purchasing building maintenance and dry-cleaning services still have experiences, albeit less exciting ones than customers of entertainment or travel services. All services *are* experiences – some are long in duration and some are short; some are complex and others are simple; some are mundane, whereas others are exciting and unique. Creating and managing effective processes and experiences are always essential management tasks for service organizations. Many subsequent chapters in this book will provide you with tools and approaches for managing specific elements of the customer experience – the heart of services marketing and management.

Services as processes

Because services are actions or performances done for and with customers, they typically involve a sequence of steps, actions and activities. Consider medical services. Some of the steps in medical care involve customers interacting with providers (e.g. patients interacting with their doctor), other steps may be carried out by the customers themselves (e.g. 'following the doctor's orders', taking medications) and other steps may involve third parties (e.g. going to a hospital for tests). The combination of these steps, and many others along the way, constitute a process, a service experience that is evaluated by the consumer. It is the combination of steps, the flow of the activities or the 'experience' that is evaluated by the customer. In many cases, the customer's experience comprises interactions with multiple, interconnected organizations, as in the case of medical services, car insurance or home buying. Diverse sets of experiences across the network of firms (e.g. a doctor's office, a pharmacy, hospital and physiotherapy clinic) will likely influence consumers' overall impressions of their experience. Whether or not the provider acknowledges it or seeks to control this experience in a particular way, it is inevitable that the customer will have an experience – good, bad or indifferent.

Service provision as drama

The metaphor of **service as theatre** is a useful framework for describing and analysing service performances. Both the theatre and service organizations aim to create and maintain a desirable impression before an audience and recognize that the way to accomplish this is by carefully managing the actors and the physical setting of their behaviour.[13] The service marketer must play many drama-related roles – including director, choreographer and writer – to be sure the performances of the actors are pleasing to the audience. The Walt Disney Company (Figure 2.4) explicitly considers its service provision a 'performance', even using show business terms such as *cast member*, *onstage* and *show* to describe the operations at Disneyland Paris.[14]

The skill of the service *actors* in performing their routines, the way they appear and their commitment to the 'show' are all essential to service delivery. Although service actors are present in most service performances, their importance increases in three conditions. First, service actors are critical when the degree of direct personal contact is high. Consider the difference between a visit to see a lawyer in comparison to a visit to a fast-food restaurant. The second condition in which service actors' skills are critical is when the services involve repeat contact. Nurses in hospitals, favourite waiters or tennis coaches in resorts or captains on cruises are essential characters in service theatre, and their individual performances can make or break the success of the services. The third condition in which contact personnel are critical is when they have discretion in determining the nature of the service and how it is delivered. When you consider the quality of the education you are receiving in college, you are certain to focus much of your evaluation on

FIGURE 2.4 At Disneyland the delivery of service is conceived as drama
Source: Freelance Consulting Services/Corbis

your professors' delivery of classes. In education, as in other services such as medical and legal services, the professional is the key actor in the performance.[15]

Ray Fisk and Steve Grove, two experts in the area of service dramaturgy, point out that service actors' performances can be characterized as sincere or cynical.[16] A sincere performance occurs when an actor becomes one with the role that he or she is playing, whereas a cynical performance occurs when an actor views a performance only as a means to an end, such as getting paid for doing the job. When a service employee takes the time to listen and help, the performance is sincere and often noteworthy. Unfortunately, too many examples of cynical performances exist in which front-line 'actors' seem to care little about the 'audience' of customers. As Grove and Fisk point out, a single employee can ruin the service experience by ridiculing other cast members' efforts, failing to perform his or her role correctly or projecting the wrong image. To create the right impression, three characteristics are necessary: loyalty, discipline and circumspection.[17]

The physical setting of the service can be likened to the staging of a theatrical production, including scenery, props and other physical cues to create desired impressions. Among a setting's features that may influence the character of a service are the colours or brightness of the service's surroundings; the volume and pitch of sounds in the setting; the smells, movement, freshness and temperature of the air; the use of space; the style and comfort of the furnishings; and the setting's design and cleanliness.[18] As an example, the service provided by a cruise ship features its layout (broad and open), decor and comfort (large, cushioned deckchairs), furnishings (lots of polished wood and brass) and cleanliness ('shipshape'). The setting increases in importance when the environment distinguishes the service. Consider how critical the setting is for a city-centre law firm, which must appear professional, capable, even imposing.[19] In essence, the delivery of service can be conceived as drama, where service personnel are the actors, service customers are the audience, physical evidence of the service is the setting and the process of service assembly is the performance. The drama metaphor offers a useful way to improve service performances.[20] Selection of personnel can be viewed as auditioning the actors. An actor's personal appearance, manner, facial expression, gestures, personality and demographic profile can be determined in large part in the interview or audition. Training of personnel can become rehearsing. Clearly defining the role can be seen as scripting the performance. Creation of the service environment involves setting the stage. Finally, deciding which aspects of the service should be performed in the presence of the customer (onstage) and which should be performed in the back room (backstage) helps define the performances the customer experiences.

Service roles and scripts

Service roles are combinations of social cues that guide and direct behaviour in a given setting.[21] Just as there are roles in dramatic performances, there are roles in service delivery. For example, the role of a hostess in a restaurant is to acknowledge and greet customers, find out how many people are in their group, and then lead them to a table where they will eat. The success of any service performance depends in part on how well the role is performed by the service actor and how well the team of players – the 'role set' of both service employees and customers – act out their roles.[22] Service employees need to perform their roles according to the expectations of the customer; if they do not, the customer may be frustrated and disappointed. If customers are informed and educated about their roles and if they cooperate with the provider in following the script, successful service provision is likely.

One factor that influences the effectiveness of role performance is the **service script** – the logical sequence of events expected by the customer, involving him or her as either a participant or an observer.[23] Service scripts consist of sequences of actions associated with actors and objects that, through repeated involvement, define what the customer expects.[24] Receiving a dental check-up is a service experience for which a well-defined script exists. For a check-up the consumer expects the following sequence: enter the reception area, greet a receptionist, sit in a waiting room, follow the dental nurse to a separate room, recline in a chair while teeth are examined by the dentist, then pay for the services. When the service conforms to this script, the customer has a feeling of confirmed expectations and satisfaction. Deviations from the service script lead to confusion and dissatisfaction. Suppose, on moving to a new town, you went to a dentist who had no receptionist and no waiting area, only a doorbell in a cubicle. Suppose, on answering the doorbell, an employee in shorts took you to a large room where all patients were in a dental chairs facing each other. These actions and objects are certainly not in the traditional service script for dentistry and might create considerable uncertainty and doubt in patients.

Some services are more scripted than others. Customers would expect very expensive, customized services such as spa vacations to be less scripted than mass-produced services such as fast food ('Have a nice day!') and airline travel.

The compatibility of service customers

We have just discussed the roles of employees and customers receiving service. We now want to focus on the role of *other customers* receiving service at the same time. Consider how central the mere presence of other customers is in churches, restaurants, dances, bars, clubs and spectator sports: if no one else shows up, customers will not get to socialize with others, one of the primary expectations in these types of services. However, if customers become so dense that crowding occurs, customers may also be dissatisfied.[25] The way other customers behave with many services – such as airlines, education, clubs and social organizations – also exerts a major influence on a customer's experience.[26] In general, the presence, behaviour and similarity of other customers receiving services has a strong impact on the satisfaction and dissatisfaction of any given customer.[27]

Customers can be incompatible for many reasons – differences in beliefs, values, experiences, ability to pay, appearance, age and health, to name just a few. The service marketer must anticipate, acknowledge and deal with heterogeneous consumers who have the potential to be incompatible. The service marketer can also bring homogeneous customers together and solidify relationships between them, which increases the cost to the customer of switching service providers.[28] Customer compatibility is a factor that influences customer satisfaction, particularly in high-contact services.

Customer co-production

In addition to being audience members, as suggested by the drama metaphor, service users also play a **customer co-production** role that can have profound influence on the service experience.[29] For example, counselling, personal training or educational services have little value without the full participation of the client, who will most likely have extensive work to do between sessions. In this sense, the client co-produces the service. In business-to-business contexts such as consulting, architecture, accounting and almost any outsourced service, customers also co-produce the service.[30] It has been suggested that customers therefore need to understand their roles and be 'trained' in ways that are similar to the training of service employees, so that they will have the motivation, ability and role clarity to perform.[31]

The idea of customers as 'partners' in the co-creation of products is gaining ground across all industries, not just services.[32] Postmodern consumer behaviour experts propose an even broader interpretation of this idea. They suggest that a fundamental characteristic of the postmodern era is consumers' assertiveness as active participants in creating their world – often evidenced in their demands to adjust, change and use products in customized ways.[33]

Emotion and mood

Emotion and mood are feeling states that influence people's (and therefore customers') perceptions and evaluations of their experiences. Moods are distinguished from emotions in that *moods* are transient feeling states that occur at specific times and in specific situations, whereas *emotions* are more intense, stable and pervasive.[34]

Because services are experiences, **moods and emotions** are critical factors that shape the perceived effectiveness of service encounters. If a service customer is in a bad mood when he or she enters a service establishment, service provision will likely be interpreted more negatively than if he or she were in a buoyant, positive mood. Similarly, if a service provider is irritable or sullen, his or her interaction with customers will likely be coloured by that mood. Furthermore, when other customers in a service establishment are cranky or frustrated, whether from problems with the service or from existing emotions unrelated to the service, their mood affects the provision of service for all customers who sense the negative mood. In sum, any service characterized by human interaction is strongly dependent on the moods and emotions of the service provider, the service customer and other customers receiving the service at the same time.

In what specific ways can mood affect the behaviour of service customers? First, positive moods can make customers more obliging and willing to participate in behaviours that help service encounters succeed.[35] Customers in a good emotional state are probably more willing to follow an exercise regimen prescribed by a personal trainer, clear their own dishes at a fast-food restaurant and overlook delays in service. Customers in a negative mood may be less likely to engage in behaviours essential to the effectiveness of the service: abstaining from chocolates when on a diet programme with Weight Watchers, taking frequent aerobic classes from a health club or completing homework assigned in a class.

A second way that moods and emotions influence service customers is to bias the way they judge service encounters and providers. Mood and emotions enhance and amplify experiences, making them either more positive or more negative than they might seem in the absence of the moods and emotions.[36] After losing a big account, a salesperson catching an airline flight will be more incensed with delays and crowding than he or she might be on a day when business went

FIGURE 2.5 Positive moods of customers in a dance club heighten their service experiences
Source: Mark Richards/Photo Edit

well. Conversely, the positive mood of a services customer at a dance or restaurant will heighten the experience, leading to positive evaluations of the service establishment (Figure 2.5). The direction of the bias in evaluation is consistent with the polarity (positive or negative) of the mood or emotion.

Finally, moods and emotions affect the way information about service is absorbed and retrieved in memory. As memories about a service are encoded by a consumer, the feelings associated with the encounter become an inseparable part of the memory. If travellers fall in love during a vacation in the Greece, they may hold favourable assessments of the destination due more to their emotional state than to the destination itself. Conversely, if a customer first becomes aware of his or her poor level of fitness when on a guest pass in a health club, the negative feelings may be encoded and retrieved every time he or she thinks of the health club or, for that matter, any health club.

Because emotions and moods play such important roles in influencing customer experiences, 'organizations must manage the emotional component of experiences with the same rigour they bring to the management of product and service functionality'.[37] Organizations may observe customers' emotional responses and attempt to create places, processes and interactions to enhance certain emotions. Some firms believe that consumers' emotional responses may be the best predictors of their ultimate loyalty. Thus, many companies are now beginning to measure emotional responses and connections as well – going beyond traditional measures of satisfaction and behavioural loyalty.

Post-experience evaluation

Following the service experience, customers form an evaluation that determines to a large degree whether they will return or continue to patronize the service organization (see Figure 2.2). Historically within the field of marketing, much more attention has been paid to pre-purchase evaluations and consumer choice. Yet, post-purchase and post-experience evaluations are typically most important in predicting subsequent consumer behaviours and repurchase, particularly for services.

Post-experience evaluation is captured by companies in measures of satisfaction, service quality, loyalty and, sometimes, emotional engagement. We devote an entire chapter (Chapter 4) to exploring the specifics of customer satisfaction and service quality. Another chapter (Chapter 7) examines the topic of relationships and loyalty.

Word-of-mouth communication

Post-experience evaluations will significantly impact what consumers tell others about the service. Because service consumers are strongly influenced by the personal opinions of others, understanding and controlling **word-of-mouth communication** becomes even more important for service companies. The best way to get positive word of mouth is, of course, to create memorable and positive service experiences. When service is dissatisfactory, it is critical to have an effective service recovery strategy (see Chapter 15) to curb negative word of mouth.

Attribution of dissatisfaction

When consumers are disappointed with purchases – because the products did not fulfil the intended needs, did not perform satisfactorily or were not worth the price – their **attribution of dissatisfaction** may be to a number of different sources, among them the producers, the retailers,

Post-experience evaluation **43**

or themselves. Because consumers participate to a greater extent in the definition and production of services, they may feel more responsible for their dissatisfaction when they purchase services than when they purchase goods. As an example, consider a consumer purchasing a haircut; receiving the cut he or she desires depends in part on clear specifications of his or her needs to the stylist. If disappointed, he or she may blame either the stylist (for lack of skill) or himself or herself (for choosing the wrong stylist or for not communicating his or her own needs clearly).

The quality of many services depends on the information the customer brings to the service encounter: a pharmacist's accurate diagnosis requires a conscientious case history and a clear articulation of symptoms; a dry cleaner's success in removing a spot depends on the consumer's knowledge of its cause; and a tax adviser's satisfactory performance relies on the receipts saved by the consumer. Failure to obtain satisfaction with any of these services may not be blamed completely on the retailer or producer, because consumers must adequately perform their part in the production process also.

With products, on the other hand, a consumer's main form of participation is the act of purchase. The consumer may attribute failure to receive satisfaction to his or her own decision-making error, but he or she holds the producer responsible for product performance. Goods usually carry warranties or guarantees with purchase, emphasizing that the producer believes that if something goes wrong, it is not the fault of the consumer. With services, consumers attribute some of their dissatisfaction to their own inability to specify or perform their part of the service. They also may complain less frequently about services than about goods because of their belief that they themselves are partly responsible for their dissatisfaction.

Positive or negative biases

There is a long history of research in psychology and consumer behaviour that suggests that people remember negative events and occurrences more than positive ones and are more influenced by negative information than by positive information. Research and personal observation suggest that it is easier for consumers to remember the negative service experiences they have than to think of the many routine, or even positive, experiences.

There is also a long stream of research that says that customers will weigh negative information about a product attribute more heavily than positive information in forming their overall brand attitudes. Yet some very interesting and recent research suggests 'positivity bias' for services.[38] The research showed that consumers tend to infer positive qualities for the firm and its employees if they have a good experience with one service employee. When individual service providers are regarded positively, customers' positive perceptions of other service providers in the company are also raised. On the other hand, customers who have a negative experience with one employee are less likely to draw a negative inference about all employees or the firm. That is, customers are more likely to attribute that negative experience to the individual provider, not the entire firm. Although this study is just one piece of research, the results and implications are very intriguing.

Brand loyalty

The degree to which consumers are committed to particular brands of goods or services depends on a number of factors: the cost of changing brands (switching cost), the availability of substitutes, social ties to the company, the perceived risk associated with the purchase, and the satisfaction obtained in the past. Because it may be more costly to change brands of services, because awareness of substitutes is limited and because higher risks may accompany services, consumers are more likely to remain customers of particular companies with services than with goods.

The difficulty of obtaining information about services means that consumers may be unaware of alternatives or substitutes for their brands, or they may be uncertain about the ability of alternatives to increase satisfaction over present brands. Monetary fees may accompany brand switching in many services: dentists sometimes demand new X-rays on the initial visit and health clubs frequently charge 'membership fees' at the outset to obtain long-term commitments from customers.

If consumers perceive greater risks with services, as is hypothesized here, they probably depend on brand names to a greater extent than when they purchase products. Brand loyalty, described as a means of economizing decision effort by substituting habit for repeated, deliberate decision, functions as a device for reducing the risks of consumer decisions.

A final reason that consumers may be more brand loyal with services is the recognition of the need for repeated patronage in order to obtain optimum satisfaction from the seller. Becoming a 'regular customer' allows the seller to gain knowledge of the customer's tastes and preferences, ensures better treatment and encourages more interest in the consumer's satisfaction. Thus a consumer may exhibit brand loyalty to cultivate a satisfying relationship with the seller.

Brand loyalty has two sides. The fact that a service provider's own customers are brand loyal is, of course, desirable. The fact that the customers of the provider's competition are difficult to capture, however, creates special challenges. The marketer may need to direct communications and strategy to the customers of competitors, emphasizing attributes and strengths that his firm possesses and the competitor lacks. Marketers can also facilitate switching from competitors' services by reducing switching costs.

Understanding differences among consumers

To this point in the chapter, we have discussed consumer decision-making and evaluation processes that are applicable across a wide range of consumers and types of services. In these last sections of the chapter, we examine two broad topics that shed light on some of the differences *among* consumers. First, we examine the role of national and ethnic cultures in shaping consumer behaviour. Then we discuss some of the unique differences in consumer decision-making for organizations and households.

Global differences: the role of culture

Culture represents the common values, norms and behaviours of a particular group and is often identified with nations or ethnicity. Culture is learned, shared, multidimensional and transmitted from one generation to the next. Understanding cultural differences is important in services marketing because of its effects on the ways that customers evaluate and use services. Culture also influences how companies and their service employees interact with customers. Culture is important in international services marketing – taking services from one country and offering them in others – but it is also critical within countries. More and more, individual countries are becoming multicultural, and organizations need to understand how this factor affects evaluation, purchase and use of services even within countries.

Research provides considerable evidence that there are differences in how consumers perceive services across cultures. For example, a study showed notable differences in how fast-food and grocery consumers in eight different countries (Australia, China, Germany, India, Morocco, the Netherlands, Sweden and the United States) evaluate these services.[39] Differences in how services are evaluated across cultures can be traced to basic factors that distinguish cultures from each other. In the next sections, we highlight some of the major differences that can influence how people choose, use and evaluate services, including values and attitudes, manners and customers, material culture, and aesthetics. Language, another obvious cultural difference particularly important for services, is discussed in Chapter 16.

Values and attitudes differ across cultures

Values and attitudes help determine what members of a culture think is right, important and/or desirable. Because behaviours, including consumer behaviours, flow from values and attitudes, services marketers who want their services adopted across cultures must understand these differences.

Service spotlight

For example, people in Greece are relaxed about eating out and treat a meal as a social occasion, and therefore service in Greek restaurants is generally much slower than it is in restaurants in Germany or the UK. British people holidaying in Greece are often impatient with the speed of restaurant service at the start of their holidays. However, this frustration regularly wears off during the holiday as the tourists also become more relaxed about time and eating.

Manners and customs

Manners and customs represent a culture's views of appropriate ways of behaving. It is important to monitor differences in manners and customs because they can have a direct effect on the service encounter.

Service spotlight

Central and Eastern Europeans are perplexed by Western expectations that unhappy workers put on a 'happy face' when dealing with customers. As an example, McDonald's requires Polish employees to smile whenever they interact with customers. Such a requirement strikes many employees as artificial and insincere. The fast-food giant has learned to encourage managers in Poland to probe employee problems and to assign troubled workers to the kitchen rather than to the food counter.[40]

Habits are similar to customs, and these tend to vary by culture. Japanese take very few vacations, and when they do they like to spend seven to 10 days. Their vacations are unusually crammed with activities – Rome, Geneva, Paris and London in 10 days is representative.[41] The travel industry has been responsive to the special preferences of these big-spending Japanese tourists. The Four Seasons Hotel chain provides special pillows, kimonos, slippers and teas for Japanese guests. Virgin Atlantic Airways and other carriers have interactive screens available for each passenger, allowing viewing of Japanese (or American, French and so on) movies, television and even gambling if regulators approve.

Country	Year to which data refers	% of dwellings owner-occupied
Romania	2002	97
Bulgaria	2002	96
Lithuania	2002	87
Estonia	2000	85
Slovenia	2002	82
Spain	2001	81
Italy	2001	80
Ireland	2002	77
Portugal	2001	76
Slovakia	2001	76
Luxembourg	2001	70
United Kingdom	2001	69
Belgium	2001	68
Turkey	2000	64
Cyprus	2000	64
Latvia	2000	60
Finland	1999	58
Austria	2002	57
France	2002	56
Poland	2002	55
Netherlands	2002	54
Denmark	2003	51
Czech Republic	2001	47
Germany	2002	43
Sweden	2002	38

TABLE 2.1 Housing ownership in European countries

Source: Norris, M. and Shiels, P., 'Regular national report on housing developments in European countries – synthesis report', The Housing Unit, Dublin, 2004

Material culture

Material culture consists of the tangible products of culture. What people own and how they use and display material possessions vary around the world. Cars, houses, clothes and furniture are examples of material culture.

The importance of owning your own home varies significantly from country to country reflecting the different cultural traditions existing within each society. Table 2.1 shows the percentage of residential dwellings that are owner-occupied in a number of European countries. The difference between Sweden and Romania is particularly striking. Such differences will impact on property-related services such as decorating, garden maintenance, estate agents, lawyers, architects (for extensions/home improvements) and even do-it-yourself (DIY) retailers

Aesthetics

Aesthetics refers to cultural ideas about beauty and good taste. These ideas are reflected in music, art, drama and dance as well as the appreciation of colour and form (Figure 2.6).

Attitudes towards style in clothing, cars, restaurants, retail stores and hotels vary internationally relating to the expectations of local culture. A French café is very different from a Starbucks in terms of atmosphere. Many Scandinavian hotels have very clean lines with utilitarian furniture supported by decor that is striking but simple. The internal design of a French car is generally more 'chic' or quirky than would be the case for a German-built car. These all reflect the aesthetic characteristics of the culture they serve. Care must therefore be taken in designing service environments to ensure that the target market is comfortable with the aesthetic qualities being presented.

FIGURE 2.6 Ideas about aesthetics differ across cultures

Source: Ryan McVay/Photodisc/Getty Images

Group decision-making

A group is defined as two or more individuals who have implicitly or explicitly defined relationships to one another such that their behaviour is interdependent.[42] When groups make decisions about services – a household purchasing a family vacation or a kitchen redesign, or an organization purchasing information technology consulting or marketing research services – many of the same issues arise as for individuals. Groups purchasing services encounter greater perceived risk, more reliance on word-of-mouth communication, greater difficulty in comparing alternatives and often a higher level of customer participation than do groups purchasing goods. For example, although many large organizations have very clear evaluation processes for buying goods, their processes and decision rules for purchasing services are often not as well defined. The intangibility and variability of business services make them more risky and often difficult to compare. Thus, organizations often rely on established partnerships, long-term relationships or referrals from others when it comes to major service purchases. Similar issues arise for households who rely heavily on personal referrals in making significant services purchases such as home repair, landscaping and annual vacations. Even smaller household decisions – where to eat dinner or the choice of a dry cleaner – may be influenced by referrals and may involve a great deal of risk, depending on the occasion. A special anniversary or birthday dinner or where to have Grandmother's 40-year-old wedding dress dry cleaned can be decisions that carry considerable personal risk.

Despite these similarities, some differences in group decision-making should be considered for a fuller understanding of consumer behaviour in services. Among the aspects that are different for group buying are collective decision-making, mixed motives or goals, roles in the purchasing process, and group culture. We will highlight some of these differences for two major groups: households and organizations.

Households

When a family makes a service purchase decision, it has a collective style of decision-making that often differs from what any of the individuals would use if making an independent choice. When a family chooses a vacation destination, for example, its style may involve one of the following: (1) one parent makes a unilateral decision that the family will go on vacation to Disneyland Paris; (2) the family discusses possible vacation destinations at the dinner table, taking each person's ideas and suggestions into account, and selects three locations that a parent will investigate further; (3) the parents provide a budget and a list of the destinations that can be visited within that budget, then allow the children to choose among them. Once a destination has been chosen, the mix of motives or goals of the group comes into play. The mother may want to sightsee, the father to rest and the children to visit local theme parks. In this and other group purchasing decisions, the needs and goals of the various members must be balanced so that the service (in this case the vacation) delivers optimal satisfaction for as many members as possible. Group roles are also a key consideration. In a household, one individual often identifies a need and initiates the purchase, someone else may influence which service provider is selected, someone else may pay and someone else may become the ultimate user of the service. For example, the father may decide that the family needs to visit an optician for an eye test, a teenager may recommend an optician that a friend uses, the mother may pay the bills, and all the family members may go to get their eyes tested. Finally, national and ethnic culture affects household purchase and consumption behaviours. For example, ethnic groups vary, with some being very patriarchal, others egalitarian and still others autocratic.

Organizations

Organizational consumers are a special category of group consumers. These days, companies spend millions on information technology services, call centres, travel management, payroll services and outsourced services for human resource management. Making the right decision on service purchases can be absolutely critical for an organization's success. How do companies make these important decisions? How, for example, do certain companies choose to outsource their call-centre operations to a company in India?

For routine and even complex purchases, organizations often rely on a small number of buyers within the company, many of whom specialize in purchasing. These buyers are typically organized either formally or informally into **buying centres**, which include all people involved in the decision process.[43] Each of these roles may be taken by a different person, or one person may assume all roles in some cases.

- The *initiator* identifies the organization's service needs.
- The *gatekeeper* collects and controls information about the purchase.
- The *decider* determines what service to purchase.
- The *buyer* or purchasing agent physically acquires the service.

◆ The *user* consumes the service and may or may not have any influence over the purchase decision.

Among the characteristics that distinguish organizational from individual decision-making are economic forces such as current business climate and technology trends; organizational strategies and culture; whether purchasing is a centralized or decentralized function; and the group forces that influence purchasing decisions.[44] Organizational purchases also tend to differ by magnitude and include new task purchases (large purchases that require careful consideration of needs and evaluation of alternative), straight rebuys (simple reorders of past service purchases) and modified rebuys (a mix of new and straight rebuy features).[45]

As companies outsource more services and particularly when these services are outsourced around the globe, purchase decisions become complex and difficult. Often companies must rely on outside consultants such as Accenture or PriceWaterhouseCoopers to help them with these multifaceted and financially risky decisions.

Organizational purchasers also rely on references and the experience of other organizations in making their service purchase decisions. Referrals and testimonials can be very helpful to other organizations considering similar business service purchases. In fact, many business service providers have customer stories, cases and testimonials on their websites to help reduce the risk of these complex decisions.

Summary

The intent of this chapter was to provide understanding for how consumers choose and evaluate services. Services possess high levels of experience and credence properties, which in turn make them challenging to evaluate, particularly prior to purchase. The chapter isolated and discussed three stages of consumer behaviour for services, and it looked at how experience and credence properties result in challenges and opportunities in all three stages. The three stages are consumer choice (including need recognition, information search, evaluation of alternatives and service purchase); consumer experience; and post-experience evaluation. Consumer behaviour theories, current research and insights for managers were highlighted in each of these sections.

Although the three stages are relevant for all types of consumer behaviour in services, important differences exist in behaviour across global cultures and for groups versus individuals. Global differences in consumer behaviour were presented, particularly as they relate to service consumption. The chapter ended with a discussion of the differences in group versus individual consumer decision-making related to households and organizations.

Key concepts

Attribution of dissatisfaction	42	Self-service technologies	35
Buying centres	48	Service roles	39
Culture, values and attitudes	44	Service script	39
Customer co-production	41	Service as theatre	38
Information search	31	Search v. experience v. credence qualities	30
Moods and emotions	41	Time deficiency	29
Need recognition	31	Word-of-mouth communication	42
Perceived risk	34		

Further reading

Bamossy, G.J., Askegaard, S., Solomon, M. and Hogg, M. (2006) *Consumer Behaviour: A European Perspective*, 3rd edn. London: FT Prentice Hall.

Bettman, J.R., Luce, M.F. and Payne, J.W. (1998) 'Constructive consumer choice processes', *Journal of Consumer Research*, 25(3), 187–217.

Fitsimmons, J.A., Noh, J. and Theis, E. (1998) 'Purchasing business services', *Journal of Business and Industrial Marketing*, 13(3/4), 370–80.

Gabbott, M. and Hogg, G. (1994) 'Consumer behaviour and services: a review', *Journal of Marketing Management*, 10(4), 311–24.

Gabbott, M. and Hogg, G. (1998) *Consumers and Services*. Chichester: John Wiley & Sons.

Hofstede, G. (2003) *Culture's Consequences: Comparing Values, Behaviours, Institutions and Organisations across Nations*, 2nd edn. London: Sage Publications.

McKoll-Kennedy, J.R. and Fetter, R. (1999) 'Dimensions of consumer search behaviour in services', *Journal of Services Marketing*, 13(3), 242–63.

Murray, K. and Schlacter, J. (1990) 'The impact of goods versus services on consumers' assessments of perceived risk and variability', *Journal of the Academy of Marketing Science*, 18(1), 51–65.

Tanner, J.F. (1999) 'Organisational buying theories: a bridge to relationship theory', *Industrial Marketing Management*, 28(3), 245–55.

Discussion questions

1 Based on the chapter, which aspects of consumer behaviour are similar and which are different for services versus goods?

2 Where does a college or university education fit on the continuum of evaluation for different types of products? Where does computer software fit? Consulting? Retailing? Fast food? What are the implications for consumer behaviour?

3 What are examples (other than those given in the chapter) of services that are high in credence properties? How do high credence properties affect consumer behaviour for these services?

4 For what types of services might consumers depend on mass communication (non-personal sources of information, including the Internet) in the purchase decision?

5 Which of the aspects discussed in the chapter describe your behaviour when it comes to purchasing services? Does your behaviour differ for different types of services?

6 Why are consumer experiences so important in the evaluation process for services?

7 Using the service drama metaphor, describe the services provided by a health club, a fine restaurant or a cruise liner.

8 What are some differences in service choice, purchase and consumption processes for organizations and households compared with individuals? What are some similarities?

Exercises

1 Choose a particular end-consumer services industry and one type of service provided in that industry (such as the financial services industry for mortgage loans, the legal services industry for wills or the travel industry for a holiday package). Talk to five customers who have purchased that service and determine to what extent the information in this chapter described their behaviour in terms of consumer choice, consumer experience and post-experience evaluation for that service.

2 Choose a particular business-to-business service industry and one type of service provided in that industry (such as the information services industry for computer maintenance services or the consulting industry for management consulting). Talk to five customers in that industry and determine to what extent the information in this chapter described their behaviour in terms of consumer choice, consumer experience and post-experience evaluation for that service.

3 Visit a service provider of your choice. Experience the service at first-hand if possible and observe other customers for a period of time. Describe the consumer (service) experience in detail in terms of what happened throughout the process and how customers, including yourself, felt about it. How could the service experience be improved?

4 Interview three people who come from countries other than your own. Ask them about their consumer behaviour patterns. Note the differences and similarities to your own consumer behaviour. What are possible causes of the differences?

Notes

[1] M.J. Dorsch, S.J. Grove and W.R. Darden, 'Consumer intentions to use a service category', *Journal of Services Marketing* 14, no. 2 (2000), pp. 92–117.

[2] P. Nelson, 'Information and consumer behaviour', *Journal of Political Economy* 78, no. 20 (1970), pp. 311–29.

[3] M.R. Darby and E. Karni, 'Free competition and the optimal amount of fraud', *Journal of Law and Economics* 16 (April 1973), pp. 67–86.

[4] 'USA snapshots: a look at statistics that shape our lives,' *USA Today*, 1 November 1998, p. D-1

[5] T.S. Robertson, *Innovative Behavior and Communication* (New York: Holt, Rinehart & Winston, 1971).

[6] P. Berthon, L. Pitt, C.S. Katsikeas, and J.P. Berthon, 'Virtual services go international: international services in the marketspace', *Journal of International Marketing* 7, no. 3 (1999), pp. 84–105.

[7] J.C. Ward and A.L. Ostrom, 'Online complaining via customer-created web sites: a protest framing perspective', working paper, W.P. Carey School of Business, Arizona State University, 2004.

[8] M. Laroche, G.H.G. McDougall, J. Bergeron and Z. Yang, 'Exploring how intangibility affects perceived risk,' *Journal of Service Research* 6, no. 4 (May 2004), pp. 373–89; K.B. Murray and J.L. Schlacter, 'The impact of services versus goods on consumers' assessment of perceived risk and variability', *Journal of the Academy of Marketing Science* 18 (Winter 1990), pp. 51–65; M.

Laroche, J. Bergeron and C. Goutaland, 'How intangibility affects perceived risk: the moderating role of knowledge and involvement', *Journal of Services Marketing* 17, no. 2 (2003), pp. 122–40.

9 M. Laroche et al., 'Exploring how intangibility affects perceived risk'.

10 R.F. Lusch, S.W. Brown and G.J. Brunswick, 'A general framework for explaining internal vs. external exchange', *Journal of the Academy of Marketing Science* 10, (Spring 1992), pp. 119–34; Dorsch, Grove and Darden, 'Consumer intentions to use a service category'.

11 J.H. Gilmore and B.J. Pine II, 'The experience is the marketing', report from Strategic Horizons LLP (2002).

12 See, for example, B.J. Pine II and J.H. Gilmore, *The Experience Economy* (Boston, MA: Harvard Business School Press, 1999); B.H. Schmitt, *Experiential Marketing* (New York: Free Press, 1999); B.H. Schmitt, *Customer Experience Management* (Hoboken, NJ: John Wiley & Sons, 2003).

13 S.J. Grove and R.P. Fisk, 'Service theater: an analytical framework for services marketing', in *Services Marketing*, 4th ed, ed. C. Lovelock (Englewood Cliffs, NJ: Prentice Hall, 2001), pp. 83–92.

14 S.J. Grove, R.P. Fisk and M.J. Bitner, 'Dramatizing the service experience: a managerial approach', in *Advances in Services Marketing and Management*, vol. 1, eds T.A. Swartz, D.E. Bowen and S.W. Brown (Greenwich, CT: JAI Press, 1992), pp. 91–121.

15 Grove, Fisk and Bitner, 'Dramatizing the service experience'.

16 Grove and Fisk, 'Service theater'.

17 Ibid.

18 Grove, Fisk and Bitner, 'Dramatizing the service experience'. Ibid.

19 Ibid.

20 Ibid.

21 M.R. Solomon, C. Surprenant, J.A. Czepiel and E.G. Gutman, 'A role theory perspective on dyadic interactions: the service encounter', *Journal of Marketing* 49 (Winter 1985), pp. 99–111.

22 Ibid.

23 R.F. Abelson, 'Script processing in attitude formation and decision making', in *Cognition and Social Behavior,* eds J.S. Carroll and J.S. Payne (Hillsdale, NJ: Erlbaum, 1976).

24 R.A. Smith and M.J. Houston, 'Script-based evaluations of satisfaction with services', in *Emerging Perspectives on Services Marketing*, eds. L. Berry, G.L. Shostack and G. Upah (Chicago, IL: American Marketing Association, 1982), pp. 59–62.

25 J.E.G. Bateson and M.K.M. Hui, 'Crowding in the service environment', in *Creativity in Services Marketing: What's New, What Works, What's Developing*, eds M. Venkatesan, D.M. Schmalensee and C. Marshall (Chicago, IL: American Marketing Association, 1986), pp. 85–8.

26 J. Baker, 'The role of the environment in marketing services: the consumer perspective', in *The Services Challenge: Integrating for Competitive Advantage,* eds J.A. Czepiel, C.A. Congram and J. Shanahan (Chicago, IL: American Marketing Association, 1987), pp. 79–84.

27 C.L. Martin and C.A. Pranter, 'Compatibility Management: customer-to-customer relationships in service environments', *Journal of Services Marketing* 3 (Summer 1989), pp. 43–53.

28 Ibid.

29 N. Bendapudi and R.P. Leone, 'Psychological implications of customer participation in co-production', *Journal of Marketing* 67 (January 2003), pp.14–28.

30 L.A. Bettencourt, A.L. Ostrom, S.W. Brown and R.I. Roundtree, 'Client co-production in knowledge-intensive business services', *California Management Review* 44, no. 4 (Summer 2002), pp. 100–28.

31 S. Dellande, M.C. Gilly and J.L. Graham, 'Gaining compliance and losing weight: the role of the service provider in health care services', *Journal of Marketing* 68 (July 2004), pp. 78–91; M.L. Meuter, M.J. Bitner, A.L. Ostrom and S.W. Brown, 'Choosing among alternative service delivery modes: an investigation of customer trials of self-service technologies', *Journal of Marketing* (2005), pp. 61–83.

32 C.K. Prahalad and V. Ramaswamy, 'The new frontier of experience innovation', *Sloan Management Review* (Summer 2003), pp. 12–18.

33 A.F. Firat and A. Venkatesh, 'Liberatory postmodernism and the reenchantment of consumption', *Journal of Consumer Research* 22, no. 3 (December 1995), pp. 239–67.

34 M.P. Gardner, 'Mood states and consumer behavior: a critical review', *Journal of Consumer Research* 12 (December 1985), pp. 281–300.

35 Ibid., p. 288.

36 S.S. Tomkins, 'Affect as amplification: some modifications in theory,' in *Emotion: Theory, Research, and Experience*, eds R. Plutchik and H. Kellerman (New York: Academic Press, 1980), pp. 141–64.

37 L.L. Berry, L.P. Carbone and S.H. Haeckel, 'Managing the total customer experience', *Sloan Management Review* (Spring 2002), pp. 85–9.

38 V.S. Folkes and V.M. Patrick, 'The positivity effect in perceptions of services: seen one, seen them all?', *Journal of Consumer Research* 30 (June 2003), pp. 125–37.

39 B.D. Keillor, G.T.M. Hult and D. Kandemir, 'A study of the service encounter in eight countries', *Journal of International Marketing* 12, no. 1 (2004), pp. 9–35.

40 D.E. Murphy, 'New East Europe retailers told to put on a happy face', *Los Angeles Times*, 26 November 1994, pp. A1, A18.

41 'Japanese put tourism on a higher plane', *International Herald Tribune*, 3 February 1992, p. 8.

42 E. Arnould, L. Price and G. Zinkhan, *Consumers*, 2nd edn (New York: McGraw-Hill, 2004).

43 For excellent coverage of buyer behaviour in organizations, see M.D. Hutt and T.W. Speh, *Business Marketing Management*, 8th edn (Mason, OH: South-Western, 2004), ch. 3.

44 Ibid., pp. 68–9.

45 Ibid., pp. 62–7.

CHAPTER 03

Customer expectations of service

❖ LEARNING OBJECTIVES

This chapter's objectives are to:

1 Recognize that customers hold different types of expectations for service performance.

2 Discuss the sources of customer expectations of service, including those that are controllable and uncontrollable by marketers.

3 Acknowledge that the types and sources of expectations are similar for end consumers and business customers, for pure service and product-related service, for experienced customers and inexperienced customers.

4 Delineate the most important current issues surrounding customer expectations.

CASE STUDY: CUSTOMER EXPECTATIONS OF VIRGIN TRAINS

Virgin Trains is a brand that has had the major challenge of bringing the UK rail industry into the twentieth century. The company is responsible for linking towns and cities across the length and breadth of the country with over 35 million passenger journeys each year. It has therefore undertaken a significant level of marketing research to identify what people expect from train travel. Many passengers have now had the experience of travelling on airlines or on overseas railways and as a result their expectations from long-distance train travel have increased. The research has highlighted the significant and highly diverse expectations that customers have of train travel. No longer is a seat and access to toilets and basic refreshments acceptable; passengers now expect – demand even – a choice of on-board meals, health-conscious snacks, reading material and entertainment. Business, and increasingly leisure, travellers also want access to the Internet and emails through on-board wireless Internet and the opportunity to use and charge their laptop and mobile. This clearly demonstrates that customer expectations of service performance do not remain constant. Organizations need to be aware of how these expectations are changing and adapt their service offering accordingly.

Source: adapted from Knight, T. and Deas, S., 'Across the tracks', *Research* (February 2006)

Importance of customer expectations

Customer **expectations** are beliefs about service delivery that serve as standards or reference points against which performance is judged. Because customers compare their perceptions of performance with these reference points when evaluating service quality, thorough knowledge about customer expectations is critical to services marketers. Knowing what the customer expects is the first and possibly most critical step in delivering good quality service. Being wrong about what customers want can mean losing a customer's business when another company hits the target exactly. Being wrong can also mean expending money, time and other resources on things that do not count to the customer. Being wrong can even mean not surviving in a fiercely competitive market.

Among the aspects of expectations that need to be explored and understood for successful services marketing are the following: what types of expectation standards do customers hold about services? What factors most influence the formation of these expectations? What role do these factors play in changing expectations? How can a service company meet or exceed customer expectations?

In this chapter we provide a framework for thinking about customer expectations.[1] The chapter is divided into three main sections: (1) the meaning and types of expected service, (2) factors that influence customer expectations of service, and (3) current issues involving customer service expectations.

Meaning and types of service expectations

To say that expectations are reference points against which service delivery is compared is only a beginning. The level of expectation can vary widely depending on the reference point the customer holds. Although most everyone has an intuitive sense of what expectations are, service marketers need a far more thorough and clear definition of expectations in order to comprehend, measure and manage them.

Let us imagine that you are planning to go to a restaurant. Figure 3.1 shows a continuum along which different possible types of service expectations can be arrayed from low to high. On the left of the continuum are different types or levels of expectations, ranging from high (top) to low (bottom). At each point we give a name to the type of expectation and illustrate what it might mean in terms of a restaurant you are considering. Note how important the expectation you held will be to your eventual assessment of the restaurant's performance. Suppose you went into the restaurant for which you held the minimum tolerable expectation, paid very little money and were served immediately with good food. Next suppose that you went to the restaurant for which

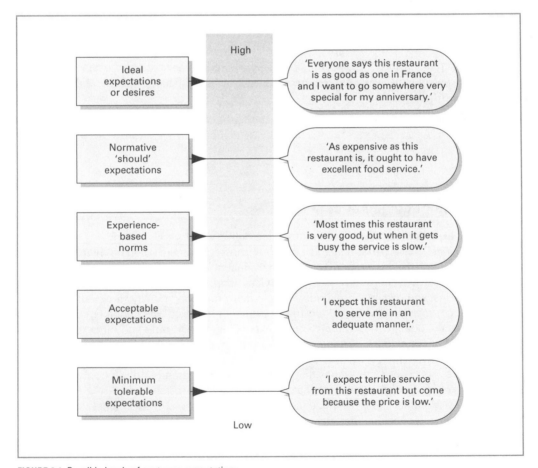

FIGURE 3.1 Possible levels of customer expectations

Source: R.K. Teas, 'Expectations, performance evaluation and consumers' perceptions of quality', *Journal of Marketing* (October 1993), pp. 18–34. Reprinted by permission of the American Marketing Association

you had the highest (ideal) expectations, paid a lot of money and were served good (but not fantastic) food. Which restaurant experience would you judge to be best? The answer is likely to depend a great deal on the reference point that you brought to the experience.

Because the idea of customer expectations is so critical to evaluation of service, we start this chapter by talking about the levels of expectations.

Expected service: levels of expectations

As we showed in Figure 3.1, customers hold different types of expectations about service. For purposes of our discussion in the rest of this chapter, we focus on two types. The highest can be termed *desired service:* the level of service the customer hopes to receive – the 'wished for' level of performance. Desired service is a blend of what the customer believes 'can be' and 'should be'. For example, consumers who sign up for a computer dating service expect to find compatible, attractive, interesting people to date and perhaps even someone to marry. The expectation reflects the hopes and wishes of these consumers; without these hopes and wishes and the belief that they may be fulfilled, consumers would probably not purchase the dating service. In a similar way, you may use an online travel-planning and flight-booking site such as Expedia to book a short holiday to Venice at Easter. What are your expectations of the service? In all likelihood you want Expedia to find you a flight exactly when you want to travel and a hotel close to the key sights in Piazza San Marco at a price you can afford – because that is what you hope and wish for.

However, you probably also see that demand at Easter may constrain the availability of airline seats and hotel rooms. And not all airlines or hotels you may be interested in may have a relationship with Expedia. In this situation and in general, customers hope to achieve their service desires but recognize that this is not always possible. We call the threshold level of acceptable service *adequate service* – the level of service the customer will accept.[2] So the customer may put up with a flight at a less than ideal time and stay at a hotel further away from the key Venetian sites, if he or she really wants to travel at Easter. Adequate service represents the 'minimum tolerable expectation',[3] the bottom level of performance acceptable to the customer.

Figure 3.2 shows these two expectation standards as the upper and lower boundaries for customer expectations. This figure portrays the idea that customers assess service performance on the basis of two standard boundaries: what they desire and what they deem acceptable.

Among the intriguing questions about service expectations is whether customers hold the same or different expectation levels for service firms in the same industry. For example, are desired service expectations the same for all restaurants? Or just for all fast-food restaurants? Do the levels of adequate service expectations vary across restaurants? Consider the following quotation:

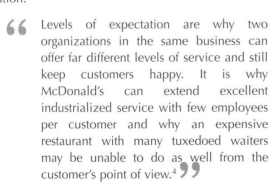 Levels of expectation are why two organizations in the same business can offer far different levels of service and still keep customers happy. It is why McDonald's can extend excellent industrialized service with few employees per customer and why an expensive restaurant with many tuxedoed waiters may be unable to do as well from the customer's point of view.[4]

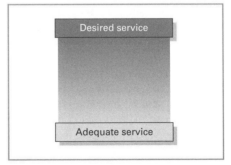

FIGURE 3.2 Dual customer expectation levels

Customers typically hold similar desired expectations across categories of service, but these categories are not as broad as whole industries. Among subcategories of restaurants are expensive restaurants, ethnic restaurants, fast-food restaurants and airport restaurants. A customer's desired service expectation for fast-food restaurants is quick, convenient, tasty food in a clean setting. The desired service expectation for an expensive restaurant, on the other hand, usually involves elegant surroundings, gracious employees, candlelight and fine food. In essence, desired service expectations seem to be the same for service providers within industry categories or subcategories that are viewed as similar by customers.

The adequate service expectation level, on the other hand, may vary for different firms within a category or subcategory. Within fast-food restaurants, a customer may hold a higher expectation for McDonald's than for Burger King, having experienced consistent service at McDonald's over time and somewhat inconsistent service at Burger King. It is possible, therefore, that a customer can be more disappointed with service from McDonald's than from Burger King even though the actual level of service at McDonald's may be higher than the level at Burger King.

The zone of tolerance

As we discussed in earlier chapters of this textbook, services are heterogeneous in that performance may vary across providers, across employees from the same provider, and even with the same service employee. The extent to which customers recognize and are willing to accept this variation is called the *zone of tolerance* and is shown in Figure 3.3. If service drops below adequate service – the minimum level considered acceptable – customers will be frustrated and their satisfaction with the company will be undermined. If service performance is higher than the zone of tolerance at the top end – where performance exceeds desired service –

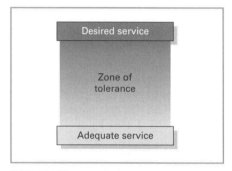

FIGURE 3.3 The zone of tolerance

customers will be very pleased and probably quite surprised as well. You might consider the zone of tolerance as the range or window in which customers do not particularly notice service performance. When it falls outside the range (either very low or very high), the service gets the customer's attention in either a positive or negative way. As an example, consider the service at a checkout queue in a grocery store. Most customers hold a range of acceptable times for this service encounter – probably somewhere between five and 10 minutes. If service consumes that period of time, customers probably do not pay much attention to the wait. If a customer enters the line and finds sufficient checkout personnel to serve him or her in the first two or three minutes, he or she may notice the service and judge it as excellent. On the other hand, if a customer has to wait in line for 15 minutes, he or she may begin to grumble and look at his or her watch. The longer the wait is below the zone of tolerance, the more frustrated the customer becomes.

Customers' service expectations are characterized by a range of levels (like those shown in Figure 3.2), bounded by desired and adequate service, rather than a single level. This tolerance zone, representing the difference between desired service and the level of service considered adequate, can expand and contract within a customer. An airline customer's zone of tolerance will narrow when he or she is running late and is concerned about making it in time for his or her plane. A minute seems much longer, and the customer's adequate service level increases. On the other hand, a customer who arrives at the airport early may have a larger tolerance zone, making the wait in line far less noticeable than when he or she is pressed for time. This example shows that the marketer must understand not just the size and boundary levels for the zone of tolerance but also when and how the tolerance zone fluctuates with a given customer.

Different customers possess different zones of tolerance

Another aspect of variability in the range of reasonable services is that different customers possess different tolerance zones. Some customers have narrow zones of tolerance, requiring a tighter range of service from providers, whereas other customers allow a greater range of service. For example, very busy customers would likely always be pressed for time, desire short wait times in general and hold a constrained range for the length of acceptable wait times. When it comes to meeting plumbers or repair personnel at their home for problems with domestic appliance, customers who work outside the home have a more restricted window of acceptable time duration for that appointment than do customers who work in their homes or do not work at all.

An individual customer's zone of tolerance increases or decreases depending on a number of factors, including company-controlled factors such as price. When prices increase, customers tend to be less tolerant of poor service. In this case, the zone of tolerance decreases because the adequate service level shifts upward. Later in this chapter we will describe many different factors, some company controlled and others customer controlled, that lead to the narrowing or widening of the tolerance zone.

Zones of tolerance vary for service dimensions

Customers' tolerance zones also vary for different service attributes or dimensions. The more important the factor, the narrower the zone of tolerance is likely to be. In general, customers are likely to be less tolerant about unreliable service (broken promises or service errors) than other service deficiencies, which means that they have higher expectations for this factor. In addition

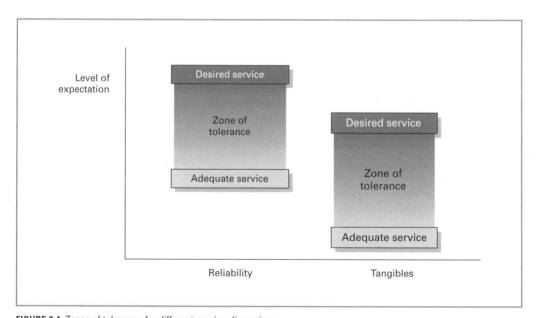

FIGURE 3.4 Zones of tolerance for different service dimensions

Source: L.L. Berry, A. Parasuraman and V.A. Zeithaml, 'Ten lessons for improving service quality', Marketing Science Institute, Report No. 93-104 (May 1993)

to higher expectations for the most important service dimensions and attributes, customers are likely to be less willing to relax these expectations than those for less important factors, making the zone of tolerance for the most important service dimension smaller and the desired and adequate service levels higher.[5] Figure 3.4 portrays the likely difference in tolerance zones for the most important and the least important factors.[6]

The fluctuation in the individual customer's zone of tolerance is more a function of changes in the adequate service level, which moves readily up and down because of situational circumstances, than in the desired service level, which tends to move upward incrementally because of accumulated experiences. Desired service is relatively idiosyncratic and stable compared with adequate service, which moves up and down and in response to competition and other factors. Fluctuation in the zone of tolerance can be likened to an accordion's movement, but with most of the movement coming from one side (the adequate service level) rather than the other (the desired service level).

In summary, we can express the boundaries of customer expectations of service with two different levels of expectations: desired service and adequate service. The desired service level is less subject to change than the adequate service level. A zone of tolerance separates these two levels. This zone of tolerance varies across customers and expands or contracts with the same customer.

Factors that influence customer expectations of service

Because expectations play such a critical role in customer evaluation of services, marketers need and want to understand the factors that shape them. Marketers would also like to have control over these factors as well, but many of the forces that influence customer expectations are uncontrollable. In this section of the chapter we try to separate the many influences on customer expectations.

Sources of desired service expectations

As shown in Figure 3.5, the two largest influences on desired service level are personal needs and philosophies about service. *Personal needs*, those states or conditions essential to the physical or psychological well-being of the customer, are pivotal factors that shape what customers desire in service. Personal needs can fall into many categories, including physical, social, psychological and functional. A cinema-goer who regularly goes to see films straight from work, and is therefore thirsty and hungry, hopes and desires that the food and drink counters at the cinema will have short queues and attentive staff, whereas a cinema-goer who regularly has dinner elsewhere has a low or zero level of desired service from the food and drink counters. A customer with high social and dependency needs

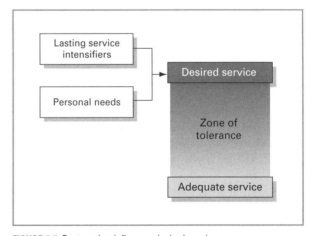

FIGURE 3.5 Factors that influence desired service

may have relatively high expectations for a hotel's ancillary services, hoping, for example, that the hotel has a bar with live music and dancing.

Some customers are more demanding than others, having greater sensitivity to, and higher expectations of, service. ***Lasting service intensifiers*** are individual, stable factors that lead the customer to a heightened sensitivity to service. One of the most important of these factors can be called *derived service expectations*, which occur when customer expectations are driven by another person or group of people. A niece from a big family who is planning a ninetieth birthday party for a favourite aunt is representing the entire family in selecting a restaurant for a successful celebration. Her needs are driven in part by the derived expectations from the other family members. A parent choosing a vacation for the family, a spouse selecting a home-cleaning service, an employee choosing an office for the firm – all these customers' individual expectations are intensified because they represent and must answer to other parties who will receive the service. In the context of business-to-business service, customer expectations are driven by the expectations of their own customers. The head of an information technology department in an insurance company, who is the business customer of a large computer company, has expectations based on those of the insurance customers he or she serves: when the computer equipment is down, his or her customers complain. The need to keep the system up and running is not just his or her own expectation but is derived from the pressure of customers.

Business-to-business customers may also derive their expectations from their managers and supervisors. Employees of a marketing research department may speed up project cycles (increase their expectations for speed of delivery) when pressured by their management to deliver the study results. Purchasing agents may increase demands for faster delivery at lower costs when company management is emphasizing cost reduction in the company.

Another lasting service intensifier is *personal service philosophy* – the customer's underlying generic attitude about the meaning of service and the proper conduct of service providers. If you have ever been employed as a member of waiting staff in a restaurant, you are likely to have standards for restaurant service that were shaped by your training and experience in that role. You might, for example, believe that waiters should not keep customers waiting longer than 15 minutes to take their orders. Knowing the way a kitchen operates, you may be less tolerant of lukewarm food or errors in the order than customers who have not held the role of waiter or waitress. In general, customers who are themselves in service businesses or have worked for them in the past seem to have especially strong service philosophies.

To the extent that customers have personal philosophies about service provision, their expectations of service providers will be intensified. Personal service philosophies and derived service expectations elevate the level of desired service.

Sources of adequate service expectations

A different set of determinants affects adequate service, the level of service the customer finds acceptable. In general, these influences are short term and tend to fluctuate more than the factors that influence desired service. In this section we explain the five factors shown in Figure 3.6 that influence adequate service: (1) **temporary service intensifiers**, (2) perceived service alternatives, (3) customer **self-perceived service role**, (4) situational factors, and (5) predicted service.

The first set of elements, *temporary service intensifiers*, consists of short-term, individual factors that make a customer more aware of the need for service. Personal emergency situations in which service is urgently needed (such as an accident and the need for car insurance or a breakdown in office equipment during a busy period) raise the level of adequate service expectation, particularly the level of responsiveness required and considered acceptable. A mail-order company that depends on freephone numbers for receiving all customer orders will tend to be

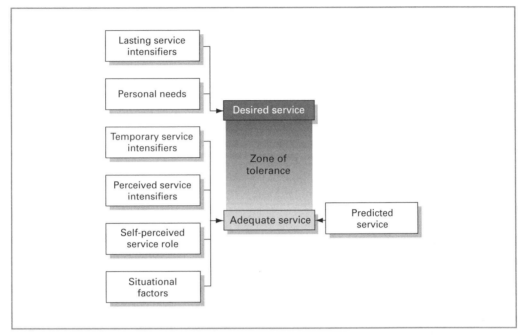

FIGURE 3.6 Factors that influence adequate service

more demanding of the telephone service during peak periods of the week, month and year. Any system breakdown or lack of clarity on the lines will be tolerated less during these intense periods than at other times.

Problems with the initial service can also lead to heightened expectations. Performing a service right the first time is very important because customers value service reliability above all other dimensions. If the service fails in the recovery phase, putting it right the second time (that is, being reliable in service recovery) is even more critical than it was the first time. Car repair service provides a case in point. If a problem with your car's brakes sends you to a car repair provider, you expect the company to fix the brakes. If you experience further problems with the brakes after the repair (a not uncommon situation with car repairs), your adequate service level will increase. In these and other situations where temporary service intensifiers are present, the level of adequate service will increase and the zone of tolerance will narrow.

Perceived service alternatives are other providers from whom the customer can obtain service. If customers have multiple service providers to choose from, or if they can provide the service for themselves (such as lawn care or personal grooming), their levels of adequate service are higher than those of customers who believe it is not possible to get better service elsewhere. An airline customer who lives in a provincial town with a small airport, for example, has a reduced set of options in airline travel. This customer will be more tolerant of the service performance of the carriers in the town because few alternatives exist. He or she will accept the scheduling and lower levels of service more than will the customer in a big city who has myriad flights and airlines to choose from. The customer's perception that service alternatives exist raises the level of adequate service and narrows the zone of tolerance.

It is important that service marketers fully understand the complete set of options that customers view as perceived alternatives. In the provincial town, small airport example just discussed, the set of alternatives from the customer's point of view is likely to include more than just other airlines: taxi service to a nearby large city, rail service or driving. In general, service marketers must discover the alternatives that the customer views as comparable rather than those in the company's competitive set.

A third factor affecting the level of adequate service is the *customer's self-perceived service role*. We define this as customer perceptions of the degree to which customers exert an influence on the level of service they receive. In other words, customers' expectations are partly shaped by how well they believe they are performing their own roles in service delivery.[7] One role of the customer is to specify the level of service expected. A customer who is very explicit with a waiter about how rare he or she wants his or her steak cooked in a restaurant will probably be more dissatisfied if the meat comes to the table overcooked than a customer who does not articulate the degree of cooking expected. The customer's active participation in the service also affects this factor. A customer who does not get his or her car serviced regularly is likely to be more lenient on the car manufacturer when he or she experiences problems than one who conscientiously follows the manufacturers service schedules.

A final way the customer defines his or her role is in assuming the responsibility for complaining when service is poor. A dissatisfied customer who complains will be less tolerant than one who does not voice his or her concerns. A car insurance customer acknowledged responsibility in service provision this way: 'You can't blame it all on the insurance broker. You need to be responsible too and let the broker know what exactly you want.'

Customers' zones of tolerance seem to expand when they sense they are not fulfilling their roles. When, on the other hand, customers believe they are doing their part in delivery, their expectations of adequate service are heightened and the zone of tolerance contracts. The comment of a car repair customer illustrates this: 'Service staff don't listen when you tell them what is wrong. I now prepare a written list of problems in advance, take it to the car dealership, and tell them to fix these.' This customer will expect more than one who did not prepare so well.

Levels of adequate service are also influenced by *situational factors*, defined as service performance conditions that customers view as beyond the control of the service provider. For example, where personal emergencies such as serious car accidents would likely intensify customer service expectations of insurance companies (because they are temporary service intensifiers), catastrophes that affect a large number of people at one time (floods or storms) may lower service expectations because customers recognize that insurers are inundated with demands for their services. Customers who recognize that situational factors are not the fault of the service company may accept lower levels of adequate service given the context. In general, situational factors temporarily lower the level of adequate service, widening the zone of tolerance.

The final factor that influences adequate service is *predicted service* (Figure 3.7), the level of service that customers believe they are likely to get. This type of service expectation can be viewed as predictions made by customers about what is likely to happen during an impending transaction or exchange. Predicted service performance implies some objective calculation of the probability of performance or estimate of anticipated service performance level. If customers predict good service, their levels of adequate service are likely to be higher than if they predict poor service. For example, travellers may expect poorer service from some of the no-frills airlines such as Ryanair or easyJet in comparison to some of the full-cost airlines (British Airways, KLM, Air France). This prediction will mean that higher standards for adequate service will exist in the full-cost airlines. On the other hand, customers of mobile phone companies may know that the companies' call centre operations will provide poor service around Christmas time when myriad people are setting up the mobiles that they have received as gifts. In this case, levels of adequate service decrease and zones of tolerance widen.

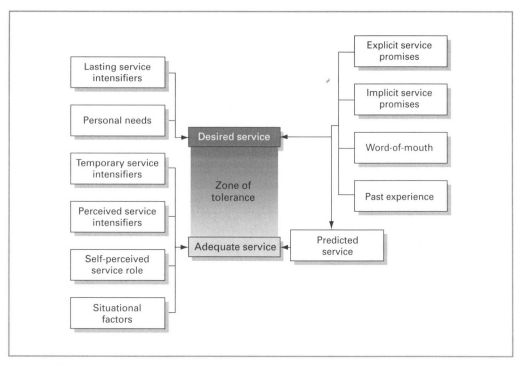

FIGURE 3.7 Factors that influence desired and predicted service

Predicted service is typically an estimate or calculation of the service that a customer will receive in an individual transaction rather than in the overall relationship with a service provider. Whereas desired and adequate service expectations are global assessments comprising many individual service transactions, predicted service is almost always an estimate of what will happen in the next service encounter or transaction that the customer experiences. For this reason, predicted service is viewed in this model as an influencer of adequate service.

Because predictions are about individual service encounters, they are likely to be more concrete and specific than the types of expectation levels customers hold for adequate service or desired service. For example, your predicted service expectations about the length of time you will spend in the waiting room the next time you visit your doctor will likely be expressed in terms of the number of minutes or hours you have spent in the waiting room on your last visit.

Service encounter expectations versus overall service expectations

In Chapter 4 we discuss the difference between overall service quality and service encounter quality, viewing the service encounter as a discrete event occurring over a definable period of time (such as a particular hotel stay or a particular check-in experience at the hotel). Customers hold expectations of the quality of each service encounter, just as they hold expectations about the overall service quality of a firm. When the expectations are about individual service encounters, they are likely to be more specific and concrete (such as the number of minutes one must wait for a receptionist) than the expectations about overall service quality (like speedy service).

Sources of both desired and predicted service expectations

When consumers are interested in purchasing services, they are likely to seek or take in information from several different sources. For example, they may call a store, ask a friend or deliberately track newspaper advertisements to find the needed service at the lowest price. They may also receive service information by watching television or hearing an unsolicited comment from a colleague about a service that was performed well. In addition to these active and passive types of external search for information, consumers may conduct an internal search by reviewing the information held in their memory about the service. This section discusses one internal and three external factors that influence both desired service and predicted service expectations: (1) **explicit service promises**, (2) **implicit service promises**, (3) word-of-mouth communications and (4) past experience.

Explicit service promises are personal and non-personal statements about the service made by the organization to customers. The statements are personal when they are communicated by salespeople or service or repair personnel; they are non-personal when they come from advertising, brochures and other written publications. Explicit service promises are one of the few influences on expectations that are completely in the control of the service provider.

Promising exactly what will ultimately be delivered would seem a logical and appropriate way to manage customer expectations and ensure that reality fits the promises. However, companies and the personnel who represent them often deliberately over-promise to obtain business or inadvertently over-promise by stating their best estimates about delivery of a service in the future. In addition to over-promising, company representatives simply do not always know the appropriate promises to make because services are often customized and therefore not easily defined and repeated; the representative may not know when or in what final form the service will be delivered.

All types of explicit service promises have a direct effect on desired service expectation. If the sales visit portrays a banking service that is available 24 hours a day, the customer's desires for that service (as well as the service of competitors) will be shaped by this promise.

Service spotlight

The Ibis hotel chain promises to solve any problem you have with your room or hotel in 15 minutes otherwise they will not charge you for your stay.

Read their Quality Commitment on line at www.ibishotels.com.

Explicit service promises influence the levels of both desired service and predicted service. They shape what customers desire in general as well as what they predict will happen in the next service encounter from a particular service provider or in a certain service encounter.

Implicit service promises are service-related cues other than explicit promises that lead to inferences about what the service should and will be like. These quality cues are dominated by price and the tangibles associated with the service. In general, the higher the price and the more impressive the tangibles, the more a customer will expect from the service. Consider a customer who shops for insurance, finding two firms charging radically different prices. He or she may infer that the firm with the higher price should and will provide higher-quality service and better coverage. Similarly, a customer who stays at a five-star hotel is likely to desire and predict a higher standard of service than from a hotel with less impressive facilities.

The importance of *word-of-mouth communication* in shaping expectations of service is well documented.[8] These personal and sometimes non-personal statements made by parties other than the organization convey to customers what the service will be like and influence both predicted and desired service. Word-of-mouth communication carries particular weight as an information source because it is perceived as unbiased. Word of mouth tends to be very important in services that are difficult to evaluate before purchase and before direct experience of them. Experts (including *consumer reports,* friends and family) are also word-of-mouth sources that can affect the levels of desired and predicted service.

Past experience, the customer's previous exposure to service that is relevant to the focal service, is another force in shaping predictions and desires. The service relevant for prediction can be previous exposure to the focal firm's service. For example, you probably compare each stay in a particular hotel with all previous stays in that hotel. But past experience with the focal hotel is likely to be a very limited view of your past experience. You may also compare each stay with your experiences in other hotels and hotel chains. Customers also compare across industries: hospital patients, for example, compare hospital stays against the standard of hotel visits. In a general sense, past experience may incorporate previous experience with the focal brand, typical performance of a favorite brand, experience with the brand last purchased or the top-selling brand, and the average performance a customer believes represents a group of similar brands.[9]

How might a manager of a service organization use the information we have developed in this chapter to create, improve, or market services? First, managers need to know the pertinent expectation sources and their relative importance for a customer population, a customer segment and, perhaps, even a particular customer. They need to know, for instance, the relative weight of word of mouth, explicit service promises and implicit service promises in shaping desired service and predicted service. Some of these sources are more stable and permanent in their influence (such as lasting service intensifiers and personal needs) than the others, which fluctuate considerably over time (like perceived service alternatives and situational factors).

The different sources vary in terms of their credibility as well as their potential to be influenced by the marketer. Table 3.1 shows the breakdown of various factors and how services marketers can influence them. Chapter 16 details these and other strategies that services marketers can use to match delivery to promises and thereby manage expectations.

Factor	Possible influence strategies
Explicit service promises	Make realistic and accurate promises that reflect the service actually delivered rather than an idealized version of the service.
	Ask contact people for feedback on the accuracy of promises made in advertising and personal selling.
	Avoid engaging in price or advertising wars with competitors because they take the focus off customers and escalate promises beyond the level at which they can be met.
	Formalize service promises through a service guarantee that focuses company employees on the promise and that provides feedback on the number of times promises are not fulfilled.
Implicit service promises	Ensure that service tangibles accurately reflect the type and level of service provided.
	Ensure that price premiums can be justified by higher levels of performance by the company on important customer attributes.
Lasting service intensifiers	Use market research to determine sources of derived service expectations and their requirements. Focus advertising and marketing strategy on ways the service allows the focal customer to satisfy the requirements of the influencing customer.
	Use market research to profile personal service philosophies of customers and use this information in designing and delivering services.
Personal needs	Educate customers on ways the service addresses their needs.
Temporary service intensifiers	Increase service delivery during peak periods or in emergencies.
Perceived service alternatives	Be fully aware of competitive offerings, and where possible and appropriate, match them.
Self-perceived service role	Educate customers to understand their roles and perform them better.
Word-of-mouth communications	Simulate word of mouth in advertising by using testimonials and opinion leaders.
	Identify influencers and opinion leaders for the service and concentrate marketing efforts on them.
	Use incentives with existing customers to encourage them to say positive things about the service.
Past experience	Use marketing research to profile customers' previous experience with similar services.
Situational factors	Use service guarantees to assure customers about service recovery regardless of the situational factors that occur.
Predicted service	Tell customers when service provision is higher than what can normally be expected so that predictions of future service encounters will not be inflated.

TABLE 3.1 How services marketers can influence factors

Issues involving customer service expectations

The following issues represent current topics of particular interest to service marketers about customer expectations. In this section we discuss five of the most frequently asked questions about customer expectations:

1 What does a service marketer do if customer expectations are 'unrealistic'?

2 Should a company try to delight the customer?

3 How does a company exceed customer service expectations?

4 Do customer service expectations continually escalate?

5 How does a service company stay ahead of competition in meeting customer expectations?

What does a services marketer do if customer expectations are 'unrealistic'?

One inhibitor to learning about customer expectations is management's and employees' fear of asking. This apprehension often stems from the belief that customer expectations will be extravagant and unrealistic and that by asking about them a company will set itself up for even loftier expectation levels (that is, 'unrealistic' levels). Compelling evidence, shown in Table 3.2, suggests that customers' main expectations of service are quite simple and basic: 'Simply put, customers expect service companies to do what they are supposed to do. They expect fundamentals, not fanciness; performance, not empty promises.'[10] Customers want service to be delivered as promised. They want planes to take off on time, hotel rooms to be clean, food to be hot and service providers to show up when scheduled. Unfortunately, many service customers are disappointed and let down by companies' inability to meet these basic service expectations.

Asking customers about their expectations does not so much raise the levels of the expectations themselves but rather heightens the belief that the company will do something with the information that surfaces. Arguably the worst thing a company can do is show a strong interest in understanding what customers expect and then never act on the information. At a minimum, a company should acknowledge to customers that it has received and heard their input and that it will expend effort trying to address their issues. The company may not be able to – and indeed does not always have to – deliver to expressed expectations. An alternative and appropriate response would be to let customers know the reasons that desired service is not being provided at the present time and describe the efforts planned to address them. Another approach could be a campaign to educate customers about ways to use and improve the service they currently receive. Giving customers progress updates as service is improved to address their needs and desires is sensible because it allows the company to get credit for incremental efforts to improve service.

Some observers recommend deliberately under-promising the service to increase the likelihood of meeting or **exceeding customer expectations**.[11] While under-promising makes service expectations more realistic, thereby narrowing the gap between expectations and perceptions, it also may reduce the competitive appeal of the offer. Some research has indicated that under-promising may also have the inadvertent effect of lowering customer *perceptions* of service, particularly in situations in which customers have little experience with a service.[12] In these situations customer expectations may be self-fulfilling; that is, if the customer goes into the service experience expecting good service, he or she will focus on the aspects of service provision that are positive, but if he or she expects low service she may focus on the negative. Thus a sales-

Type of service	Type of customer	Principal expectations
Car repair	Consumers	Be competent. ('Fix it right the first time.')
		Explain things. ('Explain why I need the suggested repairs – provide an itemized list.')
		Be respectful. ('Don't treat me like a dumb female.')
Car insurance	Consumers	Keep me informed. ('I shouldn't have to learn about insurance law changes from the newspaper.')
		Be on my side. ('I don't want them to treat me like a criminal just because I have a claim.')
		Play fair. ('Don't drop me when something goes wrong.')
		Protect me from catastrophe. ('Make sure my family is provided for in the event of a major accident.')
		Provide prompt service. ('I want fast settlement of claims.')
Hotel	Consumers	Provide a clean room. ('Don't have a deep-pile carpet that can't be completely cleaned … you can literally see germs down there.')
		Provide a secure room. ('Good bolts and peephole on door.') Treat me like a guest. ('It is almost like they're looking you over to decide whether they're going to let you have a room.')
		Keep your promise. ('They said the room would be ready, but it wasn't at the promised time.')
Property and accident insurance	Business customers	Fulfil obligations. ('Pay up.')
		Learn my business and work with me. ('I expect them to know me and my company.')
		Protect me from catastrophe. ('They should cover my risk exposure so there is no single big loss.')
		Provide prompt service. ('Fast claim service.')
Equipment repair	Business customers	Share my sense of urgency. ('Speed of response. One time I had to buy a second piece of equipment because of the huge downtime with the first piece.')
		Be competent. ('Sometimes you are quoting stuff from their instruction manuals to their own people and they don't even know what it means.')
		Be prepared. ('Have all the parts ready.')
Vehicle rental/leasing	Business customers	Keep the equipment running. ('Need to have equipment working all of the time – that is the key.')
		Be flexible. ('The leasing company should have the flexibility to rent us equipment when we need it.')
		Provide full service. ('Get rid of all the paperwork and headaches.')

TABLE 3.2 Service customers want the basics

Source : adapted from 'Understanding customer expectations of service' by A. Parasuraman, L.L. Berry and V.A. Zeithaml, MIT Sloan Management Review (Spring 1991), pp. 33–46, by permission of publisher. Copyright © 1991 by Massachusetts Institute of Technology. All rights reserved

person who sells to a customer with a realistic promise may lose the sale to another who inflates the offering. In Chapter 16 we describe various techniques for controlling a firm's promises, but for now consider two options. First, if the salesperson knows that no competitor can meet an inflated sales promise in an industry, he or she could point that fact out to the customer, thereby refuting the promise made by competitive salespeople.

The second option is for the provider to follow a sale with a 'reality check' about service delivery. I bought a new house from a builder. Typical sales promises were made about the quality of the home, some less than accurate, in order to make the sale. Before being given the keys to the new house, the builder and I conducted a final check on everything. At the front door, the builder turned to me and pointed out that each new home has between 3000 and 5000 individual elements and that in his experience the typical new home had 100 to 150 defects. Armed with this reality check, I thought the 32 defects found in my house seemed minor. Consider my response in the absence of that reality check.

Should a company try to delight the customer?

Some management consultants urge service companies to 'delight' customers to gain a competitive edge. The *delight* that they refer to is a profoundly positive emotional state that results from having one's expectations exceeded to a surprising degree.[13] One author describes the type of service that results in delight as 'positively outrageous service' – that which is unexpected, random, extraordinary and disproportionately positive.[14]

A way that managers can conceive of delight is to consider product and service features in terms of concentric rings.[15] The innermost bull's-eye refers to attributes that are central to the basic function of the product or service, called *musts*. Their provision is not particularly noticeable, but their absence would be. Around the musts is a ring called *satisfiers*: features that have the potential to further satisfaction beyond the basic function of the product. At the next and final outer level are *delights*, or product features that are unexpected and surprisingly enjoyable. These features are things that consumers would not expect to find and they are therefore highly surprised and sometimes excited when they receive them. For example, a student may consider the musts to consist of lecturers, rooms, class outlines and lectures/seminars. Satisfiers might include lecturers who are entertaining or friendly, interesting lectures and good audiovisual aids. A delight might include a free textbook for students signing up for the course.

Delighting customers may seem like a good idea, but this level of service provision comes with extra effort and cost to the firm. Therefore, the benefits of providing delight must be weighed. Among the considerations are the staying power and competitive implications of delight.

Staying power involves the question of how long a company can expect an experience of delight to maintain the consumer's attention. If it is fleeting and the customer forgets it immediately, it may not be worth the cost. Alternatively, if the customer remembers the delight and adjusts his or her level of expectation upward accordingly, it will cost the company more just to satisfy, effectively raising the bar for the future. Recent research indicates that delighting customers does in fact raise expectations and make it more difficult for a company to satisfy customers in the future.[16]

The competitive implication of delight relates to its impact on expectations of other firms in the same industry. If a competitor in the same industry is unable to copy the delight strategy, it will be disadvantaged by the consumer's increased expectations. If students were offered that free textbook in one of their classes, they might then expect to receive one in each of their classes. Those classes not offering the free textbook might not have high enrolment levels compared with the delighting class. If a competitor can easily copy the delight strategy, however, neither firm benefits (although the consumer does!), and all firms may be hurt because their costs increase and profits erode. The implication is that if companies choose to delight, they should do so in areas that cannot be copied by other firms.

How does a company exceed customer service expectations?

Many companies today talk about exceeding customer expectations – delighting and surprising them by giving more than they expect. This philosophy raises the question, Should a service provider try simply to meet customer expectations or to exceed them?

First, it is essential to recognize that exceeding customer expectations of the basics is virtually impossible. Honouring promises – having the reserved room available, meeting deadlines, showing up for meetings, delivering the core service – is what the company is supposed to do. Companies are *supposed* to be accurate and dependable and provide the service they promised to provide.[17] As you examine the examples of basic expectations of customers in Figure 3.9, ask yourself if a provider doing any of these things would delight you. The conclusion you should reach is that it is very difficult to surprise or delight customers consistently by delivering reliable service.

How, then, does a company delight its customers and exceed their expectations? In virtually any service, developing a customer relationship is one approach for exceeding service expectations. Ritz-Carlton Hotels provides highly personalized attention to its customers. In each hotel within the chain, a special organization exists called guest recognition. This special function uses the CLASS database to remember over 800 000 guests and generate information for all appropriate staff. It stores: likes/dislikes; previous difficulties; family interests; personal interests; preferred credit card; recency/frequency of use of the hotel; lifetime usage/amount of purchase. In this way staff are able to understand what is 'new or different' about an individual customer.[18]

Another way to exceed expectations is to deliberately under-promise the service to increase the likelihood of exceeding customer expectations. The strategy is to under-promise and over-deliver. If every service promise is less than what will eventually happen, customers can be delighted frequently. Although this reasoning sounds logical, a firm should weigh two potential problems before using this strategy.

First, customers with whom a company interacts regularly are likely to notice the under-promising and adjust their expectations accordingly, negating the desired benefit of delight. Customers will recognize the pattern of under-promising when time after time a firm promises one delivery time (we cannot get that to you before 5 p.m. tomorrow) yet constantly exceeds it (by delivering at noon).

Service spotlight

easyJet produces a timetable that suggests that flights will be longer than they actually are, allowing them to give the impression that their timekeeping is good as most flights will arrive early or on time. However, over time regular customers may come to expect an early arrival and be disappointed when this does not happen.

Second, under-promising in a sales situation potentially reduces the competitive appeal of an offering and must be tempered by what competition is offering. When competitive pressures are high, presenting a cohesive and honest portrayal of the service both explicitly (through advertising and personal selling) and implicitly (such as through the appearance of service facilities and the price of the service) may be wiser. Controlling the firm's promises, making them consistent with the deliverable service, may be a better approach.

A final way to exceed expectations without raising them in the future is to position unusual service as unique rather than the standard. Emphasizing that because of special circumstances or a special situation, the service will be altered from the norm. For example, a restaurant may offer customers a free dessert by claimimg that the chef is trying out some new recipes/creations.

Do customer service expectations continually escalate?

As we illustrated in the beginning of this chapter, customer service expectations are dynamic. In the credit card industry, as in many competitive service industries, battling companies seek to outdo each other and thereby raise the level of service above that of competing companies. Service expectations – in this case adequate service expectations – rise as quickly as service delivery or promises rise. In a highly competitive and rapidly changing industry, expectations can thus rise quickly. For this reason companies need continually to monitor adequate service expectations – the more turbulent the industry, the more frequent the monitoring needed.

Desired service expectations, on the other hand, are far more stable. Because they are driven by more enduring factors, such as personal needs and lasting service intensifiers, they tend to be high to begin with and remain high.

How does a service company stay ahead of competition in meeting customer expectations?

All else being equal, a company's goal is to meet customer expectations better than its competitors can. Given the fact that adequate service expectations change rapidly in a turbulent environment, how can a company ensure that it stays ahead of competition?

The adequate service level reflects the minimum performance level expected by customers after they consider a variety of personal and external factors (Figure 3.6), including the availability of service options from other providers. Companies whose service performance falls short of this level are clearly at a competitive disadvantage, with the disadvantage escalating as the gap widens. These companies' customers may well be 'reluctant' customers, ready to take their business elsewhere the moment they perceive an alternative.

If they are to use service quality for competitive advantage, companies must perform above the adequate service level. This level, however, may signal only a temporary advantage. Customers' adequate service levels, which are less stable than desired service levels, will rise rapidly when competitors promise and deliver a higher level of service. If a company's level of service is barely above the adequate service level to begin with, a competitor can quickly erode that advantage. Companies currently performing in the region of competitive advantage must stay alert to the need for service increases to meet or beat competition.

To develop a true customer franchise – immutable customer loyalty – companies must not only consistently exceed the adequate service level but also reach the desired service level. Exceptional service can intensify customers' loyalty to a point at which they are impervious to competitive options.

Summary

Using a conceptual framework of the nature and determinants of customer expectations of service, we showed in this chapter that customers hold different types of service expectations: (1) desired service, which reflects what customers want; (2) adequate service, or what customers are willing to accept; and (3) predicted service, or what customers believe they are likely to get. These different levels of service are reflected within the customer's zone of tolerance which establishes the variability in the service delivery that the customer is willing to accept.

Customer expectations and tolerance levels are influenced by a variety of factors. The types and sources of these are the same for end consumers and business customers, for pure service and product-related service, and for experienced customers and inexperienced customers.

Key concepts

Exceeding customer expectations	68
Expectations	55
Explicit and implicit service promises	65
Self-perceived service role	61
Temporary and lasting service intensifiers	61
Zone of tolerance	58

Further reading

Anderson, E. and Sullivan, M. (1993) 'The antecedents and consequences of customer satisfaction', *Marketing Science*, 12, 125–43.

Bebko, C.P. (2000) 'Service intangibility and its impact on customer expectations of service quality', *Journal of Services Marketing*, 14(1), 9–26.

Hubbert, A.R., Sehorn, A.G. and Brown, S.W. (1995) 'Service expectations: the consumer versus the provider', *International Journal of Service Industries Journal*, 6(1), 6–21.

Johnson, C. and Mathews, B.P. (1997) 'The influence of experience on service expectations', *International Journal of Service Industries Management*, 8(4), 290–305.

O'Neill, M., Wright, C. and Palmer, A. (2003) 'Disconfirming user expectations of the online service experience: inferred versus direct disconfirmation modeling', *Internet Research*, 13(4), 281–296.

Yap, K.B. and Sweeney, J.C. (2007) 'Zone of tolerance moderates the service quality–outcome relationship?', *Journal of Services Marketing*, 21(2), 137–48.

Discussion questions

1 What is the difference between desired service and adequate service? Why would a services marketer need to understand both types of service expectations?

2 Consider a recent service purchase that you have made. Which of the factors influencing expectations were the most important in your decision? Why?

3 Why are desired service expectations more stable than adequate service expectations?

4 How do the technology changes influence customer expectations?

5 Describe several instances in which a service company's explicit service promises were inflated and led you to be disappointed with the service outcome.

6 Consider a small business preparing to buy a computer system. Which of the influences on customer expectations do you believe will be pivotal? Which factors will have the most influence? Which factors will have the least importance in this decision?

7 Do you believe that any of your service expectations are unrealistic? Which ones? Should a service marketer try to address unrealistic customer expectations?

8 In your opinion, what service companies have effectively built customer franchises (immutable customer loyalty)?

9 Intuitively, it would seem that managers would want their customers to have wide tolerance zones for service. But if customers do have these wide zones of tolerance for service, is it more difficult for firms with superior service to earn customer loyalty? Would superior service firms be better off to attempt to narrow customers' tolerance zones to reduce the competitive appeal of mediocre providers?

10 Should service marketers delight their customers?

 ## Exercises

1 Keep a service journal for a day and document your use of services. Ask yourself before each service encounter to indicate your predicted service of that encounter. After the encounter, note whether your expectations were met or exceeded. How does the answer to this question relate to your desire to do business with that service firm again?

2 List five incidents in which a service company has exceeded your expectations. How did you react to the service? Did these incidents change the way you viewed subsequent interactions with the companies? In what way?

Notes

[1] The model on which this chapter is based is taken from V.A. Zeithaml, L.L. Berry and A. Parasuraman, 'The nature and determinants of customer expectations of service', *Journal of the Academy of Marketing Science* 21, no. 1 (1993), pp. 1–12.

[2] R.B. Woodruff, E.R. Cadotte and R.L. Jenkins, 'Expectations and norms in models of consumer satisfaction', *Journal of Marketing Research* 24 (August 1987), pp. 305–14.

3 J.A. Miller, 'Studying satisfaction, modifying models, eliciting expectations, posing problems, and making meaningful measurements', in *Conceptualization and Measurement of Consumer Satisfaction and Dissatisfaction*, ed. H.K. Hunt (Bloomington, IN: Indiana University School of Business, 1977), pp. 72–91.

4 W.H. Davidow and B. Uttal, 'Service companies: focus or falter', *Harvard Business Review* (July–August 1989), pp. 77–85.

5 A. Parasuraman, L.L. Berry and V.A. Zeithaml, 'Understanding customer expectations of service', *Sloan Management Review* 32 (Spring 1991), p. 42.

6 L.L. Berry, A. Parasuraman and V.A. Zeithaml, 'Ten lessons for improving service quality', *Marketing Science Institute*, Report No. 93–104 (May 1993).

7 D. Bowen, 'Leadership aspects and reward systems of customer satisfaction', speech given at CTM Customer Satisfaction Conference, Los Angeles, 17 March 1989.

8 D.L. Davis, J.G. Guiltinan and W.H. Jones, 'Service characteristics, consumer research, and the classification of retail services', *Journal of Retailing* 55 (Fall 1979), pp. 3–21; and W.R. George and L.L. Berry, 'Guidelines for the advertising of services', *Business Horizons* 24 (May–June 1981), pp. 52–6.

9 E.R. Cadotte, R.B. Woodruff and R.L. Jenkins, 'Expectations and norms in models of consumer satisfaction', *Journal of Marketing Research* 14 (August 1987), pp. 353–64.

10 Parasuraman, Berry and Zeithaml, 'Understanding customer expectations', p. 40.

11 Davidow and Uttal, 'Service Companies'.

12 W. Boulding, A. Kalra, R. Staelin and V.A. Zeithaml, 'A dynamic process model of service quality: from expectations to behavioral intentions', *Journal of Marketing Research* 30 (February 1993), pp. 7–27.

13 R.T. Rust and R.L. Oliver, 'Should we delight the customer?', *Journal of the Academy of Marketing Science* 28 (Winter 2000), pp. 86–94.

14 T.S. Gross, *Positively Outrageous Service* (New York: Warner Books, 1994).

15 J. Clemmer, 'The three rings of perceived value', *Canadian Manager* (Summer 1990), pp. 30–2.

16 Rust and Oliver, 'Should we delight the customer?'.

17 Parasuraman, Berry and Zeithaml, 'Understanding customer expectations', p. 41.

18 See http://corporate.ritzcarlton.com

Customer perceptions of service

❖ *LEARNING OBJECTIVES*

This chapter's objectives are to:

1 Provide a solid basis for understanding what influences customer perceptions of service and the relationships among customer satisfaction, service quality and individual service encounters.

2 Demonstrate the importance of customer satisfaction – what it is, the factors that influence it and the significant outcomes resulting from it.

3 Develop critical knowledge of service quality and its five key dimensions: reliability, responsiveness, empathy, assurance and tangibles.

4 Show that service encounters or the 'moments of truth' are the essential building blocks from which customers form their perceptions.

CASE STUDY: THE CHANGING FACE OF CUSTOMER SERVICE

Excellent customer service – the daily, ongoing support of a company's offerings – is critical in creating brand identity and ultimate success. It includes answering questions, taking orders, dealing with billing issues, handling complaints, scheduling appointments, and similar activities. These essential functions can make or break an organization's relationships with its customers. The quality of customer care can significantly impact brand identity for service, manufacturing, and consumer products companies. Because of its importance in creating impressions and sustaining customer relationships, customer service has sometimes been called the 'front door' of the organization or its 'face'.

So how has the 'face' of customer service changed with the influx of technology? Long ago all customer service was provided face-to-face through direct personal interaction between employees and customers. To get service you had to visit stores or service providers in person. The telephone changed this, allowing customers to call companies and speak directly with employees, typically Monday–Friday, 8 a.m. to 5 p.m. Customer service became less personal, but without a doubt more efficient, through use of the telephone. With the evolution of computer technology, call-centre staff became even more efficient. Through computer information systems and customer data files, call-centre staff are able to call up customer records at their workstations to answer questions on the spot.

Over time, because communication and computer technologies allowed it, large organizations began to centralize their customer service functions, consolidating into a few large call centres that could be located anywhere in the country or the world.

For example, a large percentage of Norwich Union's customer service calls in the UK are handled by its sales and service centre in Bangalore, India, and calls can be handled 24 hours a day. But still, in these types of call centres, customer service is for the most part an interpersonal event with customers talking directly, one on one with an employee.

The advent and rapid proliferation of the efficient, but much maligned, automated voice response systems have changed personal customer service in many organizations into menu-driven, automated exchanges. In almost every industry and any business context, consumers encounter these types of systems, and many are quite frustrating – for example, when a system has a long, confusing set of menu options or when no menu option seems to fit the purpose of the call. Similarly, consumers become angered when they cannot get out of the automated system easily, or when there is no option to speak to a live person.

Beyond automated telecommunication systems, explosion of the Internet is also dramatically changing customer service for many companies. Service can now be provided on the Internet via emails, website robots, frequently asked questions (FAQs), and online chats. In these cases there is no direct human interaction, and customers actually perform their own service. Examples include Amazon, Expedia and many of the online banking and insurance operations.

With the relentless proliferation of technology solutions, firms are finding that expectations for customer service have changed. Customers are demanding choices in how they get customer service, whether it be via telephone, automated voice system, fax, email or Internet self-service. Although customers often enjoy technology-based service and even demand it in many cases, they dislike it when it does not work reliably (a common problem), when it does not seem to have any advantages over the interpersonal service alternatives, and when there are no systems in place to recover from failures. Interestingly, when things do not work as they are supposed to on an Internet site or through an automated response system, customers are quick to look for more traditional interpersonal (in person or via telephone) options, coming full circle to where they started!

So what is it that brings about customer satisfaction? How do customers evaluate service quality? How do they form their perceptions of service? Answers to these questions are the subjects of this chapter.

Sources: J.A. Nickell, 'To voice mail hell and back', *Business 2.0*, 10 July 2001, pp. 49–53; D. Ward, 'The web's killer app: a human being', *Revolution*, March 2000, pp. 82–8; M.L. Meuter, A.L. Ostrom, R.I. Roundtree and M.J. Bitner, 'Self-service technologies: understanding customer satisfaction with technology-based service encounters', *Journal of Marketing* 64 (July 2000), pp. 50–64.

Customer perceptions

How customers perceive services, how they assess whether they have experienced quality service, and whether they are satisfied are the subjects of this chapter. Customers perceive services in terms of the quality of the service and how satisfied they are overall with their experiences. Companies today recognize that they can compete more effectively by distinguishing themselves with respect to service quality and improved customer satisfaction.

Satisfaction versus service quality

Practitioners and writers in the popular press tend to use the terms *satisfaction* and *quality* interchangeably, but researchers have attempted to be more precise about the meanings and measurement of the two concepts, resulting in considerable debate.[1] Consensus is that the two concepts are fundamentally different in terms of their underlying causes and outcomes.[2] Although they have certain things in common, **satisfaction** is generally viewed as a broader concept, whereas **service quality** focuses specifically on dimensions of service. Based on this view, *perceived service quality* is a component of customer satisfaction. Figure 4.1 graphically illustrates the relationships between the two concepts.

As shown in Figure 4.1, service quality is a focused evaluation that reflects the customer's perception of reliability, assurance, responsiveness, empathy and tangibles.[3] Satisfaction, on the other hand, is more inclusive: it is influenced by perceptions of service quality, product quality and price as well as situational factors and personal factors. For example, *service quality* of a health club is judged on attributes such as whether equipment is available and in working order when needed, how responsive the staff are to customer needs, how skilled the trainers are and whether the facility is well maintained. *Customer satisfaction* with the health club is a broader concept that will certainly be influenced by perceptions of service quality but will also include perceptions of product quality (such as quality of products sold in the bar/restaurant), price of membership,[4] personal factors such as the consumer's emotional state, and even uncontrollable

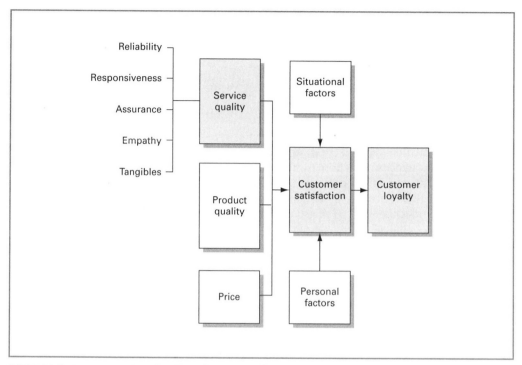

FIGURE 4.1 Customer perceptions of quality and customer satisfaction

situational factors such as weather conditions and experiences driving to and from the health club.[5]

Transaction versus cumulative perceptions

In considering perceptions, it is also important to recognize that customers will have perceptions of single, transaction-specific encounters as well as overall perceptions of a company based on all their experiences.[6] For example, a bank customer will have a perception of how he or she was treated in a particular encounter with a bank employee at a branch and will form a perception of that particular transaction based on elements of the service experienced during that specific transaction. That perception is at a very micro, transaction-specific level. That same bank customer will also have overall perceptions of the bank based on his or her encounters over a period of time. These experiences might include multiple in-person encounters at the bank branch, online banking experiences and experiences using the bank's ATMs across many different cities. At an even more general level, the customer may have perceptions of banking services or the whole banking industry as a result of all his or her experiences with banks and everything he or she knows about banking.

Research suggests that it is important to understand all these types of perceptions for different reasons and that the points of view are complementary rather than competing.[7] Understanding perceptions at the transaction-specific level is critical for diagnosing service issues and making immediate changes. These isolated encounters are also the building blocks for overall, cumulative experience evaluations, as you will learn later in this chapter. On the other hand, cumulative experience evaluations are likely to be better predictors of overall loyalty to a company. That is, customer loyalty most often results from the customer's assessment of all his experiences, not just one single encounter.

Customer satisfaction

What is customer satisfaction?

'Everyone knows what satisfaction is, until asked to give a definition. Then, it seems, nobody knows.'[8] This quote from Richard L. Oliver, respected expert and long-time writer and researcher on the topic of customer satisfaction, expresses the challenge of defining this most basic of customer concepts. Building from previous definitions, Oliver offers his own formal definition (p. 13): 'Satisfaction is the consumer's fulfillment response. It is a judgment that a product or service feature, or the product or service itself, provides a pleasurable level of consumption-related fulfillment.' In less technical terms, we interpret this definition to mean that *satisfaction* is the customer's evaluation of a product or service in terms of whether that product or service has met the customer's needs and expectations. Failure to meet needs and expectations is assumed to result in *dissatisfaction* with the product or service.

In addition to a sense of *fulfilment* in the knowledge that one's needs have been met, satisfaction can also be related to other types of feelings, depending on the particular context or type of service.[9] For example, satisfaction can be viewed as *contentment* – more of a passive response that consumers may associate with services they do not think a lot about or services that they receive routinely over time. Satisfaction may also be associated with feelings of *pleasure* for services that make the consumer feel good or are associated with a sense of happiness. For those services that really surprise the consumer in a positive way, satisfaction may mean *delight*. In some situations, where the removal of a negative leads to satisfaction, the consumer may associate a sense of *relief* with satisfaction. Finally, satisfaction may be associated with feelings of *ambivalence* when there is a mix of positive and negative experiences associated with the product or service.

Although consumer satisfaction tends to be measured at a particular point in time as if it were static, satisfaction is a dynamic, moving target that may evolve over time, influenced by a variety of factors.[10] Particularly when product usage or the service experience takes place over time, satisfaction may be highly variable depending on which point in the usage or experience cycle one is focusing on. Similarly, in the case of very new services or a service not previously experienced, customer expectations may be barely forming at the point of initial purchase; these expectations will solidify as the process unfolds and the consumer begins to form his or her perceptions. Through the service cycle the consumer may have a variety of different experiences – some good, some not good – and each will ultimately impact satisfaction.

What determines customer satisfaction?

As shown in Figure 4.1, customer satisfaction is influenced by specific product or service features, perceptions of product and service quality, and price. In addition, personal factors such as the customer's mood or emotional state and situational factors such as family member opinions will also influence satisfaction.

Product and service features

Customer satisfaction with a product or service is influenced significantly by the customer's evaluation of product or service features.[11] For a service such as a resort hotel, important features might include the pool area, access to golf facilities, restaurants, room comfort and privacy, helpfulness and courtesy of staff, room price, and so on. In conducting satisfaction studies, most firms will determine through some means (often focus groups) what the important features and attributes are for their service and then measure perceptions of those features as well as overall service satisfaction. Research has shown that customers of services will make trade-offs among different service features (for example, price level versus quality versus friendliness of personnel versus level of customization), depending on the type of service being evaluated and the criticality of the service.[12]

Consumer emotions

Customers' emotions can also affect their perceptions of satisfaction with products and services.[13] These emotions can be stable, pre-existing emotions – for example, mood state or life satisfaction. Think of times when you are at a very happy stage in your life (such as when you are on holiday), and your good, happy mood and positive frame of mind have influenced how you feel about the services you experience. Alternatively, when you are in a bad mood, your negative feelings may carry over into how you respond to services, causing you to overreact or respond negatively to any little problem.

Specific emotions may also be induced by the consumption experience itself, influencing a consumer's satisfaction with the service. Research done in a white-water rafting context showed that the guides had a strong effect on their customers' emotional responses to the trip and that those feelings (both positive and negative) were linked to overall trip satisfaction.[14] Positive emotions such as happiness, pleasure, elation and a sense of warm-heartedness enhanced customers' satisfaction with the rafting trip. In turn, negative emotions such as sadness, sorrow, regret and anger led to diminished customer satisfaction. Overall, in the rafting context, positive emotions had a stronger effect than negative ones. (These positive emotions are apparent in Figure 4.2.)

FIGURE 4.2 River rafters experience many positive emotions, increasing their satisfaction with the service
Source: River Odysseys West, www.rowinc.com

Service spotlight

Similar effects of emotions on satisfaction were found in a Finnish study that looked at consumers' satisfaction with a government labour bureau service.[15] In that study, negative emotions including anger, depression, guilt and humiliation had a strong effect on customers' dissatisfaction ratings.

Attributions for service success or failure

Attributions – the perceived causes of events – influence perceptions of satisfaction as well.[16] When they have been surprised by an outcome (the service is either much better or much worse than expected), consumers tend to look for the reasons, and their assessments of the reasons can influence their satisfaction. For example, if a customer of a weight-loss organization fails to lose weight as hoped for, he or she will likely search for the causes – was it something he or she did, was the diet plan ineffective or did circumstances simply not allow him or her to follow the diet regime – before determining his or her level of satisfaction or dissatisfaction with the weight-loss company.[17] For many services, customers take at least partial responsibility for how things turn out.

Even when customers do not take responsibility for the outcome, customer satisfaction may be influenced by other kinds of attributions. For example, research done in a travel agency context found that customers were less dissatisfied with a pricing error made by the agent if they felt that the reason was outside the agent's control or if they felt that it was a rare mistake, unlikely to occur again.[18]

Perceptions of equity or fairness

Customer satisfaction is also influenced by perceptions of **equity and fairness**.[19] Customers ask themselves: have I been treated fairly compared with other customers? Did other customers get better treatment, better prices, or better quality service? Did I pay a fair price for the service? Was I treated well in exchange for what I paid and the effort I expended? Notions of fairness are central to customers' perceptions of satisfaction with products and services, particularly in service recovery situations. As you will learn in Chapter 15, satisfaction with a service provider following a service failure is largely determined by perceptions of fair treatment.

Other consumers, family members and co-workers

In addition to product and service features and one's own individual feelings and beliefs, consumer satisfaction is often influenced by other people.[20] For example, satisfaction with a family holiday is a dynamic phenomenon, influenced by the reactions and expressions of individual family members over the duration of the holiday. Later, what family members express in terms of satisfaction or dissatisfaction with the holiday will be influenced by stories that are retold among the family and selective memories of the events. Similarly, the satisfaction of the rafters in Figure 4.2 is certainly influenced by individual perceptions, but it is also influenced greatly by the experiences, behaviour and views of the other rafters. In a business setting, satisfaction with a new service or technology – for example, a new customer relationship management software service – will be influenced not only by individuals' personal experiences with the software itself, but also by what others say about it in the company, how others use it and feel about it, and how widely it is adopted in the organization.

National customer satisfaction indices

Because of the importance of customer satisfaction to firms and overall quality of life, many countries have a national index that measures and tracks customer satisfaction at a macro level.[21] Many public policy-makers believe that these measures could and should be used as tools for evaluating the health of the nation's economy, along with traditional measures of productivity and price. **National customer satisfaction indices** begin to get at the *quality* of economic output, whereas more traditional economic indicators tend to focus only on *quantity*. The first such measure was the Swedish Customer Satisfaction Barometer introduced in 1989.[22] Throughout the 1990s similar indices were introduced in Germany (Deutsche Kundenbarometer, or DK, in

1992), the United States (American Customer Satisfaction Index, ACSI, in 1994), Norway (Norsk Kundebarometer, in 1996) and Switzerland (Swiss Index of Customer Satisfaction, SWICS, in 1998).[23] These indices measure customer satisfaction over a wide range of different industries and organizations including public sector organizations. They are intended to be complementary to productivity measures, with productivity reflecting the quantity of output and customer satisfaction measuring the customers' view of quality of output. The research is carried out through interviews with hundreds of current customers. Each of the organizations involved receives a satisfaction score computed from its customers' perceptions of quality, value, satisfaction, expectations, complaints and future loyalty. A benchmark pan-European customer satisfaction survey was undertaken in 2005 covering 10 European countries (Estonia, Latvia, Lithuania, Denmark, Finland, Norway, Sweden, Greece, Portugal and Iceland) to examine differences in satisfaction across a number of service sectors.[24]

Service quality

We now turn to *service quality*, a critical element of customer perceptions. In the case of pure services (e.g. health care, financial services, education), service quality will be the dominant element in customers' evaluations. In cases in which customer service or services are offered in combination with a physical product (e.g. IT services, car repairs), service quality may also be very critical in determining customer satisfaction. Figure 4.1 highlighted these relationships. We will focus here on the left-hand side of Figure 4.1, examining the underlying factors that form perceptions of service quality. First we discuss *what* customers evaluate; then we look specifically at the five dimensions of service that customers rely on in forming their judgements.

Outcome, interaction and physical environment quality

What is it that consumers evaluate when judging service quality? Over the years, services researchers have suggested that consumers judge the quality of services based on their perceptions of the technical outcome provided, the process by which that outcome was delivered, and the quality of the physical surroundings where the service is delivered.[25] For example, in the case of a lawsuit, a client will judge the quality of the technical outcome, or how the court case was resolved, and the quality of the interaction. Interaction quality would include such factors as the lawyer's timeliness in returning telephone calls, his or her empathy for the client, and his or her courtesy and listening skills. Similarly, a restaurant customer will judge the service on his or her perceptions of the meal (technical outcome quality) and on how the meal was served and how the employees interacted with him or her (interaction quality). The decor and surroundings (physical environment quality) of the restaurant will also impact on the customer's perceptions of overall service quality.

This depiction of service quality as outcome quality, interaction quality and physical environment quality is most recently captured by Michael Brady and Joseph Cronin in their empirical research published in the *Journal of Marketing*.[26] Other researchers have defined similar aspects of service in their examinations of service quality.[27]

Service quality dimensions

Research suggests that customers do not perceive quality in a unidimensional way but rather judge quality based on multiple factors relevant to the context. The dimensions of service quality have been identified through the pioneering research of Parsu Parasuraman, Valarie Zeithaml and

Leonard Berry. Their research identified five specific dimensions of service quality that apply across a variety of service contexts.[28] The five dimensions defined here are shown in Figure 4.1 as drivers of service quality. These five dimensions appear again in Chapter 6, along with the scale developed to measure them, SERVQUAL.

- **Reliability**: ability to perform the promised service dependably and accurately
- **Responsiveness**: willingness to help customers and provide prompt service
- **Assurance**: employees' knowledge and courtesy and their ability to inspire trust and confidence
- **Empathy**: caring, individualized attention given to customers
- **Tangibles**: appearance of physical facilities, equipment, personnel and written materials.

These dimensions represent how consumers organize information about service quality in their minds. On the basis of exploratory and quantitative research, these five dimensions were found relevant for banking, insurance, appliance repair and maintenance, securities brokerage, long-distance telephone service, car repairs and others. The dimensions are also applicable to retail and business services, and logic suggests they would be relevant for internal services as well. Sometimes customers will use all the dimensions to determine service quality perceptions, at other times not. For example, for an ATM, empathy is not likely to be a relevant dimension. And in a telephone encounter to schedule a repair, tangibles will not be relevant. Research suggests that cultural differences may also affect the relative importance placed on the five dimensions in different countries. In the following pages we expand on each of the dimensions and provide illustrations of how customers judge them.

Reliability: delivering on promises

Of the five dimensions, reliability has been consistently shown to be the most important determinant of perceptions of service quality.[29] **Reliability** is defined as the ability to perform the promised service dependably and accurately. In its broadest sense, reliability means that the company delivers on its promises – promises about delivery, service provision, problem resolution and pricing. Customers want to do business with companies that keep their promises, particularly their promises about the service outcomes and core service attributes.

Service spotlight

One company that effectively communicates and delivers on the reliability dimension is TNT Express, the express parcel service. The reliability message of TNT Express is evident in its aim: 'To satisfy customers every time' – this reflects the company's service positioning. But even when firms do not choose to position themselves explicitly on reliability, as TNT has, this dimension is extremely important to consumers.

All firms need to be aware of customer expectations of reliability. Firms that do not provide the core service that customers think they are buying fail their customers in the most direct way.

Responsiveness: being willing to help

Responsiveness is the willingness to help customers and to provide prompt service. This dimension emphasizes attentiveness and promptness in dealing with customer requests, questions, complaints and problems. Responsiveness is communicated to customers by the length of time they have to wait for assistance, answers to questions, or attention to problems. Responsiveness also captures the notion of flexibility and ability to customize the service to customer needs.

To excel on the dimension of responsiveness, a company must view the process of service delivery and the handling of requests from the customer's point of view rather than from the company's point of view. Standards for speed and promptness that reflect the company's view of internal process requirements may be very different from the customer's requirements for speed and promptness. To truly distinguish themselves on responsiveness, companies need well-staffed customer service departments as well as responsive front-line people in all contact positions. Responsiveness perceptions diminish when customers wait to get through to a company by telephone, are put on hold, are put through to a complex voice mail system, or have trouble accessing the firm's website.

Assurance: inspiring trust and confidence

Assurance is defined as employees' knowledge and courtesy and the ability of the firm and its employees to inspire trust and confidence. This dimension is likely to be particularly important for services that customers perceive as high risk or for services of which they feel uncertain about their ability to evaluate outcomes – for example, banking, insurance, medical and legal services.

Service spotlight

In other situations, trust and confidence are embodied in the organization itself. Financial services companies such as AXA Insurance ('Be Life Confident') and ING Direct ('It's Your Money We're Saving') illustrate efforts to create trusting relationships between customers and the company as a whole.

Trust and confidence may be embodied in the person who links the customer to the company, such as insurance agents, lawyers or advisers. In such service contexts the company seeks to build trust and loyalty between key contact people and individual customers. The 'personal banker' concept captures this idea: customers are assigned to a banker who will get to know them individually and who will coordinate all their banking services.

Empathy: treating customers as individuals

Empathy is defined as the caring, individualized attention that the firm provides its customers. The essence of empathy is conveying, through personalized or customized service, that customers are unique and special and that their needs are understood. Customers want to feel understood by and important to firms that provide service to them. Personnel at small service firms often know customers by name and build relationships that reflect their personal knowledge of customer requirements and preferences. When such a small firm competes with larger firms, the ability to be empathetic may give the small firm a clear advantage.

In business-to-business services, customers want supplier firms to understand their industries and issues. Many small computer consulting firms successfully compete with large vendors by positioning themselves as specialists in particular industries. Even though larger firms have superior resources, the small firms are perceived as more knowledgeable about customers' issues and needs and are able to offer more customized services.

Tangibles: representing the service physically

Tangibles are defined as the appearance of physical facilities, equipment, personnel and communication materials. Tangibles provide physical representations or images of the service that customers, particularly new customers, will use to evaluate quality. Service industries that emphasize tangibles in their strategies include hospitality services in which the customer visits the establishment to receive the service, such as restaurants and hotels, retail stores and entertainment companies.

Although tangibles are often used by service companies to enhance their image, provide continuity and signal quality to customers, most companies combine tangibles with another dimension to create a service quality strategy for the firm.

Service spotlight

For example, KwikFit tyre and exhaust centres emphasize both responsiveness and tangibles – providing fast, efficient service and a comfortable, clean waiting area.

In contrast, firms that do not pay attention to the tangibles dimension of the service strategy can confuse and even destroy an otherwise good strategy.

Table 4.1 provides examples of how customers judge each of the five dimensions of service quality across a variety of service contexts.

	Reliability	**Responsiveness**	**Assurance**	**Empathy**	**Tangibles**
Car repair (consumer)	Problem fixed the first time and ready when promised	Accessible; no waiting; responds to requests	Knowledgeable mechanics	Acknowledges customer by name; remembers previous problems and preferences	Repair facility; waiting area; uniforms; equipment
Airline (consumer)	Flights to promised destinations depart and arrive on schedule	Prompt and speedy system for ticketing, in-flight baggage handling	Trusted name; good safety record; competent employees	Understands special individual needs; anticipates customer needs	Aircraft; ticketing counters; baggage area; uniforms
Dental care (consumer)	Appointments are kept on schedule; diagnoses prove accurate	Accessible; no waiting; willingness to listen	Knowledge; skills; credentials; reputation	Acknowledges patient as a person; remembers previous problems; listens well; has patience	Waiting room; examination room; equipment; written materials
Architecture (business)	Delivers plans when promised and within budget	Returns telephone calls; adapts to changes	Credentials; reputation; name in the community; knowledge and skills	Understands client's industry; acknowledges and adapts to specific client needs; gets to know the client	Office area; reports; plans themselves; billing statements; dress of employees
Information processing (internal)	Provides needed information when requested	Prompt response to requests; not 'bureaucratic'; deals with problems promptly	Knowledgeable staff; well trained; credentials	Knows internal customers as individuals; understands individual and departmental needs	Internal reports; office area; dress of employees
Internet brokerage (consumer and business)	Provides correct information and executes customer requests accurately	Quick website with easy access and no down time	Credible information sources on the site; brand recognition; credentials apparent on site	Responds with human interaction as needed	Appearance of the website and collateral

TABLE 4.1 Examples of how customers judge the five dimensions of service quality

Dimensions in the nordic model of service quality

Gronroos's[30] 1984 **Nordic model** of the service experience categorized the dimensions into those relating to technical quality and those relating to functional quality. Technical quality relates to the outcome of the service process such as the meal in the restaurant or the haircut in the hairdresser. Functional quality relates to the manner in which the service is delivered in terms of the interactions during the service encounter relating to friendliness, care and attention, etc. The model emphasizes that the interaction between the buyer and the seller in a service setting is as important as the eventual outcome. Staff may need to be trained in technical aspects to ensure the correct outcome and may also require training on softer issues relating to customer care. Rust and Oliver[31] developed these two dimensions further into a three-component model consisting of service product, service delivery and service environment. The service product relates to the service offering and outcome, service delivery relates to the process of consuming the service and the service environment relates to the internal culture and external physical environment associated with the supplier. Other researchers[32] have built on this three-dimensional model to conceptualize expectations. There is overlap across the dimensions used by all of the researchers; the arguments tend to arise around whether each set of dimensions is applicable in all situations. One area that is perceived to be different relates to the delivery of a service over the Internet.

E-service quality

The growth of e-tailing and e-services has led many companies to wonder how consumers evaluate service quality on the Web and whether the criteria are different from those used to judge the quality of non-Internet services.[33] Some commercial groups, such as UK.BizRate.com and Kelkoo.co.uk, capture customer perceptions of specific sites. A more systematic study, sponsored by the Marketing Science Institute, has been conducted to understand how consumers judge **e-service quality** (e-SQ).[34] In that study, e-SQ is defined as the extent to which a website facilitates efficient and effective shopping, purchasing and delivery. Through exploratory focus groups and two phases of empirical data collection and analysis, this research identified seven dimensions that are critical for core service evaluation (four dimensions) and service recovery evaluation (three dimensions).

The four core dimensions that customers use to judge websites at which they experience no questions or problems are:

1 *Efficiency*: the ability of customers to get to the website, find their desired product and information associated with it, and check out with minimal effort.

2 *Fulfilment*: the accuracy of service promises, having products in stock, and delivering the products in the promised time.

3 *Reliability*: the technical functioning of the site, particularly the extent to which it is available and functioning properly.

4 *Privacy*: the assurance that shopping behaviour data are not shared and that credit information is secure.

The study also revealed three dimensions that customers use to judge recovery service when they have problems or questions:

1 *Responsiveness*: the ability of e-tailers to provide appropriate information to customers when a problem occurs, to have mechanisms for handling returns, and to provide online guarantees.

2 *Compensation*: the degree to which customers are to receive money back and are reimbursed for shipping and handling costs.

3 *Contact*: the availability of live customer service agents online or by telephone.

In comparing the dimensions of traditional service quality and e-service quality, we can make several observations. First, the traditional dimensions can and should be considered for e-tailing and Internet-based services, as illustrated by the Internet brokerage example in Table 4.1. However, both similar and different dimensions emerge in the research on e-tailing. Reliability and responsiveness are shared dimensions, but new Internet-specific dimensions appear to be critical in that context. Efficiency and fulfilment are core dimensions in e-service quality, and both share some elements of the traditional reliability and responsiveness dimensions. The personal (that is, friendly, empathetic and understanding) flavour of perceived service quality's empathy dimension is not required on the Internet except as it makes transactions more efficient or in non-routine or problem situations. While not emerging as a dimension of e-service quality, tangibles are clearly relevant given that the entire service is delivered through technology. The tangible, visual elements of the site will be critical to efficiency as well as to overall perceptions of the firm and the brand.

Service encounters: the building blocks for customer perceptions

We have just finished a discussion of customer perceptions, specifically customer satisfaction and service quality. Here we turn to what have been termed the building blocks for customer perceptions – **service encounters**, or '**moments of truth**'. Service encounters are where promises are kept or broken and where the proverbial rubber meets the road – sometimes called 'real-time marketing'. It is from these service encounters that customers build their perceptions.

Service encounters or moments of truth

From the customer's point of view, the most vivid impression of service occurs in the *service encounter* or '*moment of truth*',[35] when the customer interacts with the service firm. For example, among the service encounters that a hotel customer experiences are checking into the

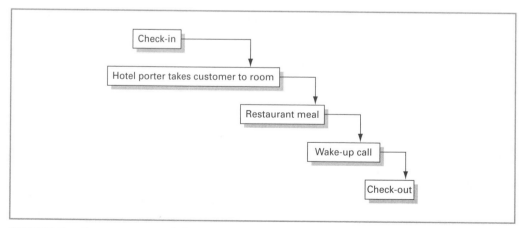

FIGURE 4.3 A service encounter cascade for a hotel visit

hotel, being taken to a room by a hotel porter, eating a restaurant meal, requesting a wake-up call and checking out. You could think of the linking of these moments of truth as a **service encounter cascade** (see Figure 4.3). It is in these encounters that customers receive a snapshot of the organization's service quality, and each encounter contributes to the customer's overall satisfaction and willingness to do business with the organization again. From the organization's point of view, each encounter thus presents an opportunity to prove its potential as a quality service provider and to increase customer loyalty.

Some services have few service encounters, and others have many. The Disney Corporation estimates that each of its amusement park customers experiences about 74 service encounters and that a negative experience in any one of them can lead to a negative overall evaluation. Mistakes or problems that occur in the early levels of the service cascade may be particularly critical. Marriott Hotels learned this through their extensive customer research to determine what service elements contribute most to customer loyalty. They found that four of the top five factors came into play in the first 10 minutes of the guest's stay.[36]

The importance of encounters

Although early events in the encounter cascade are likely to be especially important, *any* encounter can potentially be critical in determining customer satisfaction and loyalty. If a customer is interacting with a firm for the first time, that initial encounter will create a first impression of the organization. In these first encounter situations, the customer frequently has no other basis for judging the organization, and the initial telephone contact or face-to-face experience with a representative of the firm can take on excessive importance in the customer's perceptions of quality. A customer calling for a repair service on a household appliance may well hang up and call a different company if he or she is treated rudely by a customer service representative, put on hold for a lengthy period or told that two weeks is the soonest someone can be sent out to make the repair. Even if the technical quality of the firm's repair service is superior, the firm may not get the chance to demonstrate it if the initial telephone encounter drives the customer away.

Even when the customer has had multiple interactions with a firm, each individual encounter is important in creating a composite image of the firm in the customer's memory. Many positive experiences add up to a composite image of high quality, whereas many negative interactions will have the opposite effect. On the other hand, a combination of positive and negative interactions will leave the customer feeling unsure of the firm's quality, doubtful of its consistency in service delivery and vulnerable to the appeals of competitors. For example, a large corporate customer of a commercial catering company that provides food service in all its employee canteens and cafeterias could have a series of positive encounters with the account manager or salesperson who handles the account. These experiences could be followed by positive encounters with the operations staff who actually set up the food service facilities. However, even with these positive encounters, later negative experiences with the staff who serve the food or the accounting department that administers the billing procedures can result in a mixture of overall quality impressions. This variation in experiences could result in the corporate customer wondering about the quality of the organization and unsure of what to expect in the future. Each encounter with different people and departments representing the food service provider adds to or detracts from the potential for a continuing relationship.

Logic suggests that not all encounters are equally important in building relationships. For every organization, certain encounters are probably key to customer satisfaction. For Marriott Hotels, as noted, the early encounters are most important. In a hospital context, a study of patients revealed that encounters with nursing staff were more important in predicting satisfaction than were encounters with catering or administrative staff.[37]

In addition to these key encounters, there are some momentous encounters that, like the proverbial 'one bad apple', simply ruin the rest and drive the customer away no matter how many or what type of encounters have occurred in the past. These momentous encounters can occur in connection with very important events (such as the failure to deliver an essential piece of equipment before a critical deadline). Similarly, momentous positive encounters can sometimes bind a customer to an organization for life.

Types of service encounters

A service encounter occurs every time a customer interacts with the service organization. There are three general types of service encounters: *remote encounters, telephone encounters* and *face-to-face encounters.*[38] A customer may experience any of these types of encounters, or a combination of all three, in his or her relations with a service firm.

First, encounters can occur without any direct human contact (**remote encounters**), such as when a customer interacts with a bank through the ATM system, with a car park management company through an automated ticketing machine, with a retailer through its Internet website or with a mail-order service through automated touch-tone telephone ordering. Remote encounters also occur when the firm sends its billing statements or communicates other types of information to customers by mail. Although there is no direct human contact in these remote encounters, each represents an opportunity for the firm to reinforce or establish quality perceptions in the customer. In remote encounters the tangible evidence of the service and the quality of the technical processes and systems become the primary bases for judging quality.

More and more services are being delivered through technology, particularly with the advent of Internet applications. Retail purchases, airline ticketing, repair and maintenance troubleshooting, and package and shipment tracking are just a few examples of services available via the Internet. All these types of service encounters can be considered remote encounters.

In many organizations (such as insurance companies, utilities and telecommunications), the most frequent type of encounter between an end customer and the firm occurs over the telephone (*telephone encounters*). Almost all firms (whether goods manufacturers or service businesses) rely on telephone encounters to some extent for customer service, general inquiry or order-taking functions. The judgement of quality in telephone encounters is different from remote encounters because there is greater potential variability in the interaction.[39] Tone of voice, employee knowledge and effectiveness/efficiency in handling customer issues become important criteria for judging quality in these encounters.

A third type of encounter is the one that occurs between an employee and a customer in direct contact (*face-to-face encounters*). At Disney theme parks, face-to-face encounters occur between customers and ticket-takers, maintenance personnel, actors in Disney character costumes, ride personnel, food and beverage servers, and others. For a company such as Ericsson, in a business-to-business setting direct encounters occur between the business customer and salespeople, delivery personnel, maintenance representatives and professional consultants. Determining and understanding service quality issues in face-to-face contexts is the most complex of all. Both verbal and non-verbal behaviours are important determinants of quality, as are tangible cues such as employee dress and other symbols of service (equipment, informational brochures, physical setting). In face-to-face encounters the customer also plays a role in creating quality service for himself or herself through his or her own behaviour during the interaction.

Sources of pleasure and displeasure in service encounters

Because of the importance of service encounters in building perceptions, researchers have extensively analysed service encounters in many contexts to determine the sources of customers'
favourable and unfavourable impressions. The research uses the **critical incident technique** to
get customers and employees to provide verbatim stories about satisfying and dissatisfying
service encounters they have experienced.[40] With this technique, customers (either internal or
external) are told, 'Think of a time when, as a custsomer, you had a particularly *satisfying* (or *dissatisfying*) interaction with _____', and are asked the following questions:

- When did the incident happen?
- What specific circumstances led up to this situation?
- Exactly what did the employee (or firm member) say or do?
- What resulted that made you feel the interaction was *satisfying* (or *dissatisfying*)?
- What could or should have been done differently?

Sometimes contact employees are asked to put themselves in the shoes of a customer and
answer the same questions: 'Put yourself in the shoes of *customers* of your firm. In other words,
try to see your firm through your customers' eyes. Now think of a recent time when a customer
of your firm had a particularly *satisfying/unsatisfying* interaction with you or a fellow employee.'
The stories are then analysed to determine common themes of satisfaction/dissatisfaction underlying the events. On the basis of thousands of service encounter stories, four common themes –
service recovery (after failure), adaptability, spontaneity and coping – have been identified as the
sources of customer satisfaction/dissatisfaction in memorable service encounters.[41] Each of the
themes is discussed here, and sample stories of both satisfying and dissatisfying incidents for
each theme are given in Table 4.2. The themes encompass service behaviours in encounters
spanning a wide variety of industries.

Recovery – employee response to service delivery system failures

The first theme includes all incidents in which there has been a failure of the service delivery
system and an employee is required to respond in some way to consumer complaints and dis-
appointments. The failure may be, for example, a hotel room that is not available, a flight that is
delayed six hours, an incorrect item sent from a mail-order company or a critical error on an
internal document. The content or form of the employee's response is what causes the customer
to remember the event either favourably or unfavourably.

Adaptability – employee response to customer needs and requests

A second theme underlying satisfaction/dissatisfaction in service encounters is how adaptable
the service delivery system is when the customer has special needs or requests that place
demands on the process. In these cases, customers judge service encounter quality in terms of
the flexibility of the employees and the system. Incidents categorized within this theme all
contain an implicit or explicit request for customization of the service to meet a need. Much of
what customers see as special needs or requests may actually be rather routine from the
employee's point of view; what is important is that the customer perceives that something special
is being done for him or her based on his or her own individual needs. External customers and
internal customers alike are pleased when the service provider makes an effort to accommodate
and adjust the system to meet their requirements. On the flip side, they are angered and frustrated by an unwillingness to try to accommodate and by promises that are never followed
through. Contact employees also see their abilities to adapt the system as being a prominent

THEME 1: RECOVERY

Satisfactory	Dissatisfactory
They lost my room reservation but the manager gave me the top suite for the same price. Even though I did not make any complaint about the hour-and-a-half wait, the waitress kept apologizing and said the bill was on the house.	We had made advance reservations at the hotel. When we arrived we found we had no room – no explanation, no apologies and no assistance in finding another hotel. One of my suitcases was damaged and looked like it had been dropped from 30 000 feet. When I tried to make a claim for the damage, the employee insinuated that I was lying and trying to cheat them.

THEME 2: ADAPTABILITY

Satisfactory	Dissatisfactory
I did not have an appointment to see a doctor; however, the practice nurse spoke to the doctor's receptionist and worked me into the schedule. I received treatment after a 10-minute wait. I was very satisfied with the special treatment I received, the short wait and the quality of the service. It was snowing outside – my car had broken down. I checked 10 hotels and there were no rooms. Finally, one understood my situation and offered to rent me a bed and set it up in a small banquet room.	My young son, flying alone, was to be assisted by the flight attendant from start to finish. At Heathrow airport she left him alone in the airport with no one to escort him to his connecting flight. Despite our repeated requests, the hotel staff would not deal with the noisy people partying in the corridor at 3 a.m.

THEME 3: SPONTANEITY

Satisfactory	Dissatisfactory
Our children always travel with their teddy bears. When we got back to our room at the hotel we saw that the cleaning person had arranged the bears very comfortably in a chair. The bears were holding hands. The medical staff took extra time to explain exactly what I would be aware of and promised to take special care in making sure I did not wake up during the surgical operation.	The lady at the front desk acted as if we were bothering her. She was watching television and paying more attention to the television than to the hotel guests. I needed a few more minutes to decide on a dinner. The waitress said, 'If you would read the menu and not the road map, you would know what you want to order'.

THEME 4: COPING

Satisfactory	Dissatisfactory
A person who became intoxicated on a flight started speaking loudly, annoying the other passengers. The flight attendant asked the passenger if he would be driving when the plane landed and offered him coffee. He accepted the coffee and became quieter and friendlier.	An intoxicated man began pinching the female flight attendants. One attendant told him to stop, but he continued and then hit another passenger. The co-pilot was called and asked the man to sit down and leave the others alone, but the passenger refused. The co-pilot then 'decked' the man, knocking him into his seat.

TABLE 4.2 Service encounter themes

source of customer satisfaction, and often they are equally frustrated by constraints that keep them from being flexible.

Spontaneity – unprompted and unsolicited employee actions

Even when there is no system failure and no special request or need, customers can still remember service encounters as being very satisfying or very dissatisfying. Employee spontaneity in delivering memorably good or poor service is the third theme. Satisfying incidents in this group represent very pleasant surprises for the customer (special attention, being treated like royalty, receiving something nice but not requested), whereas dissatisfying incidents in this group represent negative and unacceptable employee behaviours (rudeness, stealing, discrimination, ignoring the customer).

Coping – employee response to problem customers

The incidents categorized in this group came to light when employees were asked to describe service encounter incidents in which customers were either very satisfied or dissatisfied. In addition to describing incidents of the types outlined under the first three themes, employees described many incidents in which customers were the cause of their own dissatisfaction. Such customers were basically uncooperative – that is, unwilling to cooperate with the service provider, other customers, industry regulations and/or laws. In these cases nothing the employee could do would result in the customer feeling pleased about the encounter. The term *coping* is

Theme	Do	Don't
Recovery	Acknowledge problem Explain causes Apologize Compensate/upgrade Lay out options Take responsibility	Ignore customer Blame customer Leave customer to fend for himself or herself Downgrade Act as if nothing is wrong Blame the problem on someone else
Adaptability	Recognize the seriousness of the need Acknowledge Anticipate Attempt to accommodate Adjust the system Explain rules/policies Take responsibility	Ignore Promise, but fail to follow through Show unwillingness to try Embarrass the customer Laugh at the customer Avoid responsibility Blame the problem on someone else
Spontaneity	Take time Be attentive Anticipate needs Listen Provide information Show empathy	Exhibit impatience Ignore Yell/laugh/swear Steal from customers Discriminate
Coping	Listen Try to accommodate Explain Let go of the customer	Take customer's dissatisfaction personally Let customer's dissatisfaction affect others

TABLE 4.3 General service behaviours based on service encounter themes – dos and don'ts

used to describe these incidents because coping is the behaviour generally required of employees to handle problem customer encounters. Rarely are such encounters satisfying from the customer's point of view.[42] Also of interest is that customers themselves did not relate any 'problem customer' incidents. That is, customers either do not see, or choose not to remember or retell, stories of the times when they themselves were unreasonable to the point of causing their own dissatisfactory service encounter.

Table 4.3 summarizes the specific employee behaviours that cause satisfaction and dissatisfaction in service encounters according to the four themes just presented: recovery, adaptability, spontaneity and coping. The left-hand side of the table suggests what employees do that results in positive encounters, whereas the right-hand side summarizes negative behaviours within each theme.

Technology-based service encounters

All the research on service encounters described thus far and the resulting themes underlying service encounter evaluations are based on interpersonal services – that is, face-to-face encounters between customers and employees of service organizations. Recently researchers have begun to look at the sources of pleasure and displeasure in technology-based service encounters.[43] These types of encounters involve customers interacting with Internet-based services, automated telephone services, kiosk services and services delivered via CD or video technology. Often these systems are referred to as *self-service technologies* (SSTs) because the customer essentially provides his or her own service.

The research on SSTs reveals some different themes in terms of what drives customer satisfaction and dissatisfaction. The following themes were identified from analysis of hundreds of critical incident stories across a wide range of contexts, including Internet retailing, Internet-based services, ATMs, automated telephone systems, and others.

For satisfying self-service technologies

1 *Solved an intensified need.* Customers in this category were thrilled that the technology could bail them out of a difficult situation – for example, a cash machine that came to the rescue, allowing the customer to get cash to pay a taxi driver and get to work on time when a car had broken down.

2 *Better than the alternative.* Many SST stories related to how the technology-based service was in some way better than the alternative – easy to use, saved time, available when and where the customer needed it, saved money.

3 *Did its job.* Because there are so many failures of technology, many customers are simply thrilled when the SST works as it should!

For dissatisfying self-service technologies

1 *Technology failure.* Many dissatisfying SST stories relate to the technology simply not working as promised – it is not available when needed, PIN numbers do not work, or systems are off-line.

2 *Process failure.* Often the technology seems to work, but later the customer discovers that a back office or follow-up process, which the customer assumed was connected,

does not work. For example, a product order seems to be placed successfully, but it never arrives or the wrong product is delivered.

3 *Poor design.* Many stories relate to the customer's dissatisfaction with how the technology is designed, in terms of either the technical process (technology is confusing, menu options are unclear) or the actual service design (delivery takes too long, service is inflexible).

4 *Customer-driven failure.* In some cases the customers told stories of their own inabilities or failures to use the technology properly. These types of stories are (of course) much less common than stories blaming the technology or the company.

For all of the dissatisfying SST stories, there is clearly an element of service failure. Interestingly, the research revealed little attempt in these technology-based encounters to recover from the failure – unlike the interpersonal service encounters described earlier, where excellent service recovery can be a foundation for retaining and even producing very satisfied customers. As companies progress further with SSTs and become better at delivering service this way, we expect that growing numbers will be able to deliver superior service via technology. In the future we believe that many firms will be able to deliver highly reliable, responsive, customized services via technology and will offer easy and effective means for service recovery when failure does occur.[44]

The evidence of service

Because services are intangible, customers are searching for evidence of service in every interaction they have with an organization.[45] Figure 4.4 depicts the three major categories of evidence as experienced by the customer: people, process and physical evidence. These categories together represent the service and provide the evidence that makes the offering tangible. The new mix elements essentially *are* the evidence of service in each moment of truth.

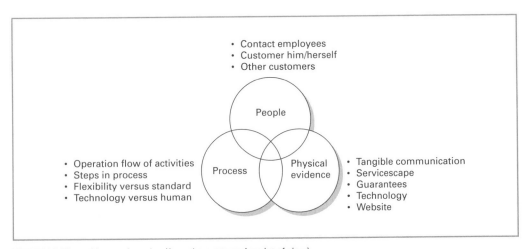

FIGURE 4.4 The evidence of service (from the customer's point of view)

Source: from 'Managing the evidence of service' by M.J. Bitner from *The Service Quality Handbook*, eds E.E. Scheuing and W.F. Christopher. Reprinted by permission of the American Marketing Association

All these evidence elements, or a subset of them, are present in every service encounter a customer has with a service firm and are critically important in managing service encounter quality and creating customer satisfaction. For example, when a dental patient has an appointment with a local dentist, the first encounter of the visit is frequently with a receptionist in a dental waiting area. The quality of that encounter will be judged by how the appointment registration *process* works (Is there a queue? How long is the wait? Is the registration system computerized and accurate?), the actions and attitude of the *people* (Is the receptionist courteous, helpful, knowledgeable? Does he or she treat the patient as an individual? Does he or she handle enquiries fairly and efficiently?) and the *physical evidence* of the service (Is the waiting area clean and comfortable? Is the signage clear?). The three types of evidence may be differentially important depending on the type of service encounter (remote, telephone, face-to-face). All three types will operate in face-to-face service encounters like the one just described.

Summary

This chapter described customer perceptions of service by first introducing you to two critical concepts: customer satisfaction and service quality. These critical customer perceptions were defined and discussed in terms of the factors that influence each of them. You learned that customer satisfaction is a broad perception influenced by features and attributes of the product as well as by customers' emotional responses, their attributions and their perceptions of fairness. Service quality, the customer's perception of the service component of a product, is also a critical determinant of customer satisfaction. Sometimes, as in the case of a pure service, service quality may be the *most* critical determinant of satisfaction. You learned that perceptions of service quality are based on five dimensions: reliability, assurance, empathy, responsiveness and tangibles.

Another major purpose of the chapter was to introduce the idea of service encounters, or 'moments of truth', as the building blocks for both satisfaction and quality. You learned that every service encounter (whether remote, over the telephone or in person) is an opportunity to build perceptions of quality and satisfaction. The underlying themes of pleasure and displeasure in service encounters were also described. The importance of managing the evidence of service in each and every encounter was discussed.

Key concepts

Assurance	85	Reliability	84
Critical incident technique (CIT)	92	Remote encounters	91
		Responsiveness	85
E-service quality	88	Satisfaction	78
Empathy	86	Self-service technologies	95
Equity and fairness	82	Service encounter	89
Moment of truth	89	Service encounter cascade	90
National customer satisfaction indices	82	Service quality	78
		Service recovery	92
Nordic model of service quality	88	Tangibles	86

Further reading

Beatson, A., Lee, N. and Coote, L.V. (2007) 'Self-service technology and the service encounter', *Service Industries Journal*, 27(1), 75–82.

Brady, M. and Cronin, J. (2001) 'Some new thoughts on conceptualising perceived service quality: a hierarchical approach', *Journal of Marketing*, 65(2), 34–49.

Chandon, J.-L., Leo, P.-Y. and Philippe, J. (1997) 'Service encounter dimensions – a dyadic perspective: measuring the dimensions of service encounters as perceived by customers and personnel', *Journal of Service Industry Management*, 8(1), 65–86.

De Ruyter, K., Bloemer, J. and Peeters, P. (1997) 'Merging service quality and service satisfaction: an empirical test of an integrative model', *Journal of Economic Psychology*, 18, 387–406.

Hennig-Thurau, T. and Klee, A. (1997) 'The impact of customer relationship quality on customer retention – a critical reassessment and model development', *Psychology and Marketing*, 14(8), 737–65.

Johnson, M.D., Gustafsson, A., Andreassen, T.W., Leavik, L. and Cha, J. (2001) 'The evolution and future of national customer satisfaction indices', *Journal of Economic Psychology*, 22(2), 217–45.

 ## Discussion questions

1 What is customer satisfaction, and why is it so important? Discuss how customer satisfaction can be influenced by each of the following: product attributes and features, customer emotions, attributions for success or failure, perceptions of fairness, and family members or other customers.

2 Discuss the differences between perceptions of service quality and customer satisfaction.

3 List and define the five dimensions of service quality. Describe the services provided by a firm you do business with (your bank, your dentist, your favourite restaurant) on each of the dimensions. In your mind, has this organization distinguished itself from its competitors on any particular service quality dimension?

4 Describe a remote encounter, a telephone encounter and a face-to-face encounter that you have had recently. How did you evaluate the encounter, and what were the most important factors determining your satisfaction/dissatisfaction in each case?

5 Describe an 'encounter cascade' for a flight. In your opinion, what are the most important encounters in this cascade for determining your overall impression of the quality of the airline?

6 Assume that you are a manager of a health club. Discuss general strategies you might use to maximize customers' positive perceptions of your club. How would you know if you were successful?

Chapter 4. Customer's Perception of Service

Customers perceive services in terms of quality of the service and how satisfied they are overall with their experiences.

Customer satisfaction is the customer's evaluation of a product or service in terms of whether that product or service has met the customer's needs and expectations.

→ Satisfaction is dynamic, and evolves overtime.

→ Influenced by:
   · features

· emotional state.

Service Quality is a focused evaluation that reflects the customers' perception of reliability, assurance, responsiveness, empathy, and tangibles.

Service encounters are where promises are kept or broken and where the proverbial rubber meets the road ('real time marketing)

→ Sounds of pleasure / displeasure.

Every encounter is an opportunity to build perceptions of quality + satisfaction.

Exercises

1 Keep a journal of your service encounters with different organizations (at least five) during the week. For each journal entry, ask yourself the following questions: what circumstances led up to this encounter? What did the employee say or do? How did you evaluate this encounter? What exactly made you evaluate the encounter that way? What should the organization have done differently (if anything)? Categorize your encounters according to the four themes of service encounter satisfaction/dissatisfaction (recovery, adaptability, spontaneity, coping).

2 Interview someone with a non-European cultural background. Ask the person about service quality, whether the five dimensions of quality are relevant and which are most important in determining quality of banking services (or some other type of service) in the person's country.

3 Think of an important service experience you have had in the last several weeks. Analyse the encounter according to the evidence of service provided (see Figure 4.4). Which of the three evidence components was (or were) most important for you in evaluating the experience, and why?

4 Interview an employee of a local service business. Ask the person to discuss each of the five dimensions of quality with you as it relates to the person's company. Which dimensions are most important? Are any dimensions *not* relevant in this context? Which dimensions does the company do best? Why? Which dimensions could benefit from improvement? Why?

5 Interview a manager, owner or director of a business. Discuss with this person the strategies he or she uses to ensure customer satisfaction. How does service quality enter into the strategies, or does it not? Find out how this person measures customer satisfaction and/or service quality.

6 Visit the Amazon website. Visit a traditional bookstore. How would you compare the two experiences? Compare and contrast the factors that most influenced your satisfaction and perceptions of service quality in the two different situations. When would you choose to use one versus the other?

Notes

[1] For more discussion of the debate on the distinctions between quality and satisfaction, see A. Parasuraman, V.A. Zeithaml and L.L. Berry, 'Reassessment of expectations as a comparison standard in measuring service quality: implications for future research', *Journal of Marketing* 58 (January 1994), pp. 111–24; R.L. Oliver, 'A conceptual model of service quality and service satisfaction: compatible goals, different concepts', in *Advances in Services Marketing and Management*, vol. 2, eds T.A. Swartz, D.E. Bowen and S.W. Brown (Greenwich, CT: JAI Press, 1994), pp. 65–85; M.J. Bitner and A.R. Hubbert, 'Encounter satisfaction vs. overall satisfaction vs. quality: the customer's voice', in *Service Quality: New Directions in Theory and Practice*, eds R.T. Rust and R.L. Oliver (Newbury Park, CA: Sage, 1993), pp. 71–93; and D.K. Iacobucci, A. Grayson and A.L. Ostrom, 'The calculus of service quality and customer satisfaction: theory and empirical differentiation and integration', in *Advances in Services Marketing and Management*, vol. 3, eds T.A. Swartz, D.E. Bowen and S.W. Brown (Greenwich, CT: JAI Press, 1994), pp. 1–67;

P.A. Dabholkar, C.D. Shepherd and D.I. Thorpe, 'A comprehensive framework for service quality: an investigation of critical conceptual and measurement issues through a longitudinal study', *Journal of Retailing* 7, no. 2 (Summer 2000), pp. 139–73; J.J. Cronin Jr, M.K. Brady and G.T.M. Hult, 'Assessing the effects of quality, value, and customer satisfaction on consumer behavioral intentions in service environments', *Journal of Retailing* 7 (Summer 2000), pp. 193–218.

2 See in particular, Parasuraman, Zeithaml and Berry, 'Reassessment of expectations'; Oliver, 'A conceptual model of service quality'; and M.K. Brady and J.J. Cronin Jr, 'Some new thoughts on conceptualizing perceived service quality: a hierarchical approach', *Journal of Marketing* 65 (July 2001), pp. 34–49.

3 A. Parasuraman, V.A. Zeithaml and L.L. Berry, 'SERVQUAL: a multiple-item scale for measuring consumer perceptions of service quality', *Journal of Retailing* 64 (Spring 1988), pp. 12–40.

4 Parasuraman, Zeithaml, and Berry, 'Reassessment of expectations'.

5 Oliver, 'A conceptual model of service quality'.

6 See V. Mittal, P. Kumar and M. Tsiros, 'Attribute-level performance, satisfaction, and behavioral intentions over time', *Journal of Marketing* 63 (April 1999), pp. 88–101; L.L. Olsen and M.D. Johnson, 'Service equity, satisfaction, and loyalty: from transaction-specific to cumulative evaluations', *Journal of Service Research* 5 (February 2003), pp. 184–95.

7 Olsen and Johnson, 'Service equity, satisfaction, and loyalty'.

8 R.L. Oliver, *Satisfaction: A Behavioral Perspective on the Consumer* (New York: McGraw-Hill, 1997).

9 For a more detailed discussion of the different types of satisfaction, see E. Arnould, L. Price and G. Zinkhan, *Consumers*, 2nd edn, (New York: McGraw-Hill, 2004), pp. 754–96.

10 S. Fournier and D.G. Mick, 'Rediscovering satisfaction', *Journal of Marketing* 63 (October 1999), pp. 5–23.

11 Oliver, *Satisfaction*, ch. 2.

12 A. Ostrom and D. Iacobucci, 'Consumer trade-offs and the evaluation of services', *Journal of Marketing* 59 (January 1995), pp. 17–28.

13 For more on emotions and satisfaction, see Oliver, *Satisfaction*, ch. 11; and L.L. Price, E.J. Arnould and S.L. Deibler, 'Consumers' emotional responses to service encounters', *International Journal of Service Industry Management* 6, no. 3 (1995), pp. 34–63.

14 L.L. Price, E.J. Arnould, and P. Tierney, 'Going to extremes: managing service encounters and assessing provider performance', *Journal of Marketing* 59 (April 1995), pp. 83–97.

15 V. Liljander and T. Strandvik, 'Emotions in service satisfaction', *International Journal of Service Industry Management* 8, no. 2 (1997), pp. 148–69.

16 For more on attributions and satisfaction, see V.S. Folkes, 'Recent attribution research in consumer behavior: a review and new directions', *Journal of Consumer Research* 14 (March 1988), pp. 548–65; and Oliver, *Satisfaction*, ch. 10.

17 A.R. Hubbert, 'Customer co-creation of service outcomes: effects of locus of causality attributions', doctoral dissertation, Arizona State University, Tempe, Arizona (1995).

18 Ibid.

19 For more on fairness and satisfaction, see E.C. Clemmer and B. Schneider, 'Fair service', in *Advances in Services Marketing and Management*, vol. 5, eds T.A. Swartz, D.E. Bowen and S.W.

Brown (Greenwich, CT: JAI Press, 1996), pp. 109–26; Oliver, *Satisfaction*, ch. 7; and Olsen and Johnson, 'Service equity, satisfaction, and loyalty'.

20 Fournier and Mick, 'Rediscovering satisfaction'.

21 See, for example: C. Fornell, M.D. Johnson, E.W. Anderson, J. Cha and B.E. Bryant, 'The American Customer Satisfaction Index: nature, purpose, and findings', *Journal of Marketing* 60 (October 1996), pp. 7–18; C. Fornell, 'A national customer satisfaction barometer: the Swedish experience', *Journal of Marketing* 56 no. 1 (1992), pp. 6–21.

22 E.W. Anderson, C. Fornell and D.R. Lehmann, 'Customer satisfaction, market share, and profitability: findings from Sweden', *Journal of Marketing* 58 (July 1994), pp. 53–66.

23 M. Bruhn and M.A. Grund, 'Theory, development and implementation of national customer satisfaction indices: the Swiss index of customer satisfaction (SWICS)', *Total Quality Management* 11, no. 7 (2000), pp. S1017–S1028; A. Meyer and F. Dornach, 'The German customer barometer', (http://www.servicebarometer.de.or); Norwegian customer satisfaction barometer (www.kundebarometer.com).

24 See www.epsi-rating.com

25 Brady and Cronin, 'Some new thoughts on conceptualizing perceived service quality'.

26 Ibid.

27 See C. Gronroos, 'A service quality model and its marketing implications', *European Journal of Marketing* 18, no. 4 (1984), pp. 36–44; R.T. Rust and R.L. Oliver, 'Service quality insights and managerial implications from the frontier', in *Service Quality: New Directions in Theory and Practice*, eds R.T. Rust and R.L. Oliver (Thousand Oaks, CA: Sage, 1994), pp. 1–19; M.J. Bitner, 'Managing the evidence of service', in *The Service Quality Handbook*, eds E.E. Scheuing and W.F. Christopher (New York: AMACOM, 1993), pp. 358–70.

28 Parasuraman, Zeithaml and Berry, 'SERVQUAL: a multiple-item scale'. Details on the SERVQUAL scale and the actual items used to assess the dimensions are provided in Chapter 6.

29 Ibid.

30 C. Gronroos, 'A service quality model and its marketing implications' *European Journal of Marketing* 18 (1984), pp. 36–44.

31 R. Rust and R. Oliver, 'Service quality: insights and managerial implications from the frontier', in *Service Quality: New Directions in Theory and Practice*, eds R.T. Rust and R.L. Oliver (Thousand Oaks, CA: Sage, 1994)

32 E.g. J.H. McAlexander, D.O. Kaldenberg and H.F. Koenig, 'Service quality measurement: examination of dental practices sheds more light on the relationships between service quality, satisfaction, and purchase intentions in a health care setting', *Journal of Health Care Marketing* 14 (Fall 1994), pp. 34–40; G.H. McDougall and T.J. Levesque, 'Benefit segmentation using service quality dimensions: an investigation in retail banking', *International Journal of Bank Marketing* 12, no. 2 (1994), pp. 15–23; Brady and Cronin, 'Some new thoughts on conceptualizing perceived service quality'.

33 For a review of what is known about service quality delivery via the Web see, V.A. Zeithaml, A. Parasuraman and A. Malhotra, 'Service quality delivery through web sites: a critical review of extant knowledge', *Journal of the Academy of Marketing Science* 30, no. 4 (2002), pp. 362–75.

34 V. Zeithaml, A. Parasuraman and A. Malhotra, 'A conceptual framework for understanding

e-service quality: implications for future research and managerial practice', Marketing Science Institute Working Paper, Report No. 00-115 (2001).

35 R. Normann, *Service Management: Strategy and Leadership in the Service Business*, 3rd edn (Chichester: John Wiley & Sons, 2000).

36 'How Marriott makes a great first impression', *The Service Edge* 6, no. 5 (May 1993), p. 5.

37 A.G. Woodside, L.L. Frey and R.T. Daly, 'Linking service quality, customer satisfaction, and behavioral intention', *Journal of Health Care Marketing* 9 (December 1989), pp. 5–17.

38 G.L. Shostack, 'Planning the service encounter', in *The Service Encounter*, eds J.A. Czepiel, M.R. Solomon and C.F. Surprenant (Lexington, MA: Lexington Books, 1985), pp. 243–54.

39 Ibid.

40 For detailed discussions of the critical incident technique, see J.C. Flanagan, 'The critical incident technique', *Psychological Bulletin* 51 (July 1954), pp. 327–58; M.J. Bitner, J.D. Nyquist and B.H. Booms, 'The critical incident as a technique for analyzing the service encounter', in *Services Marketing in a Changing Environment*, eds T.M. Bloch, G.D. Upah and V.A. Zeithaml (Chicago, IL: American Marketing Association, 1985), pp. 48–51; S. Wilson-Pessano, 'Defining professional competence: the critical incident technique 40 years later', paper presentation to the Annual Meeting of the American Educational Research Association, New Orleans (1988); I. Roos, 'Methods of investigating critical incidents', *Journal of Service Research* 4 (February 2002), pp. 193–204; D.D. Gremler, 'The critical incident technique in service research', *Journal of Service Research* 7 (August 2004), pp. 65–89.

41 For a complete discussion of the research on which this section is based, see M.J. Bitner, B.H. Booms and M.S. Tetreault, 'The service encounter: diagnosing favorable and unfavorable incidents', *Journal of Marketing* 54 (January 1990), pp. 71–84; M.J. Bitner, B.H. Booms and L.A. Mohr, 'Critical service encounters: the employee's view', *Journal of Marketing* 58, no. 4 (1994), pp. 95–106; D. Gremler and M.J. Bitner, 'Classifying service encounter satisfaction across industries', in *Marketing Theory and Applications*, eds C.T. Allen et al. (Chicago, IL: American Marketing Association, 1992), pp. 111–18; and D. Gremler, M.J. Bitner and K.R. Evans, 'The internal service encounter', *International Journal of Service Industry Management* 5, no. 2 (1994), pp. 34–56.

42 Bitner, Booms and Mohr, 'Critical service encounters'.

43 This discussion is based on research and results presented in M.L. Meuter, A.L. Ostrom, R.I. Roundtree and M.J. Bitner, 'Self-service technologies: understanding customer satisfaction with technology-based service encounters', *Journal of Marketing* 64 (July 2000), pp. 50–64.

44 M.J. Bitner, S.W. Brown and M.L. Meuter, 'Technology infusion in service encounters', *Journal of the Academy of Marketing Science* 28, no. 1 (2000), pp. 138–49.

45 Bitner, 'Managing the evidence of service'.

CHAPTER 05

Conceptual framework of the book: the gaps model of service quality

❖ **LEARNING OBJECTIVES**

This chapter's objectives are to:

1 Introduce a framework, called the gaps model of service quality, which is used to organize the remainder of this textbook.

2 Demonstrate that the gaps model is a useful framework for understanding service quality in an organization.

3 Demonstrate that the most critical service quality gap to close is the customer gap, the difference between customer expectations and perceptions.

4 Show that four gaps that occur in companies, which we call provider gaps, are responsible for the customer gap.

5 Identify the factors responsible for each of the four provider gaps.

CASE STUDY: SERVICE QUALITY IN RITZ-CARLTON HOTELS

The Ritz-Carlton group of hotels places service at the forefront of its activities. The organization aims for a gold standard of service which is communicated to staff and reinforced through tools and messages such as the Ritz-Carlton credo, motto and service values.

THE CREDO

- The Ritz-Carlton is a place where the genuine care and comfort of our guests is our highest mission.

- We pledge to provide the finest personal service and facilities for our guests who will always enjoy a warm, relaxed, yet refined ambience.

- The Ritz-Carlton experience enlivens the senses, instils well-being, and fulfils even the unexpressed wishes and needs of our guests.

MOTTO

At The Ritz-Carlton Hotel Company, L.L.C., 'We are ladies and gentlemen serving ladies and gentlemen'. This motto exemplifies the anticipatory service provided by all staff members.

SERVICE VALUES: I AM PROUD TO BE RITZ-CARLTON

1 I build strong relationships and create Ritz-Carlton guests for life.

2 I am always responsive to the expressed and unexpressed wishes and needs of our guests.

3 I am empowered to create unique, memorable and personal experiences for our guests.

4 I understand my role in achieving the Key Success Factors and creating The Ritz-Carlton Mystique.

5 I continuously seek opportunities to innovate and improve The Ritz-Carlton experience.

6 I own and immediately resolve guest problems.

7 I create a work environment of teamwork and lateral service so that the needs of our guests and each other are met.

8 I have the opportunity to continuously learn and grow.

9 I am involved in the planning of the work that affects me.

10 I am proud of my professional appearance, language and behaviour.

11 I protect the privacy and security of our guests, my fellow employees and the company's confidential information and assets.

12 I am responsible for uncompromising levels of cleanliness and creating a safe and accident-free environment.

The Ritz-Carlton hotel is not alone in attempting to deliver a gold service to its customers. Many organizations train and encourage their staff and manage their operations in such a way that exceptional service should be delivered. However, this objective is not always achieved. This chapter introduces you to some of the ways that organizations fall short in delivering quality service and to the underlying reasons why these gaps occur. Delivering high-quality service is not easy. You probably do not yet realize how many different factors must be organized and managed to deliver what a hotel or any service delivers. This chapter provides that perspective.

Source: http://www.ritzcarlton.com/corporate/about_us/gold_standards.asp

Effective services marketing is a complex undertaking that involves many different strategies, skills and tasks. Executives of service organizations have long been confused about how to approach this complicated topic in an organized manner. This textbook is designed around one approach: viewing services in a structured, integrated way called the ***gaps model*** *of service quality*.[1] This model positions the key concepts, strategies and decisions in services marketing and is used to guide the structure of the rest of this book; sections of the book are tied to each of the gaps described in this chapter.

The customer gap

The ***customer gap*** is the difference between customer expectations and perceptions (see Figure 5.1). Customer expectations are standards or reference points that customers bring to the service experience, whereas customer perceptions are subjective assessments of actual service experiences. Customer expectations often consist of what a customer believes should or will happen. For example, when you visit an expensive restaurant, you expect a high level of service, one that is considerably superior to the level you would expect in a fast-food restaurant. Closing the gap between what customers expect and what they perceive is critical to delivering quality service; it forms the basis for the gaps model.

Because customer satisfaction and customer focus are so critical to competitiveness of firms, any company interested in delivering quality service must begin with a clear understanding of its customers. This understanding is relatively easy for a small organization where the owner/manager comes into direct contact with each customer but very difficult for a large organization in which managers are not in direct contact with customers. As stated in Chapter 3, the sources of customer expectations are marketer-controlled factors (such as pricing, advertising, sales promises) as well as factors that the marketer has limited ability to affect (innate personal needs, word-of-mouth communications, competitive offerings). In a perfect world, expectations and perceptions would be identical: customers would perceive that they have received what they thought they would and should. In practice these concepts are often, even usually, separated by some distance. Broadly,

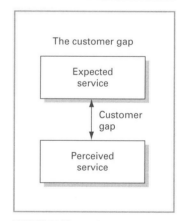

FIGURE 5.1 The customer gap

it is the goal of services marketing to bridge this distance, and we devote the remainder of the textbook to describing strategies and practices designed to close this customer gap.

The provider gaps

To close the all-important customer gap, the gaps model suggests that four other gaps – the *provider gaps* – need to be closed. These gaps occur within the organization providing the service (hence the term *provider gaps*) and include

- *Gap 1*: Not knowing what customers expect
- *Gap 2*: Not selecting the right service designs and standards
- *Gap 3*: Not delivering to service designs and standards
- *Gap 4*: Not matching performance to promises.

The rest of this chapter is devoted to a description of the full gaps model. Alternative views of the gaps model can be found in the list of further reading at the end of this chapter.

Provider gap 1: Not knowing what customers expect

Provider gap 1 is the difference between customer expectations of service and company understanding of those expectations. A primary cause in many firms for not meeting customers' expectations is that the firm lacks accurate understanding of exactly what those expectations are. Many reasons exist for managers not being aware of what customers expect: they may not

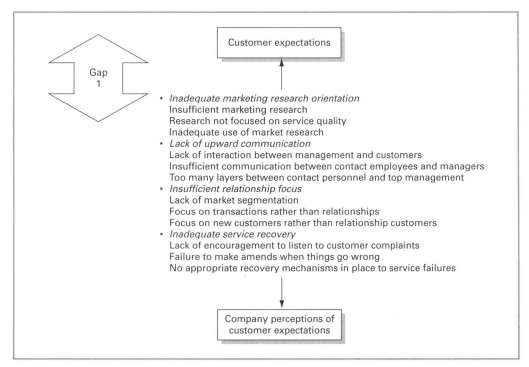

FIGURE 5.2 Key factors leading to provider gap 1

interact directly with customers, they may be unwilling to ask about expectations or they may be unprepared to address them. When people with the authority and responsibility for setting priorities do not fully understand customers' service expectations, they may trigger a chain of bad decisions and suboptimal resource allocations that results in perceptions of poor service quality. In this text, we broaden the responsibility for the first provider gap from managers alone to any employee in the organization with the authority to change or influence service policies and procedures. In today's changing organizations, the authority to make adjustments in service delivery is often delegated to empowered teams and front-line people. In business-to-business situations, in particular, account teams make their own decisions about how to address their clients' unique expectations.

Figure 5.2 shows the key factors responsible for provider gap I. An inadequate marketing research orientation is one of the critical factors. When management or empowered employees do not acquire accurate information about customers' expectations, provider gap I is large. Formal and informal methods to capture information about customer expectations must be developed through marketing research. Techniques involving a variety of traditional research approaches – among them customer interviews, survey research, complaint systems and customer panels – must be used to stay close to the customer. More innovative techniques, such as structured brainstorming and service quality gap analysis, are often needed.

Another key factor that is related to provider gap 1 is lack of upward communication. Front-line employees often know a great deal about customers; if management is not in contact with front-line employees and does not understand what they know, the gap widens.

Also related to provider gap I is a lack of company strategies to retain customers and strengthen relationships with them, an approach called relationship marketing. When organizations have strong relationships with existing customers, provider gap I is less likely to occur. Relationship marketing is distinct from transactional marketing, the term used to describe the more conventional emphasis on acquiring new customers rather than on retaining them. Relationship marketing has always been a practice with large clients of business-to-business firms (such as IBM or Siemens), but firms that sell to end customers often view such situations as sales or transactions rather than as ongoing customers. When companies focus too much on attracting new customers, they may fail to understand the changing needs and expectations of their current customers. Technology affords companies the ability to acquire and integrate vast quantities of data on customers that can be used to build relationships. Frequent-flyer travel programmes conducted by airlines, car rental companies and hotels are among the most familiar programmes of this type.

To address the factors in provider gap I, this text will cover topics that include how to understand customers through multiple research strategies (Chapter 6), and how to build strong relationships and understand customer needs over time (Chapter 7). Through these strategies, provider gap 1 can be minimized.

Provider gap 2: Not selecting the right service quality designs and standards

Accurate perceptions of customers' expectations are necessary, but not sufficient, for delivering superior quality service. Another prerequisite is the presence of service designs and performance standards that reflect those accurate perceptions. A recurring theme in service companies is the difficulty experienced in translating customer expectations into service quality specifications that employees can understand and execute. These problems are reflected in provider gap 2, the difference between company understanding of customer expectations and development of customer-driven service designs and standards. Customer-driven standards are different from the conventional performance standards that companies establish for service in that they are based

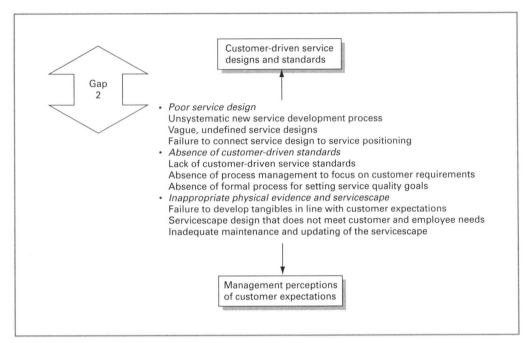

FIGURE 5.3 Key factors leading to provider gap 2

on pivotal customer requirements that are visible to and measured by customers. They are operations standards set to correspond to customer expectations and priorities rather than to company concerns such as productivity or efficiency.

As shown in Figure 5.3, provider gap 2 exists in service organizations for a variety of reasons. Those people responsible for setting standards, typically management, sometimes believe that customer expectations are unreasonable or unrealistic. They may also believe that the degree of variability inherent in service defies standardization and therefore that setting standards will not achieve the desired goal. Although some of these assumptions are valid in some situations, they are often only rationalizations of management's reluctance to tackle head-on the difficult challenges of creating service standards to deliver excellent service.

Because services are intangible, they are difficult to describe and communicate. This difficulty becomes especially evident when new services are being developed. It is critical that all people involved (managers, front-line employees and behind-the-scenes support staff) are working with the same concepts of the new service, based on customer needs and expectations. For a service that already exists, any attempt to improve it will also suffer unless everyone has the same vision of the service and associated issues. One of the most important ways to avoid provider gap 2 is clearly to design services without oversimplification, incompleteness, subjectivity and bias. To do so, tools are needed to ensure that new and existing services are developed and improved in as careful a manner as possible. Chapter 8 describes the tools that are most effective in service development and design, including service blueprinting, a unique tool for services.

The quality of service delivered by customer-contact personnel is critically influenced by the standards against which they are evaluated and compensated. Standards signal to contact personnel what the management priorities are and which types of performance really count. When service standards are absent or when the standards in place do not reflect customers' expectations, quality of service as perceived by customers is likely to suffer. When standards do reflect what customers expect, the quality of service they receive is likely to be enhanced. Chapter 9 develops further the topic of customer-defined service standards and shows that if they are developed appropriately they can have a powerful positive impact on closing both provider gap 2 and the customer gap.

In Chapter 10 we focus on the roles of physical evidence in service design and in meeting customer expectations. By *physical evidence*, we mean everything from business cards to reports, signage, Internet presence, equipment, and facilities used to deliver the service. The *servicescape*, the physical setting where the service is delivered, is a particular focus of Chapter 10. Think of a restaurant, a hotel, a theme park, a health club, a hospital or a university. The servicescape – the physical facility – is critical in these industries in terms of communicating about the service and making the entire experience pleasurable. In these cases the servicescape plays a variety of roles, from serving as a visual metaphor for what the company stands for to actually facilitating the activities of both consumers and employees. In Chapter 10 we explore the importance of physical evidence, the variety of roles it plays, and strategies for effectively designing physical evidence and the servicescape to meet customer expectations.

Provider gap 3: Not delivering to service designs and standards

Once service designs and standards are in place, it would seem that the firm is well on its way to delivering high-quality services. This assumption is true, but is still not enough to deliver excellent service. The firm must have systems, processes and people in place to ensure that service delivery actually matches (or is even better than) the designs and standards in place.

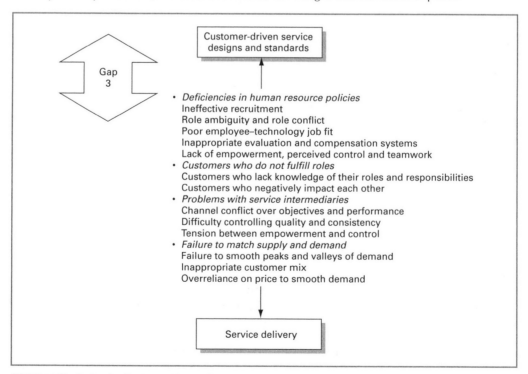

FIGURE 5.4 Key factors leading to provider gap 3

Provider gap 3 is the discrepancy between development of customer-driven service standards and actual service performance by company employees. Even when guidelines exist for performing services well and treating customers correctly, high-quality service performance is not a certainty. Standards must be backed by appropriate resources (people, systems and technology) and must be enforced to be effective – that is, employees must be measured and compensated on the basis of performance along those standards. Thus, even when standards accurately reflect customers' expectations, if the company fails to provide support for those standards – if it does not facilitate, encourage and require their achievement – standards do no good. When the level of service delivery falls short of the standards, it falls short of what customers expect as well. Narrowing gap 3 – by ensuring that all the resources needed to achieve the standards are in place – reduces the customer gap.

Research has identified many of the critical inhibitors to closing gap 3 (see Figure 5.4). These factors include employees who do not clearly understand the roles they are to play in the company, employees who experience conflict between customers and company management, poor employee selection, inadequate technology, inappropriate compensation and recognition, and lack of empowerment and teamwork. These factors all relate to the company's human resource function and involve internal practices such as recruitment, training, feedback, job design, motivation and organizational structure. To deliver better service performance, these issues must be addressed across functions (such as with both marketing and human resources).

Another important variable in provider gap 3 is the customer. Even if contact employees and intermediaries are 100 per cent consistent in their service delivery, the uncontrollable variables of the customer can introduce variability in service delivery. If customers do not perform their roles appropriately – if, for example, they fail to provide all the information necessary to the provider or neglect to read and follow instructions – service quality is jeopardized. Customers can also negatively influence the quality of service received by others if they are disruptive or take more than their share of a service provider's time. Understanding customer roles and how customers themselves can influence service delivery and outcomes is critical.

A third difficulty associated with provider gap 3 involves the challenge in delivering service through such intermediaries as retailers, franchisees, agents and brokers. Because quality in service occurs in the human interaction between customers and service providers, control over the service encounter by the company is crucial, yet it rarely is fully possible. Most service (and many manufacturing) companies face an even more formidable task: attaining service excellence and consistency in the presence of intermediaries who represent them and interact with their customers yet are not under their direct control. Franchisers of services depend on their franchisees to execute service delivery as they have specified it. And it is in the execution by the franchisee that the customer evaluates the service quality of the company. With franchises and other types of intermediaries, someone other than the producer is responsible for the fulfilment of quality service. For this reason, a firm must develop ways to either control or motivate these intermediaries to meet company goals.

Another issue in provider gap 3 is the need in service firms to synchronize demand and capacity. Because services are perishable and cannot be inventoried, service companies frequently face situations of over-demand or under-demand. Lacking inventories to handle over-demand, companies lose sales when capacity is inadequate to handle customer needs. On the other hand, capacity is frequently underutilized in slow periods. Most companies rely on operations strategies such as cross-training or varying the size of the employee pool to synchronize supply and demand. Marketing strategies for managing demand – such as price changes, advertising, promotion and alternative service offerings – can supplement approaches for managing supply.

The final key factor associated with provider gap 3 is lack of service recovery. Even the best companies, with the best of intentions and clear understanding of their customers' expectations, sometimes fail. It is critical for an organization to understand the importance of service recovery – why people complain, what they expect when they complain, and how to develop effective service recovery strategies for dealing with inevitable service failures. Such strategies might involve a well-defined complaint-handling procedure and an emphasis on empowering employees to react on the spot, in real time, to fix the failure; other times it involves a service guarantee or ways to compensate the customer for the unfulfilled promise.

We will discuss strategies to deal with the roles of employees in Chapter 11, customers in Chapter 12, intermediaries in Chapter 13, demand and capacity in Chapter 14 and service recovery in Chapter 15.

Provider gap 4: Not matching performance to promises

Provider gap 4 illustrates the difference between service delivery and the service provider's external communications. Promises made by a service company through its media advertising, sales force and other communications may potentially raise customer expectations, the standards against which customers assess service quality. The discrepancy between actual and promised service therefore has an adverse effect on the customer gap. Broken promises can occur for many reasons: over-promising in advertising or personal selling, inadequate coordination between operations and marketing, and differences in policies and procedures across service outlets. Figure 5.5 shows the key factors that lead to provider gap 4.

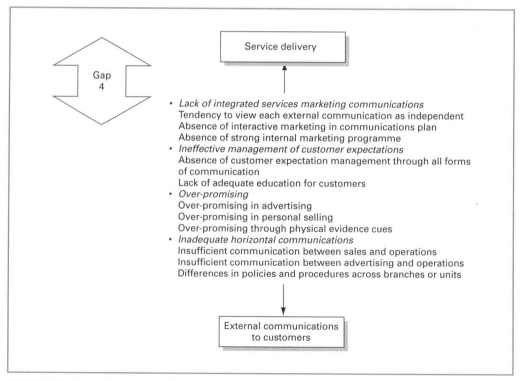

FIGURE 5.5 Key factors leading to provider gap 4

In addition to unduly elevating expectations through exaggerated claims, there are other, less obvious ways in which external communications influence customers' service quality assessments. Service companies frequently fail to capitalize on opportunities to educate customers to use services appropriately. They also neglect to manage customer expectations of what will be delivered in service transactions and relationships.

One of the major difficulties associated with provider gap 4 is that communications to consumers involve issues that cross organizational boundaries. Because service advertising promises what people do, and because what *people* do cannot be controlled like machines that produce physical goods can be controlled, this type of communication involves functions other than the marketing department. This type of marketing is what we call *interactive marketing* – the marketing between contact people and customers – and it must be coordinated with the conventional types of *external marketing* used in product and service firms. When employees who promote the service do not fully understand the reality of service delivery, they are likely to make exaggerated promises or fail to communicate to customers aspects of the service intended to serve them well. The result is poor service quality perceptions. Effectively coordinating actual service delivery with external communications, therefore, narrows provider gap 4 and favourably affects the customer gap as well.

Another issue in provider gap 4 is associated with the pricing of services. In packaged goods (and even in durable goods), customers possess enough price knowledge before purchase to be able to judge whether a price is fair or in line with competition. With services, customers often have no internal reference points for prices before purchase and consumption. Pricing strategies such as discounting, 'everyday prices', and couponing obviously need to be different in service cases in which the customer has no initial sense of prices. Techniques for developing prices for services are more complicated than those for pricing tangible goods.

In summary, external communications – whether from marketing communications or pricing – can create a larger customer gap by raising expectations about service delivery. In addition to improving service delivery, companies must also manage all communications to customers so that inflated promises do not lead to higher expectations. Chapter 16 will discuss integrated services marketing communications, and Chapter 17 will cover pricing to accomplish these objectives.

CASE STUDY: AMAZON CLOSES THE GAPS

Can an online company be an excellent service provider, identifying customer expectations and meeting them by closing the four provider gaps? Amazon is a company that exemplifies the use of the strategies needed to provide consistent, accurate, and even personalized service.

Understanding customer expectations is a strategy that Amazon begins when a customer first starts shopping at its online store. From the very first time customers make choices, the company's computers begin profiles on them, offering selections based on a database of previous customers that read similar books or listened to similar music. In the beginning some offerings may not seem on target, but the longer customers shop at Amazon, the more accurately the company identifies their preferences and the more appropriate suggestions become. In time, the company even begins to send emails that are so specific ('We noticed that you purchased the last book by Jonathan Kellerman and we want you to know that he has just published a new book.') that it almost seems like the local librarian is calling to let you know your new book is in. One of the company's unique features is 'Your Store', a tab on the home page that sends customers to a selection of items that past purchases indicate would be of interest to them.

Customer-defined standards exist for virtually all activities at Amazon, from delivery to communication to service recovery. When you buy a product from Amazon, you select the mode of delivery and the company tells you the expected number of days it will take to receive your merchandise. Standard shipping is three to five days, but two- and one-day shipping are also available. The company has standards for how quickly you are informed when a product is unavailable (immediately), how fast you find out whether an out-of-print book can be located (three weeks), how long you can return items (30 days) and whether you pay return shipping costs (not if it is Amazon's error).

Service performance is where Amazon excels. Orders almost always arrive ahead of the promised date, are accurate and are in excellent condition because of careful shipping practices. The company's copyrighted One-click Ordering allows regular customers to make purchases instantaneously without creating a shopping cart. Customers can track packages and review previous orders at any time. Amazon also makes sure that all its partners, who sell used and new books and other items direct to customers, perform to Amazon's standards. The company verifies performance of each purchase by asking the customer how well the merchant performed, then it posts scores where customers can see them easily.

Managing promises is handled by clear and careful communication on the website. Virtually every page is easy to understand and navigate. For example, the page dealing with returns eliminates customer misunderstanding by clearly spelling out what can be returned (almost everything) and what cannot (items that are gas powered or have flammable liquids, large televisions, opened CDs). The page describes how to repack items and when refunds are given. The page dealing with a customer's account shows all previous purchases and exactly where every ordered item is in the shipping process.

Amazon's strategies have been well received by its customers and the Amazon brand is known worldwide.

Source: www.Amazon.co.uk

Putting it all together: closing the gaps

The full conceptual model shown in Figure 5.6 conveys a clear message to managers wishing to improve their quality of service: the key to closing the customer gap is to close provider gaps l through 4 and keep them closed. To the extent that one or more of provider gaps l through 4 exist, customers perceive service quality shortfalls. The gaps model of service quality serves as a framework for service organizations attempting to improve quality service and services marketing.

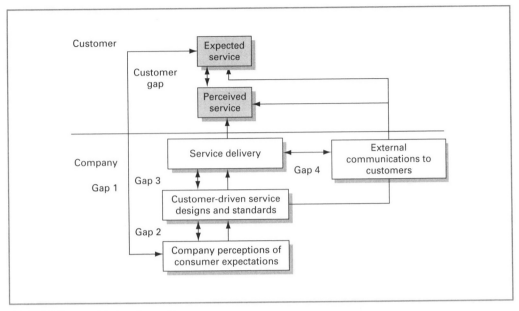

FIGURE 5.6 Gaps model of service quality

CASE STUDY: USING THE GAPS MODEL TO ASSESS AN ORGANIZATION'S SERVICE STRATEGY

The gaps model featured in this chapter and used as a framework for this textbook is a useful way to audit the service performance and capabilities of an organization. The model has been used by many companies as an assessment or service audit tool because it is comprehensive and offers a way for companies to examine all the factors that influence service quality. To use the tool, a company documents what it knows about each gap and the factors that affect the size of the gap. Although you will learn much more about each of these gaps throughout the book, we provide here a basic gaps audit. In Exercise 1 at the end of the chapter, we propose that you use this audit with a company to determine its service quality gaps.

Service quality gaps model audit
For each of the following factors in the gaps, indicate the effectiveness of the organization on that factor. Use a 1 to 10 scale where l is 'poor' and 10 is 'excellent'.

Customer gap 1
1 How well does the company understand customer expectations of service quality?
2 How well does the company understand customer perceptions of service?

1 = poor
10 = excellent

Provider gap 1

1 Market research orientation

Is the amount and type of market research adequate to understand customer expectations of service?

Does the company use this information in decisions about service provision?

2 Upward communication

Do managers and customers interact enough for management to know what customers expect?

Do contact people tell management what customers expect?

3 Relationship focus

To what extent does the company understand the expectations of different customer segments?

To what extent does the company focus on relationships with customers rather than transactions?

Score for provider gap 1

1 = poor
10 = excellent

Provider gap 2

4 Systematic service design

How effective is the company's service development process?

How well are new services defined for customers and employees?

5 Presence of customer-defined standards

How effective are the company's service standards?

Are they defined to correspond to customer expectations?

How effective is the process for setting and tracking service quality goals?

6 Appropriate physical evidence and servicescape

How appropriate, attractive and effective are the company's physical facilities, equipment and other tangibles?

Score for provider gap 2

1 = poor
10 = excellent

Provider gap 3

7 Effective human resource policies

How effectively does the company recruit, hire, train, compensate and empower employees?

Is service quality delivery consistent across employees, teams, units and branches?

8 Effective role fulfilment by customers

Do customers understand their roles and responsibilities?

▶ Does the company manage customers to fulfill their roles, especially customers that are incompatible?

9 Effective alignment with service intermediaries

How well are service intermediaries aligned with the company?

Is there conflict over objectives and performance, costs and rewards?

Is service quality delivery consistent across the outlets?

10 Alignment of supply and demand

How well is the company able to match supply with demand fluctuations?

11 Service recovery

How effective are the service recovery efforts of the organization?

How well does the organization plan for service failures?

Score for provider gap 3

1 = poor
10 = excellent

Provider gap 4

12 Integrated services marketing communications

How well do all company communications – including the interactions between company employees and customers – express the same message and level of service quality?

13 Effective management of customer expectations

How well does the company communicate to customers about what will be provided to them?

14 Accurate promising in advertising and personal selling

Does the company avoid overpromising and overselling?

15 Adequate horizontal communications

How well do different parts of the organization communicate with each other so that service quality equals what is promised?

Score for provider gap 4

1 = poor
10 = excellent

The score for each gap should be compared to the maximum score possible. Are particular gaps weaker than others? Which areas in each gap need attention? As you go through the rest of the book, we will provide more detail about how to improve the factors in each of the gaps.

The model begins where the process of improving service quality begins: with an understanding of the nature and extent of the customer gap. Given the service organization's need to focus on the customer and to use knowledge about the customer to drive business strategy, we believe that this foundation of emphasis is warranted.

Summary

This chapter presented the integrated gaps model of service quality (shown in Figure 5.6), a framework for understanding and improving service delivery. The remainder of the text will be organized around this model of service quality, which focuses on the four provider gaps in delivering and marketing a service:

- *Provider gap 1*: Not knowing what customers expect
- *Provider gap 2*: Not selecting the right service designs and standards
- *Provider gap 3*: Not delivering to service designs and standards
- *Provider gap 4*: Not matching performance to promises.

The gaps model positions the key concepts, strategies and decisions in services marketing in a manner that begins with the customer and builds the organization's tasks around what is needed to close the gap between customer expectations and perceptions. The final chapter in the book, Chapter 18, discusses the financial implications of service quality, reviewing the research and company data that indicate linkages between service quality and financial performance.

Key concepts

Customer gap	105
Gaps model	105
Provider gaps	106

Further reading

For an alternative view of the gaps model, see:

Asubonteng, P., McCleary, C. and Swan, J. (1996) 'SERVQUAL revisited: a critical review of service quality', *The Journal of Services Marketing*, 10(6), 62–81.

Brady, M. and Cronin, J. (2001) 'Some new thoughts on conceptualising perceived service quality: a hierarchical approach', *Journal of Marketing*, 65(2), 34–49.

Teas, K. (1993) 'Expectations, performance evaluation and consumers perception of quality', *Journal of Marketing*, 57(4), 18–34.

Discussion questions

1 Think about a service you receive. Is there a gap between your expectations and perceptions of that service? What do you expect that you do not receive?

2 Think about a service that you receive regularly. How would you change the service and the way it is provided to make it better for the customer?

3 If you were the manager of a service organization and wanted to apply the gaps model

to improve service, which gap would you start with? Why? In what order would you proceed to close the gaps?

4 Can provider gap 4 be closed prior to closing any of the other three provider gaps? How?

5 Which of the four provider gaps do you believe is hardest to close? Why?

Exercises

1 Choose an organization to interview, and use the integrated gaps model of service quality as a framework. Ask the manager whether the organization suffers from any of the factors listed in the figures in this chapter. Which factor in each of Figures 5.2 through to 5.5 does the manager consider the most troublesome?

2 What does the company do to try to address the problems?

3 Use the Internet to locate the website of Ritz-Carlton, IKEA, KLM or any other well-known, service organization. Which provider gaps has the company closed? How can you tell?

4 Interview a non-profit or public sector organization in your area (it could be some part of your university or college). Find out if the integrated gaps model of service quality framework makes sense in the context of its organization.

Note

1 The gaps model of service quality that provides the structure for this text was developed by and is fully presented in V.A. Zeithaml, A. Parasuraman and L.L. Berry, *Delivering Quality Service: Balancing Customer Perceptions and Expectations* (New York: Free Press, 1990).

PART 2
Understanding Customer Requirements

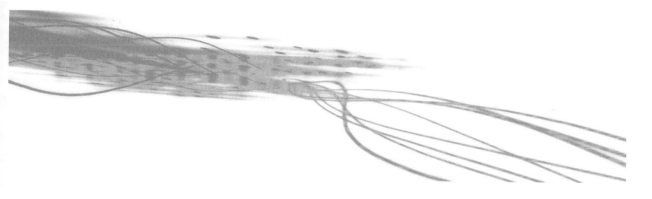

The listening gap

Not knowing what customers expect is one of the root causes of not delivering to customer expectations. Provider gap 1 is the difference between customer expectations of service and company understanding of those expectations. Note that in the accompanying figure we created a link between the customer and the company, showing customer expectations above the line that dissects the model and provider perceptions of those expectations below the line. This alignment signifies that what customers expect is not always the same as what companies believe they expect.

Part 2 describes two ways to close provider gap 1. In Chapter 6, we detail ways that companies listen to customers through research. Both formal and informal methods of customer research are described, including surveys, critical incident studies and complaint solicitation. Upward communication

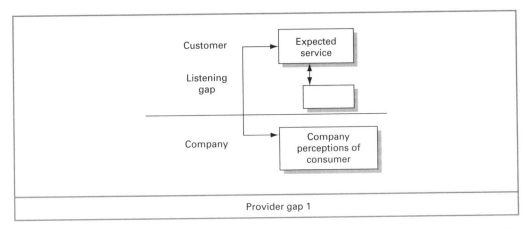

from front-line employees to managers, another key factor in listening to customers, is also discussed.

Chapter 7 covers company strategies to retain customers and strengthen relationships with them, an approach called relationship marketing. Relationship marketing is distinct from transactional marketing, the more conventional approach that tends to focus on acquiring new customers rather than retaining them. When organizations have strong relationships with existing customers, opportunities for in-depth listening increase over time and provider gap 1 is less likely to occur. A variety of strategies, including the creation of switching barriers and the development of relationship bonds, are suggested as a means of relationship development and, ultimately, the cultivation of customer loyalty.

CHAPTER 06

Listening to customers through research

This chapter's objectives are to:

1 Present the types of and guidelines for marketing research in services.

2 Show how marketing research information can and should be used for services.

3 Describe the strategies by which companies can facilitate interaction and communication between management and customers.

4 Present ways that companies can and do facilitate interaction between contact people and management.

CASE STUDY: LONDON UNDERGROUND LISTENS

The growth in London's night time economy has meant that more people now travel later at night. Over the past five years London's night bus services have been significantly expanded. However, running the Underground later would represent a significant improvement in service, helping people get home safely, quickly and conveniently at these times. The Mayor of the city, Ken Livingstone, asked Transport for London (TfL), the body responsible for London Underground, to investigate what could be done to deliver later Underground (the Tube) services.

A proposal was developed to provide services later at night without impacting on the time period required to undertake engineering works (normally carried out during the night). This comprised running the Tube one hour later on Friday and Saturday nights, and starting the service one hour later on Saturday and Sunday mornings. Initial research from TfL indicated that around 140 000 more people per week would use the Tube if the service ran later. However, around 55 000 trips being made in the early mornings at weekends would be adversely affected, particularly on Sunday mornings as the Tube would not reach most destinations until 8.30 a.m. The people that would be most affected would be those travelling to work and to or from airports. Transport for London and the Mayor of London therefore decided that it was important to seek public views on the proposal before deciding whether to proceed. The consultation exercise comprised three elements:

♦ *Public consultation* – a questionnaire formed the key method for people to give their feedback. This was available in a leaflet and on the TfL website and asked people to describe their travel patterns, both early morning and late at night. It also asked whether people would use the Tube if it ran one hour later and whether they supported or opposed the proposal. A major publicity campaign drew attention to the proposal and this generated considerable media coverage. People could also participate by writing emails and letters

♦ *Market research* – MORI asked a representative sample of 1000 Londoners about the proposal. Several other pieces of market research were also undertaken

♦ *Stakeholder engagement* – TfL contacted a wide range of stakeholders (airports/airline industry, business, the health service, local government and trade unions) to seek comments on particular issues or aspects of the proposal that may affect the members they represent: 106 replied.

A total of 54 419 questionnaire responses were received – the largest response to any London Underground consultation. Seventy-three per cent of respondents supported the proposal to run the Underground one hour later on Friday and Saturday nights and one hour later on

Saturday and Sunday mornings. This compares with 22 per cent opposing the proposal, and 15 per cent strongly opposing.

Key reasons for supporting the proposal are that the Tube is perceived to be more convenient, cheaper and safer than the alternatives. Conversely, over half of those opposing the proposal based this on the difficulty that would be caused to early morning work journeys. People were also concerned about connections to mainline train stations and airports. The stakeholder groups, in particular, were concerned about the unsatisfactory nature of alternative public transport provision in the early morning period, causing difficulties for weekend employees, especially those in low-paid employment, being able to get to work.

Having listened to the views of their customers and stakeholders, TfL are now developing proposals to put to the Mayor.

Source: adapted from Transport for London (2005) 'One hour later tube: public consultation results – executive summary', August (also available at: www.tfl.gov.uk/onehourlater)

Despite a genuine interest in meeting customer expectations, many companies miss the mark by thinking inside out – they believe they know what customers *should* want and deliver that, rather than finding out what they *do* want. When this happens, companies provide services that do not match customer expectations: important features are left out, and the levels of performance on features that are provided are inadequate. Because services have few clearly defined and tangible cues, this difficulty may be considerably larger than it is in manufacturing firms. A far better approach involves thinking outside in – determining customer expectations and then delivering to them. Thinking outside in uses **marketing research** to understand customers and their requirements fully. Marketing research, the subject of this chapter, involves far more than conventional surveys. It consists of a portfolio of listening strategies that allow companies to deliver service to meet customer expectations. It also has to be integrated with other information sources such as customer databases. Over the past 10 years, significant improvements in computerization, database management and data capture have meant that many organizations now hold significant amounts of data on their customers. For example, an airline operating a loyalty card scheme will have details on each cardholder relating to:

- Their home address
- The frequency with which they fly
- The days and times they fly
- The value of their annual flights
- The range of destinations they visit
- Their seating and check-in preferences
- The frequency with which they respond to promotional offers
- Their price sensitivity.

In addition, the booking information may indicate whether they always travel alone, travel on business or for pleasure, and use secretaries or travel agents to book their flights.

The availability of both customer databases and marketing research means that many organizations are starting to adopt an integrated approach to the collection, recording, analysing and interpreting of information on customers, competitors and markets.[1]

Using marketing research to understand customer expectations

Although behavioural information may be available from customer databases, finding out what customers expect is essential to providing service quality, and marketing research is the key vehicle for understanding customer expectations and perceptions of services. In services, as with any offering, a firm that does no marketing research at all is unlikely to understand its customers. A firm that does marketing research, but not on the topic of customer expectations, may also fail to know what is needed to stay in tune with changing customer requirements. Marketing research must focus on service issues such as what features are most important to customers, what levels of these features customers expect, and what customers think the company can and should do when problems occur in service delivery. Even when a service firm is small and has limited resources to conduct research, avenues are open to explore what customers expect.

In this section we discuss the elements of services marketing **research programmes** that help companies identify customer expectations and perceptions. In the sections that follow, we will discuss ways in which the tactics of general marketing research may need to be adjusted to maximize its effectiveness in services.

Research objectives for services

The first step in designing services marketing research is without doubt the most critical: defining the problem and **research objectives**. This is where the services marketer poses the questions to be answered or problems to be solved with research. Does the company want to know how customers view the service provided by the company, what customer requirements are, how customers will respond to a new service introduction or what customers will want from the company five years from now? Each of these research questions requires a different research strategy. Thus it is essential to devote time and resources to define the problem thoroughly and accurately. In spite of the importance of this first stage, many marketing research studies are initiated without adequate attention to objectives.

Research objectives translate into action questions. While many different questions are likely to be part of a marketing research programme, the following are the most common research objectives in services:

- To discover customer requirements or expectations for service
- To develop customer-defined standards for service delivery (see Chapter 9)
- To monitor and track service performance
- To assess overall company performance compared with that of competition
- To assess gaps between customer expectations and perceptions
- To identify dissatisfied customers, so that service recovery can be attempted
- To gauge effectiveness of changes in service delivery
- To appraise the service performance of individuals and teams for evaluation, recognition and rewards
- To determine customer expectations for a new service
- To monitor changing customer expectations in an industry
- To forecast future expectations of customers.

Type of information	Primary objectives
Complaint solicitation	To identify/attend to dissatisfied customers
	To identify common service failure points
Critical incident studies	To identify 'best practices' at transaction level
	To identify customer requirements as input for quantitative studies
	To identify common service failure points
	To identify systemic strengths and weaknesses in customer-contact services
Researching customer needs **Customer satisfaction surveys and SERVQUAL surveys**	To identify customer requirements as input for quantitative research
	To monitor and track service performance
	To assess overall company performance compared with that of competition
	To determine links between satisfaction and behavioural intentions
	To assess gaps between customer expectations and perceptions
Database marketing research	To identify the individual requirements of customers using information technology and database information
Exit surveys	To obtain immediate feedback on performance of service transactions
	To measure effectiveness of changes in service delivery
	To assess service performance of individuals and teams
	To use as input for process improvements
	To identify common service failure points
Service expectation meetings and reviews	To create dialogue with important customers
	To identify what individual large customers expect and then to ensure that it is delivered
	To close the loop with important customers
Market-oriented ethnography	To research customers in natural settings
	To study customers while they are in a service encounter
Mystery shopping	To measure individual employee performance for evaluation, recognition and rewards
	To identify systemic strengths and weaknesses in customer-contact services
Customer panels	To monitor changes in customer expectations over time
	To provide a forum for customers to suggest and evaluate new service ideas
Lost customer follow-up	To identify reasons for customer defection
	To assess gaps between customer expectations and perceptions
Future expectations research	To forecast future expectations of customers
	To develop and test new service ideas

TABLE 6.1 Elements in an effective marketing information-gathering and research programme for services

These research objectives are similar in many ways to the research conducted for physical products: both aim to assess customer requirements, dissatisfaction, and demand. Services research, however, incorporates additional elements that require specific attention.

Services research must continually monitor and track service performance because performance is subject to human variability and heterogeneity. Conducting performance research at a single point in time, as might be done for a physical product such as a car, would be insufficient in services. A major focus of services research involves capturing human performance – at the level of individual employee, team, branch, organization as a whole and competition. Another focus of services research involves documenting the process by which service is performed. Even when service employees are performing well, a service provider must continue to track performance because the potential for variation in service delivery always exists.

Table 6.1 lists a number of services research objectives. Once objectives such as these have been identified, they will point the way to decisions about the most appropriate type of research, methods of data collection, and ways to use the information. The additional columns in this figure are described in later sections of this chapter.

Criteria for an effective services research programme

A *services research programme* can be defined as the composite of separate research studies and information gathering needed to address research objectives and execute an overall measurement strategy. Many types of research could be considered in a research programme. Understanding the criteria for an effective services research programme and the information needs of the key decision-makers within a service organization will help an organization evaluate the different types of information source and choose those most appropriate to address the decisions that have to be undertaken. In this section we discuss these criteria (Figure 6.1).

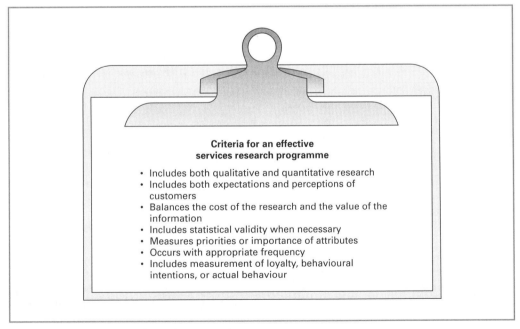

Criteria for an effective services research programme

- Includes both qualitative and quantitative research
- Includes both expectations and perceptions of customers
- Balances the cost of the research and the value of the information
- Includes statistical validity when necessary
- Measures priorities or importance of attributes
- Occurs with appropriate frequency
- Includes measurement of loyalty, behavioural intentions, or actual behaviour

FIGURE 6.1 Criteria for an effective services research programme

Includes qualitative and quantitative research

Marketing research is not limited to surveys and statistics. Some forms of research, called ***qualitative research***, are exploratory and preliminary and are conducted to clarify problem definition, to prepare for more formal research or to gain insight when more formal research is not necessary.

Service spotlight

Asda, part of the Walmart group, has trained its staff to undertake informal group discussions with customers as well as accompany individual shoppers as they proceed around a store. The organization perceives this as a very powerful way of getting the service personnel to think about the customer. Usually staff see the store from an operational perspective, rather than a customer's perspective; accompanying customers on a shopping trip changes the perspective.

Insights gained through one-to-one interactions like those at Asda, customer focus groups, critical incidents research (described in Chapter 4 and discussed more fully later in this chapter) and direct observation of service transactions also show the marketer the right questions to ask of consumers. Because the results of qualitative research play a major role in designing **quantitative research**, it is often the first type of research done. Qualitative research can also be conducted after quantitative research to make the numbers in computer printouts meaningful by giving managers the perspective and sensitivity that are critical in interpreting data and initiating improvement efforts.[2]

Quantitative research in marketing is designed to describe empirically the nature, attitudes or behaviours of customers and to test specific hypotheses that a services marketer wants to examine. Quantitative research clearly is essential to assessing and improving service delivery and design, for it provides managers with data from which they can make inferences about customer groups. These studies are key for quantifying the customers' satisfaction, the importance of service attributes, the extent of service quality gaps and perceptions of value. Such studies also provide managers with benchmarks for evaluating competitors. Finally, results from quantitative studies can highlight specific service deficiencies that can be more deeply probed through follow-up qualitative research.

Includes both perceptions and expectations of customers

As we discussed in Chapter 3, expectations serve as standards or reference points for customers. In evaluating service quality, customers compare what they perceive they get in a service encounter with their expectations of that encounter. For this reason, a measurement programme that captures only perceptions of service may be missing a critical part of the service quality equation. Companies need also to incorporate measures of customer expectations.

Measurement of expectations can be included in a research programme in multiple ways. First, basic research that relates to customers' requirements – that identifies the service features or attributes that matter to customers – can be considered expectation research. In this form, the *content* of customer expectations is captured, initially in some form of qualitative research such as focus group interviews. Research on the *levels* of customer expectations is also needed. Some organizations use research to quantitatively assess the levels of customer expectations and compare these with perception levels, usually by calculating the gap between expectations and perceptions.

Balances the cost of the research and the value of the information

An assessment of the cost of research compared with its benefits or value to the company is another key criterion. One cost is monetary, including direct costs to marketing research companies, payments to respondents and internal company costs incurred by employees collecting the information. Time costs are also important, including the time commitment needed internally by employees to administer the research and the interval between data collection and availability for use by the firm. These and other costs must be weighed against the gains to the company in improved decision-making, retained customers and successful new product launches. As in many other marketing decisions, costs are easier to estimate than the value of the information. In later chapters we describe approaches to estimating the value of customers to a company, approaches that are useful as input to the trade-off analysis needed to address this criterion.

Includes statistical validity when necessary

We have already shown that research has multiple and diverse objectives. These objectives determine the appropriate type of research and methodology. To illustrate, some research is used by companies not so much to measure as to build relationships with customers – to allow contact employees to find out what customers desire, to diagnose the strengths and weaknesses of their and the firm's efforts to address the desires, to prepare a plan to meet requirements, and to confirm after a period of time (usually one year) that the company has executed the plan. The underlying objective of this type of research is to allow contact people to identify specific action items that will gain the maximum return in customer satisfaction for individual customers. This type of research does not need sophisticated quantitative analysis, anonymity of customers, careful control of sampling or strong statistical validity.

On the other hand, research used to track overall service quality or customer satisfaction over time that may also be used for determining bonuses and salary increases of front-line service personnel must be carefully controlled for sampling bias and statistical validity. Not all forms of research have statistical validity, and not all forms need it. Most forms of qualitative research, for example, do not possess statistical validity.

Measures priorities or importance

Customers have many service requirements, but not all are equally important. One of the most common mistakes managers make in trying to improve service is spending resources on the wrong initiatives, only to become discouraged because the firm's service does not improve! Measuring the relative importance of service dimensions and attributes helps managers to channel resources effectively; therefore, research must document the priorities of the customer. Prioritization can be accomplished in multiple ways. *Direct importance measures* ask customers to prioritize items or dimensions of service. Several alternatives are available for measuring importance directly, among them asking respondents to rank-order service dimensions or attributes, or to rate them on a scale from 'not at all important' to 'extremely important'. One effective approach involves asking respondents to allocate a total of 100 points across the various service dimensions. *Indirect importance measures* are estimated using the statistical procedures of correlation and regression analysis, which show the relative contribution of questionnaire items or requirements to overall service quality. Both indirect and direct importance measures provide evidence of customer priorities, and the technique that is chosen depends on the nature of the study and the number of dimensions or attributes that are being evaluated (see customer defined service standards in Chapter 9).

Occurs with appropriate frequency

Because customer expectations and perceptions are dynamic, companies need to institute a service quality research process, not just do isolated studies. A single study of service provides only a 'snapshot' view of one moment in time. For full understanding of the marketplace's acceptance of a company's service, marketing research must be ongoing. Without a pattern of studies repeated with appropriate frequency, managers cannot tell whether the organization is moving forward or falling back and which of their service improvement initiatives are working. Just what does 'ongoing research' mean in terms of frequency? The answer is specific to the type of service and to the purpose and method of each type of service research a company might do. As we discuss the different types in the following section, you will see the frequency with which each type of research could be conducted.

Includes measures of loyalty, behavioural intentions or behaviour

An important trend in services research involves measuring the positive and negative consequences of service quality along with overall satisfaction or service quality scores. Among the most important generic behavioural intentions are willingness to recommend the service to others and repurchase intent. These behavioural intentions can be viewed as positive and negative consequences of service quality. Positive behavioural intentions include saying positive things about the company, recommending the company to others, remaining loyal, spending more with the company and paying a price premium. Negative behavioural intentions include saying negative things to others, doing less business with the company, switching to another company and complaining to consumer pressure groups. Other more specific behaviours differ by service; for example, behaviours related to medical care include following instructions from the doctor, taking medications and returning for follow-up. Tracking these areas can help a company estimate the relative value of service improvements to the company and can also identify customers who are in danger of defecting.

Elements in an effective services marketing research programme

A good services marketing research programme includes multiple types of information source and research studies. The composite of information and types of research will differ by company because the range of uses for service quality research – from employee performance assessment to advertising campaign development to strategic planning – requires a rich, multi-faceted flow of information. If an organization were to engage in virtually all types of service research, the portfolio would look like Figure 6.1, but few organizations do all types of research. The particular portfolio for any organization will match organization resources and address the key areas needed to understand the customers of the business. So that it will be easier for you to identify the appropriate type of research for different research objectives, we list the objectives in column 2 of Table 6.1. In the following sections we describe each major type of research and show the way each type addresses the criteria associated with it.

Complaint solicitation

Many of you have complained to employees of service organizations, only to find that nothing happens with your complaint. No one rushes to solve it, and the next time you experience the service the same problem is present. How frustrating! Good service organizations take complaints seriously. Not only do they listen to complaints – they also seek complaints as communications about what can be done to improve their service and their service employees.

> ## Service spotlight
>
> Scandinavian Airlines collect customers' opinions daily through a wide range of channels, including the Internet, letters, paper-based forms and the telephone. In Scandinavia alone, the company has a total of 55 people working on processing around 50 000 spontaneous customer comments a year. The data are presented in a portal environment on the airline's intranet, which means that all employees can access any of the feedback. Customized reports for a large number of department managers are also created, which allows them to see exactly how the areas they are responsible for are experienced and perceived by customers. For example, the data can be interogated with questions such as 'What can we do to improve the flights between Stockholm and Paris?'

Firms that use complaints as research collect and document them, then use the information to identify dissatisfied customers, correct individual problems where possible and identify common service failure points. Although this research is used for both goods and services, it has a critical real-time purpose in services – to improve failure points and to improve or correct the performance of contact personnel. Research on complaints is one of the easiest types of research for firms to conduct, leading many companies to depend solely on complaints to stay in touch with customers. Unfortunately, convincing research provides evidence that customer complaints alone are a woefully inadequate source of information: only a small percentage of customers with problems actually complain to the company. The rest will stay dissatisfied, telling other people about their dissatisfaction.

To be effective, **complaint solicitation** requires rigorous recording of numbers and types of complaints through many channels, and then working to eliminate the most frequent problems. Complaint channels include employees at the front line, intermediary organizations like retailers who deliver service, managers, and complaints to third parties such as consumer pressure groups. Companies must both solve individual customer problems and seek overall patterns to eliminate failure points. More sophisticated forms of complaint resolution define 'complaint' broadly to include all comments – both negative and positive – as well as questions from customers. Firms should build depositories for this information and report results frequently, perhaps weekly or monthly.

Critical incident studies

In Chapter 4, we discussed the **critical incident technique** (CIT), a qualitative interview procedure in which customers are asked to provide verbatim stories about satisfying and dissatisfying service encounters they have experienced. According to a recent summary of the use of the technique in services, CIT has been reported in hotels, restaurants, airlines, amusement parks, car repair, retailing, banking, cable television, public transportation and education.[3] The studies have explored a wide range of service topics: consumer evaluation of services, service failure and recovery, employees, customer participation in service delivery, and service experience.

Critical incident technique has many benefits. First, data are collected from the respondent's perspective and are usually vivid because they are expressed in consumers' own words and reflect the way they think. Second, the method provides concrete information about the way the company and its employees behave and react, thereby making the research easy to translate into action. Third, like most qualitative methods, the research is particularly useful when the topic or service is new and very little other information exists. Finally, the method is well suited for assessing perceptions of customers from different cultures because it allows respondents to share their perceptions rather than answer researcher-defined questions.[4]

Researching customer needs

Researching customer needs involves identifying the benefits and attributes that customers expect in a service. This type of research is very basic and essential because it determines the type of questions that will be asked in surveys and ultimately the improvements that will be attempted by the firm. Because these studies are so foundational, qualitative techniques are appropriate to begin them. Quantitative techniques may follow, usually during a pre-test stage of survey development. Unfortunately, many companies do superficial research, often developing surveys on the basis of intuition or company direction rather than through customer probing.

Service spotlight

An example of this type of research is that undertaken for Moto, the UK's largest provider of motorway service stations. The research was aimed at redesigning its service stations and food offerings. Focus groups were held with Moto's three major customer groups: families, business users and the haulage community. The business users wanted an 'office on the road', the families needed a place where 'the kids could be let loose' and the haulage users wanted separate areas in which to take their breaks. Moto is now dividing its stations into three zones. The research project is expected to continue tracking response from customers as the new design is rolled out.[5]

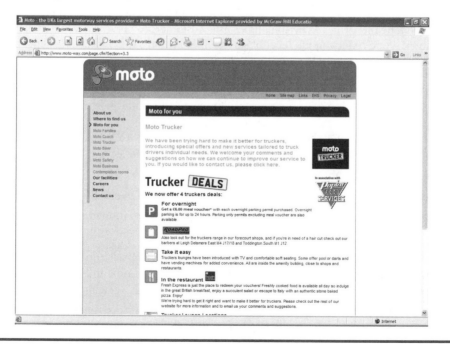

Another approach to researching customer needs that has been effective in services industries is to examine existing research about customer requirements in similar service industries. The five dimensions of quality service are generalizable across industries, and sometimes the way these dimensions are manifest is also remarkably similar. Customers of travel agencies and customers of banks, for example, expect many of the same features when using these two services. Besides expert advice, customers in travel agents expect short queues, brochures, informative websites and a friendly empathetic service – the same features that are salient to bank customers. In these and other industries that share common customer expectations, managers may find it helpful to seek knowledge from existing research in a related service industry.

Relationship and SERVQUAL surveys

One category of surveys could appropriately be named *relationship surveys* because they pose questions about all elements in the customer's relationship with the company (including service, product and price). This comprehensive approach can help a company diagnose its relationship strengths and weaknesses. These surveys typically monitor and track service performance annually with an initial survey providing a baseline. Relationship surveys are also effective in comparing company performance with that of competitors, often focusing on the best competitor's performance as a benchmark. When used for this purpose, the sponsor of the survey is not identified and questions are asked about both the company and one or more competitors.

A sound measure of service quality is necessary for identifying the aspects of service needing performance improvement, assessing how much improvement is needed on each aspect, and evaluating the impact of improvement efforts. Unlike goods quality, which can be measured objectively by such indicators as durability and number of defects, service quality is abstract and is best captured by surveys that measure customer evaluations of service. One of the first measures to be developed specifically to measure service quality was the **SERVQUAL** survey.

The SERVQUAL scale involves a survey containing 21 service attributes, grouped into the five service quality dimensions (discussed in Chapter 4) of reliability, responsiveness, assurance, empathy and tangibles. The survey sometimes asks customers to provide two different ratings on each attribute – one reflecting the level of service they would expect from excellent companies in a sector and the other reflecting their perception of the service delivered by a specific company within that sector. The difference between the expectation and perception ratings constitutes a quantified measure of service quality. Figure 6.2 shows the items on the basic SERVQUAL scale as well as the phrasing of the expectations and perceptions portions of the scale.

Data gathered through a SERVQUAL survey can be used for a variety of purposes:

- To determine the average gap score (between customers' perceptions and expectations) for each service attribute
- To assess a company's service quality along each of the five SERVQUAL dimensions
- To track customers' expectations and perceptions (on individual service attributes and/or on the SERVQUAL dimensions) over time
- To compare a company's SERVQUAL scores against those of competitors
- To identify and examine customer segments that differ significantly in their assessments of a company's service performance
- To assess internal service quality (that is, the quality of service rendered by one department or division of a company to others within the same company).

The SERVQUAL scale was first published in 1988 and has undergone numerous improvements and revisions since then. The scale currently contains 21 perception items that are distributed throughout the five service quality dimensions. The scale also contains expectation items. Although many different formats of the SERVQUAL scale are now in use, we show here the basic 21 perception items as well as a sampling of ways the expectation items have been posed.

PERCEPTIONS

Perceptions Statements in the Reliability Dimension

	Strongly disagree				Strongly agree		
1. When XYZ Company promises to do something by a certain time, it does so.	1	2	3	4	5	6	7
2. When you have a problem, XYZ Company shows a sincere interest in solving it.	1	2	3	4	5	6	7
3. XYZ Company performs the service right the first time.	1	2	3	4	5	6	7
4. XYZ Company provides its services at the time it promises to do so.	1	2	3	4	5	6	7
5. XYZ Company insists on error-free records.	1	2	3	4	5	6	7

Statements in the Responsiveness Dimension

1. XYZ Company keeps customers informed about when services will be performed.	1	2	3	4	5	6	7
2. Employees in XYZ Company give you prompt service.	1	2	3	4	5	6	7
3. Employees in XYZ Company are always willing to help you.	1	2	3	4	5	6	7
4. Employees in XYZ Company are never too busy to respond to your request.	1	2	3	4	5	6	7

Statements in the Assurance Dimension

1. The behaviour of employees in XYZ Company instills confidence in you.	1	2	3	4	5	6	7
2. You feel safe in your transactions with XYZ Company.	1	2	3	4	5	6	7
3. Employees in XYZ Company are consistently courteous with you.	1	2	3	4	5	6	7
4. Employees in XYZ Company have the knowledge to answer your questions.	1	2	3	4	5	6	7

Statements in the Empathy Dimension

1. XYZ Company gives you individual attention.	1	2	3	4	5	6	7
2. XYZ Company has employees who give you personal attention.	1	2	3	4	5	6	7
3. XYZ Company has your best interests at heart.	1	2	3	4	5	6	7
4. Employees of XYZ Company understand your specific needs.	1	2	3	4	5	6	7
5. XYZ Company has operating hours that are convenient to all its customers.	1	2	3	4	5	6	7

Statements in the Tangibles Dimension

1. XYZ Company has modern-looking equipment.	1	2	3	4	5	6	7
2. XYZ Company's physical facilities are visually appealing.	1	2	3	4	5	6	7
3. XYZ Company's employees appear neat.	1	2	3	4	5	6	7
4. Materials associated with the service (such as pamphlets or statements) are visually appealing at XYZ Company.	1	2	3	4	5	6	7

EXPECTATIONS: Several Formats for Measuring Customer Expectations Using Versions of SERVQUAL

Matching Expectations Statements (Paired with the Previous Perceptions Statements)

	Strongly disagree				Strongly agree		
When customers have a problem, excellent firms will show a sincere interest in solving it.	1	2	3	4	5	6	7

FIGURE 6.2 continued overleaf

Referent Expectations Formats

1. Considering a 'world class' company to be a '7,' how would you rate XYZ Company's performance on the following service features?

	Low						High
Sincere, interested employees	1	2	3	4	5	6	7
Service delivered right the first time	1	2	3	4	5	6	7

2. Compared with the level of service you expect from an excellent company, how would you rate XYZ Company's performance on the following?

	Low						High
Sincere, interested employees	1	2	3	4	5	6	7
Service delivered right the first time	1	2	3	4	5	6	7

Combined Expectations/Perceptions Statements

For each of the following statements, circle the number that indicates how XYZ Company's service compares with the level you expect:

	Lower than my desired service level			The same as my desired service level			Higher than my desired service level		
1. Prompt service	1	2	3	4	5	6	7	8	9
2. Courteous employees	1	2	3	4	5	6	7	8	9

Expectations Distinguishing between Desired Service and Adequate Service

For each of the following statements, circle the number that indicates how XYZ Company's performance compares with your minimum service level and with your desired service level.

	Compared with my minimum service level XYZ's service performance is:								Compared with my desired service level XYZ's service performance is:								
When it comes to . . .	Lower			Same			Higher			Lower			Same			Higher		
1. Prompt service	1	2	3	4	5	6	7	8	9	1	2	3	4	5	6	7	8	9
2. Employees who are consistently courteous	1	2	3	4	5	6	7	8	9	1	2	3	4	5	6	7	8	9

FIGURE 6.2 SERVQUAL: a multidimensional scale to capture customer perceptions and expectations of service quality
Source: A. Parasuraman, V.A. Zeithaml and L.L. Berry, 'SERVQUAL: a multiple-item scale for measuring consumer perceptions of service quality', *Journal of Retailing* 64, no. 1 (Spring 1988). Reprinted by permission of C. Samuel Craig

This instrument spawned many studies focusing on service quality assessment and is used all over the world in service industries. Despite the fact that SERVQUAL has been productively used in multiple contexts, cultures and countries for measuring service quality, the SERVQUAL instrument has been the centre of criticism from a range of academic researchers. The main criticisms identified by Buttle[6] relate to the instrument's dimensions and shortcomings associated with the **disconfirmation paradigm.**

Dimensions

There are concerns that the dimensions used in the SERVQUAL instrument are not appropriate for all service offerings and need to be contextualized to reflect different service activities. Therefore as with any method, care must be taken to ensure it is appropriate to the situation in which it is to be used. It may be necessary to add or delete dimensions from the SERVQUAL instrument; however, the original dimensions do provide a valuable starting point for the development of an appropriate tool.

Disconfirmation paradigm

Gronroos[7] suggested three problems when measuring comparisons between expectations and experiences over a number of attributes:

1 If expectations are measured after the service experience has taken place, which frequently happens for practical reasons, then what is measured is not really expectation but something which has been influenced by the service experience.

2 It may not make sense to measure expectations prior to the service experience either, because the expectations that exist before a service is delivered may not be the same as the factors that a person uses when evaluating their experiences. For example, a customer in a restaurant may place no importance on the background music in a restaurant before a meal, but the quality or volume of the music experienced during the meal may alter a customer's view of the factors to consider in evaluating the quality of a dining experience.

3 A customer's view of their experience in a service encounter is influenced by their prior expectations. Consequently, if expectations are measured and then experiences are measured, then the measures are not independent of each other and the expectations are actually being measured twice.

These issues do not necessarily invalidate the measurement of service quality however, it has led to researchers looking for alternative ways of measuring service quality. One of the better known alternatives is the **SERVPERF** instrument, developed by Cronin and Taylor,[8] which measures experiences only and does not ask respondents about their expectations. Experiences are measured over a range of attributes that the researcher has developed to describe the service as conclusively as possible. The resultant instrument may be easier to administer and the data may be easier to analyse, however it has not reached the same level of popularity as exists for SERVQUAL.

Exit surveys or post-transaction surveys

Whereas the purpose of SERVQUAL surveys is usually to gauge the overall relationship with the customer, the purpose of transaction surveys is to capture information about one or all of the key service encounters with the customer. In this method, customers are asked a short list of questions immediately after a particular transaction (hence the name *exit surveys*) about their satisfaction with the transaction and contact personnel with whom they interacted. Because the surveys are administered continuously to a broad spectrum of customers, they are more effective than complaint solicitation (where the information comes only from dissatisfied customers).

Service spotlight

Sport and Leisure Management,[9] which provides leisure management services for the public sector in the UK, needed to change its collection of customer feedback in order to improve its decision-making. Rather than paper-based systems, it has installed user-friendly computer terminals in the foyer of leisure centres. These collect customer attitudes about the service experience from users before they leave the premises.

In other companies, transaction surveys are administered by telephone several days after a transaction such as installation of durable goods or claims adjustment in insurance. Because they are timed to occur close to service transactions, these surveys are useful in identifying sources of dissatisfaction and satisfaction.

Service spotlight

For example Kwik Fit, which sells car exhausts and tyres, often calls customers a day after a car has been repaired to ensure that customers are satisfied with the repair. A strong benefit of this type of research is that it often appears to customers that the call is following up to ensure that they are satisfied; consequently, the call does double duty as a market research tool and as customer service.

This type of research is simple and fresh and provides management with continuous information about interactions with customers. Further, the research allows management to associate service quality performance with individual contact personnel so that high performance can be rewarded and low performance corrected. It also serves as an incentive for employees to provide better service because they understand how and when they are being evaluated. One type of **post-transaction survey** that is becoming more familiar is on websites following online purchases. When a consumer makes a purchase a message automatically pops up on the site and invites consumers to fill out a survey. Consumers who agree are asked questions about ease of ordering, product selection, website navigation and customer support.

Service expectation meetings and reviews

In business-to-business situations when large accounts are involved, a form of customer research that is highly effective involves eliciting the expectations of the client at a specified time of the year and then following up later (usually after a year) to determine whether the expectations were fulfilled. Even when the company produces a physical product, the meetings deal almost completely with the service expected and provided by an account or sales team assigned to the client. Unlike other forms of research we have discussed, these meetings are not conducted by objective and unbiased researchers but are instead initiated and facilitated by senior members of the account team so that they can listen carefully to the client's expectations. You may be surprised to find that such interaction does not come naturally to sales teams who are used to talking *to* clients rather than listening carefully to their needs. Consequently, teams have to be carefully trained not to defend or explain but instead to comprehend. One company found that the only way it could teach its salespeople not to talk on these interviews was to take a marketing researcher along to gently kick the salesperson under the table whenever he or she strayed from the format!

The format, when appropriate, consists of (1) asking clients what they expect in terms of eight to 10 basic requirements determined from focus group research, (2) enquiring what particular aspects of these requirements the account team performed well in the past and what aspects need improvement, and (3) requesting that the client rank the relative importance of the requirements. After getting the input, senior account members go back to their teams and plan their goals for the year around client requirements. The next step is verifying with the client that the account plan will satisfy requirements or, when it will not, managing expectations to let the client know what cannot be accomplished. After executing the plan for the year, the senior account personnel then return to the client, determine whether the plan has been successfully executed and expectations met, then establish a new set of expectations for the coming year.

Process checkpoint evaluations

With professional services such as consulting, construction and architecture, services are provided over a long period, and there are no obvious ways or times to collect customer information. Waiting until the entire project is complete – which could be years – is undesirable because myriad unresolvable problems could have occurred by then. But discrete service encounters to calibrate customer perceptions are also not usually available. In these situations, the smart service provider defines a process for delivering the services and then structures the feedback around the process, checking in at frequent points to ensure that the client's expectations are being met. For example, a management consulting firm might establish the following process for delivering its services to clients: (1) collect information, (2) diagnose problems, (3) recommend alternative solutions, (4) select alternatives, and (5) implement solutions. Next, it could agree with the client up front that it will communicate at major process checkpoints – after diagnosing the problem, before selecting the alternative, and so on – to make certain that the job is progressing as planned.

Market-oriented ethnography

Structured questionnaires make key assumptions about what people are conscious of or can recall about their behaviour and what they are willing to explain to researchers about their opinions. Even focus group interviews depend on norms of participation, or what people are willing

Service spotlight

Best Western International used this technique to better understand its senior market. Rather than bringing participants into focus-group facilities and asking them questions, the company paid 25 over-55 couples to videotape themselves on their travels. The firm was able to listen to how couples actually made decisions rather than the way they reported them. The insights they gained from this research were decidedly different from what they would have learned otherwise. Most noteworthy was the finding that seniors who talked hotel receptionists into better deals on rooms did not need the lower price to afford staying at the hotel – they were simply after the thrill of the deal, as illustrated in this description:

> The 60-ish woman caught on the grainy videotape is sitting on her hotel bed, addressing her husband after a long day spent on the road. 'Good job!' she exults. 'We beat a great deal out of that receptionist and got a terrific room.'

These customers then spent their discount money on better dinners elsewhere, contributing nothing to Best Western. 'The degree of discount clearly isn't what it used to be in importance – and we got that right out of the research,' claimed the manager of programmes for Best Western.[10] This finding would be highly unlikely using traditional research and asking customers directly, for few customers would admit to being willing to pay a higher price for a service!

to say in front of others and to researchers. To fully understand how customers assess and use services, it may be necessary and effective to use other approaches, such as market-oriented **ethnography**. This set of approaches allows researchers to observe consumption behaviour in natural settings. The goal is to enter the consumer's world as much as possible – observing how and when a service is used in an actual home environment or consumption environment, such as watching consumers eat in restaurants or attend concerts. Among the techniques used are observation, interviews, documents and examination of material possessions such as artefacts. Observation involves entering the experience as a participant observer and watching what occurs rather than asking questions about it. Such approaches provide valuable insights, especially about lifestyles and usage patterns.[11]

Mystery shopping[12]

In this form of research, which is unique to services, companies employ outside research organizations to send people into service establishments and experience the service as if they were customers. These 'mystery' shoppers are trained in the criteria important to customers of the establishment. They deliver objective assessments about service performance by completing questionnaires about service standards. Questionnaires contain items that represent important quality or service issues to customers.

In Europe, **mystery shopping** is used quite extensively by organizations in financial services, retailing, motor dealerships, hotels and catering, passenger transportation, public utilities and, even, government departments. Unlike customer satisfaction surveys, the mystery shopping approach is being used to measure the process rather than the outcomes of a service encounter. The emphasis is on the service experience as it unfolds, looking at which activities and procedures do or do not happen rather than gathering opinions about the service experience. Mystery shopping studies are used for three main purposes:

- To act as a diagnostic tool, identifying failings and weak points in an organization's service delivery
- To encourage, develop and motivate service personnel by linking with appraisal, training and reward mechanisms
- To assess the competitiveness of an organization's service provision by benchmarking it against the offerings of others in an industry.

Mystery shopping aims to collect facts rather than perceptions. These facts can relate to basic enquiries, purchases and transactions covering topics such as:

- How many rings before the telephone was answered?
- How long was the queue?
- What form of greeting was used?

They can also relate to more complex encounters such as in the purchase of a mortgage where the procedures adopted in a two-hour fact-finding meeting can be assessed in terms of service quality and financial compliance.

All the areas on which shoppers need to report are highly structured to minimize the impact of the shoppers' own preferences in terms of areas such as service or cleanliness. Shoppers are often shown videos or photographs of service environments or encounters to illustrate the appropriate rating for a specific type of encounter. Shoppers also receive a detailed briefing on the scenario that they are to enact, focusing on their personal characteristics, the questions they should ask and the behaviours they should adopt. They are then tested on these elements to ensure that the service encounter is realistic and to reduce the opportunity for the true identity of the mystery shopper to be detected by the service personnel.

Mystery shopping keeps workers alert because they know they may be evaluated at any time. They know they are being judged on the company's service standards and therefore carry out the standards more consistently than if they were not going to be judged. Mystery shopping can be a very effective way of reinforcing service standards.

Customer panels

Customer **panels** are ongoing groups of customers assembled to provide attitudes and perceptions about a service over time. They offer a company regular and timely customer information – virtually a pulse on the market. Firms can use customer panels to represent large segments of end-customers.

Customer panels are used in the entertainment industry to screen movies before they are released to the public. After a rough cut of a film has been created, the movie is viewed by a panel of consumers that matches the demographic target. In the most basic of these panels, consumers participate in post-screening interviews or focus groups in which they report on their responses to the movie. They may be asked questions as general as their reactions to the ending of the movie and as specific as whether they understood different aspects of the plot line. Based on these panels, movies are revised and edited to ensure that they are communicating the desired message and that they will succeed in the marketplace. In extreme situations, entire endings of movies have been changed to be more consistent with customer attitudes. In some of the most sophisticated consumer panel research on movies (also used for television shows and commercials) consumers have digital devices in their seats through which they indicate their responses as they watch films. This instantaneous response allows the producers, directors and editors to make changes at the appropriate places in the film to ensure that the story line, characters and scenery are 'tracking'.

Lost customer research

This type of research involves deliberately seeking customers who have dropped the company's service to inquire about their reasons for leaving. Some **lost customer research** is similar to exit interviews with employees in that it asks open-ended, in-depth questions to expose the reasons for defection and the particular events that led to dissatisfaction. It is also possible to use more standard surveys on lost customers. For example, many utility companies (e.g. Eon), mobile phone operators (e.g. Vodafone) and bank customers (e.g. BNP Paribas) contact former customers asking them about their performance during different stages of the customer–vendor relationship. The surveys also seek specific reasons for customers' defections and ask customers to describe the problems that triggered the move.

One benefit of this type of research is that it identifies failure points and common problems in the service, and can help establish an early-warning system for future defectors. Another benefit is that the research can be used to calculate the cost of lost customers.

Future expectations research

Customer expectations are dynamic and can change very rapidly in markets that are highly competitive and volatile. As competition increases, as tastes change and as consumers become more knowledgeable, companies must continue to update their information and strategies. One such 'industry' is interactive video, representing the merger of computer, telecommunications and cable television. The technologies available in this industry are revolutionary. In dynamic market situations, companies want to understand not just current customer expectations but also future expectations – the service features desired in the future. Future expectations research is new and includes different types. First, *features research* involves environmental scanning and querying of customers about desirable features of possible services. *Lead user research* brings in customers who are opinion leaders/innovators and asks them what requirements are not currently being met by existing products or services. Another form of this research is the *synectics approach*, which defines lead users more broadly than in standard lead user research.

The question of customer involvement in expectation studies is often debated. Designers and developers claim that consumers do not know what they might want, especially in industries or services that are new and rapidly changing. Consumers and marketing researchers, on the other hand, counter that services developed independent of customer input are likely to be targeted at needs that do not exist. To study this question, researchers assessed the contributions made by users compared with professional developers for end-user telecom services. Three groups were studied: users alone, developers alone and users with a design expert present to provide information on feasibility. Findings showed that users created more original but less producible ideas. However, inviting users to test and explore possibilities once a prototype has been created can produce positive results.[13]

Analysing and interpreting marketing research findings

One of the biggest challenges facing a marketing researcher is converting a complex set of data to a form that can be read and understood quickly by executives, managers and other employees who will make decisions from the research. Many of the people who use marketing research findings have not been trained in statistics and have neither the time nor the expertise to analyse computer printouts and other technical research information. The goal in this stage of the marketing research process is to communicate information clearly to the right people in a timely fashion. Among considerations are the following: who gets this information? Why do they need it? How will they use it? When users feel confident that they understand the data, they are far more likely to apply it appropriately. When managers do not understand how to interpret the data, or when they lack confidence in the research, the investment of time, skill and effort will be lost.

Depicting marketing research findings graphically is a powerful way to communicate research information. Here are a sample of graphic representations of the types of marketing research data we have discussed throughout this chapter.

Tracking of performance, gap scores and competition

A simple way of tracking performance is shown in Figure 6.3. Both expectations and perceptions are plotted, and the gap between them shows the service quality shortfall. Although any attribute or dimension of service can be tracked, Figure 6.3 shows the scores for service reliability. Competitor service performance is another frequently tracked service quality measurement. It allows managers to have a better grasp of service improvement priorities for their firm by comparing the firm's service strengths and weaknesses against those of key competitors.[14]

Zones of tolerance charts

When companies collect data on the dual expectation levels described in Chapter 3 – desired service and adequate service – and performance data, they can convey the information concisely

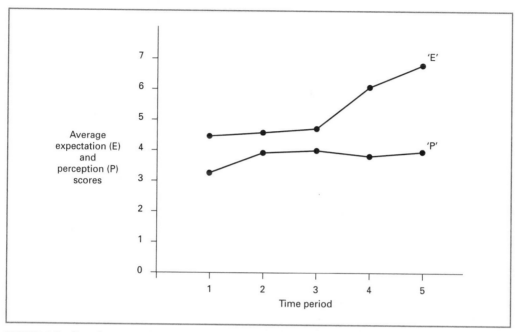

FIGURE 6.3 Tracking of customer expectations and perceptions of service reliability

Source: E. Sivadas, 'Europeans have a different take on CS [Customer Satisfaction] programs', *Marketing News*, 26 October 1998, p. 39. Reprinted by permission of the American Marketing Association

on **zones of tolerance charts**. Figure 6.4 plots customer service quality perceptions relative to customers' zones of tolerance. Perceptions of company performance are indicated by the circles, and the zones of tolerance boxes are bounded at the top by the desired service score and at the bottom by the adequate service score. When the perception scores are within the boxes, the

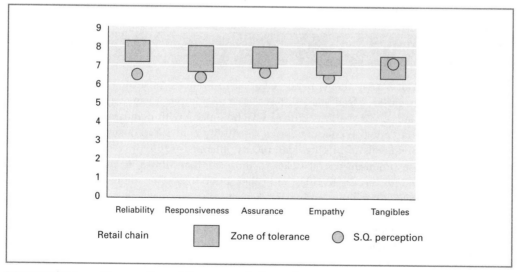

FIGURE 6.4 Service quality perceptions relative to zones of tolerance by dimensions

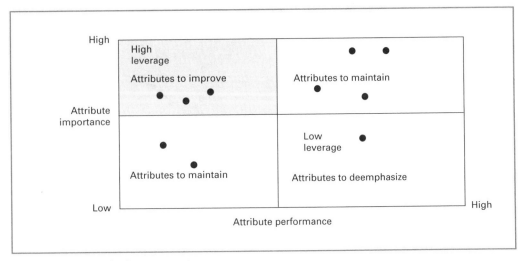

FIGURE 6.5 Importance/performance matrix

company is delivering service that is above customers' minimum level of expectations. When the perception scores are below the boxes, the company's service performance is lower than the minimum level, and customers are dissatisfied with the company's service.[15]

Importance/performance matrices

One of the most useful forms of analysis in marketing research is the importance/performance matrix. This chart combines information about customer perceptions and importance ratings. An example is shown in Figure 6.5. Attribute importance is represented on the vertical axis from high (top) to low (bottom). Performance is shown on the horizontal axis from low (left) to high (right). There are many variations of these matrices: some companies define the horizontal axis as the gap between expectations and perceptions, or as performance relative to competition. The shading on the chart indicates the area of highest leverage for service quality improvements –

Service spotlight

Most visitors to Walt Disney theme parks, whether in France or elsewhere in the world, see magic, but the magic is based on solid research discipline. Disney conducts over 200 different external surveys a year, tracking satisfaction along with demographic profiles of its customers. The company also conducts price sensitivity analysis to determine the tolerance of guests for various levels of pricing. One recent outcome of this price sensitivity analysis was the FastPass, a premium-priced ticket to the park that allows its purchasers to avoid lines and expedite their access to rides and other attractions. The company also has guests evaluate its different attractions, noting the aspects that are pleasing or troublesome, and changing aspects to ensure that the attractions run as smoothly as possible. In addition, the company monitors tens of thousands of letters and comment cards it receives and practises 'management by walking around'. By doing so, Disney gathers critical information that enables the design of a service experience that delights its guests.[16]

where importance is high and performance is low. In this quadrant are the attributes that most need to be improved. In the adjacent upper quadrant are attributes to be maintained, those that a company performs well and that are very important to customers. The lower two quadrants contain attributes that are less important, some of which are performed well and others poorly. Neither of these quadrants merit as much attention in terms of service improvements as the upper quadrants because customers are not as concerned about the attributes that are plotted in them as they are the attributes in the upper quadrants.

Using marketing research information

Conducting research about customer expectations is only the first part of understanding the customer, even if the research is appropriately designed, executed and presented. A service firm must also use the research findings in a meaningful way – to drive change or improvement in the way service is delivered. The misuse (or even non-use) of research data can lead to a large gap in understanding customer expectations. When managers do not read research reports because they are too busy dealing with the day-to-day challenges of the business, companies fail to use the resources available to them. And when customers participate in marketing research studies but never see changes in the way the company does business, they feel frustrated and annoyed with the company. Understanding how to make the best use of research – to apply what has been learned to the business – is a key way to close the gap between customer expectations and management perceptions of customer expectations. Managers must learn to turn research information and insights into action, to recognize that the purpose of research is to drive improvement and customer satisfaction.

The research plan should specify the mechanism by which customer data will be used. The research should be actionable, timely, specific and credible. It can also have a mechanism that allows a company to respond immediately to dissatisfied customers.

Upward communication

In some service firms, especially small and localized firms, owners or managers may be in constant contact with customers, thereby gaining first-hand knowledge of customer expectations and perceptions. But in large service organizations, managers do not always get the opportunity to experience at first hand what their customers want.

The larger a company is, the more difficult it will be for managers to interact directly with the customer and the less first-hand information they will have about customer expectations. Even when they read and digest research reports, managers can lose the reality of the customer if they never get the opportunity to experience the actual service. A theoretical view of how things are supposed to work cannot provide the richness of the service encounter. To truly understand customer needs, management benefits from hands-on knowledge of what really happens in stores, on customer service telephone lines, in service queues and in face-to-face service encounters.

Objectives for upward communication

Table 6.2 shows the major research objectives for improving **upward communication** in an organization. These objectives include gaining first-hand knowledge about customers, improving internal service quality, gaining first-hand knowledge of employees and obtaining ideas for service improvement. These objectives can be met by two types of interactive activities in the

Type of interaction or research	Research objective	Qualitative/ quantitative	Cost of information		
			Money	Time	Frequency
Executive visits to customers	To gain first-hand knowledge about customers	Qualitative	Moderate	Moderate	Continuous
Executive listenings	To gain first-hand knowledge about customers	Qualitative	Low	Low	Continuous
Research on intermediate customers	To gain in-depth information on end customers	Quantitative	Moderate	Moderate	Annual
Employee internal satisfaction surveys	To improve internal service quality	Quantitative	Moderate	Moderate	Annual
Employee visits or listenings	To gain first-hand knowledge about employees	Qualitative	Moderate	Moderate	Continuous
Employee suggestions	To obtain ideas for service improvements	Qualitative	Low	Low	Continuous

TABLE 6.2 Elements in an effective programme of upward communication

organization: one designed to improve the type and effectiveness of communications from customers to management, and the other designed to improve communications between employees and management.

Research for upward communication

Executive or management listening to customers

This approach is frequently used in business-to-business services marketing. In some visits, executives of the company make sales or service calls with customer contact personnel (salespeople). In other situations, executives of the selling company arrange meetings with executives at a

Service spotlight

Asda, part of the Walmart Group, has been running a customer listening programme for over 14 years where managers from head office and from individual stores accompany shoppers around their stores. 'It is tremendously powerful in getting your managers to think about the customer,' says Asda's head of market research. 'What better way to see the customer's perspective than to accompany them on a shopping trip.'[17]

similar level in client companies. When Lou Gerstner became CEO of IBM, one of his first actions was to arrange a meeting with 175 of the company's biggest customers for a discussion of how IBM can better meet their needs. The meeting was viewed as a signal that the new IBM would be more responsive and focused on the customer. Alternatively, for a consumer business, senior managers can spend time in their branches or outlets talking to customers in an informal manner.

With the growth in online communities and blogs where consumers post comments about products, services and organizations, it is important for an organization to monitor such communication. This will give another insight into how customers perceive an organization's offering. Travel sites, in particular, have consumer-generated reviews on hotels, airlines and visitor attractions which may influence the purchasing decisions of new customers. Self-publishing tools and enhanced/user-friendly communication technologies have made consumer-generated content increasingly popular. It is important that managers are aware of the content of such communications. Some organizations may establish their own blogging site, where they treat contributors as VIPs with exclusive previews and consultation on areas such as new products and plans and opportunities to air their views. Software providers such as Microsoft have been doing this for some time but now companies such as BT, Accenture, Thomson Holidays, Benetton and, even, local and national governments are establishing communication channels of this type.

Research on intermediate customers

Intermediate customers (such as contact employees, dealers, distributors, agents and brokers) are people the company serves who serve the end-customer. Researching the needs and expectations of these customers *in serving the end-customer* can be a useful and efficient way to both improve service to and obtain information about end-users. The interaction with intermediate customers provides opportunities for understanding end-customers' expectations and problems. It can also help the company learn about and satisfy the service expectations of intermediate customers, a process critical in their providing quality service to end customers.

Research on internal customers

Employees who perform services are themselves customers of internal services on which they depend heavily to do their jobs well. There is a strong and direct link between the quality of internal service that employees receive and the quality of service they provide to their own customers. For this reason it is important to conduct employee research that focuses on the service that internal customers give and receive. In many companies this focus requires adapting existing employee opinion research to focus on service satisfaction. Employee research complements customer research when service quality is the issue being investigated. Customer research provides insight into what is occurring, whereas employee research provides insight into why. The two types of research play unique and equally important roles in improving service quality. Companies that focus service quality research exclusively on external customers are missing a rich and vital source of information.[18]

Executive or management listening approaches to employees

Employees who actually perform the service have the best possible vantage point for observing the service and identifying impediments to its quality. Customer contact personnel are in regular contact with customers and thereby come to understand a great deal about customer expectations and perceptions.[19] If the information they know can be passed on to top management, top managers' understanding of the customer may improve. In fact, it could be said that in many companies, top management's understanding of the customer depends largely on the extent and types of communication received from customer contact personnel and from non-company contact personnel (like independent insurance agents and retailers) who represent the company and its services. When these channels of communication are closed, management may not get feedback about problems encountered in service delivery and about how customer expectations are changing.

Upward communication provides information to upper-level managers about activities and performances throughout the organization. Specific types of communication that may be relevant are formal (such as reports of problems and exceptions in service delivery) and informal (like discussions between contact personnel and upper-level managers). Managers who stay close to their contact people benefit not only by keeping their employees happy, but also by learning more about their customers.[20] These companies encourage, appreciate and reward upward communication from contact people. Through this important channel, management learns about customer expectations from employees in regular contact with customers and can thereby reduce the size of gap 1.

Employee suggestions

Most companies have some form of employee suggestion programme whereby contact personnel can communicate to management their ideas for improving work. Suggestion systems have come a long way from the traditional suggestion box. Effective suggestion systems are those in which employees are empowered to see their suggestions through, where supervisors can implement proposals immediately, where employees participate for continuous improvement in their jobs, where supervisors respond quickly to ideas, and where coaching is provided in ways to handle suggestions.[21] In today's companies, suggestions from employees are facilitated by self-directed work teams that encourage employees to identify problems and then work to develop solutions to those problems.

Summary

This chapter discussed the role of marketing research in understanding customer perceptions and expectations. After first describing criteria for effective services research, the chapter defined key forms of services research including critical incidents studies, mystery shopping, service expectation meetings and reviews, process checkpoint evaluations and database research. Important topics in researching services – including developing research objectives and presenting data – were also described. Finally, upward communication, ways in which management obtains and uses information from customers and customer contact personnel, was discussed. These topics combine to close gap 1 between customer expectations and company understanding of customer expectations, the first of four provider gaps in the gaps model of service quality.

Key concepts

Complaint solicitation	130	Qualitative research	127
Critical incident technique	130	Quantitative research	127
Disconfirmation paradigm	134	Research objectives	124
Ethnography	138	Research programme	124
Lost customer research	139	SERVPERF	135
Marketing research	123	SERVQUAL	132
Mystery shopping	138	Upward communication	143
Panels	139	Zones of tolerance charts	141
Post-transaction/exit survey	136		

Further reading

Buttle, F. (1996) 'SERVQUAL: review, critique, research agenda', *European Journal of Marketing*, 30(1), 8–32.

Cronin, J. and Taylor S. (1992) 'Measuring service quality: a re-examination and extension', *Journal of Marketing*, 56, 55–68.

Cronin, J. and Taylor, S.A. (1994) 'SERVPERF versus SERVQUAL: reconciling performance based and perceptions-minus expectations measurement of service quality', *Journal of Marketing*, 58, 125–31.

Parasuraman, A., Berry, L.L. and Zeithanl, V.A. (1991) 'Refinement and reassessment of the SERVQUAL scale', *Journal of Retailing*, 67(4), 420–50.

Wilson, A. (2006) *Marketing Research: An Integrated Approach*, 2nd edn, London: FT Prentice Hall.

Wilson, A.M. (1998) 'The use of mystery shopping in the measurement of service delivery', *The Service Industries Journal*, 18(3), 148–63.

Discussion questions

1 Give five reasons why research objectives must be established before marketing research is conducted.

2 Why are both qualitative and quantitative research methods needed in a services marketing research programme?

3 Why does the frequency of research differ across the research methods shown in Figure 6.1?

4 Compare and contrast the types of research that help a company identify common failure points (see column 2 in Figure 6.1). Which of the types do you think produces better information? Why?

5 In what situations does a service company need requirements research?

6 What reasons can you give for companies' lack of use of research information? How might you motivate managers to use the information to a greater extent? How might you motivate front-line workers to use the information?

7 Given a specific marketing research budget, what would be your recommendations for the percentage to be spent on customer research versus upward communication? Why?

8 What kinds of information could be gleaned from research on intermediate customers? What would intermediate customers know that service providers might not?

9 For what types of products and services would research on the Internet be preferable to traditional research?

Exercises

1 Choose a local services organization to interview about marketing research. Find out what the firm's objectives are and the types of marketing research it currently uses. Using the information in this chapter, think about the effectiveness of its marketing research. What are the strengths? Weaknesses?

2 Choose one of the services you consume. If you were in charge of creating a survey for that service, what questions would you ask on the survey? Give several examples. What type of survey (relationship versus transaction based) would be most appropriate for the service? What recommendations would you give to management of the company about making such a survey actionable?

3 If you were the marketing director of your college or university, what types of research (see Figure 6.1) would be essential for understanding both external and internal customers? If you could choose only three types of research, which ones would you select? Why?

4 Using the SERVQUAL scale in this chapter, create a questionnaire for a service firm that you use. Give the questionnaire to 10 people, and describe what you learn.

5 To get an idea of the power of the critical incidents technique, try it yourself with reference to restaurant service. Think of a time when, as a customer, you had a particularly satisfying interaction with a restaurant. Follow the instructions here, which are identical to the instructions in an actual study, and observe the insights you obtain about your requirements in restaurant service:

   a When did the incident happen?

   b What specific circumstances led up to this situation?

   c Exactly what did the employee (or firm) say or do?

   d What resulted that made you feel the interaction was satisfying?

   e What could or should have been done differently?

Notes

1 A. Wilson, *Marketing Research: An Integrated Approach*, 2nd edn (London: FT Prentice-Hall, 2006).

2 A. Parasuraman, L.L. Berry and V.A. Zeithaml, 'Guidelines for conducting service quality research', *Marketing Research: A Magazine of Management and Applications*, December 1990, pp. 34–44.

3 This section is based on a comprehensive assessment of the critical incident technique in D.D. Gremler, 'The critical incident technique in service research', *Journal of Service Research* 7 (August 2004), pp. 65–89.

4 Ibid.

5 Research-Live.com. Research Drives Moto's Appetitite for Healthy Food, 8 September 2005.

6 F. Buttle, 'SERVQUAL: review, critique, research agenda', *European Journal of Marketing* 30, no.1 (1996), pp. 8–32.

7 C. Gronroos *Service Management and Marketing*, 3rd edn (Chichester: John Wiley & Son, 2007).

8 J. Cronin and S. Taylor, 'Measuring service quality: a re-examination and extension', *Journal of Marketing* 56 (1992), pp. 55–68.

9 See http://www.slm-leisure.co.uk

10 G. Khermouch, 'Consumers in the mist', *Business Week,* 26 February 2001, pp. 92–3.

11 E. Day, 'Researchers must enter consumer's world', *Marketing News,* 17 August 1998, p. 17.

12 Adapted from A.M. Wilson, 'The use of mystery shopping in the measurement of service delivery', *The Service Industries Journal* 18, no. 3 (1998), pp. 148–63.

13 P.R. Magnusson, J. Mathing and P. Kristensson, 'Managing user involvement in service innovation: experiments with innovating end users', *Journal of Service Research* 6 (November 2003), pp. 111–24.

14 V.A. Zeithaml, A. Parasuraman and L.L. Berry, *Delivering Quality Service: Balancing Customer Perceptions and Expectations* (New York: Free Press, 1990), p. 28.

15 A. Parasuraman, V.A. Zeithaml and L.L. Berry, 'Moving forward in service quality research', Marketing Science Institute Report No. 94–114, (September 1994).

16 R. Johnson, 'A strategy for service – Disney style', *Journal of Business Strategy* (September–October 1991), pp. 38–43.

17 See Wilson, *Marketing Research*, pp. 352–53.

18 'Baldridge winner co-convenes quality summit', *Executive Report on Customer Satisfaction,* 30 October 1992.

19 M.J. Bitner, B. Booms and L. Mohr, 'Critical service encounters: the employee's viewpoint', *Journal of Marketing* 58 (October 1994), pp. 95–106.

20 Zeithaml, Parasuraman and Berry, *Delivering Quality Service,* p. 64.

21 'Empowerment is the strength of effective suggestion systems', *Total Quality Newsletter,* August 1991.

Building customer relationships

This chapter's objectives are to:

1 Explain relationship marketing, its goals, and the benefits of long-term relationships for firms and customers.

2 Explain why and how to estimate customer relationship value.

3 Introduce the concept of customer profitability segments as a strategy for focusing relationship marketing efforts.

4 Present relationship development strategies – including quality core service, **switching barriers** and **relationship bonds**.

5 Identify challenges in relationship development, including the somewhat controversial idea that 'the customer is not always right'.

CASE STUDY: TESCO FOCUSES ON LONG-TERM RELATIONSHIPS

Tesco, the supermarket giant, launched its loyalty card scheme in 1995. Tesco was aware that at any of its stores, the top 5 per cent of customers accounted for 20 per cent of sales, with the bottom 25 per cent accounting for only 2 per cent of sales. The company recognized the importance of giving extra attention and rewards to the top customers if sales and profitability were to be maintained and increased. The loyalty card allowed Tesco to capture details of over 8 million transactions per week and relate them to specific shoppers. Based on the amount spent and the frequency of shopping, customers were classified into four broad types: Premium, Standard, Potential and Uncommitted.

Shopping frequency/ expenditure	Frequent daily/ twice weekly	Infrequent weekly/stop-start	Rare now and then/hardly ever
High spend	Premium	Standard	Potential
Medium spend	Standard	Potential	Uncommited
Low spend	Potential	Uncommited	Uncommited

Tesco also identified over 5000 need segments based on customers' purchasing behaviour with each of these segments offering the potential to target individual shoppers with tailor-made campaigns and advertisements. Every three months, millions of Tesco customers in the UK receive a magazine which has been mass-customized to suit each customer's lifestyle and buying behaviour. The articles cover issues that should interest them and discount vouchers are included for the products/services that they are most likely to purchase. Tesco also holds 'customer evenings' for interacting with customers and gathering more information about their attitudes and requirements. Such interaction has been instrumental in the design of Tesco's online shopping service and the development of its range of financial service products.

The loyalty card and customer feedback resulted in Tesco identifying that around 25 per cent of its premium customers were defecting to Marks and Spencer for special occasion purchases; it responded by developing a totally new product range, 'Tesco Finest', to lure back these customers. This range was then promoted to affluent customers through personalized promotions reducing the defection of customers considerably.

Customer Relationship Management at Tesco does not simply rely on loyalty cards, it also focuses on customer service enhancement. Tesco requires all employees including top management to spend some time each year in the stores to get better acquainted with the service levels that customers are seeking. As a result improvements have been introduced through better staff training, better management of the supply chain and changes to the scheduling of work patterns for store employees.

The commitment to long-term relationships is reflected in what Tesco refers to as its core purpose: '**to create value for customers to earn their lifetime loyalty**'.

Sources: Tesco.com website; Mukund, A. (2003) 'Tesco: the customer relationship management champion', Case Study, ICFAI Centre for Management Research, India.

Tesco provides a strong example of a company that has focused on keeping its customers and building long-term relationships with them. Unlike the Tesco example, however, many companies fail to understand customers accurately because they fail to focus on customer relationships. They tend to fixate on acquiring new customers rather than viewing customers as assets that they need to nurture and retain. By concentrating on new customers, firms can easily fall into the traps of short-term promotions, price discounts or catchy advertisements that bring customers in but are not enough to bring them back. By adopting a relationship philosophy, on the other hand, companies begin to understand customers over time and in great depth, and are better able to meet their changing needs and expectations.

Marketing strategies for understanding customers over time and building long-term relationships are the subjects of this chapter.

Relationship marketing

> " There has been a shift from a transactions to a relationship focus in marketing. Customers become partners and the firm must make long-term commitments to maintaining those relationships with quality, service, and innovation.[1] "

Relationship marketing essentially represents a paradigm shift within marketing – away from an acquisitions/transaction focus toward a retention/relationship focus.[2] Relationship marketing (or relationship management) is a philosophy of doing business, a strategic orientation, that focuses on *keeping and improving* relationships with current customers rather than on acquiring new customers. This philosophy assumes that many consumers and business customers prefer to have an ongoing relationship with one organization than to switch continually among providers in their search for value. Building on this assumption and the fact that it is usually much cheaper to keep a current customer than to attract a new one, successful marketers are working on effective strategies for retaining customers. Our opening example showed how Tesco has built its business around a relationship philosophy.

It has been suggested that firms frequently focus on attracting customers (the 'first act') but then pay little attention to what they should do to keep them (the 'second act').[3] Ideas expressed in an interview with James L. Schorr, then executive vice president of marketing at Holiday Inns, illustrate this point.[4] In the interview he stated that he was famous at Holiday Inns for what is called the 'bucket theory of marketing'. By this he meant that marketing can be thought of as a big bucket: it is what the sales, advertising and promotion programmes do that pours business into the top of the bucket. As long as these programmes are effective, the bucket stays full. However, 'There's only one problem,' he said, 'there's a hole in the bucket.' When the business is running well and the hotel is delivering on its promises, the hole is small and few customers are leaving. When the operation is weak and customers are not satisfied with what they get, however, people start falling out of the bucket through the holes faster than they can be poured in through the top.

The bucket theory illustrates why a relationship strategy that focuses on plugging the holes in the bucket makes so much sense. Historically, marketers have been more concerned with acquisition of customers, so a shift to a relationship strategy often represents changes in mindset, organizational culture and employee reward systems. For example, the sales incentive systems in many organizations are set up to reward bringing in new customers. There are often fewer (or no) rewards for retaining current accounts. Thus, even when people see the logic of customer retention, the existing organizational systems may not support its implementation.

Customers as ...	Strangers	Acquaintances	Friends	Partners
Product offering	Attractive relative to competitive offerings or alternative purchases.	Parity product as a form of industry standard.	Differentiated product adapted to specific market segments.	Customized product and dedicated resources adapted to an individual customer or organization.
Source of competitive advantage	Attractiveness.	Satisfaction.	Satisfaction and trust.	Satisfaction and trust and commitment.
Buying activity	Interest, exploration, and trial.	Satisfaction facilitates and reinforces buying activity and reduces need to search for market information.	Trust in firm is needed to continue the buying activity without perfect information.	Commitment in the form of information sharing and idiosyncratic investments is needed to achieve customized product and to adjust product continuously to changing needs and situations.
Focus of selling activities	Awareness of firm's offerings (encouraging trial) facilitates initial selling.	Familiarity and general knowledge of customer (identification) facilitates selling.	Specific knowledge of customer's connection to segment need and situation facilitates selling.	Specific knowledge of customer's need and situation and idiosyncratic investments facilitates selling.
Relationship time horizon	None: buyer may have had no previous interactions with or knowledge of the firm.	Short: generally short because the buyer can often switch firms without much effort or cost.	Medium: generally longer than acquaintance relationships because trust in a differentiated position takes a longer time to build and imitate.	Long: generally long because it takes time to build and replace inter-connected activities and to develop a detailed knowledge of a customer's needs and the unique resources of a supplier to commit resources to the relationship.
Sustainability of competitive advantage	Low: generally low, as firm must continually find ways to be attractive, in terms of the value offered, in order to induce trial.	Low: generally low, but competitors can vary in how they build unique value into selling and serving even if the product is a form of industry standard.	Medium: generally medium but depends on competitors' ability to understand heterogeneity of customer needs and situations and the ability to transform this knowledge into meaningful, differentiated products.	High: generally high but depends on how unique and effective the interconnected activities between customer and supplier are organized.
Primary relationship marketing goal	*Acquire* customer's business.	*Satisfy* customer's needs and wants.	*Retain* customer's business.	*Enhance* relationship with customer.

TABLE 7.1 A typology of exchange relationships

Source: adapted from M.D. Johnson and F. Seines, 'Customer portfolio management: toward a dynamic theory of exchange relationships', *Journal of Marketing* 68 (April 2004), p. 5. Reprinted by permission of the American Marketing Association

The evolution of customer relationships

Firms' relationships with their customers, like other social relationships, tend to evolve over time. Scholars have suggested that marketing exchange relationships between providers and customers often have the potential to evolve from strangers to acquaintances to friends to partners. Table 7.1 illustrates different issues at each successive level of the relationship.[5]

Customers as strangers

Strangers are those customers who are not aware of or, perhaps, those who have not yet had any transactions (interactions) with a firm. At the industry level, strangers may be conceptualized as customers who have not yet entered the market; at the firm level, they may include customers of competitors. Clearly the firm has no relationship with the customer at this point. Consequently, the firm's primary goal with these potential customers ('strangers') is to initiate communication with them in order to *attract* them and *acquire* their business. Thus, the primary marketing efforts directed towards such customers deal with familiarizing those potential customers with the firm's offerings and, subsequently, encouraging them to give the firm a try.

Customers as acquaintances

Once customer awareness and trial are achieved, familiarity is established and the customer and the firm become acquaintances, creating the basis for an exchange relationship. A primary goal for the firm at this stage of the relationship is *satisfying* the customer. In the acquaintance stage, firms are generally concerned about providing a value proposition to customers that is comparable with that of competitors. For a customer, an acquaintanceship is effective as long as the customer is relatively satisfied and what is being received in the exchange is perceived as fair value. With repetitive interactions, the customer gains experience and becomes more familiar with the firm's product offerings. These encounters can help reduce uncertainty about the benefits expected in the exchange and, therefore, increase the attractiveness of the company relative to the competition. Repetitive interactions improve the firm's knowledge of the customer, helping to facilitate marketing, sales and service efforts. Thus, an acquaintance relationship facilitates transactions primarily through the reduction of the customer's perceived risk and the provider's costs.

In acquaintance relationships, firms generally focus on providing value comparable to the competition, often through the repetitive provision of standardized offerings. As a result, for a firm in such a relationship with a customer, the potential to develop a sustainable competitive advantage through relationship activities is limited. However, firms that have many such relationships with their customers can create value for acquaintances by learning from all their transactions. For example, Amazon has created value for its acquaintances through a highly developed order-processing system. By processing and organizing historical transaction data from a customer and comparing it with data from other customers demonstrating similar purchase behaviours, the system is able to identify additional products of potential interest to the acquaintance customer and to generate cross-selling opportunities.

Customers as friends

As a customer continues to make purchases from a firm and to receive value in the exchange relationship, the firm begins to acquire specific knowledge of the customer's needs, allowing it to create an offering that directly addresses the customer's situation. The provision of a unique offering, and thus differential value, transforms the exchange relationship from acquaintance to friendship. This transition from acquaintanceship to friendship, particularly in service exchange relationships, requires the development of trust.[6] As discussed in an earlier chapter, customers may not be able to assess a service outcome prior to purchase and consumption, and for those services high in credence qualities, customers may not be able to discern service performance even after experiencing it. Therefore, customers must trust the provider to do what is promised. As customers become friends they not only become familiar with the company but also come to trust that it provides superior value.

A primary goal for firms at the friendship stage of the relationship is customer *retention*. Given their likelihood of past satisfying experiences and repeated purchases, these customers ('friends') are more likely to appreciate the firm's product offerings and are, perhaps, more open to other related services. A firm's potential to develop sustainable competitive advantage through friends should be higher than for acquaintances, because the offering is more unique (and more difficult for competition to imitate) and the customer comes to trust that uniqueness.[7]

Customers as partners

As a customer continues to interact with a firm, the level of trust often deepens and the customer may receive more customized product offerings and interactions. The trust developed in the friendship stage is a necessary but not sufficient condition for a customer–firm partnership to develop.[8] That is, the creation of trust leads to (ideally) the creation of commitment – and that is the condition necessary for customers to extend the time perspective of a relationship.[9] The deepening of trust and the establishment of commitment reduce the customer's need to solve problems in the traditional sense of 'finding a better alternative'. Thus, in order to move the relationship into a partner relationship, a firm must use customer knowledge and information systems to deliver highly personalized and customized offerings.

The key to success in the partnership stage is the firm's ability to organize and use information about individual customers more effectively than competitors. Customers benefit from, and therefore desire to commit to, relationships with firms whose knowledge of their needs enables them to deliver highly personalized and customized offerings.[10] Over time, the customer–firm relationship may evolve through continuous adaptation and commitment, and the parties may become increasingly interdependent. At this point the relationship has advanced from having the purpose of merely meeting the customer's needs to a situation in which both parties sense a deep appreciation of each other. However, in order to continue to receive such benefits, customers generally must be willing to pay a price premium or to commit themselves to the firm for an extended period of time.

Service spotlight

For an annual membership fee of 130 euros, Accor Hotel Group customers can become 'Favourite Guests' and have their personal data and travelling preferences stored in the Accor database. Among the many benefits 'Favourite Guest' customers receive are guaranteed priority booking and reduced rates at Sofitel, Novotel, Mercure and Ibis hotels, late checking out times, reduced car hire charges, free reward nights in selected hotels and a personal welcome at each hotel.

At the partnership stage, the firm is concerned with *enhancing* the relationship. Customers are more likely to stay in the relationship if they feel that the company understands their changing needs and is willing to invest in the relationship by constantly improving and evolving its product and service mix. By enhancing these relationships, the firm expects such customers to be less likely to be lured away by competitors and more likely to buy additional products and services from the company over time. These loyal customers not only provide a solid base for the organization, they may represent growth potential. Examples include: a bank current account customer becomes a better customer when he or she sets up a savings account, takes out a loan and/or uses the financial advisory services of the bank; and a corporate account becomes a better customer when it chooses to do 75 per cent of its business with a particular supplier rather than splitting the business equally among three suppliers. In recent years, in fact, many companies have aspired to be the 'exclusive supplier' of a particular product or service for their customers. Over time these enhanced relationships can increase market share and profits for the organization.

However, it is important to note that all customers may not be interested in forming relationships with their suppliers or service providers. Depending on the product or service, the level of interest from some customers may vary from a situation where they only want to transact the business, to those who want the service provider to have ongoing knowledge of their changing requirements. Gronroos divided customer expectations into three types:[11]

1 Transactional expectations – where the customer is looking for solutions to their needs at an acceptable price, and they do not appreciate contacts from the supplier or service provider in between purchases.

2 Active relational expectations – where the customer is looking for opportunities to interact with the supplier or service provider in order to get additional value. A lack of such contacts makes them disappointed, because the value inherent in the relationship is missing.

3 Passive relational expectations – where customers are looking for the knowledge that they could contact the service provider if they wanted to. In this sense, they are also seeking contact, but they seldom respond to invitations to interact.

It is important for a service provider to be aware of the relationship expectations of their customers, if the most appropriate relationship management strategy is to be adopted.

The goal of relationship marketing

The discussion of the evolution of customer relationships demonstrates how a firm's relationship with its customers might be enhanced as customers move further along this relationship continuum. As the relationship value of a customer increases, the provider is more likely to pursue a closer relationship. Thus, the primary goal of relationship marketing is *to build and maintain a base of committed customers who are profitable for the organization.* Figure 7.1 graphically illustrates the goals of relationship marketing. The overriding goal is to move customers up the ladder (that is, along the relationship continuum) from the point at which they are strangers that need to be attracted through to the point at which they are highly valued, long-term customers whose relationship with the firm has been enhanced. From a customer's problem-solving perspective, the formation of satisfaction, trust and commitment corresponds to the customer's willingness to engage in an exchange relationship as an acquaintance, friend and partner, respectively. From a firm's resource-allocation perspective, the delivery of differential, and perhaps customized, value corresponds to the extent of its ability and/or desire to create an acquaintance, friend or partner relationship with the customer. As customers make the transition from satisfaction-based acquaintanceships to trust-based friendships to commitment-based partnerships, increases are required in both the value received and the level of cooperation.

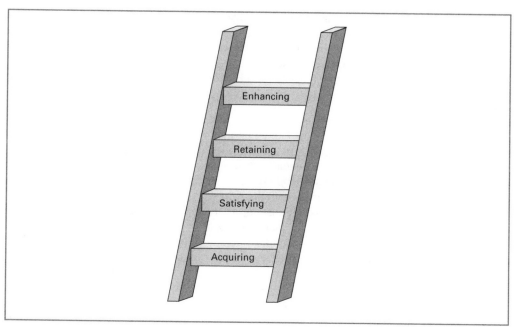

FIGURE 7.1 Customer goals of relationship marketing: acquiring customers, satisfying customers, retaining customers and enhancing customers

Benefits for customers and firms

Both parties in the customer–firm relationship can benefit from customer retention. That is, it is not only in the best interest of the organization to build and maintain a loyal customer base, but customers themselves also benefit from long-term associations.

Benefits for customers

Assuming they have a choice, customers will remain loyal to a firm when they receive greater value relative to what they expect from competing firms. *Value* represents a trade-off for the consumer between the 'give' and the 'get' components. Consumers are more likely to stay in a relationship when the gets (quality, satisfaction, specific benefits) exceed the gives (monetary and non-monetary costs). When firms can consistently deliver value from the customer's point of view, clearly the customer benefits and has an incentive to stay in the relationship.

Beyond the specific inherent benefits of receiving service value, customers also benefit in other ways from long-term associations with firms. Sometimes these relationship benefits keep customers loyal to a firm more than the attributes of the core service. Research has uncovered specific types of relational benefits that customers experience in long-term service relationships, including confidence benefits, social benefits and special treatment benefits.[12]

Confidence benefits

Confidence benefits comprise feelings of trust or confidence in the provider along with a sense of reduced anxiety and comfort in knowing what to expect. Across all the services studied in the research just cited, confidence benefits were the most important to customers.

Human nature is such that most consumers would prefer not to change service providers, particularly when there is a considerable investment in the relationship. The costs of switching are frequently high in terms of monetary costs of transferring business and the associated psychological and time-related costs. Most consumers (whether individuals or businesses) have many competing demands for their time and money, and are continually searching for ways to balance and simplify decision-making to improve the quality of their lives. When they can maintain a relationship with a service provider, they free up time for other concerns and priorities.

Social benefits

Over time, customers develop a sense of familiarity and, even, a social relationship with their service providers. These ties make it less likely that they will switch, even if they learn about a competitor that might have better quality or a lower price. This customer's description of her hair stylist illustrates the concept of social benefits: 'I like him . . . . He's really funny and always has lots of good jokes. He's kind of like a friend now . . . . It's more fun to deal with somebody that you're used to. You enjoy doing business with them.'

In some long-term customer–firm relationships, a service provider may actually become part of the consumer's social support system.[13] Hairdressers, as in the example just cited, often serve as personal confidants. Less common examples include proprietors of local retail stores who become central figures in local communities; the health club or restaurant manager who knows his or her customers personally; the pharmacist who knows an entire family and its special needs; or the tour guide who befriends passengers on a long coach tour.[14]

These types of personal relationships can develop for business-to-business customers as well as for end consumers of services. The social support benefits resulting from these relationships are important to the consumer's quality of life (personal and/or work life) above and beyond the technical benefits of the service provided. Many times the close personal and professional relationships that develop between service providers and clients are the basis for the customer's loyalty. The flip side of this customer benefit is the risk to the firm of losing customers when a valued employee leaves the firm and takes customers with him or her.[15]

Special treatment benefits

Special treatment includes getting the benefit of the doubt, being given a special deal or price, or getting preferential treatment as exemplified by the following quote from the research:

> You should get the benefit of the doubt in many situations. For example, I always pay my VISA bill on time, before a service charge is assessed. One time my payment didn't quite arrive on time. When I called them, by looking at my past history, they realized that I always make an early payment. Therefore, they waived the service charge.

Interestingly, the special treatment benefits, while important, were less important than the other types of benefits received in service relationships. Although special treatment benefits can clearly be critical for customer loyalty in some industries (think of frequent-flyer benefits in the airline industry), they seem to be less important to customers overall.

Benefits for firms

The benefits to organizations of maintaining and developing a loyal customer base are numerous. In addition to the economic benefits that a firm receives from cultivating close relationships with its customers, a variety of customer behaviour benefits and human resource management benefits are also often received.

Economic benefits

One of the most commonly cited economic benefits of customer retention is increased purchases over time, as illustrated in Figure 7.2. The figure summarizes results of studies showing that

	Year				
	1	2	3	4	5
Credit card	23	32	33	37	41
Industrial laundry	108	125	144	167	192
Industrial distribution	34	74	91	108	126
Car servicing	19	26	53	66	66

FIGURE 7.2 Profit (in euros) generated by a customer over time

Source: adapted and reprinted by permission of *Harvard Business Review*. An exhibit from 'Zero defection: quality comes to services', by F.F. Reichheld and W.E. Sasser Jr (September–October 1990). Copyright © 1990 by the Harvard Business School Publishing Corporation; all rights reserved

across industries customers generally spent more each year with a particular relationship partner than they did in the preceding period.[16] As customers get to know a firm and are satisfied with the quality of its services relative to that of its competitors, they tend to give more of their business to the firm.

Another economic benefit is lower costs. Some estimates suggest that repeat purchases by established customers require as much as 90 per cent less marketing expenditure.[17] Many start-up costs are associated with attracting new customers, including advertising and other promotion costs, the operating costs of setting up new accounts and time costs of getting to know the customers. Sometimes these initial costs can outweigh the revenue expected from the new customers in the short term, so it is to the firm's advantage to cultivate long-term relationships. Even ongoing relationship maintenance costs are likely to drop over time. For example, early in a relationship a customer is likely to have questions and encounter problems as he or she learns to use the service; an experienced customer will likely have fewer problems and questions, and the firm will incur fewer costs in serving the customer. In Chapter 18 we will provide more specifics on the financial impact of customer retention.

Customer behaviour benefits

The contribution that loyal customers make to a service business can go well beyond their direct financial impact on the firm.[18] The first, and maybe the most easily recognized, customer behaviour benefit that a firm receives from long-term customers is the free advertising provided through word-of-mouth communication. When a product is complex and difficult to evaluate and when risk is involved in the decision to buy it – as is the case with many services – consumers often look to others for advice on which providers to consider. Satisfied, loyal customers are likely to provide a firm with strong word-of-mouth endorsements. Such endorsements may also take the form of online reviews or blogs. This form of communication can be more effective than any paid advertising that the firm might use, and it has the added benefit of reducing the costs of attracting new customers. Indeed, loyal customers often talk a great deal about a company and may be responsible for generating much new business over the years.

In addition to word-of-mouth communication, a second consumer behaviour benefit is one that is sometimes labelled customer voluntary performance.[19] In a restaurant, such behaviour might include customers clearing their own tables, reporting messy washrooms to an employee or picking up litter in the car park. Such behaviours support the firm's ability to deliver quality services. Although customer voluntary performance could be engaged in by anyone, those customers who have a long-term relationship with the firm are perhaps more likely to do so because they may want to see the provider do well. Third, for some services loyal customers may provide social benefits to other customers in the form of friendships or encouragement. At a health club, for example, a new member is likely to think more highly of the club when fellow members provide encouragement and guidance during fitness sessions and classes. Finally, loyal customers may serve as mentors and, because of their experience with the provider, help other customers understand the explicitly or implicitly stated rules of conduct.[20]

Human resource management benefits

Loyal customers may also provide a firm with human resource management benefits. First, loyal customers may, because of their experience with and knowledge of the provider, be able to contribute to the co-production of the service by assisting in service delivery; often the more experienced customers can make the service employees' job easier. For example, a regular patient of a medical clinic is likely to know how the system works; she would know to bring her medication with her on a visit, and to schedule an annual mammogram without waiting for her doctor to prompt her. A second benefit relates to one of the benefits for customers that we have already discussed. We noted that loyal customers receive social benefits as a result of being in a relationship with a firm; employees who regularly interact with the same customers may also receive similar social benefits.[21] A third benefit of customer retention is employee retention. It is easier for a firm to retain employees when it has a stable base of satisfied customers. People like to work for companies whose customers are happy and loyal. Their jobs are more satisfying, and they are able to spend more of their time fostering relationships than scrambling for new customers. In turn, customers are more satisfied and become even better customers – a positive upward spiral. Because employees stay with the firm longer, service quality improves and costs of turnover are reduced, adding further to profits.

Relationship value of customers

Relationship value of a customer is a concept or calculation that looks at customers from the point of view of their lifetime revenue and/or profitability contributions to a company. This type of calculation is obviously needed when companies start thinking of building long-term relationships with their customers. Just what is the potential financial value of those long-term relationships? And what are the financial implications of *losing* a customer? Here we will first summarize the factors that influence a customer's relationship value, and then show some ways it can be estimated. In Chapter 18 we provide more detail on lifetime value financial calculations.

Factors that influence relationship value

The lifetime or relationship value of a customer is influenced by the length of an average 'lifetime', the average revenues generated per relevant time period over the lifetime, sales of additional products and services over time, referrals generated by the customer over time, and costs associated with serving the customer. **Lifetime value** sometimes refers to lifetime revenue stream only; but most often when costs are considered, lifetime value truly means 'lifetime profitability'.

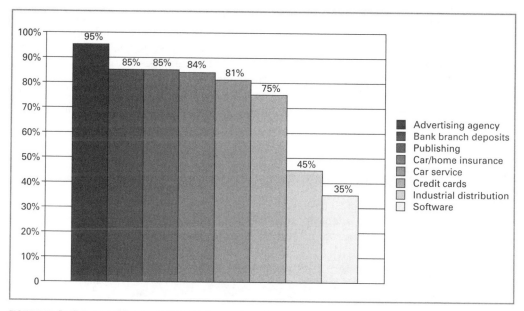

FIGURE 7.3 Profit impact of 5 per cent increase in retention rate

Source: reprinted with permission of the American Marketing Association. From F.F. Reichheld, 'Loyalty and the renaissance of marketing', *Marketing Management*, vol. 2, no. 4 (1994), p. 15

Estimating customer lifetime value

If companies knew how much it really costs to lose a customer, they would be able accurately to evaluate investments designed to retain customers. One way of documenting the value of loyal customers is to estimate the increased value or profits that accrue for each additional customer who remains loyal to the company rather than defecting to the competition. This is what Bain & Co. has done for a number of industries, as shown in Figure 7.3.[22] The figure shows the percentage of increase in total firm profits when the retention or loyalty rate rises by 5 percentage points. The increases are dramatic, ranging from 35 to 95 per cent. These increases were calculated by comparing the net present values of the profit streams for the average customer life at current retention rates with the net present values of the profit streams for the average customer life at 5 per cent higher retention rates.

With sophisticated accounting systems to document actual costs and revenue streams over time, a firm can be quite precise in documenting the value and costs of retaining customers. These systems attempt to estimate the value of *all* the benefits and costs associated with a loyal customer, not just the long-term revenue stream. The value of word-of-mouth advertising, employee retention and declining account maintenance costs can also enter into the calculation.[23]

Linking customer relationship value to firm value

The emphasis on estimating the relationship value of customers has increased substantially in the past decade. Part of this emphasis has resulted from an increased appreciation of the economic benefits that firms accrue with the retention of loyal customers. Interestingly, recent research suggests that customer retention has a large impact on firm value and that relationship value calculations can also provide a useful proxy for assessing the value of a firm.[24] That is, a firm's market value can be roughly determined by carefully calculating customer lifetime value. The approach is straightforward: estimate the relationship value of a customer, forecast the future growth of the number of customers and use these figures to determine the value of a company's current and future base. To the extent that the customer base forms a large part of a company's overall value, such a calculation can provide an estimate of a firm's value – a particularly useful figure for young, high-growth firms for which traditional financial methods (e.g. discounted cash flow) do not work well.

Customer profitability segments

Companies may want to treat all customers with excellent service, but they generally find that customers differ in their relationship value and that it may be neither practical nor profitable to meet (and certainly not to exceed) *all* customers' expectations.[25]

Service spotlight

Federal Express has categorized its customers internally as the good, the bad, and the ugly – based on their profitability. Rather than treating all its customers the same, the company pays particular attention to enhancing their relationships with the good, tries to move the bad to the good and discourages the ugly.[26]

As shown in the Tesco example at the start of this chapter, other companies also try to identify segments – or, more appropriately, tiers of customers – that differ in current and/or future profitability to a firm. This approach goes beyond usage or volume segmentation because it tracks costs and revenues for segments of customers, thereby capturing their financial worth to companies. After identifying profitability bands, the firm offers services and service levels in line with the identified segments. Building a high-loyalty customer base of the right customers increases profits.

Profitability tiers – the customer pyramid

Virtually all firms are aware at some level that their customers differ in profitability, in particular, that a minority of their customers accounts for the highest proportion of sales or profit. This finding has often been called the '80/20 rule' – 20 per cent of customers produce 80 per cent of sales or profit.

In this version of tiering, 20 per cent of the customers constitute the top tier, those who can be identified as the most profitable in the company. The rest are indistinguishable from each other but differ from the top tier in profitability. Most companies realize that there are differences among customers within this tier but do not possess the data or capabilities to analyse the distinctions. The 80/20 two-tier scheme assumes that consumers within the two tiers are similar, just as conventional market segmentation schemes typically assume that consumers within segments are similar.

However, more than two tiers are likely and can be used if the company has sufficient data to analyse customer tiers more precisely. Different systems and labels can be helpful. One useful four-tier system, shown in Figure 7.4, includes the following:

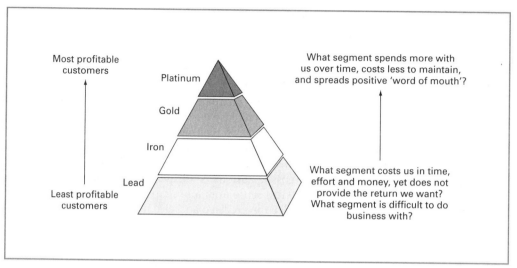

FIGURE 7.4 The customer pyramid

1 The *platinum tier* describes the company's most profitable customers, typically those who are heavy users of the product, are not overly price sensitive, are willing to invest in and try new offerings, and are committed customers of the firm.

2 The *gold tier* differs from the platinum tier in that profitability levels are not as high, perhaps because the customers want price discounts that limit margins or they are not as loyal. They may be heavy users who minimize risk by working with multiple vendors rather than just the focal company.

3 The *iron tier* contains essential customers who provide the volume needed to utilize the firm's capacity, but their spending levels, loyalty and profitability are not substantial enough for special treatment.

4 The *lead tier* consists of customers who are costing the company money. They demand more attention than they are due given their spending and profitability, and are sometimes problem customers – complaining about the firm to others and tying up the firm's resources.

Note that this classification is superficially reminiscent of, but very different from, traditional usage segmentation performed by airlines such as British Airways. Two differences are obvious. First, in the **customer pyramid** profitability rather than usage defines all levels. Second, the lower levels actually articulate classes of customers who require a different sort of attention. The firm must work either to change the customers' behaviour – to make them more profitable through increases in revenue – or to change the firm's cost structure to make them more profitable through decreases in costs.

Once a system has been established for categorizing customers, the multiple levels can be identified, motivated, served and expected to deliver differential levels of profit. Companies improve their opportunities for profit when they increase shares of purchases by customers who either have the greatest need for the services or show the greatest loyalty to a single provider. By strengthening relationships with the loyal customers, increasing sales with existing customers and increasing the profitability on each sale opportunity, companies thereby increase the potential of each customer.

The customer's view of profitability tiers

Whereas **profitability tiers** make sense from the company's point of view, customers are not always understanding, nor do they appreciate being categorized into a less desirable segment.[27] For example, at some companies the top clients have their own individual account representative whom they can contact personally. The next tier of clients may be handled by representatives who each have 100 clients. Meanwhile, most clients are served by a call centre, an automated voice response system or referral to a website. Customers are aware of this unequal treatment, and many resist and resent it. It makes perfect sense from a business perspective, but customers are often disappointed in the level of service they receive and give firms poor marks for quality as a result.

Therefore, it is increasingly important that firms communicate with customers so they understand the level of service they can expect and what they would need to do or pay to receive faster or more personalized service. The most significant issues result when customers do not understand and believe they have been singled out for poor service, or feel that the system is unfair. Although many customers refuse to pay for quality service, they react negatively if they believe it has been taken away from them unfairly.

The ability to segment customers narrowly, based on profitability implications, also raises questions of privacy for customers. In order to know who is profitable and who is not, companies must collect large amounts of individualized behavioural and personal data on consumers. Many consumers today resent what they perceive as an intrusion into their lives in this way, especially when it results in differential treatment that they perceive is unfair.

Making business decisions using profitability tiers

Prudent business managers are well aware that past customer purchase behaviour, although useful in making predictions, can be misleading.[28] What a customer spends today, or has spent in the past, may not necessarily be reflective of what he or she will do (or be worth) in the future. Banks serving students know this well – a typical student generally has minimal financial services needs (i.e. a current account) and tends not to have a high level of deposits. However, within a few years that student may embark on a professional career, start a family and/or purchase a house, and thus require several financial services and become a potentially very profitable customer to the bank. Generally, a firm would like to keep its consistent big spenders and lose the erratic small spenders. But all too often a firm also has two other groups they must consider: erratic big spenders and consistent small spenders. So, in some situations where consistent cash flow is a concern, it may be helpful to a firm to have a portfolio of customers that includes steady customers, even if they have a history of being less profitable. Some service providers have actually been quite successful in targeting customers who were previously considered to be unworthy of another firm's marketing efforts.[29] Firms, therefore, need to be cautious in blindly applying customer value calculations without thinking carefully about the implications.

Endsleigh Insurance became very successful in selling insurance to students and young people, a group that most of the competition did not feel had a sufficient relationship value. Their sales message to students emphasizes:

Recognised – We are the only insurance provider endorsed by the National Union of Students.

Trusted – We insure more student rooms in the UK than anyone else.

Proven track record – Endsleigh have been the market leaders in student insurance for over four decades.

For students – We operate a network of campus branches throughout the UK.

In tune with student lifestyles – You do not need locks on your door and we even cover you if there is no sign of break-in. Your parents' home insurance may not cover this and over a third of our claims are paid on this basis.

Not just a student insurer – We not only cover more students than anyone else but we have special policies for when you graduate.

Source: www.endsleigh.co.uk

Relationship development strategies

To this point in the chapter, we have focused on the rationale for relationship marketing, the benefits (to both firms and customers) of the development of strong exchange relationships, and an understanding of the relationship value of a customer. In this section we examine a variety of factors that influence the development of strong customer relationships, including the customer's overall evaluation of a firm's offering, bonds created with customers by the firm, and barriers that the customer faces in leaving a relationship. These factors, illustrated in Figure 7.5, provide the rationale for specific strategies that firms often use to keep their current customers.

Core service provision

Retention strategies will have little long-term success unless the firm has a solid base of service quality and customer satisfaction on which to build. The firm does not necessarily have to be the very best among its competitors or be world-class in terms of quality and customer satisfaction. It must be competitive, however, and frequently better than that. All the retention strategies that we describe in this section are built on the assumption of competitive quality and value being offered. Clearly, a firm needs to begin the relationship development process by providing a good core service delivery that, at a minimum, meets customer expectations; it does no good to design relationship strategies for inferior services. The earlier example of Tesco provides convincing support for the argument that excellence in the core service or product offered is essential to a successful relationship strategy. Tesco has benefited tremendously from its loyal customer base; it offers excellent quality and uses relationship strategies to enhance its success.

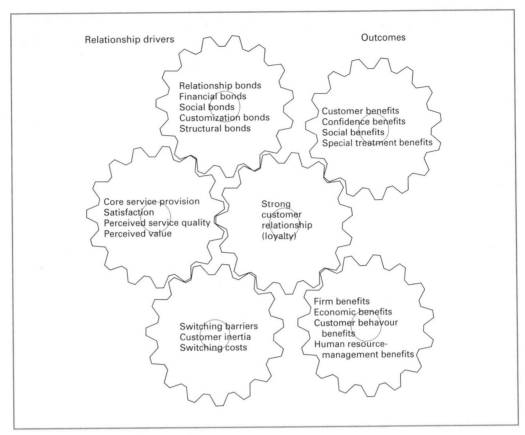

FIGURE 7.5 Relationship development model

Source: adapted from D.D. Gremler and S.W. Brown, 'Service loyalty: antecedents, components, and outcomes', in *1998 AMA Winter Educators'*
Conference: Marketing Theory and Applications, vol. 9, D. Grewal and C. Pechmann, eds. Chicago, IL: American Marketing Association, pp. 165–6

Switching barriers

When considering a switch in service providers, a customer may face a number of barriers that make it difficult to leave one service provider and begin a relationship with another. Literature suggests that switching barriers influence consumers' decisions to exit from relationships with firms and, therefore, help to facilitate customer retention.[30]

Customer inertia

One reason that customers commit to developing relationships with firms is that a certain amount of effort may be required to change firms. Sometimes consumers simplistically state that 'it's just not worth it' to switch providers. Inertia may even explain why some dissatisfied customers stay with a provider. In discussing why people remain in relationships (in general) that they no longer find satisfying, scholars suggest that people may stay because breaking the relationship would require them to restructure their life – to develop new habits of living, to refashion old friendships and to find new ones.[31] In other words, people do not like to change their behaviour.

To retain customers, firms might consider increasing the perceived effort required on the part of the customer to switch service providers. If a customer believes that a great deal of effort is needed to change companies, the customer is more likely to stay put. For example, car repair facilities might keep a complete and detailed maintenance history of a customer's vehicle. These records remove from the customer the burden of having to remember all the services performed on the vehicle and would force the customer to expend considerable effort in providing a complete maintenance history if the vehicle is taken to a new mechanic. Conversely, if a firm is looking to attract a competitor's customers, it might automate the process for switching providers as much as possible in order to reduce the effort required to switch. Utility companies supplying electricity and gas generally make switching providers as simple as saying 'yes' on the Internet or to a company representative – thereby removing any action required of the customer.

Switching costs

In many instances, customers develop loyalty to an organization in part because of costs involved in changing to and purchasing from a different firm. These costs, both real and perceived, monetary and non-monetary, are termed *switching costs*. Switching costs include investments of time, money or effort – such as set-up costs, search costs, learning costs and contractual costs – that make it challenging for the customer to move to another provider.[32] To illustrate, a patient may incur *set-up costs* such as paying for new X-rays when switching dentists or paying for a property survey when changing mortgage/housing loan provider. Because services often have characteristics that make them difficult to evaluate – including intangibility, non-standardization, inseparability of production and consumption, as well as high experience and credence qualities – high *search costs* may be required to obtain suitable information about alternative services. *Learning costs* are those costs associated with learning the idiosyncrasies of how to use a product or service; in many situations, a customer who wishes to switch firms may need to accumulate new user skills or customer know-how. *Contractual costs* arise when the customer is required to pay a penalty to switch providers (e.g. penalty charges for customer-initiated switching of mortgage companies or mobile phone services), making it financially difficult, if not impossible, for the customer to initiate an early termination of the relationship.

In order to retain customers, firms might consider increasing their switching costs to make it difficult for customers to exit the relationship (or at least create the perception of difficulty). Indeed, many firms explicitly specify such costs in the contracts that they require their customers to sign (e.g. mobile phone services, health clubs). In order to attract new customers, a service provider might consider implementing strategies designed to *lower* the switching costs of customers not currently using the provider. To reduce the set-up costs involved when switching, providers could complete the paperwork required from the customer. Banks, for example, could offer to do all the paperwork to set up a current account, including direct debits and standing orders.

Relationship bonds

Switching barriers tend to serve as constraints that keep customers in relationships with firms because they 'have to'.[33] However, firms can engage in activities that encourage customers to remain in the relationship because they 'want to'. Leonard Berry and A. Parasuraman have developed a framework for understanding the types of retention strategies that focus on developing bonds with customers.[34] The framework suggests that relationship marketing can occur at different levels and that each successive level of strategy results in ties that bind the customer a little closer to the firm. At each successive level, the potential for sustained competitive advantage is also increased. Building on the levels of the retention strategy idea, Figure 7.6 illustrates four types of retention strategies, which are discussed in the following sections. Recall, however, that the most successful retention strategies will be built on foundations of core service excellence.

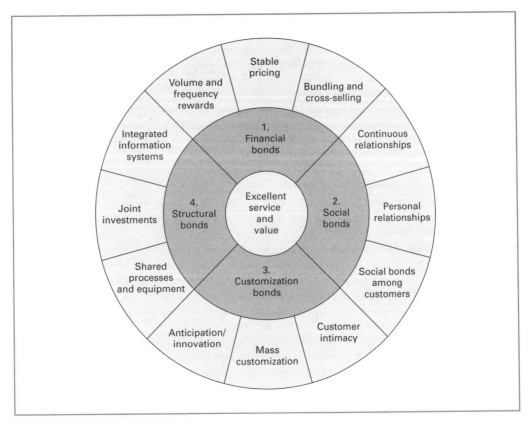

FIGURE 7.6 Levels of relationship strategies

Level 1 – Financial bonds

At level 1, the customer is tied to the firm primarily through financial incentives – lower prices for greater volume purchases or lower prices for customers who have been with the firm a long time. Examples of level 1 relationship marketing are not hard to find. Think about the airline industry and related travel service industries like hotels and car rental companies. Frequent-flyer programmes provide financial incentives and rewards for travellers who bring more of their business to a particular airline. Hotels and car rental companies do the same. Mobile phone companies have engaged in a similar battle, trying to provide volume discounts and other price incentives to retain market share and build a loyal customer base. One reason these financial incentive programmes proliferate is that they are not difficult to initiate and frequently result in at least short-term profit gains. Unfortunately, financial incentives do not generally provide long-term advantages to a firm because, unless combined with another relationship strategy, they do not differentiate the firm from its competitors in the long run. Many travellers belong to several frequent-flyer programmes and do not hesitate to trade off among them. Although price and other financial incentives are important to customers, they are generally not difficult for competitors to imitate because the primary customized element of the marketing mix is price.

Other types of retention strategies that depend primarily on financial rewards are focused on bundling and cross-selling of services. Frequent-flyer programmes again provide a common example. Many airlines link their reward programmes with hotel chains, car rental and, in some cases, credit card usage. By linking airline mileage points earned to usage of other firms' services, customers can enjoy even greater financial benefits in exchange for their loyalty.

In other cases, firms aim to retain their customers by simply offering their most loyal customers the assurance of stable prices, or at least lower price increases than those paid by new customers. In this way firms reward their loyal customers by sharing with them some of the cost savings and increased revenue that the firm receives through serving them over time.

Although widely and increasingly used as retention tactics, loyalty programmes based on financial rewards merit caution.[35] These programmes are often easily imitated. Thus, any increased usage or loyalty from customers may be short-lived. Second, these strategies are not likely to be successful unless they are structured so that they truly lead to repeat or increased usage rather than serving as a means to attract new customers and potentially causing endless switching among competitors.

Level 2 – Social bonds

Level 2 strategies bind customers to the firm through more than financial incentives. Although price is still assumed to be important, level 2 retention marketers build long-term relationships through social and interpersonal as well as financial bonds. Customers are viewed as 'clients', not nameless faces, and become individuals whose needs and wants the firm seeks to understand.

Social, interpersonal bonds are common among professional service providers (lawyers, accountants, architects) and their clients as well as among personal care providers (hairdressers, counsellors, health-care

FIGURE 7.7 Harley Davidson riders develop customer-to-customer bonds through Harley Owners Group (HOG) activities
Source: EyeWire Collection/Getty Images

providers) and their clients. A dentist who takes a few minutes to review his or her patient's file before an appointment jogs his or her memory on personal facts about the patient (occupation, family details, interests, dental health history). By bringing these personal details into the conversation, the dentist reveals a genuine interest in the patient as an individual and builds social bonds. Interpersonal bonds are also common in business-to-business relationships in which customers develop relationships with salespeople and/or relationship managers working with their firms.

Sometimes relationships are formed with the organization because of the social bonds that develop *among customers* rather than between customers and the provider of the service. Such bonds are often formed in health clubs, country clubs, educational settings and other service environments where customers interact with each other. Over time the social relationships they have with other customers are important factors that prevent them from switching to another organization. One company that has built a significant strategy around customer-to-customer bonds is Harley Davidson, with its local Harley Owners Groups (HOGs). Harley Owners Groups throughout Europe (in Belgium, Germany, Spain, France, Italy, Luxembourg, Netherlands, Austria, Switzerland and the UK) are involved in local rallies, tours and parties as well as in national HOG events organized by the company. Through the HOGs, Harley customers come to know each other and develop a sense of community around their common interest – motorcycle riding – as illustrated in Figure 7.7.

Social bonds alone may not tie the customer permanently to the firm, but they are much more difficult for competitors to imitate than are price incentives. In the absence of strong reasons to shift to another provider, interpersonal bonds can encourage customers to stay in a relationship.[36] In combination with financial incentives, social bonding strategies may be very effective.

Level 3 – Customization bonds

Level 3 strategies involve more than social ties and financial incentives, although there are common elements of level 1 and 2 strategies encompassed within a customization strategy and vice versa. For example, Royal Bank of Scotland branch managers are relied on not just to form strong personal commitments to customers, but also to feed information back into the bank to help customize services to fit developing customer needs.

Two commonly used terms fit within the customization bonds approach: *mass customization* and *customer intimacy*. Both these strategies suggest that customer loyalty can be encouraged through intimate knowledge of individual customers and through the development of one-to-one solutions that fit the individual customer's needs.

Mass customization has been defined as 'the use of flexible processes and organizational structures to produce varied and often individually customized products and services at the price of standardized, mass-produced alternatives'.[37] Mass customization does not mean providing customers with endless solutions or choices that only make them work harder for what they want; rather, it means providing them through little effort on their part with tailored services to fit their individual needs. Boots The Chemists in the UK has used technology to understand its customers and build one of the world's largest smart card loyalty scheme.

Service spotlight

Boots The Chemists is one of the best-known and trusted brands in the UK and is the UK's leading health and beauty retailer. The company, founded in 1887, spans three centuries of successful operations. Currently it offers its products through 1400 retail stores as well as an online store at www.wellbeing.com. On its website, the Boots Company states that it intends to become the global leader in well-being products and services and is expanding globally through Boots Healthcare International.

A foundation for Boots's success in recent years is its increased focus on the customer and a desire to develop customer loyalty through a number of retention and relationship strategies. At the heart of the company's loyalty strategy is its Advantage Card, started in 1997. The Advantage Card is right now the world's largest smart card loyalty scheme, with close to 13 million members. Over 50 per cent of Boots's current sales are now linked to the card. The card offers a number of benefits

Service spotlight (continued)

to customers and has helped the company increase sales but, more than that, it has been the foundation for building greater loyalty among its best customers.

Using the card for purchases, Boots's customers receive 4 points for every £1 spent. These points can be redeemed for selected products, aimed to treat customers to something special rather than simply to offer discounts off purchases. In fact the card is *not* about discounts; rather, it is about treating oneself. Customers can use their points to treat themselves to a simple lunch or to a full day of pampering at a spa. From a financial perspective, the company has seen increasing average transaction values among higher-spending customers. Boots managers say that they have increased loyalty and spending from people who were already good and profitable customers – a clear win for the company.

A number of initiatives are tied to the Advantage Card, taking it beyond a pure points reward programme from the customer's perspective. For example, Boots now mails a first-class health and beauty magazine to the top-spending 3 million Advantage Card holders. The magazine is Britain's biggest health and beauty magazine; it is not viewed as a 'Boots' magazine but as a health and beauty magazine sent by Boots. Cardholders also have access to additional benefits and discounts using interactive kiosks in over 380 stores. The card can be used for purchases at the online store through the www.wellbeing.com site that was launched jointly with Granada Media in 2001. Many products are offered on the site that are not available in Boots stores. In addition, the site provides access to an online magazine, answers to questions, a chat room, and other features and services. A credit card version of the Advantage Card was launched in 2001. And Boots joined with the Department of Health to enable Advantage Card holders to register with the National Health Service Organ Donor programme and to carry an Advantage Card featuring the programme's logo.

From the company's perspective as well, the card is much more than a reward programme. Data generated through the card is used to understand customers and to anticipate and identify individual needs in health and beauty care products. In fact, the goals with the Advantage Card programme back in 1997 were to gain customer insight, build a database that would allow the company to tailor offerings to individual customers' needs, develop incremental sales by building customer loyalty, and use the customer knowledge to develop and introduce new products and services. A great deal of planning and testing went into developing the programme, and this planning paid off in customer loyalty. Buy-in from the company's 60 000 staff members also aided in the rapid success of the programme. All associates were signed up as members six months before the launch of the card. After experiencing the benefits of the card first hand, they became enthusiastic advocates, encouraging customers to sign up.

Through the programme, Boots has learned that the more broadly customers buy, in more categories over time, the more they increase visits to Boots stores. The result has been customization of product and service offerings, and more sales and greater loyalty from its best customers.

Sources: Frederick Newell, *Loyalty.com* (New York: McGraw-Hill, 2000), pp. 239–45; www.boots-plc.com (2002); www.wellbeing.com (2002)

Level 4 – Structural bonds

Level 4 strategies are the most difficult to imitate; they involve structural as well as financial, social and customization bonds between the customer and the firm. Structural bonds are created by providing services to the client that are frequently designed right into the service delivery system for that client. Often, structural bonds are created by providing customized services to the client that are technology based and make the customer more productive.

Service spotlight

An example of structural bonds can be seen in a business-to-business context with Gist who manages the UK supply chain and logistics of food products for M&S (Marks and Spencer), duty free products for British Airways, retail products for Woolworths and beer for Carlsberg. By working closely with its retail and service customers, it has developed ways to improve supply ordering, delivery and billing that have greatly enhanced its value as a supplier. For example, Gist can manage physical stock replenishment in such a way that products are delivered to stores (or aeroplanes!) in shop-floor condition. In other words they manage the whole process of packaging, sorting, tagging and hanging items for a retailer in addition to dealing with returned goods, invoicing, etc. There is therefore a strong structural bond between the retailer and a company; for example, M&S have been using this same supplier for over 35 years.

But there is also a potential downside to this arrangement from the customer's perspective. Customers may fear that tying themselves too closely to one provider may not allow them to take advantage of potential price savings from other providers in the future.

Relationship challenges

Given the many benefits of long-term customer relationships, it would seem that a company would not want to refuse or terminate a relationship with any customer. Yet, situations arise in which either the firm, the customer or both want to end (or have to end) their relationship. This final section of the chapter discusses situations in which the firm might actually consider ending the relationship and how that might occur.

The customer is *not* always right

The assumption that all customers are good customers is very compatible with the belief that 'the customer is always right', an almost sacrosanct tenet of business. Yet any service worker can tell you that this statement is *not* always true, and in some cases it may be preferable for the firm and the customer to not continue their relationship. The following discussion presents a view of customer relationships that suggests that all relationships may not be beneficial and that every customer is not right all the time.

The wrong segment

A company cannot target its services to all customers; some segments will be more appropriate than others. It would not be beneficial to either the company or the customer for a company to establish a relationship with a customer whose needs the company cannot meet. For example, a business school offering a daytime MBA programme would not encourage full-time working people to apply for its programme, nor would a law firm specializing in government issues establish a relationship with individuals seeking advice on trusts and estates. These examples seem obvious. Yet firms frequently do give in to the temptation to make a sale by agreeing to serve a customer who would be better served by someone else.

Similarly, it would not be wise to forge relationships simultaneously with incompatible market segments. In many service businesses (such as restaurants, hotels, tour package operators, entertainment and education), customers experience the service together and can influence each other's perceptions about value received. Thus, to maximize service to core segments, an organization may choose to turn away marginally profitable segments that would be incompatible. For example, a conference hotel may find that mixing senior managers in the hotel for a serious training programme with students in the hotel for an end-of-year student ball may not be wise. If the senior management group is a key long-term customer, the hotel may choose to pass up the students in the interest of retaining the corporate business.

Not profitable in the long term

In the absence of ethical or legal mandates, organizations will prefer *not* to have long-term relationships with unprofitable customers. Some segments of customers will not be profitable for the company even if their needs can be met by the services offered. Some examples of this situation are when there are not enough customers in the segment to make it profitable to develop a marketing approach, when the segment cannot afford to pay the cost of the service, or when the projected revenue flows from the segment would not cover the costs incurred to originate and maintain the business. For example, in the banking industry it has been estimated that 40 to 70 per cent of customers served in a typical bank are not profitable in the sense that the costs of serving these customers exceed the revenues generated.[38]

At the individual customer level, it may not be profitable for a firm to engage in a relationship with a particular customer who has bad credit or who is a poor risk for some other reason. Retailers, banks and credit card companies routinely refuse to do business with individuals whose credit histories are unreliable. Although the short-term sale may be beneficial, the long-term risk of non-payment makes the relationship unwise from the company's point of view. Similarly, some car rental companies check into the driving records of customers and reject bad-risk drivers.[39] This practice, while controversial, is logical from the car rental companies' point of view because they can cut back on insurance costs and accident claims (thus reducing rental costs for good drivers) by not doing business with accident-prone drivers.

Beyond the monetary costs associated with serving the wrong customers, there can be substantial time investments in some customers that, if actually computed, would make them unprofitable for the organization. Everyone has had the experience of waiting in a bank, a retail store or, even, in an education setting while a particularly demanding customer seems to use more than his share of the service provider's time. The monetary value of the time spent with a specific customer is typically not computed or calculated into the price of the service.

In a business-to-business relationship, the variability in time commitment to customers is even more apparent. Some customers may use considerable resources of the supplier organization through inordinate numbers of telephone calls, excessive requests for information and other time-consuming activities. In the legal profession, clients are billed for every hour of the firm's time that they use in this way because time is essentially the only resource the firm has. Yet in other service businesses, all clients essentially pay the same regardless of the time demands they place on the organization.

Difficult customers

Managers have repeated the phrase 'the customer is always right' so often that you would expect it to be accepted by every employee in every service organization. So why is it not? Perhaps because it simply is not true. The customer is not always right. No matter how frequently it is said, repeating that mantra does not make it become reality, and service employees know it.

In many situations, firms have service encounters that fail because of *dysfunctional customers.* Dysfunctional customer behaviour refers to actions by customers who intentionally, or perhaps unintentionally, act in a manner that in some way disrupts otherwise functional service encounters.[40] Such customers have been described as 'customers from hell' or 'problem customers'. One of us was awakened during a recent hotel stay at 4.00 a.m. by drunk customers who were arguing with each other in a room above; management eventually called the police and asked them to escort the customers off the property. An Enterprise Rent-A-Car customer demanded that she not be charged for any of the two weeks that she had a car because, near the end of the rental period, she found a small stain in the back seat.[41] These customers often have the objective of gaining faster, superior or perhaps free service, but their behaviour is considered dysfunctional from the perspective of the service provider and perhaps fellow customers.

Dysfunctional customer behaviour can affect employees, other customers and the organization. Research suggests that exposure to dysfunctional customer behaviour can have psychological, emotional, behavioural and physical effects on employees.[42] For example, customer-contact employees who are exposed to rude, threatening, obstructive, aggressive or disruptive behaviour by customers often have their mood or temper negatively affected as well as their motivation and morale. Such customers are difficult to work with and often create stress for employees. Dysfunctional customers can also have an impact on other customers: such behaviour can spoil the service experience for other customers, and the dysfunctional customer behaviour may become contagious for other customers witnessing it, particularly if it includes vociferous or illegitimate complaining. Finally, dysfunctional customer behaviour can create both direct costs and indirect costs for the organization. Direct costs of such behaviour can include the expense of restoring damaged property, increased insurance premiums, property loss by theft, costs incurred in compensating customers affected by the dysfunctional behaviour of others, and the costs incurred through illegitimate claims by dysfunctional customers. Additionally, indirect costs might include increased workloads for staff required to deal with dysfunctional behaviour as well as increased costs for attracting and retaining appropriate personnel and, perhaps, for absenteeism payments.

Although often these difficult customers will be accommodated and employees can be trained to recognize and deal with them appropriately, at times the best choice may be to not maintain the relationship at all – especially at the business-to-business level, where long-term costs to the firm can be substantial.

Service spotlight

For example, it is quite common for European marketing research agencies to choose not to work for certain clients. Difficult clients paralyse a marketing research agency for a variety of reasons. Some ask for complex research projects to be undertaken on limited budgets. Others require so much up-front work and the development of creative research ideas before selecting an agency that much of the preliminary research design work is essentially done for free by those agencies not selected. Other clients are stingy; require many meetings before settling on an agency; or require a lot of direct, frequently disruptive, involvement in the design of questionnaires or the operations of a group discussion. As a result, agencies have become more wary of chasing every client that comes along.

Ending business relationships

For the effective management of service relationships, managers should not only know how to establish a relationship but also how to end one. As suggested earlier in this chapter, firms may identify some customers who are not in their targeted segment, who are not profitable in the long run, or who are difficult to work with or dysfunctional. A company may *not* want to continue in a relationship with every customer. However, gracefully exiting a relationship may not be easy. Customers may end up feeling disappointed, confused or hurt if a firm attempts to terminate the relationship.

Relationship endings

Relationships end in different ways – depending on the type of relationship in place.[43] In some situations, a relationship is established for a certain purpose and/or time period and then dissolves when it has served its purpose or the time frame has elapsed. For example, a house-painting service may be engaged with the customer for four days while painting the house exterior, but both parties understand that the end of the relationship is predetermined – the end occurs when the house has been painted and the customer has paid for the service. Sometimes a relationship has a natural ending. Piano lessons for children, for example, often cease as the child gets older and develops interests in other musical areas (such as singing or playing the clarinet); in such situations, the need for the relationship has diminished or become obsolete. In other situations, an event may occur that forces the relationship to end; a provider who relocates to the other side of town may force some customers to select a different company. Or a **relationship ending** may occur because the customer is not fulfilling his or her obligations. For example, a bank may choose to end the relationship with a customer who regularly has insufficient funds in their account. Whatever the reason for ending the relationship, firms should clearly communicate their reasons for wanting (or needing) to terminate it so that customers understand what is occurring and why.

Should firms fire their customers?

A logical conclusion to be drawn from the discussion of the challenges firms face in customer relationships is that perhaps firms should seek to get rid of those customers who are not right for the company. More and more companies are making these types of decisions based on the belief that troublesome customers are usually less profitable and less loyal, and that it may be counterproductive to attempt to retain their business.[44] Another reason for 'firing' a customer is the negative effect that these customers can have on employee quality of life and morale. Troublesome airline passengers who are disruptive on a flight may find that the airline refuses to carry them on any future flight.

Service spotlight

One company took reducing its customer base to the extreme. Nypro – a global, employee-owned company with operations in Europe and North America specializing in moulded plastics applications for such clients as Gillette, Abbott Laboratories, Hewlett-Packard and other large organizations[45] – reduced its customer base in the 1980s from 800 to approximately 30 clients in the belief that it could better serve those clients and grow more effectively if it focused on fewer relationships. Nypro adopted a customer intimacy strategy and tied itself closely to this much smaller number of clients. Some of these clients have now been with Nypro for more than 40 years. Over time Nypro has selectively added clients to this base, and the company has enjoyed 18 consecutive years of record sales and profit growth.

Although it may sound like a good idea, firing customers is not that simple and needs to be done in a way that avoids negative publicity or negative word of mouth. Sometimes raising prices or charging for services that previously had been given away for free can move unprofitable customers out of the company. Helping a client find a new supplier who can better meet its needs is another way to gracefully exit a non-productive relationship. If the customer has become too demanding, the relationship may be salvaged by negotiating expectations or finding more efficient ways to serve the client. If not, both parties may find an agreeable way to end the relationship.

Summary

In this chapter we focused on the rationale for, benefits of, and strategies for developing long-term relationships with customers. It should be obvious by now that organizations that focus only on acquiring new customers may well fail to understand their current customers; thus, while a company may be bringing customers in through the front door, equal or greater numbers may be exiting. Estimates of lifetime relationship value accentuate the importance of retaining current customers.

The particular strategy that an organization uses to retain its current customers can and should be customized to fit the industry, the culture and the customer needs of the organization. However, in general, customer relationships are driven by a variety of factors that influence the development of strong customer relationships, including (1) the customer's overall evaluation of the quality of a firm's core service offering, (2) the switching barriers that the customer faces in leaving a relationship, and (3) the relationship bonds developed with that customer by the firm. By developing strong relationships with customers and by focusing on factors that influence customer relationships, the organization will accurately understand customer expectations over time and consequently will narrow service quality gap 1.

The chapter concluded with a discussion of the challenges that firms face in developing relationships with customers. Although long-term customer relationships are critical and can be very profitable, firms should not attempt to build relationships with just any customer. In other words, 'the customer is not always right'. Indeed, in some situations it may be best for firms to discontinue relationships with some customers – for the sake of the customer, the firm, or both.

Key concepts

Customer pyramid	163	Relationship endings	175
Lifetime value	160	Relationship marketing	152
Profitability tiers	164	Retention	165
Relationship bonds	150	Switching barriers	150

Further reading

Egan, J. and Harker, M. (2005) *Relationship Marketing.* London: Sage Publications.

Grayson, K. and Ambler, T. (1999) 'The dark side of long-term relationships in marketing services', *Journal of Marketing Research,* 36 (February), 132–41.

Gummesson, E. (2002) *Total Relationship Marketing, Rethinking Marketing Management: from 4Ps to 30Rs.* Oxford: Butterworth-Heinemann.

Kavall, S.G., Tzokas, N.X. and Saren, M.J. (1999) 'Relationship marketing as an ethical approach: philosophical and managerial considerations', *Management Decision,* 37(7), 573–81.

Payne, C.M., Payne, A. and Ballantyne, D. (1991) *Relationship Marketing: Bringing Quality, Customer Service and Marketing Together.* Oxford: Butterworth-Heinemann.

Storbacka, K. and Lehtinen, J.R. (2001) *Customer Relationship Management.* Singapore: McGraw-Hill.

Zineldin, M. (2000) *Total Relationship Management.* Lund: Studentlitteratur.

Discussion questions

1 Discuss how relationship marketing or retention marketing is different from the traditional emphasis in marketing.

2 Describe how a firm's relationships with customers may evolve over time. For each level of relationship discussed in the chapter, identify a firm with which you have that level of relationship and discuss how its marketing efforts differ from other firms'.

3 Think about a service organization that retains you as a loyal customer. Why are you loyal to this provider? What are the benefits to you of staying loyal and not switching to another provider? What would it take for you to switch?

4 With regard to the same service organization, what are the benefits to the organization of keeping you as a customer? Calculate your 'lifetime value' to the organization.

5 Describe the logic behind 'customer profitability segmentation' from the company's point of view. Also discuss what customers may think of the practice.

6 Describe the various switching barriers discussed in the text. What switching barriers might you face in switching banks? Mobile phone service providers? Universities?

7 Describe the four levels of retention strategies, and give examples of each type. Again, think of a service organization to which you are loyal. Can you describe the reason(s) you are loyal in terms of the different levels? In other words, what ties you to the organization?

8 Have you ever worked as a front-line service employee? Can you remember having to deal with difficult or 'problem' customers? Discuss how you handled such situations. As a manager of front-line employees, how would you help your employees deal with difficult customers?

Exercises

1 Interview the manager of a local service organization. Discuss with the manager the target market(s) for the service. Estimate the lifetime value of a customer in one or more of the target segments. To do this estimate, you will need to get as much information from the manager as you can. If the manager cannot answer your questions, make some assumptions.

2 In small groups in class, debate the question, 'Is the customer always right?' In other words, are there times when the customer may be the wrong customer for the organization?

3 Design a customer appreciation programme for the organization with whom you currently work. Why would you have such a programme, and to whom would it be directed?

4 Choose a specific company context (your class project company, the company you work for or a company in an industry you are familiar with). Calculate the lifetime value of a customer for this company. You will need to make assumptions to do this calculation, so make your assumptions clear. Using ideas and concepts from this chapter, describe a relationship marketing strategy to increase the number of lifetime customers for this firm.

Notes

1 F.E. Webster Jr, 'The changing role of marketing in the corporation', *Journal of Marketing* (October 1992), pp. 1–17.

2 For discussions of relationship marketing and its influence on the marketing of services, consumer goods, strategic alliances, distribution channels and buyer–seller interactions, see *Journal of the Academy of Marketing Science*, Special Issue on Relationship Marketing, 23 (Fall 1995). Some of the early roots of this paradigm shift can be found in C. Gronroos, *Service Management and Marketing* (New York: Lexington Books, 1990); and E. Gummesson, 'The new marketing – developing long-term interactive relationships', *Long Range Planning* 20 (1987), pp. 10–20. For current thinking and excellent reviews of relationship marketing across a spectrum of topics, see J.N. Sheth, *Handbook of Relationship Marketing* (Thousand Oaks, CA: Sage Publications, 2000).

3 L.L. Berry and A. Parasuraman, *Marketing Services* (New York: Free Press, 1991), ch. 8.

4 G. Knisely, 'Comparing marketing management in package goods and service organizations', a series of interviews appearing in *Advertising Age*, 15 January, 19 February, 19 March and 14 May 1979.

5 This discussion is based on M.D. Johnson and F. Selnes, 'Customer portfolio management: toward a dynamic theory of exchange relationships', *Journal of Marketing* 68 (April 2004), pp. 1–17.

6 R.M. Morgan and S.D. Hunt, 'The commitment-trust theory of relationship marketing', *Journal of Marketing* 58 (July 1994), pp. 20–38; N. Bendapudi and L.L. Berry, 'Customers' motivations for maintaining relationships with service providers', *Journal of Retailing* 73 (Spring 1997), pp. 15–37.

7 Johnson and Selnes, 'Customer portfolio management'.

8   Ibid.

9   See also D. Siredeshmukh, J. Singh and B. Sabol, 'Customer trust, value, and loyalty in relational exchanges', *Journal of Marketing* 66 (January 2002), pp. 15–37.

10 See C. Huffman and B. Kahn, 'Variety for sale: mass customization or mass confusion?' *Journal of Retailing* 74 (Winter 1998), pp. 491–513; B.J. Pine and J.H. Gilmore, 'Welcome to the experience economy', *Harvard Business Review* 76 (July–August 1998), pp. 97–105; B.J. Pine, D. Peppers and M. Rodgers, 'Do you want to keep your customers forever?', *Harvard Business Review* 73 (March–April 1995), pp. 103–14.

11 C. Gronroos, *Service Management and Marketing* 3rd edn (Chichester: John Wiley & Sons, 2007).

12 The three types of relational benefits discussed in this section are drawn from K.P. Gwinner, D.D. Gremler and M.J. Bitner, 'Relational benefits in service industries: the customer's perspective', *Journal of the Academy of Marketing Science* 26 (Spring 1998), pp. 101–14.

13 See M.B. Adelman, A. Ahuvia and C. Goodwin, 'Beyond smiling: social support and service quality', in *Service Quality: New Directions in Theory and Practice*, eds R.T. Rust and R.L. Oliver (Thousand Oaks, CA: Sage Publications, 1994), pp. 139–72; and C. Goodwin, 'Private roles in public encounters: communal relationships in service exchanges', unpublished manuscript, University of Manitoba (1993).

14 E.J. Arnould and L.L. Price, 'River magic: extraordinary experience and the extended service encounter', *Journal of Consumer Research* 20 (June 1993), pp. 24–45.

15 N. Bendapudi and R.P. Leone, 'How to lose your star performer without losing customers, too', *Harvard Business Review* (November 2001), pp. 104–15.

16 F.F. Reichheld and W.E. Sasser Jr, 'Zero defections: quality comes to services', *Harvard Business Review* (September–October 1990), pp. 105–11; and F.F. Reichheld, *The Loyalty Effect* (Boston, MA: Harvard Business School Press, 1996).

17 R. Dhar and R. Glazer, 'Hedging customers', *Harvard Business Review* 81 (May 2003), pp. 86–92.

18 D.D. Gremler and S.W. Brown, 'The loyalty ripple effect: appreciating the full value of customers', *International Journal of Service Industry Management* 10, no. 3 (1999), pp. 271–91.

19 L.A. Bettencourt, 'Customer voluntary performance: customers as partners in service delivery', *Journal of Retailing* 73 (Fall 1997), pp. 383–406.

20 S.J. Grove and R.P. Fisk, 'The impact of other customers on service experiences: a critical incident examination of "getting along"', *Journal of Retailing* 73 (Spring 1997), pp. 63–85.

21 L.L. Price, E.J. Arnould and A. Hausman, 'Commercial friendships: service provider–client relationship dynamics', in *Frontiers in Services*, eds R.T. Rust and R.L. Oliver (Nashville, TN: Vanderbilt University, 1996).

22 Reichheld and Sasser, 'Zero defections'.

23 Additional frameworks for calculating lifetime customer value that include a variety of other variables can be found in W.J. Reinartz and V. Kumar, 'The impact of customer relationship characteristics on profitable lifetime duration', *Journal of Marketing* 67 (January 2003), pp. 77–99; Dhar and Glazer, 'Hedging customers'; H.K. Stahl, K. Matzler and H.H. Hinterhuber, 'Linking customer lifetime value with shareholder value', *Industrial Marketing Management* 32, no. 4 (2003), pp. 267–79.

[24] S. Gupta, D.R. Helmann and J.A. Stuart, 'Valuing customers', *Journal of Marketing Research* 41 (February 2004), pp. 7–18.

[25] For more on customer profitability segments and related strategies, see V.A. Zeithaml, R.T. Rust and K.N. Lemon, 'The customer pyramid: creating and serving profitable customers', *California Management Review* 43 (Summer 2001), pp. 118–42.

[26] R. Brooks, 'Alienating customers isn't always a bad idea, many firms discover', *The Wall Street Journal*, 7 January 1999, p. A1.

[27] D. Brady, 'Why service stinks', *BusinessWeek*, 23 October 2000, pp. 118–28.

[28] Dhar and Glazer, 'Hedging customers'.

[29] D. Rosenblum, D. Tomlinson and L. Scott, 'Bottom-feeding for blockbuster businesses', *Harvard Business Review* 81 (March 2003), pp. 52–9.

[30] See T.A. Burnham, J.K. Frels and V. Mahajan, 'Consumer switching costs: a typology, antecedents, and consequences', *Journal of the Academy of Marketing Science* 32 (Spring 2003), pp. 109–26; F. Selnes, 'An examination of the effect of product performance on brand reputation, satisfaction, and loyalty', *European Journal of Marketing* 27, no. 9 (2003), pp. 19–35; P. Klemperer, 'The competitiveness of markets with switching costs', *Rand Journal of Economics* 18 (Spring 1987), pp. 138–50.

[31] T.L. Huston and R.L. Burgess, 'Social exchange in developing relationships: an overview', in *Social Exchange in Developing Relationships*, eds R.L. Burgess and T.L. Huston (New York: Academic Press, 1979), pp. 3–28; L. White and V. Yanamandram, 'Why customers stay: reasons and consequences of inertia in financial services', *Managing Service Quality* 14, nos. 2/3 (2004), pp. 183–94.

[32] See J.P. Guiltinan, 'A classification of switching costs with implications for relationship marketing', in *Marketing Theory and Practice*, eds Terry L. Childers et al. (Chicago, IL: American Marketing Association, 1989), pp. 216–20; Klemperer, 'The competitiveness of markets with switching costs'; C. Fornell, 'A national customer satisfaction barometer: the Swedish experience', *Journal of Marketing* 56 (January 1992), pp. 6–21; P.G. Patterson and T. Smith, 'A cross-cultural study of switching barriers and propensity to stay with service providers', *Journal of Retailing* 79 (Summer 2003), pp. 107–20.

[33] See Bendapudi and Berry, 'Customers' motivations for maintaining relationships with service providers'; H.S. Bansal, P.G. Irving and S.F. Taylor, 'A three-component model of customer commitment to service providers', *Journal of the Academy of Marketing Science* 32 (Summer 2004), pp. 234–50.

[34] Berry and Parasuraman, *Marketing Services*, pp. 136–42.

[35] For more information on cautions to be considered in implementing rewards strategies, see L. O'Brien and C. Jones, 'Do rewards really create loyalty?', *Harvard Business Review* (May–June 1995), pp. 75–82; and G.R. Dowling and M. Uncles, 'Do customer loyalty programs really work?', *Sloan Management Review* (Summer 1997), pp. 71–82.

[36] D.D. Gremler and S.W. Brown, 'Service loyalty: its nature, importance, and implications', in *Advancing Service Quality: A Global Perspective*, eds B. Edvardsson, S.W. Brown, R. Johnston and E.E. Scheuing (Jamaica, NY: International Service Quality Association, 1996), pp. 171–80; H. Hansen, K. Sandvik and F. Selnes, 'Direct and indirect effects of commitment to a service employee on the intention to stay', *Journal of Service Research* 5 (May 2003), pp. 356–68.

[37] C.W. Hart, 'Made to order', *Marketing Management* 5 (Summer 1996), pp. 11–23.

38 R. Brooks, 'Alienating customers isn't always a bad idea', P. Carroll and S. Rose, 'Revisiting customer retention', *Journal of Retail Banking* 15, no. 1 (1993), pp. 5–13.

39 J. Dahl, 'Rental counters reject drivers without good records', *The Wall Street Journal*, 23 October 1992, p. B1.

40 See L.C. Harris and K.L. Reynolds, 'The consequences of dysfunctional customer behavior', *Journal of Service Research* 6 (November 2003), p. 145 for cites; also, see A.A. Grandey, D.N. Dickter and H.P. Sin, 'The customer is *not* always right: customer aggression and emotion regulation of service employees', *Journal of Organizational Behavior* 25 (2004), pp. 397–418.

41 K. Ohnezeit, recruiting supervisor for Enterprise Rent-A-Car, personal communication, 12 February 2004.

42 See Harris and Reynolds, 'The consequences of dysfunctional customer behavior'.

43 For a detailed discussion on relationship ending, see A. Halinen and J. Tähtinen, 'A process theory of relationship ending', *International Journal of Service Industry Management* 13, no. 2 (2002), pp. 163–80.

44 M. Schrage, 'Fire your customers', *The Wall Street Journal*, 16 March 1992, p. A8.

45 'Service with Soul' video, hosted by Tom Peters (Chicago, IL: Video Publishing House, 1995); and http://www.nypro.com.

PART 3
Aligning Service Design and Standards

Part Contents	

Meeting customer expectations of service requires not only understanding what the expectations are, but also taking action on that knowledge. Action takes several forms: designing services based on customer requirements, setting service standards to ensure that employees perform as customers expect, and providing physical evidence that creates the appropriate cues and ambience for service. When action does not take place, there is a gap – service design and standards gap – as shown in the accompanying figure. In this section you will learn to identify the causes of gap 2 as well as effective strategies for closing this gap.

Chapter 8 describes the tools that are most effective in service development and design, especially a tool called service blueprinting. Chapter 9 helps you differentiate between company-defined standards and customer-defined standards, and to recognize how they can be developed. Chapter 10 explores the strategic importance of physical evidence, the variety of roles it plays, and strategies for effectively designing physical evidence and the servicescape to meet customer expectations.

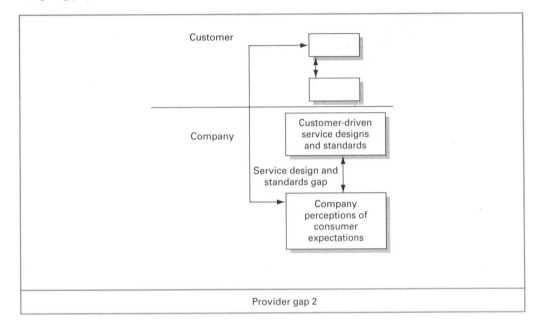

CHAPTER 08

Service development and design

❖ LEARNING OBJECTIVES

This chapter's objectives are to:

1 Describe the challenges inherent in service design.

2 Present the stages and unique elements of the new-service development process.

3 Demonstrate the value of service blueprinting and how to develop and read service blueprints.

4 Present lessons learned in choosing and implementing high-performance service innovations.

CASE STUDY: INNOVATIVE NEW SERVICES AT VOLVO TRUCK

Have you ever considered starting your own service business? What type of service would it be? What would you do first? Assuming you understood your market and had a good feel for potential customers' needs and expectations, how would you go about designing the service to meet those needs? If you were starting a business to manufacture a new product, you would most likely begin by designing and building a prototype of your new product. But how could you do this for a service?

Volvo, headquartered in Sweden, is one of the world's largest producers of trucks. In fact, approximately two-thirds of Volvo's total sales come from its Global Trucks group. But, like many manufacturers worldwide, Volvo is much more than an equipment company. It views itself as a total customer solution company offering a variety of services to enhance the value of its products and to provide revenue growth.

By listening to its truck fleet customers, Volvo has identified ideas for new services that can enhance the value of its trucks. The physical product, the truck, has become a component of Volvo's service concept, and the company is moving in the direction of becoming a service company instead of purely a heavy truck manufacturer.

One of Volvo's recent service offerings, Dynafleet 2.0, provides a good example of how Volvo is enhancing the value it offers to its business customers. Dynafleet 2.0 is an extensive transportation information system that Volvo can customize for its truck transportation business customers. The system is composed of three separate modules that are installed in the company's fleet of trucks to provide exact information and direct communication resulting in more efficient operations and reduced costs for the company. One of the modules is the 'logger tool' that gathers information on a vehicle and its driver. Some information is stored on the driver's smart card, and some information is logged in by the driver. The second module is the 'communication tool', which transmits and receives text messages, and sends information about the vehicle's location, fuel consumption and other details to the company's fleet office. Drivers can also communicate directly with the office or send messages to other drivers through this communication system. The third module is the 'information tool', which provides maps and traffic information to the driver of the vehicle via a colour display.

Back in the office, the fleet manager utilizes a 'logger manager' that provides reports on vehicle fuel consumption, hour-by-hour information on work-day activities of each vehicle and driver, and start and stop times. This information is useful for wage calculations and keeping track of work hours. The 'transport manager', used to track exactly where each vehicle is at all times, generates reports that can be used in traffic planning and other operational decisions.

Volvo has expanded far beyond simply providing trucks for its business customers. Other services, such as maintenance agreements, training and financing, further enhance Dynafleet's offering.

The services available through Dynafleet address more fully the total customer value chain, allowing Volvo to move towards its goal of being a customer solution provider rather than a truck manufacturer. The benefits accrue directly to the drivers of the trucks as well as the transportation companies that buy the trucks. Administrative work is simplified, and fleet managers and traffic planners become more efficient. Volvo aims to maintain its leadership and compete effectively through offering Dynafleet 2.0 and other services aimed at improving its customers' efficiency, service reliability and economic returns.

Sources: 'Volvo Dynafleet 2.0 – Applying a service perspective', in B. Edvardsson, A. Gustafsson, M.D. Johnson and B. Sanden, *New Service Development and Innovation in the New Economy* (Lund: Studentlitteratur AB, 2000), pp. 52–5; www.volvo.com, 2002

So what causes new products and services such as those offered by Volvo Truck to fail or succeed? If you decide to start your own business, what can you do to protect yourself as much as possible from failure?

A study of 11 000 new products launched by 77 manufacturing, service and consumer products companies found that only 56 per cent of new offerings are still on the market five years later.[1] Failures can be traced to a number of causes: no unique benefits offered, insufficient demand, unrealistic goals for the new product/service, poor fit between the new service and others within the organization's portfolio, poor location, insufficient financial backing or failure to take the necessary time to develop and introduce the product.[2] An analysis of over 60 studies on new product and service success showed that the dominant and most reliable predictors of success for new introductions relate to *product/service characteristics* (product meeting customer needs, product advantage over competing products, technological sophistication); *strategy characteristics* (dedicated human resources to support the initiative, dedicated research and development (R&D) focused on the new product initiative); *process characteristics* (marketing, pre-development, technological and launch proficiencies); and *marketplace characteristics* (market potential).[3]

Frequently a good service idea fails because of development, design and specification flaws, topics that are emphasized in this chapter. As more firms, across industries, move into services as a growth strategy, the challenges and opportunities of developing and delivering service offerings become a reality.

Challenges of service design

Because services are largely intangible and process oriented (such as a visit to the dentist, a golf lesson or a Champions League football game), they are difficult to describe and communicate. When services are delivered over a long period – a week's vacation, a six-month consulting engagement, 10 weeks on a Weight Watchers programme – their complexity increases, and they become even more difficult to define and describe. Further, because services are delivered by employees to customers, they are variable. Rarely are two services alike or experienced in the same way. These characteristics of services, which we explored in the first chapter of this book, are the heart of the challenge involved in designing services.

Because services cannot be touched, examined or tried out, people frequently resort to words in their efforts to describe them. Lynn Shostack, a pioneer in developing design concepts

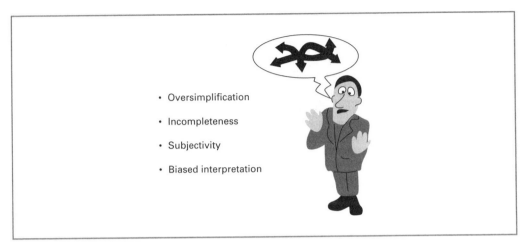

FIGURE 8.1 Risks of relying on words alone to describe services

for services, has pointed out four risks of attempting to describe services in words alone (see Figure 8.1). The first risk is *oversimplification*. Shostack points out that 'to say that "portfolio management" means "buying and selling stocks" is like describing the space shuttle as "something that flies." Some people will picture a bird, some a helicopter, and some an angel.'[4] Words are simply inadequate to describe a complex service system.

The second risk is *incompleteness*. In describing services, people (employees, managers, customers) tend to omit details or elements of the service with which they are not familiar. A person might do a fairly credible job of describing how a discount stockbroker service takes orders from customers. But would that person be able to describe fully how the monthly statements are created, how the interactive computer system works, and how these two elements of the service are integrated into the order-taking process?

The third risk is *subjectivity*. Any one person describing a service in words will be biased by personal experiences and degree of exposure to the service. There is a natural (and mistaken) tendency to assume that because all people have gone to a fast-food restaurant, they all understand what that service is. Persons working in different functional areas of the same service organization (a marketing person, an operations person, a finance person) are likely to describe the service very differently as well, biased by their own functional background.

A final risk of describing services using words alone is *biased interpretation*. No two people will define 'responsive', 'quick' or 'flexible' in exactly the same way. For example, a supervisor or manager may suggest to a front-line service employee that the employee should try to be more flexible or responsive in providing service to the customer. Unless the term 'flexibility' is further defined, the employee is likely to interpret the word differently from the manager.

All these risks become very apparent in the new service development process, when organizations may be attempting to design services never before experienced by customers. It is critical that all involved (managers, front-line employees and behind-the-scenes support staff) be working with the same concepts of the new service, based on customer needs and expectations. For a service that already exists, any attempt to improve it will also suffer unless everyone has a shared vision of the service and associated issues.

In the following sections of this chapter, we present approaches for new service development and design to address these unique challenges.

New service development

Research suggests that products that are designed and introduced via the steps in a structured planning framework have a greater likelihood of ultimate success than those not developed within a framework.[5] The fact that services are intangible makes it even more imperative for a **new-service development** system to have four basic characteristics. (1) It must be objective, not subjective. (2) It must be precise, not vague. (3) It must be fact driven, not opinion driven. (4) It must be methodological, not philosophical.[6] Although the process of developing new services should be structured and should follow a set of defined stages, it should not become overly rigid or bureaucratized. Such structure taken to an extreme can result in a rigid and plodding approach that could waste time and/or allow competitors to get out in front. Thus, common sense must dictate when flexibility and speed will override the structure.

Often new services are introduced on the basis of managers' and employees' subjective opinions about what the services should be and whether they will succeed, rather than on objective designs incorporating data about customer perceptions, market needs and feasibility. A new-service design process may be imprecise in defining the nature of the service concept because the people involved believe either that intangible processes cannot be defined precisely or that 'everyone knows what we mean'. Neither of these explanations or defenses for imprecision is justifiable, as we illustrate in this chapter's model for new service development.[7]

Because services are produced and consumed simultaneously and often involve interaction between employees and customers, it is also critical that the new-service development process involve both employees and customers. Employees frequently *are* the service, or at least they perform or deliver the service, and thus their involvement in choosing which new services to develop and how these services should be designed and implemented can be very beneficial. Contact employees are psychologically and physically close to customers and can be very helpful in identifying customer needs for new services. Involving employees in the design and development process also increases the likelihood of success of the new service because employees can identify the organizational issues that need to be addressed to support the delivery of the service to customers.[8] Many organizations develop cross-functional teams comprising representatives from a variety of teams to ensure that all aspects of the service and delivery process are considered before full-scale development of a new-service concept begins.

Because customers often actively participate in service delivery, they too should be involved in the new service development process. Beyond just providing input on their own needs, customers can help design the service concept and the delivery process, particularly in situations in which the customer personally carries out part of the service process.

Service spotlight

IKEA is well known for involving its customers in the design of its stores to ensure that the layout will work for the shoppers and not just for the staff or the architects who design the stores. A significant amount of market research was undertaken by Abbey, the UK arm of Banco Santander, in determining the future of its retail banking branches. As a result, new designs have been developed, some of which incorporate Costa Coffee outlets.

Types of new services

As we describe the new-service development process, remember that not all new services are 'new' to the same degree. New service options can run the gamut from major innovations to minor style changes:[9]

- *Major or radical innovations* are new services for markets as yet undefined. Past examples include the first broadcast television services and the creation of eBay Internet-based auction sites. Many of these innovations evolve from information, computer and Internet-based technologies.

- *Start-up businesses* consist of new services for a market that is already served by existing products that meet the same generic needs. Service examples include the creation of Amazon to provide an alternative to book stores, online banking for financial transactions and door-to-door airport shuttle services that compete with traditional taxi and limousine services.

- *New services for the currently served market* represent attempts to offer existing customers of the organization a service not previously available from the company (although it may be available from other companies). Examples include Tesco offering insurance services, a health club offering nutrition classes and airlines offering telephone and Internet service during flights.

- *Service line extensions* represent augmentations of the existing service line, such as a restaurant adding new menu items, an airline offering new routes, a law firm offering additional legal services and a university adding new courses or degrees.

- *Service improvements* represent perhaps the most common type of service innovation. Changes in features of services that are already offered might involve faster execution of an existing service process, extended hours of service, or augmentations such as added amenities in a hotel room (e.g. the addition of wireless Internet connections).

- *Style changes* represent the most modest service innovations, although they are often highly visible and can have significant effects on customer perceptions, emotions and attitudes. Changing the colour scheme of a restaurant, revising the logo for an organization, redesigning a website or painting aircraft a different colour all represent style changes. These innovations do not fundamentally change the service, only its appearance, similar to how packaging changes are used for consumer products.

Stages in new service development

In this section we focus on the actual steps to be followed in new service development. The steps can be applied to any type of new service. Much of what is presented in this section has direct parallels in the new product development process for manufactured goods. Because of the inherent characteristics of services, however, the development process for new services requires adaptations.[10] Figure 8.2 shows the basic principles and steps in new service development. Although these steps may be similar to those for manufactured goods, their implementation is significantly different.[11] The challenges typically lie in defining the concept in the early stages of the development process and again at the prototype development stage. Partly because of these

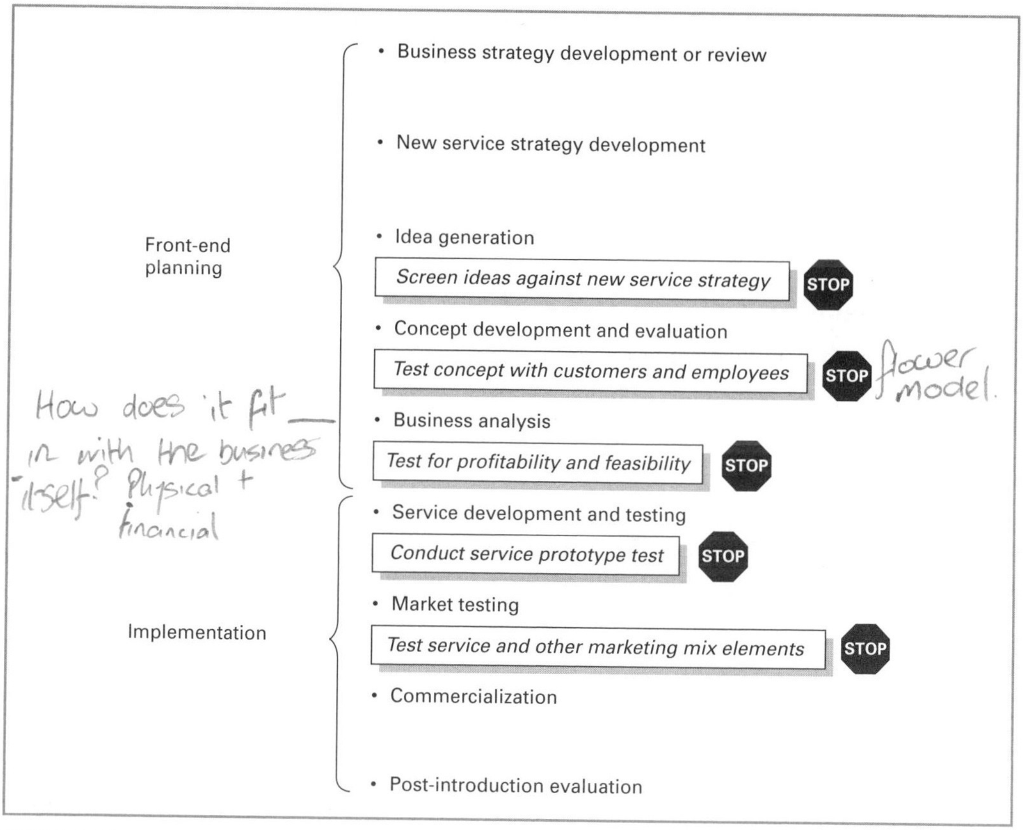
Front-end planning
Business strategy development or review
New service strategy development
Idea generation
Screen ideas against new service strategy
STOP
Concept development and evaluation
Test concept with customers and employees
STOP
Business analysis
Test for profitability and feasibility
STOP
Implementation
Service development and testing
Conduct service prototype test
STOP
Market testing
Test service and other marketing mix elements
STOP
Commercialization
Post-introduction evaluation

FIGURE 8.2 New service development process

Sources: Booz-Allen & Hamilton, *New Product Management for the 1980s* (New York: Booz-Allen & Hamilton, 1982); M.J. Bowers, 'An exploration into new service development: organization, process, and structure', doctoral dissertation, Texas A&M University, 1985; A. Khurana and S.R. Rosenthal, 'Integrating the fuzzy front end of new product development', *Sloan Management Review* (Winter 1997), pp. 103–20; and R.G. Cooper, *Winning at New Products*, 3rd edn (Cambridge, MA: Perseus Publishing, 2001)

challenges, service firms are generally less likely to carry out a structured development process for new innovations than are their manufacturing and consumer-goods counterparts.[12]

An underlying assumption of new product development process models is that new product ideas can be dropped at any stage of the process if they do not satisfy the criteria for success at that particular stage.[13] Figure 8.2 shows the checkpoints (represented by stop signs) that separate critical stages of the development process. The checkpoints specify requirements that a new service must meet before it can proceed to the next stage of development.

New service or product development is rarely a completely linear process. Many companies are finding that to speed up new service development, some steps can be worked on simultaneously, and in some instances a step may even be skipped. The overlapping of steps and simultaneous development of various pieces of the new service/product development process has been referred to as 'flexible product development'. This type of flexible, speedy process is particularly important in technology industries, in which products and services evolve extremely quickly. In these environments, computer technology lets companies monitor customer opinions and needs during development and change the final offering right up until it is launched. Often, the next version of the service is in planning stages at the same time that the current version is being launched.[14] However, even if the stages are handled simultaneously, the important check-points noted in Figure 8.2 must be assessed to maximize chances of success.

The process shown in Figure 8.2 is divided into two sections: front-end planning and implementation. The front end determines what service concepts will be developed, whereas the back end executes or implements the service concept. When asked where the greatest weaknesses in product and service innovation occur, managers typically report problems with the 'fuzzy front end'.[15] The front end is called 'fuzzy' because of its relative abstractness, which is even more apparent with intangible and variable services than with manufactured products.

Front-end planning

Business strategy development or review

It is assumed that an organization will have an overall strategic orientation, vision and mission. Clearly a first step in new service development is to review that mission and vision. The new service strategy and specific new service ideas must fit within the larger strategic mission and vision of the organization.

Service spotlight

The Virgin Group sets its mission to be the consumer champion through delivering to its brand values, which are: value for money; good quality; brilliant customer service; innovative; competitively challenging; and fun. This mission has led to the development of a host of new services, such as holidays, mobile phones, financial services, cosmetics, health clubs and Internet access.

In addition to its strategic mission, the company's underlying orientation toward growth will affect how it defines its new services strategy. Becoming aware of the organization's overall strategic orientation is fundamental to plotting a direction for growth. Noted strategy researchers suggest four primary strategic orientations that are taken by companies:[16] (1) *prospectors* seek to be innovative, searching out new opportunities and taking on risks; (2) *defenders* are experts in their own areas and tend not to seek new opportunities outside their domain of expertise; (3) *analysers* maintain stability in certain areas of operation but are open to experimenting and seeking out opportunities on the margin; (4) *reactors* seldom make adjustments unless forced to do so by environmental pressures. Another noted management strategist suggests that firms can be distinguished by whether they primarily pursue a cost-leadership strategy, a differentiation strategy or a focused strategy.[17] An organization's strategic orientation will affect how it views growth through new service development.

New-service strategy development

Research suggests that without a clear new product or service strategy, a well-planned portfolio of new products and services, and an organizational structure that facilitates product development via ongoing communications and cross-functional sharing of responsibilities, front-end decisions become ineffective.[18] Thus a product portfolio strategy and a defined organizational structure for new product or service development are critical – and are the foundations – for success.

The types of new services that will be appropriate will depend on the organization's goals, vision, capabilities and growth plans. By defining a new service strategy (possibly in terms of

Offerings	Markets	
	Current customers	New customers
Existing services	Share building	Market development
New services	Service development	Diversification

FIGURE 8.3 New service strategy matrix for identifying growth opportunities
Sources: adapted from H.I. Ansoff, *Corporate Strategy* (New York: McGraw-Hill, 1965)

markets, types of services, time horizon for development, profit criteria or other relevant factors), the organization will be in a better position to begin generating specific ideas. For example, it may focus its growth on new services at a particular level of the described continuum from major innovations to style changes. Or the organization may define its new service strategy even more specifically in terms of particular markets or market segments or in terms of specific profit generation goals.

One way to begin formulating a new service strategy is to use the framework shown in Figure 8.3 for identifying growth opportunities. The framework allows an organization to identify possible directions for growth and can be helpful as a catalyst for creative ideas. The framework may also later serve as an initial idea screen if, for example, the organization chooses to focus its growth efforts on one or two of the four cells in the matrix. The matrix suggests that companies can develop a growth strategy around current customers or for new customers, and can focus on current offerings or new service offerings.

Idea generation

The next step in the process is the formal solicitation of new ideas. The ideas generated at this phase can be passed through the new service strategy screen described in the preceding step. Many methods and avenues are available for services **idea generation**. Formal brainstorming, solicitation of ideas from employees and customers, lead user research and learning about competitors' offerings are some of the most common approaches. Some companies are even collaborating with outsiders (e.g. competitors, vendors, alliance partners) or developing licensing agreements and joint ventures in an effort to exploit all possible sources of new ideas.[19]
Observing customers and how they use the firm's products and services can also generate creative ideas for new innovations. Sometimes referred to as *empathic design*, observation is particularly effective in situations in which customers may not be able to recognize or verbalize their needs.[20] In service businesses, contact personnel, who actually deliver the services and interact directly with consumers, can be particularly good sources of ideas for complementary services and ways to improve current offerings.

Whether the source of a new idea is inside or outside the organization, some established mechanism should exist for ensuring an ongoing stream of new service possibilities. This mechanism might include a formal new-service development department or function with responsibility for generating new ideas, suggestion boxes for employees and customers, new-service development teams that meet regularly, surveys and focus groups with customers and employees, or formal competitive analysis to identify new services. Although new service ideas may arise outside the formal mechanism, total dependence on luck is not a good strategy.

In listening to their customers, many firms around the world have discovered ideas for new *services* rather than product enhancements. These new services allow the firm to move in the direction of becoming a solutions provider, as is the case with Volvo Truck, discussed at the beginning of this chapter

Service concept development and evaluation

Once an idea surfaces that is regarded as a good fit with both the business and the new service strategies, it is ready for initial development. In the case of a tangible product, this next step in **service concept development and evaluation** would mean formulating the basic product definition and then presenting consumers with descriptions and drawings to get their reactions.

The inherent characteristics of services, particularly intangibility and simultaneous production and consumption, place complex demands on this phase of the process. Drawing pictures and describing an intangible service in concrete terms are difficult. It is therefore important that agreement be reached at this stage on exactly what the concept is. The service concept is made up of the core benefit provided to the customer supported by a variety of tangible and intangible elements that assist in the delivery of that benefit. The core benefit of a passenger flight is getting a customer to a particular destination, but the service concept also involves: booking and check-in procedures; service frequency in-flight service; the design of the aeroplane; the configuration of the seating; food and drink, etc. The service concept for no-frills airlines is very different from that of the traditional carriers even though the core benefit is the same. It may be necessary to involve multiple parties in sharpening the definitionn of the service concept. For example, Lynn Shostack relates that the design and development of a new discount share dealing service was initially described by the bank as a way 'to buy and sell stocks for customers at low prices'.[21] Through the initial concept development phase it became clear that not everyone in the organization had the same idea about how this description would translate into an actual service and that there were a variety of ways the concept could be developed. Only through multiple iterations of the service – and the raising of hundreds of issues, large and small – was an agreement finally reached on the discounted share dealing concept.

After clear definition of the concept, it is important to produce a description of the service that represents its specific features and characteristics and then to determine initial customer and employee responses to the concept. The service design document would describe the problem addressed by the service, discuss the reasons for offering the new service, itemize the service process and its benefits and provide a rationale for purchasing the service.[22] The roles of customers and employees in the delivery process would also be described. The new service concept would then be evaluated by asking employees and customers whether they understand the idea of the proposed service, whether they are favourable to the concept and whether they feel it satisfies an unmet need.

Business analysis

Assuming that the service concept is favourably evaluated by customers and employees at the concept development stage, the next step is to estimate its economic feasibility and potential profit implications. Demand analysis, revenue projections, cost analyses and operational feasibility are assessed at this stage. Because the development of service concepts is so closely tied to the operational system of the organization, this stage will involve preliminary assumptions about the costs of staff recruitment and training, delivery system enhancements, facility changes and any other projected operations costs. The organization will pass the results of the **business analysis** through its profitability and feasibility screen to determine whether the new service idea meets the minimum requirements.

Implementation

Once the new service concept has passed all the front-end planning hurdles, it is ready for the implementation stages of the process.

Service development and testing

In the development of new tangible products, the development and testing stage involves construction of product prototypes and testing for consumer acceptance. Again, because services are intangible and largely produced and consumed simultaneously, this step presents unique challenges. To address these challenges, this stage of service development should involve all who have a stake in the new service: customers and contact employees as well as functional representatives from marketing, operations and human resources. During this phase, the concept is refined to the point at which a detailed **service blueprint** representing the implementation plan for the service can be produced. The blueprint is likely to evolve over a series of iterations on the basis of input from all the involved parties.

A final step is for each area involved in rendering the service to translate the final blueprint into specific implementation plans for its part of the service delivery process. Because service development, design and delivery are so intricately intertwined, all parties involved in any aspect of the new service must work together at this stage to delineate the details of the new service. If not, seemingly minor operational details can cause an otherwise good new service idea to fail.

Service spotlight

Careful service development and lots of testing are the rules at Expedia.com, the giant travel information and transportation-booking website. Customers who use Expedia's website potentially have a lot to lose – over 1000 euros per trip may be at stake, or it may be the only week of holiday the person has in a whole year. So before launching any new software onto the site or redesigning the site itself, Expedia holds many meetings with the design team to consider customer requirements. It then builds and tests prototypes of the software or website changes, conducts usability tests and gathers customer feedback on designs. Feedback is reviewed and integrated into the design constantly before, during and after the launch.[23]

Market testing

At the **market testing** stage of the development process, a tangible product might be test marketed in a limited number of trading areas to determine marketplace acceptance of the product as well as other marketing mix variables such as promotion, pricing and distribution systems. Again, the standard approach for a new manufactured product is typically not possible for a new service because of its inherent characteristics. Because new service offerings are often intertwined with the delivery system for existing services, it is difficult to test new services in isolation. And in some cases, such as a one-site retailer, it may not be possible to introduce the service to an isolated market area because the organization has only one point of delivery. There are alternative ways of testing the response to marketing mix variables, however. The new service might be offered to employees of the organization and their families for a time to assess their responses to variations in the marketing mix. Or the organization might decide to test variations in pricing and promotion in less realistic contexts by presenting customers with hypothetical mixes and getting their responses in terms of intention to try the service under varying circumstances. This approach certainly has limitations compared with an actual market test, but it is better than not assessing market response at all.

It is also extremely important at this stage in the development process to do a pilot run of the service to be sure that the operational details are functioning smoothly. Frequently this step is overlooked, and the actual market introduction may be the first test of whether the service system functions as planned. By this point, mistakes in design are harder to correct. As one noted service expert says, 'There is simply no substitute for a proper rehearsal' when introducing a new service.[24] In the case of the discount share dealing service described earlier, the bank ran a pilot test by offering employees a special price for one month. The offer was marketed internally, allowing the bank to observe the service process in action before it was actually introduced to the external market.

Commercialization

During the commercialization stage, the service goes live and is introduced to the marketplace. This stage has two primary objectives. The first is to build and maintain acceptance of the new service among large numbers of service delivery personnel who will be responsible day to day for service quality. This task is made easier if acceptance has been built in by involving key groups in the design and development process all along. However, it will still be a challenge to maintain enthusiasm and communicate the new service throughout the system; excellent internal marketing will help.

The second objective is to monitor all aspects of the service during introduction and through the complete service cycle. If the customer needs six months to experience the entire service, then careful monitoring must be maintained through at least six months. Every detail of the service should be assessed – telephone calls, face-to-face transactions, billing, complaints and delivery problems. Operating efficiency and costs should also be tracked.

Post-introduction evaluation

At this point, the information gathered during commercialization of the service can be reviewed and changes made to the delivery process, staffing or marketing mix variables on the basis of actual market response to the offering.

Service spotlight

Expedia.com, the travel website, realized that despite pre-launch testing, restrictions on Expedia bargain fares were confusing to customers. A 'hot fix' team was called in to repair the problem.[25] Within a day, the project team redesigned the presentation of information so that the fare restrictions would be clear to customers.

No service will ever stay the same. Whether deliberate or unplanned, changes will always occur. Therefore, formalizing the review process to make those changes that enhance service quality from the customer's point of view is critical. The service blueprint serves a valuable purpose in providing a focal point for discussing and planning changes in the offering.

Service blueprinting

A stumbling block in developing new services (and in improving existing services) is the difficulty of describing and depicting the service at the concept development, service development and market test stages. One of the keys to matching service specifications to customer expectations is the ability to describe critical service process characteristics objectively and to depict them so that employees, customers and managers alike know what the service is, can see their role in its delivery and understand all the steps and flows involved in the service process. In this section we look in depth at service blueprinting, a useful tool for designing and specifying intangible service processes.[26]

What is a service blueprint?

The manufacturing and construction industries have a long tradition of engineering and design. Can you imagine a house being built without detailed plans? Can you imagine a car, a computer or, even, a simple product like a child's toy or a shampoo being produced without concrete and detailed plans, written specifications and engineering drawings? Yet services commonly lack concrete specifications. A service, even a complex one, might be introduced without any formal, objective depiction of the process.

A service blueprint is a picture or map that accurately portrays the service system so that the different people involved in providing it can understand and deal with it objectively regardless of their roles or their individual points of view. Blueprints are particularly useful at the design stage of service development. A service blueprint visually displays the service by simultaneously depicting the process of service delivery, the points of customer contact, the roles of customers and employees, and the visible elements of the service (see Figure 8.4). It provides a way to break down a service into its logical components and to depict the steps or tasks in the process, the means by which the tasks are executed and the evidence of service as the customer experiences it.

Blueprinting has its origins in a variety of fields and techniques, including logistics, industrial engineering, decision theory and computer systems analysis – all of which deal with the definition and explanation of processes.[27] Because services are 'experiences' rather than objects, blueprinting is a particularly useful tool for describing them.

Blueprint components

The key components of service blueprints are shown in Figure 8.5.[28] They are customer actions, 'onstage' contact employee actions, 'backstage' contact employee actions, and support

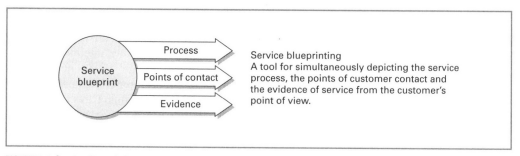

FIGURE 8.4 Service blueprinting

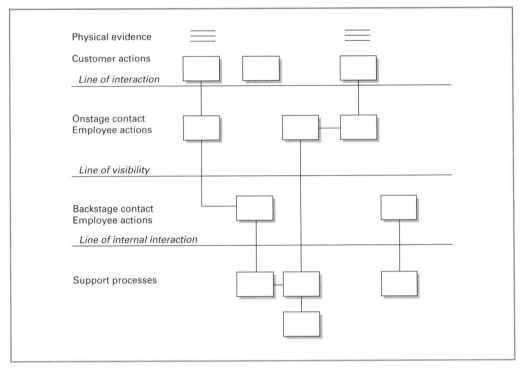

FIGURE 8.5 Service blueprint components

processes. The conventions for drawing service blueprints are not rigidly defined, and thus the particular symbols used, the number of horizontal lines in the blueprint, and the particular labels for each part of the blueprint may vary somewhat depending on what you read and the complexity of the blueprint being described. These variations are not a problem as long as you keep in mind the purpose of the blueprint and view it as a useful tool rather than as a set of rigid rules for designing services.

The *customer actions* area encompasses the steps, choices, activities and interactions that the customer performs in the process of purchasing, consuming and evaluating the service. The total customer experience is apparent in this area of the blueprint. In a legal services example, the customer actions might include a decision to contact a lawyer, telephone calls to the lawyer, face-to-face meetings, receipt of documents and receipt of a bill.

In parallel to the customer actions are two areas of contact employee actions. The steps and activities that the contact employee performs that are visible to the customer are the *onstage contact employee actions*. In the legal services setting, the actions of the lawyer (the contact employee) that are visible to the client are, for example, the initial interview, intermediate meetings and final delivery of legal documents.

Those contact employee actions that occur behind the scenes to support the onstage activities are the *backstage contact employee actions*. In the example, anything the lawyer does behind the scenes to prepare for the meetings or to prepare the final documents will appear in this section of the blueprint, together with telephone call contacts the customer has with the attorney or other front-line staff in the firm. All *non-visible* contact employee actions are shown in this area of the blueprint.

The *support processes* section of the blueprint covers the internal services, steps and interactions that take place to support the contact employees in delivering the service. Again, in our legal example, any service support activities such as legal research by staff, preparation of documents and secretarial support to set up meetings will be shown in the support processes area of the blueprint.

At the very top of the blueprint you see the *physical evidence* of the service. Typically, above each point of contact the actual physical evidence of the service is listed. In the legal example, the physical evidence of the face-to-face meeting with the lawyer would be such items as office decor, written documents, lawyer's clothing, and so on.

The four key action areas are separated by three horizontal lines. First is the *line of interaction*, representing direct interactions between the customer and the organization. Whenever a vertical line crosses the horizontal line of interaction, a direct contact between the customer and the organization, or a service encounter, has occurred. The next horizontal line is the critically important *line of visibility*. This line separates all service activities that are visible to the customer from those that are not visible. In reading blueprints it is immediately obvious whether the consumer is provided with much visible evidence of the service simply by analysing how much of the service occurs above the line of visibility versus the activities carried out below the line. This line also separates what the contact employees do onstage from what they do backstage. For example, in a medical examination situation, the doctor would perform the actual examination and answer the patient's questions above the line of visibility, or onstage, whereas he or she might read the patient's chart in advance and dictate notes following the examination below the line of visibility, or backstage. The third line is the *line of internal interaction*, which separates contact employee activities from those of other service support activities and people. Vertical lines cutting across the line of internal interaction represent internal service encounters.

One of the most significant differences between service blueprints and other process flow diagrams is the inclusion of customers and their views of the service process. In fact, in designing effective service blueprints it is recommended that the diagramming start with the customer's view of the process and work back into the delivery system. The boxes shown within each action area depict steps performed or experienced by the actors at that level.

Service blueprint examples

Figures 8.6 and 8.7 show service blueprints for two different services: express mail delivery and an overnight hotel stay.[29] These blueprints are deliberately kept very simple, showing only the most basic steps in the services. Complex diagrams could be developed for each step, and the internal processes could be much more fully developed. In addition to the four action areas separated by the three horizontal lines, these blueprints also show the physical evidence of the service from the customer's point of view at each step of the process.

Examine the express mail delivery blueprint in Figure 8.6. It is clear that from the customer's point of view there are only three steps in the service process: the telephone call, the package pick-up and the package delivery. The process is relatively standardized; the people who perform the service are the call-centre order-taker and the delivery person; and the physical evidence is the document package, the shipment forms, the truck and the handheld computer. In some cases the customer may also engage the online or telephone-based package tracking system. The complex process that occurs behind the line of visibility is of little interest or concern to the customer. However, for the three visible-to-the-customer steps to proceed effectively, invisible internal services are needed. What these steps are and the fact that they support the delivery of the service to the external customer are apparent from the blueprint.

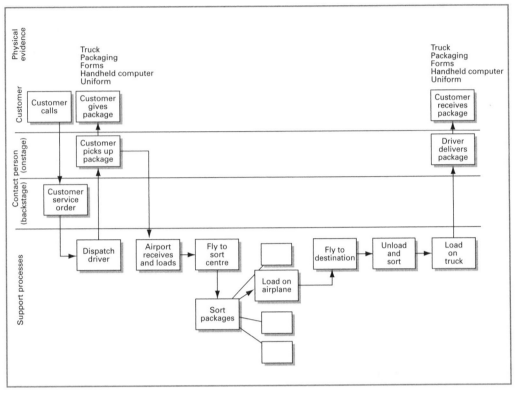

FIGURE 8.6 Blueprint for express mail delivery service

Source: The Service Quality Handbook by E.E. Scheuing and W.J. Christopher, eds. Copyright 1993 by AM MGMT ASSN/AMACOM (B). Reproduced with permission of AM MGMT ASSN/AMACOM (B) in the format Textbook via Copyright Clearance Center

Any of the steps in the blueprint could be exploded into a detailed blueprint if needed for a particular purpose. For example, if the delivery company learned that the 'unload and sort' step was taking too long and causing unacceptable delays in delivery, that step could be blueprinted in much greater detail to isolate the problems.

In the case of the overnight hotel stay depicted in Figure 8.7, the customer is more actively involved in the service than he or she is in the express mail service. The guest first checks in, then goes to the hotel room where a variety of steps take place (receiving bags, sleeping, showering, eating breakfast, and so on) and, finally, checks out. Imagine how much more complex this process could be and how many more interactions might occur if the service blueprint depicted a week-long vacation at the hotel, or even a three-day business conference. The service blueprint makes clear also (by reading across the line of interaction) those employees with whom the guest interacts and thus those employees who provide evidence of the service to the customer. Several interactions occur with a variety of hotel employees including the bellperson, the front desk clerk, the food service order-taker and the food delivery person. Each step in the customer action area is also associated with various forms of physical evidence, from the hotel parking area and hotel exterior and interior to the forms used at guest registration, the lobby, the room and the food. The hotel facility itself is critical in communicating the image of the hotel company, in providing satisfaction for the guest through the manner in which the hotel room is designed and maintained, and in facilitating the actions and interactions of both the guest and the employees

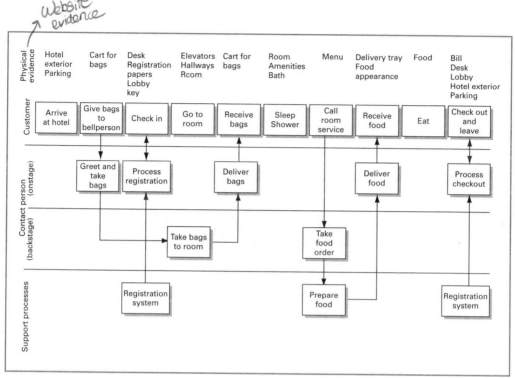

FIGURE 8.7 Blueprint for overnight hotel stay service

Source: The Service Quality Handbook by E.E. Scheuing and W.F. Christopher, eds. Copyright 1993 by AM MGMT ASSN/AMACOM (B). Reproduced with permission of AM MGMT ASSN/AMACOM (B) in the format Textbook via Copyright Clearance Center

of the hotel. In the hotel case, the process is relatively complex (although again somewhat standardized), the people providing the service are a variety of front-line employees, and the physical evidence includes everything from the guest registration form to the design of the lobby and room to the uniforms worn by front-line employees.

Blueprints for technology-delivered self-service

Up to this point all our discussion of service blueprints has related to services that are delivered in person, services in which employees interact directly with customers at some point in the process. But what about technology-delivered services like self-service websites (Expedia's travel information site, Dell's customer self-service site) and interactive kiosks (ATMs, airline self-check-in machines)? Can service blueprinting be used effectively to design these types of services? Certainly it can, but the lines of demarcation change, and some blueprint labels may need to be adapted.

If no employees are involved in the service (except when there is a problem or the service does not function as planned), the contact person areas of the blueprint are not needed. Instead, the area above the line of visibility can be used to illustrate the interface between the customer and the computer website or the physical interaction with the kiosk. This area can be relabelled onstage technology. The backstage contact person actions area would be irrelevant in this case.

If the service involves a combination of human and technology interfaces, as with airline computerized check-in, the onstage area can be cut into two distinct spaces divided by an additional horizontal line. In the airline computerized check-in example, the human contact with the airline employee who takes the bags and checks identification would be shown in one area and the technology interactions with the check-in computer kiosk would be shown in the second area, both above the line of visibility.

Reading and using service blueprints

A service blueprint can be read in a variety of ways, depending on the purpose. If the purpose is to understand the customer's view of the process or the customer experience, the blueprint can be read from left to right, tracking the events in the customer action area. Questions that might be asked include these: how is the service initiated by the customer? What choices does

---

Service spotlight

A blueprinting application in the design of a new rapid train service in Sweden illustrated a number of benefits:[30]

1   Provides an overview so employees can relate 'what I do' to the service viewed as an integrated whole, thus reinforcing a customer-oriented focus among employees.
2   Identifies fail points – that is, weak links of the chain of service activities, which can be the target of continuous quality improvement.
3   Line of interaction between external customers and employees illuminates the customer's role and demonstrates where the customer experiences quality, thus contributing to informed service design.
4   Line of visibility promotes a conscious decision on what customers should see and which employees will be in contact with customers, thus facilitating rational service design.
5   Line of internal interaction clarifies interfaces across departmental lines, with their inherent interdependencies, thus strengthening continuous quality improvement.
6   Stimulates strategic discussions by illuminating the elements and connections that constitute the service. Those who participate in strategic sessions tend to exaggerate the significance of their own special function and perspective unless a common ground for an integrated view of the service is provided.
7   Provides a basis for identifying and assessing cost, revenue and capital invested in each element of the service.
8   Constitutes a rational basis for both external and internal marketing. For example, the service map [blueprint] makes it easier for an advertising agency or an in-house promotion team to overview a service and select essential messages for communication.
9   Facilitates top-down, bottom-up approach to quality improvement. It enables managers to identify, channel and support quality improvement efforts of grass-roots employees working on both front-line and support teams. Employee work teams can create service maps [blueprints] and thus more clearly apply and communicate their experience and suggestions for improvements.

Source: reprinted with permission, from E. Gummesson and J. Kingman-Brundage, 'Service design and quality: applying service blueprinting and service mapping to railroad services', in *Quality Management in Services*, eds P. Kunst and J. Lemmink (Assen/Maastricht: Van Gorcum, 1991).

the customer make? Is the customer highly involved in creating the service, or are few actions required of the customer? What is the physical evidence of the service from the customer's point of view? Is the evidence consistent with the organization's strategy and positioning?

If the purpose is to understand contact employees' roles, the blueprint can also be read horizontally but this time focusing on the activities directly above and below the line of visibility. Questions that might be asked include: how rational, efficient and effective is the process? Who interacts with customers, when and how often? Is one person responsible for the customer, or is the customer passed off from one contact employee to another?

If the purpose is to understand the integration of the various elements of the service process, or to identify where particular employees fit into the bigger picture, the blueprint can be analysed vertically. In this analysis, it becomes clear what tasks and which employees are essential in the delivery of service to the customer. The linkages from internal actions deep within the organization to front-line effects on the customer can also be seen in the blueprint. Questions that might be asked include: what actions are being performed backstage to support critical customer interaction points? What are the associated support actions? How are handoffs from one employee to another taking place?

If the purpose is service redesign, the blueprint can be looked at as a whole to assess the complexity of the process, how it might be changed, and how changes from the customer's point of view would impact the contact employee and other internal processes, and vice versa. Blueprints can also be used to assess the overall efficiency and productivity of the service system and to evaluate how potential changes will impact the system.[31] The blueprint can also be analysed to determine likely failure points or bottlenecks in the process. When such points are discovered, a firm can introduce measures to track failures, or that part of the blueprint can be exploded so that the firm can focus in much greater detail on that piece of the system.

One of the greatest benefits of blueprinting is education.[32] When people begin to develop a blueprint, it quickly becomes apparent what is actually known about the service. Sometimes the shared knowledge is minimal. Biases and prejudices are made explicit, and agreements and compromises must be reached. The process itself promotes cross-functional integration and understanding. In the attempt to visualize the entire service system, people are forced to consider the service in new and more comprehensive ways.

Building a blueprint

Recall that many of the benefits and purposes of building a blueprint evolve from the process of doing it. Thus the final product is not necessarily the only goal. Through the process of

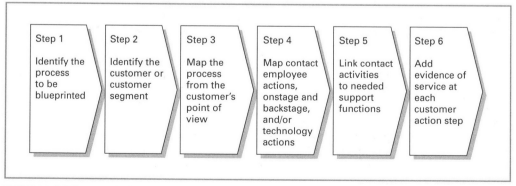

FIGURE 8.8 Building a service blueprint

developing the blueprint, many intermediate goals can be achieved: clarification of the concept, development of a shared service vision, recognition of complexities and intricacies of the service that are not initially apparent, and delineation of roles and responsibilities, to name a few. The development of the blueprint needs to involve a variety of functional representatives as well as information from customers. Drawing or building a blueprint is not a task that should be assigned to one person or one functional area. Figure 8.8 identifies the basic steps in building a blueprint.

The following provides answers to frequently asked questions about service blueprints.

CASE STUDY: FREQUENTLY ASKED QUESTIONS ABOUT SERVICE BLUEPRINTING

What process should be blueprinted?
What process to map depends on the team or organization's objectives. If these are not clearly defined, then identifying the process can present a challenge. Questions to ask: why are we blueprinting the service? What is our objective? Where does the service process begin and end? Are we focusing on the entire service, a component of the service, or a period of time?

Can multiple market segments be included on one blueprint?
Generally the answer to this question is no. Assuming that market segments require different service processes or attributes, the blueprint for one segment may look very different from the blueprint for another. Only at a very high level (sometimes called a *concept blueprint*) might it be relevant to map multiple segments simultaneously.

Who should 'draw' the blueprint?
A blueprint is a team effort. It should not be assigned as an individual task, certainly not in the development stages. All relevant parties should be involved or represented in the development effort. The task might include employees across multiple functions in the organization (marketing, operations, human resources, facilities design) as well as customers in some cases.

Should the actual or desired service process be blueprinted?
If a new service is being designed, then clearly it is important to start with the desired service process. However, in cases of service improvement or service redesign, it is very important to map (at least at a conceptual level) the actual service process first. Once the group knows how the service is actually functioning, then the blueprint can be modified or used as a base for changes and improvements.

Should exceptions or recovery processes be incorporated within the blueprint?
It may be possible to map relatively simple, commonly occurring recovery processes onto a blueprint, assuming there are not a lot of these. However, this process can quickly become complex and cause the blueprint to be confusing or unreadable. Often a better strategy is to indicate common fail points on the blueprint and, if needed, develop sub-blueprints for the service recovery processes.

What is the appropriate level of detail?
The answer to this question depends again on the objective or purpose for doing the blueprint in the first place. If it is to be used primarily to communicate the general nature of the service, then a concept blueprint with few details is best. If it is being used to focus on diagnosing and improving the service process, then more detail is needed. Because some people are more detail

oriented than others, this particular question will always arise and needs to be resolved in any team blueprinting effort.

What symbols should be used?

At this point in time, there is not a lexicon of blueprinting symbols that is commonly used or accepted across companies. What is most important is that the symbols be defined, be kept relatively simple, and be used consistently by the team and across the organization if blueprints are being shared internally.

Should time or financial costs be included on the blueprint?

Blueprints are very versatile. If reducing the time taken for various parts of the service process is an objective of the blueprinting effort, then time can definitely be included. The same is true for financial costs or anything else that is relevant as an objective. However, it is not advisable to put such information on the blueprint unless it is of central concern.

Step 1: Identify the service process to be blueprinted

Blueprints can be developed at a variety of levels, and there needs to be agreement on the starting point. For example, the express mail delivery blueprint shown in Figure 8.7 is at the basic service concept level. Little detail is shown, and variations based on market segment or specific services are not shown. Specific blueprints could be developed for two-day express mail, large accounts, Internet-facilitated services and/or high street drop-off centres. Each of these blueprints would share some features with the concept blueprint but would also include unique features. Or if the 'sort packages' and 'loading' elements of the process were found to be problem areas or bottlenecks that were slowing service to customers, a detailed blueprint of the sub-processes at work in those two steps could be developed. A firm can identify the process to be mapped once it has determined the underlying purpose for building the blueprint.

Step 2: Identify the customer or customer segment experiencing the service

A common rationale for market segmentation is that each segment's needs are different and therefore will require variations in the service or product features. Thus, blueprints are most useful when developed for a particular customer or customer segment, assuming that the service process varies across segments. At a very abstract or conceptual level it may be possible to combine customer segments on one blueprint. However, once almost any level of detail is reached, separate blueprints should be developed to avoid confusion and maximize their usefulness.

Step 3: Map the service process from the customer's point of view

Step 3 involves charting the choices and actions that the customer performs or experiences in purchasing, consuming and evaluating the service. Identifying the service from the customer's point of view first will help avoid focusing on processes and steps that have no customer impact. This step forces agreement on who the customer is (sometimes no small task) and may involve considerable research to determine exactly how the customer experiences the service.

Sometimes the beginning and ending of the service from the customer's point of view may not be obvious. For example, research in a haircutting context revealed that customers viewed the process as beginning with the telephone call to the salon and making the appointment, whereas the hairstylists did not typically view the making of appointments as part of the service process.[33] Similarly, in a mammography screening service, patients viewed driving to the clinic, parking and locating the screening office as part of the service experience. If the blueprint is being developed for an existing service, it may be helpful at this point in the process to video-tape or photograph the service process from the customer's point of view. Managers, and others who are not on the front line, often do not actually know what the customers are experiencing.

Step 4: Map contact employee actions, both onstage and backstage, and/or technology actions

First the lines of interaction and visibility are drawn, and then the process from the customer-contact person's point of view is mapped, distinguishing visible or onstage activities from invisible backstage activities. For existing services this step involves questioning front-line oper-ations employees to learn what they do and which activities are performed in full view of the customer versus which activities are carried out behind the scenes.

For technology-delivered services or those that combine technology and human delivery, the required actions of the technology interface will be mapped above the line of visibility as well. If no employees are involved in the service, the area can be relabelled 'onstage technology actions'. If both human and technology interactions are involved, an additional horizontal line can separate 'onstage contact employee actions' from 'onstage technology actions'. Using the additional line will facilitate reading and interpretation of the service blueprint.

Step 5: Link contact activities to needed support functions

The line of internal interaction can then be drawn and linkages from contact activities to internal support functions can be identified. In this process, the direct and indirect impact of internal actions on customers becomes apparent. Internal service processes take on added importance when viewed in connection with their link to the customer. Alternatively, certain steps in the process may be viewed as unnecessary if there is no clear link to the customer's experience or to an essential internal support service.

Step 6: Add evidence of service at each customer action step

Finally, the evidence of service can be added to the blueprint to illustrate what the customer sees and receives as tangible evidence of the service at each step in the customer experience. A photographic blueprint, including photos, slides or video of the process, can be very useful at this stage to aid in analysing the impact of tangible evidence and its consistency with the overall strategy and service positioning.

Quality function deployment

In addition to service blueprinting, another approach that can be used to develop a service architecture is *quality function deployment* (QFD). Quality function deployment has been defined as 'a system for translating customer requirements into appropriate company require-ments at every stage, from research through production design and development to manufacture; distribution; installation; and marketing, sales, and services'.[34] Because QFD is used as a means of integrating marketing and engineering personnel in the development process, it has more applications in manufacturing than in services. Its ideas are also applicable to services, however. Quality function deployment is implemented via what is known as the 'house of quality', which links customer requirements to design characteristics of the product or service.[35] These are then

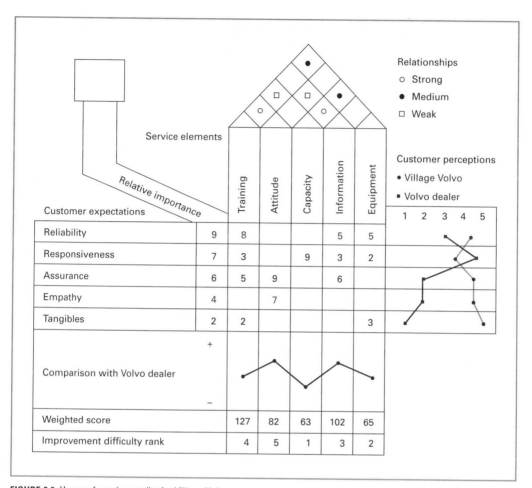

FIGURE 8.9 House of service quality for Village Volvo

Source: reprinted from J.A. Fitzsimmons and M.J. Fitzsimmons, *Service Management*, 3rd edn (New York: Irwin McGraw-Hill, 2000), p. 58. © 2000 by The McGraw-Hill Companies, Inc. Reprinted by permission of The McGraw-Hill Companies

linked to internal processes such as product planning, process planning, production planning and parts deployment. The house of quality is a diagrammatic representation of the service, its attributes, the customers' requirements and the company's capabilities.

For services, the concept of service quality deployment has been suggested as a means of adapting QFD tools for service development and design.[36] The resulting **house of service quality** (see Figure 8.9 for an example) comprises three distinct sections: customer quality criteria (what customers perceive), service company facets (how these criteria are created by the firm) and the relationship grid (how the two are related). This matrix is extended to include quantitative information so that relative importance of relationships among different functions of the firm can be highlighted.

Service spotlight

Figure 8.9 provides an example of QFD applied to Village Volvo, a Volvo service garage, to create a house of service quality.[37] The following list explains elements of the house of service quality shown in Figure 8.9.

1 *Customer expectations.* On the far left of the house are listed the customers' expectations of Village Volvo's customer service. In this case the customers' expectations correspond to the five service quality dimensions presented in Chapter 5. This is generally the first part of the house matrix to be constructed, it documents a structured list of a service's customer requirements.

2 *Importance of expectations.* Next to each expectation (on the chimney of the house) is listed the importance of that particular attribute to customers on a scale from 1 to 9, with 9 being the most important. These importance weights are determined by customer research.

3 *Controllable elements of service.* The columns of the house represent the elements of service that the company has control over, such as training, capacity, equipment, attitude and information.

4 *Relationship among elements.* The relationships among the elements of service are shown in the roof of the house. The relationship among elements can be strong, medium or weak. For example, the relationship between training and attitude is strong, whereas the relationship between training and capacity is weak.

5 *Association between expectations and service elements.* In the body of the matrix are numbers representing the strength of the relationship between each expectation and the related service element. The numbers reflect (from the service team's perspective) how various elements affect the company's ability to satisfy the particular customer expectation. A 0 suggests no effect, whereas a 9 suggests a very strong effect.

6 *Overall importance of service elements for meeting customer expectations.* The weighted score on the floor of the house represents the total points for each element, calculated by multiplying the importance weights by the element association ratings and adding all the scores for each element together [e.g. training = (9)(8) + (7)(3) + (6)(5) + (4)(0) + (2)(2) = 127]. These scores should be treated relatively, however, and not as absolutes because they are based on some subjectivity and judgement.

7 *Difficulty rankings.* In the basement of the house are listed the difficulty rankings assigned to each element in terms of how difficult it would be to make improvements in that element, with the ranking of 1 being the most difficult.

8 *Competitive assessment.* Two areas of the house suggest some comparisons of Village Volvo with the competing Volvo dealership. On the right are shown comparisons of the two on the dimensions of service quality. Just above the floor of the house are shown relative ratings comparing Village Volvo with the Volvo dealership on the elements of service.

The house of service quality in Figure 8.9 can be used to make preliminary service design decisions based on the relative importance of various attributes to customers, Village Volvo's relative competitive position, the weighting of the elements in terms of their contribution overall to customer satisfaction, and the difficulty of implementing change. In this example it would appear that training would be a good investment because it has the strongest weight, is rated relatively weak with respect to competition, and is relatively less difficult to change.

High-performance service innovations

Up to this point in the chapter, we have discussed approaches and tools for developing and designing new services. A dilemma in most companies is that there are too many new ideas from which to choose. New technologies, changing customer needs, deregulation, competitors' actions – all these areas result in myriad potential new offerings to consider. The question is which to pursue. How can a company decide which new offerings will likely be major successes, and which may be less successful or even fail?

In this section we summarize some of what has been learned about successful new services in terms of measures of success, the key success drivers and the importance of integrating new services.

Choose the right projects

Success with new services is going to be determined by two things: choosing the right projects and doing the projects right.[38] Researchers confirm that following the new service development process discussed earlier in the chapter and illustrated in Figure 8.2 will help with both these goals.[39] Service blueprinting and QFD, also presented in this chapter, will help as well, primarily with the second goal.

Another concept, *portfolio management for new products*, is very useful in helping companies choose the right projects in the first place.[40] Using this approach, companies manage their product portfolio like they manage their financial portfolio. The approach helps companies prioritize projects, choose which ones to accelerate, and determine the best balance between risk versus return, maintenance versus growth and short-term versus long-term projects. Methods for portfolio management include financial models, scoring models and checklists, mapping approaches, and behavioural approaches.[41]

Integrate new services

Because of the nature of services – they are processes, typically delivered at least in part by people, consumed and produced simultaneously – any new service introduction will affect the existing systems and services. Unlike when a manufacturer adds a new product to its production facility, new service introductions are frequently visible to customers and may even require their participation. Explicit recognition of these potential impacts, and planning for the integration of people, processes and physical evidence, will facilitate success.[42] This recognition will help in both (1) deciding which projects to pursue – sometimes the disruptive effect on existing systems is too great to warrant the investment – and (2) knowing how to proceed with implementation – what elements of existing processes, people and physical facilities will need to be adjusted, added or changed.

Consider multiple measures of success

In predicting the success of a new service, multiple performance measures may be considered.[43] First, and most commonly used, is near-term *financial performance* including revenue growth, profitability, market share and return on investment (ROI). In other cases, *relationship enhancement* may be a more appropriate measure of success. This measurement might include (1) the new service's effect on customer loyalty, (2) image enhancement and (3) the effect on the success of other products and services. Or success may be measured in terms of *market development* – the degree to which the new service opens up new markets or new customer segments. Successful projects will lead to increases in one, or perhaps more than one, of these measures.

Learn from major successes

In investing in new products and services, most companies are looking for big winners rather than modest improvements.[44] In a study of financial services, the following factors were found to distinguish major successes from moderate or small successes:[45]

- *Market synergy.* A strong fit exists between the new service and the company's marketing, promotion, sales and distribution expertise and resources.

- *Market-driven new product process.* The company has a well-planned and executed new service development process including customer input, research and development, customer testing and competitive analysis.

- *Effective marketing communications.* The company has an effective strategy for raising customer awareness, explaining service benefits, and establishing a unique positioning and distinct brand image.

- *Customer service.* The most successful new financial products were linked to excellent customer service support.

- *Managerial and financial synergy.* A strong fit exists between the new project and the company's management and financial expertise and resources.

- *Launch preparation.* The company provides extensive training and preparation of front-line personnel to support the product prior to launch.

- *Product responsiveness.* Major successes are new services that truly offer improvements from the customers' point of view – better than competition, responsive to a new need or offering greater flexibility.

- *Product advantage.* Major successes are better than alternatives in terms of benefits, quality and distinct branding.

- *Innovative technology.* Technology is instrumental in providing a superior product, or it provides innovation for the delivery system or the company uses hardware and software to develop significant new offerings. (This factor is particularly important for market development.)

Maintain some flexibility

New service success depends on (1) market-driven, customer-focused new product processes, (2) emphasis on planning for and executing the launch, (3) integration of services within existing processes (including staff training) and (4) strong marketing communications, both external and internal. Yet, firms must be cautioned about being too rigid in the new service development approach. Steps in the development process should be allowed some flexibility, and there will no doubt be overlapping processes. Initial service development, for example, can be occurring simultaneously with additional gathering of customer information. Because services, particularly business-to-business services, are often very complex, some creativity and 'out of order' decisions will be needed. There must be some elements of improvisation, anarchy and internal competition in the development of new services. 'Consequently, the innovation and adoption of new services must be both a planned process and a happening!'[46]

Summary

Service providers must effectively match customer expectations to new service innovations and actual service process designs. However, because of the very nature of services – their intangibility and variability specifically – the design and development of service offerings are complex and challenging. Many services are only vaguely defined before their introduction to the marketplace. This chapter has outlined some of the challenges involved in designing services and some strategies for effectively overcoming the challenges.

Through adaptations of the new product development process that is commonplace in goods production and manufacturing companies, service providers can begin to not only make their offerings more explicit but also avoid failures. The new service development process presented in the chapter includes nine stages, beginning with the development of a business and new service strategy and ending with post-introduction evaluation of the new service. Between these initial and ending stages are a number of steps and checkpoints designed to maximize the likelihood of new service success. Carrying out the stages requires the inclusion of customers, contact employees and anyone else who will affect or be affected by the new service. Because successful new service introduction is often highly dependent on service employees (often they are the service), integration of employees at each stage is critical.

Service blueprinting is a particularly useful tool in the new service development process. A blueprint can make a complex and intangible service concrete through its visual depiction of all the steps, actors, processes and physical evidence of the service. The key feature of service blueprints is their focus on the customer – the customer's experience is documented first and is kept fully in view as the other features of the blueprint are developed. This chapter has provided the basic tools needed to build, use and evaluate service blueprints. Quality function deployment was introduced as another tool for linking customer requirements to internal elements of service design.

The final section of the chapter summarized some of the key factors driving successful new service innovations, including the need for portfolio planning and integration of new services with existing processes and systems. The need to consider multiple measures of success was highlighted as well as the importance of maintaining flexibility in the new service development process.

Key concepts

Business analysis	195	Quality function development	206
House of service quality	207	Service blueprint	195
Idea generation	193	Service concept development and evaluation	194
Market testing	195		
New service development	189		

Further reading

Akao, Y. (2004) *Quality Function Deployment*. Shelton, CTL Productivity Press.

Berry, L.L. and Kampo, S.K. (2000) 'Teaching an old service new tricks: the promise of service redesign', *Journal of Service Research*, 2(2), 265–75.

Cohen, L. (1995) *Quality Function Deployment: How to Make QFD Work for You*. New York: Addison-Wesley Prentice Hall.

Edvardsson, B., Enquist, B. and Johnston, R. (2005) 'Cocreating customer value through hyperreality in the prepurchase service experience', *Journal of Service Research*, 8(2), 149–61.

Edvardsson, B., Gustafsson, A. and Johnson, M.D. (2002) *New Service Development and Innovation in the New Economy*. Lund: Studentlitteratur.

Johne, A. and Storey, C. (1998) 'New service development: a review of the literature and annotated bibliography', *European Journal of Marketing*, 32(3/4), 184–251.

Shostack, G.L. (1984) 'Designing services that deliver', *Harvard Business Review*, (January/February), 133–9.

Discussion questions

1 Why is it challenging to design and develop services?

2 What are the risks of attempting to describe services in words alone?

3 Compare and contrast the blueprints in Figures 8.6 and 8.7.

4 How might a service blueprint be used for marketing, human resource and operations decisions? Focus on one of the blueprint examples shown in the text as a context for your answer.

5 Assume that you are a multi-product service company that wants to grow through adding new services. Describe a logical process you might use to introduce a new service to the marketplace. What steps in the process might be most difficult and why? How might you incorporate service blueprinting into the process?

6 Discuss Figure 8.3 in terms of the four types of opportunities for growth represented there. Choose a company or service, and explain how it could grow by developing new services in each of the four cells.

7 Explain the house of service quality that is shown in Figure 8.9. Based on the information in that figure for Village Volvo, what might you do to improve service if you were the manager of that organization?

Exercises

1 Think of a new service you would like to develop if you were an entrepreneur. How would you go about it? Describe what you would do and where you would get your information.

2 Find a new and interesting service in your local area, or a service offered on your campus. Document the service process via a service blueprint. To do this exercise, you will probably need to interview one of the service employees. After you have documented the existing service, use blueprinting concepts to redesign the service or change it in some way.

3 Choose a service you are familiar with and document the customer action steps through a blueprint. What is the 'evidence of service' from your point of view as a customer?

4 Develop a service blueprint for a technology-delivered service (such as an Internet-based travel service). Compare and contrast this blueprint to one for the same service delivered via more traditional channels (such as a personal travel agent).

5 Interview customers and employees of a service of your choice. Construct a basic house of service quality. What would you recommend to the manager of the service based on your analysis?

6 Compare two services on the Internet. Discuss the design of each in terms of whether it meets your expectations. How could the design or the service process be changed? Which one is most effective, and why?

Notes

[1] 'Flops, too many new products fail. Here's why – and how to do better', cover story, *BusinessWeek*, 16 August 1993, pp. 76–82.

[2] Ibid.; R.G. Cooper, *Winning at New Products*, 3rd edn (Cambridge, MA: Perseus Publishing, 2001); R.G. Cooper and S.J. Edgett, *Product Development for the Service Sector* (Cambridge, MA: Perseus Books, 1999); C.M. Froehle, A.V. Roth, R.B. Chase and C.A. Voss, 'Antecedents of new service development effectiveness', *Journal of Service Research* 3 (August 2000), pp. 3–17.

[3] D.H. Henard and D.M. Szymanski, 'Why some new products are more successful than others', *Journal of Marketing Research* (August 2001), pp. 362–75.

[4] G.L. Shostack, 'Understanding services through blueprinting', in *Advances in Services Marketing and Management*, vol. 1, eds T.A. Swartz, D.E. Bowen and S.W. Brown (Greenwich, CT: JAI Press, 1992), pp. 75–90, quote from p. 76.

[5] Cooper, *Winning at New Products*; Cooper and Edgett, *Product Development for the Service Sector*; Henard and Szymanski, 'Why some new products are more successful than others'.

[6] G.L. Shostack, 'Service design in the operating environment', in *Developing New Services*, eds W.R. George and C. Marshall (Chicago, IL: American Marketing Association, 1984), pp. 27–43.

[7] For excellent reviews of research and issues in new services development see *Journal of Operations Management* 20 (2002), special issue on New Issues and Opportunities in Service Design Research; A. Johne and C. Story, 'New service development: a review of the literature and annotated bibliography', *European Journal of Marketing* 32, no. 3–4 (1998), pp. 184–251; B. Edvardsson, A. Gustafsson, M.D. Johnson and B. Sanden, *New Service Development and Innovation in the New Economy* (Lund: Studentlitteratur AB, 2000).

[8] B. Schneider and D.E. Bowen, 'New services design, development and implementation and the employee', in *Developing New Services*, eds W.R. George and C. Marshall (Chicago, IL: American Marketing Association, 1984), pp. 82–101.

9 Adapted from D.F. Heany, 'Degrees of product innovation', *Journal of Business Strategy* (Spring 1983), pp. 3–14, appearing in C.H. Lovelock, 'Developing and implementing new services', in *Developing New Services*, eds W.R. George and C. Marshall (Chicago, IL: American Marketing Association, 1984), pp. 44–64.

10 For a discussion of these adaptations and related research issues, see M.V. Tatikonda and V.A. Zeithaml, 'Managing the new service development process: synthesis of multidisciplinary literature and directions for future research', in *New Directions in Supply Chain Management: Technology, Strategy, and Implementation*, eds T. Boone and R. Ganeshan (New York: AMACOM, 2002), pp. 200–36; B. Edvardsson et al., *New Service Development and Innovation in the New Economy*.

11 The steps shown in Figure 8.2 and discussed in the text are based primarily on the model developed by M.J. Bowers, 'An exploration into new service development: organization, process, and structure', doctoral dissertation, Texas A&M University, 1985. Bowers's model is adapted from Booz-Allen & Hamilton, *New Product Management for the 1980s* (New York: Booz-Allen & Hamilton, 1982).

12 A. Griffin, 'PDMA research on new product development practices: updating trends and benchmarking best practices', *Journal of Product Innovation Management* 14 (1997), pp. 429–58; S. Thomke, 'R&D comes to services: Bank of America's pathbreaking experiments', *Harvard Business Review*, 81 (April 2003), pp. 70–9.

13 R.G. Cooper, 'Stage gate systems for new product success', *Marketing Management* 1, no. 4 (1992), pp. 20–9.

14 M. Iansiti and A. MacCormack, 'Developing products on Internet time', *Harvard Business Review* (September–October 1997), pp. 108–17.

15 A. Khurana and S.R. Rosenthal, 'Integrating the fuzzy front end of new product development', *Sloan Management Review* (Winter 1997) pp. 103–20.

16 Iansiti and MacCormack, 'Developing products on Internet time'.

17 M.E. Porter, *Competitive Strategy* (New York: Free Press, 1980).

18 Khurana and Rosenthal, 'Integrating the fuzzy front end'; see also R.G. Cooper, S.J. Edgett and E.J. Kleinschmidt, *Portfolio Management for New Products* (Reading, MA: Addison-Wesley, 1998).

19 D. Rigby and C. Zook, 'Open-market innovation', *Harvard Business Review* (October 2002), pp. 80–9.

20 D. Leonard and J.F. Rayport, 'Spark innovation through empathic design', *Harvard Business Review* (November–December 1997), pp. 103–13.

21 Shostack, 'Service design'.

22 E.E. Scheuing and E.M. Johnson, 'A proposed model for new service development', *Journal of Services Marketing* 3, no. 2 (1989), pp. 25–34.

23 D. Maxey, 'Testing, testing, testing', *The Wall Street Journal*, 10 December 2001, p. R8.

24 Shostack, 'Service design', p. 35.

25 Maxey, 'Testing, testing, testing'.

26 The service blueprinting section of the chapter draws from the pioneering works in this area: G.L. Shostack, 'Designing services that deliver', *Harvard Business Review* (January–February 1984),

pp. 133–9; G.L. Shostack, 'Service positioning through structural change', *Journal of Marketing* 51 (January 1987), pp. 34–43; J. Kingman-Brundage, 'The ABCs of service system blueprinting', in *Designing a Winning Service Strategy*, eds M.J. Bitner and L.A. Crosby (Chicago, IL: American Marketing Association, 1989), pp. 30–3.

27 Shostack, 'Understanding services through blueprinting', pp. 75–90.

28 These key components are drawn from Kingman-Brundage, 'The ABCs'.

29 The text explaining Figures 8.6 and 8.7 relies on M.J. Bitner, 'Managing the evidence of service', in *The Service Quality Handbook*, eds E.E. Scheuing and W.F. Christopher (New York: American Management Association, 1993), pp. 358–70.

30 E. Gummesson and J. Kingman-Brundage, 'Service design and quality: applying service blueprinting and service mapping to railroad services', in *Quality Management in Services*, eds P. Kunst and J. Lemmink (Assen/Maastricht: Van Gorcum, 1991).

31 S. Flieb and M. Kleinaltenkamp, 'Blueprinting the service company: managing service processes efficiently', *Journal of Business Research* 57 (2004), pp. 392–404.

32 Shostack, 'Understanding services through blueprinting'.

33 D. Getz, M. O'Neill and J. Carlsen, 'Service quality evaluation at events through service mapping', *Journal of Travel Research* 39 (May 2001), pp. 380–90.

34 American Supplier Institute (1987), as quoted in R.S. Behara and R.B. Chase, 'Service quality deployment: quality service by design', in *Perspectives in Operations Management: Essays in Honor of Elwood Buffa*, ed. R. V. Sarin (Norwell, MA: Kluwer Academic, 1993).

35 J.R. Hauser and D. Clausing, 'The house of quality', *Harvard Business Review*, (May–June 1988), pp. 63–73.

36 Behara and Chase, 'Service quality deployment'. See also F.I. Stuart and S.S. Tax, 'Planning for service quality: an integrative approach', *International Journal of Service Industry Management* 7, no. 4 (1996), pp. 58–77.

37 J.A. Fitzsimmons and M.J. Fitzsimmons, *Service Management*, 4th edn (New York: McGraw-Hill/Irwin, 2004), pp. 144–6.

38 Cooper et al., *Portfolio Management for New Products*.

39 Froehle et al., 'Antecedents of new service development effectiveness'; Henard and Szymanski, 'Why some new products are more successful than others'; Edvardsson et al., *New Service Development and Innovation in the New Economy*.

40 Cooper et al., *Portfolio Management for New Products*.

41 See ibid. for an excellent discussion and coverage of multiple methods for managing product and service portfolios.

42 S.S. Tax and I. Stuart, 'Designing and implementing new services: the challenges of integrating service systems', *Journal of Retailing* 73 (Spring 1977), pp. 105–34.

43 R.G. Cooper, C.J. Easingwood, S. Edgett, E.J. Kleinschmidt, and C. Storey, 'What distinguishes the top performing new products in financial services?', *Journal of Product Innovation Management* 11 (1994), pp. 281–99.

44 For information on success and failure of new services, see Cooper et al., 'What distinguishes the top performing new products'; Ulrike de Brentani, 'New industrial service development: scenarios for success and failure', *Journal of Business Research* 32 (1995), pp. 93–103; C.R.

Martin Jr and D.A. Horne, 'Services innovation: successful versus unsuccessful firms', *International Journal of Service Industry Management* 4, no. 1 (1993), pp. 49–65; B. Edvardsson, L. Haglund and J. Mattsson, 'Analysis, planning, improvisation, and control in the development of new services', *International Journal of Service Industry Management* 6, no. 2 (1995), pp. 24–35; Froele et al., 'Antecedents of new service development effectiveness'; Henard and Szymanski, 'Why some new products are more successful than others'; Cooper and Edgett, *Product Development for the Service Sector.*

[45] Cooper et al., 'What distinguishes the top performing new products in financial services'.

[46] Edvardsson, Haglund and Mattsson, 'Analysis, planning, improvisation, and control', p. 34.

CHAPTER 09

Customer-defined service standards

❖ LEARNING OBJECTIVES

This chapter's objectives are to:

1 Distinguish between company-defined and customer-defined service standards.

2 Differentiate among one-time service fixes and 'hard' and 'soft' customer-defined standards.

3 Explain the critical role of the service encounter sequence in developing customer-defined standards.

4 Illustrate how to translate customer expectations into behaviours and actions that are definable, repeatable and actionable.

5 Explain the process of developing customer-defined service standards.

6 Emphasize the importance of service performance indexes in implementing strategy for service delivery.

CASE STUDY: ISS SETS STANDARDS THROUGHOUT THE WORLD

Integrated Service Solutions (ISS) headquartered in Denmark is one of the world's largest facility service providers, with market presence in Europe, Asia, South America and Australia employing more than 390 000 people to satisfy more than 100 000 business-to-business customers. It offers services such as catering, office support, cleaning and property services. It has to meet standards of service set by its customers. For example, in Singapore, where the company cleans the Raffles Link shopping area, the standards for cleanliness may be among the most challenging in the world. ISS Singapore uses the most modern and environmentally friendly cleaning equipment, chemicals and methods to serve their demanding Singapore customers.

'First of all, managing demanding customer expectations means understanding the customer's requirements and needs. When I come here early in the morning, I have to ensure that all areas are attended to and cleaned before my client arrives. The result at the end of the day matters a lot to me,' explains Project Manager Jason Foo of ISS Singapore.

Jason heads the 60 employees in the shopping and office area connected to the Raffles Link Station. They have more than 300 000 square metres to clean.

The work to be done at Raffles Link Station is not only cleaning. Jason and his staff also segregate the waste, look for security breaches and watch out for building defects to be reported to the customer, Hongkong Land, a major property owner.

'When I first worked with this client, he used a white handkerchief to check the cleanliness of surfaces. As time has passed, he found less and less dirt on his handkerchief. In the past year, we managed to gain his trust and confidence, and he no longer uses his handkerchief when inspecting our work,' explains Jason.

At National University Hospital in Singapore, the demand for quality is also high. To manage the expectations of their customer is a full-time job, and it is hardly a joke when Project Manager Peter Sim Aik Khia of ISS Singapore calls the hospital his second home.

Peter manages 150 employees who clean about 180 000 square metres every day in order to maintain a healthy and clean environment at the 935-bed National University Hospital.

Every day, ISS inspectors use a laptop computer to check whether the customer's standards are being met. Like Jason, Peter emphasized the necessity of earning the confidence of the customer by doing a quality job.

Source: adapted from www.issworld.com

As we saw in Chapters 6, and 7, understanding customer requirements is the first step in delivering high service quality. Once managers of service businesses accurately understand what customers expect, they face a second critical challenge: using this knowledge to set service quality standards and goals for the organization. Service companies often experience difficulty in setting standards to match or exceed customer expectations partly because doing so requires that the marketing and operations departments within a company work together. In most service companies, integrating the work of the marketing function and the operations function (appropriately called *functional integration*) is not a typical approach; more frequently these two functions operate separately – setting and achieving their own internal goals – rather than pursuing a joint goal of developing the operations standards that best meet customer expectations.

Creating service standards that address customer expectations is not a common practice in service firms. Doing so often requires altering the very process by which work is accomplished, which is ingrained in tradition in most companies. Often change requires new equipment or technology. Change also necessitates aligning executives from different parts of the firm to understand collectively the comprehensive view of service quality from the customer's perspective. And almost always, change requires a willingness to be open to different ways of structuring, calibrating and monitoring the way service is provided.

Factors necessary for appropriate service standards

Standardization of service behaviours and actions

The translation of customer expectations into specific service quality standards depends on the degree to which tasks and behaviours to be performed can be standardized or routinized. Some executives and managers believe that services cannot be standardized – that customization is essential for providing high-quality service. Managers also may feel that standardizing tasks is inconsistent with employee empowerment – that employees will feel controlled by the company if tasks are standardized. Further, they feel that services are too intangible to be measured. This view leads to vague and loose standard setting with little or no measurement or feedback.

In reality, many service tasks are routine (such as those needed for opening cheque accounts or servicing domestic gas central heating boilers) and, for these, specific rules and standards can be fairly easily established and effectively executed. Employees may welcome knowing how to perform actions most efficiently: it frees them to use their ingenuity in the more personal and individual aspects of their jobs.

According to one long-term observer of service industries, standardization of service can take three forms: (1) substitution of technology for personal contact and human effort, (2) improvement in work methods, and (3) combinations of these two methods.[1] Examples of technology substitution include automatic teller machines, automatic car washes and airport X-ray machines. Improvements in work methods are illustrated by restaurant salad bars and routinized tax and accounting services developed by firms such as Pizza Hut and Sage Accounting software.

Technology and work improvement methods facilitate the standardization of service necessary to provide consistent delivery to customers. By breaking tasks down and providing them efficiently, technology also allows the firm to calibrate **service standards** such as the length of time a transaction takes, the accuracy with which operations are performed and the number of problems that occur. In developing work improvements, the firm comes to understand completely the process by which the service is delivered. With this understanding, the firm more easily establishes appropriate service standards.

Standardization, whether accomplished by technology or by improvements in work processes, reduces gap 2. Standardization does not mean that service is performed in a rigid, mechanical way. Customer-defined standardization ensures that the most critical elements of a service are performed as expected by customers, not that every action in a service is executed in a uniform manner. Using customer-defined standardization can, in fact, allow for and be compatible with employee empowerment. One example of this compatibility involves the time limits many companies establish for customer service calls. If their customers' highest priorities involve feeling good about the call or resolving problems, then setting a limit for calls would be decidedly company defined and not in customers' best interests.

Service spotlight

Companies such as Barclaycard, in using customer priorities rather than company priorities, have no set standard for the amount of time an employee spends on the telephone with a customer. Instead, they have standards that focus on making the customer satisfied and comfortable, allowing telephone representatives to use their own judgement about the time limits. Standardization of service is not appropriate in some situations.

When is the strategy of customization better than standardization?

This chapter focuses on the benefits of customer-defined standards in the context of situations – hotels, retail stores, service outlets – in which it is important to provide the same service to all or most customers. In these situations, standards establish strong guidelines for technology and employees in order to ensure consistency and reliability. In other services, providing **standardization** is neither appropriate nor possible, and **customization** – providing unique types and levels of service to customers – is a deliberate strategy.

In most 'expert' services – such as accounting, consulting, engineering and dentistry, for example – professionals provide customized and individualized services; standardization of the tasks is perceived as being impersonal, inadequate and not in the customer's best interests. Because patient and client needs differ, these professionals offer very customized services that address individual requirements. They must adapt their offerings to the particular needs of each customer because each situation is different. Even within a given medical specialty, few patients have the same illness with precisely the same symptoms and the same medical history. Therefore, standardizing the amount of time a doctor spends with a patient is rarely possible, one of the reasons why patients usually must wait before receiving medical services even though they have advance appointments. Because professionals such as accountants and lawyers cannot usually standardize what they provide, they often charge by the hour rather than by the job, which allows them to be compensated for the customized periods of time they spend with clients. It is important to recognize, however, that even in highly customized services, some aspects of service provision can be routinized. Physiotherapists and dentists, for example, can and do standardize recurring and non-technical aspects such as checking patients in, weighing patients, taking routine measurements, billing patients and collecting payment. In delegating these routine tasks to assistants, the professional staff can spend more of their time on the expert service of diagnosis or patient care.

Another situation in which customization is the chosen strategy is in business-to-business contexts, particularly with key accounts. When accounts are large and critical to a provider, most aspects of service provision are customized. At a very basic level, this customization takes the form of service contracts such as those described for ISS at the start of this chapter in which the client and the provider agree on issues such as cleaning standards, speed of response, etc. At a higher level, customization involves creative problem-solving and innovative ideas (as in consulting services).

Finally, many consumer services are designed to be (or appear) very customized. These services include spa and upmarket hotel visits, exotic vacations such as safaris, and even haircuts from expensive salons. In these situations, the steps taken to ensure the successful delivery of service is often standardized behind the scenes but appears to the customer to be very individualized. Even Disney theme parks use this approach, employing hundreds of standards to ensure the delivery of 'magic' to each individual customer.

Formal service targets and goals

Companies that have been successful in delivering consistently high service quality are noted for establishing formal standards to guide employees in providing service. These companies have an accurate sense of how well they are performing service that is critical to their customers – how long it takes to conduct transactions, how frequently service fails, how quickly they settle customer complaints – and strive to improve by defining goals that lead them to meet or exceed customer expectations.

One type of formal **goal-setting** that is relevant in service businesses involves specific targets for individual behaviours or actions. As an example, consider the behaviour 'calls the customer back quickly', an action that signals responsiveness in contact employees. If the service goal for employee behaviour is stated in such a general term as 'call the customer back quickly', the standard provides little direction for service employees. Different employees will interpret this vague objective in their own ways, leading to inconsistent service: some may call the customer back in 10 minutes whereas others may wait two to four days. And the firm itself will not be able to determine when or if individual employees meet the goal because its expression is not measurable – one could justify virtually any amount of time as 'quickly'. On the other hand, if the individual employee's service goal is to call each customer back within four hours, employees have a specific, unambiguous guideline about how quickly they should execute the action (four hours). Whether the goal is met is also unequivocal: if the call occurs within four hours the company meets the goal; otherwise it does not.

Another type of formal goal setting involves the overall department or company target, most frequently expressed as a percentage, across all executions of the behaviour or action. For example, a department might set as its overall goal 'to call the customer back within four hours 97 per cent of the time' and collect data over a month's or year's time to evaluate the extent to which it meets the target.

Service firms that produce consistently excellent service – firms such as Disneyland Paris, DHL and British Airways – have very specific, quantified, measurable service goals. Disneyland calibrates employee performance on myriad behaviours and actions that contribute to guest perceptions of high service quality. Whether they are set and monitored using audits (such as timed actions) or customer perceptions (such as opinions about courtesy), service standards provide a means for formal goal setting.

Customer- not *company-*defined standards

Virtually all companies possess service standards and measures that are *company defined* – they are established to reach internal company goals for productivity, efficiency, cost or technical quality. A current company-defined standard that does not meet customer expectations is the common practice of voice-activated telephone support systems that do not allow consumers to speak to humans. Because these systems save companies money (and actually provide faster service to some customers), many organizations have switched from the labour-intensive practice of having customer representatives to using these systems. To close gap 2, standards set by companies must be based on customer requirements and expectations (identified using some of the methods outlined in Chapter 6) rather than just on internal company goals. In this chapter we make the case that company-defined standards are not typically successful in driving behaviours that close provider gap 2. Instead, a company must set *customer-defined standards*: operational standards based on pivotal customer requirements that are visible to and measured by customers. These standards are deliberately chosen to match customer expectations and to be calibrated the way the customer views and expresses them. Because these goals are essential to the provision of excellent service, the rest of this chapter focuses on customer-defined standards.

Knowing customer requirements, priorities and expectation levels can be both effective and efficient. Anchoring service standards on customers can save money by identifying what the customer values, thus eliminating activities and features that the customer either does not notice or will not pay for. Through precise measurement of expectations, the company often discovers that it has been overdelivering to many customer needs.

Service spotlight

A bank might add several extra tellers and reduce the average peak waiting time in line from seven minutes to five minutes. If customers expect, however, to wait up to eight minutes during peak time, the investment in extra tellers may not be effective. An opportunity thus exists to capture the value of this information through reduced teller costs and higher profits.[2]

Although customer-defined standards need not conflict with productivity and efficiency, they are not developed for these reasons. Rather, they are anchored in and steered by customer perceptual measures of service quality or satisfaction. The service standards that evolve from a customer perspective are likely to be different from company-defined service standards.

Virtually all organizations have lists of actions that they measure regularly, most of which fall into the category of company-defined standards. Often these standards deal with activities or actions that reflect the history of the business rather than the reality of today's competitive marketplace or the needs of current customers.

Types of customer-defined service standards

The type of standards that close provider gap 2 are *customer-defined standards*: operational goals and measures based on pivotal customer requirements that are visible to and measured by customers rather than on company concerns such as productivity or efficiency. Take a typical operations standard such as inventory control. Most firms control inventory from the company's point of view.

However, supermarkets such as Tesco and Sainsbury's capture every single service measurement related to inventory control *from the customer's point of view*. The companies begin with the question, 'What does the customer see?' and answer, 'The average number of stockouts per week'. These supermarkets then design a customer-focused measurement system based on measures such as the number of empty shelves, the number of unfulfilled product requests and complaints as well as transaction-based data linked to the use of customer loyalty cards at the tills. These and other customer-defined standards allow for the translation of customer requirements into goals and guidelines for employee performance. Two major types of customer-defined service standards can be distinguished: 'hard' and 'soft'. These standards are discussed in the following two sections.

Hard customer-defined standards

As we stressed in Chapter 3, customer expectations of reliability – fulfilment of service promises – are high. A series of 35 studies across numerous industries from the Arthur D. Little management consulting firm found that the most frequently cited customer complaint was late product and service delivery (44 per cent), followed by product and service quality mistakes (31 per cent).[3]

To address the need for reliability, companies can institute a 'do it right the first time' and an 'honour your promises' value system by establishing reliability standards. An example of a generic reliability standard that would be relevant to virtually any service company is 'right first time', which means that the service performed is done correctly the first time according to the customer's assessment. If the service involves delivery of products, 'right first time' to the customer might mean that the shipment is accurate – that it contains all that the customer ordered and nothing that the customer did not order. If the service involves installation of equipment, 'right first time' would likely mean that the equipment was installed correctly and was able to be used immediately by the customer. Another example of a reliability standard is 'right on time', which means that the service is performed at the scheduled time. The company representative arrives when promised or the delivery is made at the time the customer expects it. In more complex services, such as disaster recovery or systems integration in computer service, 'right on time' would likely mean that the service was completed by the promised date.

Reliability is the single most important concern of service customers. In online retailing, on-time and accurate fulfilment of orders is one of the most important aspects of reliability. One of the best examples of **hard customer-defined service standards** in the Internet context is the set of summary metrics that Dell Computer uses for fulfilment.[4] They include:

- *Ship to target* (STT) – the percentage of orders delivered on time with complete accuracy
- *Initial field incident rate* (IFIR) – the frequency of customer problems
- *On time first time fix* (OTFTF) – the percentage of problems fixed on the first visit by a service representative arriving at the time promised.

Dell tracks its performance to these standards and rewards employees on the basis of their 'met promises' or reliability, which is often higher than 98 per cent.

Hard service standards for responsiveness are set to ensure the speed or promptness with which companies deliver products (within two working days), handle complaints (by sundown each day), answer questions (within two hours), answer the telephone and arrive for repair calls (within 30 minutes of the estimated time). In addition to standard-setting that specifies levels of response, companies must have well-staffed customer service departments. Responsiveness perceptions diminish when customers wait to get through to the company by telephone, are put on hold, or are dumped into a telephone mail system.

Examples of hard standards include:

Company	Customer priorities	Customer-defined standards
DHL	On-time delivery	Number of packages right day late
		Number of packages wrong day late
		Number of missed pickups
Dell Computer	On-time delivery	Ship to target
	Computer works properly	Initial field incident rate
		Missing, wrong, and damaged rate

Soft customer-defined standards

Not all customer priorities can be counted, timed or observed through audits. As Albert Einstein once said, 'Not everything that counts can be counted, and not everything that can be counted, counts'. For example, 'understanding and knowing the customer' is not a customer priority that can be adequately captured by a standard that counts, times or observes employees. In contrast to hard measures, soft measures are those that must be documented using perceptual data. We call the second category of customer-defined standards *soft standards and measures* because they are opinion-based measures and cannot be directly observed. They must be collected by talking to customers, employees or others. **Soft customer-defined service standards** provide direction, guidance and feedback to employees in ways to achieve customer satisfaction and can be quantified by measuring customer perceptions and beliefs. Soft standards are especially important for person-to-person interactions such as the selling process and the delivery process for professional services. Examples of soft customer-defined standards include:

Company	Customer priorities	Customer-defined standards
Ritz-Carlton*	Being treated with respect	'Gold Standards' Uniforms are to be immaculate Wear proper and safe footwear Wear name tag Adhere to grooming standards Notify supervisor immediately of hazards Use proper telephone etiquette Ask the caller, 'May I place you on hold?' Do not screen calls Eliminate call transfers when possible
American Express	Resolution of problems	Resolve problem at first contact (no transfers, other calls or multiple contacts); communicate and give adequate instructions; take all the time necessary
	Treatment	Listen; do everything possible to help; be appropriately reassuring (open and honest)
	Courtesy of representative	Put card member at ease; be patient in explaining billing process; display sincere interest in helping card member; listen attentively; address card member by name; thank card member at end of call

Source: 'The Ritz-Carlton Basics', flyer distributed by the Ritz-Carlton to all employees

The Ritz-Carlton, winner of a Malcolm Baldrige Award, uses a set of 'Gold Standards' to drive the service performance it wants (see table).

One-time fixes

When customer research is undertaken to find out what aspects of service need to be changed, requirements can sometimes be met using **one-time fixes**. One-time fixes are *technology, policy or procedure changes that, when instituted, address customer requirements*. We further define one-time fixes as those company standards that can be met by an outlet (a franchisee, for example) making a one-time change that does not involve employees and therefore does not require motivation and monitoring to ensure compliance. We include one-time fixes in our discussion of standards because organizations with multiple outlets often must clearly define these standards to ensure consistency.

Examples of successful one-time fixes include Europcar and other car rental companies' express check-in, Tesco's self-scanning tills, KLM's online check-in facility. In each of these examples, customers expressed a desire to be served in ways different from the past. All had clearly indicated their frustration at waiting in long lines. Whereas most companies in these industries decided for various reasons not to address these customer requirements, Europcar, Tesco and KLM each responded with one-time fixes that virtually revolutionized the service quality delivered by their companies. One-time fixes are often accomplished by technology. Technology can simplify and improve customer service, particularly when it frees company personnel by handling routine, repetitive tasks and transactions. Customer service employees can then spend more time on the personal and possibly more essential portions of the job. Some technology, in particular computer databases that contain information on individual needs and interests of customers, allows the company to standardize the essential elements of service delivery.

One-time fixes also deal with the aspects of service relating to rules and policies, operating hours, product quality and price. An example of a one-time fix involving a policy change is that of allowing front-line employees to refund money to dissatisfied customers. An example of operating-hour changes is extending the operating-hours of your call centre to include Sundays.

Development of customer-defined service standards

Basing standards on the service encounter sequence

A customer's overall service quality evaluation is the accumulation of evaluations of multiple service experiences. Service encounters are the component pieces needed to establish service standards in a company. In establishing standards we are concerned with service encounter quality, because we want to understand for each service encounter the specific requirements and priorities of the customer. When we know these priorities, we can focus on them as the aspects of service encounters for which standards should be established. Therefore, one of the first steps in establishing customer-defined standards is to delineate the service encounter sequence. Identifying the sequence can be done by listing the sequential steps and activities that the customer experiences in receiving the service. Alternatively, service blueprints (see Chapter 8) can be used to identify the sequence by noting all the customers' activities across the top of the blueprint. Vertical lines from customer activities into the lower levels of the blueprint signal the points at which service encounters take place. Standards that meet customer expectations can then be established.

Because many services have multiple encounters, companies and researchers have examined whether some encounters (for example, the first or the last) are more important than others. The Marriott Corporation identified the encounters that occur in the first 10 minutes of a hotel stay as the most critical, leading the hospitality company to focus on hotel front-desk experiences (such as express check-in) when making improvements. Although service practice and management literature have emphasized strong starts, recent research indicates that strong finishes in the final event of the encounter have a greater impact on overall satisfaction. Further, the research shows that consistent performance throughout the encounter – widely believed to produce the most favorable evaluations – is not as effective as a pattern of improving performance that culminates in a strong finish.[5] An implication of this research for hotels is that managers should focus on the 'back end' of the hotel experience – checkout, parking, concierge services – to leave a strong final impression.

Expressing customer requirements as specific behaviours and actions

Setting a standard in broad conceptual terms, such as 'improve skills in the company', is ineffective because the standard is difficult to interpret, measure and achieve. When a company collects data, it often captures customer requirements in very abstract terms. In general, contact or field people often find that data are not diagnostic – they are too broad and general. Research neither tells them specifically what is wrong and right in their customer relationships nor helps them understand what activities can be eliminated so that the most important actions can be accomplished. In most cases, field people need help translating the data into specific actions to deliver better customer service.

Effective service standards are defined in very specific ways that enable employees to understand what they are being asked to deliver. At best, these standards are set and measured in terms of specific responses of human behaviours and actions.

Figure 9.1 shows different levels of abstraction/concreteness for standards in a service firm, arrayed from top (most abstract) to bottom (most concrete and specific). At the very abstract level are customer requirements that are too general to be useful to employees: customers want satisfaction, value and relationships. One level under these very general requirements are abstract dimensions of service quality already discussed in this text: reliability, responsiveness, empathy, assurance and tangibles. One level further are attributes more specific in describing requirements. If we dig still deeper beneath the attribute level, we get to specific behaviours and actions that are at the right level of specificity for setting standards.

A real-world example of the difference in requirements across these levels will illustrate their practical significance. In a traditional measurement system for a major company's training division, only one aspect of the instructor was included in its class evaluation: ability of instructor. During qualitative research relating to the attributes that satisfy students, three somewhat more specific requirements were elicited: (1) instructor's style, (2) instructor's expertise and (3) instructor's management of class. Although the articulation of the three attributes was more helpful to instructors than the broad 'ability of instructor', management found that the attributes

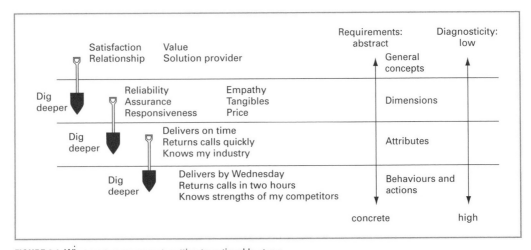

FIGURE 9.1 What customers expect: getting to actionable steps

were still too broad to help instructors wanting to improve their course delivery. When the company invested in a customer-defined standards project, the resulting measurement system was far more useful in diagnosing student requirements because the research focused on *specific behaviours and actions* of instructors that met student requirements. Instead of a single broad requirement or three general attributes, the requirements of students were articulated in 14 specific behaviours and actions that related to the instructor and 11 specific behaviours and actions that related to the course content. These behaviours and actions were clearly more diagnostic for communicating what was good and bad in the courses. An additional benefit of this approach was that feedback on behaviours and actions was less personal than feedback on traits or personal characteristics. It was also easier for employees of the company to make changes that related to behaviours rather than to personality traits.

Measuring behaviours and actions

Hard measurements

Hard measurements for **measuring behaviour and actions** consist of counts or audits or timed actions that provide feedback about the operational performance of a service standard. What distinguishes these data from soft measurements is that they can be captured continuously and operationally without asking the customer's opinion about them.

Service spotlight

Here are some of the actual hard measurements used by Federal Express in its international operations:

- *Missing proofs of delivery*: the number of invoices that do not include proof-of-delivery paperwork
- *Overgoods*: lost and found packages that lack, or have lost, identifying labels for the sender and the addressee and are sent to the Overgoods Department
- *Wrong day late deliveries*: number of packages delivered after the commitment date
- *Traces*: the number of 'proof of performance' requests from customers that cannot be answered through data contained in the computer system.[6]

In these and other hard measurements, the actual gauge involves a count of the number and type of actions or behaviours that are correct or incorrect. Somewhere in the operation system these actions and behaviours are tabulated, frequently through information technology. Other gauges of hard measures include service guarantee lapses (the number of times a service guarantee is invoked because the service did not meet the promise), amounts of time (as in the number of hours or days to respond to a question or complaint or minutes waited in line) and frequencies associated with relevant standards (such as the number of visits made to customers).

The appropriate hard measure to deliver to customer requirements is not always intuitive or obvious, and the potential for counting or tracking an irrelevant aspect of operations is high. For this reason it is desirable to link the measure of operational performance with soft measures (relationship surveys or follow-up satisfaction surveys) to be sure that they are strongly correlated.

Soft measurements

Two types of perceptual measurement that were described in Chapter 6 can document customers' opinions about whether performance met the standards established: satisfaction surveys and relationship surveys. Relationship and SERVQUAL surveys cover all aspects of the customer's relationship with the company, are typically expressed in attributes, and are usually completed once a year. Follow-up satisfaction surveys are associated with specific service encounters, are short (approximately six or seven questions) and are administered as close in time to a specific service encounter as possible. Such surveys can be administered in various ways: company-initiated telephone calls following the interactions, postcards to be mailed, letters requesting feedback, customer-initiated calls to a freephone number or online electronic surveys. For requirements that are longer term and at a higher level of abstraction (such as at the attribute level), annual relationship surveys can document customer perceptions on a periodic basis. Follow-up satisfaction surveys are administered continuously, whenever a customer experiences a service encounter of the type being considered, and they provide data on a continuous basis. The company must decide on a survey strategy combining relationship surveys and follow-up satisfaction surveys to provide soft measurement feedback.

Adapting standards globally or locally

How do companies adjust for cultural or local differences in service standards if they recognize that these geographic differences are related to varying customer expectations? Companies with worldwide brands have much to lose if their service standards vary too much across countries, and therefore they must find ways to achieve universally high quality while still allowing for local differences.

Service spotlight

As one of the world's leading operators of luxury hotels and resorts, Four Seasons manages 63 properties in 29 countries, and successfully accomplishes this goal by balancing universal services standards with standards that vary by country.[7] The company owes much of its success to its seven 'service culture standards' expected of *all* staff *all* over the world at *all* times. The seven standards, which form the acrostic SERVICE, are:

1 **S**mile: employees will actively greet guests, smile and speak clearly in a friendly manner
2 **E**ye: employees will make eye contact, even in passing, with an acknowledgement
3 **R**ecognition: all staff will create a sense of recognition by using the guest's name, when known, in a natural and discreet manner
4 **V**oice: staff will speak to guests in an attentive, natural and courteous manner, avoiding pretension and in a clear voice
5 **I**nformed: all guest contact staff will be well informed about their hotel, their product, will take ownership of simple requests, and will not refer guests elsewhere
6 **C**lean: staff will always appear clean, crisp, well groomed and well fitted
7 **E**veryone: everyone, everywhere, all the time, shows their care for our guests.

In addition to these culture standards that are expected of all staff all over the world, the hotel has 270 core standards that apply to different aspects of service provision (examples include 'the staff will be aware of arriving vehicles and will move toward them, opening

Service spotlight (continued)

doors within 30 seconds' and 'unanswered guest room phones will be picked up within 5 rings, or 20 seconds'). Exceptions to these 270 standards are allowed if they make local or cultural sense. For example, in the United States, coffee pots are left on tables at breakfast; in many parts of Europe, including France, customers perceive this practice as a lack of service and servers personally refill coffee cups as needed. Standards for uniforms and decor differ across cultures, but minimum expectations must be met everywhere.

Developing customer-defined standards

Figure 9.2 shows the general process for setting customer-defined service standards.

Step 1: Identify existing or desired service encounter sequence

The first step involves delineating the service encounter sequence. In many cases a service blueprint may be used to identify the service encounter sequence. Ideally, the company would be open to discovering customers' desired service encounter sequences, exploring the ways customers want to do business with the firm.

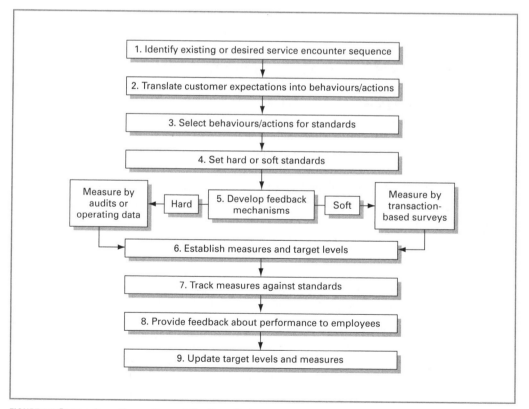

FIGURE 9.2 Process for setting customer-defined standards

Step 2: Translate customer expectations into behaviours and actions for each service encounter

The input to step 2 is existing research on customer expectations. In this step, abstract customer requirements and expectations must be translated into concrete, specific behaviours and actions associated with each service encounter. Abstract requirements (like reliability) can call for a different behaviour or action in each service encounter, and these differences must be probed. Eliciting these behaviours and actions is likely to require additional qualitative research because in most service companies, marketing information has not been collected for this purpose.

Information on behaviours and actions must be gathered and interpreted by an objective source such as a research firm or an internal department with no stake in the ultimate decisions. If the information is filtered through company managers or front-line people with an internal bias, the outcome would be company-defined rather than customer-defined standards.

Research techniques discussed in Chapter 6 that are relevant for eliciting behaviours and actions include in-depth interviewing of customers and focus group interviews.

Step 3: Select behaviours and actions for standards

This stage involves prioritizing the behaviours and actions, of which there will be many, into those for which customer-defined standards will be established. The following are the most important criteria for creation of the standards.

1 *The standards are based on behaviours and actions that are very important to customers.* Customers have many requirements for the products and services that companies provide. Customer-defined standards need to focus on what is *very important* to customers. Unless very important behaviours/actions are chosen, a company could show improvement in delivering to standards with no impact on overall customer satisfaction or business goals.

2 *The standards cover performance that needs to be improved or maintained.* Customer-defined standards should be established for behaviour that needs to be improved or maintained. The company gets the highest leverage or biggest impact from focusing on behaviours and actions that need to be improved. Figure 9.3 shows an importance/performance matrix for a computer manufacturer. It combines the importance and performance criteria and indicates them by the shading in the cell in the matrix where behaviours and actions should be selected to meet those criteria.

3 *The standards cover behaviours and actions employees can improve.* Employees perform consistently according to standards only if they understand, accept and have control over the behaviours and actions specified in the standards. Holding contact people to standards that they cannot control (such as product quality or time lag in introduction of new products) does not result in improvement. For this reason, service standards should cover controllable aspects of employees' jobs.

4 *The standards are accepted by employees.* Employees will perform to standards consistently only if they understand and accept the standards. Imposing standards on unwilling employees often leads to resistance, resentment, absenteeism, even turnover. Many companies establish standards for the amount of time it should take (rather than for the time it does take) for each service job and gradually cut back on the time to reduce labour costs. This practice inevitably leads to increasing tensions among

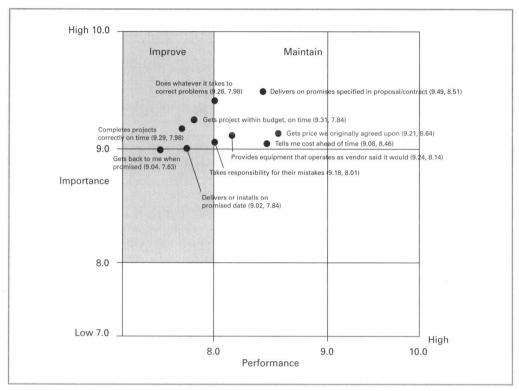

FIGURE 9.3 Importance/performance matrix: delivery, installing, performing

employees. In these situations, managers, financial personnel and union representatives can work together to determine new standards for the tasks.

5   *The standards are predictive rather than reactive.* Customer-defined standards should not be established on the basis of complaints or other forms of reactive feedback. Reactive feedback deals with past concerns of customers rather than with current and future customer expectations. Rather than waiting for dissatisfied customers to complain, the company should actively seek both positive and negative perceptions of customers in advance of complaints.

6   *The standards are challenging but realistic.* A large number of studies on goal-setting show that highest performance levels are obtained when standards are challenging but realistic. If standards are not challenging, employees get little reinforcement for mastering them. On the other hand, unrealistically high standards leave an employee feeling dissatisfied with performance and frustrated by not being able to attain the goal.

Table 9.1 shows an example of the set of behaviours and actions selected by a company for its complaint-handling service encounter. Some of these are different across the two segments of customers for which standards were set (small and large customers). Three other behaviours were chosen for standards across all customers.

Large customers	All complaint-handling personnel trained to
Are assigned an individual to call with complaints	Paraphrase problems
Have a four-hour standard for resolving problems	Ask customers what solution they prefer
Small customers	
Can call service centre or individual	Verify that problem has been fixed
Have an eight-hour standard for resolving problems	

TABLE 9.1 Customer-defined standards for complaint handling by segment

Step 4: Decide whether hard or soft standards are appropriate

The next step involves deciding whether hard or soft standards should be used to capture the behaviour and action. One of the biggest mistakes companies make in this step is to choose a hard standard hastily. Companies are accustomed to operational measures and have a bias towards them. However, unless the hard standard adequately captures the expected behaviour and action, it is not customer defined. The best way to decide whether a hard standard is appropriate is first to establish a soft standard by means of follow-up satisfaction surveys and then determine over time which operational aspect most correlates to this soft measure. Figure 9.4 shows the linkage between speed of complaint handling (a hard measure) and satisfaction (a soft measure), and illustrates that satisfaction strongly depends on the number of hours it takes to resolve a complaint.

Step 5: Develop feedback mechanisms for measurement to standards

Once companies have determined whether hard or soft standards are appropriate and which specific standards best capture customer requirements, they must develop feedback mechanisms that adequately capture the standards. Hard standards typically involve mechanical counts or technology-enabled measurement of time or errors. Soft standards require perceptual measure-

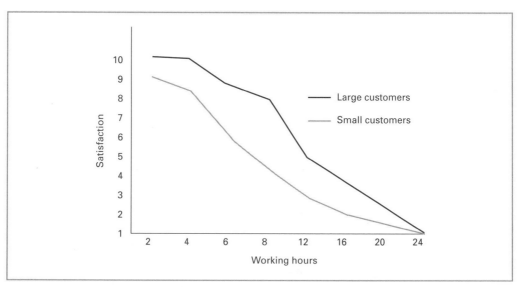

FIGURE 9.4 Linkage between soft and hard measures for speed of complaint handling

ments through the use of follow-up satisfaction surveys or employee monitoring. Employee monitoring is illustrated by the practice of supervisors listening in on employee calls. You may have experienced this practice when you called customer service numbers for many organizations and noticed that the voice prompts tell you that calls may be monitored for quality purposes. The purpose of this monitoring is to provide feedback on employee performance to the standards set by the organization to meet customer needs. One critical aspect of developing feedback mechanisms is ensuring that performance captures the process from the customer's view rather than the company's perspective. A supervisor monitoring an employee's handling of a customer service call, for example, should focus not so much on how quickly the employee gets the customer off the telephone as with how adequately he or she handles the customer's request.

Step 6: Establish measures and target levels

The next step requires that companies establish target levels for the standards. Without this step the company lacks a way to quantify whether the standards have been met. Figure 9.4 provided a good example of the approach used to set standards for timeliness in a service company. Each time a complaint was made to the company, and each time a complaint was resolved, employees logged in the times. They also asked each customer his or her satisfaction with the performance in resolving the complaint. The company was then able to plot the information from each complaint on the chart to determine how well the company was performing as well as where the company wished to be in the future. The vertical axis in Figure 9.4 shows the satisfaction levels of customers, and the horizontal axis shows the number of hours it took the company to resolve customer problems. This technique is one of several for determining the target level.

Another technique is a simple perception–action correlation study. When the service consists of repetitive processes, companies can relate levels of customer satisfaction with actual performance of a behaviour or task. Consider, for example, a study to determine the standard for customers' wait time in a line. The information needed includes customer perceptions of their wait in line (soft perceptual measure) and the amount of time they actually stand in line (hard operations measure). The joint collection of these data over many transactions provides evidence of the sensitivity of customers to different wait times.

An airline conducted precisely this study by having airline staff intercept customers as they approached the check-in counter. As each customer entered the line, the attendant stamped the entry time on a ticket and handed the customer the stamped ticket. As the customer exited the line at the end of the transaction, airline staff restamped the ticket with the exit time and asked the customer three or four questions about perceptions of the wait in line and satisfaction with the transaction. Aggregating the individual customer data provided a graph that allowed the company to evaluate the impact on perceptions of various levels of line waits.

Step 7: Track measures against standards

Since the quality movement of the 1980s, many techniques have been developed to track measures against standards. W. Edwards Deming, one of the most influential leaders of the quality movement, developed an approach called the P-D-C-A cycle (Plan-Do-Check-Act) that is applied to processes to measure and continuously improve their performance. Joseph Juran, another founder of the quality movement, was one of the first to apply statistical methods to improvement, leading to the widespread use of statistical process control as a way to measure performance to standards.

Step 8: Provide feedback about performance to employees

Data and facts need to be analysed and distributed to support evaluation and decision-making at multiple levels within the company. The data also must be deployed quickly enough that the people who need it to make decisions about service or processes can do so. Responsibility for meeting service requirements must also be communicated throughout the organization. All parts of the organization must be measuring their services to internal customers and, ultimately, measuring how that performance relates to external customer requirements.[8]

Step 9: Periodically update target levels and measures

The final step involves revising the target levels, measures and, even, customer requirements regularly enough to keep up with customer expectations.

Developing service performance indices

One outcome from following the process for developing customer-defined standards is a service performance index. *Service performance indices* are comprehensive composites of the most critical performance standards. Development of an index begins by identifying the set of customer-defined standards that the company will use to drive behaviour. Not all service performance indices contain customer-defined standards, but the best are based on them. Most companies build these indices by (1) understanding the most important requirements of the customer, (2) linking these requirements to tangible and measurable aspects of service provision, and (3) using the feedback from these indices to identify and improve service problems. The most progressive companies also use the feedback for reward and recognition systems within the company. Here are a few examples of service performance indices in some major companies.

Service spotlight

The Royal Bank of Scotland

Uses customer satisfaction, actual performance and operational measures as the drivers of service performance measurement. Qualitative research involving trade-off analysis was used to identify customers' perceptions of the key service attributes from a bank. These attributes were then established as service standards which were measured through an index which was constructed from scores relating to:

- Customer satisfaction questionnaire (70 per cent)
- Mystery shopping activity (20 per cent)
- An inventory of tangibles relating to physical aspects of each branch (10 per cent).

The attributes that were measured by each method are shown below:

Attributes	Satisfaction questionnaire	Mystery shopping	Inventory
Courtesy	X	X	
Telephone handling	X	X	
Queuing	X	X	
Product/service knowledge	X	X	
Problem-solving	X		
Efficiency	X		
Appearance	X	X	
Loyalty	X		
Tangibles			X

Service spotlight continued

London Underground

Measures service quality through customer satisfaction surveys, mystery shopping activities and the monitoring of complaints. However, the quality of service is also measured through operational information relating to areas such as:

♦ Percentage of trains cancelled
♦ Percentage of ticket offices open
♦ Percentage of ticket machines in operation
♦ Average journey times
♦ Headway: the average time between each train arriving at a platform.

These combine with the other service quality measures to provide guidance for management priorities and investment decisions.

Ritz-Carlton

Has created a service quality indicator (SQI). The Ritz's SQI spells out the 12 most serious defects that can occur in the operation of a hotel and weights them by their seriousness. The defects and points associated with them include:

1   Missing guest preferences (10 points)
2   Unresolved difficulties (50 points)
3   Inadequate guest-room housekeeping (1 point)
4   Abandoned reservation calls (5 points)
5   Guest-room changes (5 points)
6   Inoperable guest-room equipment (5 points)
7   Unready guest-room (10 points)
8   Inappropriate hotel appearance (5 points)
9   Meeting event difficulties (5 points)
10 Inadequate food/beverage (1 point)
11 Missing/damaged guest property/accidents (50 points)
12 Invoice adjustment (3 points).

The hotel calculates the SQI by multiplying the total number of occurrences by their points, totals the points and divides by the number of working days to get an average daily point value. This value is communicated every day to employees.[9]

Among the issues that companies must tackle when developing service performance indices are (1) the number of components to be contained, (2) what overall or summary measures will be included, (3) whether the index should be weighted or unweighted (to put greater emphasis on the performance of the attributes considered most important to customers), and (4) whether all parts of the business (departments, sectors or business units) will be held to the same performance measures. One of the most important goals of an index is to simply and clearly communicate business performance in operational and perceptual terms. Companies must develop the rigour in these measurement areas that they have in financial performance.

Summary

This chapter discussed the discrepancy between company perceptions of customer expectations and the standards they set to deliver to these expectations. Among the major causes for provider gap 2 are inadequate standardization of service behaviours and actions, absence of formal processes for setting service quality goals, and lack of customer-defined standards. These problems were discussed and detailed, along with strategies to close the gap.

Customer-defined standards are at the heart of delivery of service that customers expect: they are the link between customers' expressed expectations and company actions to deliver to those expectations. Creating these service standards is not always done by service organizations. Doing so requires that companies' marketing and operations departments work together by using the marketing research as input for operations design. Unless the operations standards are defined by customer priorities, they are not likely to have an impact on customer perceptions of service.

Key concepts

Customization v. standardization	220	One-time fixes	224
		Service performance indices	234
Goal-setting	221	Service standards	219
Hard customer-defined service standards	223	Soft customer-defined service standards	224
Measuring behaviours and attitudes	227		

Further reading.

Johnston, R. (1999) 'Service operations management: return to roots', *International Journal of Operations and Production Management*, 19(2), 104–24.

Kontoghiorges, C. (2003) 'Examining the association between quality and productivity performance in a service organization', *The Quality Management Journal*, 10(1), 32–42.

Parasuraman, A. (2002) 'Service quality and productivity: a synergistic perspective', *Managing Service Quality*, 12(1), 6–9.

Wilson, A. (2000) 'The use of performance information in the management of service delivery', *Marketing Intelligence and Planning*', 18(3), 127–34.

Discussion questions

1 How does the service measurement that we describe in this chapter differ from the service measurement in Chapter 6? Which of the two types do you think is most important? Why?

2 In what types of service industries are standards most difficult to develop? Why? Recommend three standards that might be developed in one of the firms from the industries you specify. How would employees react to these standards? How could you gain buy-in for them?

3 Given the need for customer-defined service standards, do firms need company-defined standards at all? Could all standards in a company be customer defined? Why or why not? What functional departments in a firm would object to having all standards customer defined?

4 What is the difference between hard and soft standards? Which do you think would be more readily accepted by employees? By management? Why?

5 Consider the university or college you currently attend. What are examples of hard standards, soft standards and one-time fixes that would address student requirements? Does the university or college currently use these standards for delivery of service to students? Why or why not? Do you think your reasons would apply to private sector companies as well? To public or non-profit companies?

6 Think about a service that you currently use, then map out the service encounter sequence for that service. What is your most important requirement in each interaction? Document these requirements, and make certain that they are expressed at the concrete level of behaviours and actions.

 ## Exercises

1 Select a local service firm. Visit the firm and ascertain the service measurements that the company tracks. What hard measures does it monitor? Soft measures? On the basis of what you find, develop a service performance index.

2 Choose one of the peripheral services (such as computer, library, placement) provided by your university or college. What hard standards would be useful to track to meet student expectations? What soft standards? What one-time fixes would improve service?

3 Think about a specific service that you have delivered or received. Using Figure 9.1, write in the customer requirements at each of the levels. How far down in the chart can you describe requirements? Is that far enough? What would you need to do to find out more?

4 Look at three websites from which you can order products (such as amazon.co.uk or tesco.com). What are the companies' delivery promises? What types of standards might they set for these promises? Are these customer- or company-defined standards?

Notes

[1] T. Levitt, 'Industrialization of service', *Harvard Business Review* (September–October 1976), pp. 63–74.

[2] B.S. Lunde and S.L. Marr, 'Customer satisfaction measurement: does it pay off?' (Indianapolis, IN: Walker Customer Satisfaction Measurements, 1990).

3 'Fast, reliable delivery processes are cheered by time-sensitive customers', *The Service Edge* 4, no. 3 (1993), 1.

4 F. Reichheld, 'e-loyalty', *Harvard Business Review* (July–August 2000), pp. 105–13.

5 D.E. Hansen and P.J. Danaher, 'Inconsistent performance during the service encounter: what's a good start worth?', *Journal of Service Research* 1 (February 1999), pp. 227–35.

6 'Taking the measure of quality', *Service Savvy* (March 1992), p. 3.

7 This discussion about the Four Seasons is based on R. Hallowell, D. Bowen and C. Knoop, 'Four Seasons goes to Paris', *Academy of Management Executive* 16, no. 4 (2002), pp. 7–24.

8 'Taking the measure of quality', p. 3.

9 1999 application summary for The Ritz-Carlton Hotel Company, Malcolm Baldrige National Quality Award, 2000.

Physical evidence and the servicescape

This chapter's objectives are to:

1 Explain the profound impact of physical evidence, particularly the servicescape, on customer perceptions and experiences.

2 Illustrate differences in types of servicescapes, the roles played by the servicescape, and the implications for strategy.

3 Explain *why* the servicescape affects customer and employee behaviour, using a framework based in marketing, organizational behaviour and environmental psychology.

4 Present elements of an effective physical evidence strategy.

CASE STUDY: MCDONALD'S ADAPTS SERVICESCAPES TO FIT THE CULTURE

People's reactions to elements of the physical environment and design are shaped to a large degree by culture and expectations they have formed through their life experiences, dominated by the culture they live in. Just think of one design element – colour – and the variety of uses it has across cultures. Consider the commonly used earth tones in the decor of Japanese restaurants around the world compared with the glossy reds that are so evident in Chinese restaurants. Other cultural differences – personal space requirements, social distance preferences, sensitivity to crowding – can affect how consumers experience servicescapes around the world.

McDonald's Corporation recognizes these culturally defined expectations in allowing its franchisees around the world tremendous freedom in designing their servicescapes. In most McDonald's franchises, a large percentage of the ownership is retained locally. Employees are nationals, and marketing strategies reflect local consumers' buying and preference patterns. In all cases, the restaurant is a 'community institution', involved in social causes as well as local events.

McDonald's strategy is to have its restaurants worldwide reflect the cultures and communities in which they are found – to mirror the communities they serve. At the same time that it allows this creative energy to flourish in design and marketing strategies, McDonald's is extremely tight on its operating procedures and menu standards.

Although the golden arches are always present, a brief tour around the globe shows the wide variation in McDonald's face to the community:

♦ Bologna, Italy: in Bologna, known as the 'City of Arches' for hundreds of years, McDonald's has taken on the weathered, crafted look of the neighbouring historic arches. Even the floor in the restaurant was done by hand, using old-world techniques. The restaurant used local architects and artists to bring the local architectural feel to the golden arches.

♦ Paris, France: near the Sorbonne in Paris, the local McDonald's reflects its studious neighbour. The servicescape there has the look of a leather-bound library with books, statues and heavy wood furniture.

♦ Salen, Sweden: on the slopes of Lindvallen Resort in Salen, you can find the world's first 'ski-thru' restaurant, named McSki, located next to the main ski lift. The building is different from any other McDonald's restaurant, built in a typical mountain style with wood panels and natural stone from the surroundings. Skiers can simply glide to the counter without taking off their skis, or they can be seated indoors or out.

♦ Beijing, China: McDonald's restaurants here have become a 'place to hang out', very different from the truly 'fast-food' role they play in the United States. They are part of the community, serving young and old, families and couples. Customers can be seen lingering for long periods of time, relaxing, chatting, reading, enjoying the music or celebrating birthdays. Teenagers and young couples even find the restaurants to be very romantic environments. The emphasis on a Chinese-style family atmosphere is apparent from the interior walls of local restaurants, which are covered by posters emphasizing family values.

♦ Tokyo, Japan: although some McDonald's restaurants in Japan are located in prime real-estate districts such as the Ginza in Tokyo, many others are situated near major train stations or other high-traffic locations. The emphasis at these locations is on convenience and speed, not on comfort or socializing. Many of these locations have little frontage space and limited seating. Customers frequently stand while eating, or they may sit on stools at narrow counters. Even the elite Ginza location has few seats. Some locations have a small ordering and service area on the first floor, with limited seating (still primarily stools rather than tables and chairs) on the second floor. Young people – from teenagers to schoolchildren – are a common sight in Japanese McDonald's.

Sources: *Golden Arches East: McDonald's in East Asia*, ed. J.L. Watson (Stanford, CA: Stanford University Press, 1997); 'A unique peak', *Franchise Times* 3, no. 4 (1997), p. 46; 'McDonald's turns up the heat on fast food', Video Case Series accompanying C.L. Bovee, M.J. Houston and J.V. Thill, *Marketing*, 2nd edn (New York: McGraw-Hill, 1995).

In this chapter we explore the importance of physical evidence for communicating service quality attributes, setting customer expectations, and creating the service experience. In Chapter 1, when we introduced the expanded marketing mix for services, we defined physical evidence as *the environment in which the service is delivered and in which the firm and the customer interact, and any tangible commodities that facilitate performance or communication of the service*. The first part of this definition encompasses the actual physical facility in which the service is performed, delivered and consumed; throughout this chapter the physical facility is referred to as the ***servicescape***[1].

Physical evidence is particularly important for communicating about credence services (such as hairstyling), but it is also important for services such as hotels, hospitals and theme parks that are dominated by experience attributes. Think of how effectively Disney uses the physical evidence of its service to excite its customers. The brightly coloured displays, the music, the fantastic rides and the costumed characters all reinforce the feelings of fun and excitement that Disney seeks to generate in its customers. Think also of how effective Disney is in portraying consistent physical evidence that is compatible with its goals. The physical evidence and servicescape, or the 'stage' in Disney's terms, is always stimulating to the extreme, is always clean, is always in top repair and never fails to deliver what it has promised to consumers, and more. In this chapter we present many examples of how physical evidence communicates with customers and how it can play a role in creating the service experience, in satisfying customers, and in enhancing customers' perceptions of quality.

Physical evidence

What is physical evidence?

Because services are intangible, customers often rely on tangible cues, or physical evidence, to evaluate the service before its purchase and to assess their satisfaction with the service during and after consumption. Effective design of physical, tangible evidence is important for closing gap 2.

General elements of physical evidence are shown in Table 10.1. They include all aspects of the organization's physical facility (the servicescape) as well as other forms of tangible communication. Elements of the servicescape that affect customers include both exterior attributes (such as signage, parking, and the landscape) and interior attributes (such as design, layout, equipment and decor). Note that web pages and **virtual servicescapes** conveyed over the Internet are more recent forms of physical evidence that companies can use to communicate about the service experience, making services more tangible for customers both before and after purchase. For example, travellers can now preview destinations, view hotels and their rooms, tour natural environments and 'experience' entertainment venues online before booking their trips or even deciding where to travel. Virtual tours and 360-degree views can allow the potential guests to view the exterior of the facilities as well as the actual rooms available.

Service spotlight

Sofitel, the upmarket hotel chain owned by the French company Accor allows potential guests to undertake a virtual visit to each of their hotels on their website (www.sofitel.com) using 360-degree views of their public rooms and bedrooms. Users can move around the individual images by clicking on the left-hand button of their mouse. They can also zoom in by pushing their mouse cursor towards the centre of the screen.

Servicescape	Other tangibles
Facility exterior	Business cards
Exterior design	Stationery
Signage	Billing statements
Parking	Reports
Landscape	Employee dress
Surrounding environment	Uniforms
Facility interior	Brochures
Interior design	Web pages
Equipment	Virtual servicescape
Signage	
Layout	
Air quality/temperature	
Lighting	
Floor coverings	
Aromas/scents	

TABLE 10.1 Elements of physical evidence

Internet technology clearly provides tremendous opportunities for firms to communicate about their services. Tangible images on the Web create expectations for customers that set standards for service delivery, and it is critical that the actual services live up to these expectations. Images and virtual service tours presented on the Internet also need to support the positioning of the service brand and be consistent with other marketing messages.

Physical evidence examples from different service contexts are given in Table 10.2. It is apparent that some services (like hospitals, resorts and child care) rely heavily on physical evidence to communicate and create customer experiences. Others (insurance, express mail) provide limited physical evidence for customers. All the elements of evidence listed for each service communicate something about the service to consumers, facilitate performance of the service and/or add to the customer's total experience. Although we focus in this chapter primarily

	Physical evidence	
Service	**Servicescape**	**Other tangibles**
Insurance	Not applicable	Policy itself
		Billing statements
		Periodic updates
		Company brochure
		Letters/cards
		Website
Hotel	Building exterior	Uniforms
	Parking	Reports/stationery
	Reception area	Billing statements
	Lift/corridors	Website
	Bedroom	
	Bathroom	
	Restaurant layout	
	Bar	
	Leisure facilities	
Airline	Airline check-in area	Tickets
	Airline gate area	Food
	Airplane exterior	Uniforms
	Airplane interior (decor, seats, air quality)	Website
Express mail	Not applicable	Packaging
		Vehicles
		Uniforms
		Computers
		Website
Sporting event	Parking	Signs
	Stadium exterior	Tickets
	Ticketing area	Programmes
	Entrance	Uniforms
	Seating	Website
	Toilets	
	Catering outlets	
	Playing field	

TABLE 10.2 Examples of physical evidence from the customer's point of view

on the servicescape and its effects, keep in mind that what is said applies to the other forms of evidence as well.

How does physical evidence affect the customer experience?

Physical evidence, particularly the servicescape, can have a profound effect on the customer experience. This is true whether the experience is mundane (e.g. a bus or train ride), personally meaningful (e.g. a wedding or a birthday celebration), or spectacular (e.g. a week-long travel adventure). In all cases, the physical evidence of the service will influence the flow of the experience, the meaning customers attach to it, their satisfaction and their emotional connections with the organization delivering the experience.

As marketers and corporate strategists begin to pay more attention to experiences, they have recognized the impact of physical space and tangibles in creating those experiences. Lewis Carbone, a leading consultant on experience management, has developed an entire lexicon and management process around the basic idea of 'experience engineering' through '**clue management**'.[2] *Clue management* refers to the process of clearly identifying and managing *all* the various clues that customers use to form their impressions and feelings about the company. Included in this set of clues are what Carbone refers to as *mechanics clues*, or the physical and tangible clues that we focus on in this chapter. Other writers and consultants who focus on managing customer experiences also zero in on the importance of tangible evidence and physical facilities in shaping those experiences.[3] Throughout this chapter are numerous examples of how physical evidence communicates with customers and shapes their experiences.

Types of servicescapes

In this chapter we explain the roles played by the servicescape and how it affects employees and customers and their interactions. The chapter relies heavily on ideas and concepts from **environmental psychology**, a field that encompasses the study of human beings and their relationships with built (human-made), natural and social environments.[4] The physical setting may be more or less important in achieving the organization's marketing and other goals depending on certain factors. Table 10.3 is a framework for categorizing service organizations on two dimensions that capture some of the key differences that will impact the management of the servicescape. Organizations that share a cell in the matrix will face similar issues and decisions regarding their physical spaces.

Servicescape usage

First, organizations differ in terms of *who* the servicescape will actually affect. That is, who actually comes into the service facility and thus is potentially influenced by its design – customers, employees, or both groups? The first column of Table 10.3 suggests three types of service organizations that differ on this dimension. At one extreme is the *self-service* environment, in which the customer performs most of the activities and few if any employees are involved. Examples of self-service environments include ATMs, cinemas, self-service entertainment such as golf courses and theme parks, and online Internet services. In these primarily self-service environments the organization can plan the servicescape to focus exclusively on marketing goals such as attracting the right market segment, making the facility pleasing and easy to use, and creating the desired service experience.

	Complexity of the servicescape	
Servicescape usage	**Elaborate**	**Lean**
Self-service (customer only)	Golf course eBay	ATM Car wash Simple Internet services
Interpersonal services (both customer and employee)	Hotel Restaurant Health clinic Hospital Bank Airline School	Dry cleaner Hair salon
Remote service (employee only)	Telephone company Insurance company Utility Many professional services	Telephone mail-order desk Automated voice-messaging services

TABLE 10.3 Typology of service organizations based on variations in form and use of the servicescape
Source: From M.J. Bitner, 'Servicescapes: the impact of physical surroundings on customers and employees', *Journal of Marketing* 56 (April 1992), pp. 57–71. Reprinted with permission of the American Marketing Association

At the other extreme of the use dimension is the *remote service*, which has little or no customer involvement with the servicescape. Telecommunications, utilities, financial consultants and mail-order services are examples of services that can be provided without the customer ever seeing the service facility. In fact, the facility may be in a different region or a different country. In remote services, the facility can be set up to keep employees motivated and to facilitate productivity, teamwork, operational efficiency or whatever organizational behaviour goal is desired without any consideration of customers because they will never need to see the servicescape.

In Table 10.3, *interpersonal services* are placed between the two extremes and represent situations in which both the customer and the employee are present and active in the servicescape. Examples abound, such as hotels, restaurants, hospitals, educational settings and banks. In these situations the servicescape must be planned to attract, satisfy and facilitate the activities of both customers and employees simultaneously. Special attention must also be given to how the servicescape affects the nature and quality of the social interactions between and among customers and employees. A cruise ship provides a good example of a setting in which the servicescape must support customers and the employees who work there, and facilitate interactions between the two groups.

Servicescape complexity

The horizontal dimension of Table 10.3 suggests another factor that will influence servicescape management. Some service environments are very simple, with few elements, few spaces and few pieces of equipment. Such environments are termed *lean*. Shopping-centre information kiosks and ATMs would be considered lean environments because both provide service from one simple structure. For lean servicescapes, design decisions are relatively straightforward, especially in self-service or remote service situations in which there is no interaction among employees and customers.

Other servicescapes are very complicated, with many elements and many forms. They are termed *elaborate* environments. An example is a hotel with its many floors and rooms, sophisticated equipment and complex variability in functions performed within the physical facility. In such an elaborate environment, the full range of marketing and organizational objectives theoretically can be approached through careful management of the servicescape. For example, a guest's hotel room can be designed to enhance comfort and satisfaction while simultaneously facilitating low-energy usage and costs. Firms such as hotels that are positioned in the elaborate interpersonal service cell face the most complex servicescape decisions.

Strategic roles of the servicescape

Within the cells of the typology, the servicescape can play many strategic roles simultaneously. An examination of the variety of roles and how they interact makes clear how strategically important it is to provide appropriate physical evidence of the service. In fact, the servicescape is frequently one of *the* most important elements used in positioning a service organization.

Package

Similar to a tangible product's package, the servicescape and other elements of physical evidence essentially 'wrap' the service and convey to consumers an external image of what is 'inside'. Product packages are designed to portray a particular image as well as to evoke a particular sensory or emotional reaction. The physical setting of a service does the same thing through the interaction of many complex stimuli. The servicescape is the outward appearance of the organization and thus can be critical in forming initial impressions or setting up customer expectations – it is a visual metaphor for the intangible service. This packaging role is particularly important in creating expectations for new customers and for newly established service organizations that are trying to build a particular image. The physical surroundings offer an organization the opportunity to convey an image in a way not unlike the way an individual chooses to 'dress for success'. The packaging role extends to the appearance of contact personnel through their uniforms or dress and other elements of their outward appearance.[5]

Service spotlight

Metropolitano de Lisboa is the underground railway network of Lisbon, the capital of Portugal. With an environment that was austere and basic, it was a system tolerated rather than loved. In 1998, Lisbon was to host Expo '98, resulting in the prospect of 12 million extra passengers on the underground. Design consultants were brought in to create a fresh up-to-date style for the network. The Metro's original architectural strategy was to build each new station with a strong individual character. Wolff Olins worked to create a simpler experience for the traveller. They developed a family of standard elements common to all stations, so that the Metro identity was expressed throughout the system. These elements included a pylon and illuminated symbol to identify the stations at street level and, within stations, ticket sales booths, ticket machines, barriers and platform furniture.[6]

Interestingly, the same care and resource expenditures given to **package** design in product marketing are often not provided for services, even though the service package serves a variety of important roles. There are many exceptions to this generality, however. Smart companies like H&M, KLM and Novotel spend a lot of time and money relating their servicescape design to their brand, providing their customers with strong visual metaphors and 'service packaging' that conveys the brand positioning.

Facilitator

The servicescape can also serve as a **facilitator** in aiding the performance of persons in the environment. How the setting is designed can enhance or inhibit the efficient flow of activities in the service setting, making it easier or harder for customers and employees to accomplish their goals. A well-designed, functional facility can make the service a pleasure to experience from the customer's point of view and a pleasure to perform from the employee's. On the other hand, poor and inefficient design may frustrate both customers and employees. For example, an international air traveller who finds him or herself in a poorly designed airport with few signs, poor ventilation and few places to sit or eat will find the experience quite dissatisfying, and employees who work there will probably be unmotivated as well. The same international traveller will appreciate seats on the aeroplane that are conducive to work and sleep. The seating itself, part of the physical surroundings of the service, has been improved over the years to better facilitate travellers' needs to sleep. In fact, the competition for better seat design continues as a major point of contention among the international airline carriers, and the results have translated into greater customer satisfaction for business travellers.[7] British Airways has even seen its market share increase on some routes as a direct result of its award-winning Club-World seat.[8] As hotels begin development of new prototype rooms in the early 2000s, they are focusing on making the rooms more useful to their guests who are spending more time in their hotel rooms than they used to. Rooms are being designed with colours, fabrics and textures that have a homelike look, and the new hotels are putting in bigger desks, more high-speed Internet connections, and larger flat screen televisions.[9] All these examples emphasize the facilitator role of the servicescape.

Socializer

The design of the servicescape aids in the socialization of both employees and customers in the sense that it helps convey expected roles, behaviours and relationships. For example, a new employee in a professional services firm would come to understand his or her position in the hierarchy partly through noting the office he or she has been allocated, the quality of the office furnishings and his or her location relative to others in the organization.

The design of the facility can also suggest to customers what their role is relative to employees, what parts of the servicescape they are welcome in and which are for employees only, how they should behave while in the environment and what types of interactions are encouraged. For example, consider a Club Med vacation environment that is set up to facilitate customer–customer interactions as well as guest interactions with Club Med staff. The organization also recognizes the need for privacy, providing areas that encourage solitary activities. To illustrate further, in many Starbucks locations, the company has shifted to more of a traditional coffeehouse environment in which customers spend social time rather than coming in for a quick cup of coffee on the run. To encourage this type of socializing, these Starbucks locations have comfortable lounge chairs and tables set up to encourage customers to interact and to stay longer.

Differentiator

The design of the physical facility can differentiate a firm from its competitors and signal the market segment that the service is intended for. Given its power as a **differentiator**, changes in the physical environment can be used to reposition a firm and/or to attract new market segments. In shopping malls the signage, colours used in decor and displays, and type of music wafting from a store signal the intended market segment.

Service spotlight

In the banking industry, Omega Bank, a private bank with branches across Greece, has designed its branch interiors to communicate a feeling of 'understated quality', avoiding ostentation and short-lived trendiness. Instead of using Greek marble and granite, they imported honed green slate from the Lake District in the UK for the flooring which better matched the 'understated quality' image. The teller desks were designed in etched glass and steel, with maple timber slab ends. Aesthetically, they are meant to be very open and welcoming in appearance, accentuated by 'floating' all the surface planes on stainless steel spacers, so that none of the major elements actually touch each other.

The same design system is incorporated into graphic and print items such as banking and ATM cards, promotional leaflets and private banking communication and print items.[10]

The design of a physical setting can also differentiate one area of a service organization from another. For example, in the hotel industry, one large hotel may have several levels of dining possibilities, each signalled by differences in design. Price differentiation is also often partly achieved through variations in physical setting. Bigger rooms with more physical amenities cost more, just as larger seats with more leg room (generally in first class) are more expensive on an airline.

Framework for understanding servicescape effects on behaviour

Although it is useful from a strategic point of view to think about the multiple roles of the servicescape and how they interact, making actual decisions about servicescape design requires an understanding of why the effects occur and how to manage them. The next sections of the chapter present a framework or model of environment and behaviour relationships in service settings.

The underlying framework

The framework for understanding servicescape effects on behaviour follows from basic **stimulus–organism–response theory**. In the framework the multidimensional environment is the *stimulus*, consumers and employees are the *organisms* that respond to the stimuli, and behaviours directed at the environment are the *responses*. The assumptions are that dimensions of the servicescape will impact customers and employees and that they will behave in certain ways depending on their internal reactions to the servicescape.

A specific example will help illustrate the theory in action. Assume there is a fresh coffee

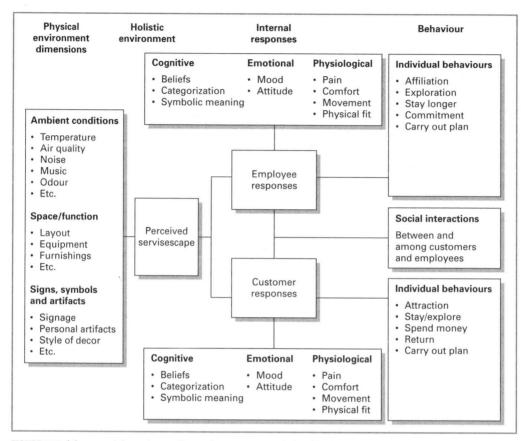

FIGURE 10.1 A framework for understanding environment–user relationships in service organizations

Source: adapted from M.J. Bitner, 'Servicescapes: the impact of physical surroundings on customers and employees', *Journal of Marketing* 56 (April 1992), pp. 57–71. Reprinted with permission of the American Marketing Association

outlet close to the lecture theatres on a university campus. The coffee outlet has large comfortable sofas, and an aroma of fresh coffee wafts from it. The design and the aroma are two elements of the servicescape that will impact customers in some way. Now assume you are a tired student, just out of class, strolling across campus. The comfortable sofas attract your attention, and simultaneously you smell the coffee. The furniture and the delicious smell cause you to feel happy, relaxed and thirsty at the same time. You are attracted to the coffee outlet and decide to buy a coffee and cookie because you have another class to attend before lunch. The movement toward the outlet and the purchase of a coffee are behaviours directed at the servicescape. Depending on how much time you have, you may even choose to relax in a sofa and read a newspaper with your coffee, other forms of behaviour directed at the servicescape.

The framework shown in Figure 10.1 is detailed in the next sections. It represents a comprehensive stimulus–organism–response model that recognizes complex dimensions of the environment, impacts on multiple parties (customers, employees and their interactions), multiple types of internal responses (cognitive, emotional and physiological) and a variety of individual and social behaviours that can result.

Our discussion of the framework begins on the right side of the model with *behaviours*. Next we explain and develop the *internal responses* portion of the model. Finally we turn to the dimensions of the *environment* and the holistic perception of the environment.

Behaviours in the servicescape

That human behaviour is influenced by the physical setting in which it occurs is essentially a truism. Interestingly, however, until the 1960s psychologists largely ignored the effects of physical setting in their attempts to predict and explain behaviour. Since that time, a large and steadily growing body of literature within the field of environmental psychology has addressed the relationships between human beings and their built environments. Recent marketing focus on the customer experience has also drawn attention to the effects of physical spaces and design on customer behaviour.[11]

Individual behaviours

Environmental psychologists suggest that individuals react to places with two general, and opposite, forms of behaviour: approach and avoidance. Approach behaviours include all positive behaviours that might be directed at a particular place, such as desire to stay, explore, work and affiliate.[12] Avoidance behaviours reflect the opposite – a desire not to stay, to explore, to work or to affiliate. In a study of consumers in retail environments, researchers found that approach behaviours (including shopping enjoyment, returning, attraction and friendliness towards others, spending money, time spent browsing, and exploration of the store) were influenced by perceptions of the environment.[13] At one 7-Eleven store the owners played 'easy-listening music' to drive away the youthful market segment that was detracting from the store's image. And our coffee outlet example is reminiscent of bakeries in supermarkets that attract patrons through the power of smell.

In addition to attracting or deterring entry, the servicescape can actually influence the degree of success that consumers and employees experience in executing their plans once inside. Each individual comes to a particular service organization with a goal or purpose that may be aided or hindered by the setting. Sports fans are aided in their enjoyment of the game by adequate and easy-access parking, clear signage directing them to their seats, efficient food service and clean washrooms. The ability of employees to do their jobs effectively is also influenced by the servicescape. Adequate space, proper equipment, and comfortable temperature and air quality all contribute to an employee's comfort and job satisfaction, causing him or her to be more productive, stay longer and affiliate positively with co-workers.

FIGURE 10.2 Social interactions are defined partly by the configuration of the servicescape
Source: Carnival Cruise Lines

Social interactions

In addition to its effects on their individual behaviours, the servicescape influences the nature and quality of customer and employee interactions, most directly in interpersonal services. It has been stated that 'all social interaction is affected by the physical container in which it occurs'.[14] The 'physical container' can affect the nature of social interaction in terms of the duration of interaction and the actual progression of events. In many service situations, a firm may want to ensure a particular progression of events (a 'standard script') and limit the duration of the service. Environmental variables such as physical proximity, seating arrangements, size and flexibility can define the possibilities and limits of social episodes such as those occurring between customers and employees, or customers and other customers. The Carnival Cruise Line photograph shown in Figure 10.2 illustrates how the design of the servicescape can help define the social rules, conventions and expectations in force in a given setting, thus serving to define the nature of social interaction.[15] The close physical proximity of passengers on the sunbathing deck will in and of itself prescribe certain patterns of behaviour. This vacation is not designed for a social recluse! Some researchers have implied that recurring social behaviour patterns are associated with particular physical settings and that when people encounter typical settings, their social behaviours can be predicted.[16]

Service spotlight: Nike Town, London

> ❝ 'Nike Town', a retail concept that exists in London and fifteen other locations around the world, is built as a theatre, where our consumers are the audience participating in the production. Nike Town gives us the opportunity to explore and experiment with innovative ways to connect with our consumers. (Nike press release) ❞

Nike Towns epitomize the role of servicescape design in building the brand, providing customers with a way to interact with the brand, and making Nike come alive. Nike Town represents the height of retail theatre.

So what is so special about Nike Town? What sets it apart from other retail environments? First, it is a showcase for the full range of Nike products. A common reaction of consumers is that they had no idea Nike made and carried all of the products displayed. And every designed element of the servicescape encourages impulsive behaviour, inviting instant gratification. But the prices are very high – higher than prices on the same items in other stores. This is by design. Here the servicescape and the experience of Nike Town are meant to build the brand – not necessarily to sell the products and especially not to compete with other Nike stores and dealers.

The Nike Town store in London is a concept 'town'. Buildings, each housing a specific sport, surround a central square, the store's focal point. In its centre sits the core – a three-storey high, 360-degree projector screen – which springs to life every 20 minutes; as window blinds are snapped shut, customers are then surrounded by Nike sports images. Nike Town is more than just a shop; each week there are special events, athletes come in for interviews, they even organize a running club. With 70 000 square foot of shopping space they manage to fit everything in, and more besides. The store boasts the largest women's sports clothing and footwear area in Europe.[17]

Examples of how environments shape social interactions – and how these interactions in turn influence the environment – are abundant.[18] Even casual observation of the retail phenomenon 'Nike Town' shows how this form of 'entertainment retail' shapes the behaviours of consumers but at the same time allows them to interpret and create their own realities and experiences.[19] In a white-water rafting trip, the 'wilderness servicescape' profoundly influences the behaviours, interactions and total experiences of rafting consumers and their guides. In this case the natural, and for the most part uncontrollable, environment is the setting for the service.[20]

Internal responses to the servicescape

Employees and customers respond to dimensions of their physical surroundings cognitively, emotionally and physiologically, and those responses are what influence their behaviours in the environment (as shown in the middle portion of Figure 10.1). In other words, the perceived servicescape does not directly *cause* people to behave in certain ways. Although the internal responses are discussed independently here, they are clearly interdependent: a person's beliefs about a place, a cognitive response, may well influence the person's emotional response, and vice versa. For example, patients who come into a dentist's waiting room that is designed to calm and sooth their anxieties (emotional responses) may believe as a result that the dentist is caring and competent (cognitive responses).

Environment and cognition

The perceived servicescape can have an effect on people's beliefs about a place and their beliefs about the people and products found in that place. In a sense the servicescape can be viewed as a form of non-verbal communication, imparting meaning through what is called 'object language'.[21] For example, particular environmental cues such as the type of office furniture and decor and the clothing worn by the lawyer may influence a potential client's beliefs about whether the lawyer is successful, expensive and trustworthy. In a consumer study, variations in descriptions of store atmospheres were found to alter beliefs about a product (perfume) sold in the store.[22] Another study showed that a travel agent's office decor affected customer attributions and beliefs about the travel agent's behaviour.[23] Travel agents whose facilities were more organized and professional were viewed more positively than were those whose facilities were disorganized and unprofessional.

In other cases, perceptions of the servicescape may simply help people distinguish a firm by influencing how it is categorized. The overall perception of the servicescape enables the consumer or employee to categorize the firm mentally. Research shows that in the restaurant industry a particular configuration of environmental cues such as hard furnishings suggests 'fast food', whereas another configuration (soft furnishings) suggests 'elegant sit-down restaurant'.[24] In such situations, environmental cues serve as a shortcut device that enables customers to categorize and distinguish among types of restaurants.

Environment and emotion

In addition to influencing beliefs, the perceived servicescape can directly elicit emotional responses that, in turn, influence behaviours. Just being in a particular place can make a person feel happy, light-hearted and relaxed, whereas being in another place may make that person feel sad, depressed and gloomy. The colours, decor, music and other elements of the atmosphere can have an unexplainable and sometimes subconscious effect on the moods of people in the place. For some people, certain environmental stimuli (noises, smells) common in a dental office can bring on immediate feelings of fear and anxiety. In very different contexts, the marble interior and grandeur of a government building or palace may call up feelings of pride and respect; lively music and bright decor in a local night spot may cause people to feel excited and happy. In all these examples, the response from the consumer probably does not involve thinking but, rather, is just an unexplained feeling. Consumers' responses to Nike Town (on page 251) are in large part emotional.

Service spotlight

Tiso Outdoor Experience stores in the UK provide another example of emotional connection through architectural design and the servicescape. At its flagship store in Glasgow, the company has created an experience for consumers that includes a climbing mountain, a bicycle track and walking trails.

Environmental psychologists have researched people's emotional responses to physical settings.[25] They have concluded that any environment, whether natural or engineered, will elicit emotions that can be captured by two basic dimensions: (1) pleasure/displeasure and (2) degree of arousal (amount of stimulation or excitement). Servicescapes that are both pleasant and arousing would be termed *exciting*, whereas those that are pleasant and non-arousing, or sleepy, would be termed *relaxing*. Unpleasant servicescapes that are arousing would be called *distressing*, whereas unpleasant, sleepy servicescapes would be *gloomy*. These basic emotional responses to environments can be used to begin predicting the expected behaviours of consumers and employees who find themselves in a particular type of place.

Environment and physiology

The perceived servicescape may also affect people in purely physiological ways. Noise that is too loud may cause physical discomfort, the temperature of a room may cause people to shiver or perspire, the air quality may make it difficult to breathe, and the glare of lighting may decrease ability to see and may cause physical pain. All these physical responses may, in turn, directly influence whether people stay in and enjoy a particular environment. It is well known that the comfort of seating in a restaurant influences how long people stay. The hard seats in a fast-food restaurant cause most people to leave within a predictable period of time, whereas the soft, cozy chairs in some Starbucks coffee shops have the opposite effect, encouraging people to stay. Similarly, environmental design and related physiological responses affect whether employees can perform their job functions well.

A vast amount of research in engineering and design has addressed human physiological responses to ambient conditions as well as physiological responses to equipment design.[26] Such research fits under the rubric of *human factors design* or *ergonomics*. Human factors research systematically applies relevant information about human capabilities and limitations to the design of items and procedures that people use. For example, First Group, one of the largest bus operators in the UK, has introduced new low-floor buses to offer easier access for parents with pushchairs, wheelchairs and the elderly.

Variations in individual responses

In general, people respond to the environment in the ways just described – cognitively, emotionally, physiologically – and their responses influence how they behave in the environment. However, the response will not be the same for every individual, every time. Personality differences as well as temporary conditions such as moods or the purpose for being there can cause variations in how people respond to the servicescape.[27]

One personality trait that has been shown to affect how people respond to environments is *arousal-seeking*. Arousal-seekers enjoy and look for high levels of stimulation, whereas arousal-avoiders prefer lower levels of stimulation. Thus an arousal-avoider in a loud, bright disco with flashing lights might show strong dislike for the environment, whereas an arousal-seeker would be very happy. In a related vein, it has been suggested that some people are better *screeners* of environmental stimuli than others.[28] Screeners of stimuli would be able to experience a high level of stimulation but not be affected by it. Non-screeners would be highly affected and might exhibit extreme responses even to low levels of stimulation.

The particular purpose for being in a servicescape can also affect a person's response to it. A person who is on an aeroplane for a one-hour flight will likely be less affected by the atmosphere on the plane than will the traveller who is embarking on a 14-hour long-haul flight. Similarly, a day-surgery hospital patient will likely be less sensitive and demanding of the hospital environment than would a patient who is spending two weeks in the hospital. And a person who is staying at a hotel for a business meeting will respond differently to the environment than will a couple on their honeymoon.

Temporary mood states can also cause people to respond differently to environmental stimuli. A person who is feeling frustrated and fatigued after a long day at work is likely to be affected differently by a highly arousing restaurant than the person would be after a relaxing three-day weekend.

Environmental dimensions of the servicescape

The preceding sections have described customer and employee behaviours in the servicescape and the three primary responses – cognitive, emotional and physiological – that lead to those behaviours. In this section we turn to the complex mix of environmental features that influence these responses and behaviours (the left-hand portion of Figure 10.1). Specifically, **environmental dimensions** of the physical surroundings can include all the objective physical factors that can be controlled by the firm to enhance (or constrain) employee and customer actions. There is an endless list of possibilities: lighting, colour, signage, textures, quality of materials, style of furnishings, layout, wall decor, temperature, and so on. In Figure 10.1 and in the discussion that follows here, the hundreds of potential elements have been categorized into three composite dimensions: *ambient conditions*; *spatial layout and functionality*; and *signs, symbols and artifacts*.

Although we discuss the three dimensions separately, environmental psychology explains that people respond to their environments holistically. That is, although individuals perceive discrete stimuli (for example, they can perceive noise level, colour and decor as distinct elements), it is the total configuration of stimuli that determines their reactions to a place. Hence, though the dimensions of the environment are defined independently in the following sections, it is important to recognize that they are perceived by employees and customers as a holistic pattern of interdependent stimuli. The holistic response is shown in Figure 10.1 as the 'perceived servicescape'.

Ambient conditions

Ambient conditions include background characteristics of the environment such as temperature, lighting, noise, music, scent and colour. All these factors can profoundly affect how people feel, think, and respond to a particular service establishment. For example, a number of studies have documented the effects of music on consumers' perceptions of products, their perceptions of how long they have waited for service, and the amount of money they spend.[29] When there is music, shoppers tend to perceive that they spend less time shopping or in queues than when there is no music. Slower music tempos at lower volumes tend to make people shop more leisurely and, in some cases, they spend more. Shoppers also spend more time when the music 'fits' the product or matches their musical tastes. Other studies have similarly shown the effects of scent on consumer responses.[30] Scent in bakeries, coffee shops and cheese shops, for example, can be used to draw people in, and pleasant scents can increase lingering time. The presence of a scent can reduce perceptions of time spent and improve store evaluations.

The effects of ambient conditions are especially noticeable when they are extreme. For example, people attending a music concert in a hall in which the air conditioning has failed and the air is hot and stuffy will be uncomfortable, and their discomfort will be reflected in how they feel about the concert. If the temperature and air quality were within a comfort tolerance zone, these ambient factors would probably go unnoticed. Ambient conditions also have a greater effect when the customer or employee spends considerable time in the servicescape. The impact of temperature, music, odours and colours builds over time. Another instance in which ambient conditions will be particularly influential is when they conflict with what the customer or employee expects. As a general rule, ambient conditions affect the five senses. Sometimes such dimensions may be totally imperceptible (gases, chemicals, equipment noise) yet have profound effects, particularly on employees who spend long hours in the environment.

Spatial layout and functionality

Because service environments generally exist to fulfil specific purposes or needs of customers, spatial layout and functionality of the physical surroundings are particularly important. *Spatial layout* refers to the ways in which machinery, equipment and furnishings are arranged, the size and shape of those items, and the spatial relationships among them. *Functionality* refers to the ability of the same items to facilitate the accomplishment of customer and employee goals. The spatial layout and functionality of the environment are particularly important for customers in self-service environments, where they must perform the service on their own and cannot rely on employees to assist them. Thus the functionality of an ATM machine and of self-serve restaurants, service stations and Internet shopping are critical to success and customer satisfaction.

The importance of facility layout is particularly apparent in retail, hospitality and leisure settings, where research shows it can influence customer satisfaction, store performance and consumer search behaviour.[31]

Signs, symbols and artefacts

Many items in the physical environment serve as explicit or implicit signals that communicate about the place to its users. Signs displayed on the exterior and interior of a structure are examples of explicit communicators. They can be used as labels (name of company, name of department, and so on), for directional purposes (entrances, exits) and to communicate rules of behaviour (no smoking, children must be accompanied by an adult). Adequate signs have even been shown to reduce perceived crowding and stress.

Other environmental symbols and artefacts may communicate less directly than signs, giving implicit cues to users about the meaning of the place and norms and expectations for behaviour in the place. Quality construction materials, artwork, certificates and photographs, floor coverings, and personal objects displayed in the environment can all communicate symbolic meaning and create an overall aesthetic impression. Restaurant managers, for example, know that white tablecloths and subdued lighting symbolically convey full service and relatively high prices, whereas counter service, plastic furnishings and bright lighting symbolize the opposite. In office environments, certain cues such as desk size and placement symbolize status and may be used to reinforce professional image.[32]

Signs, symbols and artefacts are particularly important in forming first impressions and for communicating service concepts. When customers are unfamiliar with a particular service establishment, they look for environmental cues to help them categorize the place and form their expectations. A study of dentists' offices found that consumers use the environment, in particular its style of decoration and level of quality, as a cue to the competence and manner of the service provider.[33]

Guidelines for physical evidence strategy

To this point in the chapter we have presented ideas, frameworks and psychological models for understanding the effects of physical evidence and most specifically the effects of the physical facility or servicescape. In this section we suggest some general guidelines for an effective physical evidence strategy.[34]

Recognize the strategic impact of physical evidence

Physical evidence can play a prominent role in determining service quality expectations and perceptions. For some organizations, just acknowledging the impact of physical evidence is a major first step. After this step they can take advantage of the potential of physical evidence and plan strategically.

For an evidence strategy to be effective, it must be linked clearly to the organization's overall goals and vision. Thus planners must know what those goals are and then determine how the physical evidence strategy can support them. At a minimum, the basic service concept must be defined, the target markets (both internal and external) identified and the firm's broad vision of its future known. Because many evidence decisions are relatively permanent and costly (particularly servicescape decisions), they must be planned and executed deliberately.

Blueprint the physical evidence of service

The next step is to map the service. Everyone should be able to see the service process and the existing elements of physical evidence. An effective way to depict service evidence is through the service blueprint. (Service blueprinting was presented in detail in Chapter 8.) Although service blueprints clearly have multiple purposes, they can be particularly useful in visually capturing physical evidence opportunities. People, process and physical evidence can all be seen in the blueprint. Firms can read the actions involved in service delivery, the complexity of the process, the points of human interaction that provide evidence opportunities and the tangible representations present at each step. To make the blueprint even more useful, photographs or videotape of the process can be added to develop a photographic blueprint that provides a vivid picture of physical evidence from the customer's point of view.

Clarify strategic roles of the servicescape

Early in the chapter we discussed the varying roles played by the servicescape and how firms could locate themselves in the typology shown in Table 10.3 to begin to identify their roles. For example, a child-care company would locate itself in the 'elaborate, interpersonal' cell of the matrix and quickly see that its servicescape decisions would be relatively complex and that the servicescape strategy (1) would have to consider the needs of both the children and the service providers, and (2) could impact on marketing, organizational behaviour and consumer satisfaction goals.

Sometimes the servicescape may have no role in service delivery or marketing from the customer's point of view, such as in telecommunications services or utilities. Clarifying the roles played by the servicescape in a particular situation will aid in identifying opportunities and deciding who needs to be consulted in making facility design decisions. Clarifying the strategic role of the servicescape also forces recognition of the importance of the servicescape in creating customer experiences.

Assess and identify physical evidence opportunities

Once the current forms of evidence and the roles of the servicescape are understood, possible changes and improvements can be identified. One question to ask is, are there missed opportunities to provide service evidence? The service blueprint of an insurance or utility service may show that little if any evidence of service is ever provided to the customer. A strategy might then be developed to provide more evidence of service to show customers exactly what they are paying for.

Or it may be discovered that the evidence provided is sending messages that do not enhance the firm's image or goals or that do not match customer expectations. For example, a restaurant might find that its high-price menu cues are not consistent with the design of the restaurant, which suggests 'family dining' to its intended market segment. Either the pricing or the facility design would need to be changed, depending on the restaurant's overall strategy.

Another set of questions addresses whether the current physical evidence of service suits the needs and preferences of the target market. To begin answering such questions, the framework for understanding environment–user relationships (Figure 10.1) and the research approaches suggested in this chapter could be employed. Finally, does the evidence strategy take into account the needs (sometimes incompatible) of both customers and employees? This question is particularly relevant in making decisions regarding the servicescape.

Be prepared to update and modernize the evidence

Some aspects of the evidence, particularly the servicescape, require frequent or at least periodic updating and modernizing. Even if the vision, goals and objectives of the company do not change, time itself takes a toll on physical evidence, necessitating change and modernization. Clearly, an element of fashion is involved, and over time different colours, designs and styles may come to communicate different messages. Organizations obviously understand this concept when it comes to advertising strategy, but sometimes they overlook other elements of physical evidence.

Work cross-functionally

In presenting itself to the consumer, a service firm is concerned with communicating a desired image, with sending consistent and compatible messages through all forms of evidence, and with providing the type of service evidence the target customers want and can understand. Frequently, however, physical evidence decisions are made over time and by various functions within the organization. For example, decisions regarding employee uniforms may be made by the human resources area, servicescape design decisions may be made by the facilities management group, process design decisions are most frequently made by operations managers, and advertising and pricing decisions may be made by the marketing department. Thus it is not surprising that the physical evidence of service may at times be less than consistent. Service blueprinting can be a valuable tool for communicating within the firm, identifying existing service evidence and providing a springboard for changing or providing new forms of physical evidence.

A multifunction team approach to physical evidence strategy is often necessary, particularly for making decisions about the servicescape. It has been said that 'Facility planning and management ... is a problem-solving activity that lies on the boundaries between architecture, interior space planning and product design, organizational [and consumer] behavior, planning and environmental psychology'.[35]

Summary

In this chapter we explored the roles of physical evidence in forming customer and employee perceptions and shaping customer experiences. Because services are intangible and because they are often produced and consumed at the same time, they can be difficult to comprehend or evaluate before their purchase. The physical evidence of the service thus serves as a primary cue for setting customer expectations before purchase. These tangible cues, particularly the servicescape, also influence customers' responses as they experience the service. Because customers and employees often interact in the servicescape, the physical surroundings also influence employees and the nature of employee–customer interactions.

The chapter focused primarily on the servicescape – the physical surroundings or the physical facility where the service is produced, delivered and consumed. We presented a typology of servicescapes that illustrated their range of complexity and usage. By locating itself in the appropriate cell of the typology, an organization can quickly see who needs to be consulted regarding servicescape decisions, what objectives might be achieved through careful design of the facility, and how complex the decisions are likely to be. General strategic roles of the servicescape were also described. The servicescape can serve as a package (a 'visual metaphor' for the service itself), a facilitator in aiding the accomplishment of customer and employee goals, a socializer in prescribing behaviours in the environment and a differentiator to distinguish the organization from its competitors.

With this grounding in the importance of physical evidence, in particular the servicescape, we presented a general framework for understanding servicescape effects on employee and customer behaviours. The servicescape can affect the approach and avoidance behaviours of individual customers and employees as well as their social interactions. These behavioural responses come about because the physical environment influences (1) people's beliefs or cognitions about the service organization, (2) their feelings or emotions in response to the place, and (3) their actual physiological reactions while in the physical facility. The chapter also pointed out that individuals may respond differently to the servicescape depending on their personality traits, the mood they are in or the goals they are trying to accomplish.

Three categories of environmental dimensions capture the complex nature of the servicescape: ambient conditions; spatial layout and functionality; and signs, symbols and artefacts. These dimensions affect people's beliefs, emotions and physical responses, causing them to behave in certain ways while in the servicescape.

Given the importance of physical evidence and its potentially powerful influence on both customers and employees, it is important for firms to think strategically about the management of the tangible evidence of service. The impact of physical evidence and design decisions needs to be researched and planned as part of the marketing strategy. The chapter concluded with specific guidelines for physical evidence strategy. If physical evidence is researched, planned and implemented effectively, key problems leading to service quality shortcomings can be avoided. Through careful thinking about physical evidence decisions, an organization can avoid miscommunicating to customers via incompatible or inconsistent evidence or overpromising and raising customer expectations unrealistically. Beyond its role in helping avoid these negative outcomes, an effective physical evidence strategy can play a critically important role in communicating to customers and in guiding them in understanding the firm's offerings and setting up accurate expectations. During the service experience, physical evidence plays a major role in creating memorable outcomes and emotional connections with customers.

Key concepts

Clue management	244	Servicescape	241
Environmental psychology	244	Stimulus–organism–response	
Environmental dimensions	254	theory	248
Package v. facilitator v.		Virtual servicescapes	242
differentiator	247		

Further reading

Bitner, M.J. (1992) 'Servicescapes: the impact of physical surroundings on customers and employees', *Journal of Marketing*, 56 (April), 57–71.

Hoffman, K.D. and Turley, L.W. (2002) 'Atmospherics, service encounters and consumer decision-making: an integrative perspective', *Journal of Marketing Theory and Practice*, 10(3), 33–47.

Marila, A.S. and Wirtz, J. (2001) 'Congruency of scent and music as a driver of in-store evaluations and behaviour', *Journal of Retailing*, 77 (Summer), 273–89.

Oakes, S. (2000) 'The influence of the musicscape within service environments', *Journal of Services Marketing*, 14(7), 539–56.

Sundaram, D.S. and Webster, C. (2000) 'The role of nonverbal communication in service encounters', *Journal of Services Marketing*, 14(5), 378–91.

 ## Discussion questions

1 What is physical evidence, and why have we devoted an entire chapter to it in a marketing text?

2 Describe and give an example of how servicescapes play each of the following strategic roles: package, facilitator, socializer and differentiator.

3 Imagine that you own an independent copying and printing shop. In which cell would you locate your business in the typology of servicescapes shown in Table 10.3? What are the implications for designing your physical facility?

4 How can an effective physical evidence strategy help close provider gap 2? Explain.

5 Why are both customers and employees included in the framework for understanding

servicescape effects on behaviour (Figure 10.1)? What types of behaviours are influenced by the servicescape according to the framework? Think of examples.

6 Using your own experiences, give examples of times when you have been affected cognitively, emotionally and physiologically by elements of the servicescape (in any service context).

7 Why is everyone not affected in exactly the same way by the servicescape?

8 Describe the physical environment of your favourite restaurant in terms of the three categories of servicescape dimensions: ambient conditions; spatial layout and functionality; and signs, symbols and artefacts.

9 Imagine that you are serving as a consultant to a local health club. How would you advise the health club to begin the process of developing an effective physical evidence strategy?

 Exercises

1 Choose two very different firms (different market segments or service levels) in the same industry. Observe both establishments. Describe the service 'package' in both cases. How does the package help distinguish the two firms? Do you believe that the package sets accurate expectations for what the firm delivers? Is either firm over-promising through the manner in which its servicescape (or other types of physical evidence) communicates with customers?

2 Think of a particular service organization (it can be a class project company, the company you work for or some other organization) for which you believe physical evidence is particularly important in communicating with and satisfying customers. Prepare the text of a presentation you would give to the manager of that organization to convince him or her of the importance of physical evidence in the organization's marketing strategy.

3 Choose a service organization and collect all forms of physical evidence that the organization uses to communicate with its customers. If customers see the firm's facility, also take a photograph of the servicescape. Analyse the evidence in terms of compatibility, consistency and whether it over-promises or under-promises what the firm can deliver.

4 Visit the websites of several service providers. Does the physical evidence of the website portray an image consistent with other forms of evidence provided by the organizations?

Notes

1 The term *servicescape* used throughout this chapter, and much of the content of this chapter, are based, with permission, on M.J. Bitner, 'Servicescapes: the impact of physical surroundings on customers and employees', *Journal of Marketing* 56 (April 1992), pp. 57–71. For recent contributions to this topic, see *Servicescapes: The Concept of Place in Contemporary Markets*, ed. J.F. Sherry Jr (Chicago, IL: NTC/Contemporary Publishing, 1998); and M.J. Bitner, 'The servicescape', in *Handbook of Services Marketing and Management*, eds T.A. Swartz and D. Iacobucci (Thousand Oaks, CA: Sage Publications, 2000), pp. 37–50.

2 L.P. Carbone, *Clued In: How to Keep Customers Coming Back Again and Again* (Upper Saddle River, NJ: Prentice Hall, 2004). See also L.L. Berry and N. Bendapudi, 'Clueing in customers', *Harvard Business Review* (February 2003), pp. 100–6.

3 J.H. Gilmore and B.J. Pine II, 'The experience is the marketing', *Strategic Horizons* (2002), an e-Doc; B.J. Pine II and J.H. Gilmore, *The Experience Economy: Work Is Theater and Every Business Is a Stage* (Boston, MA: Harvard Business School Press, 1999); B.H. Schmitt, *Experiential Marketing* (New York: Free Press, 1999).

4 For reviews of environmental psychology, see D. Stokols and I. Altman, *Handbook of Environmental Psychology* (New York: John Wiley, 1987); S. Saegert and G.H. Winkel, 'Environmental psychology', *Annual Review of Psychology* 41 (1990), pp. 441–77; and E. Sundstrom, P.A. Bell, P.L. Busby and C. Asmus, 'Environmental psychology 1989–1994', *Annual Review of Psychology* 47 (1996), pp. 485–512.

5 See M.R. Solomon, 'Dressing for the part: the role of costume in the staging of the servicescape', in *Servicescapes: The Concept of Space in Contemporary Markets*, ed. J.F. Sherry Jr (Chicago, IL: NTC/Contemporary Publishing, 1998), pp. 81–108; and A. Rafaeli, 'Dress and behavior of customer contact employees: a framework for analysis', in *Advances in Services Marketing and Management*, vol. 2, eds T.A. Swartz, D.E. Bowen and S.W. Brown (Greenwich, CT: JAI Press, 1993), pp. 175–212.

6 Adapted from http://www.wolff-olins.com

7 D. Michaels, 'Business-class warfare: rival airlines scramble to beat BA's reclining bed seats', *The Wall Street Journal*, 16 March 2001, p. B1.

8 Ibid.; and British Airways' website, www.britishairways.com

9 R. Chittum, 'New concepts in lodging', *The Wall Street Journal*, 8 October 2003, p. B1.

10 Adapted from http://www.creativematch.co.uk/viewnews/€88220

11 Carbone, *Clued In*; Berry and Bendapudi, 'Clueing in customers'; Gilmore and Pine, 'Experience is the marketing'; Pine and Gilmore, *The Experience Economy*; Schmitt, *Experiential Marketing*.

12 A. Mehrabian and J.A. Russell, *An Approach to Environmental Psychology* (Cambridge, MA: Massachusetts Institute of Technology, 1974).

13 R. Donovan and J. Rossiter, 'Store atmosphere: an environmental psychology approach', *Journal of Retailing* 58 (Spring 1982), pp. 34–57.

14 D.J. Bennett and J.D. Bennett, 'Making the scene', in *Social Psychology through Symbolic Interactionism*, eds G. Stone and H. Farberman (Waltham, MA: Ginn-Blaisdell, 1970), pp. 190–6.

15 J.P. Forgas, *Social Episodes* (London: Academic Press, 1979).

16 R.G. Barker, *Ecological Psychology* (Stanford, CA: Stanford University Press, 1968).

17 Adapted from J.F. Sherry Jr, 'The soul of the company store: Nike Town Chicago and the emplaced brandscape', in *Servicescapes: The Concept of Place in Contemporary Markets*, ed. J.F. Sherry Jr (Chicago: NTC/Contemporary Publishing Company, 1998), pp. 109–46. Copyright © 1998 by NTC Business Books. Reprinted by permission of NTC Contemporary Books. The initial quotation is from 'Nike Town Comes to Chicago,' Nike press release, 2 July 1992, as quoted in ibid., p. 109.

18 For a number of excellent papers on this topic spanning a range from toy stores to bridal salons

to cybermarketspaces to Japanese retail environments and others, see J.F. Sherry Jr, ed., *Servicescapes: The Concept of Place in Contemporary Markets.*

19 Sherry, 'The soul of the company store: Nike Town Chicago and the emplaced brandscape', in *Servicescapes: The Concept of Place in Contemporary Markets*, ed. J.F. Sherry Jr (Chicago, IL: NTC/Contemporary Publishing, 1998), pp. 109–46.

20 E.J. Arnould, L.L. Price and P. Tierney, 'The wilderness servicescape: an ironic commercial landscape', in *Servicescapes: The Concept of Place in Contemporary Markets*, ed. J.F. Sherry Jr (Chicago, IL: NTC/Contemporary Publishing, 1998), pp. 403–38.

21 A. Rapoport, *The Meaning of the Built Environment* (Beverly Hills, CA: Sage Publications, 1982); R.G. Golledge, 'Environmental cognition', in *Handbook of Environmental Psychology*, vol. 1, eds D. Stokols and I. Altman (New York: John Wiley, 1987), pp. 131–74.

22 M.P. Gardner and G. Siomkos, 'Toward a methodology for assessing effects of in-store atmospherics', in *Advances in Consumer Research*, vol. 13, ed. R.J. Lutz (Ann Arbor, MI: Association for Consumer Research, 1986), pp. 27–31.

23 M.J. Bitner, 'Evaluating service encounters: the effects of physical surroundings and employee responses', *Journal of Marketing* 54 (April 1990), pp. 69–82.

24 J.C. Ward, M.J. Bitner and J. Barnes, 'Measuring the prototypicality and meaning of retail environments', *Journal of Retailing* 68 (Summer 1992) pp. 194–220.

25 See, for example, Mehrabian and Russell, *An Approach to Environmental Psychology*; J.A. Russell and U.F. Lanius, 'Adaptation level and the affective appraisal of environments', *Journal of Environmental Psychology* 4, no. 2 (1984), pp. 199–235; J.A. Russell and G. Pratt, 'A description of the affective quality attributed to environments', *Journal of Personality and Social Psychology* 38, no. 2 (1980), pp. 311–22; J.A. Russell and J. Snodgrass, 'Emotion and the environment', in *Handbook of Environmental Psychology*, vol. 1, eds D. Stokols and I. Altman (New York: John Wiley, 1987), pp. 245–81; J.A. Russell, L.M. Ward and G. Pratt, 'Affective quality attributed to environments', *Environment and Behavior* 13 (May 1981), pp. 259–88.

26 See, for example, M.S. Sanders and E.J. McCormick, *Human Factors in Engineering and Design*, 7th edn (New York: McGraw-Hill, 1993); and D.J. Osborne, *Ergonomics at Work*, 2nd edn (New York: John Wiley, 1987).

27 Mehrabian and Russell, *An Approach to Environmental Psychology*; Russell and Snodgrass, 'Emotion and the environment'.

28 A. Mehrabian, 'Individual differences in stimulus screening and arousability', *Journal of Personality* 45, no. 2 (1977), pp. 237–50.

29 For recent research documenting the effects of music on consumers, see J. Baker, D. Grewal and A. Parasuraman, 'The influence of store environment on quality inferences and store image', *Journal of the Academy of Marketing Science* 22 (Fall 1994), pp. 328–39; J.C. Chebat, C. Gelinas-Chebat and P. Filliatrault, 'Interactive effects of musical and visual cues on time perception: an application to waiting lines in banks', *Perceptual and Motor Skills* 77 (1993), pp. 995–1020; L. Dube, J.C. Chebat and S. Morin, 'The effects of background music on consumers' desire to affiliate in buyer–seller interactions', *Psychology and Marketing* 12, no. 4 (1995), pp. 305–19; J.D. Herrington and L.M. Capella, 'Effects of music in service environments: a field study', *Journal of Services Marketing* 10, no. 2 (1996), pp. 26–41; J.D. Herrington and L.M. Capella, 'Practical applications of music in service settings', *Journal of Services Marketing* 8, no. 3 (1994), pp. 50–65; M.K. Hui, L. Dube and J.C. Chebat, 'The impact of music on consumers' reactions to waiting for services', *Journal of Retailing* 73 (Spring 1997) pp. 87–104;

A.S. Matila and J. Wirtz, 'Congruency of scent and music as a driver of in-store evaluations and behavior', *Journal of Retailing* 77 (Summer 2001), pp. 273–89; L. Dube and S. Morin, 'Background music pleasure and store evaluation: intensity effects and psychological mechanisms', *Journal of Business Research* 54 (November 2001), pp. 107–13; J. Bakec, A. Parasuraman, D. Grewal and G.B. Voss, 'The influence of multiple store environment cues as perceived merchandise value and patronage intentions', *Journal of Marketing* 66 (April 2002), pp. 120–41.

[30] For recent research documenting the effects of scent on consumer responses, see D.J. Mitchell, B.E. Kahn and S.C. Knasko, 'There's something in the air: effects of congruent and incongruent ambient odor on consumer decision making', *Journal of Consumer Research* 22 (September 1995), pp. 229–38; and E.R. Spangenberg, A.E. Crowley and P.W. Henderson, 'Improving the store environment: do olfactory cues affect evaluations and behaviors?' *Journal of Marketing* 60 (April 1996), pp. 67–80.

[31] See J.M. Sulek, M.R. Lind and A.S. Marucheck, 'The impact of a customer service intervention and facility design on firm performance', *Management Science* 41, no. 11 (1995), pp. 1763–73; P.A. Titus and P.B. Everett, 'Consumer wayfinding tasks, strategies, and errors: an exploratory field study', *Psychology and Marketing* 13, no. 3 (1996), pp. 265–90; C. Yoo, J. Park and D.J. MacInnis, 'Effects of store characteristics and in-store emotional experiences on store attitude', *Journal of Business Research* 42 (1998), pp. 253–63; K.L. Wakefield and J.G. Blodgett, 'The effect of the servicescape on customers' behavioral intentions in leisure service settings', *Journal of Services Marketing* 10, no. 6 (1996), pp. 45–61.

[32] T.R.V. Davis, 'The influence of the physical environment in offices', *Academy of Management Review* 9, no. 2 (1984), pp. 271–83.

[33] J.C. Ward and J.P. Eaton, 'Service environments: the effect of quality and decorative style on emotions, expectations, and attributions', in *Proceedings of the American Marketing Association Summer Educators' Conference*, eds. R. Achrol and A. Mitchell (Chicago, IL: American Marketing Association 1994), pp. 333–4.

[34] This section is adapted from M.J. Bitner, 'Managing the evidence of service', in *The Service Quality Handbook*, eds E.E. Scheuing and W.F. Christopher (New York: AMACOM, 1993), pp. 358–70.

[35] F.D. Becker, *Workspace* (New York: Praeger, 1981).

PART 4
Delivering and Performing Service

In the gaps model of service quality, provider gap 3 (the service performance gap) is the discrepancy between customer-driven service standards and actual service delivery (see the accompanying figure). Even when guidelines exist for performing service well and treating customers correctly, high-quality service performance is not a certainty. Part 4 deals with all the ways in which companies ensure that services are performed according to customer-defined designs and standards.

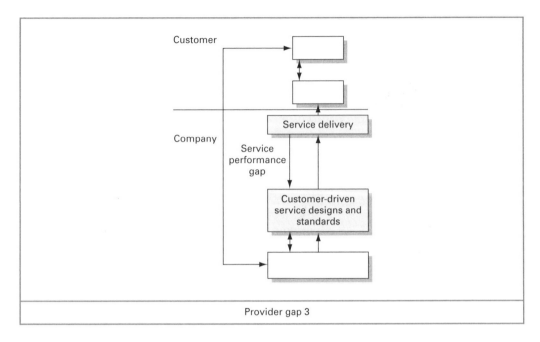

Provider gap 3

In Chapter 11, we focus on the key roles that employees play in service delivery and strategies that ensure they are effective in their roles. Issues of particular concern include employees who feel in conflict between customers and company management, the wrong employees, inadequate technology, inappropriate compensation and recognition, and lack of empowerment and teamwork.

In Chapter 12, we discuss the variability caused by customers. If customers do not perform appropriately – if they do not follow instructions or if they disturb other customers receiving service at the same time – service quality is jeopardized. Effective service organizations acknowledge the role of customer variability and develop strategies to teach customers to perform their roles appropriately.

Chapter 13 describes service delivery through electronic channels and intermediaries such as retailers, franchisees, agents and brokers. Although some service companies have control over the delivery channel, many service companies depend on other organizations to provide service to the end-customer. For this reason, firms must develop ways to either control or motivate these intermediaries to meet company goals and deliver consistent quality service.

Chapter 14 emphasizes the need to synchronize demand and capacity in service organizations in order to deliver consistent, high-quality service. Service organizations often face situations of over- or under-demand because they lack inventories to smooth demand. Marketing strategies for managing demand, such as price changes, advertising, promotion and alternative service offerings, can help this challenge.

Chapter 15 describes service recovery management, which involves understanding why customers complain, what they expect when they complain, and how to deal with service failures. Firms engaged in service recovery must, along with other approaches, create a complaint-handling procedure, empower employees to react in real time to fix failures and guarantee service.

CHAPTER 11

Employees' roles in service delivery

❖ LEARNING OBJECTIVES

This chapter's objectives are to:

1 Demonstrate the importance of creating a service culture in which providing excellent service to both internal and external customers is a way of life.

2 Illustrate the critical importance of service employees in creating customer satisfaction and service quality.

3 Demonstrate the linkages in the service profit chain.

4 Identify the challenges inherent in boundary-spanning roles.

5 Provide examples of strategies for creating customer-oriented service delivery through hiring the right people, developing employees to deliver service quality, providing needed support systems and retaining the best service employees.

CASE STUDY: EMPLOYEES ARE THE SERVICE AND THE BRAND

Noted service expert Leonard Berry has documented that investments in employee success are key drivers of sustained business success.[1] Why is this true? Why do service companies choose to invest heavily in their employees?

For clues, consider the following true stories:

◆ On a long overseas Singapore Airlines flight, a restless toddler repeatedly dropped his dummy. Every time the child would cry, and someone (the mother, another passenger or a flight attendant) would retrieve the dummy. Finally, one of the attendants picked up the dummy, attached it to a ribbon, and sewed it to the child's shirt. The child and mother were happy, and passengers seated nearby gave the attendant a standing ovation.[2]

◆ A call-centre operator at a leading credit card company received a call from a husband whose wife, suffering from Alzheimer's disease, had vanished. The husband hoped that he could find his wife through tracing her use of her credit card. The call-centre operator placed a hold on the card and arranged to be called personally the moment there was any activity on the card. When it happened, about a week later, the associate contacted the husband, the doctor and the police, who were then able to assist the missing woman and get her home.[3]

◆ A computer programmer made a room reservation at a major hotel for a discounted price. On arrival he discovered that all rooms were filled. The front desk clerk responded by sending him to a competing hotel and picking up his bill, which was more than twice what he originally paid. The clerk also paid for the guest's taxi fare to the new hotel, and threw in a free meal at the hotel as well.[4]

These stories illustrate the important roles played by service employees in creating satisfied customers and in building customer relationships. The front-line service providers in each example are enormously important to the success of the organizations they represent. They are responsible for understanding customer needs and for interpreting customer requirements in real time. Leonard Berry has documented that, in case after case, companies that represent sustained service success all recognize the critical importance of their employees.[5]

In this chapter we focus on service employees and human resource practices that facilitate delivery of quality services. The assumption is that even when customer expectations are well understood (gap 1) and services have been designed and specified to conform to those expectations (gap 2), there may still be discontinuities in service quality when the service is not delivered as specified. These discontinuities are labelled gap 3 – the service performance gap – in the service quality framework. Because employees frequently deliver or perform the service, human resource issues are a major cause of this gap. By focusing on the critical role of service employees and by developing strategies that will lead to effective customer-oriented service, organizations can begin to close the service delivery gap.

The failure to deliver services as designed and specified can result from a number of employee and human performance factors: ineffective recruitment of service-oriented employees; role ambiguity and role conflict among contact employees; poor employee–technology–job fit; inappropriate evaluation and compensation systems; and lack of empowerment, perceived control and teamwork. Prior to examining these factors and strategies for overcoming them, we begin the chapter with a discussion of service culture and its influence on employee behaviour.

Service culture

Before addressing the role of the employee in service delivery, we should look at the bigger picture. The behaviour of employees in an organization will be heavily influenced by the culture of an organization, or the pervasive norms and values that shape individual and group behaviour. *Corporate culture* has been defined as 'the pattern of shared values and beliefs that give the members of an organization meaning, and provide them with the rules for behavior in the organization'.[6] *Culture* has been defined more informally as 'the way we do things around here'.

To understand at a personal level what corporate culture is, think of different places you have worked or organizations you have been a member of, such as sports clubs, schools or associations. Your behaviour and the behaviours of others were no doubt influenced by the underlying values, norms and culture of the organization. Even when you attend an interview for a new job, you can begin to get a sense of the culture through talking to a number of employees and observing behaviour. Once you are on the job, your formal training as well as informal observation of behaviour will work together to give you a better picture of the organization's culture.

Experts have suggested that a customer-oriented, service-oriented organization will have at its heart a *service culture*, defined as 'a culture where an appreciation for good service exists, and where giving good service to internal as well as ultimate, external customers is considered a natural way of life and one of the most important norms by everyone'.[7] This very rich definition has many implications for employee behaviours. First, a service culture exists if there is an 'appreciation for good service'. This phrase does not mean that the company has an advertising campaign that stresses the importance of service, but 'in that underneath sort of way' people know that good service is appreciated and valued. A second important point in this definition is that good service is given to internal as well as external customers.[8] It is not enough to promise excellent service to final customers; all people within the organization deserve the same kind of service. Finally, in a service culture good service is 'a way of life' and it comes naturally because it is an important norm of the organization.

Service culture has been linked to competitive advantage in companies.[9] Why is it so important? No realistic amount of supervision would allow a firm to exercise sufficient control over *all* employee behaviour. In many service settings, employees interact with customers with no management present. In such instances, the firm must rely on its service culture to influence employee thoughts, feelings and behaviours.

Exhibiting service leadership

A strong service culture begins with leaders in the organization who demonstrate a passion for service excellence. Leonard Berry suggests that leaders of successful service firms tend to have similar core values, such as integrity, joy and respect, and they 'infuse those values into the fabric of the organization'.[10] **Service leadership** does not consist of bestowing a set of commands from a thick rulebook but, rather, the regular and consistent demonstration of one's values. Employees are more likely to embrace a service culture when they see management living out these values. Espoused values – what managers *say* the values are – tend to have less impact on employees than enacted values – what employees believe the values to be because of what they observe management actually *doing*.[11] That is, culture is what employees perceive that management *really* believes, and employees gain an understanding of what is important in the organization through the daily experiences they have with those people in key roles throughout the organization.

Service spotlight

The Virgin Group, driven by Sir Richard Branson, has the following brand values: quality; innovation; value for money; fun; and sense of challenge. These values reflect those of Sir Richard himself, for example the sense of challenge is evident in his world record-breaking attempts at crossing the Atlantic and Pacific in fast boats and hot air balloons. In terms of innovation, he is involved in organizing the first passenger flights into space and in terms of fun he is regularly involved in the activities of the Comic Relief charity and has undertaken stunts involving him dressing up as an air hostess, shaving off his beard, etc. He has also positioned himself as a campaigner against big business, placing an emphasis on quality and value for money for the customer.

Developing a service culture

A service culture cannot be developed overnight, and there is no magic, easy way to sustain a service culture. The human resource and internal marketing practices discussed later in the chapter can help develop a service culture over time. If, however, an organization has a culture that is rooted in product- or operations-oriented government regulation or traditions, no single strategy will change it overnight. Hundreds of little (but significant) factors, not just one or two big factors, are required to build and sustain a service culture.[12] Successful companies such as Hilton Hotels and IBM Global Services have all found that it takes years of consistent, concerted effort to build a service culture and to shift the organization from its old patterns to new ways of doing business. Even for companies such as Eurostar, Disney and the Ritz-Carlton that started out with a strong service and customer focus, sustaining their established service cultures still takes constant attention to hundreds of details.

Transporting a service culture

Transporting a service culture through international business expansion is also very challenging. Attempting to 'export' a corporate culture to another country creates additional issues. For instance, will the organization's service culture clash with a different *national* culture? If there is a clash, is it over *what* the actual values are or over *how* they are to be enacted? If the issue is over what the values are, and they are core values critical to the firm's competitive advantage, then perhaps the company cannot be successful in that setting. Although tremendous opportunities exist in the global marketplace, the many legal, cultural and language barriers become particularly evident for services that depend on human interaction.

Service spotlight: Americans in Europe

McDonald's approach

McDonald's has been very successful in its international expansion. In some ways it has remained very 'American' in everything it does – people around the world want an American experience when they go to McDonald's. However, the company is sensitive to cultural differences as well. This subtle blending of the 'McDonald's way' with adaptations to cultural nuances has resulted in great success. One way that McDonald's maintains its standards is through its Hamburger University (HU), which is required training for *all* McDonald's employees worldwide before they can become managers. Each year approximately 3000 employees from nearly 100 countries enrol and attend the Advanced Operations Course at HU, located in Oak Brook, Illinois. The curriculum is 80 per cent devoted to communications and human relations skills. Because of the international scope of McDonald's, translators and electronic equipment enable professors to teach and communicate in 22 languages at one time. The result is that all managers in all countries have the same 'ketchup in their veins', and the restaurant's basic human resources and operating philosophies remain fairly stable from operation to operation. Certain adaptations in decor, menu and other areas of cultural differences are then allowed (see Chapter 10 for some specific examples).

Disney in Europe

When Disney first expanded into Europe by opening EuroDisney near Paris, it also faced challenges and surprises. The highly structured, scripted and customer-oriented approach that Disney used in the United States was not easily duplicated with European employees. In attempting to transport the Disney culture and experience to Europe, the company confronted clashing values and norms of behaviour in the workplace that made the expansion difficult. Customers also needed to be 'trained' in the Disney way – not all cultures are comfortable with waiting in long queues, for example. And not all cultures treat their children the same. For example, in the United States, families will spend lots of money at Disneyland on food, toys and other things that their children 'must' have. Some European cultures view this behaviour as highly indulgent, so families will visit the park without buying much beyond the ticket for admission.

The critical importance of service employees

An often heard quotation about service organizations goes like this: 'In a service organization, if you're not serving the customer, you'd better be serving someone who is.'[13] People – front-line employees and those supporting them from behind the scenes – are critical to the success of any service organization. The importance of people in the marketing of services is captured in the *people* element of the services marketing mix, which we described in Chapter 1 *as all the human actors who play a part in service delivery and thus influence the buyer's perceptions; namely, the firm's personnel, the customer, and other customers in the service environment.*

The key focus in this chapter is on customer-contact service employees because:

- Employees *are* the service.
- Employees *are* the organization in the customer's eyes.
- **Employees *are* the brand.**
- **Employees *are* marketers.**

In many cases, the contact employee *is the service* – there is nothing else. For example, in most personal and professional services (like haircutting, personal trainers, child care, cleaning/maintenance, limousine services, counselling and legal services) the contact employee provides the entire service singlehandedly. The offering *is* the employee. Thus, investing in the employee to improve the service parallels making a direct investment in the improvement of a manufactured product.

Even if the contact employee does not perform the service entirely, he or she may still *personify the firm in the customer's eyes.* All the employees of a law firm or a health clinic – from the professionals who provide the service to the receptionists and office staff – represent the firm to the client, and everything these individuals do or say can influence perceptions of the organization. Even off-duty employees, such as flight attendants or restaurant employees on a break, reflect on the organizations they represent. If they are unprofessional or make rude remarks about or to customers, customers' perceptions of the organization will suffer even though the employee is not on duty.

Service spotlight

Disneyland Paris insists that its employees maintain 'onstage' attitudes and behaviours whenever they are in front of the public and that they relax these behaviours only when they are truly behind the scenes or 'backstage' in underground tunnels where guests cannot see them in their off-duty times.

Service employees *are the brand*. A Barclays Bank financial adviser, an IKEA sales assistant, a KLM flight attendant – in each case, the primary image that a customer has of the firm is formed by the interactions the customer has with the employees of that firm. A customer sees Barclays Bank as a good provider of financial services if the employees he or she interacts with are knowledgeable, understanding and concerned about her financial situation and goals. Similarly, a customer sees IKEA as a professional and empathetic company because of interactions he or she has with its sales assistants.

Service spotlight

Even in a non-service setting, Audi, a car manufacturer, recognizes the importance of its employees in representing and reinforcing the brand image of the company. As a result, Audi recruits service personnel at all levels whose psychological traits parallel and support the Audi image.[14] For example, Audi looks to hire employees who are not afraid to develop a personal relationship with customers. When looking for a technician, they are not just looking for someone who repairs cars well but also someone who is inclined to spend time interacting with customers and demonstrating empathy – characteristics that they want customers to associate with Audi. At Audi the brand image is not just built and maintained by the cars themselves and the advertising: it is a function of the people who work at Audi.

Because contact employees represent the organization and can directly influence customer satisfaction, they *perform the role of marketers*. They physically embody the product and are walking billboards from a promotional standpoint. Some service employees may also perform more traditional selling roles. For example, bank tellers are often called on to cross-sell bank products, a departure from the traditional teller role of the operations function only. Whether acknowledged or not, whether actively selling or not, service employees perform marketing functions. They can perform these functions well, to the organization's advantage, or poorly, to the organization's detriment. In this chapter we examine frameworks, tools and strategies for ensuring that service employees perform their marketing functions well.

Employee satisfaction, customer satisfaction and profits

Satisfied employees make for satisfied customers (and satisfied customers can, in turn, reinforce employees' sense of satisfaction in their jobs). Some researchers have even gone so far as to suggest that unless service employees are happy in their jobs, customer satisfaction will be difficult to achieve.[15]

Through their research with customers and employees in 28 different bank branches, Benjamin Schneider and David Bowen have shown that both a *climate for service* and a *climate for employee well-being* are highly correlated with overall customer perceptions of service quality.[16] That is, both service climate and human resource management experiences that *employees* have within their organizations are reflected in how *customers* experience the service. Other research suggests that employees who feel they are treated fairly by their organizations will treat customers better, resulting in greater customer satisfaction.[17]

The underlying logic connecting employee satisfaction and loyalty to customer satisfaction and loyalty and ultimately profits is illustrated by the **service profit chain** shown in Figure 11.1.[18] In earlier chapters we focused on customer satisfaction and retention; here we focus on **employee satisfaction** and **employee retention**. The service profit chain suggests that there are critical linkages among internal service quality; employee satisfaction/productivity; the value of services provided to the customer; and, ultimately, customer satisfaction, retention and profits.

Service profit chain researchers are careful to point out that the model does not suggest causality. That is, employee satisfaction does not *cause* customer satisfaction; rather the two are interrelated and feed off each other. The model does imply that companies that exhibit high levels of success on the elements of the model will be more successful and profitable than those that do not. This finding is borne out in other research, which reports that companies that manage people right will outperform by 30 to 40 per cent companies that do not.[19]

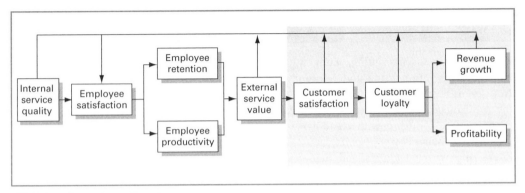

FIGURE 11.1 The service profit chain

The effect of employee behaviours on service quality dimensions

Customers' perceptions of service quality will be impacted by the customer-oriented behaviours of employees.[20] In fact, all of the five dimensions of service quality (reliability, responsiveness, assurance, empathy and tangibles) can be influenced directly by service employees.

Delivering the service as promised – *reliability* – is often totally within the control of front-line employees. Even in the case of automated services (such as ATMs, automated ticketing machines or self-serve service stations), behind-the-scenes employees are critical for making sure all the systems are working properly. When services fail or errors are made, employees are essential for setting things right and using their judgement to determine the best course of action for service recovery.

Front-line employees directly influence customer perceptions of *responsiveness* through their personal willingness to help and their promptness in serving customers. Consider the range of responses you receive from different retail staff when you need help finding a particular item of clothing. One employee may ignore your presence, whereas another offers to help you search and calls other stores to locate the item. One may help you immediately and efficiently, whereas another may move slowly in accommodating even the simplest request.

The *assurance* dimension of service quality is highly dependent on employees' ability to communicate their credibility and to inspire trust and confidence. The reputation of the organization will help, but in the end, individual employees with whom the customer interacts confirm and build trust in the organization or detract from its reputation and ultimately destroy trust. For startup or relatively unknown organizations, credibility, trust and confidence will be tied totally to employee actions.

It is difficult to imagine how an organization would deliver 'caring, individualized attention' to customers independent of its employees. *Empathy* implies that employees will pay attention, listen, adapt and be flexible in delivering what individual customers need.[21] For example, research documents that when employees are customer oriented, have good rapport with customers and exhibit perceptive and attentive listening skills, customers will evaluate the service more highly and be more likely to return.[22] Employee appearance and dress are important aspects of the *tangibles* dimension of quality, along with many other factors that are independent of service employees (the service facility, decor, brochures, signage, and so on).

Boundary-spanning roles

Our focus in this chapter is on front-line service employees who interact directly with customers, although much of what is described and recommended can be applied to internal service employees as well. The front-line service employees are referred to as **boundary spanners** because they operate at the organization's boundary. As indicated in Figure 11.2, boundary spanners provide a link between the external customer and environment and the internal operations of the organization. They serve a critical function in understanding, filtering and interpreting information and resources to and from the organization and its external constituencies.

Who are these boundary spanners? What types of people and positions comprise critical boundary-spanning roles? Their skills and experience cover the full spectrum of jobs and careers. In industries such as fast food, hotels, telecommunication and retail, the boundary spanners are the least skilled, lowest-paid employees in the organization. They are order-takers, front-desk employees, telephone operators, store clerks, truck drivers and delivery people. In other industries, boundary spanners are well-paid, highly educated professionals – for example, doctors, lawyers, accountants, consultants, architects and teachers.

No matter what the level of skill or pay, boundary-spanning positions are often high-stress jobs. In addition to mental and physical skills, these positions require extraordinary levels of **emotional labour**, frequently demand an ability to handle interpersonal and interorganizational conflict, and call on the employee to make real-time trade-offs between quality and productivity on the job. These stresses and trade-offs can result in failure to deliver services as specified, which widens gap 3.

Emotional labour

The term *emotional labour* was coined by Arlie Hochschild to refer to the labour that goes beyond the physical or mental skills needed to deliver quality service.[23] It means delivering smiles, making eye contact, showing sincere interest and engaging in friendly conversation with people who are essentially strangers and who may or may not ever be seen again. Friendliness, courtesy, empathy and responsiveness directed towards customers all require huge amounts of

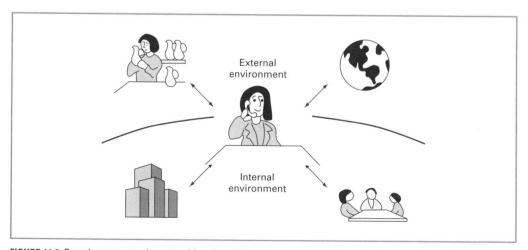

FIGURE 11.2 Boundary spanners interact with and provide information to both internal and external constituents

emotional labour from the front-line employees who shoulder this responsibility for the organization. Emotional labour draws on people's feelings (often requiring them to suppress their true feelings) to be effective in their jobs. A front-line service employee who is having a bad day or is not feeling just right is still expected to put on the face of the organization when dealing with customers. One of the clearest examples of emotional labour is the story (probably apocryphal) of the flight attendant who was approached by a businessman who said, 'Let's have a smile.' 'Okay,' she replied, 'I'll tell you what, first you smile and then I'll smile, okay?' He smiled. 'Good,' she said. 'Now hold that for 15 hours,' and walked away.[24]

Many of the strategies we will discuss later in the chapter can help organizations and employees deal with the realities of emotional labour on the job. For the organization, such strategies include carefully selecting people who can handle emotional stress, training them in needed skills (like listening and problem-solving) and teaching or giving them coping abilities and strategies (via job rotation, scheduled breaks, teamwork or other techniques).[25]

Strategies for managing emotional labour

Customer-contact employees in service positions are often required to display (or, conversely, to withhold display of) a variety of emotions. Such employees are increasingly being required to invest personal identity and expression into their work in many situations. The following description suggests how the experience of the service employee, even in the most routine of occupations, is markedly different from that of the traditional manufacturing worker:

 The assembly-line worker could openly hate his job, despise his supervisor, and even dislike his co-workers, and while this might be an unpleasant state of affairs, if he [completes] his assigned tasks efficiently, his attitude [is] his own problem. For the service worker, inhabiting the job means, at the very least, pretending to like it, and, at most, actually bringing his whole self into the job, liking it, and genuinely caring about the people with whom he interacts.[26]

Emotional labour occurs more often when the job requires frequent contact and long durations of voice contact or face-to-face contact with customers. These employees often need emotional management to deal with such situations. Later in this chapter we suggest many strategies for organizations to create an environment that helps employees deal with the realities of emotional labour on the job.

Screening for emotional labour abilities

Many firms look to hire employees who are well suited to meet the emotional labour requirements of the job. Retailers such as Marks and Spencer or Asda (Wal-mart) put prospective employees through simulated customer contact exercises to see the kind of friendliness and warmth they naturally communicate. Such practices help in identifying employees whose values, background and personalities match the job's emotional labour requirements.

Teaching emotional management skills and appropriate behaviours

Most customer-contact employees are taught that they need to be courteous to customers. However, customers have no obligation to return empathy or courtesy. In situations in which customers exercise the privilege of 'the customer is always right', employees face real challenges in suppressing their true feelings. Seldom do firms provide much training to assist employees in facing these challenges. Arlie Hochschild identifies two forms of emotional labour: *surface acting*, in which employees pretend to feel emotions that are not really present and, in doing so, deliberately and consciously create an outward appearance in order to deceive others; and *deep acting*, in which employees attempt to experience the real feelings they must express to the customer, including the active invocation of 'thoughts, images, and memories to induce the associated emotion'.[27] Hair salon stylists and airline flight attendants are often encouraged to engage in deep-acting strategies such as imagining that the client is a friend or that the passenger is a frightened little child flying for the first time. Often, in order to persuade clients to buy hair products or colour their hair, stylists have to moderate their language or behaviour; they may use deep acting to justify these behaviours to themselves. Companies may also train employees in how to avoid absorbing a customer's bad mood, perhaps by having employees spend hours role-playing to suppress their natural reaction to return negative customer emotions with their own negative emotions.

Carefully constructing the physical work environment

As we discussed in Chapter 10, the environment in which the service is delivered can have an impact on employee behaviours and emotions. Many of the better call centres working for insurance companies or banks attempt to reduce staff stress and boredom through bright airy decoration with windows that allow employees to see the weather, trees, grass, people and cars driving by.

Allowing employees to air their views

Employees who must exert emotional labour often need to have an outlet to 'let off steam'. Allowing employees to air their views lets them get rid of their frustrations. If such venting is done in a group setting, it can provide emotional support and encouragement as well as allowing employees to see that others are experiencing the same problems and that they are not alone. If part of the work day (or week) is explicitly set aside to allow employees to share their frustrations, it delivers a message to employees that the company is aware of and acknowledges the emotional contribution that they have made. Ritz-Carlton, Wal-Mart and other companies regularly set aside time for such venting. In addition to the cathartic benefit this experience can provide, other employees may reveal coping strategies that they have found useful.

Putting management on the front line

Customer-contact employees often feel that management does not truly understand or appreciate the emotional labour they must expend. Managers should regularly be required to interact with customers. Scottish and Southern Energy has its management team work alongside its customer service representatives in fielding customers' telephone calls. In addition to understanding what the issues are, managers are truly able to empathize with employees. Managers who do so not only have an appreciation for the emotional labour requirements of their employees, but they are also in a better position to serve as role models and mentors in using emotional management skills.

Giving employees a break

In situations in which an employee has just handled a particularly tough customer, especially if the employee has frequent and long durations of voice or face-to-face contact with customers, a particularly helpful strategy is to allow the employee a short break to regroup. Retailers rotate employees into different positions throughout the day so that they do not spend the entire time working on checkouts. Customer contact employees can be reenergized and refreshed after spending a little time away from the situation, even if they take only a few minutes to finish paperwork or complete some other job responsibility.

Handing off demanding customers to managers

Some customers may be too much for an employee to handle. In such situations, to alleviate pressure on the customer-contact employee, firms may shift responsibility for the interaction to managers. Norwich Union Insurance call-centre operators are trained to pass difficult customers to supervisors or managers.

Sources of conflict

Front-line employees often face interpersonal and interorganizational conflicts on the job. Their frustration and confusion can, if left unattended, lead to stress, job dissatisfaction, a diminished ability to serve customers and burnout.[28] Because they represent the customer to the organization and often need to manage a number of customers simultaneously, front-line employees inevitably have to deal with conflicts, including person/role conflicts, organization/client conflicts and inter-client conflicts, as suggested by Figure 11.3 and discussed in the next sections.[29]

Person/role conflicts

In some situations, boundary spanners feel conflicts between what they are asked to do and their own personalities, orientations or values. Service workers may feel role conflict when they are required to subordinate their feelings or beliefs, as when they are asked to live by the motto 'The customer is always right – even when he [or she] is wrong'. Sometimes there is a conflict between role requirements and the self-image or self-esteem of the employee.

Person/role conflict also arises when employees are required to wear specific clothing or change some aspect of their appearance to conform to the job requirements. A young lawyer, just out of school, may feel an internal conflict with his new role when his employer requires him to cut his long hair and trade his casual clothes for a suit.

Organization/client conflict

A more common type of conflict for front-line service employees is the conflict between their two bosses, the organization and the individual customer. Service employees are typically rewarded for following certain standards, rules and procedures. Ideally these rules and standards are customer based, as described in Chapter 10. When they are not, or when a customer makes

FIGURE 11.3 Boundary-spanning workers juggle many issues

excessive demands, the employee has to choose whether to follow the rules or satisfy the demands. The conflict is greatest when the employee believes the organization is wrong in its policies and must decide whether to accommodate the client and risk losing a job, or to follow the policies. These conflicts are especially severe when service employees depend directly on the customer for income. For example, employees who depend on tips or commissions are likely to face greater levels of organization/client conflict because they have even greater incentives to identify with the customer.

Inter-client conflict

Sometimes conflict occurs for boundary spanners when incompatible expectations and requirements arise from two or more customers. This situation occurs most often when the service provider is serving customers in turn (a bank teller, a supermarket checkout operator, a doctor) or is serving many customers simultaneously (teachers, entertainers).

When serving customers in turn, the provider may satisfy one customer by spending additional time, customizing the service, and being very flexible in meeting the customer's needs. Meanwhile, waiting customers are becoming dissatisfied because their needs are not being met in a timely way. Beyond the timing issue, different clients may prefer different modes of service delivery. Having to serve one client who prefers personal recognition and a degree of familiarity in the presence of another client who is all business and would prefer little interpersonal interaction can also create conflict for the employee.

When serving many customers at the same time, employees often find it difficult or impossible simultaneously to serve the full range of needs of a group of heterogeneous customers. This type of conflict is readily apparent in any classroom in which the teacher must meet a multitude of expectations and different preferences for formats and style.

Quality/productivity trade-offs

Front-line service workers are asked to be both effective and efficient: they are expected to deliver satisfying service to customers and at the same time to be cost-effective and productive in what they do. A dentist, for example, is expected to deliver caring, quality, individualized service to his or her patients but at the same time to serve a certain number of patients within a specified time frame. A checkout operator at a grocery store is expected to know his or her customers and to be polite and courteous, yet also to process the groceries accurately and move people through the line quickly. An architectural draftsperson is expected to create quality drawings, yet to produce a required quantity of drawings in a given period of time. These essential trade-offs between quality and quantity and between maximum effectiveness and efficiency place real-time demands and pressures on service employees.

Research suggests that these trade-offs are more difficult for service businesses than for manufacturing and packaged goods businesses, and that pursuing goals of customer satisfaction and productivity simultaneously is particularly challenging in situations in which service employees are required to customize service offerings to meet customer needs.[30]

Jagdip Singh, a noted services researcher, has studied productivity and quality as two types of performance inherent in front-line service jobs.[31] He explains the difficult trade-offs that employees face and has developed ways to measure these two types of performance together with a theoretical model to predict the causes and consequences of these trade-offs. He finds that quality of job performance is particularly susceptible to burnout and job stress. He also finds that internal support from understanding managers and control over the job tasks can help employees in making quality and productivity trade-offs, avoiding burnout and maintaining their performance. Technology is being used to an ever-greater degree to balance the quality/quantity trade-off to increase productivity of service workers and at the same time free them to provide higher-quality service for the customer. Through software applications, calls coming into call centres are identified (by telephone number and market segment) and routed to the right customer segment personnel even before the calls are answered. Employees get the calls that they are trained for and best able to handle. The software also allows the employee to view the entire account history of the caller, and this information is available on the employee's computer screen simultaneously with the incoming call. Employees have at their fingertips information on the wide variety of services on offer and other options available to customers. The person who answers the call is empowered to make decisions, answer questions and encourage sales in ways that were totally impractical prior to this technology.

Although front-office customer relationship management (CRM) systems hold great promise and have provided tremendous bottom-line benefits for companies already, they come with their own, often significant, challenges. They can require major monetary and human investments. They often mandate integration of incompatible information systems, significant internal training costs and incentives to be sure they are used effectively. Frequently they fail, at least on the initial try, for a variety of reasons. Some companies do not anticipate the amount of work involved, and many do not realize how resistant their employees will be to making the necessary changes. Even giant Microsoft faced significant challenges when it attempted to integrate all of its 36 distinct customer information applications worldwide. Microsoft underestimated the internal demands of such a large deployment and cut back on end-user training at the wrong time. It learned that training (of employees and, sometimes, customers) is critical to the success of the technology. Despite some difficulties, however, the system soon began to pay for itself, allowing Microsoft service staff and salespeople to make decisions better and in a more timely fashion, satisfying customers and building the business.

Strategies for delivering service quality through people

A complex combination of strategies is needed to ensure that service employees are willing and able to deliver quality services and that they stay motivated to perform in customer-oriented, service-minded ways. These strategies for enabling service promises are often referred to as **internal marketing**, as shown in the service triangle (Figure 1.3) in Chapter 1.[32] Even during slow economic times, the importance of attracting, developing and retaining good people in knowledge- and service-based industries cannot be overemphasized, as *Fast Company* magazine suggested: 'When it comes to building great companies, the most urgent business challenge is finding and keeping great people. Sure a Web strategy is important, and the stock market is scary, but still the best companies know that people are the foundation of greatness.'[33]

By approaching human resource decisions and strategies from the point of view that the primary goal is to motivate and enable employees to deliver successfully customer-oriented promises, an organization will move towards delivering service quality through its people. The strategies presented here are organized around four basic themes. To build a customer-oriented, service-minded workforce, an organization must (1) hire the right people, (2) develop people to deliver service quality, (3) provide the needed support systems, and (4) retain the best people. Within each of these basic strategies are a number of specific substrategies for accomplishing the goal, as shown in Figure 11.4.

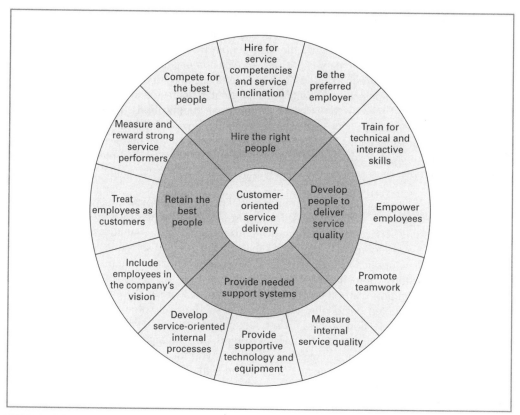

FIGURE 11.4 Human resource strategies for delivering service quality through people

Hire the right people

To effectively deliver service quality, considerable attention should be focused on recruiting and **hiring service employees**. Such attention is contrary to traditional practices in many service industries, where service personnel are the lowest on the corporate ladder and work for a minimum wage. At the other end of the spectrum, in the professional services, the most important recruiting criteria are typically technical training, certifications and expertise. However, many organizations are now looking above and beyond the technical qualifications of applicants to assess their customer and service orientation as well. Figure 11.4 shows a number of ways to go about hiring the right people.

Compete for the best people

To get the best people, an organization needs to identify them and compete with other organizations to hire them. Leonard Berry and A. Parasuraman refer to this approach as 'competing for talent market share'.[34] They suggest that firms act as marketers in their pursuit of the best employees, just as they use their marketing expertise to compete for customers. Firms that think of recruiting as a marketing activity will address issues of market (employee) segmentation, product (job) design and promotion of job availability in ways that attract potential long-term employees.

Hire for service competencies and service inclination

Once potential employees have been identified, organizations need to be conscientious in interviewing and screening to truly identify the best people from the pool of candidates. Service employees need two complementary capacities: *service competencies* and *service inclination.*[35]

Service competencies are the skills and knowledge necessary to do the job. In many cases, employees validate competencies by achieving particular degrees and certifications, such as attaining a degree and passing the relevant professional qualifications. These are required of doctors, airline pilots, university professors, teachers and many other job seekers before they are ever interviewed for service jobs in their fields. In other cases, service competencies may not be degree related but may instead relate to basic intelligence or physical requirements. A checkout assistant, for example, must possess basic mathematical skills and the potential to operate a cash register.

Given the multidimensional nature of service quality, service employees should be screened for more than their service competencies. They must also be screened for *service inclination* – their interest in doing service-related work – which is reflected in their attitudes towards service and orientation toward serving customers and others on the job. Self-selection suggests that most service jobs will draw applicants with some level of service inclination and that most employees in service organizations are inclined towards service. However, some employees clearly have a greater service inclination than others. Research has shown that service effectiveness is correlated with service-oriented personality characteristics such as helpfulness, thoughtfulness and sociability.[36] An ideal selection process for service employees assesses both service competencies and service inclination, resulting in employee hires who are high on both dimensions.[37]

In many cases a component of the selection process will include a form of work simulation that allows employees to demonstrate how they would actually perform on the job. A simulation may take the form of role-playing or a series of exercises that parallel the demands of the actual job. In addition to being a good way to assess potential employee abilities, simulations can give the potential recruit a better view of what the job is actually like. Those candidates who do not like what they experience can back out of the applicant pool before being hired and then finding out the job is not what they had expected.

Be the preferred employer

One way to attract the best people is to be known as the preferred employer in a particular industry or in a particular location. This is achieved through extensive training, career and advancement opportunities, excellent internal support, attractive incentives, and quality goods and services that employees are proud to be associated with. Organizations such as Marks and Spencer, British Airways, Hilton, Ritz-Carlton, Mercedes and Accenture would all be seen as preferred employers in their sector.

Develop people to deliver service quality

To grow and maintain a workforce that is customer oriented and focused on delivering quality, an organization must develop its employees to deliver service quality. That is, once it has hired the right employees, the organization must train and work with these individuals to ensure service performance.

Train for technical and interactive skills

To provide quality service, employees need ongoing training in the necessary technical skills and knowledge and in process or interactive skills.[38] Examples of technical skills and knowledge are working with accounting systems in hotels, cash machine procedures in a retail store, underwriting procedures in an insurance company and any operational rules the company has for running its business. Most service organizations are quite conscious of, and relatively effective at, training employees in technical skills. These skills may be taught through formal education, as is the case at McDonald's Hamburger University, which trains McDonald's managers from all over the world. Additionally, technical skills are often taught through on-the-job training, as when education students work with experienced teachers in internship programmes or when telephone service trainees listen in on the conversations of experienced employees. Companies are increasing their use of information technology to train employees in the technical skills and knowledge needed on the job.

Service employees also need training in interactive skills that allow them to provide courteous, caring, responsive and empathetic service. Successful companies invest heavily in training and make sure that the training fits their business goals and strategies.

Service spotlight

At the Ritz-Carlton, all employees go through extensive initial training and are given pocket-sized, laminated credo cards to carry in their wallets. The credo card specifies the three steps of service, Ritz-Carlton's well-known motto 'We are Ladies and Gentlemen Serving Ladies and Gentlemen', and the credo itself. Further, employees in every hotel attend a brief standing staff meeting each day to review one of Ritz-Carlton's 'Gold Standards: The 20 Basics' so as to continually reinforce earlier training.

Empower employees

Many organizations have discovered that to be truly responsive to customer needs, front-line providers need to be empowered to accommodate customer requests and to recover on the spot when things go wrong. ***Empowerment*** means giving employees the desire, skills, tools and authority to serve the customer. Although the key to empowerment is giving employees authority to make decisions on the customer's behalf, authority alone is not enough. Employees need the knowledge and tools to be able to make these decisions, and they need incentives that encourage them to make the right decisions. Organizations do not succeed in empowering their employees if they simply tell them, 'You now have the authority to do whatever it takes to satisfy the customer'. First, employees often do not believe this statement, particularly if the organization has functioned hierarchically or bureaucratically in the past. Second, employees often do not know what it means to 'do whatever it takes' if they have not received training, guidelines and the tools needed to make such decisions.

Research suggests positive benefits to empowering front-line service workers. Some of these benefits include reduction in job-related stress, improved job satisfaction, greater adaptability and better outcomes for customers.[39] But such success does not come easily. In fact, some experts have concluded that few organizations have truly taken advantage of, or properly implemented, successful empowerment strategies.[40] Nor is empowerment the answer for all organizations. David Bowen and Edward Lawler,[41] experts on this subject, suggest that organizations well suited to empowerment strategies are ones in which (1) the business strategy is one of differentiation and customization, (2) customers are long-term relationship customers, (3) technology is non-routine or complex, (4) the business environment is unpredictable, and (5) managers and employees have high growth and social needs and strong interpersonal skills. They also enumerate the costs and benefits of empowerment as:[42]

Benefits

- *Quicker online responses to customer needs during service delivery.* Employees who are allowed to make decisions on behalf of the customer can make decisions more quickly, bypassing what in the past might have meant a long chain of command, or at least a discussion with an immediate supervisor.

- *Quicker online responses to dissatisfied customers during service recovery.* When failures occur in the delivery system, customers hope for an immediate recovery effort on the part of the organization. Empowered employees can recover on the spot, and a dissatisfied customer can potentially be turned into a satisfied, even loyal, one.

- *Employees feel better about their jobs and themselves.* Giving employees control and authority to make decisions makes them feel responsible and gives them ownership for the customer's satisfaction. Decades of job design research suggest that when employees have a sense of control and of doing meaningful work, they are more satisfied. The result is lower turnover and less absenteeism.

- *Employees will interact with customers with more warmth and enthusiasm.* Employees feel better about themselves and their work, and these attitudes will spill over into their feelings about customers and will be reflected in their interactions.

- *Empowered employees are a great source of service ideas.* When employees are empowered, they feel responsible for the service outcome and they will be excellent sources of ideas about new services or how to improve current offerings.

- *Great word-of-mouth advertising from customers.* Empowered employees do special and unique things that customers will remember and tell their friends, family and associates about.

Costs

- *A potentially greater investment in selection and training.* To find employees who will work well in an empowered environment requires creative, potentially more costly selection procedures. Training will also be more expensive in general because employees need more knowledge about the company, its products and how to work in flexible ways with customers.

- *Higher labour costs.* The organization may not be able to use as many part-time or seasonal employees, and it may need to pay more for asking employees to assume responsibility.

- *Potentially slower or inconsistent service delivery.* If empowered employees spend more time with all, or even some, customers, then service overall may take longer and may annoy customers who are waiting. Empowerment also means that customers will get what they need or request. When decisions regarding customer satisfaction are left to the discretion of employees, there may be inconsistency in the level of service delivered.

- *May violate customers' perceptions of fair play.* Customers may perceive that sticking to procedures with every customer is fair. Thus, if they see that customers are receiving different levels of service or that employees are cutting special deals with some customers, they may believe that the organization is not fair.

- *Employees may 'give away the store' or make bad decisions.* Many people fear that empowered employees will make costly decisions that the organization cannot afford. Although this situation can happen, good training and appropriate guidelines will help.

Promote teamwork

The nature of many service jobs suggests that customer satisfaction will be enhanced when employees work as teams. Because service jobs are frequently frustrating, demanding and challenging, a teamwork environment will help alleviate some of the stresses and strains. Employees who feel supported and feel that they have a team backing them up will be better able to maintain their enthusiasm and provide quality service.[43] 'An interactive community of co-workers who help each other, commiserate and achieve together is a powerful antidote to service burnout',[44] and, we would add, an important ingredient for service quality. By promoting teamwork, an organization can enhance the employees' *abilities* to deliver excellent service while the camaraderie and support enhance their *inclination* to be excellent service providers.

One way of promoting teamwork is to encourage the attitude that 'everyone has a customer'. That is, even when employees are not directly responsible for or in direct interaction with the final customer, they need to know whom they serve directly and how the role they play in the total service picture is essential to the final delivery of quality service. If each employee can see how he or she is somehow integral in delivering quality to the final customer and if each employee knows who to support to make service quality a reality, teamwork will be enhanced. Service blueprints, described in Chapter 8, can serve as useful tools to illustrate for employees their integral roles in delivering service quality to the ultimate customer.

Team goals and rewards also promote teamwork. When a firm rewards teams of individuals rather than basing all rewards on individual achievements and performance, team efforts and team spirit are encouraged.

Provide needed support systems

To be efficient and effective in their jobs, service workers require internal support systems that are aligned with their need to be customer focused. This point cannot be overemphasized. In fact, without customer-focused internal support and customer-oriented systems, it is nearly impossible for employees to deliver quality service no matter how much they want to. For example, a bank teller who is rewarded for customer satisfaction as well as for accuracy in bank transactions needs easy access to up-to-date customer records, a well-staffed branch (so that he or she is not constantly facing a long line of impatient customers), and supportive customer-oriented supervisors and back-office staff. In examining customer service outcomes in Australian call centres, researchers found that internal support from supervisors, teammates and other departments as well as evaluations of technology used on the job were all strongly related to employee satisfaction and ability to serve customers.[45] The following sections suggest strategies for ensuring customer-oriented internal support.

Measure internal service quality

One way to encourage supportive internal service relationships is to measure and reward internal service. By first acknowledging that everyone in the organization has a customer and then measuring customer perceptions of internal service quality, an organization can begin to develop an internal quality culture. **Internal customer service audits** can be used to implement a culture of internal service quality. Through the audit, internal organizations identify their customers, determine their needs, measure how well they are doing and make improvements. The process parallels market research practices used for external customers.

CASE STUDY: STEPS IN CONDUCTING AN INTERNAL CUSTOMER SERVICE AUDIT[46]

1 *Define your customer.*

  a List all the people or departments in the organization who need help from you or your department in any way. This list may include specific departments, particular staff people, the CEO, certain executives or the board of directors.

  b Prioritize the names on the list, placing the people or departments that rely on you the most at the top.

2 *Identify your contribution.*

  a For each of these customers, specify the primary need you think they have to which you can contribute. Talk to your internal customers about what problems they are trying to solve and think about how you can help.

3 *Define service quality.*

  a What are the critical moments of truth that really define the department–internal customer interface from your customer's point of view? Blueprint the process and list the moments of truth.

  b For each major internal customer, design a customer report card (based on customer input) and a set of evaluation criteria for your department's service package, as seen through the eyes of that customer. The criteria might include such dimensions as timeliness, reliability and cost.

4 *Validate your criteria.*

  a Talk to your customers. Allow them to revise, as necessary, how you saw their needs and the criteria they used in assessing your performance. This dialogue itself can go a long way toward building internal service teamwork.

5 *Measure service quality.*

  a Evaluate your service (using internal measures and/or customer surveys) against the quality criteria you established in talking to your customers. See how you score. Identify opportunities for improvement. Set up a process and timetable for following through.

6 *Develop a mission statement based on what you contribute.*

  a Consider drafting a brief, meaningful service mission statement for your operation. Be certain to frame it in terms of the value you *contribute*, not what you *do*. For example, the mission of the HR department should not be 'to deliver training' (the action); it would be 'to create competent people' (the contribution).

One risk of measuring and focusing on internal service quality and internal customers is that people can sometimes get so involved in meeting the needs of internal customers that they forget they are in business to serve the ultimate, external customers.[47] In measuring internal service quality, therefore, it is important to constantly draw the linkages between what is being delivered internally and how it supports the delivery of the final service to customers. Service blueprinting, introduced in Chapter 8, can help to illustrate these critical linkages.

Provide supportive technology and equipment

When employees do not have the right equipment or their equipment fails them, they can be easily frustrated in their desire to deliver quality service. To do their jobs effectively and efficiently, service employees need the right equipment and technology. Having the right technology and equipment can extend into strategies regarding workplace and workstation design.

Service spotlight

In designing their corporate headquarters offices, Scandinavian Airline Systems identified particular service-oriented goals that it wished to achieve, among them teamwork and open, frequent communication among managers. An office environment was designed with open spaces (to encourage meetings) and internal windows in offices (to encourage frequent interactions). In this way the work space facilitated the internal service orientation.

Develop service-oriented internal processes

To best support service personnel in their delivery of quality service on the front line, an organization's internal processes should be designed with customer value and customer satisfaction in mind. In other words, internal procedures must support quality service performance. In many companies internal processes are driven by bureaucratic rules, tradition, cost efficiencies or the needs of internal employees. Providing service- and customer-oriented internal processes can therefore imply a need for total redesign of systems. This kind of wholesale redesign of systems and processes has become known as 'process re-engineering'. Although developing service-oriented internal processes through re-engineering sounds sensible, it is probably one of the most difficult strategies to implement, especially in organizations that are steeped in tradition. Refocusing internal processes and introducing large amounts of new, supportive technology were among the changes made by British Telecom in its transition from a traditional, operations-driven company to a customer-focused one.

Retain the best people

An organization that hires the right people, trains and develops them to deliver service quality, and provides the needed support must also work to retain them. Employee turnover, especially when the best service employees are leaving, can be very detrimental to customer satisfaction, employee morale and overall service quality. And, just as they do with customers, some firms spend a lot of time attracting employees but then tend to take them for granted (or even worse), causing these good employees to search for alternative jobs. Although all the strategies depicted in Figure 11.4 will support the retention of the best employees, here we focus on some strategies that are particularly aimed at this goal.

Include employees in the company's vision

For employees to remain motivated and interested in sticking with the organization and supporting its goals, they need to share an understanding of the organization's vision. People who deliver service day after day need to understand how their work fits into the big picture of the organization and its goals. They will be motivated to some extent by their pay and other benefits, but the best employees will be attracted away to other opportunities if they are not committed to the vision of the organization. They cannot be committed to the vision if that vision is kept secret from them. What this strategy means in practice is that the vision is communicated frequently to employees and that it is communicated by top managers, often by the CEO.[48] Respected CEOs such as Richard Branson of the Virgin Group and Ingvar Kamprad of IKEA are known for communicating their visions clearly and often to employees. When the vision and direction are clear and motivating, employees are more likely to remain with the company through the inevitable rough spots along the path to the vision.

Treat employees as customers

If employees feel valued and their needs are taken care of, they are more likely to stay with the organization. Many companies have adopted the idea that employees are also customers of the organization and that basic marketing strategies can be directed at them.[49] The products that the organization has to offer its employees are a job (with assorted benefits) and quality of work life. To determine whether the job and work-life needs of employees are being met, organizations conduct periodic internal marketing research to assess employee satisfaction and needs.

In addition to basic internal research, organizations can apply other marketing strategies to their management of employees. For example, segmentation of the employee population is apparent in many of the flexible benefit plans and career path choices now available to employees. Organizations that are set up to meet the needs of specific segments and to adjust as people proceed through their lives will benefit from increased employee loyalty. Advertising and other forms of communication directed at employees can also increase their sense of value and enhance their commitment to the organization.[50]

Measure and reward strong service performers

If a company wants the strongest service performers to stay with the organization, it must reward and promote them. This strategy may seem obvious, but often the reward systems in organizations are not set up to reward service excellence. Reward systems may value productivity, sales or some other dimension that can potentially work *against* good service. Even those service workers who are intrinsically motivated to deliver high service quality will become discouraged at some point and start looking elsewhere if their efforts are not recognized and rewarded.

Reward systems need to be linked to the organization's vision and to outcomes that are truly important. For instance, if customer satisfaction and retention are viewed as critical outcomes, service behaviours that increase those outcomes need to be recognized and rewarded. In the Royal Bank of Scotland and National Westminster Bank, employees in branches do not receive their sales bonuses unless their branch has achieved the required customer service scores.

Service spotlight

At Intel, the 'Vender of Choice' (VOC) customer retention measure is incorporated into all employees' incentive systems. For example, in January 2002 when VOC was 96 per cent across the entire company, all employees received an extra day of pay, costing the company millions of dollars. The VOC score is calculated from customers' statements as to whether Intel is their first-choice vendor for a particular product or service. The measure itself, along with all the analyses and service improvement initiatives that are behind it, is intended to align employee behaviour around retaining customers.

Companies with a goal of customer satisfaction in every service encounter often need to adjust the criteria by which employee performance is judged. Mystery shopping scores may be used in determining rewards for staff in organizations such as Burger King.

Aligning reward systems with customer outcomes can be challenging. Reward systems are usually well entrenched, and employees have learned over time how they need to perform within the old structures. Change is difficult both for the managers who may have created and still may believe in the old systems and for employees who are not sure what they need to do to succeed under the new rules. In many organizations, however, reward and incentive systems are still not matched with customer satisfaction and loyalty goals.[51]

In developing new systems and structures to recognize customer focus and customer satisfaction, organizations have turned to a variety of rewards. Traditional approaches such as higher pay, promotions and one-off monetary awards or prizes can be linked to service performance. Other types of rewards include special organizational and team celebrations for achieving improved customer satisfaction or for attaining customer retention goals. In most service organizations it is not only the major accomplishments but the daily perseverance and attention to detail that move the organization forward, so recognition of the 'small wins' is also important.

In many situations, a customer's relationship is with a specific employee and may be stronger with the *employee* than with the firm. If this employee leaves the firm and is no longer available to the customer, the firm's relationship with the customer may be jeopardized.[52] Clearly, a firm should make great efforts to retain such employees; however, in spite of the firm's best efforts, some good employees are going to leave. If the firm is not successful at retaining a key customer-contact employee, what can it do to reduce the impact on the customer? Employees could be rotated occasionally in order to ensure that the customer has exposure to and is comfortable with more than one employee. Firms might also form teams of employees who are responsible for interacting with each customer. In both cases, the idea is that the customer would have multiple contacts with several employees in the organization, thus reducing the firm's vulnerability to losing the customer should any one employee leave. Emphasis should also be placed on creating a positive firm image in the minds of its customers and in so doing convey that *all* its employees are capable.[53]

Customer-oriented service delivery

As indicated by the examples presented in this chapter, specific approaches for hiring and energizing front-line workers take on a different look and feel across companies, based on the organization's values, culture, history and vision.[54] For example, 'developing people to deliver service quality' is accomplished quite differently at TGIF restaurants than at Disney. At Disney the orientation and training process is highly structured, scripted and standardized. At TGIF restaurants, the emphasis is more on developing needed skills but then empowering employees to be spontaneous and non-scripted in their approach to customers. Although the style and culture of the two organizations are different, both pay special attention to all four basic themes shown in Figure 11.4. Both have made significant investments in their people, recognizing the critical roles they play.

Throughout this book we have advocated a strong customer focus. Firms that have a strong service culture clearly put an emphasis on the customer and the customer's experience. In order to do so, firms must also create an environment that staunchly supports the customer-contact employee, because this person in the organization is frequently most responsible for ensuring that the customer's experience is delivered as designed. Historically, many firms have viewed

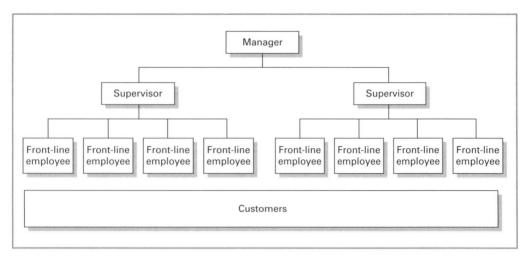

FIGURE 11.5 Traditional organizational chart

senior management as the most important people in the firm and, indeed, organizational charts reflect this view in their structure. Such an approach, as suggested in Figure 11.5, places management at the top of the structure and (implicitly) the customer at the bottom, with customer-contact employees just above them. If the organization's most important people are customers, they should be at the top of the chart, followed by those with whom they have contact. Such a view, illustrated in Figure 11.6, is more consistent with a customer-oriented focus. In effect, the role of top-level management changes from that of commanding employees to that of facilitating and supporting employees in the organization who are closest to the customer. The human resource strategies that we have offered in this chapter are suggested as a means to support the customer contact employee. A statement by Michel Bon, CEO of France Telecom, succinctly summarizes the philosophy behind this approach: 'If you sincerely believe that "the customer is king," the second most important person in this kingdom must be the one who has a direct interaction on a daily basis with the one who is king.'[55]

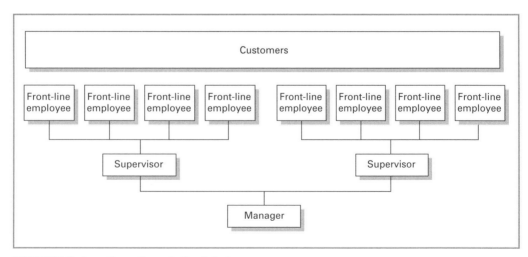

FIGURE 11.6 Customer-focused organizational chart

Summary

Because many services are delivered by people in real time, closing the service performance gap is heavily dependent on human resource strategies. The successful execution of such strategies begins with the development and nurturing of a true service culture in which 'an appreciation for good service exists, and where giving good service to internal as well as ultimate, external customers is considered a natural way of life and one of the most important norms by everyone'.[56]

Often, service employees are the service, and in all cases they represent the organization in customers' eyes. They affect service quality perceptions to a large degree through their influence on the five dimensions of service quality: reliability, responsiveness, empathy, assurance and tangibles. It is essential to match what the customer wants and needs with service employees' abilities to deliver.

In this chapter we focused on service employees to provide you with an understanding of the critical nature of their roles and appreciation of the inherent stresses and conflicts they face. You learned that front-line service jobs demand significant investments of emotional labour and that employees confront a variety of on-the-job conflicts. Sometimes service employees are personally uncomfortable with the roles they are asked to play; other times the requirements of the organization may conflict with client expectations, and employees must resolve the dilemma on the spot. Sometimes there are conflicting needs among customers who are being served in turn (such as in a bank teller line) or among customers being served simultaneously (as in a college classroom). At other times a front-line employee may be faced with a decision about whether to satisfy a customer or meet productivity targets (such as a dentist who is required to see a certain number of patients in a defined period of time).

Grounded in this understanding of the importance of service employees and the nature of their roles in the organization, you learned strategies for integrating appropriate human resource practices into service firms. The strategies are aimed at allowing employees to effectively satisfy customers as well as be efficient and productive in their jobs. The strategies were organized around four major human resource goals in service organizations: to hire the right people, to develop people to deliver service quality, to provide needed support systems, and to retain the best people. A company that works toward implementing these strategies is well on its way to delivering service quality through its people, thereby diminishing gap 3.

Key concepts

Boundary spanners	275	Hiring service employees	281
Corporate culture	269	Internal customer service audit	285
Emotional labour	275		
Employee retention	273	Internal marketing	280
Employee satisfaction	273	Service culture	269
Employees are marketers	272	Service leadership	270
Employees are the brand	272	Service profit chain	273
Empowerment	283		

Further reading

Argyris, C. (1998) 'Empowerment: the emperor's new clothes', *Harvard Business Review*, 76, 98–105.

Bowen, D.A., Schneider, B. and Kim, S.S. (2000) 'Shaping service cultures through strategic human resource management', in T.A. Swartz and D. Iacobucci (eds), *Handbook of Services Marketing and Management*. Thousand Oaks, CA: Sage Publications, pp. 439–54.

Chebat, J.C. and Kollias P. (2000) 'The impact of empowerment on customer contact employees' roles in service organisations', *Journal of Service Research*, 3, 66–81.

Edvardsson, B. and Enqvist, B. (2002) 'The IKEA saga: how service culture drives service strategy', *The Service Industries Journal*, 22(4), 153–66.

Hesket, J.L., Earl Sasser Jr, W. and Schlesinger L.L. (1997) *The Service Profit Chain*. New York: Free Press.

Schein, E.H. (1992) *Organizational Culture and Leadership*, 2nd edn. San Francisco, CA: Jossey-Bass.

Scheider, B., Hayes, S.C., Lim, B.-C. and Raver, J.L. (2003) 'The human side of strategy: employee experiences of strategic alignment in service organization', *Organizational Dynamics*, 32(2), 122–38.

Wilson, A.M. (1997), 'The nature of corporate culture within a service delivery environment', *International Journal of Service Industry Management*, 8(1), 87–102.

Wilson, A.M. (2001) 'Understanding organisational culture and the implications for corporate marketing', *European Journal of Marketing*, 35(4), 353–68.

Wilson, A.M. and Frimpong, J. (2004), 'Towards an integrated conceptualisation of the determinants of employee service orientation', *Journal of Services Marketing*, 18(6), 471–81.

Discussion questions

1 Define *service culture*. Why is service culture so important? Can a manufacturing firm have a service culture? Why or why not?

2 Why are service employees critical to the success of any service organization? Why do we include an entire chapter on service employees in a marketing course?

3 What is emotional labour? How can it be differentiated from physical or mental labour?

4 Reflect on your own role as a frontline service provider, whether in a current job or in any full- or part-time service job you have had in the past. Did you experience the kinds of conflicts described in the boundary-spanning roles section of the chapter? Be prepared with some concrete examples for class discussion.

5 Select a service provider (your dentist, doctor, lawyer, hair stylist) with whom you are familiar, and discuss ways this person could positively influence the five dimensions of

service quality in the context of delivering his or her services. Do the same for yourself (if you are currently a service provider).

6 Describe the four basic human resource strategy themes and why each plays an important role in building a customer-oriented organization.

7 What is the difference between technical and interactive service skills? Provide examples (preferably from your own work context or from another context with which you are familiar). Why do service employees need training in both?

8 Is empowerment always the best approach for effective service delivery? Why is employee empowerment so controversial?

 ## Exercises

1 Visit the websites of companies with known world-class service cultures (such as Ritz-Carlton, FedEx or SAS airlines). How does the information conveyed on the website reinforce the company's service culture?

2 Review the section of the chapter on boundary-spanning roles. Interview at least two front-line service personnel regarding the stresses they experience in their jobs. How do the examples they provide relate to the sources of conflict and trade-offs described in the text?

3 Assume that you are the manager of a team of front-line customer-service employees in a credit card company. Assume that these employees work over the telephone and that they deal primarily with customer requests, questions and complaints. In this specific context,

  (a) Define what is meant by *boundary-spanning roles*, and discuss the basic purposes or functions performed by participants in these roles.

  (b) Discuss two of the potential conflicts that your employees may face on the basis of their roles as boundary spanners.

  (c) Discuss how you, as their supervisor, might deal with these conflicts based on what you have learned.

4 Choose one or more of the human resource strategy themes (hire the right people, develop people to deliver service quality, provide needed support systems, retain the best people). Interview a manager in a service organization of your choice regarding his or her current practices within the theme you have chosen. Describe the current practices and recommend any appropriate changes for improving them.

Notes

[1] L.L. Berry, *Discovering the Soul of Service* (New York: Free Press, 1999).

[2] Interview with Singapore Airlines senior vice president of marketing services, included in 'How may I help you?', *Fast Company* (March 2000), pp. 93–126.

[3] P. Gallagher, 'Getting it right from the start', *Journal of Retail Banking* 15 (Spring 1993), pp. 39–41.

[4] J.S. Hirsch, 'Now hotel clerks provide more than keys', *The Wall Street Journal*, 5 March 1993, p. B1.

[5] Berry, *Discovering the Soul of Service.*

[6] S.M. Davis, *Managing Corporate Culture* (Cambridge, MA: Ballinger, 1985).

[7] C. Gronroos, *Service Management and Marketing* (Lexington, MA: Lexington Books, 1990), p. 244.

[8] See K.N. Kennedy, F.G. Lassk, and J.R. Goolsby, 'Customer mind-set of employees throughout the organization', *Journal of the Academy of Marketing Science*, 30 (Spring 2002), pp. 159–71.

[9] R. Hallowell, D. Bowen and C. Knoop, 'Four Seasons goes to Paris', *Academy of Management Executive* 16, no. 4 (2002), pp. 7–24; J.L. Heskett, L.A. Schlesinger and E.W. Sasser Jr, *The Service Profit Chain* (New York: Free Press, 1997); B. Schneider and D.E. Bowen, *Winning the Service Game* (Boston, MA: Harvard Business School Press, 1995).

[10] Berry, *Discovering the Soul of Service*, p. 40.

[11] Hallowell, Bowen and Knoop, 'Four Seasons goes to Paris'.

[12] For an excellent discussion of the complexities involved in creating and sustaining a service culture, see Schneider and Bowen, *Winning the Service Game*, ch. 9. See also M.D. Hartline, J.G. Maxham III and D.O. McKee, 'Corridors of influence in the dissemination of customer-oriented strategy to customer-contact service employees', *Journal of Marketing* 64 (April 2000), pp. 35–50.

[13] This quote is most frequently attributed to J. Carlzon of Scandinavian Airline Systems.

[14] J. Garrett, 'The human side of brand: why Audi hires workers with the same traits as its luxury cars', *Gallup Management Journal* (Summer 2001), pp. 4–5.

[15] See, for example, H. Rosenbluth, 'Tales from a nonconformist company', *Harvard Business Review* (July–August 1991), pp. 26–36; and L.A. Schlesinger and J.L. Heskett, 'The service-driven service company', *Harvard Business Review* (September–October 1991), pp. 71–81.

[16] B. Schneider and D.E. Bowen, 'The service organization: human resources management is crucial', *Organizational Dynamics* 21, (Spring 1993), pp. 39–52.

[17] D.E. Bowen, S.W. Gilliland and R. Folger, 'How being fair with employees spills over to customers', *Organizational Dynamics* 27 (Winter 1999), pp. 7–23.

[18] See J.L. Heskett, T.O. Jones, G.W. Loveman, W.E. Sasser Jr and L.A. Schlesinger, 'Putting the service–profit chain to work', *Harvard Business Review* (March–April 1994), pp. 164–74; G.W. Loveman, 'Employee satisfaction, customer loyalty, and financial performance', *Journal of Service Research* 1 (August 1998), pp. 18–31; A. Rucci, S.P. Kirn and R.T. Quinn, 'The employee–customer profit chain at Sears', *Harvard Business Review* (January–February 1998), pp. 82–97; and R. Hallowell and L.L. Schlesinger, 'The service–profit chain', in *The Handbook of Services Marketing and Management*, eds T.A. Swartz and D. Iacobucci (Thousand Oaks, CA: Sage Publications, 2000), pp. 203–22.

[19] J. Pfeffer, *The Human Equation* (Boston, MA: Harvard Business School Press, 1998); and A.M. Webber, 'Danger: toxic company', *Fast Company* (November 1998), pp. 152–62.

[20] M.K. Brady and J.J. Cronin Jr, 'Customer orientation: effects on customer service perceptions and outcome behaviors', *Journal of Service Research* 3 (February 2001), pp. 241–51.

[21] L.A. Bettencourt and K. Gwinner, 'Customization of the service experience: the role of the frontline employee', *International Journal of Service Industry Management* 7, no. 2 (1996), pp. 3–20.

22 For research on the influence of frontline employee behaviours on customers, see D.D. Gremler and K.P. Gwinner, 'Customer–employee rapport in service relationships', *Journal of Service Research* 3 (August 2000), pp. 82–104; K. de Ruyter and M.G.M. Wetzels, 'The impact of perceived listening behavior in voice-to-voice service encounters', *Journal of Service Research* 2 (February 2000), pp. 276–84; T.J. Brown, J.C. Mowen, D.T. Donavan and J.W. Licata, 'The customer orientation of service workers: personality trait effects of self- and supervisor performance ratings', *Journal of Marketing Research* 39 (February 2002), pp. 110–19.

23 A. Hochschild, *The Managed Heart: Commercialization of Human Feeling* (Berkeley, CA: University of California Press, 1983).

24 A. Hochschild, 'Emotional labor in the friendly skies', *Psychology Today* (June 1982), pp. 13–15.

25 For additional discussion on emotional labour strategies, see R. Leidner, 'Emotional labor in service work', *Annals of the American Academy of Political and Social Science* 561, no. 1 (1999), pp. 81–95.

26 Quoted from C.L. Macdonald and C. Sirianni, *Working in the Service Society* (Philadelphia: Temple University Press, 1996), p. 4.

27 Quoted from B.F. Ashforth and R.H. Humphrey, 'Emotional labor in service roles: the influence of identity', *Academy of Management Review* 18 (1993), p. 93.

28 M.D. Hartline and O.C. Ferrell, 'The management of customer-contact service employees: an empirical investigation', *Journal of Marketing* 60 (October 1996), pp. 52–70; J. Singh, J.R. Goolsby and G.K. Rhoads, 'Burnout and customer service representatives', *Journal of Marketing Research* 31 (November 1994), pp. 558–69; L.A. Bettencourt and S.W. Brown, 'Role stressors and customer-oriented boundary-spanning behaviors in service organizations', *Journal of the Academy of Marketing Science* 31 (Fall 2003), pp. 394–408.

29 B. Shamir, 'Between service and servility: role conflict in subordinate service roles', *Human Relations* 33, no. 10 (1980), pp. 741–56.

30 E.W. Anderson, C. Fornell and R.T. Rust, 'Customer satisfaction, productivity, and profitability: differences between goods and services', *Marketing Science* 16, no. 2 (1997), pp. 129–45.

31 J. Singh, 'Performance productivity and quality of frontline employees in service organizations', *Journal of Marketing* 64 (April 2000), pp. 15–34.

32 For discussions of internal marketing, see L.L. Berry and A. Parasuraman, 'Marketing to employees', in *Marketing Services*, L.L. Berry and A. Parasuraman, (New York: Free Press, 1991) ch. 9; C. Gronroos, 'Managing internal marketing: a prerequisite for successful external marketing', in *Service Management and Marketing*, C. Gronroos (Lexington, MA: Lexington Books, 1990), ch. 10.

33 B. Breen and A. Muoio, 'PeoplePalooza 2001', *Fast Company* (January 2001), cover and feature article.

34 Berry and Parasuraman, 'Marketing to employees', p. 153.

35 This section on hiring for service competencies and service inclination draws from work by B. Schneider and colleagues, specifically, B. Schneider and D. Schechter, 'Development of a personnel selection system for service jobs', in *Service Quality: Multidisciplinary and Multinational Perspectives*, eds S.W. Brown, E. Gummesson, B. Edvardsson and B. Gustavsson (Lexington, MA: Lexington Books, 1991), pp. 217–36.

36 J. Hogan, R. Hogan and C.M. Busch, 'How to measure service orientation', *Journal of Applied Psychology* 69, no. 1 (1984), pp. 167–73. See also Brown et al., 'The customer orientation of service workers'; and D.T. Donovan, T.J. Brown and J.C. Mowen, 'Internal benefits of service-

worker customer orientation: job satisfaction, commitment, and organizational citizenship behaviors', *Journal of Marketing* 68 (January 2004), pp. 128–46.

37 For a detailed description of a model selection system for telephone sales and service people, see Schneider and Schechter, 'Development of a personnel selection system'.

38 R. Normann, 'Getting people to grow', *Service Management* (New York: John Wiley, 1984), pp. 44–50.

39 J.C. Chebat and P. Kollias, 'The impact of empowerment on customer contact employees' roles in service organizations', *Journal of Service Research* 3 (August 2000), pp. 66–81.

40 C. Argyris, 'Empowerment: the emperor's new clothes', *Harvard Business Review* 76 (May–June 1998), pp. 98–105.

41 D.E. Bowen and E.E. Lawler III, 'The empowerment of service workers: what, why, how, and when', *Sloan Management Review* (Spring 1992), pp. 31–9.

42 Reprinted from 'The empowerment of service workers: what, why, how, and when', by D.E. Bowen and E.E. Lawler, *Sloan Management Review* (Spring 1992), pp. 31–9, by permission of the publisher. Copyright 1992 by Massachusetts Institute of Technology. All rights reserved.

43 J.H. Gittell, 'Relationships between service providers and their impact on customers', *Journal of Service Research* 4 (May 2002), pp. 299–311.

44 Berry and Parasuraman, 'Marketing to employees', p. 162.

45 A. Sergeant and S. Frenkel, 'When do customer-contact employees satisfy customers?', *Journal of Service Research* 3 (August 2000), pp. 18–34.

46 Reprinted from K. Albrecht, *At America's Service* (Homewood, IL: Dow-Jones-Irwin, 1988), pp. 139–42, as discussed in B. Schneider and D.E. Bowen, *Winning at the Service Game* (Boston, MA: Harvard Business School Press, 1995), pp. 231–2. © 1988 by Dow-Jones-Irwin. Reprinted by permission of The McGraw-Hill Companies.

47 Scheider and Bowen, *Winning the Service Game*, pp. 230–4.

48 O. Gadiesh and J.L. Gilbert, 'Transforming corner-office strategy into frontline action', *Harvard Business Review* (May 2001), pp. 73–9.

49 L.L. Berry, 'The employee as customer', *Journal of Retail Banking* 3 (March 1981), pp. 33–40.

50 M.C. Gilly and M. Wolfinbarger, 'Advertising's internal audience', *Journal of Marketing* 62 (January 1998), pp. 69–88.

51 See Schneider and Bowen, *Winning the Service Game*, ch. 6, for an excellent discussion of the complexities and issues involved in creating effective reward systems for service employees.

52 N. Bendapudi and R.P. Leone, 'Managing business-to-business customer relationships following key contact employee turnover in a vendor firm', *Journal of Marketing* 66 (April 2002), pp. 83–101.

53 Ibid.

54 J.R. Katzenbach and J.A. Santamaria, 'Firing up the front line', *Harvard Business Review* (May–June 1999), pp. 107–17.

55 Quoted in D. Stauffer, 'The art of delivering great customer service', *Harvard Management Update* 4, no. 9 (September 1999), pp. 1–3.

56 Gronroos, *Service Management and Marketing*, p. 244.

CHAPTER 12

Customers' roles in service delivery

❖ LEARNING OBJECTIVES

This chapter's objectives are to:

1 Illustrate the importance of customers in successful service delivery and co-creation of service experiences.

2 Discuss the variety of roles that service customers play: productive resources for the organization; contributors to quality and satisfaction; competitors.

3 Explain strategies for involving service customers effectively to increase both quality and productivity.

CASE STUDY: AT IKEA, CUSTOMERS CREATE VALUE FOR THEMSELVES[1]

Source: Michael Newman/Photo Edit

IKEA of Sweden has managed to transform itself from a small mail-order furniture company in the 1950s into the world's largest retailer of home furnishings. In 2006 over 200 stores in 35 countries around the world generated more than 17 500 million euros in revenues. The company sells simple Scandinavian design furnishings, charging 25 to 50 per cent less than its competitors.

A key to IKEA's success is the company's relationship with its customers. IKEA has drawn the customer into its production system: 'If customers agree to take on certain key tasks traditionally done by manufacturers and retailers – the assembly of products and their delivery to customers' homes – then IKEA promises to deliver well-designed products at substantially lower prices.' In effect, IKEA's customers become essential contributors to value – they create value for themselves through participating in the manufacturing, design and delivery processes.

IKEA has made being part of the value creation process an easy, fun and pleasant experience for customers. The stores are set up with 'inspirational displays', including realistic room settings and real-life homes that allow customers to get comfortable with the furnishings, try them out and visualize the possibilities in their own homes. To make shopping easy, free pushchairs and supervised child care are provided as well as wheelchairs for those who need them.

When customers enter the store they are given catalogues, tape measures, pens and notepaper to use as they shop, allowing them to perform functions commonly done by sales and service staff. After payment, customers take their purchases to their cars on trolleys; if necessary they can rent or buy a roof rack to carry larger purchases. Thus customers also provide furniture loading and delivery services for themselves. At home, IKEA customers then take on the role of manufacturer in assembling the new furnishings following carefully written, simple and direct instructions.

IKEA prints catalogues in more than 17 different languages, making its products and instructions for their use accessible worldwide. In addition to tailoring its catalogues, another key to IKEA's successful global expansion has been the company's policy of allowing each store to tailor its mix according to the local market needs and budgets. For example, in its China stores, layouts reflect the design of many Chinese apartments. Because many of the apartments have balconies, the stores have a selection of balcony furnishings and displays. And because Chinese kitchens are generally small, fewer kitchen items and furnishings are shown. Even IKEA's famous 'do it yourself' (DIY) assembly concept has also been adapted to some extent in China. Because fewer people have cars and therefore use public transport, IKEA has a more extensive delivery service in China than in most countries. And because labour is cheaper in China, many customers choose to have their furniture assembled for them rather than doing it themselves. Although IKEA has not abandoned its DIY strategy, it has been somewhat more flexible in China to suit customer realities in that country.

IKEA's success is attributable in part to recognizing that customers can be part of the business system, performing roles they have never performed before. The company's flexible implementation of this idea through clearly defining customers' new roles and making it fun to perform these roles is the genius of its strategy. Through the process, customers co-create their own experiences and contribute to their own satisfaction.

In this chapter we examine the unique roles played by customers in service delivery situations. Service customers are often present in the 'factory' (the place the service is produced and/or consumed), interacting with employees and with other customers. For example, in a classroom or training situation, students (the customers) are sitting in the factory interacting with the instructor and other students as they consume and co-create the educational services. Because they are present during service production, customers can contribute to or detract from the successful delivery of the service and to their own satisfaction. In a manufacturing context, rarely does the production facility contend with customer presence on the factory floor, nor does it rely on the customer's immediate real-time input to manufacture the product. As our opening vignette illustrates, service customers can actually produce the service themselves and to some extent are responsible for their own satisfaction. Buying IKEA furniture, customers co-create value for themselves and in the process also reduce the prices they pay for printing services.

Because customers are participants in service production and delivery, they can potentially contribute to the widening of gap 3. That is, customers themselves can influence whether the delivered service meets customer-defined specifications. Sometimes customers contribute to gap 3 because they lack understanding of their roles and exactly what they should do in a given situation, particularly if the customer is confronting a service concept for the first time. Customers visiting IKEA for the first time need detailed, but simple, instructions to help them understand how to use the service effectively and get the greatest value.

At other times customers may understand their roles but be unwilling or unable to perform for some reason. In a health club context, members may understand that to get into good physical shape they must follow the workout guidelines set up by the trainers. If work schedules or illness keep members from living up to their part of the guidelines, the service will not be successful because of customer inaction. In a different service situation, customers may choose not to perform the roles defined for them because they are not rewarded in any way for contributing their effort. When service customers are enticed through price reductions, greater convenience or some other tangible benefit, they are more likely to perform their roles willingly, as in the case of our opening vignette about IKEA.

Finally, gap 3 may be widened not through actions or inactions on the part of the customer, but because of what *other* customers do. Other customers who are in the service factory either receiving the service simultaneously (passengers on an aeroplane flight) or waiting their turn to receive the service sequentially (bank customers waiting in a queue, Disneyland customers waiting to go on one of the rides) can influence whether the service is effectively and efficiently delivered.

This chapter focuses on the roles of customers in service delivery and co-creation of service experiences as well as strategies to effectively manage them.

The importance of customers in service delivery

Customer participation at some level is inevitable in service delivery and co-creation. Services are actions or performances, typically produced and consumed simultaneously. In many situations employees, customers and, even, others in the service environment interact to produce the ultimate service outcome. Because they participate, customers are indispensable to the production process of service organizations, and they can actually control or contribute to their own satisfaction.[2]

The importance of customers in successful service delivery is obvious if service performances are looked at as a form of drama. The drama metaphor for services (discussed in Chapter 2) suggests the reciprocal, interactive roles of employees (actors) and customers (audience) in creating the service experience. The service actors and audience are surrounded by the service setting or the servicescape (discussed in Chapter 10). The drama metaphor argues that the development and maintenance of an interaction (a service experience) relies on the audience's input as well as the actors' presentation. Through this **services as drama** metaphor, service performances or service delivery situations are viewed as tenuous, fragile processes that can be influenced by behaviours of customers as well as by employees.[3] Service performance results from actions and interactions among individuals in both groups.

Consider the services provided by a cruise ship company. The actors (ship's personnel) provide the service through interactions with their audience (the passengers) and among each other. The audience also produces elements of the service through interactions with the actors and other audience members. Both actors and audience are surrounded by an elaborate setting (the cruise ship itself) that provides a context to facilitate the service performance. The drama metaphor provides a compelling frame of reference for recognizing the interdependent roles of actors and audience in service delivery.[4]

Recognition of the role of customers is also reflected in the definition of the *people* element of the services marketing mix given in Chapter 1: *all human actors who play a part in service delivery and thus influence the buyer's perceptions; namely, the firm's personnel, the customer, and other customers in the service environment.* Chapter 11 thoroughly examined the role of the firm's employees in delivering service quality. In this chapter we focus on the customer receiving the service and on fellow customers in the service environment.

Customer receiving the service

Because the customer receiving the service participates in the delivery process, he or she can contribute to narrowing or widening gap 3 through behaviours that are appropriate or inappropriate, effective or ineffective, productive or unproductive. Even in a relatively simple service such as retail mail order, customers' actions and preparation can have an effect on service delivery. Customers who are unprepared in terms of what they want to order can soak up the customer service representative's time as they seek advice. Similarly, shoppers who are not prepared with their credit card numbers can put the representative on hold while they search for their cards or retrieve them from another room or their cars. Meanwhile, other customers and calls are left unattended, causing longer wait times and potential dissatisfaction.

The level of customer participation – low, medium or high – varies across services, as shown in Table 12.1. In some cases, all that is required is the customer's physical presence (*low level of participation*), with the employees of the firm doing all the service production work, as in the example of a orchestral concert. Concert-goers must be present to receive the entertainment service, but little else is required once they are seated. In other situations, consumer inputs are required to aid the service organization in creating the service (*moderate level of participation*). Inputs can include *information, effort* or *physical possessions.* All three of these are required for an accountant to prepare effectively a client's tax return: information in the form of tax history, marital status and number of dependents; effort in putting the information together in a useful fashion; and physical possessions such as receipts and past tax returns. In some situations, customers are truly co-creators of the service (*high level of participation*). For these services, customers have mandatory production roles that, if not fulfilled, will affect the nature of the service outcome. In a complex or long-term business-to-business consulting engagement, the client can be involved in activities such as identification of issues, shared problem-solving, ongoing communication, provision of equipment and work space, and implementation of solutions.

Low: consumer presence required during service delivery	Moderate: consumer inputs required for service creation	High: customer co-creates the service product
Products are standardized	Client inputs (information, materials) customize a standard service	Active client participation guides the customized service
Service is provided regardless of any individual purchase	Provision of service requires customer purchase	Service cannot be created apart from the customer's purchase and active participation
Payment may be the only required customer input	Customer inputs are necessary for an adequate outcome, but the service firm provides the service	Customer inputs are mandatory and co-create the outcome
End consumer examples		
Airline travel	Haircut	Marriage counselling
Motel stay	Tax advice	Personal training
Fast-food restaurant	Full-service restaurant	Weight reduction programme
Business-to-business customer examples		
Office cleaning services	Agency-created advertising campaign	Management consulting
Pest control	Payroll service	Executive management seminar
Photocopier maintenance	Freight transportation	Installation of computer network

TABLE 12.1 Levels of customer participation across different services

Source: adapted from A.R. Hubbert, 'Customer co-creation of service outcomes: effects of locus of causality attributions', doctoral dissertation, Arizona State University, Tempe, Arizona (1995)

Table 12.1 provides several examples of each level of participation for both consumer and business-to-business services. The effectiveness of customer involvement at all the levels will impact organizational productivity and, ultimately, quality and customer satisfaction.

Fellow customers

In many service contexts, customers receive the service simultaneously with other customers or must wait their turn while other customers are being served. In both cases 'fellow customers' are present in the service environment and can affect the nature of the service outcome or process. Fellow customers can either *enhance* or *detract* from customer satisfaction and perceptions of quality.[5] Some of the ways fellow customers can negatively affect the service experience are by exhibiting disruptive behaviours, causing delays, excessively crowding and manifesting incompatible needs. In restaurants, hotels, aeroplanes and other environments in which customers are in very close proximity to each other as they receive the service, crying babies, smoking patrons and loud unruly groups can be disruptive and detract from the experiences of their fellow customers. The customer is disappointed through no direct fault of the provider. In other cases, overly demanding customers (even customers with legitimate problems) can cause a delay for others while their needs are met. This occurrence is common in banks, post offices and customer service counters in retail stores. Excessive crowding or overuse of a service can also affect the nature of the customer's experience. For example the quality of mobile phone networks and the ability to make a call can suffer on special holidays such as Christmas and New Year's Eve when large numbers of customers all try to use the service at the same time.

Finally, customers who are being served simultaneously but who have incompatible needs can negatively affect each other. This situation can occur in restaurants, university lecture theatres, hospitals and any service establishment in which multiple segments are served simultaneously. In a study of critical service encounters occurring in tourist attractions, researchers found that customers negatively affected each other when they failed to follow either explicit or implicit 'rules of conduct'. Customers reported such negative behaviours as shoving, smoking, drinking alcohol, being verbally abusive or pushing into the line. Other times, dissatisfaction resulted when other customers were impersonal, rude, unfriendly or, even, spiteful.[6]

We can offer just as many examples of other customers enhancing satisfaction and quality for their fellow customers as detracting from them. Sometimes the mere presence of other customers enhances the experience, for example, at sporting events, in cinemas and in other entertainment venues. The presence of other patrons is essential for true enjoyment of these experiences. In other situations, fellow customers provide a positive social dimension to the service experience. At health clubs, churches and resorts such as Club Med, other customers provide opportunities to socialize and build friendships.

In some situations, customers may actually help each other achieve service goals and outcomes. The success of the Weight Watchers organization, for example, depends significantly on the camaraderie and support that group members provide each other. The study of tourist attractions mentioned earlier found that customers increased the satisfaction of others by having friendly conversations while waiting in line, by taking photographs, by assisting with children and by returning dropped or lost items.[7] An ethnographic study that observed hundreds of hours of customer interactions among travellers on the UK rail system found that customers often helped each other by (1) providing important service-related information (e.g. schedules, interesting features en route) that can reduce trip-related anxiety; (2) engaging in enjoyable conversation, thus making the trip more pleasant; and (3) serving as someone to complain to when mishaps and service failures occurred.[8]

Customers helping each other is not limited to consumer services. Computer and software suppliers often have user groups who share ideas and solutions to issues and problems with fellow users.

Customers' roles

The following subsections examine in more detail three major roles played by customers in service delivery: customers as productive resources; customers as contributors to quality and satisfaction; and **customers as competitors**.

Customers as productive resources

Service customers have been referred to as 'partial employees' of the organization – human resources who contribute to the organization's productive capacity.[9] Some management experts have suggested that the organization's boundaries be expanded to consider the customer as part of the service system. In other words, if customers contribute effort, time or other resources to the service production process, they should be considered as part of the organization. (Later in the chapter we devote a section to defining customers' jobs and strategies for managing them effectively.)

Customer inputs can affect the organization's productivity through both the quality of what they contribute and the resulting quality and quantity of output generated. In a business-to-business services context, the contributions of the client can enhance the overall productivity of the firm in both quality and quantity of service.[10]

Service spotlight

easyJet depends on customers to perform critical service roles for themselves, thus increasing the overall productivity of the airline. Passengers are asked to carry their own bags when transferring to other airlines, get their own food and seat themselves.

Customer participation in service production raises a number of issues for organizations. Because customers can influence both the quality and quantity of production, some experts believe the delivery system should be isolated as much as possible from customer inputs in order to reduce the uncertainty they can bring into the production process. This view sees customers as a major source of uncertainty – in the timing of their demands and the uncontrollability of their attitudes and actions. The logical conclusion is that any service activities that do not require customer contact or involvement should be performed away from customers: the less direct contact there is between the customer and the service production system, the greater the potential for the system to operate at peak efficiency.[11]

Other experts believe that services can be delivered most efficiently if customers are truly viewed as partial employees and their co-production roles are designed to maximize their contributions to the service creation process. The logic behind this view is that organizational productivity can be increased if customers learn to perform service-related activities they currently are not doing or are educated to perform more effectively the tasks they are already doing.[12]

For example, when self-service service stations first came into being, customers were asked to fill their own tanks. With customers performing this task, fewer employees were needed and the overall productivity of service stations improved. Now many service stations offer customers the option of paying for their fuel at the pump by popping their credit cards into a slot on the pump and leaving the station without dealing directly with a cashier. Similarly, the introduction of many automated airline services such as baggage check-in and self-ticketing are intended to speed up the process for customers while freeing employees for other tasks.[13] Organizational productivity is increased by using customers as a resource to perform tasks previously completed by employees. In both business-to-business and business-to-consumer contexts, organizations are turning to automated and online customer service. One prominent goal with online customer service is to increase organizational productivity by using the customer as a partial employee, performing his or her own service.

Although organizations derive obvious productivity benefits by involving customers as co-producers, customers do not always like or accept their new roles, especially when they perceive the purpose to be bottom-line cost savings for the company. If customers see no clear benefit to being involved in co-production (e.g. lower prices, quicker access, better quality outcome), then they are likely to resent and resist their coproduction roles.

Customers as contributors to service quality and satisfaction

Another role customers can play in services co-creation and delivery is that of contributor to their own satisfaction and the ultimate quality of the services they receive. Customers may care little that they have increased the productivity of the organization through their participation, but they likely care a great deal about whether their needs are fulfilled. Effective customer participation can increase the likelihood that needs are met and that the benefits the customer seeks are actually attained. Think about services such as health care, education, personal fitness and weight loss, in which the service outcome is highly dependent on customer participation. In these services, unless the customers perform their roles effectively, the desired service outcomes are not possible.

Research has shown that in education, active participation by students – as opposed to passive listening – increases learning (the desired service outcome) significantly.[14] The same is true in health care; patient compliance, in terms of taking prescribed medications or changing diet or other habits, can be critical to whether patients regain their health (the desired service outcome).[15] In both these examples, the customers contribute directly to the quality of the outcome and to their own satisfaction with the service. In a business-to-business context, couriers and parcel carriers have found that in many situations customers cause their own *dissatisfaction* with the service by failing to pack shipments appropriately, resulting in breakage or delays while items are repacked.

Research suggests that customers who believe they have done their part to be effective in service interactions are more satisfied with the service. In a study of the banking industry, bank customers were asked to rate themselves (on a scale from 'strongly agree' to 'strongly disagree') on questions related to their contributions to service delivery, as follows:

- *What they did – outcome quality of customer inputs*

  I clearly explained what I wanted the bank employee to do.

  I gave the bank employee proper information.

  I tried to cooperate with the bank employee.

  I understand the procedures associated with this service.

- *How they did it – interaction quality of customer inputs*

  I was friendly to the bank employee.

  I have a good relationship with the bank employee.

  I was courteous to the bank employee.

  Receiving this service was a pleasant experience.

Results of the study indicated that the customers' perceptions of both what they did and how they did it were significantly related to customers' satisfaction with the service they received from the bank.[16] That is, those customers who responded more positively to the questions listed above were also more satisfied with the bank. Research in another context showed that customers' perceptions of service quality increased with greater levels of participation. Specifically, customers (in this case members of a YMCA) who participated more in the club gave the club higher ratings on aspects of service quality than did those who participated less.[17]

Customers contribute to quality service delivery when they ask questions, take responsibility for their own satisfaction, and complain when there is a service failure. The following four scenarios illustrate the wide variations in customer participation that can result in equally wide variations in service quality and customer satisfaction.

Scenario 1: A major international hotel

Guest A called the desk right after check-in to report that his television was not working and that the light over the bed was burned out; both problems were fixed immediately. The hotel staff exchanged his television for one that worked and fixed the light bulb. Later they brought him a fruit plate to make up for the inconvenience. Guest B did not communicate to management until checkout time that his television did not work and he could not read in his bed. His complaints were overheard by guests checking in, who wondered whether they had chosen the right place to stay.

Scenario 2: Office of a tax adviser

Client A has organized into categories the information necessary to do her taxes and has provided all documents requested by the accountant. Client B has a box full of papers and receipts, many of which are not relevant to her taxes but which she brought along 'just in case'.

Scenario 3: An airline flight from London to New York

Passenger A arrives for the flight with an MP3 player and reading material and wearing warm clothes; passenger A also called ahead to order a special meal. Passenger B, who arrives empty-handed, becomes annoyed when the crew runs out of blankets, complains about the magazine selection and the meal, and starts fidgeting after the movie.

Scenario 4: Architectural consultation for remodelling an office building

Client A has invited the architects to meet with its design committee made up of managers, staff and customers in order to lay the groundwork for a major redesign job that will affect everyone who works in the building as well as customers. The committee has already formulated initial ideas and surveyed staff and customers for input. Client B has invited architects in following a decision the week previously to redesign the building; the design committee is two managers who are preoccupied with other, more immediate, tasks and have little idea what they need or what customers and staff would prefer in terms of a redesign of the office space.

Customers who take responsibility and providers who encourage their customers to become their partners in identifying and satisfying their own needs will together produce higher levels of service quality. In addition to contributing to their own satisfaction by improving the quality of service delivered to them, some customers simply enjoy participating in service delivery. These customers find the act of participating to be intrinsically attractive.[18] They enjoy using the Internet to attain airline tickets, or doing all their banking via ATMs and the Internet, or refuelling their own car. Often customers who like self-service in one setting are predisposed to serving themselves in other settings as well.

Interestingly, because service customers must participate in service delivery, they frequently blame themselves (at least partially) when things go wrong. Why did it take so long to reach an accurate diagnosis of my health problem? Why was the service contract for our company's canteen full of errors? Why was the room we reserved for our meeting unavailable when we arrived? If customers believe they are partially (or totally) to blame for the failure, they may be less dissatisfied with the service provider than when they believe the provider is responsible.[19] A recent series of studies suggests the existence of this 'self-serving bias'. That is, when services go better than expected, customers who have participated tend to take credit for the outcome and are less satisfied with the firm than are those customers who have not participated. However, when the outcome is worse than expected, customers who have chosen to participate in service production are less dissatisfied with the service than are those who choose not to participate – presumably because the participating customers have taken on some of the blame themselves.[20]

Customers as competitors

A final role played by service customers is that of potential competitor. If self-service customers can be viewed as resources of the firm, or as 'partial employees', they could in some cases partially perform the service or perform the entire service for themselves and not need the provider at all. Thus, in a sense customers are competitors of the companies that supply the service. Whether to produce a service for themselves (*internal exchange*) – for example, child care, home maintenance, car repair – or have someone else provide the service for them (*external exchange*) is a common dilemma for consumers.[21]

Similar internal versus external exchange decisions are made by organizations. Firms frequently choose to outsource service activities such as payroll, data processing, call centres, accounting, maintenance and facilities management. They find that it is advantageous to focus on their core businesses and leave these essential support services to others with greater expertise. Alternatively, a firm may decide to stop purchasing services externally and bring the service production process in-house.

Whether a household or a firm chooses to produce a particular service itself or contract externally for the service depends on a variety of factors. A proposed model of internal/external exchange suggests that such decisions depend on the following:[22]

■ *Expertise capacity*: the likelihood of producing the service internally is increased if the household or firm possesses the specific skills and knowledge needed to produce it. Having the expertise will not necessarily result in internal service production, however, because other factors (available resources and time) will also influence the decision. (For firms, making the decision to outsource is often based on recognizing that although they may have the expertise, someone else can do it better.)

■ *Resource capacity*: to decide to produce a service internally, the household or firm must have the needed resources including people, space, money, equipment and materials. If the resources are not available internally, external exchange is more likely.

- *Time capacity*: time is a critical factor in internal/external exchange decisions. Households and firms with adequate time capacity are more likely to produce services internally than are groups with time constraints.

- *Economic rewards*: the economic advantages or disadvantages of a particular exchange decision will be influential in choosing between internal and external options. The actual monetary costs of the two options will sway the decision.

- *Psychic rewards*: rewards of a non-economic nature have a potentially strong influence on exchange decisions. Psychic rewards include the degree of satisfaction, enjoyment, gratification or happiness that is associated with the external or internal exchange.

- *Trust*: in this context *trust* means the degree of confidence or certainty the household or firm has in the various exchange options. The decision will depend to some extent on the level of self-trust in producing the service versus trust of others.

- *Control*: the household or firm's desire for control over the process and outcome of the exchange will also influence the internal/external choice. Entities that desire and can implement a high degree of control over the task are more likely to engage in internal exchange.

The important thing to remember from this section is that in many service scenarios customers can, and often do, choose to fully or partially produce the service themselves. Thus, in addition to recognizing that customers can be productive resources and co-creators of quality and value, organizations also need to recognize the customer's role as a potential competitor.

Self-service technologies – the ultimate in customer participation

Self-service technologies (SSTs) are services produced entirely by the customer without any direct involvement or interaction with the firm's employees. As such, SSTs represent the ultimate form of customer participation along a continuum from services that are produced entirely by the firm to those that are produced entirely by the customer. This continuum is depicted in

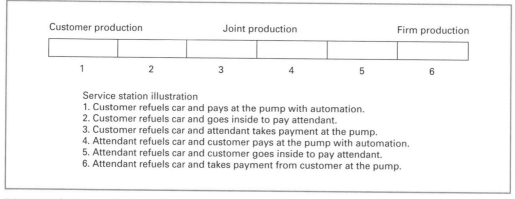

FIGURE 12.1 Services production continuum

Source: adapted from M.L. Meuter and M.J. Bitner, 'Self-service technologies: extending service frameworks and identifying issues for research', in *Marketing Theory and Applications*, eds D. Grewal and C. Pechmann (American Marketing Association Winter Educators' Conference, 1998), pp. 12–19. Reprinted by permission of the American Marketing Association

Figure 12.1, using the example of a service station to illustrate the various ways the same service could be delivered along all points on the continuum. At the far right end of the continuum, the service station attendant does everything from refuelling the car to taking payment. On the other end of the spectrum, the customer does everything; in between are various forms and levels of customer participation. Many service delivery options, across industries, could be laid out on this type of continuum from total customer production through total firm production.

A proliferation of new SSTs

Advances in technology, particularly the Internet, have allowed the introduction of a wide range of self-service technologies that occupy the far left end of the customer participation continuum in Figure 12.1. These technologies have proliferated as companies see the potential cost savings and efficiencies that can be achieved, potential sales growth, increased customer satisfaction and competitive advantage. A partial list of some of the self-service technologies available to consumers includes:

- ATMs
- Self-service petrol pumps
- Airline check-in
- Hotel check-in and check-out
- Automated car rental
- Automated filing of legal claims
- Online tax returns
- Automated betting machines
- Electronic blood pressure machines
- Various vending services
- Tax preparation software
- Self-scanning at retail stores

- Internet banking
- Vehicle registration online
- Online auctions
- Home and car buying online
- Automated investment transactions
- Insurance online
- Package tracking
- Internet shopping
- Internet information search
- Interactive voice response telephone systems
- Distance education.

Service spotlight

KLM offers online check-in for its flights which involves the passenger undertaking four steps. Step 1: entering their e-ticket number or the booking code onto the KLM website; step 2: selecting their preferred seat; step 3: printing off their boarding pass at home or using the self-service machines at the airport; step 4: checking in their baggage at a KLM drop-off point at the airport at least 40 minutes before departure.

The rapid proliferation of new SSTs is occurring for several reasons.[23] Many times firms are tempted by the cost savings that they anticipate by shifting customers to technology-based, automated systems and away from expensive personal service. If cost saving is the only reason for introducing an SST and if customers see no apparent benefits, the SST is likely to fail. Customers quickly see through this strategy and are not likely to adopt the SST if they have alternative options for service. Other times, firms introduce new SSTs based on customer demand. More and more, customers are expecting to find access to information, services and delivery options online. When they do not find what they want from a particular firm online, they are likely to choose a competitor. Thus, customer demand in some industries is forcing firms to develop and offer their services via technology. Other companies are developing SSTs in order to open up new geographic, socio-economic and lifestyle markets that were not available to them through traditional channels.

Customer usage of SSTs

Some of the SSTs listed above – ATMs, self-service fuel pumps, Internet information search – have been very successful, embraced by customers for the benefits they provide in terms of convenience, accessibility and ease of use.[24] Benefits to firms, including cost savings and revenue growth, can also result for those SSTs that succeed. Others – airline ticket kiosks, online hotel bookings, grocery self-scanning – have been less quickly embraced by customers.

Failure results when customers see no personal benefit in the new technology or when they do not have the ability to use it or know what they are supposed to do. Often, adopting a new SST requires customers to change significantly their traditional behaviours, and many are reluctant to make those changes. Research looking at customer adoption of SSTs found that 'customer readiness' was a major factor in determining whether customers would even try a new self-service option.[25] Customer readiness results from a combination of personal motivation (What is in it for me?), ability (Do I have the ability to use this SST?) and role clarity (Do I understand what I am supposed to do?). Other times customers see no value in using the technology when compared to the alternative interpersonal mode of delivery; or the SSTs may be so poorly designed that customers may prefer not to use them.[26]

Success with SSTs

Companies such as Amazon have been successful because they offer clear benefits (such as lower priced products) to customers, the benefits are well understood and appreciated compared with the alternative delivery modes, and the technology is user-friendly and reliable. In addition, customers understand their roles and have the capability to use the technology.

From a strategic perspective, research suggests that as firms move into SSTs as a mode of delivery, these questions are important to ask:[27]

- What is our strategy? What do we hope to achieve through the SST (cost savings, revenue growth, competitive advantage)?
- What are the benefits to customers of producing the service on their own through the SST? Do they know and understand these benefits?
- How can customers be motivated to try the SST? Do they understand their role? Do they have the capability to perform this role?
- How 'technology ready' are our customers?[28] Are some segments of customers more ready to use the technology than others?
- How can customers be involved in the design of the service technology system and processes so that they will be more likely to adopt and use the SST?
- What forms of customer education will be needed to encourage adoption? Will other incentives be needed?
- How will inevitable SST failures be handled to regain customer confidence?

Strategies for enhancing customer participation

The level and the nature of customer participation in the service process are strategic decisions that can impact an organization's productivity, its positioning relative to competitors, its service quality and its customers' satisfaction. In the following sections we will examine the strategies captured in Figure 12.2 for effectively involving customers in the service delivery process. The overall goals of a customer participation strategy will typically be to increase organizational productivity and customer satisfaction while simultaneously decreasing uncertainty due to unpredictable customer actions.

Define customers' jobs

In developing strategies for addressing customer involvement in service delivery, the organization first determines what type of participation it wants from customers, thus beginning to define the customer's 'job'. Identifying the current level of customer participation can serve as a starting point. Customers' roles may be partially predetermined by the nature of the service, as suggested in Table 12.1. The service may require only the customer's presence (a concert, airline travel) or it may require moderate levels of input from the customer in the form of effort or information (a haircut, tax preparation) or it may require the customer to actually co-create the service outcome (fitness training, consulting, self-service offerings).

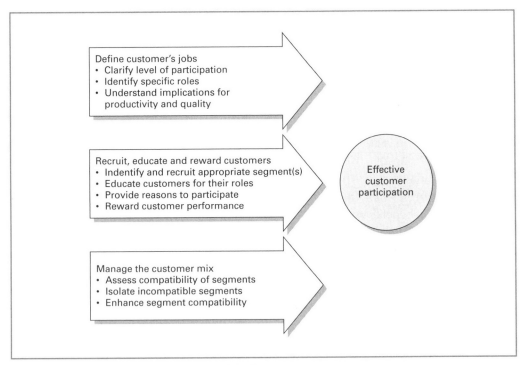

FIGURE 12.2 Strategies for enhancing customer participation

Source: adapted from M.L. Meuter and M.J. Bitner, 'Self-service technologies: extending service frameworks and identifying issues for research', in *Marketing Theory and Applications*, eds D. Grewal and C. Pechmann (American Marketing Association Winter Educators' Conference, 1998), pp. 12–19. Reprinted by permission of the American Marketing Association

The organization may decide that it is satisfied with the existing level of participation it requires from customers but wants to make the participation more effective. For example, IKEA has positioned itself as a company whose customers are highly involved in the purchase, transportation and construction of their products. It may see no added benefit in getting customers to use self-scanning equipment at the checkout or buy their restaurant products from vending machines.

Alternatively, the organization may choose to increase the level of customer participation, which may reposition the service in the customers' eyes. Experts have suggested that higher levels of customer participation are strategically advisable when service production and delivery are inseparable, marketing benefits (cross-selling, building loyalty) can be enhanced by on-site contact with the customer, and customers can supplement for the labour and information provided by employees.[29]

Finally, the organization may decide it wants to reduce customer participation owing to all the uncertainties it causes. In such situations the strategy may be to isolate all but the essential tasks, keeping customers away from the service facility and employees as much as possible.[30] Mail order is an extreme example of this form of service. Customers are in contact with the organization via telephone or the Internet, never see the organization's facility and have limited employee interactions. The customer's role is thus extremely limited and can interfere very little with the service delivery process.

Once the desired level of participation is clear, the organization can define more specifically what the customer's 'job' entails.[31] The customer's 'job description' will vary with the type of service and the organization's desired position within its industry. The job might entail helping oneself, helping others or promoting the company.

Helping oneself

In many cases the organization may decide to increase the level of customer involvement in service delivery through active participation, as shown in Figure 12.3. In such situations the customer becomes a productive resource, performing aspects of the service previously performed by employees or others. IKEA is an example of customers 'helping themselves'. The result may be increased productivity for the firm and/or increased value, quality and satisfaction for the customer.

Helping others

Sometimes the customer may be called on to help others who are experiencing the service. A child at a day-care centre might be appointed 'buddy of the day' to help a new child acclimatize into the environment. Long-time residents of retirement communities often assume comparable roles to welcome new residents. Many universities have established mentoring programmes, particularly for students from minority groups, in which experienced students with similar backgrounds help newcomers adjust and learn the system. Many membership organizations (like health clubs, churches and social organizations) also rely heavily, although often informally, on current members to help orientate new members and make them feel welcome. In engaging in these types of roles, customers are again performing productive functions for the organization, increasing customer satisfaction and retention. Acting as a mentor or facilitator can have very positive effects on the person performing the role and is likely to increase his or her loyalty as well.

Promoting the company

In some cases the customer's job may include a sales or promotional element. As you know from previous chapters, service customers rely heavily on word-of-mouth endorsements in deciding which providers to try. They are more comfortable getting a recommendation from someone who has actually experienced the service than from advertising alone. A positive recommendation from a friend, relative, colleague or an acquaintance can pave the way for a positive service experience. Many service organizations have been very imaginative in getting their current customers to work as promoters or salespeople:

FIGURE 12.3 Customers help produce the service for themselves through scanning their own groceries
Source: NCR FastLane™ self-checkout from NCR Corporation

- A dental practice encourages referrals by sending flowers or tickets to a local sports event to its patients whose names appear frequently in their 'who referred you?' database.

- A bowling alley holds a prize draw for its regular patrons. The person whose name is drawn is given a party at the bowling alley to which he or she can invite friends for free bowling. This effectively creates a 'word-of-mouth champion' who brings new people into the establishment.

- A chiropractor gives a free next examination to people who refer new patients. Patients who make referrals have their names listed on a board in the office waiting area.

- To increase membership, an insurance company published a member referral coupon in its newsletter. Those who referred new members were then given a monetary reward.

- A credit card that gives customers frequent-flyer points every time they use their credit card offers 10 000 free miles to those who solicit a new credit card customer.

- A nightclub holds regular prize draws (using business cards left by its patrons). Those whose names are drawn get a free party (no entry charge) for as many of their friends as they want to invite.

Individual differences: not everyone wants to participate

In defining customers' jobs it is important to remember that not everyone will want to participate.[32] Some customer segments enjoy self-service, whereas others prefer to have the service performed entirely for them. Companies that provide education and training services to organizations know that some customers want to be involved in designing the training and perhaps in delivering it to their employees. Other companies want to hand over the entire training design and delivery to the consulting organization, staying at arm's length with little of their own time and energy invested in the service. In health care, it is clear that some patients want lots of information and want to be involved in their own diagnosis and treatment decisions. Others simply want the doctor to tell them what to do. Despite all the customer service and purchase options now available via the Internet, many customers still prefer human, high-contact service delivery rather than self-service. Research has shown, for example, that customers with a high 'need for human interaction' are less likely to try new self-service options offered via the Internet and automated telephone systems.[33] Because of these differences in preferences, most companies find they need to provide service delivery choices for different market segments.

Often an organization can customize its services to fit the needs of these different segments – those who want to participate and those who prefer little involvement. Banks typically customize their services by offering both automated self-service options and high-touch, human delivery options. At other times, organizations such as IKEA can effectively position themselves to specifically serve segments of customers who want a high level of participation.

Recruit, educate and reward customers

Once the customer's role is clearly defined, the organization can think in terms of facilitating that role. In a sense, the customer becomes a 'partial employee' of the organization at some level, and strategies for managing customer behaviour in service production and delivery can mimic to some degree the efforts aimed at service employees discussed in Chapter 11. As with employees, customer participation in service production and delivery will be facilitated when (1) customers understand their roles and how they are expected to perform, (2) customers are able to perform as expected, and (3) customers receive valued rewards for performing as expected.[34] Through these means, the organization will also reduce the inherent uncertainty associated with the unpredictable quality and timing of customer participation.

Recruit the right customers

Before the company begins the process of educating and socializing customers for their roles, it must attract the right customers to fill those roles. The expected roles and responsibilities of customers should be clearly communicated in advertising, personal selling and other company messages. By previewing their roles and what is required of them in the service process, customers can self-select into (or out of) the relationship. Self-selection should result in enhanced perceptions of service quality from the customer's point of view and reduced uncertainty for the organization.

To illustrate, a child-care centre that requires parent participation on the site at least one-half day per week needs to communicate that expectation before it enrolls any child in its programme. For some families, this level of participation will not be possible or desirable, thus precluding them from enrolling in the centre. The expected level of participation needs to be communicated clearly in order to attract customers who are ready and willing to perform their roles. In a sense this situation is similar to a manufacturing firm exercising control over the quality of inputs into the production process.[35]

Educate and train customers to perform effectively

Customers need to be educated, or in essence 'socialized', so that they can perform their roles effectively. Through the socialization process, service customers gain an appreciation of specific organizational values, develop the abilities necessary to function within a specific context, understand what is expected of them and acquire the skills and knowledge to interact with employees and other customers.[36] Customer education programmes can take the form of formal orientation programmes, written literature provided to customers, directional cues and signage in the service environment, and information obtained from employees and other customers.

Many services offer 'customer orientation' programmes to assist customers in understanding their roles and what to expect from the process before experiencing it. For example, health clubs provide guidance on the layout of the club, details on fitness classes and training on how the different fitness machines operate.

Customer education can also be partially accomplished through written literature and customer 'handbooks'. Many hospitals have developed patient handbooks, very similar in appearance to employee handbooks, to describe what the patient should do in preparation for arrival at the hospital, what will happen when he or she arrives, and policies regarding visiting hours. The handbook may even describe the roles and responsibilities of family members.

Although formal training and written information are usually provided in advance of the service experience, other strategies can continue customer socialization during the experience itself. On site, customers require two kinds of orientation: *place orientation* (Where am I? How do I get from here to there?) and *function orientation* (How does this organization work? What am I supposed to do?).[37] Signage, the layout of the service facility and other orientation aids can help customers answer these questions, allowing them to perform their roles more effectively. Orientation aids can also take the form of rules that define customer behaviour for safety (airlines, health clubs), appropriate dress (restaurants, entertainment venues) and noise levels (hotels, classrooms, theatres). Customers may also be socialized to their expected roles through information provided by employees and by observing other customers.

Reward customers for their contributions

Customers are more likely to perform their roles effectively, or to participate actively, if they are rewarded for doing so. Rewards are likely to come in the form of increased control over the delivery process, time savings, monetary savings and psychological or physical benefits. For instance, some accountants have clients complete extensive forms before they meet with their accountants. If the forms are completed, the accountants will have less work to do and the clients will be rewarded with fewer billable hours. Those clients who choose not to perform the requested role will pay a higher price for the service. Automated teller machine customers who perform banking services for themselves are also rewarded through greater access to the bank, in terms of both locations and times. In some situations, ATM customers are also rewarded because they avoid fees that are assessed for interpersonal transactions with tellers. In healthcare contexts, patients who perform their roles effectively are likely to be rewarded with better health or quicker recovery. For a long time airlines have offered price discounts for passengers who ordered tickets online, providing a monetary incentive for customer participation.

Customers may not realize the benefits or rewards of effective participation unless the organization makes the benefits apparent to them. In other words, the organization needs to clarify the performance-contingent benefits that can accrue to customers just as it defines these types of benefits to employees. The organization also should recognize that not all customers are motivated by the same types of rewards. Some may value the increased access and time savings they can gain by performing their service roles effectively. Others may value the monetary savings. Still others may be looking for greater personal control over the service outcome.

Avoid negative outcomes of inappropriate customer participation

If customers are not effectively socialized the organization runs the risk that inappropriate customer behaviours will result in negative outcomes for customers, employees, and the organization itself:[38]

1 Customers who do not understand the service system or the process of delivery may slow down the service process and negatively affect their own as well as other customers' outcomes. In a rental car context, customers who do not understand the reservation process, the information needed from them, insurance coverage issues and the pick-up and drop-off procedures can slow the flow for employees and other customers, lowering both productivity and quality of service.

2 If customers do not perform their roles effectively, it may not be possible for employees to provide the levels of technical and process quality promised by the organization. For example, in a management consulting practice, clients who do not provide the information and cooperation needed by the consultants will likely receive inferior service

in terms of both the usefulness of the management report and the timeliness of the delivery.

3 If customers are frustrated because of their own inadequacies and incompetencies, employees are likely to suffer emotionally and be less able to deliver quality service. For example, if customers routinely enter the service delivery process with little knowledge of how the system works and their role in it, they are likely to take out their frustrations on front-line employees. This negative impact on individual employees can take its toll on the organization in the form of turnover and decreased motivation to serve.

Manage the customer mix

Because customers frequently interact with each other in the process of service delivery and consumption, another important strategic objective is to effectively **manage the mix of customers** who simultaneously experience the service. If a restaurant chooses to serve two segments during the dinner hour that are incompatible with each other – for example, students who want to party and business people who want quiet to discuss work – it may find that the two groups do not merge well. Of course it is possible to manage these segments so that they do not interact with each other by seating them in separate sections or by attracting the two segments at different times of day. Major tourism attractions around the world face the challenge of accommodating visitors who differ in the languages they speak, the foods they want to eat, their values and their perceptions of appropriate behaviours. Sometimes these visitors can clash when they do not understand and appreciate each other.

The process of managing multiple and sometimes conflicting segments is known as *compatibility management*, broadly defined as 'a process of first attracting homogeneous consumers to the service environment, then actively managing both the physical environment and customer-to-customer encounters in such a way as to enhance satisfying encounters and minimize dissatisfying encounters'.[39] Compatibility management will be critically important for some businesses (such as health clubs, public transportation and hospitals) and less important for others. Table 12.2 lists seven interrelated characteristics of service businesses that will increase the importance of compatibility management.

To manage multiple (and sometimes conflicting) segments, organizations rely on a variety of strategies. Attracting maximally homogeneous groups of customers through careful positioning and segmentation strategies is one approach.

Service spotlight

This strategy is used by the Ritz-Carlton Hotel Company, for which upmarket travellers are the primary target segment. The Ritz-Carlton is positioned to communicate that message to the marketplace, and customers self-select into the hotel. However, even in that context there are potential conflicts – for example, when the hotel is simultaneously hosting a large business convention and serving individual leisure travellers. A second strategy is often used in such cases. Compatible customers are grouped together physically so that the segments are less likely to interact directly with each other. The Ritz-Carlton keeps meetings and large group events separated from the areas of the hotel used by individual business people.

Characteristic	Explanation	Examples
Customers are in close physical proximity to each other	Customers will more often notice each other and be influenced by each other's behaviour when they are in close physical proximity	Aeroplane flights Entertainment events Sports events
Verbal interaction takes place among customers	Conversation (or lack thereof) can be a component of both satisfying and dissatisfying encounters with fellow patrons	Full-service restaurants Cocktail lounges Educational settings
Customers are engaged in numerous and varied activities	When a service facility supports varied activities all going on at the same time, the activities themselves may not be compatible	Libraries Health clubs Resort hotels
The service environment attracts a heterogeneous customer mix	Many service environments, particularly those open to the public, will attract a variety of customer segments	Public parks Public transportation Shopping centres
The core service is compatibility	The core service is to arrange and nurture compatible relationships between customers	Speed-dating events Weight-loss group programmes Mental health support groups
Customers must occasionally wait for the service	Waiting in line for service can be monotonous or anxiety producing. The boredom or stress can be magnified or lessened by other customers, depending on their compatibility	Dentists Tourist attractions Restaurants
Customers are expected to share time, space or service utensils with each other	The need to share space, time and other service factors is common in many services but may become a problem if segments are not comfortable with sharing with each other or if the need to share is intensified because of capacity constraints	Golf courses Hospitals Retirement communities Aeroplanes

TABLE 12.2 Characteristics of service that increase the importance of compatible segments
Source: adapted from C.I. Martin and C.A. Pranter, 'Compatibility management: customer-to-customer relationships in service environments', *Journal of Services Marketing* 3, no. 3 (Summer 1989), pp. 5–15. Reprinted with the permission of MCB University Press

Other strategies for enhancing customer compatibility include **customer 'codes of conduct'** such as the regulation of smoking behaviour and dress codes. Clearly such codes of conduct may vary from one service establishment to another. Finally, training employees to observe customer-to-customer interactions and to be sensitive to potential conflicts is another strategy for increasing compatibility among segments. Employees can also be trained to recognize opportunities to foster positive encounters among customers in certain types of service environments.

Summary

This chapter focused on the role of customers in service creation and delivery. The customer receiving the service and the fellow customers in the service environment can all potentially cause a widening of gap 3 if they fail to perform their roles effectively. A number of reasons why customers may widen the service delivery gap were suggested: customers lack understanding of their roles; customers are unwilling or unable to perform their roles; customers are not rewarded for good performance; other customers interfere; or market segments are incompatible.

Managing customers in the process of service delivery is a critical challenge for service firms. Whereas manufacturers are not concerned with customer participation in the manufacturing process, service managers constantly face this issue because their customers are often present and active partners in service production. As participants in service creation, production and delivery, customers can perform three primary roles, discussed and illustrated in the chapter: *productive resources* for the organization, *contributors* to service quality and satisfaction and *competitors* in performing the service for themselves.

Through understanding the importance of customers in service delivery and identifying the roles played by the customer in a particular context, managers can develop strategies to enhance customer participation. Strategies discussed in the text include defining the customers' roles and jobs, recruiting customers who match the customer profile in terms of desired level of participation, educating customers so they can perform their roles effectively, rewarding customers for their contributions, and managing the customer mix to enhance the experiences of all segments. By implementing these strategies, organizations should see a reduction in gap 3 due to effective, efficient customer contributions to service delivery.

Key concepts

Customer 'codes of conduct'	316	Managing the mix of customers	315
Customer participation	299	Self-service technologies	307
Customers as competitors	302	Services as drama	300

Further reading

Meuter, M.L., Ostrom, A.L., Roundtree, R.I. and Bitner, M.J. (2000) 'Self-service technologies: understanding customer satisfaction with technology-based service encounters', *Journal of Marketing*, 64 (July), 50–64.

Pujari, D. (2004) 'Self-service with a smile? Self-service technology (SST) encounters among Canadian business to business', *International Journal of Service Industry Management*, 15(2), 200–19.

Selnes, F. and Hansen, H. (2001) 'The potential hazard of self-service in developing customer loyalty', *Journal of Service Research*, 4(2), 79–90.

Discussion questions

1 Using your own personal examples, discuss the general importance of customers in the successful creation and delivery of service experiences.

2 Why might customer actions and attitudes cause gap 3 to occur? Use your own examples to illustrate your understanding.

3 Using Table 12.1, think of specific services you have experienced that fall within each of the three levels of customer participation: low, medium and high. Describe specifically what you did as a customer in each case. How did your involvement vary across the three types of service situations?

4 Describe a time when your satisfaction in a particular situation was *increased* because of something another customer did. Could (or does) the organization do anything to ensure that this experience happens routinely? What does it do? Should it try to make this situation a routine occurrence?

5 Describe a time when your satisfaction in a particular situation was *decreased* because of something another customer did. Could the organization have done anything to manage this situation more effectively? What?

6 Discuss the customer's role as a *productive resource* for the firm. Describe a time when you played this role. What did you do and how did you feel? Did the firm help you perform your role effectively? How?

7 Discuss the customer's role as a *contributor to service quality and satisfaction*. Describe a time when you played this role. What did you do and how did you feel? Did the firm help you perform your role effectively? How?

8 Discuss the customer's role as a potential *competitor*. Describe a time when you chose to provide a service for yourself rather than pay someone to provide the service for you. Why did you decide to perform the service yourself? What could have changed your mind, causing you to contract with someone else to provide the service?

 Exercises

1 Visit a service establishment where customers can influence each other (such as a theme park, entertainment establishment, resort, shopping mall, restaurant, airline, school or hospital). Observe (or interview) customers and record cases of positive and negative customer influence. Discuss how you would manage the situation to increase overall customer satisfaction.

2 Interview someone regarding his or her decision to outsource a service – for example, legal services, payroll, or maintenance in a company; or cleaning, child care or pet care in a household. Use the criteria for internal versus external exchange described in the text to analyse the decision to outsource.

3 Think of a service in which a high level of customer participation is necessary for the service to be successful (health club, weight loss, educational setting, health care, golf

lessons, or the like). Interview a service provider in such an organization to find out what strategies the provider uses to encourage effective customer participation.

4 Visit a service setting in which multiple types of customer segments use the service at the same time (such as a theatre, golf course, resort or theme park). Observe (or interview the manager about) the organization's strategies to manage these segments effectively. Would you do anything differently if you were in charge?

Notes

[1] Sources: www.ikea.com; R. Normann and R. Ramirez, 'From value chain to value constellation: designing interactive strategy', *Harvard Business Review* (July–August 1993), pp. 65–77; B. Edvardsson and B. Enquist, 'The IKEA saga: how service culture drives service strategy', *The Service Industries Journal* 22 (October 2002), pp. 153–86; P.M. Miller, 'IKEA with Chinese characteristics', *The China Business Review* (July–August 2004), pp. 36–8; www.ikea.com (2004).

[2] See B. Schneider and D.E. Bowen, *Winning the Service Game* (Boston, MA: Harvard Business School Press, 1995), ch. 4; L.A. Bettencourt, 'Customer voluntary performance: customers as partners in service delivery', *Journal of Retailing* 73, no. 3 (1997), pp. 383–406; P.K. Mills and J.H. Morris, 'Clients as "partial" employees: role development in client participation', *Academy of Management Review* 11, no. 4 (1986), pp. 726–35; C.H. Lovelock and R.F. Young, 'Look to customers to increase productivity', *Harvard Business Review* (Summer 1979), pp. 9–20; A.R. Rodie and S.S. Kleine, 'Customer participation in services production and delivery', in *Handbook of Services Marketing and Management*, eds T.A. Swartz and D. Iacobucci (Thousand Oaks, CA: Sage Publications, 2000), pp. 111–26; C.K. Prahalad and V. Ramaswamy, 'Co-opting customer competence', *Harvard Business Review* (January–February 2000), p. 7; N. Bendapudi and R.P. Leone, 'Psychological implications of customer participation in co-production', *Journal of Marketing* 67 (January 2003), pp. 14–28.

[3] S.J. Grove, R.P. Fisk and M.J. Bitner, 'Dramatizing the service experience: a managerial approach', in *Advances in Services Marketing and Management*, vol. 1, eds T.A. Swartz, D.E. Bowen and S.W. Brown (Greenwich, CT: JAI Press, 1992), pp. 91–122.

[4] For an interesting view of work and business as theatre, see B.J. Pine II and J.H. Gilmore, *The Experience Economy: Work Is Theatre and Every Business a Stage* (Boston, MA: Harvard Business School Press, 1999).

[5] See S.J. Grove and R.P. Fisk, 'The impact of other customers on service experiences: a critical incident examination of "Getting Along"', *Journal of Retailing* 73, no. 1 (1997), pp. 63–85; C.I. Martin and C.A. Pranter, 'Compatibility management: customer-to-customer relationships in service environments', *Journal of Services Marketing* 3 (Summer 1989), pp. 5–15.

[6] Grove and Fisk, 'The impact of other customers on service experiences'.

[7] Ibid.

[8] K. Harris and S. Baron, 'Consumer-to-consumer conversations in service settings', *Journal of Service Research* 6 (February 2004), pp. 287–303.

[9] See P.K. Mills, R.B. Chase and N. Margulies, 'Motivating the client/employee system as a service production strategy', *Academy of Management Review* 8, no. 2 (1983), pp. 301–10; D.E. Bowen, 'Managing customers as human resources in service organizations', *Human Resource Management* 25, no. 3 (1986), pp. 371–83; and Mills and Morris, 'Clients as "partial" employees'.

[10] L.A. Bettencourt, A.L. Ostrom, S.W. Brown and R.I. Rowntree, 'Client co-production in knowledge-intensive business services', *California Management Review*, 44, no. 4 (2002), pp. 100–28.

[11] R.B. Chase, 'Where does the customer fit in a service operation?', *Harvard Business Review* (November–December 1978), pp. 137–42.

[12] Mills et al., 'Motivating the client/employee system'.

[13] M. Adams, 'Tech takes bigger role in air services', *USA Today*, 18 July 2001, p. 1.

[14] See D.W. Johnson, R.T. Johnson and K.A. Smith, *Active Learning: Cooperation in the College Classroom* (Edina, MN: Interaction Book Company, 1991).

[15] S. Dellande, M.C. Gilly and J.L. Graham, 'Gaining compliance and losing weight: the role of the service provider in health care services', *Journal of Marketing* 68 (July 2004), pp. 78–91.

[16] S.W. Kelley, S.J. Skinner and J.H. Donnelly Jr, 'Organizational socialization of service customers', *Journal of Business Research* 25 (1992), pp. 197–214.

[17] C. Claycomb, C.A. Lengnick-Hall and L.W. Inks, 'The customer as a productive resource: a pilot study and strategic implications', *Journal of Business Strategies* 18 (Spring 2001), pp. 47–69.

[18] J.E.G. Bateson, 'The self-service customer – empirical findings', in *Emerging Perspectives in Services Marketing*, eds L.L. Berry, G.L. Shostack and G.D. Upah (Chicago, IL: American Marketing Association, 1983), pp. 50–3.

[19] V.S. Folkes, 'Recent attribution research in consumer behavior: a review and new directions', *Journal of Consumer Research* 14 (March 1988), pp. 548–65; and M.J. Bitner, 'Evaluating service encounters: the effects of physical surroundings and employee responses', *Journal of Marketing* 54 (April 1990), pp. 69–82.

[20] Bendapudi and Leone, 'Psychological implications of customer participation in co-production'.

[21] R.F. Lusch, S.W. Brown and G.J. Brunswick, 'A general framework for explaining internal vs. external exchange', *Journal of the Academy of Marketing Science* 10 (Spring 1992), pp. 119–34.

[22] Ibid.

[23] See M.J. Bitner, A.L. Ostrom and M.L. Meuter, 'Implementing successful self-service technologies', *Academy of Management Executive* 16 (November 2002), pp. 96–109.

[24] See P. Dabholkar, 'Consumer evaluations of new technology-based self-service options: an investigation of alternative models of service quality', *International Journal of Research in Marketing* 13 (1), pp. 29–51; F. Davis, 'User acceptance of information technology: system characteristics, user perceptions and behavioral impact', *International Journal of Man-Machine Studies* 38 (1993), pp. 475–87; L.M. Bobbitt and P.A. Dabholkar, 'Integrating attitudinal theories to understand and predict use of technology-based self-service', *International Journal of Service Industry Management* 12, no. 5 (2001), pp. 423–50; J.M. Curran, M.L. Meuter and C.F. Surprenant, 'Intentions to use self-service technologies: a confluence of multiple attitudes', *Journal of Service Research* 5, no. 3 (2003), pp. 209–24.

[25] M.L. Meuter, M.J. Bitner, A.L. Ostrom and S.W. Brown, 'Choosing among alternative service delivery modes: an investigation of customer trial of self-service technologies', *Journal of Marketing,* 69 (2005), pp. 61–83.

[26] M.L. Meuter, A.L. Ostrom, R.I. Roundtree and M.J. Bitner, 'Self-service technologies: understanding customer satisfaction with technology-based service encounters', *Journal of Marketing* 64 (July 2000), pp. 50–64.

[27] Meuter et al., 'Choosing among alternative service delivery modes'; see also Y. Moon and F.X. Frei, 'Exploding the self-service myth', *Harvard Business Review*, 78 (May–June 2000), pp. 26–7; Bitner et al., 'Implementing successful self-service technologies'.

[28] A. Parasuraman and C.L. Colby, *Techno-Ready Marketing: How and Why Your Customers Adopt Technology* (New York: Free Press, 2001).

[29] Bowen, 'Managing customers as human resources'.

[30] Chase, 'Where does the customer fit in a service operation?'

[31] See Schneider and Bowen, *Winning the Service Game*, ch. 4. The four job descriptions in this section are adapted from M.R. Bowers, C.L. Martin and A. Luker, 'Trading places, employees as customers, customers as employees', *Journal of Services Marketing* 4 (Spring 1990), pp. 56–69.

[32] Bateson, 'The self-service customer'.

[33] Meuter et al., 'Choosing among alternative service delivery modes'.

[34] Bowen, 'Managing customers as human resources'; and Schneider and Bowen, *Winning the Service Game,* ch. 4; Meuter et al., 'Choosing among alternative service delivery modes'; Dellande et al., 'Gaining compliance and losing weight'.

[35] C. Goodwin and R. Radford, 'Models of service delivery: an integrative perspective', in *Advances in Services Marketing and Management*, vol. 1, eds T.A. Swartz, D.E. Bowen and S.W. Brown (Greenwich, CT: JAI Press, 1992) pp. 231–52.

[36] S.W. Kelley, J.H. Donnelly Jr and S.J. Skinner, 'Customer participation in service production and delivery', *Journal of Retailing* 66 (Fall 1990), pp. 315–35; and Schneider and Bowen, *Winning the Service Game*, ch. 4.

[37] Bowen, 'Managing customers as human resources'.

[38] Ibid.; see also L.C. Harris and K.L. Reynolds, 'The consequences of dysfunctional customer behavior', *Journal of Service Research* 6 (November 2003), pp. 144–61.

[39] Martin and Pranter, 'Compatibility management'.

CHAPTER 13

Delivering service through technology and intermediaries

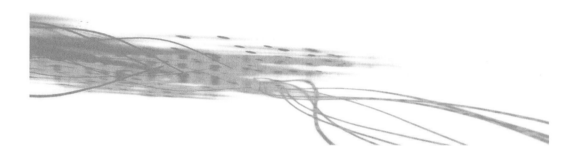

❖ *Learning Objectives*

This chapter's objectives are to:

1 Identify the primary channels through which services are delivered to end customers.

2 Examine the manner in which services can be delivered through technology and electronic channels

3 Provide examples of each of the key service intermediaries.

4 View delivery of service from two perspectives – the service provider and the service deliverer.

5 Discuss the benefits and challenges of each method of service delivery.

6 Outline the strategies that are used to manage service delivery through intermediaries.

CASE STUDY: STARBUCKS SERVICE

Source: reprinted with permission of Starbucks Coffee Company

One of the biggest marketing success stories of the last decade is Starbucks Coffee Company, although it has been in business for more than 30 years. Twenty years ago, its owner began to think of coffee not as something to retail in a store but instead as something to experience in a coffeehouse. Consistency of service and product are two of the most important reasons that Starbucks annually reports profit growth of more than 50 per cent a year. Here are some of the efforts it undertakes to ensure that the Starbucks experience is always the same, always positive.

Employee training: learning to be a barista

All employees are called partners, and those who prepare coffee are called 'baristas', the Italian name for one who prepares and serves coffee. As many as 400 to 500 employees per month nationally are carefully trained to 'call' ('triple-tall non-fat mocha'), make drinks, clean espresso machines and deliver quality customer service. Baristas are taught 'coffee knowledge', so that among other things they know how everything tastes, and 'customer service', so that they can explain the Italian drink names to customers.

Ensuring product quality

'Retail skills' are another portion of the training. Employees are taught such specifics as how to wipe oil from the coffee bin, open a giant bag of beans and clean the milk wand on the espresso machine, all of which ensures that the coffee drinks taste just right. Another part, 'brewing the perfect cup at home', helps baristas teach customers how to use the espresso machines and coffee they buy at Starbucks to replicate the product they get in the coffeehouse.

Service standards

No pot of Starbucks coffee sits on a burner for more than 20 minutes. An espresso machine with unused coffee must be purged regularly. And no one goes home at night until everything is completed, cleaned and polished according to the service standards in the manual. Using such standards ensures that both service and quality are maintained.

Star skills

To hire, keep and motivate the very best employees, Starbucks has three guidelines for on-the-job interpersonal relations: (1) maintain and enhance self-esteem, (2) listen and acknowledge, and (3) ask for help. These and other human resource practices, including higher-than-average pay, health insurance and stock options, lower barista turnover to 60 per cent compared with 140 per cent for hourly workers in the fast-food business in general.

Starbucks and the Internet

Starbucks had high hopes for the Internet, given that its shops tend to attract young, affluent, technology-aware customers, 70 per cent of whom are Internet users. However, it overestimated its ability to transition off-line success to the online environment. Several of its online initiatives failed, including Starbucks X, which was a quasi-separate division built around the Internet, and its online retail store, which once sold coffee beans, mugs and brewing machines. Now, customers who wish to purchase Starbucks products must physically visit a store; no purchases can be made via the Internet. Starbucks originally refused to offer Internet connections in the coffeeshops themselves, not wanting to create dimly lit cybercafés with people hunched over machines. The company has since changed its stance and has partnered with T-Mobile to create Wireless HotSpot Stores.

International expansion

The company now has more than 3000 outlets in 37 countries outside North America. When the company chose to go international, management realized that its best route was not to own but instead to franchise or form other types of alliances with organizations within each country. In Germany, Starbucks entered the market through a licensing deal with KarstadtQuelle. In Switzerland, Starbucks and Bon Appetit Group signed a joint venture agreement to develop Starbucks retail business in the country. In France, Starbucks is building its operation as a 50–50 joint venture with Spanish firm Grupo Vips, also the chain's partner in Spain. The same retail formula is used throughout the world, no matter who the joint venture partner is.

Sources: J. Reese, 'Starbucks: inside the coffee cult', *Fortune*, 9 December 1996, pp. 190–200; G. Anders, 'Starbucks brews a new strategy', *Fast Company* (August 2001), pp. 144–6; 'Starbucks keeps pace', *Beverage Industry* (October 2001), p. 11; www.starbucks.com

Delivering service through technology and electronic channels

Electronic channels are the only service distributors that do not require direct human interaction. What they do require is some pre-designed service (almost always information, education or entertainment) and an electronic vehicle to deliver it. You are all familiar with telephone and television channels and the Internet and the Web, and may be aware of the other electronic vehicles that are currently under development. The consumer and business services that are made possible through these vehicles include movies on demand, interactive news and music, banking and financial services, multimedia libraries and databases, distance learning, desktop videoconferencing, remote health services and interactive network-based games.

Benefits	Challenges
Consistent delivery for standardized services	Price competition
Low cost	Inability to customize with highly standardized services
Customer convenience	Lack of consistency due to customer involvement
Wide distribution	Changes in consumer behaviour
Customer choice and ability to customize	Security concerns
Quick customer feedback	Competition from widening geographies

TABLE 13.1 Benefits and challenges in electronic distribution of services

The more a service relies on technology and/or equipment for service production and the less it relies on face-to-face contact with service providers, the less the service is characterized by inseparability and non-standardization. As you will see in the following section, using electronic channels overcomes some of the problems associated with service inseparability and allows a form of standardization not previously possible in most services. Table 13.1 summarizes the benefits and challenges of electronic distribution.

Benefits of electronic channels

Consistent delivery for standardized services

Electronic channels such as the Internet do not alter the service, as channels with human interaction tend to do. Unlike delivery from a personal provider, electronic delivery does not interpret the service and execute it according to that interpretation. Its delivery is likely to be the same in all transmissions. The process of booking a flight on the easyJet website is the same for every customer, no matter where they are or who they are.

Low cost

Electronic media offer more efficient means of delivery than does interpersonal distribution. Critics could rightly claim that the personal sales interaction is more powerful and effective, but with interactive services, companies such as Amazon are able to gain some of the credibility benefits of personal interaction (such as being able to answer individual questions or tailor the service, book recommendations and website for individuals).

Customer convenience

With electronic channels, customers are able to access a firm's services when and where they want. 'Retailers still tell customers, You have to come to us. But online consumers are saying, No way – *you* have to come to *us*. My place, my time is the new mantra of consumers everywhere.'[1] Just as catalogue shopping freed working women from the perceived drudgeries of having to go to the shops, e-commerce is changing the way people shop. Many companies with call centres and telephone ordering still limit their hours of availability, a real mistake if they are going to match the customer convenience of being able to order online 24 hours a day, seven days a week. For the marketer, electronic channels allow access to a large group of customers who would otherwise be unavailable to them because of busy schedules that do not allow them to shop in other ways.

Wide distribution

Electronic channels do more than allow the service provider to interact with a large number of geographically dispersed consumers. They also allow the service provider to interact (often simultaneously) with a large number of intermediaries. The costs and effort to inform, select and motivate non-electronic channels are higher than the costs to accomplish the same activities with electronic channels. Many franchisers have found that prospecting through the Internet provides better-qualified franchisees than the traditional methods of mainstream advertising and trade shows.

Customer choice and ability to customize

Just as Dell Computer allows customers to configure entire products to their own particular needs and desires, the Internet allows many companies to design services from the beginning. Individuals who want to renovate their kitchen may now go to many Internet sites, specify their requirements and order what they wish. Whether the supplier is a large retailer such as B&Q (www.diy.com) or a small start-up company, customers get exactly what they want.

Quick customer feedback

Rapid customer feedback is without doubt one of the major strengths of e-commerce. Companies can find out immediately what customers think of services and can gain far higher participation from customers in surveys. With quick customer feedback, changes can be made rapidly to service assortments, problems can be addressed immediately and the learning cycles of companies can speed up dramatically. Online customers may not be aware that they are giving feedback, but companies can monitor which web pages they access, the length of time that they spend on each page and whether they make a purchase (or at what stage they leave the website).

Challenges in distributing services through electronic channels

Price competition

One of the traditional differences between goods and services has been the difficulty of directly comparing features and prices of services with each other. Whereas goods can typically be compared in retail settings, few retail settings exist that offer services from multiple sources. The Internet has changed all that. Services such as travelocity.com and Kelkoo.co.uk make it simple for customers to compare prices for a wide variety of services.

Service spotlight

Online travel has been one of the biggest success stories in electronic channels. The Internet has been an extremely effective channel for travel for three key reasons:

1   Prices are more competitive than offline prices, and the technology can conjure up literally thousands of providers in an instant.
2   Online travel companies have no inventory costs and therefore low cost of goods sold.
3   Sites obtain significant advertising revenue due to focused clientele, with advertisers knowing that all users are potential buyers of their travel services.

One of the most successful, profitable online travel sites is Travelocity.com. Like other online travel sites, it sells airline tickets, hotel rooms and car rentals directly to consumers, avoiding travel agents. It has been one of the top online travel sites since its inception in 1996 by Sabre Holdings. The site earned the loyalty of its users by being very customer focused in an industry that is all too often technology focused. Based on focus groups and surveys to assess site design and ease of use, the company created excellent customer service, carefully detailed explanations, and guarantees of its credit card security and privacy policies. The company has a special help desk that focuses on taking credit card numbers over the telephone for those afraid to input them online. The site also offers instantaneous price quotes and the ability to track prices to cities that customers plan to visit.[2]

Service spotlight (continued)

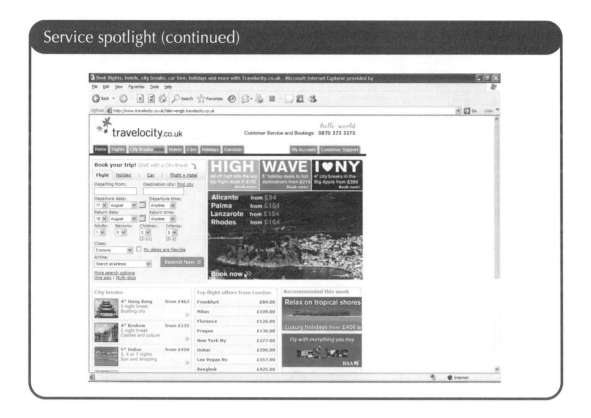

Inability to customize with highly standardized electronic services

Some of you may be on a distance learning course using video or online support materials. If you consider what you miss in learning that way compared with learning directly from a professor, you will understand this challenge. You may not be able to interact directly with the professor, ask questions, raise points for clarification or experience the connection that you receive in person. In online classes – as in videoconferences that are springing up in many businesses – the quality of the service can also be impeded by the way the audience reacts (or does not react) in those situations. People talk among themselves, leave, laugh and criticize, among other behaviours.

Lack of consistency because of customer involvement

Although electronic channels are very effective in minimizing the inconsistency from employees or providers of service, customer variability still presents a problem. Customers use the technology themselves to produce the service but often this can lead to errors or frustration unless the technology is highly user friendly. Manoeuvring online can sometimes be overwhelming, and not all websites are easy to use. Furthermore, many customers may not have computers and, even if they do, may be reluctant to use this medium.

Changes in consumer behaviour

A consumer purchasing a service through electronic channels engages in very different behaviour to a consumer entering a retail store and talking to a salesperson. Considerable changes – in the willingness to search for information, in the willingness to perform some aspects of the services themselves, in the acceptance of different levels of service – are necessary when customers use electronic channels. Behaviour change is difficult, even for a consumer wanting to make a change; therefore, marketers wishing to motivate consumers to alter long-established patterns will be challenged.

Security concerns

One issue confronting marketers using electronic channels is concern about the security of information, particularly health and financial information. Many customers are still hesitant about giving credit card numbers on the Internet. These problems can undermine consumers' trust in the Internet as a safe place to do business. Companies doing business through the Internet must continually devise ways to protect their systems from penetration, vandalism, eavesdropping and impersonation.[3] With penetration, intruders steal passwords and exploit unprotected modems and connections, actually taking over the sites. With vandalism, hackers crash corporate and other computers. To combat these problems, firewalls and other software scan for unusual activity. With eavesdropping, hackers snoop on information as it passes through multiple computers to the Internet. The typical solution is encryption software that scrambles electronic mail and other data to make it unintelligible to eavesdroppers. Finally, with impersonation, criminals steal consumers' identities in order to buy goods and services. A form of encryption technology is often used to deal with this problem, and special service companies confirm signature holders.[4]

Competition from widening geographies

Historically, many services were somewhat protected from competition because customers had limited choice among the providers they could physically drive to. Banks, for example, supplied all local customers with current accounts, savings accounts and mortgages. In fact, it used to be said that because services could not be transported they were limited in their scope. Not any longer – and not with electronic channels. Through the Internet, many services, including financial services, can be purchased from service providers far from the local area.

Other forms of service distribution

Except for situations where electronic channels can distribute services, providers and consumers come into direct contact in service provision. Because of the inseparability of production and consumption in service, providers must either be present themselves when customers receive service or find ways to involve others in distribution. Involving others can be problematic because quality in service occurs in the service encounter between company and customer. Unless the service distributor is willing and able to perform in the service encounter as the service principal would, the value of the offering decreases and the reputation of the original service may be damaged. Chapter 11 pointed out the challenges of controlling encounters within service organizations themselves, but most service (and many manufacturing) companies face an even more formidable task: attaining service excellence and consistency when intermediaries represent them to customers. As we have indicated throughout this textbook, services are generally intangible and experiential in nature. Thus, service distribution does not typically involve moving items through a chain of firms that begins with a manufacturer and ends with a consumer, as is the case for goods distribution. In fact, many services are delivered directly from the service producer to the consumer. That is, in contrast to channels for goods, channels for services are often *direct* – with the creator of the service (i.e. the service principal) selling directly to and interacting directly with the customer. Examples include air travel (easyJet), opticians

(Vision Express) and consulting services (Accenture). Because services cannot be owned, there are no titles or rights to most services that can be passed along a delivery channel. Because services are intangible and perishable, inventories cannot exist, making warehousing a dispensable function. In general, because services cannot be produced, warehoused and then retailed, as goods can, many channels available to goods producers are not feasible for service firms. Thus, many of the primary functions that distribution channels serve – inventorying, securing and taking title to goods – have no meaning in services, allowing the service principal to deliver the service directly to the customer.

Delivery of service through intermediaries

Two distinct services marketers are involved in delivering service through intermediaries: the **service principal**, or originator, and the **service deliverer**, or intermediary. The service principal is the entity that creates the service concept (whose counterpart is the manufacturer of physical goods), and the service deliverer is the entity that interacts with the customer in the actual execution of the service (whose counterpart is the distributor or wholesaler of physical goods).

Even though many of the functions that intermediaries provide for goods manufacturers are not relevant for service firms, intermediaries often deliver services and perform several important functions for service principals. First, they may co-produce the service, fulfilling service principals' promises to customers. Franchise services such as haircutting, key-making and dry-cleaning are produced by the intermediary (the franchisee) using a process developed by the service principal. Service intermediaries also make services locally available, providing time and place convenience for the customer. Because they represent multiple service principals, such intermediaries as travel and insurance agents provide a retailing function for customers, gathering together in one place a variety of choices. And in many financial or professional services, intermediaries function as the glue between the brand or company name and the customer by building the trusting relationship required in these complex and expert offerings.

The primary types of intermediaries used in service delivery are franchisees, agents and brokers. *Franchisees* are service outlets licensed by a principal to deliver a unique service concept it has created or popularized. Examples include fast-food chains (McDonald's, Burger King), video stores (Blockbuster[5]) and hotels (Holiday Inn). **Agents and brokers** are representatives who distribute and sell the services of one or more service suppliers. Examples include insurance (AA Insurance Services[6]), financial services (through any one of the many independent financial advisers) and travel services (American Express).

We do not include retailers in our short list of service intermediaries because most retailers – from department stores to discount stores – are channels for delivering physical goods rather than services. Retailers that sell only services (cinemas, film-processing kiosks, restaurants) or retail services that support physical products (car dealers, service stations) can also be described as dealers or franchises. For our purposes in this chapter, such retailers are grouped into the franchise category because they possess the same characteristics, strengths and weaknesses as franchises.

Goods retailers, by the way, are service organizations themselves; they are intermediaries for goods and perhaps services. Manufacturing companies depend on retailers to represent, explain, promote and ensure their products – all of which are pre-sale services. Manufacturers also need retailers to return, exchange, support and service products – all of which are post-sale services. These roles are increasingly critical as products become more complex, technical and expensive. For example, camera and computer firms rely on retailers carrying their products to understand and communicate highly technical information so that customers choose products that fit their needs. A retailer that leads the customer to the wrong product choice or that inadequately instructs the customer on how to use the product creates service problems that strongly influence the manufacturer's reputation.

Service principals depend on their intermediaries to deliver service to their specifications. Service intermediaries determine how the customer evaluates the quality of the company. When a McDonald's franchisee cooks the McNuggets for too short a time, the customer's perception of the company – and of other McDonald's franchisees – is tarnished. When one Holiday Inn franchisee has unsanitary conditions, it reflects on all other Holiday Inns and on the Holiday Inn brand itself. Unless service providers ensure that the intermediary's goals, incentives and motives are consistent with their own, they lose control over the service encounters between the customer and the intermediary. When someone other than the service principal is critical to the fulfilment of quality service, a firm must develop ways to either control or motivate these intermediaries to meet company goals and standards. In the sections that follow, we discuss both direct delivery of service by the service principal and indirect delivery of the service through intermediaries.

Direct or company-owned channels

Although we call this chapter 'Delivering service through technology and intermediaries', it is important to acknowledge that many services are distributed directly from provider to customer. Some of these are local services – doctors, dry-cleaners and hairstylists – whose area of distribution is limited. Others are national chains with multiple outlets but are considered direct channels because the provider owns all the outlets. HSBC bank,[7] is an example of a service provider with all company-owned outlets enabling service delivery to be controlled and managed in a consistent manner thereby maintaining the bank's image.

Perhaps the major benefit of distributing through company-owned channels is that the company has complete *control* over the outlets. One of the most critical implications of this type of control is that the owner can maintain consistency in service provision. Standards can be established and will be carried out as planned because the company itself monitors and rewards proper execution of the service. Control over hiring, firing and motivating employees is also a benefit of company-owned channels. Using company-owned channels also allows the company to expand or contract sites without being bound by contractual agreements with other entities.

A final benefit of company-owned channels is that the company owns the customer relationship. In service industries in which skilled or professional workers have individual relationships with customers, a major concern is whether the loyalty the customer feels is for the company or for the individual service employee. It is well known, for example, that most people are loyal to individual hairstylists and will follow them from one place of business to another. Therefore, one of the important issues in service delivery is who owns the customer relationship – the store or the employee. With company-owned channels, the company owns both the store and the employee, and therefore has complete control over the customer relationship.

However, several disadvantages exist with company-owned channels. First, and probably the largest impediment to most service chains, the company must bear all the financial risk. When expanding, the firm must find all the capital, sometimes using it for store proliferation rather than for other uses (such as advertising, service quality or new service development) that would be more profitable. Second, large companies are rarely experts in local markets – they know their businesses but not all markets. When adjustments are needed in business formats for different markets, they may be unaware of what these adjustments should be. This disadvantage is especially evident when companies expand into other cultures and other countries. Partnering or joint venturing is almost always preferred to company-owned channels in these situations.

When two or more service companies want to offer a service and neither has the full financial capability or expertise, they often undertake service partnerships. These partnerships operate very much like company-owned channels except that they involve multiple owners. The benefit is that risk and effort are shared, but the disadvantage is that control and returns are also distributed among the partners. Several areas in which partnerships are common are telecommunications, high-technology services, Internet-based services and entrepreneurial services. Service partnerships also proliferate when companies expand beyond their country boundaries – typically one partner provides the business format and the other provides knowledge of the local market.

Franchising

Franchising is the most common type of distribution in services in the UK, where the franchise industry is worth around 15 billion euros and employs more than 330 000 people with more than 718 franchisers licensing their brand names, business processes or formats, unique products, services or reputations in return for fees and royalties.[8] Franchising works well with services that can be standardized and duplicated through the delivery process, service policies, warranties, guarantees, promotion and branding. Body Shop[9], Domino's Pizza[10], Prontaprint[11], Toni & Guy[12] and Vision Express[13] are examples of companies that are ideal for franchise operations. At its best, franchising is a relationship or partnership in which the service provider – the franchiser – develops and optimizes a service format that it licenses for delivery by other parties – the franchisees. There are benefits and disadvantages for both the franchiser and the franchisee in this relationship (see Table 13.2).

The franchiser's perspective

A franchiser typically begins by developing a business concept that is unique in some way. Perhaps it is a fast-food concept (such as McDonald's) with unique cooking or delivery processes. Perhaps it is a hairstylist (such as Toni & Guy) with established formats for marketing to customers, pricing and hiring employees. Or maybe it is a video store (such as Blockbuster) with

Benefits	Challenges
For franchisers	
Leveraged business format for greater expansion and revenues	Difficulty in maintaining and motivating franchisees
Consistency in outlets	Highly publicized disputes and conflict
Knowledge of local markets	Inconsistent quality
Shared financial risk and more working capital	Control of customer relationship by intermediary
For franchisees	
An established business format	Encroachment
National or regional brand marketing	Disappointing profits and revenues
Minimized risk of starting a business	Lack of perceived control over operations
	High fees

TABLE 13.2 Benefits and challenges in franchising

unique store environments, employee training, purchasing and computer systems. A franchiser typically expands business through this method because it expects the following benefits:

- *A leveraged business format for greater expansion and revenues.* Most franchisers want wider distribution – and increased revenues, market share, brand name recognition and economies of scale – for their concepts and practices than they can support in company outlets.

- *Consistency in outlets.* When franchisers have strong contracts and unique formats, they can require that service be delivered according to their specifications. The introduction to this chapter, for example, shows how Starbucks is maintaining consistency across cultures and countries through franchising.

- *Knowledge of local markets.* National chains are unlikely to understand local markets as well as the business people who live in the geographic areas. With franchising, the company obtains a connection to the local market.

- *Shared financial risk and more working capital.* Franchisees must contribute their own capital for equipment and personnel, thereby bearing part of the risk of doing business.

Franchising is not without its challenges, however. Most franchisers encounter the following disadvantages:

- *Difficulty in maintaining and motivating franchisees.* Motivating independent operators to price, promote, deliver and hire according to standards the principal establishes is a difficult job, particularly when business is down.

- *Highly publicized disputes between franchisees and franchisers.* Franchisees are organizing and hiring lobbyists and lawyers to gain more economic clout. Many countries are looking at implementing legislation to boost franchisee rights.

- *Inconsistent quality.* Although some franchisees deliver the service in the manner in which the franchiser intended, other franchisees do not perform the service as well as desired. This inconsistency can undermine the company's image, reputation and brand name.

- *Customer relationships controlled by the franchisee rather than the franchiser.* The closer a company is to the customer, the better able it is to listen to that customer's concerns and ideas. When franchisees are involved, a relationship forms between the customer and the franchisee rather than between the customer and the franchiser. All customer information, including demographics, purchase history and preferences, is in the hands of the intermediary rather than the principal.

The franchisee's perspective

From the perspective of the franchisee, one of the main benefits of franchising is obtaining an established business format on which to base a business, something one expert has defined as an 'entrepreneur in a prepackaged box, a super-efficient distributor of services and goods through a decentralized web'.[14] A second benefit is receiving national or regional brand marketing. Franchisees obtain advertising and other marketing expertise as well as an established reputation. Finally, franchising minimizes the risks of starting a business.

Disadvantages for franchisees also exist. One of the most problematic is *encroachment* – the opening of new units near existing ones without compensation to the existing franchisee. When encroachment occurs, potential revenues are diminished and competition is increased. Another frequent disadvantage involves disappointment over profits and revenues which is exacerbated by having to pay fees to the franchiser (currently averaging 7.7 per cent in the UK).[15] Other disadvantages include lack of perceived control over operations and high fees. Many of these problems are due to over-promising by the franchiser, but others are caused by unrealistic expectations about what will be achieved in a franchise agreement.

Agents and brokers

An *agent* is an intermediary who acts on behalf of a service principal (such as an estate agent) or a customer and is authorized to make agreements between the principal and the customer. Some agents, called selling agents, work with the principal and have contractual authority to sell a principal's output (such as travel, insurance or financial services), usually because the principal lacks the resources or desire to do so. Other agents, called purchasing agents, often have long-term relationships with buyers and help them in evaluating and making purchases. Such agents are frequently hired by companies and individuals to find art, antiques and rare jewellery. A *broker* is an intermediary who brings buyers and sellers together while assisting in negotiation. Brokers are paid by the party who hired them, rarely become involved in financing or assuming risk and are not long-term representatives of buyers or sellers. The most familiar examples are insurance brokers.

Agents and brokers do not take title to services but instead deliver the rights to them. They have legal authority to market services as well as to perform other marketing functions on behalf of producers. The benefits and challenges in using agents and brokers are summarized in Table 13.3.

Benefits of agents and brokers

The travel industry provides an example of both agents and brokers. Three main categories of travel intermediaries exist: tour packagers, retail travel agents and specialty channellers (including incentive travel firms, meeting and convention planners, hotel representatives and corporate travel offices). You are likely to be most familiar with traditional retail travel agents. Industry convention terms the travel companies as brokers and the individuals who work for them as travel agents or sales associates. We use this industry to illustrate some of the benefits and challenges of delivering service through agents and brokers. This traditional industry is changing rapidly because of electronic channels, and we illustrate these new entrants and their impact later in the chapter.

Benefits	Challenges
Reduced selling and distribution costs	Loss of control over pricing
Intermediary's possession of special skills and knowledge	Representation of multiple service principals
Wide representation	
Knowledge of local markets	
Customer choice	

TABLE 13.3 Benefits and challenges in distributing services through agents and brokers

Reduced selling and distribution costs

Traditionally (before the Internet), if an airline or resort hotel needed to contact every potential traveller to promote its offerings, costs would be exorbitant. Because most travel services are transactional rather than long term, travellers would need to expend tremendous effort to find services that meet their needs. Travel agents and brokers accomplish the intermediary role by assembling information from travel suppliers and offering it to travellers.

Possession of special skills and knowledge

Agents and brokers have special knowledge and skills in their areas. For example, retail travel agents know the industry well and know how to access the information they do not possess, often through reference materials and online services. Tour packagers have a more specialized role – they assemble, promote and price bundles of travel services from travel suppliers, then offer these bundles either to travellers themselves or to retail travel agents. Specialty channellers have even more specialized roles. Some work in corporate travel offices to lend their skills to an entire corporation; others are business meeting and convention planners who act almost as tour packagers for whole companies or associations; and some are incentive travel firms that focus on travel recognition programmes in corporations or associations.

Wide representation

Because agents and brokers are paid by commission rather than by salary, there is little risk or disadvantage to the service principal in extending the service offerings to a wide geography. Thus companies have representatives in many places, far more than if fixed costs such as buildings, equipment and salaries were required.

Knowledge of local markets

Another key benefit of agents and brokers is that they become experts in the local markets they serve. They know or learn the unique needs of different markets, including international markets. They understand what their clients' preferences are and how to adapt the principal's services to match the needs of clients. This benefit is particularly needed and appreciated when clients are dispersed internationally. Knowing the culture and taboos of a country is critical for successful selling. Most companies find that obtaining local representation by experts with this knowledge is necessary.

Customer choice

Travel and insurance agents provide a retailing service for customers – they represent the services of multiple suppliers. If a traveller needed to visit six or eight different travel agencies, each of which carried the services of a single supplier, imagine the effort a customer would need to make to plan a trip! Similarly, independent insurance agents have the right to sell a wide variety of insurance, which allows them to offer customers a choice. These types of agents also are able to compare prices across suppliers and get the best prices for their clients.

Challenges of delivering service through agents and brokers

Loss of control over pricing

As representatives of service principals and experts on customer markets, agents and brokers are typically empowered to negotiate price, configure services and otherwise alter the marketing of a principal's service. This issue could be particularly important – and possibly detrimental – when a service provider depends on a particular (high) price to convey a level of service quality. If the price can be changed, it might drop to a level that undermines the quality image. In addition, the agent often has the flexibility to give different prices to different customers. As long as the customers are geographically dispersed, this variation will not create a problem for the service principal; however, if buyers compare prices and realize they are being given different prices, they may perceive the service principal as unfair or unethical.

Representation of multiple service principals

When independent agents represent multiple suppliers, they offer customer choice. From the perspective of the service principal, however, customer choice means that the agent represents – and in many cases advocates – a competitive service offering. This is the same challenge a manufacturer confronts when distributing products in a retail store. Only in rare cases are its products the only ones in a given category on the retail floor. In a service context, consider the use of independent insurance agents. These agents carry a range of insurance products from different companies, serving as a surrogate service retail store for customers. When they find a customer who needs insurance, they sell from their portfolio the offerings that best match the customer's requirements.

Common issues involving intermediaries

Key problems with intermediaries include conflict over objectives and performance, difficulty controlling quality and consistency across outlets, tension between empowerment and control, and **channel ambiguity**.

Channel conflict over objectives and performance

The parties involved in delivering services do not always agree about how the channel should operate. **Channel conflict** can occur between the service provider and the service intermediary, among intermediaries in a given area, and between different types of channels used by a service provider (such as when a service principal has its own outlets as well as franchised outlets). The conflict most often centres on the parties having different goals, competing roles and rights, and conflicting views of the way the channel is performing. Sometimes the conflict occurs because the service principal and its intermediaries are too dependent on each other.

Difficulty controlling quality and consistency across outlets

One of the biggest difficulties for both principals and their intermediaries involves the inconsistency and lack of uniform quality that result when multiple outlets deliver services. When poor performance occurs, even at a single outlet, the service principal suffers because the entire brand and reputation are jeopardized, and other intermediaries endure negative attributions to their outlets. The problem is particularly acute in highly specialized services such as management consulting or architecture, in which execution of the complex offering may be difficult to deliver to the standards of the principal.

Tension between empowerment and control

McDonald's and other successful service businesses were founded on the principle of performance consistency. Both they and their intermediaries have attained profits and longevity because the company controls virtually every aspect of their intermediaries' businesses. McDonald's, for example, is famous for its demanding and rigid service standards (such as 'turn, never flip, hamburgers on the grill'), carefully specified supplies, and performance monitoring. The strategy makes sense: unless an intermediary delivers service exactly the same way the successful company outlets provide it, the service may not be as desirable to customers. From the principal's point of view, its name and reputation are on the line in each outlet, making careful control a necessity.

Control, however, can have negative ramifications within intermediaries. Many service franchisees, for example, are entrepreneurial by nature and select service franchising because they can own and operate their own businesses. If they are to deliver according to consistent standards, their independent ideas must be integrated into and often subsumed by the practices and policies of the service principal. In these situations they often feel like automatons with less freedom than they have anticipated as owners of their own businesses.

Channel ambiguity

When control is not the chosen strategy, doubt exists about the roles of the company and the intermediary. Who will undertake market research to identify customer requirements, the company or an intermediary? Who owns the results and in what way are they to be used? Who determines the standards for service delivery, the franchiser or the franchisee? Who should train a dealer's customer service representatives, the company or the dealer? In these and other situations, the roles of the principal and its intermediaries are unclear, leading to confusion and conflict.

Strategies for effective service delivery through intermediaries

Service principals, of course, want to manage their service intermediaries to improve service performance, solidify their images and increase profits and revenues. The principal has a variety of choices, which range from strict contractual and measurement control to partnering with intermediaries in a joint effort to improve service to the customer. One of the biggest issues a principal faces is whether to view intermediaries as extensions of its company, as customers or as partners. We discuss three categories of intermediary management strategies: **control, empowerment and partnering strategies**.

Control strategies

In the control strategies category, the service principal believes that intermediaries will perform best when it creates standards both for revenues and service performance, measures results and compensates or rewards on the basis of performance level. To use these strategies the principal must be the most powerful participant in the channel, possessing unique services with strong consumer demand or loyalty, or other forms of economic power.

Measurement

Some franchisers maintain control of the service quality delivered by their franchisees by ongoing measurement programmes that feed data back to the principal. Virtually all car dealers' sales and service performance is monitored regularly by the manufacturer, which creates the measurement programme, administers it and maintains control of the information. The company surveys customers at key points in the service encounter sequence: after sale, 30 days out, 90 days out and after a year. The manufacturer designs the survey instruments (some of them with the assistance of dealer councils) and obtains the customer feedback directly. On the basis of this information, the manufacturer rewards and recognizes both individuals and dealerships that perform well and can potentially punish those that perform poorly. The obvious advantage to this approach is that the manufacturer retains control; however, the trust and goodwill between manufacturers and dealers can easily be eroded if dealers feel that the measurement is used to control and punish.

Review

Some franchisers control through terminations, non-renewals, quotas and restrictive supplier sources. Expansion and encroachment are two of the tactics being used today. Another means by which franchisers exert control over franchisees is through quotas and sales goals, typically by offering price breaks after a certain volume is attained.

Empowerment strategies

Empowerment strategies – in which the service principal allows greater flexibility to intermediaries based on the belief that their talents are best revealed in participation rather than acquiescence – are useful when the service principal is new or lacks sufficient power to govern the channel using control strategies. In empowerment strategies, the principal provides information, research or processes to help intermediaries perform well in service.

Help the intermediary develop customer-oriented service processes

Individual intermediaries rarely have the funds to sponsor their own customer research studies or training programmes. One way for a company to improve intermediary performance is to conduct research or standard-setting studies relating to service performance, then provide the results as a service to intermediaries. Service originators can invest in training or other forms of development to improve the skills and knowledge of intermediaries and their employees.

Provide needed support systems

Service spotlight

After Ford Motor Company conducted customer research and identified six sales standards and six service standards that address the most important customer expectations, it found that dealers and service centres did not know how to implement, measure and improve service with these standards. For example, one sales standard specified that customers be approached within the first minute they enter the dealership and be offered help when and if the customer needs it. Although dealers could see that this standard was desirable, they did not immediately know how to make it happen. Ford stepped in and provided the research and process support to help the dealers. As another form of support, the company created national advertising featuring dealers discussing the quality care standards.

In airlines and hotels as well as other travel and ticketing services, the service principal's reservation system is an important support system. Holiday Inn has a franchise service delivery system that adds value to the Holiday Inn franchise and differentiates it from competitors.

Change to a cooperative management structure

Companies such as TGI Fridays[16] use the technique of empowerment to manage and motivate franchisees. They develop worker teams in their outlets to hire, discipline and handle financial tasks such as deposits and audits.

Partnering strategies

The group of strategies with the highest potential for effectiveness involves partnering with intermediaries to learn together about end customers, set specifications, improve delivery and communicate honestly. This approach capitalizes on the skills and strengths of both principal and intermediary, and engenders a sense of trust that improves the relationship.

Alignment of goals

One of the most successful approaches to partnering involves aligning company and intermediary goals early in the process. Both the service principal and the intermediary have individual goals that they strive to achieve. If channel members can see that they benefit the ultimate consumer of services and in the process optimize their own revenues and profit, they begin the relationship with a target in mind.

Consultation and cooperation

A strategy of consultation and cooperation is not as dramatic as setting joint goals, but it does result in intermediaries participating in decisions. In this approach, which could involve virtually any issue, from compensation to service quality to the service environment, the principal makes a point of consulting intermediaries and asking for their opinions and views before establishing policy. For example, when a franchiser finds that the outlets need greater support in promotion, the company can began to make customer mailings for franchisees. This approach makes the franchisees feel that they have some control over the way they do business and also generates a steady stream of improvement ideas.

Summary

This chapter discussed the benefits and challenges of delivering service through intermediaries. Service intermediaries perform many important functions for the service principal – co-producing the service, making services locally available and functioning as the link between the principal and the customer. The focus in service distribution is on identifying ways to bring the customer and principal or its representatives together.

In contrast to channels for products, channels for services are almost always direct, if not to the customer then to the intermediary that sells to the customer. Many of the primary functions that distribution channels serve – stock-holding, securing and taking title to goods – have no meaning in services because of services' intangibility. Because services cannot be owned, most have no titles or rights that can be passed along a delivery channel. Because services are intangible and perishable, stock-holding cannot exist, making warehousing dispensable. In general, because services cannot be produced, warehoused, and then retailed as goods can, many channels available to goods producers are not feasible for service firms.

Four forms of distribution in service were described in the chapter: electronic channels, franchisees, agents/brokers and direct. The benefits and challenges of each type of intermediary were discussed, and examples of firms successful in delivering services through each type were detailed. Discussion centred on strategies that could be used by service principals to improve management of intermediaries.

Key concepts

Agents and brokers	329	Electronic channels	324
Channel ambiguity	335	Franchising	331
Channel conflict	335	Service deliverer	329
Control v. empowerment v. partnering strategies	336	Service principal	329

Further reading

Heinonen, K. (2006) 'Temporal and spatial e-service value', *International Journal of Service Industry Management*, 17(4), 380–400.

Hoffman, D. and Novak, T. (2000) 'How to acquire customers on the web', *Harvard Business Review* 78(3), 179–86.

Mendelsohn, M. (1999) *The Guide to Franchising*. London: Cassell.

Mohanned, R., Fisher, R.J., Jaworski, B.J. and Cahill, A.M. (2001) *Internet Marketing: Building Advantage in the Networked Economy*. Boston, MA: McGraw-Hill/Irwin.

Rust, R.T. and Lemon, K.N. (2001) 'E-service and the consumer', *International Journal of Electronic Commerce*, 5(3), 85–101.

 ## Discussion questions

1 In what specific ways does the distribution of services differ from the distribution of goods?

2 Identify other service firms that are company owned and see whether the services they provide are more consistent than ones provided by franchisees.

3 List five services that could be distributed on the Internet that are not mentioned in this chapter. Why are these particular services appropriate for electronic distribution? Choose two that you particularly advocate. How would you address the challenges to electronic media discussed in this chapter?

4 List services that are sold through selling agents. Why is the use of agents the chosen method of distribution for these services? Could any be distributed in the other ways described in this chapter?

5 What are the main differences between agents and brokers?

6 What types of services are bought through purchasing agents? What qualifies a purchasing agent to represent a buyer in these transactions? Why do buyers themselves not engage in the purchase, rather than hiring someone to do so?

7 Which of the reasons for channel conflict described in this chapter is the most problematic? Why? Based on the chapter, and in particular the strategies discussed at the

end of the chapter, what can be done to address the problem you selected? Rank the possible strategies from most effective to least effective.

8 Which of the three categories of strategies for effective service delivery through intermediaries do you believe is most successful? Why? Why are the other two categories less successful?

 Exercises

1 On the Internet, locate three services that you believe are interesting. What benefits does buying on the Internet have over buying those services elsewhere?

2 Develop a brief franchising plan for a service concept or idea that you believe could be successful.

3 Visit a franchisee and discuss the pros and cons of the arrangement from his or her perspective. How closely does this list of benefits and challenges fit the one provided in this chapter? What would you add to the chapter's list to reflect the experience of the franchisee you interviewed?

4 Select a service industry with which you are familiar. How do service principals in that industry distribute their services? Develop possible approaches to manage intermediaries using the three categories of strategies in the last section of this chapter. Which approach do you believe would be most effective? Why? Which approaches are currently used by service principals in the industry?

Notes

[1] G. Hamel and J. Sampler, 'The e-corporation', *Fortune, 7* December 1998, pp. 80–92.

[2] D. Coleman, 'Internet success stories: Travelocity', australia.internet.com, 12 November 2001, p. 1.

[3] D. Clark, 'Safety first', *The Wall Street Journal, 7* December 1998, p. R14.

[4] Ibid.

[5] www.blockbuster.co.uk

[6] www.theAA.com

[7] www.hsbc.com

[8] 2006 Nat West/British Franchise Association Survey.

[9] www.thebodyshop.com

[10] www.dominos.co.uk

[11] www.prontaprint.co.uk

[12] www.toniandguy.co.uk

[13] www.visionexpress.com

[14] A.E. Serwer, 'Trouble in franchise nation', *Fortune*, 6 March 1995, pp. 115–29.

[15] 2006 Nat West/ British Franchise Association Survey.

[16] www.fridays.com

CHAPTER 14

Managing demand and capacity

❖ LEARNING OBJECTIVES

This chapter's objectives are to:

1 Explain the underlying issue for capacity-constrained services: lack of inventory capability.

2 Present the implications of time, labour, equipment and facilities constraints combined with variations in demand patterns.

3 Lay out strategies for matching supply and demand through (a) shifting demand to match capacity, or (b) adjusting capacity to meet demand.

4 Demonstrate the benefits and risks of yield management strategies in forging a balance among capacity utilization, pricing, market segmentation and financial return.

5 Provide strategies for managing waiting lines for times when capacity and demand cannot be aligned.

CASE STUDY: HOW TO FILL HOTEL NOVOTEL ROOMS 365 DAYS OF THE YEAR

Occupancy rates of hotel bedrooms and function rooms are critical to the success of any hotel chain. For example, Novotel has bedrooms, restaurants and meeting facilities all available to guests 365 days and nights of the year. Yet natural demand for them varies tremendously. Because Novotels cater to business travellers and business meetings, demand has a weekly cycle in addition to any seasonal fluctuations. Business travellers do not stay over weekends. Thus, demand for rooms from the hotel's primary market segment drops on Friday and Saturday nights.

To smooth the peaks and valleys of demand for its facilities, Novotel has employed a number of strategies. Group business (primarily business conferences) is pursued throughout the year to fill the lower-demand periods. A variety of special events, weddings and getaway packages are offered year round to increase weekend demand for rooms. Most city centre hotels have tried to cater to families and children on the weekends. For many working parents, weekend getaways are a primary form of relaxation and vacation. The city centre hotels cater to these couples and families by offering discounted room rates, child-oriented activities and amenities, and an environment in which families feel comfortable. At weekends, children stay free. On arrival, each child receives a gift featuring 'Dolfi', the hotel's dolphin mascot. The hotels also do special weekend promotions with local theme parks and visitor attractions.

For Novotel and other hotels, managing demand and utilizing the hotel's fixed capacity of rooms, restaurants and meeting facilities can be a seasonal, weekly and, even, daily challenge. Although the hotel industry epitomizes the challenges of demand and capacity management, many service providers face similar problems. For example, tax advisers and air-conditioning maintenance services face seasonal demand fluctuations, whereas services such as commuter trains and restaurants face weekly and, even, hourly variations in customer demand. For some businesses, demand is predictable, as for a tax adviser. For others, such as management or technology consultants, demand may be less predictable, fluctuating based on customer needs and business cycles. Sometimes firms experience too much demand for the existing capacity and sometimes capacity sits idle.

Overuse or underuse of a service can directly contribute to gap 3: failure to deliver what was designed and specified. For example, when demand for services exceeds maximum capacity, the quality of service may drop because staff and facilities are over-taxed. And some customers may be turned away, not receiving the service at all. During periods of slow demand it may be necessary to reduce prices or cut service amenities, changing the make-up of the clientele and the nature of the service, and thus running the risk of not delivering what customers expect. At Novotel hotels mentioned in our opening vignette, older travellers or business groups who are in a hotel on a weekend may resent the invasion of families and children because it changes the nature of the service they expected. At the pool, for example, collisions can occur between adults trying to swim laps and children playing water games.

In this chapter we focus on the challenges of matching supply and demand in capacity-constrained services. Gap 3 can occur when organizations fail to smooth the peaks and valleys of demand, overuse their capacities, attract an inappropriate customer mix in their efforts to build demand or rely too much on price in smoothing demand. The chapter gives you an understanding of these issues and strategies for addressing them. The effective use of capacity is frequently a key success factor for service organizations.

The underlying issue: lack of inventory capability

The fundamental issue underlying supply and demand management in services is the lack of inventory capability. Unlike manufacturing firms, service firms cannot build up inventories during periods of slow demand to use later when demand increases. This lack of inventory capability is due to the perishability of services and their simultaneous production and consumption. An airline seat that is not sold on a given flight cannot be resold the following day. The productive capacity of that seat has perished. Similarly, an hour of a lawyer's billable time cannot be saved from one day to the next. Services also cannot be transported from one place to another or transferred from person to person. Thus Novotel's services cannot be moved to an alternative location in off-peak months – say, to a skiing area where conditions are ideal for tourists and demand for hotel rooms is high.

The lack of inventory capability combined with fluctuating demand leads to a variety of potential outcomes, as illustrated in Figure 14.1.[1] The horizontal lines in Figure 14.1 indicate

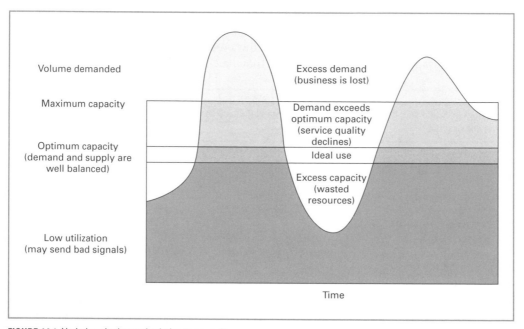

FIGURE 14.1 Variations in demand relative to capacity

Source: reprinted from C. Lovelock, 'Getting the most out of your productive capacity', in *Product Plus* (Boston, MA: McGraw-Hill, 1994), ch. 16, p. 241.
© 1994 by The McGraw-Hill Companies, Inc. Reprinted by permission of The McGraw-Hill Companies

service capacity, and the curved line indicates customer demand for the service. In many services, capacity is fixed; thus capacity can be designated by a flat horizontal line over a certain time period. Demand for service frequently fluctuates, however, as indicated by the curved line. The topmost horizontal line in Figure 14.1 represents maximum capacity. For example, it could represent all 160 rooms in a hotel or it could represent the approximately 70 000 seats in a large football stadium. The rooms and the seats remain constant, but demand for them fluctuates. The band between the second and third horizontal lines represents optimum capacity – the best use of the capacity from the perspective of both customers and the company (the difference between optimal and maximum capacity utilization is discussed later in the chapter). The areas in the middle of Figure 14.1 are labelled to represent four basic scenarios that can result from different combinations of capacity and demand:

1 *Excess demand.* The level of demand exceeds maximum capacity. In this situation some customers will be turned away, resulting in lost business opportunities. For the customers who do receive the service, its quality may not match what was promised because of crowding or overtaxing of staff and facilities.

2 *Demand exceeds optimum capacity.* No one is being turned away, but the quality of service may still suffer because of overuse, crowding or staff being pushed beyond their abilities to deliver consistent quality.

3 *Demand and supply are balanced at the level of optimum capacity.* Staff and facilities are occupied at an ideal level. No one is overworked, facilities can be maintained and customers are receiving quality service without undesirable delays.

4 *Excess capacity.* Demand is below optimum capacity. Productive resources in the form of labour, equipment and facilities are underutilized, resulting in lost productivity and lower profits. Customers may receive excellent quality on an individual level because they have the full use of the facilities, no waiting and complete attention from the staff. If, however, service quality depends on the presence of other customers, customers may be disappointed or may worry that they have chosen an inferior service provider.

Extent to which supply is constrained	Extent of demand fluctuations over time	
	Wide	**Narrow**
Peak demand can usually be met without a major delay	1 Electricity Gas Hospital maternity unit Police and fire emergencies	2 Insurance Legal services Banking Laundry and dry-cleaning
Peak demand regularly exceeds capacity	4 Accounting and tax preparation Passenger transportation Hotels Restaurants Hospital emergency rooms	3 Services similar to those in 2 that have insufficient capacity for their base level of business

TABLE 14.1 Demand versus supply

Source: C.H. Lovelock, 'Classifying services to gain strategic marketing insights', *Journal of Marketing* 47 (Summer 1983), p. 17. Reprinted by permission from the American Marketing Association

Not all firms will be challenged equally in terms of managing supply and demand. The seriousness of the problem will depend on the *extent of demand fluctuations over time* and the *extent to which supply is constrained* (Table 14.1).[2] Some types of organizations will experience wide fluctuations in demand (telecommunications, hospitals, transportation, restaurants), whereas others will have narrower fluctuations (insurance, laundry, banking). For some, peak demand can usually be met even when demand fluctuates (electricity or gas supply), but for others peak demand may frequently exceed capacity (hospital emergency rooms, restaurants, hotels). Those firms with wide variations in demand (cells 1 and 4 in Table 14.1), and particularly those with wide fluctuations in demand that regularly exceed capacity (cell 4), will find the issues and strategies in this chapter particularly important to their success. Those firms that find themselves in cell 3 need a 'one-time-fix' to expand their capacity to match regular patterns of excessive demand. The example industries in Table 14.1 are provided to illustrate where *most* firms in those industries would likely be classified. In reality, an individual firm from any industry could find itself in any of the four cells, depending on its immediate circumstances.

To identify effective strategies for managing supply and demand fluctuations, an organization needs a clear understanding of its **capacity constraints** and the underlying **demand patterns**.

Capacity constraints

Later in the chapter, we present some creative ways to expand and contract capacity in the short and long term, but for our discussion now, you can assume that service capacity is fixed. Depending on the type of service, critical fixed-capacity factors can be time, labour, equipment, facilities or (in many cases) a combination of these.

Time, labour, equipment, facilities

For some service businesses, the primary constraint on service production is *time*. For example, a lawyer, a consultant, a hairdresser, a plumber and a personal counsellor all primarily sell their time. If their time is not used productively, profits are lost. If there is excess demand, time cannot be created to satisfy it. From the point of view of the individual service provider, time is the constraint.

From the point of view of a firm that employs a large number of service providers, *labour* or staffing levels can be the primary capacity constraint. A law firm, a university department, a consulting firm, a tax accounting firm and a repair and maintenance contractor may all face the reality that at certain times demand for their organizations' services cannot be met because staff are already operating at peak capacity. However, it does not always make sense (nor may it be possible in a competitive labour market) to hire additional service providers if low demand is a reality at other times.

In other cases, *equipment* may be the critical constraint. For road transport or air-freight delivery services, the lorries or aeroplanes needed to service demand may be the capacity limitation. During the Christmas holidays, DHL, TNT and other delivery service providers face this issue. Health clubs also deal with this limitation, particularly at certain times of the day (before work, during lunch hours, after work) and in certain months of the year. For network service providers, bandwidth, servers and switches represent their perishable capacity.

Finally, many firms face restrictions brought about by their limited *facilities*. Hotels have only a certain number of rooms to sell, airlines are limited by the number of seats on the aircraft, universities are constrained by the number of rooms and the number of seats in each lecture theatre, and restaurant capacity is restricted to the number of tables and seats available.

Nature of the constraint	Type of service*
Time	Legal
	Consulting
	Accounting
	Medical
Labour	Law firm
	Accounting firm
	Consulting firm
	Health clinic
Equipment	Delivery services
	Telecommunications
	Network services
	Utilities
	Health club
Facilities	Hotels
	Restaurants
	Hospitals
	Airlines
	Schools
	Theatres
	Churches

TABLE 14.2 Constraints on capacity

* The examples illustrate the most common capacity constraint for each type of service. In reality, any of the service organizations listed can be operating under multiple constraints. For example, a law firm may be operating under constrained labour capacity (too few attorneys) and facilities constraints (not enough office space) at the same time.

Understanding the primary capacity constraint, or the combination of factors that restricts capacity, is a first step in designing strategies to deal with supply and demand issues (Table 14.2).

Optimal versus maximum use of capacity

To fully understand **capacity** issues, it is important to know the difference between **optimum** and **maximum** use of capacity. As suggested in Figure 14.1, optimum and maximum capacity may not be the same. Using capacity at an optimum level means that resources are fully employed but not overused and that customers are receiving quality service in a timely manner. Maximum capacity, on the other hand, represents the absolute limit of service availability. In the case of a football game, optimum and maximum capacity may be the same. The entertainment value of the game is enhanced for customers when every seat is filled, and obviously the profitability for the team is greatest under these circumstances (Figure 14.2). On the other hand, in a university classroom it is usually not desirable for students or faculty to have every seat filled. In this case, optimal use of capacity is less than the maximum. In some cases, maximum use of capacity may result in excessive waiting by customers, as in a popular restaurant. From the perspective of customer satisfaction, optimum use of the restaurant's capacity will again be less than maximum use.

In the case of equipment or facilities constraints, the maximum capacity at any given time is obvious. There are only a certain number of weight machines in the health club, a certain number of seats in the aeroplane and a limited amount of space in a cargo carrier. In the case of

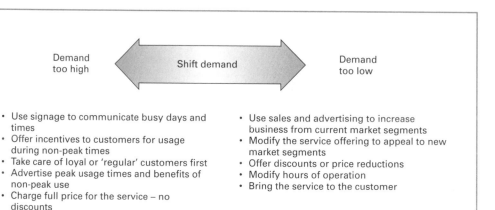

FIGURE 14.2 Strategies for shifting demand to match capacity

a bottling plant, when maximum capacity on the assembly line is exceeded, bottles begin to break and the system shuts down. Thus it is relatively easy to observe the effects of exceeding maximum equipment capacity.

When the limitation is people's time or labour, maximum capacity is harder to specify because people are in a sense more flexible than facilities and equipment. When an individual service provider's maximum capacity has been exceeded, the result is likely to cause decreased service quality, customer dissatisfaction, and employee burnout and turnover, but these outcomes may not be immediately observable even to the employee him or herself. It is often easy for a consulting firm to take on one more assignment, taxing its employees beyond their maximum capacity, or for a dental clinic to schedule a few more appointments in a day, stretching its staff and dentists beyond their maximum capacity. Given the potential costs in terms of reduced quality and customer and employee dissatisfaction, it is critical for the firm to understand optimum and maximum human capacity limits.

Demand patterns

To manage fluctuating demand in a service business, it is necessary to have a clear understanding of demand patterns, why they vary, and the market segments that comprise demand at different points in time.[3] A number of questions need to be answered regarding the predictability and underlying causes of demand.

The recording of demand patterns

First, the organization needs to record the level of demand over relevant time periods. Organizations that have good computerized customer information systems can record this information very accurately. Others may need to record demand patterns more informally. Daily, weekly and monthly demand levels should be followed, and if seasonality is a suspected problem, graphs should be drawn for data from at least the past year. In some services, such as restaurants or health care, hourly fluctuations within a day may also be relevant. Sometimes demand patterns are intuitively obvious; in other cases patterns may not reveal themselves until the data are collected.

Predictable cycles

In looking at the graphic representation of demand levels, is there a predictable cycle daily (variations occur by hours), weekly (variations occur by day), monthly (variations occur by day or week) and/or yearly (variations occur according to months or seasons)? In some cases, predictable patterns may occur at all periods. For example, in the restaurant industry, especially in seasonal tourist locations, demand can vary predictably by month, by week, by day and by hour.

If a predictable cycle is detected, what are its underlying causes? Tax advisers can predict demand based on when taxes are due. Services catering to children and families respond to variations in school hours and vacations. Retail and telecommunications services have peak periods at certain holidays and times of the week and day. When predictable patterns exist, generally one or more causes can be identified.

Random demand fluctuations

Sometimes the patterns of demand appear to be random – there is no apparent predictable cycle. Yet even in this case, causes can often be identified. For example, day-to-day changes in the weather may affect use of recreational, shopping or entertainment facilities. Although the weather cannot be predicted far in advance, it may be possible to anticipate demand a day or two ahead. Health-related events also cannot be predicted. Accidents, heart attacks and births all increase demand for hospital services, but the level of demand cannot generally be determined in advance. Natural disasters such as floods, fires and hurricanes can dramatically increase the need for such services as insurance, telecommunications, builders and health care.

Demand patterns by market segment

An organization that has detailed records on customer transactions may be able to disaggregate demand by market segment, revealing patterns within patterns. Or the analysis may reveal that demand from one segment is predictable whereas demand from another segment is relatively random. For example, for a bank, the visits from its business customers may occur daily at a predictable time, whereas personal account holders may visit the bank at seemingly random intervals. Health clinics often notice that walk-in or 'same-day requests to see a doctor' patients tend to concentrate their arrivals on Monday, with fewer needing immediate attention on other days of the week. Knowing that this pattern exists, some clinics schedule more future appointments (which they can control) for later days of the week, leaving more of Monday available for same-day appointments and walk-ins.

Strategies for matching capacity and demand

When an organization has a clear grasp of its capacity constraints and an understanding of demand patterns, it is in a good position to develop strategies for **matching capacity and demand**. There are two general approaches for accomplishing this match. The first is to smooth the demand fluctuations themselves by shifting demand to match existing supply. This approach implies that the peaks and valleys of the demand curve (Figure 14.1) will be flattened to match as closely as possible the horizontal optimum capacity line. The second general strategy is to adjust capacity to match fluctuations in demand. This implies moving the horizontal capacity lines shown in Figure 14.1 to match the ups and downs of the demand curve. Each of these two basic strategies is described next with specific examples.

Shifting demand to match capacity

With this strategy an organization seeks to shift customers away from periods in which demand exceeds capacity, perhaps by convincing them to use the service during periods of slow demand. This change may be possible for some customers but not for others. For example, many business travellers are not able to shift their needs for airline, car rental and hotel services; leisure travellers, on the other hand, can often shift the timing of their trips. Customers who cannot shift and cannot be accommodated will represent lost business for the firm.

During periods of slow demand, the organization seeks to attract more and/or different customers to utilize its productive capacity. A variety of approaches, detailed in the following sections, can be used to shift or increase demand to match capacity. Frequently, a firm uses a combination of approaches. Ideas for how to shift demand during both slow and peak periods are shown in Figure 14.2.

Vary the service offering

One approach is to change the nature of the service offering, depending on the season of the year, day of the week or time of day. For example, hotels in the Scottish Highlands for skiers in the winter offer their facilities for executive development and training programmes during the summer when snow skiing is not possible. Airlines even change the configuration of their plane seating to match the demand from different market segments. Some planes may have no first-class section. On routes with a large demand for first-class seating, a significant proportion of seats may be placed in first class. Our opening vignette featured ways in which Novotel hotels change their offerings to appeal to the family market segment on weekends. In all these examples, the service offering and associated benefits are changed to smooth customer demand for the organization's resources.

Care should be exercised in implementing strategies to change the service offering, because such changes may easily imply and require alterations in other marketing mix variables – such as promotion, pricing and staffing – to match the new offering. Unless these additional mix variables are altered effectively to support the offering, the strategy may not work. Even when done well, the downside of such changes can be a confusion in the organization's image from the customers' perspective, or a loss of strategic focus for the organization and its employees.

Communicate with customers

Another approach for shifting demand is to communicate with customers, letting them know the times of peak demand so they can choose to use the service at alternative times and avoid crowding or delays. For example, signs in banks and post offices that let customers know their busiest hours and busiest days of the week can serve as a warning, allowing customers to shift their demand to another time if possible. Forewarning customers about busy times and possible waits can have added benefits. Many customer service telephone lines provide a similar warning by informing waiting customers of approximately how long it will be until they are served. Those who do not want to wait may choose to call back later when the lines are less busy or to visit the company's website for faster service. Research in a bank context found that customers who were forewarned about the bank's busiest hours were more satisfied even when they had to wait than were customers who were not forewarned.[4]

In addition to signage that communicates peak demand times to customers, advertising and other forms of promotion can emphasize different service benefits during peak and slow periods. Advertising and sales messages can also remind customers about peak demand times.

Modify timing and location of service delivery

Some firms adjust their hours and days of service delivery to more directly reflect customer demand. Historically, UK banks were open only during 'bankers' hours' from 10 a.m. to 3 p.m. every weekday. Obviously these hours did not match the times when most people preferred to do their personal banking. Now UK banks open earlier, stay open until 5 p.m. many days, and are open on Saturdays, better reflecting customer demand patterns. Online banking has also shifted demand from branches to 'anytime, anywhere' websites. Theatres accommodate customer schedules by offering matinees on weekends and holidays when people are free during the day for entertainment. Cinemas are sometimes rented during weekdays by business groups – an example of varying the service offering during a period of low demand.

Differentiate on price

A common response during slow demand is to discount the price of the service. This strategy relies on basic economics of supply and demand. To be effective, however, a price differentiation strategy depends on solid understanding of customer price sensitivity and demand curves. For example, business travellers are far less price sensitive than are families travelling for pleasure. For Novotel group (our opening vignette), lowering prices during the slow summer months is not likely to increase dramatically bookings from business travellers. However, lower summer prices attract considerable numbers of families and local guests who want an opportunity to experience a good quality hotel but are not able to afford the rooms during peak season.

The maximum capacity of any hotel, airline, restaurant or other service establishment could be reached if the price were low enough. But the goal is always to ensure the highest level of capacity utilization without sacrificing profits. We explore this complex relationship among price, market segments, capacity utilization and profitability later in the chapter in the section on **yield management**.

Heavy use of price differentiation to smooth demand can be a risky strategy. Over-reliance on price can result in price wars in an industry in which eventually all competitors suffer. Price wars are well known in the airline industry, and total industry profits often suffer as a result of airlines simultaneously trying to attract customers through price discounting. Another risk of relying on price is that customers grow accustomed to the lower price and expect to get the same deal the next time they use the service. If communications with customers are unclear, customers may not understand the reasons for the discounts and will expect to pay the same during peak demand periods. Overuse or exclusive use of price as a strategy for smoothing demand is also risky because of the potential impact on the organization's image, the potential for attracting undesired market segments, and the possibility that higher paying customers will feel they have been treated unfairly.

Adjusting capacity to meet demand

A second strategic approach to matching supply and demand focuses on adjusting capacity. The fundamental idea here is to adjust, stretch and align capacity to match customer demand (rather than working on shifting demand to match capacity, as just described). During periods of peak demand the organization seeks to stretch or expand its capacity as much as possible. During periods of slow demand it tries to shrink capacity so as not to waste resources. General strategies for adjusting the four primary service resources (time, people, equipment and facilities) are dis-

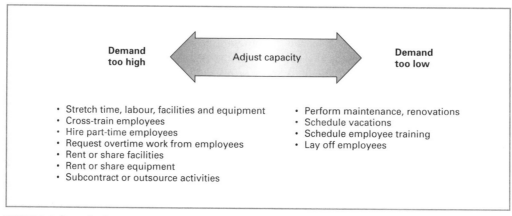

FIGURE 14.3 Strategies for adjusting capacity to match demand

cussed throughout the rest of this section. In Figure 14.3, we summarize specific ideas for adjusting capacity during periods of peak and slow demand. Often, a number of different strategies are used simultaneously.

Stretch existing capacity

The existing capacity of service resources can often be expanded temporarily to match demand. In such cases no new resources are added; rather the people, facilities and equipment are asked to work harder and longer to meet demand.

Stretch time

It may be possible to extend the hours of service temporarily to accommodate demand. A health clinic might stay open longer during flu epidemics, retailers are open longer hours during the Christmas shopping season, and accountants have extended appointment hours (evenings and Saturdays) before tax deadlines.

Stretch labour

In many service organizations, employees are asked to work longer and harder during periods of peak demand. For example, consulting organizations face extensive peaks and troughs with respect to demand for their services. During peak demand, associates are asked to take on additional projects and work longer hours, and front-line service personnel in banks, tourist attractions, restaurants and telecommunications companies are asked to serve more customers per hour during busy times than during hours or days when demand is low.

Stretch facilities

Theatres, restaurants, meeting facilities and classrooms can sometimes be expanded temporarily by the addition of tables, chairs or other equipment needed by customers. Or, as in the case of a commuter train, a carriage that holds a fixed number of people seated comfortably can 'expand' by accommodating standing passengers.

Stretch equipment

Computers, power lines and maintenance equipment can often be stretched beyond what would be considered the maximum capacity for short periods to accommodate peak demand.

In using these types of 'stretch' strategies, the organization needs to recognize the wear and tear on resources and the potential for inferior quality of service that may go with the use. These strategies should thus be used for relatively short periods in order to allow for later maintenance of the facilities and equipment, and refreshment of the people who are asked to exceed their usual capacity. Sometimes it is difficult to know in advance, particularly in the case of human resources, when capacity has been stretched too far.

Align capacity with demand fluctuations

This basic strategy is sometimes known as a 'chase demand' strategy. By adjusting service resources creatively, organizations can in effect chase the demand curves to match capacity with customer demand patterns. Time, labour, facilities and equipment are again the focus, this time with an eye towards adjusting the basic mix and use of these resources. Specific actions might include the following.[5]

Use part-time employees

In this situation the organization's labour resource is being aligned with demand. Retailers hire part-time employees during the holiday rush, tax accountants engage temporary help during the tax return season, tourist resorts bring in extra workers during peak season. Restaurants often ask employees to work split shifts (work the lunch shift, leave for a few hours, and come back for the dinner rush) during peak mealtime hours.

Outsourcing

Firms that find they have a temporary peak in demand for a service that they cannot perform themselves may choose to outsource the entire service. For example, in recent years, many firms have found they do not have the capacity to fulfil their own needs for technology support, Web design and software-related services. Rather than try to hire and train additional employees, these companies look to firms that specialize in outsourcing these types of functions as a temporary (or sometimes long-term) solution.

Rent or share facilities or equipment

For some organizations it is best to rent additional equipment or facilities during periods of peak demand. For example, express mail delivery services such as DHL rent or lease trucks during the peak holiday delivery season. It would not make sense to buy trucks that would sit idle during the rest of the year. Sometimes organizations with complementary demand patterns can share facilities. An example is a church that shares its facilities with a pre-school during the week. The school needs the facilities Monday to Friday during the day; the church needs the facilities evenings and at the weekend. There are whole businesses that have been created to satisfy other businesses' fluctuating demand. For example, a firm may offer temporary office suites and clerical support to individuals who do not need such facilities and support on a continuous basis.

Schedule downtime during periods of low demand

If people, equipment and facilities are being used at maximum capacity during peak periods, then it is imperative to schedule repair, maintenance and renovations during off-peak periods. This schedule ensures that the resources are in top condition when they are most needed. Vacations and training are also scheduled during slow demand periods.

Cross-train employees

If employees are cross-trained, they can shift among tasks, filling in where they are most needed. Cross-training increases the efficiency of the whole system and avoids underutilizing employees in some areas while others are being over-worked. Many airlines such as easyJet cross-train their employees to move from ticketing to working on boarding gates to assisting with baggage if needed. In some fast-food restaurants, employees specialize in one task (like making french fries) during busy hours, and the team of specialists may number 10 people. During slow hours the team may shrink to three, with each person performing a variety of functions. Grocery stores also use this strategy, with most employees able to move as needed from operating checkouts to stocking shelves to bagging groceries.

Modify or move facilities and equipment

Sometimes it is possible to adjust, move or creatively modify existing capacity to meet demand fluctuations. Hotels utilize this strategy by reconfiguring rooms – two rooms with a locked door between can be rented to two different parties in high demand times or turned into a suite during slow demand. The airline industry offers dramatic examples of this strategy. Using an approach known as 'demand-driven dispatch', airlines have begun to experiment with methods that assign aeroplanes to flight schedules on the basis of fluctuating market needs.[6] The method depends on accurate knowledge of demand and the ability to quickly move aeroplanes with different seating capacities to flights that match their capacity. The Boeing 777 aircraft is so flexible that it can be reconfigured within hours to vary the number of seats allocated to one, two or three classes.[7] The plane can thus be quickly modified to match demand from different market segments, essentially moulding capacity to fit demand. Another strategy may involve moving the service to a new location to meet customer demand or even bringing the service to customers. Mobile training facilities, libraries and blood donation facilities are examples of services that physically follow customers.

Combining demand and capacity strategies

Many firms use multiple strategies, combining marketing-driven demand management approaches with operations-driven capacity management strategies. Figuring out which is the best set of strategies for maximizing capacity utilization, customer satisfaction and profitability can be challenging, particularly when the service offering is a constellation of offerings within one service setting, for example, theme parks with rides, restaurants, shopping; hotel vacation villages with hotels, shopping, spas, pools, restaurants; or ski resorts with ski slopes, spas, restaurants and entertainment. Firms face complex problems in trying to balance demand across all the different offerings with an eye to quality and profitability.

Yield management

Yield management is a term that has become attached to a variety of methods, some very sophisticated, matching demand and supply in capacity-constrained services. Using yield management models, organizations find the best balance at a particular point in time among the prices charged, the segments sold to and the capacity used. The goal of yield management is to produce the best possible financial return from a limited available capacity. Specifically, yield management (also referred to as revenue management) has been defined as 'the process of allocating the right type of capacity to the right kind of customer at the right price so as to maximize revenue or yield'.[8]

Although the implementation of yield management can involve complex mathematical models and computer programs, the underlying effectiveness measure is the ratio of actual revenue to potential revenue for a particular measurement period:

$$\text{Yield} = \frac{\text{Actual revenue}}{\text{Potential revenue}}$$

where

Actual revenue = actual capacity used $\times$ average actual price

Potential revenue = total capacity $\times$ maximum price

The equations indicate that yield is a function of price and capacity used. Recall that capacity constraints can be in the form of time, labour, equipment or facilities. Yield is essentially a measure of the extent to which an organization's resources (or capacities) are achieving their full revenue-generating potential. Assuming that total capacity and maximum price cannot be changed, yield approaches 1 as actual capacity utilization increases or when a higher actual price can be charged for a given capacity used. For example, in an airline context, a manager could focus on increasing yield by finding ways to bring in more passengers to fill the capacity, or by finding higher-paying passengers to fill a more limited capacity. In reality, expert yield managers work on capacity and pricing issues simultaneously to maximize revenue across different customer segments. The following shows simple yield calculations and the inherent trade-offs for two types of services: hotel and legal.

CASE STUDY: SIMPLE YIELD CALCULATIONS: EXAMPLES FROM HOTEL AND LEGAL SERVICES

You can do basic yield calculations for any capacity-constrained service assuming you know the actual capacity, average price charged for different market segments, and maximum price that could be charged. Ideally, yield will approach the number 1, or 100 per cent, where:

Yield = Actual revenue/Potential revenue

We describe yield calculations for two simple examples – a 200-room hotel and a lawyer with a 40-hour work week – under different assumed pricing and usage situations. Although companies use much more complex mathematical models to determine yield, the underlying ideas are the same. The goal is to maximize the revenue-generating capability of the organization's capacity.

200-room hotel with maximum room rate of €100 per room per night

Potential revenue = 100 euros $\times$ 200 rooms = 20 000 euros per night

1 Assume: the hotel rents all its rooms at a discounted rate of 50 euros per night.

Yield = 50 euros $\times$ 200 rooms/20 000 euros = 50%

At this rate, the hotel is maximizing capacity utilization, but not getting a very good price.

2 Assume: the hotel charges its full rate, but can only rent 40 per cent of its rooms at that price, due to price sensitivity.

Yield = 100 euros $\times$ 80 rooms/20 000 euros = 40%

▶

In this situation the hotel has maximized the per-room price, but the yield is even lower than in the first situation because so few rooms were rented at that relatively high rate.

3 Assume: the hotel charges its full rate of 100 euros for 40 per cent of its rooms and then gives a discount of 50 euros for the remaining 120 rooms.

$$\text{Yield} = [(100 \text{ euros} \times 80) + (50 \text{ euros} \times 120)]/$$
$$20\,000 \text{ euros} = 14\,000 \text{ euros}/20\,000 \text{ euros} = 70\%$$

Clearly, the final alternative, which takes into account price sensitivity and charges different prices for different rooms or market segments, will result in the highest yield.

40 hours of a lawyer's time across a typical work week at €200 per hour maximum (private client rate)

$$\text{Potential revenue} = 40 \text{ hours} \times 200 \text{ euros per hour} = 8000 \text{ euros per week}$$

1 Assume: the lawyer is able to bill out 30 per cent of her billable time at 200 euros per hour.

$$\text{Yield} = 200 \text{ euros} \times 12 \text{ hours}/8000 \text{ euros} = 30\%$$

In this case the lawyer has maximized her hourly rate, but has only enough work to occupy 12 billable hours.

2 Assume: the lawyer decides to charge 100 euros for non-profit or government clients and is able to bill out all 40 hours at this rate for these types of clients.

$$\text{Yield} = 100 \text{ euros} \times 40 \text{ hours}/8000 \text{ euros} = 50\%$$

In this case, although she has worked a full week, yield is still not very good given the relatively low rate per hour.

3 Assume: the lawyer uses a combined strategy in which she works 12 hours for private clients and fills the rest of her time with non-profit clients at 100 euros per hour.

$$\text{Yield} = [(200 \text{ euros} \times 12) + (100 \text{ euros} \times 28)]/ 8000 \text{ euros} = 5200 \text{ euros}/8000 \text{ euros} = 65\%$$

Again, catering to two different market segments with different price sensitivities is the best overall strategy in terms of maximizing revenue-generating capacity of the lawyer's time.

Implementing a yield management system

To implement a yield management system, an organization needs detailed data on past demand patterns by market segment as well as methods of projecting current market demand. The data can be combined through mathematical programming models, threshold analysis or use of expert systems to project the best allocation of limited capacity at a particular point in time.[9] Allocations of capacity for specific market segments can then be communicated to sales representatives or reservations staff as targets for selling rooms, seats, time or other limited resources. Sometimes the allocations, once determined, remain fixed. At other times allocations change weekly, or even daily or hourly, in response to new information.

Service spotlight

Austrian Airlines

Austrian Airlines has been one of the most consistently profitable airlines in Europe. Prior to deregulation of airlines in Europe, Austrian foresaw the need to develop a competitive advantage that would carry it into the deregulated future. The airline invested in a revenue management computer system to build a two-year historical database of booking data that would monitor flights up to 250 days into the future. Using the system, Austrian saw significant improvements in both number of passengers carried and revenue. By being more selective in its discounting practices than were its competitors, Austrian Airlines achieved excellent results. Other European airlines such as easyJet and Ryanair have very sophisticated yield management systems operating their online bookings.[10]

Marriott Hotels

The hotel industry has also embraced the concept of yield management, and Marriott Hotels has been a leader. The systems at Marriott, for example, maximize profits for a hotel across full weeks rather than by day. In their hotels that target business travellers, Marriott has peak days during the middle of the week. Rather than simply sell the hotel out on those nights on a first-come, first-served basis with no discounts, the revenue management system (which is reviewed and revised daily) now projects guest demand both by price and length of stay, providing discounts in some cases to guests who will stay longer, even on a peak demand night. One early test of the system was at the Munich Marriott during Oktoberfest. Typically no discounts would be offered during this peak period. However, the yield management system recommended that the hotel offer some rooms at a discount, but only for those guests who stayed an extended period before or after the peak days. Although the average daily rate was down 11.7 per cent for the period, occupancy was up over 20 per cent, and overall revenues were up 12.3 per cent. Using yield management practices, Marriott Hotels estimates an additional 300 million euro per year in revenue.[11]

Recent research indicates that traditional yield management approaches are most profitable when (1) a service provider faces different market segments or customers, who arrive or make their reservations at different times and (2) customers who arrive or reserve early are more price sensitive than those who arrive or reserve late.[12] These criteria exactly fit the situation for airlines and many hotels – industries that have effectively and extensively used yield management techniques to allocate capacity. In other services (entertainment, sports, fashion), those customers willing to pay the higher prices are the ones who buy early rather than late. People who really want to see a particular performance reserve their seats at the earliest possible moment. Discounting for early purchases would reduce profits. In these situations, the price generally starts out high and is reduced later to fill capacity if needed.

Interestingly, some airlines now use both these strategies effectively. They start with discounted seats for customers who are willing to buy early, usually leisure and discretionary travellers. They charge a higher fare for those who want a seat at the last minute, typically the less price-sensitive business travellers whose destinations and schedules are inflexible. However, in some cases a bargain fare can be found at the last minute as well, commonly via Internet sales, to fill seats that would otherwise go unoccupied. Online auctions and services offered by companies like Internet-based Lastminute.com serve a purpose in filling capacity at the last minute, often charging much lower fares.

Challenges and risks in using yield management

Yield management programmes can significantly improve revenues. However, although yield management may appear to be an ideal solution to the problem of matching supply and demand, it is not without risks. By becoming focused on maximizing financial returns through differential capacity allocation and pricing, an organization may encounter these problems:[13]

- *Loss of competitive focus.* Yield management may cause a firm to over-focus on profit maximization and inadvertently neglect aspects of the service that provide long-term competitive success.

- *Customer alienation.* If customers learn that they are paying a higher price for service than someone else, they may perceive the pricing as unfair, particularly if they do not understand the reasons. However, a study done in the restaurant industry found that when customers were informed of different prices being charged by time of day, week or table location, they generally felt the practice was fair, particularly if the price difference was framed as a discount for less desirable times rather than a premium for peak times or table locations.[14] Customer education is thus essential in an effective yield management programme. Customers can be further alienated if they fall victim (and are not compensated adequately) to overbooking practices that are often necessary to make yield management systems work effectively.

- *Employee morale problems.* Yield management systems take much guesswork and judgement in setting prices away from sales and reservations people. Although some employees may appreciate the guidance, others may resent the rules and restrictions on their own discretion.

- *Incompatible incentive and reward systems.* Employees may resent yield management systems that do not match incentive structures. For example, many managers are rewarded on the basis of *either* capacity utilization *or* average rate charged, whereas yield management balances the two factors.

- *Lack of employee training.* Extensive training is required to make a yield management system work. Employees need to understand its purpose, how it works, how they should make decisions, and how the system will affect their jobs.

- *Inappropriate organization of the yield management function.* To be most effective with yield management, an organization must have centralized reservations. Although airlines and some large hotel chains and shipping companies do have such centralization, smaller organizations may have decentralized reservations systems and thus find it difficult to operate a yield management system effectively.

Queuing strategies

Sometimes it is not possible to manage capacity to match demand, or vice versa. It may be too costly – for example, most health clinics would not find it economically feasible to add additional facilities or physicians to handle peaks in demand during periods of flu epidemics; patients usually simply have to wait to be seen. Or demand may be very unpredictable and the service capacity very inflexible (it cannot be easily stretched to match unpredictable peaks in demand). Sometimes waits may occur when demand backs up because of the variability in length of time for service. For example, even though patients are

FIGURE 14.4 Waiting is common in many service industries.
Source: Photodisc Green/Getty Images.

scheduled by appointments in a doctor's surgery, frequently there is a wait because some patients take longer to serve than the time allotted to them.

For most service organizations, waiting customers are a fact of life at some point (see Figure 14.4). Waiting can occur on the telephone (customers put on hold when they call in to ask for information, order something or make a complaint) and in person (customers waiting in line at the bank, post office, Disneyland or a doctor's surgery). Waiting can occur even with service transactions through the mail – delays in mail-order delivery or backlogs of correspondence on a manager's desk.

In today's fast-paced society, waiting is not something most people tolerate well. As people work longer hours, as individuals have less leisure, and as families have fewer hours together, the pressure on people's time is greater than ever. In this environment, customers are looking for efficient, quick service with no wait. Organizations that make customers wait take the chance that they will lose business or at the very least that customers will be dissatisfied.[15] To deal effectively with the inevitability of waits, organizations can utilize a variety of **queuing strategies**, described next.

Employ operational logic

If customer waits are common, a first step is to analyse the operational processes to remove any inefficiencies. It may be possible to redesign the system to move customers along more quickly.

Service spotlight

Modifications in the operational system were part of the solution employed by Tesco in its efforts to reduce customer waiting and improve service. The retailer introduced self-service checkouts, hired 'peak-time' checkout operators, expanded its hours in some stores to 24-hour operations, and provided customers with alternative delivery channels (Tesco.com). Collectively these efforts reduced customer wait time, increased productivity and improved customer satisfaction.

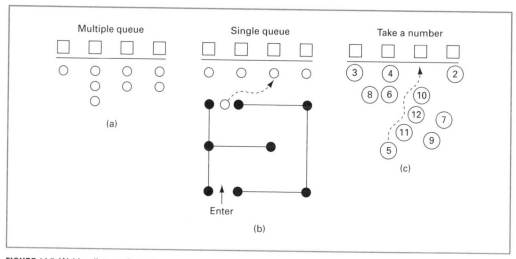

FIGURE 14.5 Waiting-line configurations

Source: J.A. Fitzsimmons and M.J. Fitzsimmons, *Service Management*, 4th edn (New York: Irwin/McGraw-Hill, 2004), ch. 11, p. 296. © 2004 by The McGraw-Hill Companies, Inc. Reprinted by permission of The McGraw-Hill Companies

When queues are inevitable, the organization faces the operational decision of what kind of queuing system to use, or how to configure the queue. Queue configuration refers to the number of queues, their locations, their spatial requirement and their effect on customer behaviour.[16] Several possibilities exist, as shown in Figure 14.5. In the multiple-queue alternative, the customer arrives at the service facility and must decide which queue to join and whether to switch later if the wait appears to be shorter in another line. In the single-queue alternative, fairness of waiting time is ensured in that the first-come, first-served rule applies to everyone; the system can also reduce the average time customers spend waiting overall. However, customers may leave if they perceive that the line is too long or if they have no opportunity to select a particular service provider. The last option shown in Figure 14.5 is the take-a-number option in which arriving customers take a number to indicate line position. Advantages are similar to the single-queue alternative with the additional benefit that customers are able to mill about, browse and talk to each other. The disadvantage is that customers must be on the alert to hear their numbers when they are called. Recent research suggests that length of the queue and perceived cost of waiting are not the only influences on customers' likelihood of staying in line. In a series of experiments and field tests, researchers showed that the larger the number of customers waiting in line *behind* a consumer, the more likely that consumer is to stay in line and wait for the service.[17]

Establish a reservation process

When waiting cannot be avoided, a reservation system can help to spread demand. Restaurants, transportation companies, theatres, doctors and many other service providers use reservation systems to alleviate long waits. The idea behind a reservation system is to guarantee that the service will be available when the customer arrives.

> ### Service spotlight
>
> Even at Disneyland Paris a FASTPASS service is used to reserve times for visitors and cut the waiting time on the most popular attractions. As a result visitors spend less time waiting in line and more time enjoying the park. Here is how it works. The visitor inserts their park entrance ticket into the FASTPASS machine at an attraction and they receive a designated ride time. Then they are free to go enjoy the rest of the park until their allotted time when they come back to the Disney's FASTPASS entrance and hop on board with no further wait.

Beyond simply reducing waiting time, a reservation system has the added benefit of potentially shifting demand to less desirable time periods. A challenge inherent in reservation systems, however, is what to do about 'no shows'. Inevitably there will be customers who reserve a time but do not show up. Some organizations deal with this problem by overbooking their service capacity on the basis of past records of no-show percentages. If the predictions are accurate, overbooking is a good solution. When predictions are inaccurate, however, customers may still have to wait and sometimes may not be served at all, as when airlines overbook the number of seats available on a flight. Victims of overbooking may be compensated for their inconvenience in such cases. To minimize the no-show problem, some organizations (such as hotels, airlines, conferences/training programmes and theatres) charge customers who fail to show up or cancel their reservations within a certain time frame.

Differentiate waiting customers

Not all customers necessarily need to wait the same length of time for service. On the basis of need or customer priority, some organizations differentiate among customers, allowing some to experience shorter waits for service than others. Known as 'queue discipline', such differentiation reflects management policies regarding whom to select next for service.[18] The most popular discipline is first-come, first-served. However, other rules may apply. Differentiation can be based on factors such as:[19]

- *Importance of the customer.* Frequent customers or customers who spend large amounts with the organization can be given priority in service by providing them with a special waiting area or segregated lines.
- *Urgency of the job.* Those customers with the most urgent need may be served first. This strategy is used in emergency health care. It is also used by maintenance services such as central-heating or air-conditioning repair that give priority to customers whose system is not functioning over those who call for routine maintenance.
- *Duration of the service transaction.* In many situations, shorter service jobs get priority through 'express lanes'. At other times, when a service provider sees that a transaction is going to require extra time, the customer is referred to a designated provider who deals only with these special-needs customers.
- *Payment of a premium price.* Customers who pay extra (first class on an airline, for example) are often given priority via separate check-in lines or express systems.

The psychology of queuing

Even when they have to wait, customers can be more or less satisfied depending on how the wait is handled by the organization. Of course, the actual length of the wait will affect how customers feel about their service experience. But it is not just the actual time spent waiting that has an impact on customer satisfaction – it is how customers feel about the wait and their perceptions during it. The type of wait (for example, a standard queue versus a wait due to a delay of service) can also influence how customers will react.[20] In a classic article entitled 'The psychology of waiting lines', David Maister proposes several principles about the **psychology of queuing**, each of which has implications for how organizations can make waiting more pleasurable or at least tolerable.[21]

Unoccupied time feels longer than occupied time

When customers are unoccupied they will likely be bored and will notice the passage of time more than when they have something to do. Providing something for waiting customers to do, particularly if the activity offers a benefit in and of itself or is related in some way to the service, can improve the customer's experience and may benefit the organization as well.[22] Examples include giving customers menus to look at while waiting in a restaurant, providing interesting information to read in a dentist's office or playing entertaining music over the telephone while customers are on hold. At Disney, customers waiting to get on a ride wind their way through a themed environment such as space tunnels or pirates' caves that become part of the total service adventure.[23]

Pre-process waits feel longer than in-process waits

If wait time is occupied with activities that relate to the upcoming service, customers may perceive that the service has started and they are no longer actually waiting. This in-process activity will make the length of the wait seem shorter and will also benefit the service provider by making the customer better prepared when the service actually does begin. Filling out medical information while waiting to see the doctor, reading a menu while waiting to be seated in a restaurant, and watching a videotape of the upcoming service event are all activities that can both educate the customer and reduce perceptions of waiting.

Research in a restaurant context found that customers reacted less negatively to in-process waits than to either pre-process or post-process waits.[24] Other researchers have found the same for waits due to routine slowness of the process. However, if the wait is due to a service failure, then the in-process wait is viewed more negatively than the pre-process wait.[25] Thus, how customers perceive pre-process, in-process and post-process waits may depend to some extent on the cause of the wait.

Anxiety makes waits seem longer

When customers fear that they have been forgotten or do not know how long they will have to wait, they become anxious, and this anxiety can increase the negative impact of waiting. Anxiety also results when customers are forced to choose in a multiple-line situation and they discover they have chosen the 'wrong line'. To combat waiting-line anxiety, organizations can provide information on the length of the wait. At its theme parks, Disney uses signs at intervals along the line that let customers know how long the wait will be from that point on. Using a single line also alleviates customer anxiety over having chosen the wrong line. Explanations and reassurances that no one has forgotten them help alleviate customer anxiety by taking away their cause for worry.

Uncertain waits are longer than known, finite waits

Anxiety is intensified when customers do not know how long they will have to wait. Health-care providers combat this problem by letting customers know when they check in how far behind the doctor is that day. Some patients resolve this uncertainty themselves by calling ahead to ask. Maister provides an interesting example of the role of uncertainty, which he terms the 'appointment syndrome'. Customers who arrive early for an appointment will wait patiently until the scheduled time, even if they arrive very early. However, once the expected appointment time has passed, customers grow increasingly anxious. Before the appointment time the wait time is known; after that, the length of the wait is not known.

Research in an airline context has suggested that as uncertainty about the wait increases, customers become more angry, and their anger in turn results in greater dissatisfaction.[26] Research also shows that giving customers information on the length of the anticipated wait and/or their relative position in the queue can result in more positive feelings and acceptance of the wait and, ultimately, more positive evaluation of the service.[27]

Unexplained waits are longer than explained waits

When people understand the causes for waiting, they frequently have greater patience and are less anxious, particularly when the wait is justifiable. An explanation can reduce customer uncertainty and may help customers estimate how long they will be delayed. Customers who do not know the reason for a wait begin to feel powerless and irritated.

Unfair waits are longer than equitable waits

When customers perceive that they are waiting while others who arrived after them have already been served, the apparent inequity will make the wait seem even longer. This situation can easily occur when there is no apparent order in the waiting area and many customers are trying to be served. Queuing systems that work on a first-come, first-served rule are best at combating perceived unfairness. However, other approaches may be required to determine who will be served next. For example, in an emergency medical care situation, the most seriously ill or injured patients would be seen first. When customers understand the priorities and the rules are clearly communicated and enforced, fairness of waiting time should not be an issue. To understand more about perceptions of fairness, see the 'Fair treatment' section in Chapter 15.

The more valuable the service, the longer the customer will wait

Customers who have substantial purchases or who are waiting for a high-value service will be more tolerant of long wait times and may even expect to wait longer. For example, in a supermarket, customers who have a full cart of groceries will generally wait longer than customers who have only a few items and expect to be checked through quickly. And diners expect to wait longer for service in an expensive restaurant than they do when eating at a 'greasy spoon'.

Solo waits feel longer than group waits

People will wait longer when they are in a group than when they are alone because of the distractions provided by other members of the group. People also feel comfort in waiting with a group rather than alone.[28] In some group waiting situations, such as at Disneyland or when patrons are waiting in long lines to purchase concert tickets, customers who are strangers begin to talk to each other and the waiting experience can actually become fun and a part of the total service experience.

Summary

Because service organizations lack the ability to inventory their products, the effective use of capacity can be critical to success. Idle capacity in the form of unused time, labour, facilities or equipment represents a direct drain on bottom-line profitability. When the capacity represents a major investment (for example, aircraft, expensive medical imaging equipment, lawyers and doctors), the losses associated with underuse of capacity are even more accentuated. Overused capacity is also a problem. People, facilities and equipment can become worn out over time when used beyond optimum capacity constraints. People can quit, facilities become run down and equipment can break. From the customer's perspective, service quality also deteriorates. Organizations focused on delivering quality service, therefore, have a natural drive to balance capacity utilization and demand at an optimum level in order to meet customer expectations.

This chapter has provided you with an understanding of the underlying issues of managing supply and demand in capacity-constrained services by exploring the lack of inventory capability, the nature of service constraints (time, labour, equipment, facilities), the differences in optimal versus maximum use of capacity, and the causes of fluctuating demand.

Based on a grounding in the fundamental issues, the chapter presented a variety of strategies for matching supply and demand. The basic strategies fall under two headings: *demand strategies* (shifting demand to match capacity) and *supply strategies* (adjusting capacity to meet demand). Demand strategies seek to flatten the peaks and valleys of demand to match the flat capacity constraint, whereas supply strategies seek to align, flex or stretch capacity to match the peaks and valleys of demand. Organizations frequently employ several strategies simultaneously to solve the complex problem of balancing supply and demand.

Yield management was presented as a sophisticated form of supply and demand management that balances capacity utilization, pricing, market segmentation and financial return. Long practised by the passenger airline industry, this strategy is growing in use by hotel, shipping, car rental and other capacity-constrained industries in which bookings are made in advance. Essentially, yield management allows organizations to decide on a monthly, weekly, daily or hourly basis to whom they want to sell their service capacity at what price.

All strategies for aligning capacity and demand need to be approached with caution. Any one of the strategies is likely to imply changes in multiple marketing mix elements to support the strategy. Such changes, even if done well, carry a risk that the firm will lose focus or inadvertently alter its image in pursuit of increased revenues. Although a different focus or image is not necessarily bad, the potential strategic impact on the total organization should be considered.

In the last section of the chapter, we discussed situations in which it is not possible to align supply and demand. In these unresolved capacity utilization situations, the inevitable result is customer waiting. We described strategies for effectively managing waiting lines, such as employing operational logic, establishing a reservation process, differentiating waiting customers and making waiting fun or at least tolerable.

Key concepts

Further reading

Adenso-Diaz, B., Gonzalez-Torre, P. and Garcia, V. (2002) 'A capacity management model in service industries', *International Journal of Service Industry Management*, 13(3/4), 286–302.

Betts, A., Meadows, M. and Walley, P. (2000) 'Call centre capacity management', *International Journal of Service Industry Management*, 11(2), 185–96.

Ingold, A., Mcmahon-Beattie, U. and Yeoman, I. (eds) (2000) *Yield Management Strategies for the Service Industries*, 2nd edn. London: Continuum.

Kimes, S.E. (2003) 'Revenue management: a retrospective', *Cornell Hotel and Restaurant Administration Quarterly*, 44(6), 131–8.

Klassen, K.J. and Rohleder, T.R. (2001) 'Combining operations and marketing to manage capacity and demand in services', *Service Industries Journal*, 21(2), 1–30.

Klassen, K.J. and Rohleder, T.R. (2002) 'Demand and capacity management decisions in services: how they impact on one another', *International Journal of Operations and Production Management*, 22(5), 527–48.

Maister, D. (1985) 'The psychology of waiting lines', in J. Czepiel, M.R. Solomon and C.F. Suprenant (eds), *The Service Encounter*. Lexington, MA: Lexington Books, 113–23.

Discussion questions

1 Discuss the four scenarios illustrated in Figure 14.1 and presented in the text (excess demand, demand exceeds optimum capacity, demand and supply are balanced, excess capacity) in the context of a football team selling seats for its games. What are the challenges for management under each scenario?

2 Discuss the four common types of constraints (time, labour, equipment, facilities) facing service businesses and give an example of each (real or hypothetical).

3 How does optimal capacity utilization differ from maximum capacity utilization? Give an example of a situation in which the two might be the same and one in which they are different.

4 Choose a local restaurant or some other type of service with fluctuating demand. What is the likely underlying pattern of demand? What causes the pattern? Is it predictable or random?

5 Describe the two basic strategies for matching supply and demand, and give at least two specific examples of each.

6 What is yield management? Discuss the risks in adopting a yield management strategy.

7 How might yield management apply in the management of the following: a major theatre? A consulting firm? A commuter train?

8 Describe the four basic waiting line strategies, and give an example of each one, preferably based on your own experiences as a consumer.

Exercises

1 Choose a local service organization that is challenged by fixed capacity and fluctuating demand. Interview the marketing manager (or other knowledgeable person) to learn (a) in what ways capacity is constrained, (b) the basic patterns of demand, and (c) strategies the organization has used to align supply and demand. Write up the answers to these questions, and make your own recommendations regarding other strategies the organization might use.

2 Assume you manage a winter ski resort. (a) Explain the underlying pattern of demand fluctuation that is likely to occur at your resort and the challenges it would present to you as a manager. Is the pattern of demand predictable or random? (b) Explain and give examples of how you might use both demand-oriented and supply-oriented strategies to smooth the peaks and troughs of demand during peak and slow periods.

3 Choose a local organization in which people have to wait in line for service. Design a waiting line strategy for the organization.

4 Visit the website of Royal Bank of Scotland (www.rbs.co.uk), a leader in online banking. What online services does the bank currently offer? How do these online services help Royal Bank of Scotland manage the peaks and troughs of customer demand? How do its strategies to use more ATMs and other alternative delivery strategies complement the online strategies?

Notes

1 C. Lovelock, 'Getting the most out of your productive capacity', in *Product Plus* (Boston, MA: McGraw-Hill, 1994), ch. 16.

2 C.H. Lovelock, 'Classifying services to gain strategic marketing insights', *Journal of Marketing* 47 (Summer 1983), pp. 9–20.

3 Portions of this section are based on C.H. Lovelock, 'Strategies for managing capacity-constrained service organizations', in *Managing Services: Marketing, Operations, and Human Resources*, 2nd edn (Englewood Cliffs, NJ: Prentice Hall, 1992), pp. 154–68.

4 E.C. Clemmer and B. Schneider, 'Toward understanding and controlling customer dissatisfaction with waiting during peak demand times', in *Designing a Winning Service Strategy*, eds M.J. Bitner and L.A. Crosby (Chicago, IL: American Marketing Association, 1989), pp. 87–91.

5 Lovelock, 'Getting the most out of your productive capacity'.

6 M.E. Berge and C.A. Hopperstad, 'Demand driven dispatch: a method for dynamic aircraft capacity assignment, models, and algorithms', *Operations Research* 41 (January–February 1993), pp. 153–68.

7 Lovelock, 'Getting the most out of your productive capacity'.

8 See S.E. Kimes, 'Yield management: a tool for capacity-constrained service firms', *Journal of Operations Management* 8 (October 1989), pp. 348–63; S.E. Kimes and R.B. Chase, 'The strategic levers of yield management', *Journal of Service Research* 1 (November 1998), pp. 156–66; S.E. Kimes, 'Revenue management: a retrospective', *Cornell Hotel and Restaurant Administration Quarterly* 44, no. 5/6 (2003), pp. 131–8.

[9] Kimes, 'Yield management'.

[10] H. Richardson, 'Simplify! Simplify! Simplify!', *Transportation and Distribution* 39 (October 1998), pp. 111–17.

[11] N. Templin, 'Your room costs $250 . . . No! $200 . . . No', *The Wall Street Journal*, 5 May 1999, p. B1.

[12] R. Desiraji and S.M. Shugan, 'Strategic service pricing and yield management', *Journal of Marketing* 63 (January 1999), pp. 44–56.

[13] Kimes, 'Yield management'.

[14] S.E. Kimes and J. Wirtz, 'Has revenue management become acceptable? Findings from an international study on the perceived fairness of rate fences', *Journal of Service Research* 6 (November 2003), pp. 125–35.

[15] For research supporting the relationship between longer waits and decreased satisfaction, quality evaluations and patronage intentions see Clemmer and Schneider, 'Toward understanding and controlling customer dissatisfaction'; A.T.H. Pruyn and A. Smidts, 'Customer evaluation of queues: three exploratory studies', *European Advances in Consumer Research* 1 (1993), pp. 371–82; S. Taylor, 'Waiting for service: the relationship between delays and evaluations of service', *Journal of Marketing* 58 (April 1994), pp. 56–69; K.L. Katz, B.M. Larson and R.C. Larson, 'Prescription for the waiting-in-line blues: entertain, enlighten, and engage', *Sloan Management Review* (Winter 1991), pp. 44–53; S. Taylor and J.D. Claxton, 'Delays and the dynamics of service evaluations', *Journal of the Academy of Marketing Science* 22 (Summer 1994), pp. 254–64; D. Grewal, J. Baker, M. Levy and G.B. Voss, 'The effects of wait expectations and store atmosphere on patronage intentions in service-intensive retail stores', *Journal of Retailing* 79 (Winter 2003), pp. 259–68.

[16] J.A. Fitzsimmons and M.J. Fitzsimmons, *Service Management*, 3rd edn (New York: Irwin/McGraw-Hill, 2000), ch. 11.

[17] R. Zhou and D. Soman, 'Looking back: exploring the psychology of queuing and the effect of the number of people behind', *Journal of Consumer Research* 29 (March 2003), pp. 517–30.

[18] Fitzsimmons and Fitzsimmons, *Service Management*, ch. 11.

[19] Lovelock, 'Getting the most out of your productive capacity'.

[20] For an excellent review of the literature on customer perceptions of and reactions to various aspects of waiting time, see S. Taylor and G. Fullerton, 'Waiting for services: perceptions management of the wait experience', in *Handbook of Services Marketing and Management*, eds T.A. Swartz and D. Iacobucci (Thousands Oaks, CA: Sage Publications, 2000), pp. 171–89.

[21] D.A. Maister, 'The psychology of waiting lines', in *The Service Encounter*, eds J.A. Czepiel, M.R. Solomon and C.F. Surprenant (Lexington, MA: Lexington Books, 1985), pp. 113–23.

[22] S. Taylor, 'The effects of filled waiting time and service provider control over the delay on evaluations of service', *Journal of the Academy of Marketing Science* 23 (Summer 1995), pp. 38–48.

[23] A. Bennett, 'Their business is on the line', *The Wall Street Journal*, 7 December 1990, p. B1.

[24] L. Dube-Rioux, B.H. Schmitt and F. Leclerc, 'Consumer's reactions to waiting: when delays affect the perception of service quality', in *Advances in Consumer Research*, vol. 16, ed. T. Srull (Provo, UT: Association for Consumer Research, 1988), pp. 59–63.

[25] M.K. Hui, M.V. Thakor and R. Gill, 'The effect of delay type and service stage on consumers' reactions to waiting', *Journal of Consumer Research* 24 (March 1998), pp. 469–79.

[26] Taylor and Fullerton, 'Waiting for services'.

[27] M.K. Hui and D.K. Tse, 'What to tell consumers in waits of different lengths: an integrative model of service evaluation', *Journal of Marketing* 60 (April 1996), pp. 81–90.

[28] J. Baker and M. Cameron, 'The effects of the service environment on affect and consumer perception of waiting time: an integrative review and research propositions', *Journal of the Academy of Marketing Science* 24 (Fall 1996), pp. 338–49.

CHAPTER 15

Service recovery

This chapter's objectives are to:

1 Illustrate the importance of recovery from service failures in keeping customers and building loyalty.

2 Discuss the nature of consumer complaints and why people do and do not complain.

3 Provide evidence of what customers expect and the kind of responses they want when they do complain.

4 Present strategies for effective service recovery, together with examples of what does and does not work.

5 Discuss service guarantees – what they are, the benefits of guarantees and when to use them – as a particular type of service recovery strategy.

CASE STUDY: THE 'WORLD'S FAVOURITE AIRLINE' WELCOMES COMPLAINTS

Advertisements for British Airways (BA) reinforce the company's branding strategy as the 'World's Favourite Airline'. Indeed, British Airways is a favourite among world travellers – but it was not always so. The success in turning BA around from a bureaucratic institution that regarded itself as doing the public a favour by allowing them to fly on its planes to a customer-responsive, world-class service provider can be attributed to its CEO at the time, Sir Colin Marshall. Marshall (former chairman of the board) was brought in to head up a major change for BA in the 1980s – and he did. His legacy has sustained and further propelled the airline to its current level of success.

A big part of this success was achieved in new ways of listening to customers and new approaches to dealing with customer complaints. One of the first things Marshall did was to install video booths at Heathrow airport so that upset customers could immediately go to the video booth while still at the airport and complain directly to him. In addition to this type of innovative action, Marshall instituted a series of systems and training changes to encourage and be responsive to customer complaints. To quote him directly, 'I ardently believe that customer complaints are precious opportunities to hold on to customers who otherwise might take their business elsewhere and to learn about problems that need to be fixed'.

Initially BA did research to understand the effect that dissatisfied or defecting customers had on the business. It learned that 50 per cent of the dissatisfied customers who did *not* tell BA about their problems left the airline for a competitor. However, of those who *did* tell the company of their problems, 87 per cent remained loyal to BA. It quickly became obvious that complaints should be encouraged! Considering that an average business class passenger has a lifetime value of €115 000, encouraging complaints and retaining their business was obviously critical.

British Airways responded by building a model for 'Making customers into champions'. Goals of the new system were to (1) use customer feedback more effectively to improve quality; (2) strive to prevent future service problems through teamwork; (3) compensate customers on their terms, not the company's; and (4) practise customer retention, not adjudication. The bottom-line objective: to prevent customer defections.

To accomplish this objective, BA set up a four-step process to guide development of its technical and human delivery systems. This process was based on knowledge of how customers would like their complaints handled. The first step in the process was to *apologize and own the customer's problem* – not to search for someone to blame but rather to become the customer's advocate. The second essential was to *respond quickly* – taking absolutely no longer than 72 hours, and preferably providing an immediate solution. The third step was to *assure the customer that the problem is being fixed*. Finally, as much as possible, *handle complaints by phone*. British Airways found that customers with problems were delighted to speak personally to a customer service representative who could solve their problems.

To facilitate the process just described required major investments in systems and people. First, BA invested in a computer system called Caress that eliminated all paper by scanning or manually entering all customer information relevant to a complaint into a customer complaint database. A particular customer's information was thus easily accessed, and the data could be analysed for patterns as well. The process for dealing with a complaint was also shortened by eliminating a number of unnecessary and redundant steps: the number of steps required to deal with a complaint was reduced from 13 to three. Further, customer service representatives were given the tools and authority – they were empowered – to use whatever resources were needed to retain the customer's business. New training on listening skills, how to handle anger and how to negotiate win–win solutions were put in place for customer service representatives. Finally, customers were encouraged to complain. Prior to the new initiatives, BA knew that only about 10 per cent of its customers ever communicated with the airline directly – whether for good or bad reasons. The airline thus worked hard to get customers to complain and provide input by establishing 12 different 'listening posts' or ways of communicating, including postage-paid cards, customer forums, surveys, and a 'Fly with Me' programme, where customer service representatives flew with customers to experience and hear their responses at first hand.

Not only did BA use the information and systems it developed to directly retain dissatisfied customers, it also built systems to use the data and information to improve systems for the future. It used the information to design out common failure patterns and to design early-warning mechanisms to alert the company to potential future failures.

British Airways found that all its efforts toward complaint management paid off. For every €1 spent in customer retention efforts, BA found it had a €2 return. British Airways continues to take great pride in delivering the highest levels of customer service. In January 2000 the company unveiled €900 000 000 worth of new customer service initiatives to be rolled out over the following two years.

Sources: J. Barlow and C. Moller, *A Complaint Is a Gift* (San Francisco, CA: Berrett-Koehler, 1996), pp. 16–18; C.R. Weiser, 'Championing the customer', *Harvard Business Review* (November–December 1995), pp. 113–15; S.E. Prokesch, 'Competing on service: an interview with British Airways' Sir Colin Marshall', *Harvard Business Review* (November–December 1995), pp. 101–16; and www.BritishAirways.com (2002).

In all service contexts – whether customer service, consumer services or business-to-business services – service failure is inevitable. Failure is inevitable even for the best of firms with the best of intentions, even for those with world-class service systems.

To fully understand and retain their customers, firms must know what customers expect when service failures occur, and must implement effective strategies for **service recovery**. Our chapter-opening vignette illustrates British Airways' approach for dealing with customer complaints.

The impact of service failure and recovery

*S*ervice recovery refers to the actions taken by an organization in response to a service failure. Failures occur for all kinds of reasons – the service may be unavailable when promised, it may be delivered late or too slowly, the outcome may be incorrect or poorly executed or employees may be rude or uncaring.[1] All these types of failures bring about negative feelings and responses from customers. Left unfixed, they can result in customers leaving, telling other customers about their negative experiences and, even, challenging the organization through consumer rights organizations or legal channels.

Service recovery effects

Research has shown that resolving customer problems effectively has a strong impact on customer satisfaction, loyalty, word-of-mouth communication and bottom-line performance.[2] That is, customers who experience service failures but who are ultimately satisfied based on recovery efforts by the firm, will be more loyal than those whose problems are not resolved. That loyalty translates into profitability, as you learned in Chapter 7. Data from the Technical Assistance Research Program (TARP) verifies this relationship, as shown in Figure 15.1.[3] Customers who complain and have their problems resolved quickly are much more likely to repurchase than are those whose complaints are not resolved. Those who never complain are *least* likely to repurchase.

An effective service recovery strategy has multiple potential impacts. It can increase customer satisfaction and loyalty and generate positive word-of-mouth communication. A well-designed, well-documented service recovery strategy also provides information that can be used to improve service as part of a continuous improvement effort. By making adjustments to service processes, systems and outcomes based on previous service recovery experiences, companies increase the likelihood of 'doing it right the first time'. In turn, this reduces costs of failures and increases initial customer satisfaction.

Unfortunately, many firms do not employ effective recovery strategies. A recent study suggests that 50 per cent of customers who experienced a serious problem received no response

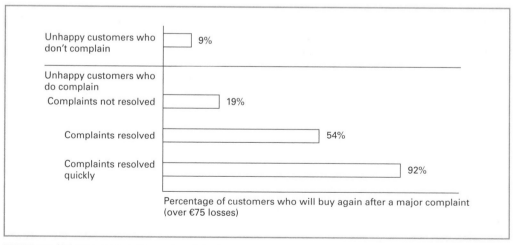

FIGURE 15.1 Unhappy customers' repurchase intentions

Source: adapted from data reported by the Technical Assistance Research Program

from the firm.[4] There are tremendous downsides to having no service recovery or ineffective service recovery strategies. Poor recovery following a bad service experience can lead to customers who are so dissatisfied that they become 'terrorists', actively pursuing opportunities to openly criticize the company.[5] When customers experience a service failure, they talk about it to others no matter what the outcome. That recent study also found that customers who were satisfied with a firm's recovery efforts talked to an average of seven people, whereas those customers who were dissatisfied with the response talked to an average of 25 people.[6] With the ability to share such stories on the Internet, the potential reach of such dissatisfied customers is even greater. Further, repeated service failures without an effective recovery strategy in place can aggravate even the best employees. The costs in employee morale and even lost employees can be huge but costs of not having an effective service recovery strategy are often overlooked.

The recovery paradox

Occasionally some businesses have customers who are initially dissatisfied with a service experience and then experience a high level of excellent service recovery, seemingly leading them to be even more satisfied and more likely to repurchase than if no problem had occurred at all; that is, they appear to be more satisfied after they experience a service failure than they otherwise would have been![7] To illustrate, consider a hotel customer who arrives to check in and finds that no room is available. In an effort to recover, the hotel front-desk person immediately upgrades this guest to a better room at the original price. The customer, thrilled with this compensation, reports that he or she is extremely satisfied with this experience, is even more impressed with the hotel than before, and vows to be loyal into the future. Although such extreme instances are relatively rare, this idea – that an initially disappointed customer who has experienced good service recovery might be even more satisfied and loyal as a result – has been labelled the *service recovery paradox*.

So, should a firm 'screw up' just a little so that it can 'fix the problem' superbly? If doing so would actually lead to more satisfied customers, is this strategy worth pursuing? The logical, but not very rational, conclusion is that companies should *plan to disappoint customers* so they can recover well and (hopefully) gain even greater loyalty from them! What are the problems with such an approach? First, as we indicated earlier in this chapter, a vast majority of customers do not complain when they experience a problem. The possibility of a recovery exists only in situations in which the firm is aware of a problem and is able to recover well; if customers do not make the firm aware of the failure – and most do not – dissatisfaction is most likely to be the result. Second, it is expensive to fix mistakes; re-creating or reworking a service may be quite costly to a firm. Third, it would appear somewhat ludicrous to encourage service failures – after all, reliability ('doing it right the first time') is the most critical determinant of service quality across industries. Finally, although the recovery paradox suggests that a customer *may* end up more satisfied after experiencing excellent recovery, there is certainly *no* guarantee that the customer actually *will* end up more satisfied. The recovery paradox is highly dependent on the context and situation; although one customer may find it easy to forgive a restaurant who provides him with a gift certificate for a later date for having lost his or her dinner reservation, another customer who had planned to propose marriage to his or her date over dinner may not be all that happy with the same recovery scenario.

The intrigue stimulated by the recovery paradox has led to empirical research specifically on this issue. Although anecdotal evidence provides limited support for the recovery paradox, research seems to indicate that this phenomenon is not pervasive. In one study, researchers found that only the very highest levels of customers' service recovery ratings resulted in increased satisfaction and loyalty.[8] This research suggests that customers weigh their most recent experiences heavily in their determination of whether to buy again. If the most recent experience is negative, overall feelings about the company will decrease and repurchase intentions will also diminish significantly. Unless the recovery effort is absolutely superlative, it cannot overcome the negative impression of the initial experience enough to build repurchase intentions beyond the point at which they would be if the service had been provided correctly in the first place. A second study found that overall satisfaction was consistently lower for those customers who had experienced a service failure than for those who had experienced no failure, no matter what the recovery effort.[9] An explanation for why no recovery paradox occurred is suggested by the magnitude of the service failure in this study – a three-hour airplane flight delay. Perhaps this type of failure may be too much to be overcome by any recovery effort. However, in this study, strong service recovery was able to mitigate, if not reverse, the effects of the failure by reducing overall dissatisfaction. Finally, a study suggests that the recovery paradox phenomenon *may* only exist after *one* service failure; however, if a customer experiences a second service failure, the likelihood of the customer's evaluations of the service being greater after the second failure is minimal.[10] That is, although satisfactory service recoveries might produce a recovery paradox after one failure, they do not trigger such paradoxical increases after two failures.

Given the mixed opinions on the extent to which the recovery paradox exists, 'doing it right the first time' is still the best and safest strategy in the long run. However, when a failure does occur, then every effort at a superior recovery should be made to mitigate its negative effects. If the failure can be fully overcome, if the failure is less critical or if the recovery effort is clearly superlative, it may be possible to observe evidence of the recovery paradox.

How customers respond to service failures

Customers who experience service failures can respond in a variety of ways, as illustrated in Figure 15.2.[11] It is assumed that following a failure, dissatisfaction at some level will occur for the customer. In fact, research suggests that a variety of negative emotions can occur following a service failure, including such feelings as anger, discontent, disappointment, self-pity and anxiety.[12] These initial negative responses will affect how customers evaluate the service recovery effort and presumably their ultimate decision to return to the provider or not.[13]

Many customers are very passive about their dissatisfaction, simply saying or doing nothing. Whether they take action or not, at some point the customers will decide whether to stay with that provider or switch to a competitor. As we have already pointed out, customers who do not complain are least likely to return. For companies, customer passivity in the face of dissatisfaction is a threat to future success.

Why people do (and do not) complain

Some customers are more likely to complain than others for a variety of reasons. These consumers believe that positive consequences may occur and that there are social benefits of complaining, and their personal norms support their complaining behaviour. They believe they should and will be provided compensation for the service failure in some form. They believe that fair treatment and good service are their due, and that in cases of service failure someone should make good. In some cases they feel a social obligation to complain – to help others avoid similar situations or to punish the service provider. A very small number of consumers have 'complaining' personalities – they just like to complain or cause trouble.

Consumers who are unlikely to take any action hold the opposite beliefs. They often see complaining as a waste of their time and effort. They do not believe anything positive will occur for

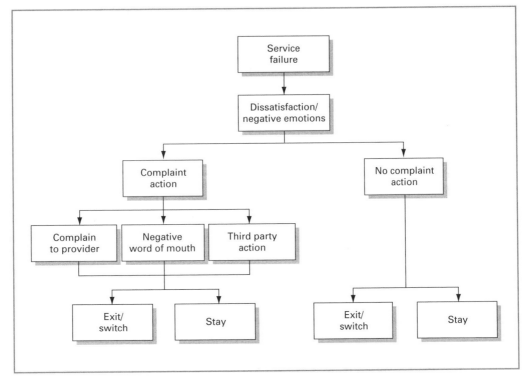

FIGURE 15.2 Customer complaint actions following service failure

them, or others, based on their actions. Sometimes they do not know how to complain – they do not understand the process or may not realize that avenues are open to them to voice their complaints. In some cases non-complainers may engage in 'emotion-focused coping' to deal with their negative experiences. This type of coping involves self-blame, denial and, possibly, seeking social support.[14] They may feel that the failure was somehow their fault and that they do not deserve redress.

Personal relevance of the failure can also influence whether people complain.[15] If the service failure is really important, if the failure has critical consequences for the consumer, or if the consumer has much ego involvement in the service experience, then he or she is more likely to complain. Consumers are more likely to complain about services that are expensive, high risk and ego-involving (like vacation packages, airline travel and medical services) than they are about less expensive, frequently purchased services (fast-food drive-through service, a taxi ride, a call to a customer service helpline). These latter services are simply not important enough to warrant the time to complain. Unfortunately, even though the experience may not be important to the consumer at that moment, a dissatisfying encounter can still drive him or her to a competitor next time the service is needed.

Types of customer complaint actions

If customers initiate actions following service failure, the **customer complaint actions** can be of various types. A dissatisfied customer can choose to complain on the spot to the service provider, giving the company the opportunity to respond immediately. This reaction is often the best-case scenario for the company because it has a second chance at that moment to satisfy the customer, keep his or her business in the future and, potentially, avoid any negative word of mouth. Customers who do not complain immediately may choose to complain later to the provider by telephone, in writing or via the Internet. Again, the company has a chance to recover. Researchers refer to these proactive types of complaining behaviour as *voice* responses or *seeking redress*.

Some customers choose not to complain directly to the provider but rather spread negative word of mouth about the company to friends, relatives and co-workers. This negative word-of-mouth communication can be extremely detrimental because it can reinforce the customer's feelings of negativism and spread that negative impression to others. Further, the company has no chance to recover unless the negative word of mouth is accompanied by a complaint directly to the company. In recent years, customers have taken to complaining via the Internet. A variety of websites, including **web-based consumer opinion platforms** (for example, www.rawcomplaints.com or www.complaints.com),[16] have been created to facilitate customer complaints and, in doing so, have provided customers with the opportunity of spreading negative word-of-mouth communication to a much broader audience. Some customers become so dissatisfied with a product or service failure that they construct websites targeting the firm's current and prospective customers. On these sites[17] angry customers convey their grievances against the firm in ways designed to convince other consumers of the firm's incompetence and evil.[18]

Finally, customers may choose to complain to third parties such as the Consumers Association, to trading standards departments of local or national government, to a licensing authority, to a professional association or to radio or television programmes that focus on consumer issues. No matter the action (or inaction), ultimately the customers determine whether to patronize the service provider again or to switch to another provider.

Types of complainers

Research suggests that people can be grouped into categories based on how they respond to failures. Four categories of response types were identified in a study that focused on grocery stores, car repair services, medical care, and banking and financial services:[20] *passives*, *voicers*, *irates* and *activists*. Although the proportion of the **types of complainers** is likely to vary across industries and contexts, it is likely that these four types of complainers will be relatively consistent and that each type can be found in all companies and industries.

Passives

This group of customers is least likely to take any action. They are unlikely to say anything to the provider, less likely than others to spread negative word of mouth and unlikely to complain to a third party. They often doubt the effectiveness of complaining, thinking that the consequences will not merit the time and effort they will expend. Sometimes their personal values or norms argue against complaining. These folks tend to feel less alienated from the marketplace than irates and activists.

Voicers

These customers actively complain to the service provider, but they are less likely to spread negative word of mouth, to switch patronage or to go to third parties with their complaints. *These customers should be viewed as the service provider's best friends!* They actively complain and thus give the company a second chance. As with the passives, these customers are less alienated from the marketplace than those in the other two groups. They tend to believe complaining has social benefits and therefore do not hesitate to voice their opinions. They believe that the

The following newspaper article demonstrates the impact of web-based complaining.

Ryanair is preparing a legal battle to shut down websites set up by disgruntled customers who are frustrated that they cannot make complaints online or over the telephone.

"The company, which this week published its monthly customer service statistics, is furious that one of the sites – Ryanair.org.uk – published the email addresses of senior executives. Ryanair customers who want to make an official complaint can only do so by either writing to its corporate head office at Dublin airport, or by fax. Unlike other low-cost airlines such as easyJet or Aer Lingus, Ryanair, whose own website address is Ryanair.com, has no online complaints form or customer service email address. It also has no customer service telephone number other than its reservations hotline, which doesn't deal with post-flight queries.

In a strongly worded letter to the website's founder – the second it has sent – Ryanair's legal team accused the site of breaching data protection legislation, saying that the email addresses, which included that of its head of customer service, are not meant for the public.

'The legal action against Ryanair.org.uk will go ahead,' said Peter Sherrard, Ryanair's head of communications. 'We have to do this to protect our business.'

Ryanair.org.uk was temporarily shut down when Ryanair's solicitors wrote to its UK internet service provider (ISP) to complain. The site reappeared shortly afterwards using what is believed to be a Canadian ISP, and has received more than 22,000 hits since January 20. It contains stories posted by anonymous site visitors detailing complaints against the airline. Ryanair says the postings are unfounded and defamatory.

'Everything we do is designed to keep our costs, and our prices, down,' said Sherrard. 'We are not interested in setting up a telephone service because it would increase costs.' However, Sherrard said the airline may look at providing an online complaints form.

Ryanair.org.uk contains a link to a second unofficial website called Ryanaircomplaints.oneuk.com, which promises to fax in complaints for customers who fill out an online form. According to this site's founder, the 'hit counter' that records the origin and location of visitors has identified two visits from Ryanair's own computer system.

The site's founder went on to say that the site will continue 'with the aim of pressuring Ryanair into setting up an online complaint mechanism'.

Paul Walsh, a Dublin-born businessman now based in Sweden, said he used Ryanaircomplaints.oneuk.com to file a complaint after his flight from Gothenburg to Stansted was delayed, and his connecting flight from Stansted to Dublin was diverted to Shannon.

'I think it is their policy to send you in circles. If you were to lose your baggage, you can ring the airport and ServisAir, but not Ryanair,' said Walsh. 'I would at least like to see a way of complaining online.'[19]"

consequences of complaining to the provider can be very positive, and they believe less in other types of complaining such as spreading word of mouth or talking to third parties. Their personal norms are consistent with complaining.

Irates

These consumers are more likely than are others to engage in negative word-of-mouth communication with friends and relatives and to switch providers. They are about average in their propensity to complain to the provider. They are unlikely to complain to third parties. These folk tend to feel somewhat alienated from the marketplace. As their label suggests, they are more angry with the provider, although they do believe that complaining to the provider can have social benefits. They are less likely to give the service provider a second chance and instead will switch to a competitor, spreading the word to friends and relatives along the way.

Activists

These consumers are characterized by above average propensity to complain on all dimensions: they will complain to the provider, they will tell others and they are more likely than any other group to complain to third parties. Complaining fits with their personal norms. As with the irates, these consumers are more alienated from the marketplace than the other groups. They have a very optimistic sense of the potential positive consequences of all types of complaining.

Customers' recovery expectations

When they take the time and effort to complain, customers generally have high **recovery expectations**. They expect the firm to be accountable. They expect to be helped quickly. They expect to be compensated for their grief and for the hassle of being inconvenienced. And they expect to be treated nicely in the process.

Understanding and accountability

In many service failure situations, customers are not looking for extreme actions from the firm; however, they are looking to understand what happened and for firms to be accountable for their actions (or inactions).[21] One study identified the seven most common 'remedies' that customers seek when they experience a serious problem;[22] three of these remedies were to have the product repaired or service fixed, to be reimbursed all their money or to be reimbursed part of their money. Interestingly, however, the other four remedies – including an apology from the firm, an explanation by the firm as to what happened, an assurance that the problem would not be repeated and an opportunity for the customer to vent his or her frustrations to the firm – cost the firm very little to provide.

These four non-monetary remedies consist primarily of affording employees the opportunity to communicate with customers. Understanding and accountability are very important to many customers after a service failure, for if they perceive an injustice has occurred, someone is to blame. Customers expect an apology when things go wrong, and a company that provides an apology demonstrates courtesy and respect; customers also want to know what the company is going to do to ensure that the problem does not reoccur.[23] Results from the study mentioned in the previous paragraph suggest that when a firm does nothing about a service failure, 86 per cent of the customers are dissatisfied with the 'response'; however, if a firm provides an apology to the customer, the percentage of dissatisfied customers drops to 20 per cent.[24] Providing customers with an opportunity to vent their frustrations has a similar effect, because doing so reduces customer dissatisfaction with the response to about 33 per cent.[25] Customer discontent can also be moderated if customers understand why the failure occurred and what specific actions were undertaken to recover.[26] Customers clearly value such communication, because these non-monetary remedies were found to be positively related to satisfaction with the complaint process, continued loyalty and positive word-of-mouth communication.[27]

Fair treatment

Customers also want justice and **fairness** in handling their complaints. Service recovery experts Steve Brown and Steve Tax have documented three specific types of justice that customers are looking for following their complaints: *outcome fairness, procedural fairness* and *interactional fairness*.[28] Outcome fairness concerns the results that customers receive from their complaints; procedural fairness refers to the policies, rules and timeliness of the complaint process; and interactional fairness focuses on the interpersonal treatment received during the complaint process.[29] Table 15.1 shows examples of each type of fairness taken from Brown and Tax's study of consumers who reported on their experiences with complaint resolution.

	Fair	Unfair
Outcome fairness: the results that customers receive from complaints	'The waitress agreed that there was a problem. She took the sandwiches back to the kitchen and had them replaced. We were also given a free drink.' 'They were very thorough with my complaint. One week later I received a coupon for a free oil change and an apology from the shop owner.'	'Their refusal to refund our money or make up for the inconvenience and cold food was inexcusable.' 'If I wanted a refund, I had to go back to the store the next day. It's a 20-minute drive; the refund was barely worth the trouble.' 'All I wanted was for the ticket agent to apologize for doubting my story. I never got the apology.'
Procedural fairness: the policies, rules and timeliness of the complaint process	'The hotel manager said that it didn't matter to her who was at fault, she would take responsibility for the problem immediately.' 'The sales manager called me back one week after my complaint to check if the problem was taken care of to my satisfaction.'	'They should have assisted me with the problem instead of giving me a phone number to call. No one returned my calls, and I never had a chance to speak to a real person.' 'I had to tell my problem to too many people. I had to become irate in order to talk with the manager, who was apparently the only one who could provide a solution.'
Interactional fairness: the interpersonal treatment received during the complaint process	'The loan officer was very courteous, knowledgeable and considerate – he kept me informed about the progress of the complaint.' 'The teller explained that they had a power outage that morning so things were delayed. He went through a lot of files [effort] so that I would not have to come back the next day.'	'The person who handled my complaint about the faulty air-conditioner repair wasn't going to do anything about it and didn't seem to care.' 'The receptionist was very rude; she made it seem like the doctor's time was important but mine was not.'

TABLE 15.1 Fairness themes in service recovery

Source: reprinted from 'Recovering and learning from service failure', by S.S. Tax and S.W. Brown, MIT *Sloan Management Review* (Fall 1998), p. 79, by permission of the publisher. Copyright © 1998 by Massachusetts Institute of Technology. All rights reserved

Outcome fairness

Customers expect outcomes, or compensation, that match the level of their dissatisfaction. This compensation can take the form of actual monetary compensation, an apology, future free services, reduced charges, repairs and/or replacements. Customers expect equity in the exchange – that is, they want to feel that the company has 'paid' for its mistakes in a manner at least equal to what the customer has suffered. The company's 'punishment should fit the crime'. Customers expect equality – that is, they want to be compensated no more or less than other customers who have experienced the same type of service failure. They also appreciate it when a company gives them choices in terms of compensation. For example, a hotel guest could be offered the choice of a refund or a free upgrade to a better room in compensation for a room not being available on arrival. Outcome fairness is especially important in settings in which customers have particularly negative emotional responses to the service failure; in such situations recovery efforts should focus on improving the outcome from the customer's point of view.[30]

However, it should also be noted that customers can feel uncomfortable if they are overly compensated.

Service spotlight

Early in its experience with service guarantees, Domino's Pizza offered not to charge for the pizza if the driver arrived after the 30-minute guaranteed delivery time. Many customers were not comfortable asking for this level of compensation, especially if the driver was only a few minutes late. In this case 'the punishment was greater than the crime'. For a while Domino's changed the compensation to a more reasonable reduced price for late deliveries. Later the time guarantee was dropped altogether because of problems it caused with employees who were driving too fast in order to make their deliveries.

Procedural fairness

In addition to fair compensation, customers expect fairness in terms of policies, rules and timeliness of the complaint process. They want easy access to the complaint process, and they want things handled quickly, preferably by the first person they contact. They appreciate companies that can be adaptable in their procedures so that the recovery effort can match their individual circumstances. In some cases, particularly in business-to-business services, companies actually ask the customer, 'What can we do to compensate you for our failure?' Many times what the customer asks for is actually less than the company might have expected.

Fair procedures are characterized by clarity, speed and absence of difficulties. Unfair procedures are those that customers perceive as slow, prolonged and inconvenient. Customers also feel it is unfair if they have to prove their case – when the assumption seems to be they are wrong or lying until they can prove otherwise.

Interactional fairness

Above and beyond their expectations of fair compensation and difficulty-free, quick procedures, customers expect to be treated politely, with care and honesty. This form of fairness can dominate the other forms if customers feel the company and its employees have uncaring attitudes and have done little to try to resolve the problem. This type of behaviour on the part of employees may seem strange – why would they treat customers rudely or in an uncaring manner under these circumstances? Often it is due to lack of training and empowerment – a frustrated front-line employee who has no authority to compensate the customer may easily respond in an aloof or uncaring manner, especially if the customer is angry and/or rude.

Switching versus loyalty following service recovery

Ultimately, how a service failure is handled and the customer's reaction to the recovery effort can influence future decisions to remain loyal to the service provider or to switch to another provider. Whether customers switch to a new provider following service failure will depend in addition on a number of other factors. The magnitude and criticality of the failure will clearly be a factor in future repurchase decisions. The more serious the failure, the more likely the customer is to switch no matter what the recovery effort.[31]

The nature of the customer's relationship with the firm may also influence whether the customer stays or switches providers. Research suggests that customers who have 'true relationships' with their service providers are more forgiving of poorly handled service failures and are less likely to switch than are those who have a 'pseudo-relationship' or a 'first-time encounter' type of relationship.[32] A true relationship is one in which the customer has had repeated contact over time with the same service provider. A first-time encounter relationship is one in which the customer has had only one contact, on a transaction basis, with the provider. A pseudo-relationship is one in which the customer has interacted many times with the same company, but with different service providers each time.

Other research reveals that the individual customer's attitude towards switching will strongly influence whether he or she ultimately stays with the provider and that this attitude toward switching will be even more influential than basic satisfaction with the service.[33] This research suggests that certain customers will have a greater propensity to switch service providers no matter how their service failure situations are handled. Research in an online service context, for example, shows that demographic factors such as age and income as well as individual factors such as risk aversion will influence whether a customer continues to use an online service or switches to another provider.[34] The profile of an 'online service switcher' emerged in the research as a person who was influenced to subscribe to the service through positive word-of-mouth communication; who used the service less; who was less satisfied and less involved with the service; who had a lower income and education level; and who also had a lower propensity for taking risks.

Finally, the decision to switch to a different service provider may not occur immediately following service failure or poor service recovery, but may follow an accumulation of events. That is, **service switching** can be viewed as a process resulting from a series of decisions and critical service encounters over time rather than one specific moment in time when a decision is made.[35] This process orientation suggests that companies could potentially track customer interactions and predict the likelihood of defection based on a series of events, intervening earlier in the process to head off the customer's decision to switch.

Although customers may decide to switch service providers for a variety of reasons, service failure and poor service recovery are often a cause of such behaviour. A study of approximately 500 service-switching incidents identified eight broad themes underlying the decision to defect.[36] These themes (pricing, inconvenience, core service failure, service encounter failure, response to service failure, competition, ethical problems and involuntary switching) are shown in Figure 15.3. In about 200 of the incidents, a single theme was identified as the cause for switching service providers, and the two largest categories were related to service failure. Core service failure was the cause of switching for 25 per cent of the respondents, and service encounter failure was the reason for switching services for an additional 20 per cent of the

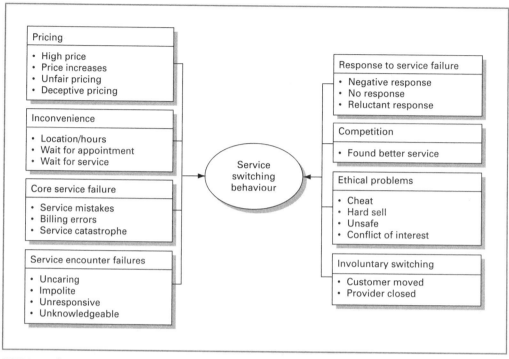

FIGURE 15.3 Causes behind service switching

Source: reprinted with permission of the American Marketing Association. From S. Keaveney, 'Customer switching behavior in service industries: an exploratory study', *Journal of Marketing* 59 (April 1995), pp. 71–82

sample. In incidents that listed two themes, 29 per cent listed core service failure and 18 per cent service encounter failure as contributing to their desire to switch providers; poor response to failure was mentioned by an additional 11 per cent of the respondents as the cause for switching. As these findings suggest, service failure can cause customers to switch companies. To minimize the impact of service failure, excellent service recovery is needed. In the next section we discuss several service recovery strategies that attempt to keep dissatisfied customers from defecting.

Service recovery strategies

Many companies have learned the importance of providing excellent recovery for disappointed customers. In this section we examine their strategies and share examples of benchmark companies and what they are doing. It will become clear that excellent service recovery is really a combination of a variety of strategies that need to work together, as illustrated in Figure 15.4. We discuss each of the strategies shown in the figure, starting with the basic 'do it right the first time'.

Make the service fail-safe – do it right the first time!

The first rule of service quality is to do it right the first time. In this way recovery is unnecessary, customers get what they expect and the costs of redoing the service and compensating for errors

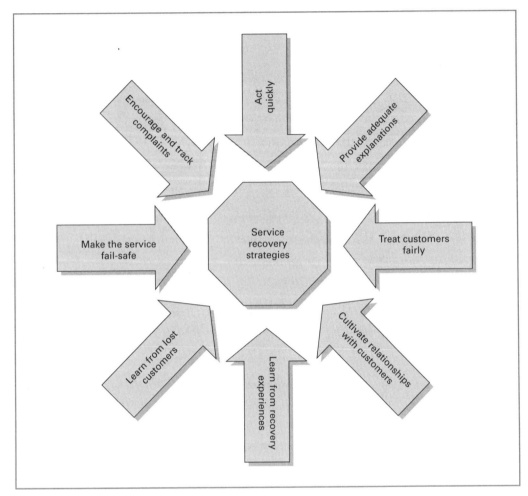

FIGURE 15.4 Service recovery strategies

can be avoided. As you have already learned, reliability, or doing it right the first time, is the most important dimension of service quality across industry contexts.[37]

What specific strategies do firms employ to achieve reliability? Total quality management or TQM, practices aimed at '**zero defects**' are commonly used. However, given the inherent differences between services and manufactured products, these tools typically require considerable adaptation to work well in service contexts. Firms that blindly adopt TQM practices without considering services implications often fail in their efforts.

Dick Chase, noted service operations expert, suggests that services adopt the TQM notion of *poka yokes* to improve service reliability.[38] Poka yokes are automatic warnings or controls in place to ensure that mistakes are not made; essentially they are quality control mechanisms, typically used on assembly lines. Chase suggests that poka yokes can be devised in service settings to 'mistake-proof' the service, to ensure that essential procedures are followed and to ensure that service steps are carried out in the proper order and in a timely manner. In a hospital setting, numerous poka yokes ensure that procedures are followed to avoid potentially life-threatening mistakes. For example, trays for surgical instruments have indentations for specific instruments, and each instrument is nested in its appropriate spot. In this way surgeons and their staff know that all instruments are in their places prior to closing the patient's incision.[39]

Similarly, poka yokes can be devised to ensure that the tangibles associated with the service are clean and well maintained, and that documents are accurate and up to date. Poka yokes can also be implemented for employee behaviours (checklists, role-playing and practice, reminder signs) and even for ensuring that customers perform effectively. Many of the strategies we discuss in Parts 3 and 4 of the text ('Aligning service design and standards' and 'Delivering and performing service') are aimed at ensuring service reliability and can be viewed as applications of the basic fail-safe notion of poka yokes.

Even more fundamentally, it is important for a firm to create a culture of zero defections to ensure doing it right the first time.[40] Within a zero defections culture, everyone understands the importance of reliability. Employees and managers aim to satisfy every customer and look for ways to improve service. Employees in a zero defections culture fully understand and appreciate the 'relationship value of a customer' concept that was presented in Chapter 7. Thus they are motivated to provide quality service *every time* and to *every customer*.

Encourage and track complaints

Even in a zero defections organization that aims for 100 per cent service quality, failures occur. A critical component of a service recovery strategy is thus to encourage and track complaints. Service failures can occur in a variety of ways and at numerous times throughout the service delivery process. However, in many cases it is difficult, if not impossible, for the firm to know that a service failure has occurred unless the customer informs the firm accordingly. Unfortunately, a relatively low percentage of customers (5–10 per cent) will actually complain to the firm. Thus, a major challenge facing management is how to get customers to complain when they experience a service failure and/or they are not satisfied with service delivery. What can a firm do to elicit complaints? Here are some issues to consider:[41]

- *Develop the mind-set that complaints are good.* Too often the complaining customer is looked on by employees in the organization as the *enemy* – someone to be conquered and subdued. The more prudent approach is to develop the mind-set that the complaining customer is the firm's *friend*. Complaints provide valuable feedback to the firm, giving it the opportunity not only to address the service failure for the complaining customer, but also to identify problems that other (less vocal) customers may also be experiencing. It has been suggested that complainers should be treated with the dignity and respect given to the best analysts and consultants. One company puts all customers who have complained on a VIP list. Accepting complaints is truly reflective of firms who are close to their customers.

- *Make complaining easy.* If the firm truly wants to hear from customers who experience poor service, it needs to make it easy for them to share their experiences with the firm. Sometimes customers have no idea whom to speak to if they have a complaint, what the process is or what will be involved. Complaining should be easy – the last thing customers want when they are dissatisfied is to face a complex, difficult-to-access process for complaining. Customers should know where to go and/or who to talk to when they encounter problems, and they should be made to feel confident that something positive will result from their efforts. Technological advances have made it possible to provide customers with multiple avenues to complain, including freephone customer call centres, company email addresses, and website feedback forms. The firm should regularly communicate to customers that complaining is easy and that it welcomes and appreciates such feedback.

- *Be an active listener.* Employees should be encouraged and trained to listen actively to customers, particularly to see if they can pick up on any cues to suggest less than ideal service. A restaurant customer might respond 'fine' to the waiter's question, 'How is your meal?' However, the customer's body language and tone of voice, or the amount of food not eaten, might indicate that all is not fine. Some customers may not be assertive in voicing their displeasure, but they may drop clues to suggest that something is amiss. Employees as well as managers should be consistently listening not only to the customer's actual words but also to what he or she may really be trying or wanting to communicate.

- *Ask customers about specific service issues.* A very simple, informal way to find out about any service failure is simply to ask. Managers at one hotel with a high percentage of business travellers make it a point to be at the front desk between 7.45 a.m. and 8.45 a.m. every day, because approximately 80 per cent of their business travellers check out at that time. During the checkout process, managers avoid questions that can be answered with a simple 'yes', 'OK', or 'fine' (e.g. 'How was your stay?') and instead ask questions that force customers to provide specific feedback (e.g. 'How could we have improved the technology accommodations in your room?' or 'What needs to be done to improve our recreation centre?'). Asking customers very specific questions that cannot be answered with a simple 'yes' or 'no' may provide customers with an easy way to point out expectations that were not fulfilled.

- *Conduct short surveys.* A follow-up telephone call to a customer still in the midst of the service experience can help to identify problems in real time and thus enable real-time recovery.

Service spotlight

Enterprise Rent-A-Car Company, for example, regularly calls customers a day after they have picked up a rental car and asks the customer if everything is OK with the car. Customers who report problems, such as a broken window or a car that smells of smoke, are brought a replacement vehicle that day without any additional questions.

As shown, firms can utilize a number of ways to encourage and track complaints. Customer research can be designed specifically for this purpose through satisfaction surveys, critical incidents studies and **lost customer research**, as discussed in Chapter 6. Freephone call centres, email and pagers are now used to facilitate, encourage and track complaints. Software applications in a number of companies also allow complaints to be analyzed, sorted, responded to and tracked automatically.[42] The case at the start of this chapter shows how a world-class airline, British Airways, encourages, facilitates and tracks customer complaints as a critical component of its effective service recovery process. It is apparent that British Airways is highly dependent on information technology to implement its strategy.

In some cases technology can anticipate problems and complaints before they happen, allowing service employees to diagnose problems before the customer recognizes they exist. At companies such as Ericsson and Siemens, information systems are being implemented to anticipate equipment failures and to send out an electronic alert to the local field technician with the nature of the problem as well as which parts and tools will be needed to make the repair – a repair the customer does not yet know is needed.

Act quickly

Complaining customers want quick responses.[43] Thus if the company welcomes, even encourages, complaints, it must be prepared to act on them quickly. Immediate response requires not only systems and procedures that allow quick action but also empowered employees.

Take care of problems on the front line

Customers want the persons who hear their complaints to solve their problems whether a complaint is registered in person, over the telephone or via the Internet.

Service spotlight

The Ritz-Carlton, for example, insists that the first person to hear a complaint from a customer 'owns' that complaint until the employee is sure it is resolved. If a maintenance employee hears a complaint from a customer while the employee is in the middle of fixing a light in the hotel corridor, he owns that complaint and must be sure that it is handled appropriately before returning to his work.

Another obvious way to speed complaint handling is to call (or in some cases electronically respond to) customers rather then send responses in the mail.

Empower employees

Employees must be trained and **empowered** to solve problems as they occur. A problem not solved can quickly escalate. Take, for example, a true story of a company director who sent an email to his bank to register a complaint while he was attempting a transaction through its Internet banking service. The email was never answered. The customer then sent an email directly to the chairman of the bank. That email was never answered either. Ultimately the customer withdrew his approximately 75 000 euro account because his complaint was not handled in a timely manner. In this case the technology was not effectively linked to other systems, nor ultimately to employees. The Internet access encouraged the complaint, but the response never occurred.

Sometimes employees can even anticipate problems before they arise and surprise customers with a solution. For example, flight attendants on a flight severely delayed because of weather anticipated everyone's hunger, particularly the young children's. Once in flight, they announced to the harried travellers, 'Thank you for your extreme patience in waiting with us. Now that we're on our way, we'd like to offer you complimentary beverages and dinner. Because we have a number of very hungry children on board, we'd like to serve them first, if that's OK with all of you'. The passengers nodded and applauded their efforts, knowing that hungry, crying children could make the situation even worse. The flight attendants had anticipated a problem and solved it before it escalated.

Service spotlight: Cisco Systems – customers recover for themselves[44]

One of the challenges of 90 per cent growth per year is learning how to handle customers' service needs quickly. This was the problem faced by Cisco Systems, a worldwide leader in the networking equipment business. Cisco provides the equipment, builds the factories and produces networking devices that keep businesses running. If the network is not working, the business is not working. Failures in this environment become extremely costly very quickly. Customers want to know that their problems can be solved immediately, and they want a sense of control over the solution.

To address these issues – extremely high growth coupled with the critical nature of the business – Cisco Systems turned to the Internet. It built a world-class model of customer service using the Internet. The system described here has set Cisco apart in its industry and helped the company build customer loyalty in a highly competitive environment.

Essentially, Cisco has put customers in charge of their own service through the Internet. In many cases customers now solve their own service problems totally, with no intervention of Cisco personnel. Access to information is immediate, and solutions can be highly customized for the individual customer. Called 'Cisco Connection Online', the system includes the following types of services:

- *Discussion forum* – a searchable database for answers to networking questions. If the question is too complex, the customer can escalate the request to a highly trained service representative. However, most questions can be answered without human intervention. Plus, the questions asked are used to further enhance and develop the information system to answer questions in the future.
- *Troubleshooting engine* – an expert system that takes the user through the problem identification and resolution process. Here customers actually solve problems and are instructed on how to fix their systems. This system saves time for customers and gives them a much greater sense of control, particularly in critical situations in which every minute of downtime is extremely costly.
- *Bug tool-kit* – collection of interactive tools for identifying, tracking and resolving software bugs.
- *Software centre* – a comprehensive vending machine for Cisco software. This system provides one-stop shopping for Cisco software and helps customers upgrade in a timely manner and be sure that they have the right release of a particular software.
- *Service order agent* – a parts information, ordering and tracking system that allows customers to conduct transactions online. This system provides fast service for orders and saves on administrative costs for both Cisco and its customers.
- *Service contract centre* – a system that allows customers to view the contents and/or status of their contracts with Cisco.

Through its continual innovation in providing service to its customers through the Internet, Cisco has recognized tremendous benefits. Currently 80 per cent of customer problems are handled via the Internet through information provided by Cisco and self-help tools that allow customers to diagnose and solve their own problems. Customer satisfaction increased with the introduction of Internet-based customer service, productivity increased at the rate of 200 per cent, and the company saves over £250 million per year. This is truly a win-win situation for Cisco's bottom line, for its employees and for its business customers.

Service employees have a specific and real need for recovery training. Because customers demand that service recovery take place on the spot and quickly, front-line employees need the skills, authority and incentives to engage in effective recovery. Effective recovery skills include hearing the customer's problems, taking initiative, identifying solutions, improvising and perhaps bending the rules from time to time.

Not only do employees need the authority to act (usually within certain defined limits), but they also should not be punished for taking action. In fact, incentives should exist that encourage employees to exercise their recovery authority. At the Ritz-Carlton, employees are authorized to spend 1500 euros on behalf of the customer to solve a problem. This amount of money is rarely needed, but knowing that they have it encourages employees to be responsive without fear of retribution.

Allow customers to solve their own problems

Another way that problems or complaints can be handled quickly is by building systems that allow customers to actually solve their own service needs and fix their own problems. Typically this approach is done through technology. Customers directly interface with the company's technology to perform their own customer service, which provides them with instant answers. DHL uses this strategy for its package tracking services, for example. Featured above is an example of a company that is a master at online customer service – Cisco Systems.

Provide adequate explanations

In many service failures, customers look to try to understand why the failure occurred. Research suggests that when the firm's ability to provide an adequate outcome is not successful, further dissatisfaction can be reduced if an adequate explanation is provided to the customer.[45] In order for an explanation to be perceived as adequate, it must possess two primary characteristics. First, the content of the explanation must be appropriate; relevant facts and pertinent information are important in helping the customer understand what occurred. Second, the style of the delivery of the explanation, or how the explanation is delivered, can also reduce customer dissatisfaction. Style includes the personal characteristics of the explanation givers, including their credibility and sincerity. Explanations perceived by customers as honest, sincere and not manipulative are generally the most effective.

Treat customers fairly

In responding quickly, it is also critical to treat each customer fairly. Customers expect to be treated fairly in terms of the outcome they receive, the process by which the service recovery takes place, and the interpersonal treatment they receive. In the section titled 'Customers' recovery expectations', we discussed examples, strategies and results of research that focused on fairness in service recovery. Here we remind you that fair treatment is an essential component of an effective service recovery strategy.

Cultivate relationships with customers

In Chapter 7 we discussed the importance of developing long-term relationships with customers. One additional benefit of relationship marketing is that if the firm fails in service delivery, those customers who have a strong relationship with the firm are often more forgiving of service failures and more open to the firm's service recovery efforts. Research suggests that strong customer–firm relationships can help shield the firm from the negative effects of failures on customer satisfaction.[46] To illustrate, one study demonstrated that the presence of rapport between customers and employees provided several service recovery benefits, including increased post-failure satisfaction, increased loyalty intentions and decreased negative word-of-mouth communication.[47] Another study found that customers who expect the relationship to continue also tend to have lower service recovery expectations and may demand less immediate compensation for a failure because they consider the balance of equity across a longer time horizon.[48] Thus, cultivation of strong customer relationships can provide an important buffer to service firms when failures occur.

Learn from recovery experiences

'Problem-resolution situations are more than just opportunities to fix flawed services and strengthen ties with customers. They are also a valuable – but frequently ignored or underutilized – source of diagnostic, prescriptive information for improving customer service.'[49] By tracking service recovery efforts and solutions, managers can often learn about systematic problems in the delivery system that need fixing. By conducting root-cause analysis, firms can identify the sources of the problems and modify processes, sometimes eliminating almost completely the need for recovery.

Service spotlight

At Ritz-Carlton Hotels, all employees carry service recovery forms called 'instant action forms' with them at all times so that they can immediately record service failures and suggest actions to address them. Each individual employee 'owns' any complaint that he or she receives and is responsible for seeing that service recovery occurs. In turn, the employees report to management these sources of service failure and the remedies. This information is then entered into the customer database and analysed for patterns and systemic service issues that need to be fixed. If common themes are observed across a number of failure situations, changes are made to service processes or attributes. In addition, the information is entered into the customer's personal data file so when that customer stays at the Ritz-Carlton again (no matter at which hotel), employees can be aware of the previous experience, ensuring that it does not happen again for that particular customer.

Learn from lost customers

Another key component of an effective service recovery strategy is to learn from the customers who defect or decide to leave. Formal market research to discover the reasons customers have left can assist in preventing failures in the future. This type of research is difficult, even painful for companies, however. No one really likes to examine their failures. Yet such examination is essential for preventing the same mistakes and losing more customers in the future.[50]

As presented in Chapter 6, lost customer research typically involves in-depth probing of customers to determine their true reasons for leaving. This information is most effectively obtained by in-depth interviews, administered by skilled interviewers who truly understand the business. It may be best to have this type of research done by senior people in the company, particularly in business-to-business contexts in which customers are large and the impact of even one lost customer is great. The type of in-depth analysis often requires a series of 'why' questions or 'tell me more about that' questions to get at the actual reason for the customer's defection.[51]

In conducting this kind of research, a firm must focus on important or profitable customers who have left – not just everyone who has left the company. An insurance company in Australia once began this type of research to learn about their lost customers, only to find that the customers they were losing tended to be their least profitable customers anyway. They quickly determined that in-depth research on how to keep these unprofitable customers would not be a good investment!

Act quickly before being forced to do so through legislation

If an industry or large organization is not seen to be responding to the complaints of customers, national or European governmental bodies may step in and impose regulations and legislation to ensure the protection of the consumer. Many utilities such as water, gas, electricity, telephone and broadcasting are controlled by regulators who set regulations and guidance for pricing and service delivery. Another example is in the airline industry where the European Union introduced legislation in February 2004 to protect air passenger rights with regard to cancellations and delays of flights. This new legislation has introduced significant improvements to the protection of air passengers' rights in the European Union. Airlines now have to pay compensation for denied boarding (250 euros for flights of less than 1500 km, 400 euros for flights of between 1500 and 3500 km and 600 euros for flights of more than 3500 km). Passengers will be compensated for late cancellation of their flight and will receive assistance in the event of long delays. There is therefore an incentive in addressing problems before the cost of addressing the issue increases as a result of responding to externally imposed regulations.

Service guarantees

A guarantee is a particular type of recovery tool. In a business context, a guarantee is a pledge or assurance that a product offered by a firm will perform as promised and, if not, then some form of reparation will be undertaken by the firm. Although guarantees are relatively common for manufactured products, they have only recently been used for services. Traditionally, many people believed that services simply could not be guaranteed given their intangible and variable nature. What would be guaranteed? With a product, the customer is guaranteed that it will perform as promised and, if not, that it can be returned. With services, it is generally not possible to take returns or to 'undo' what has been performed. The scepticism about **service guarantees** is being dispelled, however, as more and more companies find they can guarantee their services and that there are tremendous benefits for doing so.

Companies are finding that effective service guarantees can complement the company's service recovery strategy – serving as one tool to help accomplish the service recovery strategies.

Service spotlight

In Radisson SAS hotels, they operate the 100 per cent guest satisfaction guarantee. That is, if a customer complains, they will respond speedily. If the guest remains disappointed, any staff member can envoke the 100 per cent Guest Satisfaction Guarantee, and that guest will not have to pay for their room or the service in question.

Benefits of service guarantees

'Service organizations, in particular, are beginning to recognize that guarantees can serve not only as a marketing tool but as a means for defining, cultivating, and maintaining quality throughout an organization.'[52] The benefits to the company of an effective service guarantee are numerous:[53]

- *A good guarantee forces the company to focus on its customers.* To develop a meaningful guarantee, the company must know what is important to its customers – what they expect and value. In many cases 'satisfaction' is guaranteed, but in order for the guarantee to work effectively, the company must clearly understand what satisfaction means for its customers (what they value and expect).

- *An effective guarantee sets clear standards for the organization.* It prompts the company to define clearly what it expects of its employees and to communicate that expectation to them. The guarantee gives employees service-oriented goals that can quickly align employee behaviours around customer strategies.

Service spotlight

For example, Pizza Hut's guarantee that 'If you're not satisfied with your pizza, let our restaurant know. We'll make it right or give you your money back' lets employees know exactly what they should do if a customer complains. It is also clear to employees that making it right for the customer is an important company goal.

- *A good guarantee generates immediate and relevant feedback from customers.* It provides an incentive for customers to complain and thereby provides more representative feedback to the company than simply relying on the relatively few customers who typically voice their concerns. The guarantee communicates to customers that they have the right to complain.

- *When the guarantee is invoked there is an instant opportunity to recover*, thus satisfying the customer and helping retain loyalty.

- *Information generated through the guarantee can be tracked and integrated into continuous improvement efforts.* A feedback link between customers and service operations decisions can be strengthened through the guarantee.

- *Studies of the impact of service guarantees suggest that employee morale and loyalty can be enhanced as a result.* A guarantee generates pride among employees. Through feedback from the guarantee, improvements can be made in the service that benefit customers and, indirectly, employees.

- *For customers, the guarantee reduces their sense of risk* and builds confidence in the organization. Because services are intangible and often highly personal or ego-involving, customers seek information and cues that will help reduce their sense of uncertainty. Guarantees have been shown to reduce risk and increase positive evaluation of the service prior to purchase.[54]

The bottom line for the company is that an effective guarantee can affect profitability through building customer awareness and loyalty, through positive word of mouth and through reduction in costs as service improvements are made and service recovery expenses are reduced. Indirectly, the guarantee can reduce costs of employee turnover through creating a more positive service culture.

Types of service guarantees

Satisfaction versus service attribute guarantees

Service guarantees can be *unconditional satisfaction guarantees* or *service attribute guarantees*. Radisson SAS's guarantee is an unconditional satisfaction guarantee. Travelodge and Ibis offer similar types of guarantee.

In other cases, firms offer guarantees of particular aspects of the service that are important to customers. Tesco has developed a 'One in Front' policy, which ensures that each customer should have no more than one person ahead of him or her in the checkout queue. If they do, another checkout will be opened. Pizza Hut guarantees to deliver your pizza to the table in 20 minutes or the pizza is free. In both cases, the companies have guaranteed elements of the service that they know are important to customers.

External versus internal guarantees

Interestingly, guarantees do not have to be just for external customers. Some companies are finding that internal service guarantees – one part of the organization guaranteeing its services to others – are effective ways of aligning internal service operations. For example, at Embassy Suites the housekeeping supplies department guarantees its internal customer, the housekeeping staff, that they can get supplies on the day requested. If not, the supply department pays approximately 4 euros to the housekeeper. At one direct-mail firm, the sales force guarantees to give the production department all the specifications needed to provide service to the external customer, or the offending salesperson will take the production department to lunch, will sing a song at their next department meeting, or will personally input all the specifications into the computer.[55]

Characteristics of effective guarantees

No matter the type of guarantee, certain characteristics make some guarantees more effective than others. Characteristics of effective guarantees are shown in Table 15.2. The guarantee should be unconditional – no strings attached. Some guarantees can appear as if they were written by the legal department (and often are), with all kinds of restrictions, proof required and limitations. These guarantees are generally not effective. The guarantee should be meaningful. Guaranteeing what is obvious or expected is not meaningful to customers. For example, a water delivery company offered a guarantee to deliver water on the day promised, or a free jug of water would be provided next time. In that industry, delivery on the day scheduled was an expectation nearly always met by every competitor – thus the guarantee was not meaningful to the customer. It was a bit like guaranteeing four wheels on a car! The payout should also be meaningful. Customers expect to be reimbursed in a manner that fully compensates them for their dissatisfaction, their time and for the inconvenience involved. A firm's guarantee should also be easy to understand and communicate to both customers and employees. Sometimes the wording is confusing, the guarantee language is verbose or the guarantee contains so many restrictions and conditions that neither customers nor employees are certain what is being guaranteed. Similarly, the guarantee should be easy to invoke. Requiring customers to write a letter and/or provide documented proof

UNCONDITIONAL	EASY TO UNDERSTAND AND COMMUNICATE
◆ The guarantee should make its promise unconditionally – no strings attached	◆ Customers need to understand what to expect ◆ Employees need to understand what to do
MEANINGFUL	**EASY TO INVOKE AND COLLECT**
◆ The firm should guarantee elements of the service that are important to the customer ◆ The payout should cover fully the customer's dissatisfaction	◆ The firm should eliminate hoops or red tape in the way of accessing or collecting on the guarantee

TABLE 15.2 Characteristics of an effective service guarantee
Source: C.W.L. Hart, 'The Power of Unconditional Guarantees', *Harvard Business Review*, July–August 1988, pp. 54–62

of service failure are common pitfalls that make invoking the guarantee time-consuming and not worth it to the customer, particularly if the monetary value of the service is relatively low.

When to use (or not use) a guarantee

Service guarantees are not appropriate for every company and certainly not in every service situation. Before putting a guarantee strategy in place, a firm needs to address a number of important questions (see Table 15.3). A guarantee is probably *not* the right strategy when:

- *Existing service quality in the company is poor.* Before instituting a guarantee, the company should fix any significant quality problems. Although a guarantee will certainly draw attention to these failures and the poor quality, the costs of implementing the guarantee could easily outweigh any benefits. These costs include actual monetary payouts to customers for poor service as well as the costs associated with customer goodwill.

- *A guarantee does not fit the company's image.* If the company already has a reputation for very high quality, and in fact implicitly guarantees its service, then a formal guarantee is most likely unnecessary. For example, if Ritz-Carlton Hotels were to offer an explicit guarantee, it could potentially confuse customers who already expect the highest of quality, implicitly guaranteed, from this high-end hotel chain. Research suggests that the benefits of offering a guarantee for a high-end hotel like the Ritz-Carlton may be significantly less than the benefits that a hotel of lesser quality would enjoy, and in fact the benefits might not be justified by the costs.[56]

- *Service quality is truly uncontrollable.* Uncontrollable service quality is often an excuse for not employing a guarantee, but firms encounter few situations in which service quality is truly uncontrollable. Here are a couple of examples to illustrate such situations. It would not be good practice for a training organization to guarantee that all participants would pass a particular examination on completion of the training course if passing depends too much on the participants' own effort. The company could, however, guarantee satisfaction with the training or particular aspects of the training process. Similarly, a ferry company operating in the Western Isles of Scotland in the winter would probably not guarantee on-time departure because of the unpredictability and uncontrollability of the weather.

DECIDING WHO DECIDES
- ◆ Is there a guarantee champion in the company?
- ◆ Is senior management committed to a guarantee?
- ◆ Is the guarantee design a team effort?
- ◆ Are customers providing input?

WHEN DOES A GUARANTEE MAKE SENSE?
- ◆ How high are quality standards?
- ◆ Can we afford a guarantee?
- ◆ How high is customer risk?
- ◆ Are competitors offering a guarantee?
- ◆ Is the company's culture compatible with a guarantee?

WHAT TYPE OF GUARANTEE SHOULD WE OFFER?
- ◆ Should we offer an unconditional guarantee or a specific-outcome guarantee?
- ◆ Is our service measurable?
- ◆ What should our specific guarantee be about?
- ◆ What are the uncontrollables?
- ◆ Is the company particularly susceptible to unreasonable triggerings?
- ◆ What should the payout be?
- ◆ Will a refund send the wrong message?
- ◆ Could a full refund make customers feel guilty?
- ◆ Is the guarantee easy to invoke?

TABLE 15.3 Questions to consider in implementing a service guarantee
Source: A.L. Ostrom and C.W.L. Hart, 'Service guarantees: research and practice', in *Handbook of Services Marketing and Management*, eds T. Swartz and D. Iacobucci (Thousand Oaks, CA: Sage Publications, 2000). © 2000 by Sage Publications. Reprinted by permission of Sage Publications

- *Potential exists for customer abuse of the guarantee.* Fear of opportunistic customer behaviour, including customer cheating or fraudulent invocation of service guarantees, is a common reason that firms hesitate to offer guarantees.[57] For example, at one large pizza chain students occasionally 'cheated' the company by invoking the service guarantee without cause in order to receive free food.[58] In those situations in which abuse of the service guarantee can easily occur, firms should carefully consider the consequences of offering a guarantee. A recent study found that guarantees are more likely to be abused when offered in situations in which a large percentage of customers are not regular (repeat) customers.[59] In general, customer abuse of service guarantees is fairly minimal and not at all widespread.[60]

- *Costs of the guarantee outweigh the benefits.* As it would with any quality investment, the company will want to carefully calculate expected costs (payouts for failures and costs of making improvements) against anticipated benefits (customer loyalty, quality improvements, attraction of new customers, word-of-mouth advertising).

- *Customers perceive little risk in the service.* Guarantees are usually most effective when customers are uncertain about the company and/or the quality of its services. The guarantee can allay uncertainties and help reduce risk.[61] If customers perceive little risk, if the service is relatively inexpensive with lots of potential alternative providers, and if quality is relatively invariable, then a guarantee will likely produce little effectiveness for the company other than perhaps some promotional value.

- *Customers perceive little variability in service quality among competitors.* Some industries exhibit extreme variability in quality among competitors. In these cases a guarantee may be quite effective, particularly for the first company to offer one. Guarantees may also be effective in industries in which quality is perceived to be low overall across competitors. The first firm with a guarantee can often distinguish itself from competitors. A study of guarantees offered by several service firms in Singapore found that companies that were the only competitor offering a guarantee in their industry attributed more of their success to the guarantee than did companies in industries in which guarantees were more common.[62]

Summary

You learned in this chapter the importance of an effective service recovery strategy for retaining customers and increasing positive word-of-mouth communication. Another major benefit of an effective service recovery strategy is that the information it provides can be useful for service improvement. The potential downsides of poor service recovery are tremendous – negative word of mouth, lost customers and declining business when quality issues are not addressed.

In this chapter you learned how customers respond to service failures and why some complain while others do not. You learned that customers expect to be treated fairly when they complain – not just in terms of the actual outcome or compensation they receive, but also in terms of the procedures that are used and how they are treated interpersonally. We pointed out in this chapter that there is tremendous room for improvement in service recovery effectiveness across firms and industries.

The second half of the chapter focused on specific strategies that firms are using for service recovery: (1) making the service fail-safe, or doing it right the first time, (2) encouraging and tracking complaints, (3) acting quickly, (4) providing adequate explanations, (5) treating customers fairly, (6) cultivating relationships with customers, (7) learning from recovery experiences, and (8) learning from lost customers. The chapter ended with a discussion of service guarantees as a tool used by many firms to build a foundation for service recovery. You learned the benefits of service guarantees, the elements of a good guarantee, and the pros and cons of using guarantees under various circumstances.

Key concepts

Customer complaint actions	374	Service recovery paradox	372
Empowerment	385	Service switching	380
Fairness (outcome v. procedural v. interactional)	378	Types of complainers (passives v. voicers v. irates v. activists)	376
Lost customer research	384	Web-based consumer opinion platforms	376
Recovery expectations	377		
Service guarantees	389	Zero defects	382
Service recovery	370		

Further reading

Andreassen, T.W. (1999) 'What drives customer loyalty with complaint resolution', *Journal of Service Research*, 1(4), 324–32.

Boshoff, C. and Allen, J. (2000) 'The influence of selected antecedents on frontline staff's perception of service recovery performance', *International Journal of Service Industry Management*, 11(1), 63–90.

De Ruyter, K. and Wetzels, M. (2000) 'Customer equity considerations in service recovery: a cross-industry perspective', *International Journal of Service Industry Management*, 11(1), 91–108.

Hirschman, A.O. (2006) *Exit, Voice and Loyalty: Responses to Decline in Firms, Organizations and States.* Cambridge, MA: Harvard University Press.

Shoefer, K. and Ennew, C. (2005) 'The impact of perceived justice on consumers' responses to service complaint experiences', *Journal of Services Marketing*, 19(5), 261–70.

Sparks, B. and McColl-Kennedy, J.R. (2001) 'Justice strategy options for increased customer satisfaction in a service recovery setting', *Journal of Business Research*, 54, 209–18.

Tax, S.S., Brown, S.W. and Chandrashekaran, M. (1998) 'Customer evaluations of service complaint experiences: implications for relationship marketing', *Journal of Marketing*, 62 (April), 60–76.

Discussion questions

1 Why is it important for a service firm to have a strong recovery strategy? Think of a time when you received less than desirable service from a particular service organization. Was any effort made to recover? What should/could have been done differently? Do you still buy services from the organization? Why or why not? Did you tell others about your experience?

2 Discuss the benefits to a company of having an effective service recovery strategy. Describe an instance in which you experienced (or delivered as an employee) an effective service recovery. In what ways did the company benefit in this particular situation?

3 Explain the recovery paradox, and discuss its implications for a service firm manager.

4 Discuss the types of actions that customers can take in response to a service failure. What type of complainer are you? Why? As a manager, would you want to encourage your customers to be voicers? If so, how?

5 Explain the logic behind these two quotes: 'a complaint is a gift' and 'the customer who complains is your friend'.

6 Choose a firm you are familiar with. Describe how you would design an ideal service recovery strategy for that organization.

7 What are the benefits to the company of an effective service guarantee? Should every service organization have one?

8 Describe three service guarantees that are currently offered by companies or organizations in addition to the ones already described in the chapter. (Examples are readily available on the Internet.) Are your examples good guarantees or poor guarantees based on the criteria presented in this chapter?

 ## Exercises

1 Write a letter of complaint (or voice your complaint in person) to a service organization from which you have experienced less than desirable service. What do you expect the organization to do to recover? (Later, report to the class the results of your complaint, whether you were satisfied with the recovery, what could/should have been done differently and whether you will continue using the service.)

2 Interview five people about their service recovery experiences. What happened and what did they expect the firm to do? Were they treated fairly based on the definition of recovery fairness presented in the chapter? Will they return to the company in the future?

3 Interview a manager about service recovery strategies used in his or her firm. Use the strategies shown in Figure 15.5 to frame your questions.

4 Reread the example relating to Cisco Systems on page 386. Visit Cisco System's website (www.cisco.com). Review what the company is currently doing to help its customers solve their own problems. Compare what Cisco is doing with the self-service efforts of another service provider of your choice.

5 Choose a service you are familiar with. Explain the service offered and develop a good service guarantee for it. Discuss why your guarantee is a good one, and list the benefits to the company of implementing it.

Notes

1 For research that shows different types of service failures, see M.J. Bitner, B.H. Booms and M.S. Tetreault, 'The service encounter: diagnosing favorable and unfavorable incidents', *Journal of Marketing* 54 (January 1990), pp. 71–84; and S.M. Keaveney, 'Customer switching behavior in service industries: an exploratory study', *Journal of Marketing* 59 (April 1995), pp. 71–82.

2 For research on important outcomes associated with service recovery, see S.S. Tax, S.W. Brown and M. Chandrashekaran, 'Customer evaluations of service complaint experiences: implications for relationship marketing', *Journal of Marketing* 62 (April 1998), pp. 60–76; S.S. Tax and S.W. Brown, 'Recovering and learning from service failure', *Sloan Management Review* (Fall 1998), pp. 75–88; A.K. Smith and R.N. Bolton, 'An experimental investigation of customer reactions to service failure and recovery encounters', *Journal of Service Research* 1 (August 1998), pp. 65–81; S.W. Kelley, K.D. Hoffman and M.A. Davis, 'A typology of retail failures and recoveries', *Journal of Retailing* 69 (Winter 1993), pp. 429–52; R.N. Bolton, 'A dynamic model of the customer's relationship with a continuous service provider: the role of satisfaction', *Marketing Science* 17, no. 1 (1998), pp. 45–65; A.K. Smith and R.N. Bolton, 'The effect of customers' emotional responses to service failures on their recovery effort evaluations and satisfaction judgments', *Journal of the Academy of Marketing Science* 30 (Winter 2002), pp. 5–23.

[3] Technical Assistance Research Program, 'Consumer complaint handling in America: an update study' (Washington, DC: Department of Consumer Affairs, 1986).

[4] M. Granier, J. Kemp and A. Lawes, 'Customer complaint handling – the multimillion pound sinkhole: a case of customer rage unassuaged', study conducted by the Customer Care Alliance (2004).

[5] Tax and Brown, 'Recovering and learning from service failure'.

[6] Granier, Kemp and Lawes, 'Customer complaint handling – the multimillion pound sinkhole'.

[7] See C.W. Hart, J.L. Heskett and W.E. Sasser Jr, 'The profitable art of service recovery', *Harvard Business Review* 68 (July–August 1990), pp. 148–56; M.A. McCollough and S.G. Bharadwaj, 'The recovery paradox: an examination of consumer satisfaction in relation to disconfirmation, service quality, and attribution based theories', in *Marketing Theory and Applications*, eds C.T. Allen et al. (Chicago, IL: American Marketing Association, 1992), p. 119.

[8] Smith and Bolton, 'An experimental investigation of customer reactions to service failure and recovery encounters'.

[9] M.A. McCullough, L.L. Berry and M.S. Yadav, 'An empirical investigation of customer satisfaction after service failure and recovery', *Journal of Service Research* 3 (November 2000), pp. 121–37.

[10] J.G. Maxham III and R.G. Netemeyer, 'A longitudinal study of complaining customers' evaluations of multiple service failures and recovery efforts', *Journal of Marketing* 66 (October 2002), pp. 57–71.

[11] For research foundations on typologies of customer responses to failures, see R.L. Day and E.L. Landon Jr, 'Towards a theory of consumer complaining behavior', in *Consumer and Industrial Buying Behavior*, eds A. Woodside, J. Sheth and P. Bennett (Amsterdam: North-Holland, 1977); J. Singh, 'Consumer complaint intentions and behavior: definitional and taxonomical issues', *Journal of Marketing* 52 (January 1988), pp. 93–107; and J. Singh, 'Voice, exit, and negative word-of-mouth behaviors: an investigation across three service categories', *Journal of the Academy of Marketing Science* 18 (Winter 1990), pp. 1–15.

[12] Smith and Bolton, 'The effect of customers' emotional responses to service failures'.

[13] Ibid.

[14] N. Stephens and K.P. Gwinner, 'Why don't some people complain? a cognitive–emotive process model of consumer complaining behavior', *Journal of the Academy of Marketing Science* 26 (Spring 1998), pp. 172–89.

[15] Ibid.

[16] T. Hennig-Thurau, K.P. Gwinner, G. Walsh and D.D. Gremler, 'Electronic word-of-mouth via consumer-opinion platforms: what motivates consumers to articulate themselves on the Internet?', *Journal of Interactive Marketing* 18 (Winter 2004), pp. 38–52.

[17] Many such websites exist; examples include www.untied.com (for United Airlines experiences), www.starbucked.com (for Starbucks) and www.walmartsucks.com (for Wal-Mart).

[18] J.C. Ward and A.L. Ostrom, 'Online complaining via customer-created web sites: a protest framing perspective', working paper, W.P. Carey School of Business, Arizona State University (2004).

[19] Source: *Sunday Times*, 13 February 2005.

[20] J. Singh, 'A typology of consumer dissatisfaction response styles', *Journal of Retailing* 66 (Spring 1990), pp. 57–99.

[21] J.R. McColl-Kennedy and B.A. Sparks, 'Application of fairness theory to service failures and service recovery', *Journal of Service Research* 5 (February 2003), pp. 251–66; M. Davidow, 'Organizational responses to customer complaints: what works and what doesn't', *Journal of Service Research* 5 (February 2003), pp. 225–50.

[22] Granier, Kemp and Lawes, 'Customer complaint handling – the multimillion pound sinkhole'.

[23] Davidow, 'Organizational responses to customer complaints'.

[24] Granier, Kemp and Lawes, 'Customer complaint handling – the multimillion pound sinkhole'.

[25] Ibid.

[26] McColl-Kennedy and Sparks, 'Application of fairness theory to service failures and service recovery'; A.S. Mattila and P.G. Patterson, 'Service recovery and fairness perceptions in collectivist and individualist contexts', *Journal of Service Research* 6 (May 2004), pp. 336–46.

[27] Granier, Kemp and Lawes, 'Customer complaint handling – the multimillion pound sinkhole'.

[28] See Tax, Brown and Chandrashekaran, 'Customer evaluations of service complaint experiences'; Tax and Brown, 'Recovering and learning from service failure'.

[29] Tax and Brown, 'Recovering and learning from service failure'.

[30] Smith and Bolton, 'The effect of customers' emotional responses to service failures'.

[31] McCullough, Berry and Yadav, 'An empirical investigation of customer satisfaction after service failure and recovery'.

[32] A.S. Mattila, 'The impact of relationship type on customer loyalty in a context of service failures', *Journal of Service Research*, 4 (November 2001), pp. 91–101; see also R.L. Hess Jr, S. Ganesan and N.M. Klein, 'Service failure and recovery: the impact of relationship factors on customer satisfaction', *Journal of the Academy of Marketing Science* 31 (Spring 2003), pp. 127–45; R. Priluck, 'Relationship marketing can mitigate product and service failures', *Journal of Services Marketing* 17, no. 1 (2003), pp. 37–52.

[33] H.S. Bansal and S.F. Taylor, 'The service provider switching model (SPSM)', *Journal of Service Research* 2 (November 1999), pp. 200–18.

[34] S.M. Keaveney and M. Parthasarathy, 'Customer switching behavior in online services: an exploratory study of the role of selected attitudinal, behavioral, and demographic factors', *Journal of the Academy of Marketing Science* 29, no. 4 (2001), pp. 374–90.

[35] I. Roos, 'Switching processes in customer relationships', *Journal of Service Research* 2 (August 1999), pp. 68–85.

[36] Keaveney, 'Customer switching behavior in service industries'.

[37] A. Parasuraman, V.A. Zeithaml and L.L. Berry, 'SERVQUAL: a multiple-item scale for measuring consumer perceptions of service quality', *Journal of Retailing* 64 (Spring 1988), pp. 64–79.

[38] R.B. Chase and D.M. Stewart, 'Make your service fail-safe', *Sloan Management Review* (Spring 1994), pp. 35–44.

[39] Ibid.

[40] F.F. Reichheld and W.E. Sasser Jr, 'Zero defections: quality comes to services', *Harvard Business Review* (September–October 1990), pp. 105–7.

41 Sources: Tax and Brown, 'Recovering and learning from service failure'; O. Harari, 'Thank heaven for complainers', *Management Review* 81 (January 1992), p. 59.

42 L.M. Fisher, 'Here comes front-office automation', *Strategy and Business* 13 (Fourth Quarter, 1999), pp. 53–65; and R.A. Shaffer, 'Handling customer service on the web', *Fortune*, 1 March 1999, pp. 204, 208.

43 Davidow, 'Organizational responses to customer complaints'.

44 Sources: www.cisco.com (2004); 'The globally networked business', Cisco presentation at 'Activating your firm's service culture' symposium, Arizona State University (1997); R.L. Nolan, 'Cisco Systems architecture: ERP and web-enabled IT', Harvard Business School Case #9-301-099, 2001; 'Ten minutes with John Chambers', *NASDAQ: The International Magazine* 29 (January 2001).

45 J. Dunning, A. Pecotich and A. O'Cass, 'What happens when things go wrong? Retail sales explanations and their effects', *Psychology and Marketing* 21, no. 7 (2004), pp. 553–72; McColl-Kennedy and Sparks, 'Application of fairness theory to service failures and service recovery'; Davidow, 'Organizational responses to customer complaints'.

46 Hess, Ganesan and Klein, 'Service failure and recovery: the impact of relationship factors on customer satisfaction'; Priluck, 'Relationship marketing can mitigate product and service failures'.

47 T. DeWitt and M.K. Brady, 'Rethinking service recovery strategies: the effect of rapport on consumer responses to service failure', *Journal of Service Research* 6 (November 2003), pp. 193–207.

48 Hess, Ganesan and Klein, 'Service failure and recovery: the impact of relationship factors on customer satisfaction'.

49 L.L. Berry and A. Parasuraman, *Marketing Services* (New York: Free Press, 1991), p. 52.

50 F.F. Reichheld, 'Learning from customer defections', *Harvard Business Review* (March–April 1996), pp. 56–69.

51 Ibid.

52 A.L. Ostrom and C.W.L. Hart, 'Service guarantees: research and practice', in *Handbook of Services Marketing and Management*, eds T. Swartz and D. Iacobucci (Thousand Oaks, CA: Sage Publications, 2000), pp. 299–316.

53 See ibid.; C.W.L. Hart, 'The power of unconditional guarantees', *Harvard Business Review* (July–August 1988), pp. 54–62; and C.W.L. Hart, *Extraordinary Guarantees* (New York: AMACOM, 1993).

54 A.L. Ostrom and D. Iacobucci, 'The effect of guarantees on consumers' evaluation of services', *Journal of Services Marketing* 12, no. 5 (1998), pp. 362–78; S.B. Lidén and P. Skålén, 'The effect of service guarantees on service recovery', *International Journal of Service Industry Management* 14, no. 1 (2003), pp. 36–58.

55 Example cited in Ostrom and Hart, 'Service guarantees'.

56 J. Wirtz, D. Kum and K.S. Lee, 'Should a firm with a reputation for outstanding service quality offer a service guarantee?', *Journal of Services Marketing* 14, no. 6 (2000), pp. 502–12.

57 J. Wirtz, 'Development of a service guarantee model', *Asia Pacific Journal of Management* 15 (April 1998), pp. 51–75.

58 Ibid.

59 J. Wirtz and D. Kum, 'Consumer cheating on service guarantees', *Journal of the Academy of Marketing Science* 32 (Spring 2004), pp. 159–75.

60 Wirtz, 'Development of a service guarantee model'.

61 Ostrom and Iacobucci, 'The effect of guarantees'.

62 Wirtz, 'Development of a service guarantee model'.

PART 5
Managing Service Promises

The fourth provider gap, shown in the accompanying figure, illustrates the difference between service delivery and the service provider's external communications. Promises made by a service company through its media advertising, sales force and other communications may potentially raise customer expectations that serve as the standard against which customers assess service quality. Broken promises can occur for many reasons: ineffective marketing communications, over-promising in advertising or personal selling, inadequate coordination between operations and marketing, and differences in policies and procedures across service outlets.

In service companies, a fit between communications about service and actual service delivery is necessary. Chapter 16 is devoted to the topic of integrated services marketing communications – careful integration and organization of all of a service marketing organization's external and internal communications channels. The chapter describes why this com-

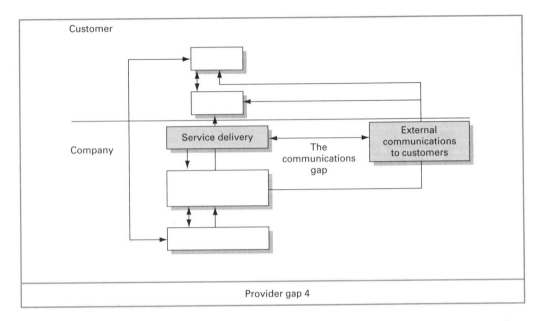

Provider gap 4

munication is necessary and how companies can do it well. Successful company communications are the responsibility of both marketing and operations: marketing must accurately but beguilingly reflect what happens in actual service encounters, and operations must deliver what is promised in advertising. If communications set up unrealistic expectations for customers, the actual encounter will disappoint the customer.

Chapter 17 deals with another issue related to managing promises, the pricing of services. In packaged goods (and even in durable goods), many customers possess enough price knowledge before purchase to be able to judge whether a price is fair or in line with competition. With services, customers often have no internal reference point for prices before purchase and consumption. Techniques for developing prices for services are more complicated than those for pricing tangible goods, and all the approaches for setting prices must be adapted for the special characteristics of services.

In summary, external communications – whether from marketing communications or pricing – can create a larger customer gap by raising expectations about service delivery. In addition to improving service delivery, companies must also manage all communications to customers so that inflated promises do not lead to higher expectations. Companies must also manage the messages conveyed by pricing so that customer expectations are in line with what they perceive that they receive.

CHAPTER 16

Integrated services marketing communications

❖ LEARNING OBJECTIVES

This chapter's objectives are to:

1 Discuss the key reasons for service communication challenges.

2 Introduce the concept of integrated service marketing communications.

3 Present four ways to integrate marketing communications in service organizations.

4 Present specific strategies for managing promises, managing customer expectations, educating customers and managing internal communications.

CASE STUDY: VIRGIN ATLANTIC AIRWAYS

Source: Courtesy Virgin Atlantic Airways

' A brand name that is known internationally for innovation, quality and a sense of fun – this is what we have always aspired to with Virgin.' (Richard Branson)

Richard Branson, first known for Virgin Records, the legendary record label that signed the Rolling Stones, Janet Jackson and The Human League, surprised the world in 1984 when he launched an upstart airline called Virgin Atlantic Airways. His vision was to create a high-quality, value-for-the-money airline to challenge the UK's market leader, British Airways. Twenty years later, Virgin Atlantic is the third-largest European carrier over the North Atlantic and flies to destinations in the United States, Caribbean, Far East, India, China, Hong Kong and Africa.

Parent company Virgin Group, with combined sales exceeding €1.5 billion, is known worldwide as an innovative global brand with megastore music retailing, book and software publishing, film and video-editing facilities, clubs, trains and financial advising through more than 100 companies in 15 countries. Virgin Atlantic Airways' brand and marketing campaign epitomizes successful global communication, with universal marketing components that are integrated in theme and design across the world as well as individual advertisements that adapt to geographies.

Virgin Atlantic Airways' common global marketing elements include its brand values, logo and distinctive airplanes. The airline's brand values – 'caring, honest, value, fun, inno-

Source: Red Advertising & Marketing, Barbados, W.I./Courtesy Virgin Atlantic Airways.

vative' – are executed in all communications and strategies. Virgin focuses on customer service and low cost while also being the first to offer up unique services. For example, Virgin was the first airline to install television screens in every seat, offer massages and beauty services in first class, and mount a gambling casino right in the plane! The red and white logo, in the shape of an airline tail fin, appears in all worldwide advertising media including television, press, magazines, price promotions, outdoor posters and taxi sides. Another common image is the company's Flying Lady, a Vargas painting of a redheaded, scantily dressed woman holding a scarf. Distinctive airplanes feature the Flying Lady on the fuselage and Union Flags on their wings in three core colours of red, purple and silver metallic. Even the paint technology – based on mica, a hard mineral that produces a pearl-like shine – is unique. When the iridescent gleam combines with the plane's vibrant colours, the aircraft stirs up memories of the 1930s, when flying was glamorous and romantic.

As shown in the accompanying international advertisement, Virgin Atlantic Airways manages to translate its brand themes in culturally specific ways while retaining its global image. The Caribbean advertisement draws in readers with its bananas. Although the text and appeal change to suit the culture, all international advertisements contain the same Virgin Atlantic Airways logo and the same company colours.

Source: www.virgin-atlantic.com

A major cause of poorly perceived service is the difference between what a firm promises about a service and what it actually delivers. **Customer expectations** are shaped by both uncontrollable and company-controlled factors. Although word-of-mouth communication, customer experiences with other service providers and customer needs are key factors that influence customer expectations, they are rarely controllable by the firm. However, controllable factors such as company **advertising**, brochures, personal selling and promises made by service personnel also influence customer expectations. In this chapter we focus on these controllable factors. Accurate, coordinated and appropriate company communication – advertising, personal selling and online and other messages that do not over-promise or misrepresent – is essential to delivering services that customers perceive as high in quality.

Because company communications about services promise what people do and because people's behaviour cannot be standardized like physical goods produced by machines, the potential for a mismatch between what is communicated and perceptions of actual service delivery (provider gap 4) is high. By coordinating communication within and outside the organization, companies can minimize the size of this gap.

The need for coordination in marketing communication

Marketing communication is more complex today than it used to be. In the past, customers received marketing information about goods and services from a limited number of sources, usually mass communication sources such as television and newspapers. With a limited number of sources, marketers could easily convey a uniform brand image and coordinate promises. However, today's consumers of both goods and services receive communications from a far richer variety of advertising vehicles – targeted magazines, websites, direct mail, cinema advertising, email solicitation and a host of sales promotions. Consumers of services receive additional communication from servicescapes, customer service departments and everyday service encounters with employees. These service interactions add to the variety, volume and complexity of information that a customer receives. Ensuring that messages from all these company sources provide a consistent message about the service brand is a major challenge for marketers of services.

Any company that disseminates information through multiple channels needs to be certain that customers receive unified messages and promises. These channels include not only advertising messages that flow directly from the company but also personal messages that employees send to customers. Figure 16.1 shows an enhanced version of the **services marketing triangle** that we presented in Chapter 1, emphasizing that the customer of services is the target of two types of communication. First, external marketing communication includes traditional channels such as advertising, **sales promotion** and **public relations**. Second, interactive marketing

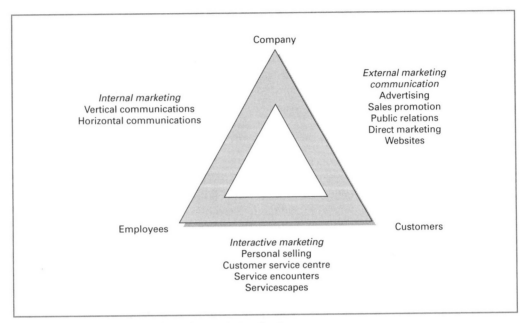

FIGURE 16.1 Communications and the services marketing triangle

Source: adapted from P. Kotler, *Marketing Management: Analysis, Planning, Implementation, and Control*, 9th edn, © 1997. Reprinted by permission of Pearson Education, Inc., Upper Saddle River, NJ

communication involves the messages that employees give to customers through such channels as personal selling, customer service interactions, service encounter interactions and servicescapes (discussed in Chapter 10). A service company must be sure that these interactive messages are consistent both among themselves and with those sent through external communications. To do so, the third side of the triangle, **internal marketing** communications, must be managed so that information from the company to employees is accurate, complete and consistent with what customers are hearing or seeing.

Consider an example from your own experience that may illustrate what happens when services marketing communications are not integrated. Have you ever seen an advertisement for a service, such as a bank product from your bank, then gone to your local branch and found it is not available there? Did the employee behind the counter offer a reason for the product not being available? Did he or she even realize that it was advertised and for sale elsewhere? In banks, this may be due to advertising being changed frequently and quickly to meet competitive offerings, but the bank tellers' training in the new offerings is failing to keep pace with the changes in advertising. As a result, customers come in expecting new accounts and rates to be available, and employees are embarrassed because they have not been informed.

This example demonstrates one of the main reasons that integrated marketing communications have not been the norm in many companies. All too often, various parts of the company are responsible for different aspects of communication. The sales department develops and executes sales communication. The marketing department prepares and disseminates advertising. A public relations firm is responsible for publicity. Functional specialists handle sales promotions, **direct marketing** and company websites. The human resources department trains front-line employees for service interactions, and still another area is responsible for the customer service department. Rarely is one person responsible for the overall communications strategy in a company, and all too often people responsible for the different communication components do not coordinate their efforts.

Today, however, more companies are adopting the concept of *integrated marketing communications* (IMC), where the company carefully integrates and organizes all of its external communications channels. As a marketing executive explained it,

> 66 Integrated marketing communications build a strong brand identity in the marketplace by tying together and reinforcing all your images and messages. IMC means that all your corporate messages, positioning and images, and identity are coordinated across all venues. It means that your PR materials say the same things as your direct mail campaign, and your advertising has the same 'look and feel' as your website.[1] 99

In this chapter we propose that a more complex type of integrated marketing communication is needed for services than for goods. External communications channels must be coordinated, as with physical goods, but both external communications and interactive communication channels must be integrated to create consistent service promises. To do that, internal marketing communications channels must be managed so that employees and the company are in agreement about what is communicated to the customer. As Figure 16.2 shows, this coordination requires both **vertical communications** – typically called *internal marketing communications* – and **horizontal communications** across departments and areas of the firm. We call this more complicated version of IMC **integrated services marketing communications** (ISMC). ISMC requires that everyone involved with communication clearly understand both the company's marketing strategy and its promises to consumers.

Key reasons for service communication challenges

Discrepancies between service delivery and external communications, in the form of exaggerated promises and/or the absence of information about service delivery aspects intended to serve customers well, can powerfully affect consumer perceptions of service quality. The factors that contribute to these communication problems include (1) inadequate management of **service promises**, (2) elevated customer expectations, (3) insufficient **customer education**, and (4) inadequate internal communications. In this chapter, we first describe the challenges stemming from these factors and then detail strategies that firms have found useful in dealing with them.

Inadequate management of service promises

A discrepancy between service delivery and promises occurs when companies fail to manage service promises – the vows made by salespeople, advertising and service personnel. One of the primary reasons for this discrepancy is that the company lacks the information and integration needed to make fulfillable promises. Salespeople often sell services, particularly new business services, before they are actually available and without having an exact date of when they will be ready for market. Demand and supply variations make service provision possible at some times, improbable at others and difficult to predict. The traditional functional structure in many companies also makes communication about promises and delivery difficult.

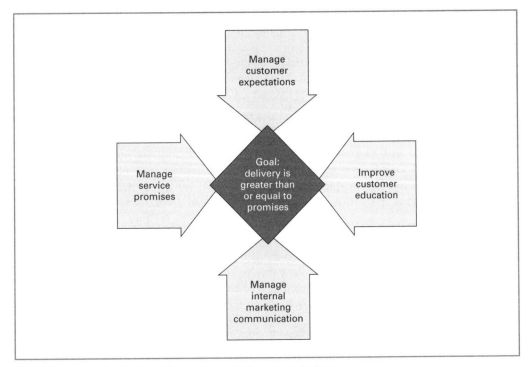

FIGURE 16.2 Approaches for integrating services marketing communication

Inadequate management of customer expectations

Appropriate and accurate communication about services is the responsibility of both marketing and operations. Marketing must accurately (if compellingly) reflect what happens in actual service encounters; operations must deliver what is promised in communications. For example, when a management consulting firm introduces a new offering, the marketing and sales departments must make the offering appealing enough to be viewed as superior to competing services. In promoting and differentiating the service, however, the company cannot afford to raise expectations above the level at which its consultants can consistently perform. If advertising, personal selling or any other external communication sets up unrealistic expectations, actual encounters will disappoint customers.

Because of increasing deregulation and intensifying competition in the services sector, many service firms feel pressure to acquire new business and to meet or beat competition. To accomplish these ends, service firms often over-promise in selling, advertising and other company communications. In the airline industry, advertising is a constant battlefield of competing offers and price reductions to gain the patronage of customers. The greater the extent to which a service firm feels pressured to generate new customers, and perceives that the industry norm is to over-promise ('everyone else in our industry over-promises'), the greater is the firm's propensity to over-promise.

If advertising shows a smiling young worker at the counter in a Carrefour commercial, the customer expects that, at least most of the time, there will be a smiling young worker in the local Carrefour. If a brochure claims that a customer's wake-up call will always be on time at an Ibis Hotel, the customer expects no mistakes. Raising expectations to unrealistic levels may lead to more initial business but invariably fosters customer disappointment and discourages repeat business.

Inadequate customer education

Differences between service delivery and promises also occur when companies do not sufficiently educate their customers. If customers are unclear about how the service will be provided, what their role in delivery involves, and how to evaluate services they have never used before, they will be disappointed. When disappointed, they will often hold the service company, not themselves, responsible. Research by a leading service research firm reveals that one-third of all customer complaints are related to problems caused by customers themselves. These errors or problems in service – even when they are 'caused' by the customer – still lead customers to defect. For this reason the firm must assume responsibility for educating customers.

For services high in credence properties – expert services that are difficult for customers to evaluate even after they have received the services – many customers do not know the criteria by which they should judge the service. For high-involvement services, such as long-term dental treatment or purchase of a first home, customers are also unlikely to comprehend and anticipate the service process. First-time home buyers rarely understand the complex set of services (surveys, conveyancing, insurance) and processes (securing a mortgage, offers and counter-offers) that will be involved in their purchases. Professionals and other providers of high-involvement services often forget that customers are novices who must be educated about each step in the process. They assume that an overview at the beginning of the service, or a manual or a set of instructions, will equip the customer. Unfortunately these steps are rarely sufficient, and customers defect because they can neither understand the process nor appreciate the value received from the service.

A final condition under which customer education can be beneficial involves services in which demand and supply are not synchronized, as discussed in Chapter 14. If the customer is not informed about peaks and troughs in demand, service overloads and failures, not to mention underutilized capacity, are likely to result.

Inadequate internal marketing communications

Multiple functions in the organization, such as marketing and operations, must be coordinated to achieve the goal of service provision. Because service advertising and personal selling promise what *people* do, frequent and effective communication across functions – horizontal communication – is critical. If internal communication is poor, perceived service quality is at risk. If company advertising and other promises are developed without input from operations, contact personnel may not be able to deliver service that matches the image portrayed in marketing efforts.

Not all service organizations advertise, but all need coordination or integration across departments or functions to deliver quality service. All need internal communication between the sales force and service providers. Horizontal communication also must occur between the human resource and marketing departments. To deliver excellent customer service, firms must be certain to inform and motivate employees to deliver what their customers expect. If marketing and sales personnel who understand customer expectations do not communicate this information to contact employees, the lack of knowledge for these employees will affect the quality of service that they deliver.

A final form of internal coordination central to providing service excellence is consistency in policies and procedures across departments and branches. If a service organization operates many outlets under the same name, whether franchised or company owned, customers expect similar performance across those outlets. If managers of individual branches or outlets have significant autonomy in procedures and policies, customers may not receive the same level of service quality across the branches.

Strategies to match service promises with delivery

Figure 16.2 shows four categories of strategies to match service delivery with promises: (1) manage service promises, (2) manage customer expectations, (3) improve customer education, and (4) manage internal marketing communication. 'Managing service promises' involves coordinating the promises made by all external and interactive marketing sources to ensure that they are consistent and feasible. 'Managing customer expectations' incorporates strategies that tell customers that the firm cannot or may not always provide the level of service they expect. 'Educating customers' means providing customers with information about the service process or evaluative criteria about important aspects of the service. Finally, 'managing internal marketing communication' means transmitting information across organizational boundaries – upward, downward and across – to align all functions with customer expectations. Strategies in each of these categories are discussed in detail in the following sections.

Manage service promises

In manufacturing physical goods, the departments that make promises and those that deliver them can operate independently. Goods can be fully designed and produced and then turned over to marketing for promotion and sale. In services, however, the sales and marketing departments make promises about what other employees in the organization will fulfil. Because what employees do cannot be standardized like physical goods produced mechanically, greater coordination and management of promises are required. Successful services advertising and personal selling become the responsibility of both marketing and operations.

Figure 16.3 shows specific strategies that are effective in managing promises.

Create effective external communications

Intangibility makes external communications about services different from communication for products. The intangible nature of services creates problems for consumers both before and after purchase. Before buying services, consumers have difficulty understanding them and coming up with sets of services to consider.[2] After buying services, consumers have trouble evaluating their

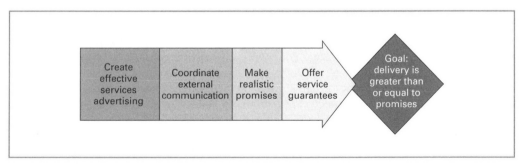

FIGURE 16.3 Approaches for managing service promises

service experiences. Various authors have suggested strategies to overcome these problems, but before we turn to them, we will discuss intangibility in greater depth.

Banwari Mittal described the difficulties associated with intangibility by dividing it into five properties, each of which has implications for external communications. In Mittal's view, intangibility involves incorporeal existence, abstractness, generality, non-searchability and mental impalpability:[3]

- *Incorporeal existence.* The service product is neither made out of physical matter nor occupies physical space. Although the delivery mechanism (such as a Kwikfit outlet) may occupy space, the service itself (car servicing and tyre change) does not. This lack of form makes showing the service difficult compared to showing a product.

- *Abstractness.* Services are considered apart from any particular instances or material objects.[4] Service benefits such as financial security, fun or health do not correspond directly with objects, making them difficult to visualize and understand. How do you communicate or advertise the value of an insurance policy?

- *Generality versus specificity. Generality* refers to a class of things, persons, events or properties, whereas *specificity* refers to particular objects, people or events. Many services and service promises are described in generalities (wonderful experience, superior education, completely satisfied customers), making them difficult to differentiate from those of competitors.

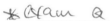

Property of intangibility	Communication strategy	Description
Incorporeal existence	Physical representation	Show physical components of service that are unique, indicate high quality and create the right association
Generality	System documentation	Objectively document physical system capacity by showing facts and figures
	Performance documentation	Document and cite past positive performance statistics
	Service performance episode	Present a vivid story of an actual service delivery incident that relates to the important service attribute
Abstractness	Service consumption episode	Capture and display typical customers benefiting from the service, evoking particular incidents
Non-searchability	Performance documentation	Cite independently audited performance
	Consumption documentation	Obtain and present customer testimonials
Impalpability	Service process episode	Present a vivid documentary on the step-by-step service process
	Case history episode	Present an actual case history of what the firm did for a specific client

TABLE 16.1 External communication strategies matched with properties of intangibility

Source: adapted from B. Mittal, 'The advertising of services: meeting the challenge of intangibility', *Journal of Service Research* 2, no. 1 (August 1999), pp. 98–116

■ *Non-searchability*. Because service is a performance, it often cannot be previewed or inspected in advance of purchase. As we discussed in Chapter 2, non-searchability is particularly true of services that are classified as either experience or credence services.

■ *Mental impalpability*. Services are often too complex, multidimensional and difficult to grasp mentally. Impalpability is the absence of prior exposure, familiarity or knowledge, which makes services difficult to interpret.

According to Mittal, only incorporeal existence is an inevitable property of services. The other four properties often tend to be present but are not intrinsic to intangibility. By following the strategies shown in Table 16.1, external communications can overcome these challenging properties. The abstract can be made concrete, the general can be made specific, the non-searchable can be made searchable and the mentally impalpable can be made palpable.

Service marketers have developed guidelines for external communication effectiveness. These guidelines include the following:

■ *Use narratives to demonstrate the service experience*. Many services are experiential, and a uniquely effective approach to communicating them involves story-based appeals. Research has concluded that consumers with relatively low familiarity with a service category prefer appeals based on stories to appeals based on lists of service attributes. Furthermore, the relative advantage of the story is intensified when the novice consumer is in a happy mood rather than a sad one.[5]

■ *Present vivid information*. Effective communication creates a strong or clear impression on the senses and produces a distinct mental picture. One way to use vivid information is to evoke strong emotion, such as in British Airways' classic 'World's Favourite Airline' advertising campaign. Vividness can also be achieved by concrete language and dramatization.

■ *Use interactive imagery*. One type of vividness involves what is called *interactive imagery*.[6] Imagery (defined as a mental event that involves the visualization of a concept or relationship) can enhance recall of names and facts about service. Interactive imagery integrates two or more items in some mutual action, resulting in improved recall. Some service companies effectively integrate their logos or symbols with an expression of what they do, such as Orange where the colour of the logo and the brand name help to maintain high awareness of the mobile phone company.

■ *Focus on the tangibles*.[7] Another way that advertisers can increase the effectiveness of services communications is to feature the tangibles associated with the service, such as showing a bank's marble columns or gold credit card. Showing the tangibles provides clues about the nature and quality of the service. Berry and Clark propose four **tangibilization strategies**: association, physical representation, documentation and visualization.[8] *Association* means linking the service to a tangible person, place or object, such as linking Alan Whicker with Travelocity or Virgin with Richard Branson. *Physical representation* means showing tangibles that are directly or indirectly part of the service, such as employees, buildings or equipment. *Documentation* means featuring objective data and factual information. *Visualization* is a vivid mental picture of a service's benefits or qualities, such as showing people on vacation having fun.

■ *Feature service employees in communication*. Customer contact personnel are an important second audience for services advertising.[9] Featuring actual employees doing their jobs or explaining their services in communications is effective for both the primary audience (customers) and the secondary audience (employees) because it communicates to employees that they are important. Furthermore, when employees who perform a service well are featured in advertising, they become standards for other employees' behaviours. B&Q has its own employees appearing in its advertisements.

- *Promise what is possible.*[10] Many companies hope to create good service by leading with good communications, but this strategy can backfire when the actual service does not live up to the promises in advertising or other communications. In line with the strategies we discuss in the next section, all service communications should promise only what is possible and not attempt to make services more attractive than they actually are.

- *Encourage word-of-mouth communication.* Because services are usually high in experience and credence properties, people frequently turn to others for information rather than to traditional marketing channels. Services advertising and other external messages can generate word-of-mouth communication that extends the investment in paid communication and improves the credibility of the messages. Communications that generate talk because it is humorous, compelling or unique can be particularly effective.

- *Feature service customers.* One way to generate positive word of mouth is to feature satisfied customers in the communications. Testimonials featuring actual service customers simulate personal communications between people and are thereby a credible way to communicate the benefits of service.

- *Use transformational advertising.*[11] Transformational advertising is image advertising that changes the experience of buying and consuming the product. Most advertising for vacation destinations is transformational: it invites the consumer to escape into a world that is necessarily subjective and perceptual. This approach involves making the advertisement vivid or rich in detail, realistic and rewarding.

Coordinate external communication

For any organization, one of the most important yet challenging aspects of managing brand image involves coordinating all the external communication vehicles that send information to customers. These communication vehicles include advertising, websites, sales promotion, public relations, direct marketing and personal selling.

Advertising is any paid form of non-personal presentation and promotion of a company's offerings by an identified sponsor. Dominant advertising vehicles include television, radio, newspapers, magazines, outdoor signage and the Internet. Because advertising is paid, marketers control the creative appeals, placement and timing. Internet advertising is becoming a more important and larger portion of companies' advertising budgets, and should be synchronized with traditional advertising vehicles. MasterCard's highly successful worldwide 'Priceless' advertising campaign lists three or four tangible items and their prices followed by a key customer benefit that is 'priceless'. The campaign is an example of solid synchronization because it is 'extraordinarily flexible, and carries a brand message that is not only relevant globally but also adapts well to different media, different payment channels, different markets'.[12] The campaign, now seen in 96 countries and 47 languages, has generated strong brand recall and has received the advertising industry's prestigious Gold Effie, Addy and Cresta awards.

Websites are the company's own online communication to customers. Often a disconnect exists between the look, feel and content of a company's website and its advertising, usually because different parts of the company (or different advertising vendors) are responsible for creating these vehicles. When websites are coordinated in theme, content and promises – as they are in DHL advertising – a company is better able to match service delivery with promises because the promises themselves are consistent. A major factor contributing to the success of Internet advertising is the availability of advertising approaches that are more popular than the **banner advertisement**, which dominated the medium for years. Banner advertisements[13] still account for the largest category of Internet advertisements, but their effectiveness as a marketing tool is being seriously questioned. Click-through rates, the most common measure of effectiveness, have dropped from 10 per cent to 0.025 per cent over the years. Analysts suggest the following reasons for the drop:

- *Banner clutter.* As spending increased, so did the number of advertisements, which reduced the novelty and created sites filled with banners that often led to no value. Just as with other advertising clutter, users learned to stop paying attention.

- *Boring banners.* Although the potential to create fun and interactive banner advertisements existed, many advertisers simply created me-too banners that were low on content and creativity.

- *Built-in banners.* Once advertisers started using animation and other colourful attention-getting devices, the advertisements became intrusive, interfering with the users' surfing stream and with the time they spent on sites. Some advertisements took so long to download that they delayed and derailed users' interactions on the Web.

Advertisers had to face the fact that their hopes for banner advertisements were not being fulfilled, at least as measured simply by click-through rates. Improved advertising approaches have been developed in the last three years, with the most significant being search-based advertising, or **paid search advertising**. In this form of advertising, which currently represents the largest share of online spending among all online advertisement formats, advertisers pay only when qualified leads are delivered to their websites. With AdWords, a pay-per-click advertising service offered by Google, advertisers buy the rights to words and terms related to their business. When a consumer searches Google using one of those keywords, the advertiser's Uniform Resource Locator (URL), along with its name and description, appears in a coloured box beside the search results. The advertiser pays only when a user clicks on the advertisement, and the going rate is as little as 5 cents per click. Marketers recognize that managing their media planning and buying strategy as a whole, rather than as segregated channels, maximizes campaign effectiveness. For this reason, more and more advertisers are adding online advertising to their traditional advertising buys. Today, online advertising accounts for a small percentage of total advertising expenditures, largely because the medium is not as costly as television or print. In the future, as consumers spend more time on the Web, Internet advertising will become even more important than before.

Sales promotion includes short-term incentives such as coupons, premiums, discounts and other activities that stimulate customer purchases and stretch media spending. The fast-food industry, including McDonald's, Burger King and Wendy's, offers premiums such as action figures that link the chains' offerings to current movies and television shows.

Public relations include activities that build a favourable company image with a firm's public through publicity, relations with the news media and community events.

Service spotlight

Richard Branson, founder of Virgin Atlantic Airways (in this chapter's opening vignette) is a master at obtaining publicity for his airline. When launching the airline, he claimed, 'I knew that the only way of competing with British Airways and the others was to get out there and use myself to promote it'.[14] In the years since the airline's launch, his publicity-winning stunts included recording the fastest time across the Atlantic Ocean in a speedboat, flying a hot-air balloon across the Atlantic Ocean and from Japan to Canada, dressing up in everything from a stewardess's uniform to a bikini on Virgin flights, and being photographed in his bath.

Direct marketing involves the use of mail, telephone, fax, email and other tools to communicate directly with specific consumers to obtain a direct response.

Service spotlight

American Express is a service company that uses direct marketing extensively and ensures that it integrates well with all other messages, including interactive messages from employees. As the executive vice president of global advertising at American Express clearly states:

'Service brands are not created solely in advertising. In fact, much of a brand's equity stems from the direct consumer experiences with the brand. We partner with a relationship marketing company to help us manage consumer experiences with our brand across all products and services – Card, Travel, Financial Services, and Relationship Services – via all direct channels, including phone, Internet, and mail.'[15]

Michael Bronner, the founder of the relationship marketing company that American Express uses, emphasizes the need for coordinating external and interactive marketing communications: 'The client [such as American Express] may spend millions on TV advertising but lose when the customer is working his way through layer upon layer of voice response options on the customer service line.'[16]

Personal selling is face-to-face presentation by a representative from the firm to make sales and build customer relationships. One way that personal selling and advertising are integrated in business-to-business companies is through the development of advertising materials that salespeople distribute to customers. This approach not only creates an integrated message to customers but also keeps salespeople fully informed of the promises the company is making.

Make realistic promises

The expectations that customers bring to the service affect their evaluations of its quality: the higher the expectation, the higher the delivered service must be to be perceived as high quality. Therefore, promising reliability in advertising is appropriate only when reliability is actually delivered. It is essential for a firm's marketing or sales department to understand the actual levels of service delivery (percentage of times the service is provided correctly, or percentage and number of problems that arise) before making promises about reliability. To be appropriate and effective, communications about service quality must accurately reflect what customers will actually receive in service encounters.

Offer service guarantees

As discussed in Chapter 15, service guarantees are formal promises made to customers about aspects of the service they will receive. Although many services carry implicit service satisfaction guarantees, the true benefits from them – an increase in the likelihood of a customer choosing or remaining with the company – come only when the customer knows that guarantees exist and trusts that the company will stand behind them.

Manage customer expectations

Many service companies find themselves in the position of having to tell customers that service previously provided will be discontinued or available only at a higher price. In the 1990s, service from large computer companies such as IBM typically included salespeople who interacted with customers in person. This level of service attention was deemed necessary (because without it customers comprehended adequately neither the options nor their needs) and worthwhile (because almost all customers were perceived to be potentially large customers for computers). When demand for computers shifted from mainframes to personal computers (PCs), the personal attention provided by direct salespeople was no longer necessary or cost-effective. Instead of the traditional face-to-face service, the companies shifted to telephone interaction alone, a distinct – and for many customers disappointing – departure from the past. Credit card companies that offer multiple value-added services when interest rates are high also find that they need to withdraw these services when interest rates drop.

How can a company gracefully give the customer news that service will not be as expected? Figure 16.4 summarizes four strategies.

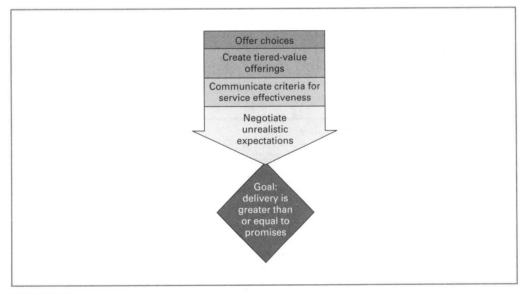

FIGURE 16.4 Approaches for managing customer expectations

Offer choices

One way to reset expectations is to give customers options for aspects of service that are meaningful, such as time and cost. A lawyer charging 100 euros per hour, for example, might offer clients the choice between a price increase of 10 euros per hour or a reduction in the number of minutes comprising the hour (such as 50 minutes). With the choice, clients can select the aspect of the trade-off (time or money) that is most meaningful to them. Making the choice solidifies the client's expectations of service.

This strategy is effective in business-to-business situations, particularly in terms of speed versus quality. Customers who are time-conscious often want reports, proposals or other written documents quickly. When asked to provide a 10-page proposal for a project within three days, an architectural firm responded that it could provide either a two-page proposal in three days or a 10-page proposal in a week. Its customer selected the latter option, recognizing that the deadline could be extended. In most business-to-business services, speed is often essential but threatens performance. If customers understand the trade-off and are asked to make a choice, they are likely to be more satisfied because their service expectations for each option become more realistic.

Create tiered-value service offerings

Product companies are accustomed to offering different versions of their products with prices commensurate with the value customers perceive. Cars with different configurations of features carry price tags that match not their cost but their perceived value to the customer. This same type of formal bundling and pricing can be accomplished in services, with the extra benefit of managing expectations.

Credit card companies offer **tiered-value service offerings**. American Express has multiple levels of credit card services based on the type of service provided: the traditional green card offers basic service features, the gold card additional benefits and the platinum card still more. Two advantages of tiered offerings are (1) the practice puts the burden of choosing the service level on the customer, thereby familiarizing the customer with specific service expectations, and (2) the company can identify which customers are willing to pay higher prices for higher service levels.

The opportunity to set expectations accurately is present when the customer makes the decision at the time of purchase when customers can be reminded of the terms of the agreement if they request support that is above the level in the contract.

Communicate the criteria and levels of service effectiveness

At times companies can establish the criteria by which customers assess service. Consider a business customer who is purchasing market research services for the first time. Because market research is an expert service, it is high in credence properties that are hard for customers to judge. Moreover, the effectiveness of this type of service differs depending on the objectives the client brings to the service. In this situation, a service provider can teach the customer the criteria by which to evaluate the service. The provider that teaches the customer in a credible manner will have an advantage in shaping the evaluation process.

As an example, consider research company A, which communicates the following criteria to the customer: (1) a low price signals low quality, (2) reputation of the firm is critical, and (3) person-to-person interviews are the only type of customer feedback that will provide accurate information. A customer who accepts these criteria will evaluate all other suppliers using them. If research company B had talked to the customer first, consider these (very different!) criteria and their impact on the buyer: (1) market research companies with good reputations are charging for their reputation, not their skill, (2) telephone interviews have been found to work as well as person-to-person interviews, and (3) price does not indicate quality level.

The same approach can be used with service *levels* rather than evaluative criteria. If research company B provides four-day turnaround on the results of the data analysis, the company has just set the customer's expectation level for all other suppliers.

Negotiate unrealistic expectations

Sometimes customers express service requests as they would their lowest bid in a negotiation. The service they request for the price they are willing to pay is unrealistic; they know it and the firm knows it. It is, in effect, a starting point for discussion, not the expected end point. In these situations successful service providers present their offerings in terms of value and not price alone. They also negotiate more realistic expectations.

Improve customer education

As discussed in Chapter 12, customers must perform their roles properly for many services to be effective. If customers forget to perform their roles, or perform them improperly, disappointment may result. For this reason, communication to customers can take the form of customer education. Figure 16.5 shows several types of customer education approaches that can help match promises with delivery.

Prepare customers for the service process

On a return trip from Singapore on Singapore Airlines, I neglected to heed the airline's warning that return flights must be confirmed 24 hours in advance. On my arrival at the airport to return home, my seat had been given to another customer who had conformed to the airline's request for confirmation. Depending on the perspective taken, you could argue that either the company or the customer was right in this situation. Whose responsibility is it to make sure that customers perform their roles properly?

Companies can avoid such situations by preparing customers for the service process. And companies may need to prepare the customer often, even every step of the way, for the subsequent actions the customer needs to take. A business-to-business example will help illustrate this strategy.

Customers of management consulting services purchase intangible benefits: marketing effectiveness, motivated workforces, culture change. The very fact that companies purchase these services usually indicates that they do not know how to perform them alone. Many clients will also not know what to look for along the way to judge progress. In management consulting and

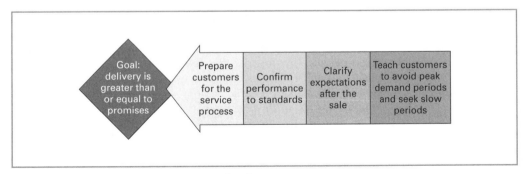

FIGURE 16.5 Approaches for improving customer education

other complex service situations, the effective provider prepares the customer for the service process and creates structure for the customer. At the beginning of the engagement, the management consulting firm establishes checkpoints throughout the process, at which times progress will be evaluated, and leads the customer to establish objectives for project completion. Because customers do not know what that progress will look like, the consulting firm takes the lead in setting goals or criteria to be examined at those times.

A similar approach is effective with individual service customers. Do you remember registration at the beginning of your first university semester or term? How aware were you of the steps in the process and where to go after each step? It is unlikely that directions, even in great detail, made you feel confident and competent in the new service experience. You may have required step-by-step – 'next call this telephone number or go to page B' – guidance.

As these examples show, whenever a customer is inexperienced or a service process is new or unique, education about what to expect is essential.

Confirm performance to standards and expectations

Service providers sometimes provide service, even explicitly requested service, yet fail to communicate to the customer that it has been accomplished. These providers stop short of getting credit for their actions when they do not reinforce actions with communication about their fulfilment of the request. This situation may happen under one or more of the following conditions:

- The customer cannot evaluate the effectiveness of a service.
- The decision-maker in the service purchase is a person different from the users of the service.
- The service is invisible.
- The provider depends on others to perform some of the actions to fulfil customer expectations.

When customers cannot evaluate service effectiveness, usually because they are inexperienced or the service is technical, the provider may fail to communicate specific actions that address client concerns because the actions seem too complex for the customer to comprehend. In this situation, the service provider can improve perceptions by translating the actions into customer-friendly terms. A personal injury lawyer who aids a client with the medical and financial implications of an accident needs to be able to tell the client in language the client can understand that the lawyer has performed the necessary actions.

When the decision-maker in service purchases is different from the users of the service, a wide discrepancy in satisfaction may exist between decision-makers and users. An example is in the purchase of information technology products and services in a company. The decision-maker – the manager of information technology or someone in a similar position – makes the purchase decisions and understands the service promises. If users are not involved in the purchase process, they may not know what has been promised and may be dissatisfied.

Customers are not always aware of everything done behind the scenes to serve them well. Most services have invisible support processes. For instance, doctors frequently request diagnostic tests to rule out possible causes for illness. When these tests come back negative, doctors may neglect to inform patients. Many hairstyling firms have guarantees that ensure customer satisfaction with haircuts, permanents and colour treatments. However, only a few of them actively communicate these guarantees in advertising because they assume customers know about them. The firm that explicitly communicates the guarantee may be selected over others by a customer who is uncertain about the quality of the service. Making customers aware of standards or efforts to improve service that are not readily apparent can improve service quality perceptions.

Clarify expectations after the sale

When service involves a handover between sales and operations, as it does in most companies, clarifying expectations with customers helps the service delivery arm of the company to align with customer expectations. Salespeople are motivated and compensated to raise customer expectations – at least to the point of making the sale – rather than to communicate realistically what the company can provide. In these situations, service providers can avoid future disappointment by clarifying what was promised as soon as the handover is made.

Teach customers to avoid peak demand periods and seek slow demand periods

Few customers want to face queues or delays in receiving services. In the words of two researchers, 'At best, waiting takes their time, and at worst, they may experience a range of unpleasant reactions – feeling trapped, tired, bored, angry, or demeaned'.[17] In a bank setting, researchers tested three strategies for dealing with customer waits: (1) giving customers prior notice of busy times, (2) having employees apologize for the delays, and (3) assigning all visible employees to serving customers. Only the first strategy focuses on educating customers; the other two involve managing employees. Researchers expected – and confirmed – that customers warned of a wait in line tended to minimize the negative effects of waiting to justify their decision to seek service at peak times. In general, customers given a card listing the branch's busiest and slowest times were more satisfied with the banking service. The other two strategies, apology and all tellers serving, showed no effects on satisfaction.[18] Educating customers to avoid peak times benefits both customers (through faster service) and companies (by easing the problem of over-demand).

Manage internal marketing communication

The fourth major category of strategies necessary to match service delivery with promises involves managing internal marketing communications (see Figure 16.6). Internal marketing

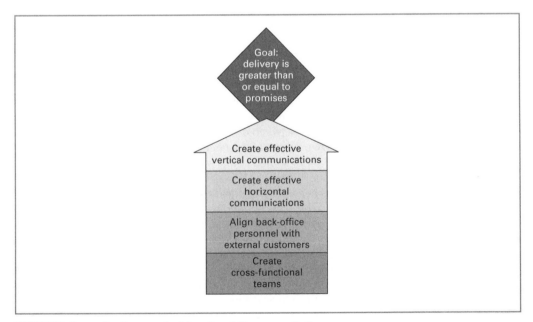

FIGURE 16.6 Approaches for managing internal marketing communications

communications can be both vertical and horizontal. *Vertical communications* are either downward, from management to employees, or upward, from employees to management. *Horizontal communications* are those across functional boundaries in an organization.

Create effective vertical communications

Companies that give customer-contact employees adequate information, tools and skills allow them to perform successful interactive marketing. Some of these skills come through training and other human resource efforts discussed in Chapter 11, but some are provided through downward communication. Among the most important forms of downward communication are company newsletters and magazines, corporate television networks, email, briefings, videotapes and internal promotional campaigns, and recognition programmes. One of the keys to successful downward communication is keeping employees informed of everything that is being conveyed to customers through external marketing. Employees should see company advertising before it is aired or published and should be familiar with the website, mailings and direct selling approaches used. If these vertical communications are not present, both customers and employees suffer – customers will not receive the same messages from employees that they hear in company external marketing, and employees will feel uninformed and not be aware of what their company is doing. Customers come to them asking for services that have been marketed externally but not internally, making the employees feel uninformed, left out and helpless.[19]

Upward communication is also necessary in closing the gap between service promises and service delivery. Employees are at the front line of service, and they know – more than anyone else in the organization – what can and cannot be delivered. They know when service breakdowns are occurring and, very often, why they are happening. Having open communication channels from employees to management can prevent service problems before they occur and minimize them when they do take place.

Create effective horizontal communications

Horizontal communication – communication across functional boundaries in an organization – facilitates coordinated efforts for service delivery. This task is difficult because functions typically differ in goals, philosophies, outlooks and views of the customer, but the payoff is high. Coordination between marketing and operations can result in communication that accurately reflects service delivery, thus reducing the gap between customer expectations and actual service delivery. Integration of effort between marketing and human resources can improve the ability of each employee to become a better marketer. Coordination between finance and marketing can create prices that accurately reflect the customer's evaluation of a service. In service firms, all these functions need to be integrated to produce consistent messages and to narrow the service gaps.

One important strategy for effective horizontal communications is to open channels of communication between the marketing department and operations personnel. For example, when a company creates advertising that depicts the service encounter, it is essential that the advertising accurately reflects what customers will experience in actual service encounters. Exaggeration puts service quality perceptions at risk, especially when the firm is consistently unable to deliver to the level of service portrayed in the advertising. Coordination and communication between advertising and service providers are pivotal in delivering service that meets expectations.

Featuring actual employees doing their jobs or explaining the services they provide, a strategy we mentioned earlier in this chapter, is one way to coordinate advertising portrayals and the reality of the service encounter. To create this type of advertising, the advertising department or agency interacts directly with service employees, facilitating horizontal communications. Similar benefits can be achieved if employees are included in the advertising process in other ways, such as by being shown advertising in its pre-test forms.

Another important strategy for horizontal communications involves opening channels of communication between sales and operations. Mechanisms for achieving this goal can be formal or informal and can include annual planning meetings, retreats, team meetings or workshops in which departments clarify service issues. In these sessions, the departments can interact to understand the goals, capabilities and constraints of the other. Some companies hold 'gap workshops' at which employees from both functions meet for a day or two to try to understand the difficulties in matching promises made through selling with delivery accomplished by operations personnel.[20]

Involving the operations staff in face-to-face meetings with external customers is also a strategy that allows operations personnel to more readily understand the salesperson's role and the needs and desires of customers. Rather than filtering customers' needs through the sales force, operations employees can witness at first hand the pressures and demands of customers. A frequent and desirable result is better service to the internal customer – the salesperson – from the operations staff as they become aware of their own roles in satisfying both external and internal customers.

Align back-office and support personnel with external customers through interaction or measurement

As companies become increasingly customer focused, front-line personnel develop improved skills in discerning what customers require. As they become more knowledgeable about and empathetic toward external customers, they also experience intrinsic rewards for satisfying customers. Back-office or support personnel, who typically do not interact directly with external customers, miss out on this bonding and, as a consequence, fail to gain the skills and rewards associated with it.

Interaction

Companies are creating ways to facilitate the interaction between back-office and support personnel and external customers.

Service spotlight

Scottish and Southern Energy, an electricity provider, regularly gets support staff (such as generating staff, finance personnel and human resource personnel) to handle customers' calls in the company's call centres.

When actual interaction is difficult or impossible, some companies videotape customers in their service facilities during the purchase and consumption process to vividly portray needs and requirements of customers and to show personnel the support that front-line people need to deliver to those expectations.

Measurement

When company measurement systems are established, employees are sometimes judged on the basis of how they perform for the next internal customer in the chain. Although this approach provides feedback in terms of how well the employees are serving the internal customer, it lacks the motivation and reward that come from seeing their efforts affect the end-customer.

Create cross-functional teams

Another approach to improving horizontal communications to better serve customers is to involve employees in cross-functional teams to align their jobs with end-customer requirements. For example, if a team of telecommunications service representatives is working to improve interaction with customers, back-office people such as computer technicians or training personnel can become part of the team. The team then learns requirements and sets goals for achieving them together, an approach that directly creates communications across the functions.

The cross-functional team approach can best be explained by the examples of an advertising agency. The individual in an advertising agency who typically interacts directly with the client is the account executive (often called a 'suit' by the creative staff). In the traditional agency, the account executive visits the client, elicits client expectations and then interacts with the various departments in the agency (art, copywriting, production, traffic and media buying) that will perform the work. All functions are specialized and, in the extreme case, get direction for their portion of the work right from the account executive. A cross-functional team approach has representatives from all the areas meet with the account executive, even the client, and collectively discuss the account and approaches to address client needs. Each team member brings his or her function's perspectives and opens communication. All members can then understand the constraints and schedules of the other groups.

Summary

Discrepancies between service delivery and external communications have a strong effect on customer perceptions of service quality. In this chapter we discussed the role of and need for integrated services marketing communications in minimizing these discrepancies. We described external, interactive and internal marketing communications using the service triangle and emphasized the need to coordinate all three forms to deliver service that meets customer expectations. We also discussed the factors that lead to problems in marketing communications and four sets of strategies to deal with them. These strategies include (1) managing service promises, (2) managing customer expectations, (3) improving customer education, and (4) managing internal marketing communications.

Key concepts

Advertising	405	Paid search advertising	414
Banner advertisements	414	Public relations	405
Customer education	407	Sales promotion	405
Customer expectations	405	Service marketing triangle	405
Direct marketing	406	Service promises	407
Horizontal communications	407	Tangibilization strategies	412
Integrated service marketing communications	407	Tiered-value service offerings	417
Internal marketing	406	Vertical communications	407

Further reading

De Chernatony, L. and McDonald, M. (2003) *Creating Powerful Brands in Consumer Service and Industrial Markets*, 3rd edn (Oxford: Butterworth Heinemann).

De Chernatony, L. and Segal-Horn, S. (2003) 'The criteria for successful services brands', *European Journal of Marketeers*, 37(7/8), 1095–118.

De Chernatony, L., Drury, S. and Segal-Horn, S. (2003) 'Building a services brand: stages, people and orientations', *The Service Industries Journal*, 23(3), 1–21.

Lindberg-Repo, K. and Gronroos, C. (2004) 'Conceptualising communications strategy from a relational perspective', *Industrial Marketing Management*, 33, 229–39.

Mittal, B. (1999) 'The advertising of services. Meeting the challenge of intangibility', *Journal of Service Research*, 2(1), 98–116.

Mortimer, K. (2000) 'Are services advertised differently? An analysis of the relationship between product and service types and the informational content of their advertisements', *Journal of Marketing Communications*, 6, 121–34.

Reichheld, F.F. (2003) 'The one number you need to grow', *Harvard Business Review*, 81(2), 46–55.

 ## Discussion questions

1 Which of the key reasons for provider gap 4 discussed in the beginning of this chapter is the easiest to address in a company? Which is the hardest to address? Why?

2 Review the four general strategies for achieving integrated services marketing communications. Would all these strategies be relevant in goods firms? Which would be most critical in goods firms? Which would be most critical in services firms? Are there any differences between those most critical in goods firms and those most critical in services firms?

3 What are the most effective Internet advertisements that you have seen? Why are they effective?

4 Using the section on managing customer expectations, put yourself in the position of your professor, who must reduce the amount of 'service' provided to the students in your class. Give an example of each strategy in this context. Which of the strategies would work best with you (the student) in managing your expectations? Why?

5 Why is internal marketing communication so important in service firms? Is it important in product firms?

6 Which form of internal marketing communication – vertical or horizontal – would you invest in if you had to select between them as an organization's CEO? Why?

7 What other strategies can you add to the four offered in the section on customer education? What types of education do you expect from service firms? Give an example of a firm from which you have received adequate education. What firm has not provided you with adequate education?

Exercises

1 Go to the DHL website. Explore each area of the site, and make a list of the types of information you can find based on the three categories of marketing communication (external, interactive, internal) discussed in this chapter. What additional information do you find useful on the site?

2 Find five effective service advertisements in newspapers and magazines. According to the criteria given in this chapter, identify why they are effective. Critique them using the list of criteria, and discuss ways they could be improved.

Notes

[1] P.G. Lindell, 'You need integrated attitude to develop IMC', *Marketing News*, 26 May 1997, p. 5.

[2] D. Legg and J. Baker, 'Advertising strategies for service firms', in *Add Value to Your Service*, ed. C. Suprenant (Chicago, IL: American Marketing Association, 1987), pp. 163–8.

[3] B. Mittal, 'The advertising of services: meeting the challenge of intangibility', *Journal of Service Research* 2 (August 1999), pp. 98–116.

[4] E. Breivik and S.V. Troye, 'Dimensions of intangibility and their impact on product evaluations', *Developments in Marketing Science*, vol. 19, eds E. Wilson and J. Hair (Miami, FL: Academy of Marketing Science, 1996), pp. 56–9.

[5] A.S. Mattila, 'The role of narratives in the advertising of experiential services', *Journal of Service Research* 3 (August 2000), pp. 35–45.

[6] K.L. Alesandri, 'Strategies that influence memory for advertising communications', in *Information Processing Research in Advertising*, ed. R.J. Harris (Hillsdale, NJ: Erlbaum, 1983).

[7] L.L. Berry and T. Clark, 'Four ways to make services more tangible', *Business* (October–December 1986), pp. 53–4.

[8] Ibid.

[9] W.R. George and L.L. Berry, 'Guidelines for the advertising of services', *Business Horizons* (May–June 1981), pp. 52–6.

[10] Ibid.

[11] Mittal, 'The advertising of services'.

[12] www.mastercardinternational.com

[13] Sources: K.J. Bannan, 'Seven ways to make online advertising work for you', *Advertising Age*, 11 October 2004, p. 11; R. Bayani, 'Banner ads – still working after all these years?', *Link-up* (November/December 2001), pp. 2, 6.

[14] P. Denoyelle and J.-C. Larreche, 'Virgin Atlantic Airways – ten years later', INSEAD Case (1995).

[15] D.E. Bell and D.M. Leavitt, 'Bronner Slosberg Humphrey', *Harvard Business School Case 9-598-136* (1998), p. 5.

[16] Ibid., p. 4

[17] E.C. Clemmer and B. Schneider, 'Managing customer dissatisfaction with waiting: applying social-psychological theory in a service setting', in *Advances in Services Marketing and*

Management, vol. 2, eds T. Schwartz, D.E. Bowen and S.W. Brown (Greenwich, CT: JAI Press, 1993), pp. 213–29.

[18] Ibid.

[19] L.L. Berry, V.A. Zeithaml and A. Parasuraman, 'Quality counts in services, too', *Business Horizons* (May–June 1985), pp. 44–52.

[20] V.A. Zeithaml, A. Parasuraman and L.L. Berry, *Delivering Quality Service: Balancing Customer Perceptions and Expectations* (New York: Free Press, 1990), p. 120.

CHAPTER 17

Pricing of services

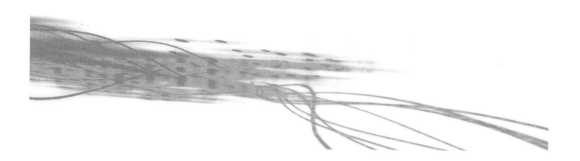

❖ LEARNING OBJECTIVES

This chapter's objectives are to:

1 Discuss three major ways that service prices are perceived differently from goods prices by customers.

2 Articulate the key ways that pricing of services differs from pricing of goods from a company's perspective.

3 Demonstrate what value means to customers and the role that price plays in value.

4 Describe strategies that companies use to price services.

5 Give examples of pricing strategy in action.

CASE STUDY: RAIL TRAVELLERS FACE 'CHAOTIC' TICKET SYSTEM

Rail travellers between Glasgow and London face a head-scratching range of prices, from only 18 euros for a cheap off-peak deal to a huge 201 euros for a first-class return.

Bosses at one of the railway companies under scrutiny, GNER, admitted its fares were difficult to understand, especially if you book via the Internet. Politicians have branded the system 'chaotic', with the confusion becoming even greater as rival companies give different names to their deals from 'apex' and 'saver' to 'value advance' and 'standard advance'. Each of the different tickets has a different price and different conditions of use in terms of flexibility, time of use, ability to get a refund for cancelled travel, etc.

Analysis of popular routes from London revealed the extent of the problems facing passengers. Journeys to Glasgow offered the most options with 45 prices available from GNER, Virgin and ScotRail. After the Glasgow route, the worst was London to Exeter with 36 options from First Great Western and South West Trains. Passengers even have to face 18 fares for the short journey from Gatwick Airport to London.

The farce has turned the official rail fares manual into an enormous document. In the late 1980s under the government-owned British Rail, the notes to the manual ran to six pages. Today, it is 202 pages.

Critics claim the system is 'dreadful' and impenetrable to all but the most experienced travellers. As well as the traditional 'full open' fare and walk-on 'saver' ticket, every major route now has several lower-priced forward-booking fares sold under a variety of different names and brands. There are thought to be about 350 different types of tickets on sale. The issue of fare structures is under investigation by the government's Transport Select Committee. Committee member Clive Efford said a passenger travelling from Penzance to Birmingham could save 16 euros by booking two singles – one from Penzance to Cheltenham and one from Cheltenham to Birmingham rather than buying one single ticket for the whole journey.

GNER chief executive Christopher Garnett admitted to the committee that it was much easier finding cheap fares on the website of low-cost airlines such as easyJet. He said passengers had to 'hunt' for low fares on the GNER website, although he claimed the company was trying to make the site more accessible.

These differences in offerings illustrate an important issue about pricing that will be made clear in this chapter: Price is not only about monetary cost. Price also involves time and convenience payments.

Source: adapted from *Daily Mail*, 20 December 2005, p. 19

According to one of the leading experts on pricing, most service organizations use a 'naive and sometimes complicated approach to pricing without regard to underlying shifts in demand, the rate that supply can be expanded, prices of available substitutes, consideration of the price–volume relationship, or the availability of future substitutes'.[1] What makes the pricing of services more difficult than pricing of goods? What approaches work well in the context of services?

This chapter builds on three key differences between customer evaluation of pricing for services and goods: (1) customers often have inaccurate or limited reference prices for services, (2) price is a key signal of quality in services, and (3) monetary price is not the only price relevant to service customers. As we demonstrate, these three differences can have a profound impact on the strategies companies use to set and administer prices for services.

The chapter also discusses common pricing structures including **cost-based**, **competition-based**, and **demand-based pricing**. One of the most important aspects of demand-based pricing is perceived value, which must be understood by service providers so that they price in line with offerings and customer expectations. For that reason we also describe how customers define value and discuss pricing strategies in the context of value.

Service prices are different for consumers

What role does price play in consumer decisions about services? How important is price to potential buyers compared with other factors and service features? Service companies must understand how pricing works, but first they must understand how customers perceive prices and price changes. The three subsections that follow describe what we know about the ways that customers perceive services, and each is central to effective pricing.

Customer knowledge of service prices

To what extent do customers use price as a criterion in selecting services? How much do consumers know about the costs of services? Before you answer these questions, take the services pricing quiz in Figure 17.1. Were you able to fill in a price for each of the services listed? If you were able to answer the questions on the basis of memory, you have internal *reference prices* for the services. A reference price is *a price point in memory for a good or a service* and can consist of the price last paid, the price most frequently paid or the average of all prices customers have paid for similar offerings.[2]

To see how accurate your reference prices for services are, you can compare them with the actual price of these services from the providers in your town or city. If you are like many consumers, you feel quite uncertain about your knowledge of the prices of services, and the reference prices you hold in memory for services are not generally as accurate as those you hold for goods. There are many reasons for this difference.

Service variability limits knowledge

Because services are not created on a factory assembly line, service firms have great flexibility in the configurations of services they offer. Firms can conceivably offer an infinite variety of combinations and permutations, leading to complex and complicated pricing structures. The vignette on UK rail services is an example of this. How did you answer the questions about prices for a dental check-up? If you are like most consumers, you probably wanted more information before you offered a reference price. You probably wanted to know what type of check-up the dentist is providing. Does it include X-rays and other diagnostic tests? What types of tests? How long

What do the following services cost in your town or city?	
	Price?
Dental check-up	
A grocery home delivery	
Legal help with a divorce	
Laundering a dress or suit	
Rental of a DVD for one night	
One hour of housecleaning	
Room at an IBIS hotel	
Haircut	
Oil change on a car	

FIGURE 17.1 What do you know about the prices of services?

does it take? What is its purpose? If the check-up is undertaken simply as a regular six-monthly check-up, you may expect to pay less than if it is for addressing some problem that you are having with your teeth or to advise you on elements of cosmetic dentistry. The point we want to illustrate here is that a high degree of variability often exists across providers of services. Not every dentist defines a check-up the same way.

Providers are unwilling to estimate prices

Another reason customers lack accurate reference prices for services is that many providers are unable or unwilling to estimate price in advance. For example, car servicing and legal service providers are rarely willing – or even able – to estimate a price in advance. The fundamental reason is that they do not know themselves what the services will involve until they have fully examined the car or the client's situation or until the process of service delivery (such as the car service or a trial) unfolds. In a business-to-business context, companies will obtain bids or estimates for complex services such as consulting or construction, but this type of price estimation is typically not undertaken with end-consumers; therefore, they often buy without advance knowledge about the final price of the service.

Individual customer needs vary

Another factor that results in the inaccuracy of reference prices is that individual customer needs vary. Some hairstylists' service prices vary across customers on the basis of length of hair, type of haircut and whether a conditioning treatment and style are included. Therefore, if you were to ask a friend what a cut costs from a particular stylist, the chances are that your cut from the same stylist may be a different price. In a similar vein, a service as simple as a hotel room will have prices that vary greatly: by size of room, time of year, type of room availability and individual versus group rate. These two examples are for very simple services. Now consider a service purchase as idiosyncratic as cosmetic surgery from a dentist or help from a lawyer. In these and many other services, customer differences in need will play a strong role in the price of the service.

Collection of price information is overwhelming in services

Still another reason customers lack accurate reference prices for services is that customers feel overwhelmed with the information they need to gather. With most goods, retail stores display the products by category to allow customers to compare and contrast the prices of different brands and sizes. Rarely is there a similar display of services in a single outlet. If customers want to compare prices (such as for dry-cleaning), they must drive to or call individual outlets.

The fact that consumers often possess inaccurate reference prices for services has several important managerial implications. Promotional pricing (as in couponing or special pricing) may be less meaningful for services, for which price anchors typically do not exist. Perhaps that is why price is not featured in service advertising as much as it is featured in advertising for goods. Promotional pricing may also create problems if the promotional price (such as a 30 euro cut and blow dry special from a salon) is the only one customers see in advertising, for it could become the customer's anchor price, making the regular price of 50 euros for a future purchase seem high by comparison.

The absence of accurate reference prices also suggests that advertising actual prices for services the customer is not used to purchasing may reduce uncertainty and overcome a customer's inflated price expectations for some services. For example, a marketing research firm's advertisements citing the price for a simple study (such as 7500 euros) would be informative to business customers who are not familiar with the costs of research studies and therefore would be guessing at the cost. By featuring price in advertising, the company overcomes the fear of high cost by giving readers a price anchor.

Prices are not visible

One requirement for the existence of customer reference prices is *price visibility* – the price cannot be hidden or implicit. In many services, particularly financial services, most customers know about only the rate of return and not the costs they pay in the form of fund management and insurance fees. American Express Financial Services discovered through research how little customers know about prices of the company's services.[3] After being told by the independent agents who sell its services to customers that its services were priced too high, the company did research to find out how much customers knew about what they pay for financial services and how much customers factor price into their value assessments.

The study surprised the company by revealing that customers knew even less than expected: Not only did they not understand *what* they were paying for many of their services, very few consumers understood *how* they pay for financial services in general. Only for financial products in which price was visible – such as with securities and term life insurance – were customers aware of fees. When price was invisible, such as in whole-life insurance and annuities, customers did not know how they were charged and what they paid. Further, when customers were asked to indicate how important 10 factors (including price) were, price ranked seventh. Finally, the company found that shopping behaviour in the category of financial services was extremely limited. Between 50 and 60 per cent of customers bought financial products from the very first person they talked to.

For all the reasons above, many customers do not see the price at all until *after* they receive certain services. Of course in situations of urgency, such as in accident or illness, customers must make the decision to purchase without respect to cost. And if cost is not known to the customer before purchase, it cannot be used as a key criterion for purchase, as it often is for goods. Price is likely to be an important criterion in *repurchase*, however. Furthermore, monetary price in repurchase may be an even more important criterion than in initial purchase.

The role of non-monetary costs

Economists have long recognized that monetary price is not the only sacrifice consumers make to obtain products and services. Demand, therefore, is not just a function of monetary price but is influenced by other costs as well. **Non-monetary costs** represent other sources of sacrifice perceived by consumers when buying and using a service. Time costs, search costs and psychological costs often enter into the evaluation of whether to buy or rebuy a service, and may at times be more important concerns than monetary price. Customers will trade money for these other costs.

- *Time costs.* Most services require direct participation of the consumer and thus consume real time: time waiting as well as time when the customer interacts with the service provider. Consider the investment you make to exercise, see a doctor or get through the crowds to watch a concert or football game. Not only are you paying money to receive these services, but you are also expending time. Time becomes a sacrifice made to receive service in multiple ways. First, because service providers cannot completely control the number of customers or the length of time it will take for each customer to be served, customers are likely to expend time waiting to receive the service. Waiting time for a service is frequently longer and less predictable than waiting time to buy goods. Second, customers often have to wait for an available appointment from a service provider. Virtually everyone has expended waiting time to receive services.

- *Search costs.* Search costs – the effort invested to identify and select among services you desire – are often higher for services than for physical goods. Prices for services are rarely displayed on shelves of service establishments for customers to examine as they shop, so these prices are often known only when a customer has decided to experience the service. As an example, how well did you estimate the costs of an hour of housecleaning in the price quiz? As a student, it is unlikely that you regularly purchase housecleaning, and you probably have not seen the price of an hour of cleaning displayed in any retail store. Another factor that increases search costs is that each service establishment typically offers only one 'brand' of a service (with the exception of brokers in insurance or financial services), so a customer must initiate contact with several different companies to get information across sellers. Price comparisons for some services (travel and hotels, for example) have been facilitated through the Internet.

- *Convenience costs.* There are also convenience (or, perhaps more accurately, inconvenience) costs of services. If customers have to travel to a service, they incur a cost, and the cost becomes greater when travel is difficult, as it is for elderly persons. Further, if service hours do not coincide with customers' available time, they must arrange their schedules to correspond to the company's schedule. And if consumers have to expend effort and time to prepare to receive a service (such as removing furniture before getting a carpet laid), they make additional sacrifices.

- *Psychological costs.* Often the most painful non-monetary costs are the psychological costs incurred in receiving some services. Fear of not understanding (insurance), fear of rejection (bank loans), fear of outcomes (medical treatment or surgery) – all these fears constitute psychological costs that customers experience as sacrifices when purchasing and using services. New services, even those that create positive change, bring about psychological costs that consumers factor into the purchase of services. When banks first introduced ATMs, customer resistance was significant, particularly to the idea of putting money into a machine: customers felt uncomfortable with the idea of letting go of their cheque and bank cards. And most customers also rejected voicemail when it was first developed.

Non-monetary cost priorities

Everybody will have different cost priorities. Some people will wait longer or travel further to get their car serviced, to save money. Others will be more concerned about convenience and will seek the nearest car service centre, no matter what the price. Quality may be more important to others and they will travel further for a car service centre that they perceive as having better quality mechanics.

Reducing non-monetary costs

The managerial implications of these other sources of sacrifice are compelling. First, a firm may be able to increase monetary price by reducing time and other costs. For example, a services marketer can reduce the perceptions of time and convenience costs when use of the service is embedded in other activities (such as when a convenience store provides utility bill payment services, sells stamps and serves coffee along with selling products). Second, customers may be willing to pay to avoid the other costs. Many customers willingly pay extra to have items delivered to their home – including restaurant meals – rather than transporting the services and products themselves. Some customers also pay a premium for fast check-in and checkout when hiring cars, for reduced waiting time in a professional's office (as in so-called executive appointments where, for a premium price, a busy executive comes early in the morning and does not have to wait) and to avoid doing the work themselves (such as paying one and one-half times the price per litre to avoid having to put fuel in a rental car before returning it). If time or other costs are pivotal for a given service, the company's advertising can emphasize these savings rather than monetary savings.

Many other services save time, thus actually allowing the customer to 'buy' time. Household cleaning services, lawn care, babysitting, online shopping, home banking, home delivery of groceries, decorating and carpet cleaning – all these services represent net gains in the discretionary time of consumers and can be marketed that way. Services that allow the customer to buy time are likely to have monetary value for busy consumers.

Price as an indicator of service quality

One of the intriguing aspects of pricing is that buyers are likely to use price as an indicator of both service costs and service quality – price is at once an attraction variable and a repellent.[4] Customers' use of price as an indicator of quality depends on several factors, one of which is the other information available to them. When service cues to quality are readily accessible, when brand names provide evidence of a company's reputation or when the level of advertising communicates the company's belief in the brand, customers may prefer to use those cues instead of price. In other situations, however, such as when quality is hard to detect or when quality or price varies a great deal within a class of services, consumers may believe that price is the best indicator of quality. Many of these conditions typify situations that face consumers when purchasing services.[5] Another factor that increases the dependence on price as a quality indicator is the risk associated with the service purchase. In high-risk situations, many of which involve credence services such as restaurants or management consulting, the customer will look to price as a surrogate for quality.

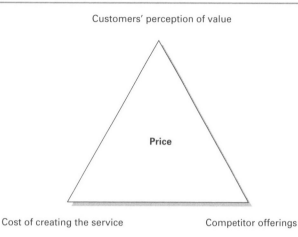

Customers' perception of value

Price

Cost of creating the service   Competitor offerings

A summary of the basics of pricing is provided here. For more details, consider looking at *Marketing Management* by Philip Kotler, the text from which we excerpted these fundamental points about pricing.

1. The firm must consider many factors in setting its pricing policy: selecting the pricing objective, determining demand, estimating costs, analysing competitors' prices and offers, selecting a pricing method, and selecting the final price.

2. Companies do not always seek to maximize profits through pricing. Other objectives they may have include survival, maximizing current revenue, maximizing sales growth, maximizing market skimming and product/quality leadership.

3. Marketers need to understand how responsive demand would be to a change in price. To evaluate this important criterion of price sensitivity, marketers can calculate the price elasticity of demand, which is expressed as

$$\text{ELASTICITY} = \frac{\text{Percentage change in quantity purchased}}{\text{Percentage change in price}}$$

4. Various types of costs must be considered in setting prices, including direct and indirect costs, fixed and variable costs, indirect traceable costs and allocated costs. If a product or service is to be profitable for a company, price must cover all costs and include a mark-up as well.

5. Competitors' prices will affect the desirability of a company's offerings and must be considered in establishing prices.

6. A variety of pricing methods exist including mark-up, target return, perceived-value, going-rate, sealed-bid and psychological.

7. After setting a price structure, companies adapt prices using geographic pricing, price discounts and allowances, promotional pricing, discriminatory pricing and product-mix pricing.

FIGURE 17.2 The pricing triangle

Because customers depend on price as a cue to quality and because price sets expectations of quality, service prices must be determined carefully. In addition to being chosen to cover costs or match competitors, prices must be selected to convey the appropriate quality signal. Pricing too low can lead to inaccurate inferences about the quality of the service. Pricing too high can set expectations that may be difficult to match in service delivery.

Strategic decisions in pricing[6]

Many of the strategic aspects of pricing of services are the same as pricing of goods. When a service provider wants to establish a market-oriented pricing policy, prices should be based on the three Cs of the **pricing triangle**. This is shown in Figure 17.2. The perceived value placed on the service by the customers will determine how much they will be willing to pay for a service. Competitor offerings and their price including the cost of customers undertaking the service themselves (such as the time and effort of valeting your own car) will impact on how the service can be positioned and priced. A service provider also needs to take account of the costs involved in creating and delivering a service; profitability can only be achieved if these costs are exceeded.

Approaches to pricing services

Building on these basic principles of pricing, we want to emphasize in this chapter the way that services prices and pricing differ from both the customer's and the company's perspective. We discuss these differences in the context of the three pricing structures typically used to set prices: (1) cost-based, (2) competition-based, and (3) demand-based pricing. These categories, as shown in Figure 17.3, are the same bases on which goods prices are set, but adaptations must be made in services. The figure shows the three structures interrelating, because companies need to consider each of the three to some extent in setting prices. In the following

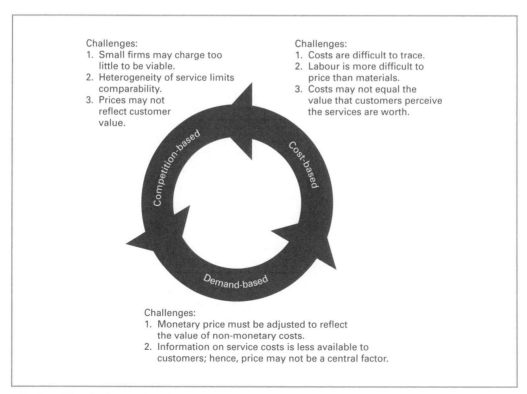

FIGURE 17.3 Three basic marketing price structures and challenges associated with their use for services

sections we describe in general each basis for pricing and discuss challenges that occur when the approach is used in services pricing. Figure 17.3 summarizes those challenges.

Cost-based pricing

In cost-based pricing, a company determines expenses from raw materials and labour, adds amounts or percentages for overhead and profit, and thereby arrives at the price. This method is widely used by industries such as utilities, contracting, wholesaling and advertising. The basic formula for cost-based pricing is

$$\text{Price} = \text{Direct costs} + \text{Overhead costs} + \text{Profit margin}$$

Direct costs involve materials and labour that are associated with delivering the service, overhead costs are a share of fixed costs, and the profit margin is a percentage of full costs (direct + overhead).

Special challenges in cost-based pricing for services

One of the major difficulties in cost-based pricing involves defining the units in which a service is purchased. Thus the price per unit – a well-understood concept in pricing of manufactured goods – is a vague entity. For this reason many services are sold in terms of input units rather than units of measured output. For example, most professional services (such as consulting, engineering, architecture, psychotherapy and tutoring) are sold by the hour.

What is unique about services when using cost-based approaches to pricing? First, costs are difficult to trace or calculate in services businesses, particularly where multiple services are provided by the firm.[7] Consider how difficult it must be for a bank to allocate teller time accurately across its current, savings and money market accounts in order to decide what to charge for the services. Second, a major component of cost is employee time rather than materials, and the value of people's time, particularly non-professional time, is not easy to calculate or estimate.

An added difficulty is that actual service costs may under-represent the value of the service to the customer. A local tailor charges 10 euros for taking in a seam on a 350-euro ladies' suit jacket and an equal 10 euros for taking in a seam on a pair of 30-euro trousers. The tailor's rationale is that both jobs require the same amount of time. What she neglects to see is that the customer would pay a higher price – and might even be happier about the alterations – for the expensive suit jacket, and that 10 euros is too high a price for the trousers.

Examples of cost-based pricing strategies used in services

Cost-plus pricing is a commonly used approach in which component costs are calculated and a mark-up added. In product pricing, this approach is quite simple; in service industries, however, it is complicated because the tracking and identification of costs are difficult. The approach is typically used in industries in which cost must be estimated in advance, such as construction, engineering and advertising. In construction or engineering, bids are solicited by clients on the basis of the description of the service desired. Using their knowledge of the costs of the components of the service (including the raw materials such as stone and timber), labour (including both professional and unskilled) and margin, the company estimates and presents to the client a price for the finished service. A contingency amount – to cover the possibility that costs may be higher than estimated – is also stated because in large projects specifications can change as the service is provided.

Fee for service is the pricing strategy used by professionals; it represents the cost of the time involved in providing the service. Consultants, psychologists, accountants and lawyers, among other professionals, charge for their services on an hourly basis. Virtually all psychologists and lawyers have a set hourly rate they charge to their clients, and most structure their time in increments of an hour.

One of the most difficult aspects of this approach is that record-keeping is tedious for professionals. Lawyers and accountants must keep track of the time they spend for a given client, often down to 10-minute increments. For this reason the method has been criticized because it does not promote efficiency and sometimes ignores the expertise of the lawyers (those who are very experienced can accomplish much more than novices in a given time period, yet billings do not always reflect this). Clients often fear padding of their legal bills, and they frequently audit them. Despite these concerns, the hourly bill dominates the industry, with the majority of revenues billed this way.[8]

Competition-based pricing

The competition-based pricing approach focuses on the prices charged by other firms in the same industry or market. Competition-based pricing does not always imply charging the identical rate others charge but rather using others' prices as an anchor for the firm's price. This approach is used predominantly in two situations: (1) when services are standard across providers, such as in the dry-cleaning industry, and (2) in oligopolies with a few large service providers, such as in the airline or rental car industry. Difficulties involved in provision of services sometimes make competition-based pricing less simple than it is in goods industries.

Special challenges in competition-based pricing for services

Small firms may charge too little and not make margins high enough to remain in business. Many family-owned service establishments – dry-cleaning, retail and tax accounting, among others – cannot deliver services at the low prices charged by chain operations.

Further, the heterogeneity of services across and within providers makes this approach complicated. Bank services illustrate the wide disparity in service prices. Customers buying current accounts, money orders or foreign currency, to name a few services, find that prices are rarely similar across providers. For example, there are likely to be major differences in overdraft charges between banks, and the commission and exchange rates quoted for foreign currency can also differ significantly. Banks claim that they set fees high enough to cover the costs of these services. The wide disparity in prices probably reflects banks' difficulty in determining prices as well as their belief that financial customers do not shop around nor discern the differences (if any) among offerings from different providers. A banking expert makes the point that 'It's not like buying a litre of milk . . . . Prices aren't standardized'.[9] Only in very standardized services (such as dry-cleaning) are prices likely to be remembered and compared.

Examples of competition-based pricing in services industries

Price signalling occurs in markets with a high concentration of sellers. In this type of market, any price offered by one company will be matched by competitors to avoid giving a low-cost seller a distinct advantage. The airline industry exemplifies price signalling in services. When any competitor drops the price of routes, others match the lowered price almost immediately.

Going-rate pricing involves charging the most prevalent price in the market.

> ## Service spotlight
>
> Rental car pricing is an illustration of this technique (and an illustration of price signalling, because the rental car market is dominated by a small number of large companies). For years, the prices set by one company (Hertz) have been followed by the other companies. When Hertz instituted a new pricing plan that involved 'no mileage charges, ever', other rental car companies imitated the policy. They then had to raise other factors such as base rates, size and type of car, daily or weekly rates and drop-off charges to continue to make profits. Prices in different geographic markets, even cities, depend on the going rate in that location, and customers often pay different rates in contiguous cities in the same country.

Demand-based pricing

The two approaches to pricing just described are based on the company and its competitors rather than on customers. Neither approach takes into consideration that customers may lack reference prices, may be sensitive to non-monetary prices and may judge quality on the basis of price. All these factors can be accounted for in a company's pricing decisions. The third major approach to pricing, *demand-based pricing,* involves setting prices consistent with customer perceptions of value: prices are based on what customers will pay for the services provided.

Special challenges in demand-based pricing for services

One of the major ways that pricing of services differs from pricing of goods in demand-based pricing is that non-monetary costs and benefits must be factored into the calculation of perceived value to the customer. When services require time, inconvenience and psychological and search costs, the monetary price must be adjusted to compensate. And when services save time, inconvenience and psychological and search costs, the customer is willing to pay a higher monetary price. The challenge is to determine the value to customers of each of the non-monetary aspects involved.

Another way services and goods differ with respect to this form of pricing is that information on service costs may be less available to customers, making monetary price not as salient a factor in initial service selection as it is in goods purchasing.

Four meanings of perceived value

One of the most appropriate ways that companies price their services is basing the price on the **perceived value** of the service to customers. Among the questions a services marketer needs to ask are the following: what do consumers mean by *value*? How can we quantify perceived monetary value so that we can set appropriate prices for our services? Is the meaning of value similar across consumers and services? How can value perceptions be influenced? To understand demand-based pricing approaches, we must fully understand what value means to customers.

This is not a simple task. When consumers discuss value, they use the term in many different ways and talk about myriad attributes or components. What constitutes value, even in a single service category, appears to be highly personal and idiosyncratic. Customers define value in four ways: (1) value is low price; (2) value is whatever I want in a product or service; (3) value is the quality I get for the price I pay; and (4) value is what I get for what I give (Figure 17.4).[10] Let us take a look at each of these definitions more carefully.

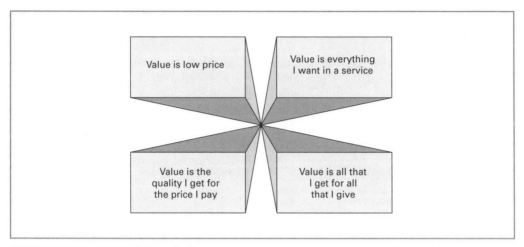

FIGURE 17.4 Four customer definitions of value

Source: N.C. Mohn, 'Pricing research for decision making', *Marketing Research: A Magazine of Management and Applications* 7, no. 1 (Winter 1995), pp. 10–19. Reprinted by permission of the American Marketing Association

Value is low price

Some consumers equate value with low price, indicating that what they have to give up in terms of money is most salient in their perceptions of value, as typified in these representative comments from customers:

- *For dry cleaning*: 'Value means the lowest price.'
- *For carpet steam-cleaning*: 'Value is price – which one is on sale.'
- *For a fast-food restaurant*: 'When I can use coupons, I feel that the service is a value.'
- *For airline travel*: 'Value is when airline tickets are discounted.'[11]

Value is whatever I want in a product or service

Rather than focusing on the money given up, some consumers emphasize the benefits they receive from a service or product as the most important component of value. In this value definition, price is far less important than the quality or features that match what the consumer wants. In the telecommunications industry, for example, business customers strongly value the reliability of the systems and are willing to pay for the safety and confidentiality of the connections. Service customers describe this definition of value as follows:

- *For an MBA degree*: 'Value is the very best education I can get.'
- *For dental services*: 'Value is high quality.'
- *For a social club*: 'Value is what makes me look good to my friends and family.'
- *For a rock or country music concert*: 'Value is the best performance.'

Value is the quality I get for the price I pay

Other consumers see value as a trade-off between the money they give up and the quality they receive.

- *For a hotel for vacation*: 'Value is price first and quality second.'
- *For a hotel for business travel*: 'Value is the lowest price for a quality brand.'

■ *For a computer services contract*: 'Value is the same as quality. No – value is affordable quality.'

Value is what I get for what I give

Finally, some consumers consider all the benefits they receive as well as all sacrifice components (money, time, effort) when describing value.

■ *For a housekeeping service*: 'Value is how many rooms I can get cleaned for what the price is.'

■ *For a hairstylist*: 'Value is what I pay in cost and time for the look I get.'

■ *For executive education*: 'Value is getting a good educational experience in the shortest time possible.'

The four consumer expressions of value can be captured in one overall definition consistent with the concept of utility in economics: *perceived value is the consumer's overall assessment of the utility of a service based on perceptions of what is received and what is given*. Although what is received varies across consumers (some may want volume, others high quality, still others convenience), as does what is given (some are concerned only with money expended, others with time and effort), value represents a trade-off of the give and get components. Customers will make a purchase decision on the basis of perceived value, not solely to minimize the price paid. These definitions are the first step in identifying the elements that must be quantified in setting prices for services.

Incorporating perceived value into service pricing

The buyer's perception of total value prompts the willingness to pay a particular price for a service. To translate the customer's value perceptions into an appropriate price for a specific service offering, the marketer must answer a number of questions. What benefits does the service provide? How important is each of these benefits? How much is it worth to the customer to receive a particular benefit from a service? At what price will the service be economically acceptable to potential buyers? In what context is the customer purchasing the service?

The most important thing a company must do – and often a difficult thing – is to estimate the value to customers of the company's services. Value may be perceived differently by consumers because of idiosyncratic tastes, knowledge about the service, buying power and ability to pay. In this type of pricing, what the consumers value – not what they pay – forms the basis for pricing. Therefore its effectiveness rests solely on accurately determining what the market perceives the service to be worth.

When the services are for the end-consumer, most often service providers will decide that they cannot afford to give each individual exactly the bundle of attributes he or she values. They will, however, attempt to find one or more bundles that address segments of the market. On the other hand, when services are sold to businesses (or to end-customers in the case of high-end services), the company can understand and deliver different bundles to each customer.

One of the most complex and difficult tasks of services marketers is setting prices internationally. If services marketers price on the basis of perceived value and if perceived value and willingness to pay differ across countries (which they often do), then service firms may provide essentially the same service but charge different prices in different countries. Here, as in pricing domestically, the challenge is to determine the perceived value not just to different customers but to customers in different parts of the world.

Pricing strategies that link to perceived value

In this section we describe the approaches to services pricing that are particularly suited to each of the four value definitions.

Pricing strategies when the customer means 'value is low price'

When monetary price is the most important determinant of value to a customer, the company focuses mainly on price. This focus does not mean that the quality level and intrinsic attributes are always irrelevant, just that monetary price dominates in importance. To establish a service price in this definition of value, the marketer must understand to what extent customers know the objective prices of services in this category, how they interpret various prices and how much is too much of a perceived sacrifice. These factors are best understood when the service provider also knows the relative monetary value of the purchase, the frequency of past price changes and the range of acceptable prices for the service. Some of the specific pricing approaches appropriate when customers define value as low price include **discounting**, **odd pricing**, **synchro-pricing** and **penetration pricing** (Figure 17.5).

Discounting

Service providers offer discounts or price cuts to communicate to price-sensitive buyers that they are receiving value. Airlines such as British Airways, easyJet and Ryanair advertise short periods of two to three months when ticket prices within Europe will be discounted. Ryanair regularly advertises free seats where the passenger only pays taxes and administration charges for a flight. These attract customers to try their flights and help fill planes during off-peak periods. It also brings traffic to the company's website which may result in flights other than the free ones being booked.

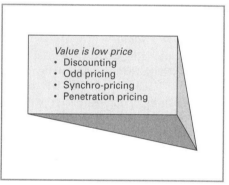

FIGURE 17.5 Pricing strategies when the customer defines value as low price

Odd pricing

Odd pricing is the practice of pricing services just below the exact dollar amount to make buyers perceive that they are getting a lower price. Dry-cleaners charge 2.98 euros for a shirt rather than 3.00 euros, health clubs have membership fees priced at 33.90 euros per month rather than 34 euros, and haircuts are 19.50 euros rather than 20.00 euros. Odd prices suggest discounting and bargains and are appealing to customers for whom value means low price.

Synchro-pricing

Synchro-pricing is the use of price to manage demand for a service by capitalizing on customer sensitivity to prices. Certain services, such as tax preparation, passenger transportation, long-distance telephone, hotels and theatres, have demand that fluctuates over time as well as constrained supply at peak times. For companies in these and other industries, setting a price that provides a profit over time can be difficult. Pricing can, however, play a role in smoothing demand and synchronizing demand and supply. Time, place, quantity and incentive differentials have all been used effectively by service firms, as discussed in Chapter 14.

Place differentials are used for services in which customers have a sensitivity to location. The front row at concerts, centre court in tennis or basketball, beach-side rooms in hotels – all these represent place differentials that are meaningful to customers and that therefore command higher prices.

Time differentials involve price variations that depend on when the service is consumed. Telephone service after 11 p.m., airline tickets that include a Saturday night stay, and health spas in the off-season are time differentials that reflect slow periods of service. By offering lower prices for underused time periods, a service company can smooth demand and also gain incremental revenue.

Quantity differentials are usually price decreases given for volume purchasing. This pricing structure allows a service company to predict future demand for its services. Customers who buy a booklet of coupons for a tanning salon or facial, a quantity of tokens for toll roads or bridges, or packages of advertising spots on radio or television are all responding to price incentives achieved by committing to future services. Corporate discounts for airlines, hotels and rental cars exemplify quantity discounts in the business context; by offering lower prices, the service provider locks in future business.

Differentials as incentives are lower prices for new or existing clients in the hope of encouraging them to be regular users or more frequent users. Some professionals – lawyers, dentists and, even, some chiropractors – offer free consultations at the front end, usually to overcome fear and uncertainty about high service prices. Other companies stimulate use by offering regular customers discounts or premiums during slow periods.

Penetration pricing

Penetration pricing is a strategy in which new services are introduced at low prices to stimulate trial and widespread use. The strategy is appropriate when (1) sales volume of the service is very sensitive to price, even in the early stages of introduction; (2) it is possible to achieve economies in unit costs by operating at large volumes; (3) a service faces threats of strong potential competition very soon after introduction; and (4) there is no class of buyers willing to pay a higher price to obtain the service.[12] Penetration pricing can lead to problems when companies then select a 'regular' increased price. Care must be taken not to penetrate with so low a price that customers feel the regular price is outside the range of acceptable prices.

Pricing strategies when the customer means 'value is everything I want in a service'

When the customer is concerned principally with the 'get' components of a service, monetary price is not of primary concern. The more desirable intrinsic attributes a given service possesses, the more highly valued the service is likely to be and the higher the price the marketer can set. Figure 17.6 shows appropriate pricing strategies.

Prestige pricing

Prestige pricing is a special form of demand-based pricing by service marketers who offer high-quality or status services. For certain services – restaurants, health clubs, airlines and hotels – a higher price is charged for the luxury end of the business. Some customers of service companies who use this approach may actually value the high price

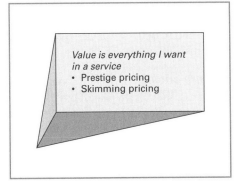

Value is everything I want in a service
- Prestige pricing
- Skimming pricing

FIGURE 17.6 Pricing strategies when the customer defines value as everything wanted in a service

because it represents prestige or a quality image. Others prefer purchasing at the high end because they are given preference in seating or accommodation and are entitled to other special benefits. In prestige pricing, demand may actually increase as price increases because the costlier service has more value in reflecting quality or prestige.

Skimming pricing

Skimming pricing, a strategy in which new services are introduced at high prices with large promotional expenditures, is an effective approach when services are major improvements over past services. In this situation customers are more concerned about obtaining the service than about the cost of the service, allowing service providers to skim the customers most willing to pay the highest prices.

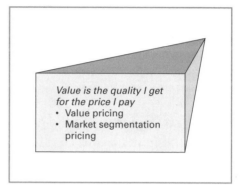

Value is the quality I get for the price I pay
- Value pricing
- Market segmentation pricing

FIGURE 17.7 Pricing strategies when the customer defines value as quality for the price paid

Pricing strategies when the customer means 'value is the quality I get for the price I pay'

Some customers primarily consider both quality and monetary price. The task of the marketer is to understand what *quality* means to the customer (or segments of customers) and then to match quality level with price level. Specific strategies are shown in Figure 17.7.

Value pricing

The widely used term **value pricing** has come to mean 'giving more for less'. In current usage it involves assembling a bundle of services that are desirable to a wide group of customers and then pricing them lower than they would cost alone.

Service spotlight

McDonald's in the UK offers value pricing with their pound saver menu, which includes a double cheeseburger at €1.78. Burger King, KFC and other fast-food restaurants have similar product ranges. easyJet also offers value pricing in its airline service: a low cost for a bundle of desirable service attributes such as frequent departures, friendly employees and on-time arrival. The airline offers consistently low fares with bare-bones service.

Market segmentation pricing

With market segmentation pricing, a service marketer charges different prices to groups of customers for what are perceived to be different quality levels of service, even though there may not be corresponding differences in the costs of providing the service to each of these groups. This form of pricing is based on the premise that segments show different price elasticities of demand and desire different quality levels.

Services marketers often price by *client category*, based on the recognition that some groups find it difficult to pay a recommended price. Health clubs will typically offer student memberships, recognizing that this segment of customers has limited ability to pay full price. In addition to the lower price, student memberships may also carry with them reduced hours of use, particularly in peak times. The same line of reasoning leads to memberships for retired people who are less able to pay full price but are willing to patronize the clubs during daytime hours when most full-price members are working.

Companies also use market segmentation by *service version*, recognizing that not all segments want the basic level of service at the lowest price. When they can identify a bundle of attributes that are desirable enough for another segment of customers, they can charge a higher price for that bundle. Companies can configure service bundles that reflect price and service points appealing to different groups in the market. Hotels, for example, offer standard rooms at a basic rate but then combine amenities and tangibles related to the room to attract customers willing to pay more for the executive floor, spa baths, additional beds and sitting areas.

Pricing strategies when the customer means 'value is all that I get for all that I give'

Some customers define value as including not just the benefits they receive but also the time, money, and effort they put into a service. Figure 17.8 illustrates the pricing strategies described in this definition of value.

Price framing

Because many customers do not possess accurate reference prices for services, services marketers are more likely than product marketers to organize price information (**price framing**) for customers so they know how to view it. Customers naturally look for price anchors as well as familiar services against which to judge focal services.

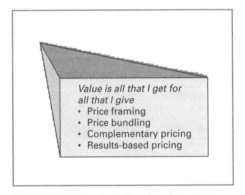

FIGURE 17.8 Pricing strategies when the customer defines value as all that is received for all that is given

---

Service spotlight

Sky satellite television in the UK has various packages putting together channels into a 'kids mix', a 'knowledge mix', a 'music mix', a 'variety mix', a 'style and culture mix' and a 'news and events mix'. Viewers are charged around 22 euros for two mixes, 27 euros for four mixes and 32 euros for six mixes. They are then charged an additional fee if they want movie or sports packages. By organizing price information in this way, consumers find it easier to select the optimum package for their household.[13]

Price bundling

Some services are consumed more effectively in conjunction with other services; other services accompany the products they support (such as extended service warranties, training and expedited delivery). When customers find value in a package of services that are interrelated, **price bundling** is an appropriate strategy. Bundling, which means pricing and selling services as a group rather than individually, has benefits to both customers and service companies. Customers find that bundling simplifies their purchase and payment, and companies find that the approach stimulates demand for the firm's service line, thereby achieving cost economies for the operations as a whole while increasing net contributions.[13] Bundling also allows the customer to pay less than when purchasing each of the services individually, which contributes to perceptions of value.

The effectiveness of price bundling depends on how well the service firm understands the bundles of value that customers or segments perceive, and on the complementarity of demand for these services. Effectiveness also depends on the right choice of services from the firm's point of view. Because the firm's objective is to increase overall sales, the services selected for bundling should be those with a relatively small sales volume without the bundling to minimize revenue loss from discounting a service that already has a high sales volume.

Approaches to bundling include mixed bundling, mixed-leader bundling and mixed-joint bundling.[14] In *mixed bundling*, the customer can purchase the services individually or as a package, but a price incentive is offered for purchasing the package. As an example, a health club customer may be able to contract for aerobics classes at 10 euros per month, weight machines at 15 euros and the swimming pool at 15 euros – or the group of three services for 27 euros (a price incentive of 13 euros per month).[15] In *mixed-leader bundling*, the price of one service is discounted if the first service is purchased at full price. For example, in DVD rental stores if customers hire one premium DVD at full price, they can acquire a second premium DVD at a reduced rate. The objective is to reduce the price of the higher-volume service to generate an increase in its volume that 'pulls' an increase in demand for a lower-volume but higher-contribution margin service. In *mixed-joint bundling*, a single price is formed for the combined set of services to increase demand for both services by packaging them together.

Complementary pricing

Services that are highly interrelated can be leveraged by using **complementary pricing**. This pricing includes three related strategies – captive pricing, two-part pricing and loss leadership.[16] In *captive pricing* the firm offers a base service or product and then provides the supplies or peripheral services needed to continue using the service. In this situation the company could offload some part of the price for the basic service to the peripherals. For example, photocopier rental services often drop the price for installation to a very low level, then compensate by charging enough for the ink, paper and maintenance contracts to make up for the loss in revenue. With service firms, this strategy is often called *two-part pricing* because the service price is broken into a fixed fee plus variable usage fees (also found in telephone services and health clubs). *Loss leadership* is the term typically used in retail stores when providers place a familiar service on special largely to draw the customer to the store and then reveal other levels of service available at higher prices.

Results-based pricing

In service industries in which outcome is very important but uncertainty is high, the most relevant aspect of value is the *result* of the service. In personal injury lawsuits, for example, clients value the settlement they receive at the conclusion of the service. From tax accountants, clients value cost savings. From universities and colleges, students most value getting a job upon graduation. In these and other situations, an appropriate value-based pricing strategy is to price on the basis of results or outcome of the service.

The most commonly known form of **results-based pricing** is a practice called *contingency pricing* used by lawyers. Contingency pricing is the major way that personal injury and certain consumer cases are billed. In this approach, lawyers do not receive fees or payment until the case is settled, when they are paid a percentage of the money that the client receives. Therefore, only an outcome in the client's favour is compensated. From the client's point of view, the pricing makes sense in part because most clients in these cases are unfamiliar with and possibly intimidated by law firms. Their biggest fears are high fees for a case that may take years to settle. By using contingency pricing, clients are ensured that they pay no fees until they receive a settlement.

In these and other instances of contingency pricing, the economic value of the service is hard to determine before the service, and providers develop a price that allows them to share the risks and rewards of delivering value to the buyer. Partial contingency pricing, now being used in commercial law cases, is a version in which the client pays a lower fee than usual but offers a bonus if the settlement exceeds a certain level.

Sealed bid contingency pricing

Companies wishing to gain the most value from their services purchases are increasingly turning to a form of results-based pricing that involves sealed bids guaranteeing results. Such **sealed bid contingency pricing** methods are frequently used by local government, hospitals, universities and large corporates when choosing suppliers for contracts involving catering, cleaning, energy supplies, security, building maintenance, construction and telephone services.

Money-back guarantees

Hotel groups such as Ibis and Travelodge offer **money-back guarantees** if customers are not 100 per cent satisfied with their stay in a hotel. This reassures potential guests that the room rates are worth paying because the quality of service is guaranteed.

Commission

Many services providers – including estate agents and advertising agencies – earn their fees through commissions based on a percentage of the selling price. In these and other industries, **commission** is paid by the supplier rather than the buyer. Advertising agencies generally obtain their revenues from the 15 per cent commission paid by the print and broadcast media (newspaper, radio, television, magazines) for the amount of advertising that they place with the media, rather than being paid by their clients. Estate agents in the UK are paid a percentage of the selling price of a house.

The commission approach to services pricing is compelling in that agents are compensated most when they find the highest rates and fares. It would seem that agents have an underlying motivation to avoid the lowest fares and rates for their clients.

Summary

This chapter began with three key differences between customer evaluation of pricing for services and goods: (1) customers often have inaccurate or limited reference prices for services, (2) price is a key signal to quality in services, and (3) monetary price is not the only relevant price to service customers. These three differences can have a profound impact on the strategies that companies use to set and administer prices for services. The chapter next discussed common pricing structures, including cost-based, competition-based and demand-based pricing. Central to the discussion were the specific challenges in each of these structures and the services pricing techniques that have emerged in practice.

Finally, the chapter defined customer perceptions of value and suggested appropriate pricing strategies that match each customer definition. Figure 17.9 summarizes these definitions and strategies. The four value definitions include (1) value is low price, (2) value is whatever I want

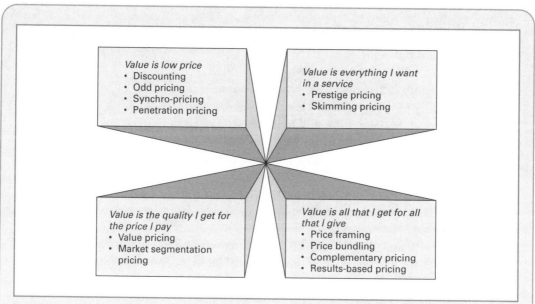

FIGURE 17.9 Summary of service pricing strategies for four customer definitions of value

in a product or service, (3) value is the quality I get for the price I pay, and (4) value is all that I get for all that I give.

Key concepts

Further reading

Avlonitis, G.J. and Indounas, K.A. (2005) 'Pricing objectives and pricing methods in the services sector', *Journal of Services Marketing*, 19(1), 47–57.

Bolton, L.E., Warlop, L. and Alba, J.W. (2003) 'Consumer perceptions of price (un)fairness', *Journal of Consumer Research*, 29(4), 474–91.

Docters, R., Reopel, M., Sun, J.-M. and Tanny, S. (2004) 'Capturing the unique value of services: why pricing services is different', *Journal of Business Strategy*, 25(2), 23–28.

Heinonen, K. (2004) 'Reconceptualising customer perceived value: the value of time and place', *Managing Service Quality*, 14(3), 205–15.

Homburg, C., Hoyer, W.D. and Koschate, N. (2005) 'Customers' reactions to price increases: do customer satisfaction and perceived motive fairness matter?', *Journal of the Academy of Marketing Science*, 33(1), 36–49.

Lin, C.-H., Sher, P.J. and Shih, H.-Y. (2005) 'Past progress and future directions in conceptualising customer perceived value', *International Journal of Service Industry Management*, 16(4), 318–36.

Xia, L., Monroe, K.B. and Cox, J.L. (2004) 'The price is unfair! A conceptual framework of price fairness perceptions', *Journal of Marketing*, 68, 1–15.

Discussion questions

1 Which approach to pricing (cost-based, competition-based or demand-based) is the most fair to customers? Why?

2 Is it possible to use all three approaches simultaneously when pricing services? If you answer yes, describe a service that is priced this way.

3 For what consumer services do you have reference prices? What makes these services different from others for which you lack reference prices?

4 Name three services you purchase in which price is a signal to quality. Do you believe that there are true differences across services that are priced high and those that are priced low? Why or why not?

5 Describe the non-monetary costs involved in the following services: getting a car loan, belonging to a health club, attending an executive education class, and getting dental braces.

6 Consider the specific pricing strategies for each of the four customer value definitions. Which of these strategies could be adapted and used with another value definition?

Exercises

1 List five services for which you have no reference price. Now put yourself in the role of the service providers for two of those services and develop pricing strategies. Be sure

to include in your description which of the value definitions you believe customers will possess and what types of strategies would be appropriate given those definitions.

2 In the next week, find three price lists for services (such as from a restaurant, dry-cleaner or hairstylist). Identify the pricing base and the strategy used in each of them. How effective is each?

3 Consider that you are the owner of a new health club and can prepare a value/price package that is appealing to students. Describe your approach. How does it differ from existing offerings?

Notes

[1] K. Monroe, 'The pricing of services', *Handbook of Services Marketing*, eds C.A. Congram and M.L. Friedman (New York: AMACOM, 1989), pp. 20–31.

[2] Ibid.

[3] M.A. Ernst, 'Price visibility and its implications for financial services', paper presentation at the Effective Pricing Strategies for Service Providers Conference, Institute for International Research, Boston, October 1994.

[4] Monroe, 'The pricing of services'.

[5] V.A. Zeithaml, 'The acquisition, meaning, and use of price information by consumers of professional services', in *Marketing Theory: Philosophy of Science Perspectives*, eds R. Bush and S. Hunt (Chicago, IL: American Marketing Association, 1982), pp. 237–41.

[6] Kotler, P., *Marketing Management*, 11th edn. (Upper Saddle River, NJ: Pearson Education, 2003).

[7] C.H. Lovelock, 'Understanding costs and developing pricing strategies', *Services Marketing* (New York: Prentice Hall, 1991), pp. 236–46.

[8] A. Stevens, 'Firms try more lucrative ways of charging for legal services', *The Wall Street Journal*, 25 November 1994, pp. B1ff.

[9] J.L. Fix, 'Consumers are snarling over charges', *USA Today*, 2 August 1994, pp. B1–B2.

[10] V.A. Zeithaml, 'Consumer perceptions of price, quality, and value: a means-end model and synthesis of evidence', *Journal of Marketing* 52 (July 1988), pp. 2–22.

[11] All comments from these four sections are based on those from Zeithaml, 'Consumer perceptions of price, quality, and value', pp. 13–14

[12] Monroe, 'The pricing of services'.

[13] Monroe, 'The pricing of services'.

[14] Ibid.

[15] J.P. Guiltinan, 'The price bundling of services: a normative framework', *Journal of Marketing* 51 (April 1987), pp. 74–85.

[16] G.J. Tellis, 'Beyond the many faces of price: an integration of pricing strategies', *Journal of Marketing* 50 (October 1986), pp. 146–60.

PART 6
Service and the Bottom Line

In this final section of the text, we discuss one of the most important questions about service that managers have been debating over the past 25 years: is excellent service profitable to an organization? We pull together research and company experience, virtually all of it from the past decade, to answer this question. We present our own model of how the relationship works and consider some alternative models that have been used. Our model shows how service quality has offensive effects (gaining new customers) and defensive effects (retaining customers).

We also discuss several important performance models in this chapter. Return on service quality (ROSQ) is a modelling approach that allows a company to gauge the return on investments in different service activities. Customer equity is an extension of the ROSQ approach that compares investments in service with expenditures on other marketing activities. The balanced scorecard is an approach that includes multiple company factors including financial, customer, operational and innovative measures. The balanced scorecard allows a company to measure performance from the cústomer's perspective (Chapter 9), from the employee's perspective (Chapter 11) and from an innovation and new service perspective (Chapter 8). Thus, in Chapter 18 we synthesize the measurement issues that underlie the provision of service and offer a way for companies to demonstrate that service is accountable financially. We also present an approach called strategic performance mapping that helps companies integrate all elements of their balanced scorecards. These models help companies understand more accurately their benefits from investments in service excellence.

The financial impact of service quality

This chapter's objectives are to:

1 Examine the direct effects of service on profits.

2 Consider the effect of service on getting new customers.

3 Evaluate the role of service in keeping customers.

4 Discuss what is known about the key service drivers of overall service quality, customer retention and profitability.

5 Discuss the balanced scorecard that allows for strategic focus on measurements other than financials.

6 Describe the role of strategy maps in implementing the balanced scorecard.

CASE STUDY: 'WHAT RETURN CAN I EXPECT ON SERVICE QUALITY IMPROVEMENTS?' (A TYPICAL CEO)

All authors of this text work with companies to improve their service quality and better meet their customers' expectations. The two questions most frequently asked by executives of these companies are:

♦ 'How do I know that service quality improvements will be a good investment?'

♦ 'Where in the company do I invest money to achieve the highest return?'

For example, a restaurant chain, after conducting consumer research, found that service quality perceptions averaged 85 per cent across the chain. The specific items receiving the lowest scores on the survey were appearance of the restaurant's exterior (70 per cent), wait time for service (78 per cent) and limited menu (76 per cent). The company's CEO wanted to know, first of all, whether making improvements in overall service quality or to any of the specific areas would result in revenues that exceeded their costs. Moreover, he wanted guidance as to which of the service aspects to tackle. He could determine how much each of the initiatives would cost to change, but that was as far as his financial estimates would take him. Clearly, the restaurant's exterior was most in need of change because it was rated lowest; but would it not also be by far the most expensive to change? What could he expect in return for improvements in each service area? Would adjustments in the other two factors be better investments? Which of the three service initiatives would generate noticeable improvements to raise the overall customer perceptions of the restaurant?

Ten years ago, these questions had to be answered on the basis of executive intuition. Today, fortunately, more analytical and rigorous approaches exist to help managers make these decisions about service quality investments. The best known and most widely respected approach is called return on service quality (ROSQ) and was developed by Roland Rust, Anthony Zahorik and Tim Keiningham, a team of researchers and consultants.[1] The ROSQ approach is based on the following assumptions:

♦ Quality is an investment.

♦ Quality efforts must be financially accountable.

♦ It is possible to spend too much on quality.

♦ Not all quality expenditures are equally valid.

Their approach looks at investments in services as a chain of effects of the following form:

1 A service improvement effort will produce an increased level of customer satisfaction at the process or attribute level. For example, expending money to refurbish the exterior of the restaurants will likely increase customers' satisfaction level from the current low rating of 70 per cent.

2 Increased customer satisfaction at the process or attribute level will lead to increased overall customer satisfaction. If satisfaction with the restaurant's exterior goes from 70 to 80 per cent, overall service quality ratings may increase from 85 to 90 per cent. (Both these per-

centage changes could be accurately measured the next time surveys are conducted and could even be projected in advance using the ROSQ model.)

3 Higher overall service quality or customer satisfaction will lead to increased behavioural intentions, such as greater repurchase intention and intention to increase usage. Customers who have not yet eaten at the restaurant will be drawn to do so, and many who currently eat there once a month will consider increasing their patronage.

4 Increased behavioural intentions will lead to behavioural impact, including repurchase or customer retention, positive word of mouth and increased usage. Intentions about patronizing the restaurant will become reality, resulting in higher revenues and more positive word-of-mouth communications.

5 Behavioural effects will then lead to improved profitability and other financial outcomes. Higher revenues will lead to higher profits for the restaurant, assuming that the original investment in refurbishing the exterior is covered.

The ROSQ methodology can help distinguish among all the company strategies, processes, approaches and tactics that can be altered. The ROSQ approach is informative because it can be applied in companies to direct their individual strategies. Software has been developed to accompany the approach, and consulting firms work with companies to apply it. No longer do firms like the restaurant discussed here have to depend on intuition alone to guide them in their service quality investments.

In the current era of accountability and streamlining, virtually all companies hunger for evidence and tools to ascertain and monitor the payoff and payback of new investments in service. Many managers still see service and service quality as costs rather than as contributors to profits, partly because of the difficulty involved in tracing the link between service and financial returns. Determining the financial impact of service parallels the age-old search for the connection between advertising and sales. Service quality's results – like advertising's results – are cumulative, and therefore, evidence of the link may not come immediately or even quickly after investments. And, like advertising, service quality is one of many variables – among them pricing, advertising, efficiency and image – that simultaneously influence profits. Furthermore, spending on service per se does not guarantee results because strategy and execution must both also be considered.

In recent years, however, researchers and company executives have sought to understand the relationship between service and profits, and have found strong evidence to support the relationship. For example, a recent study examined the comparative benefits of revenue expansion and cost reduction on return on quality. The research addressed a common strategic dilemma faced by executives: whether to reduce costs through the use of quality programmes such as Six Sigma that focus on efficiencies and cost-cutting, or to build revenues through improvements to customer service, customer satisfaction and customer retention.[2] Using managers' reports as well as secondary data on firm profitability and stock returns, the study investigated whether the highest return on quality was generated from cost-cutting, revenue expansion or a combination of the two approaches. The results suggest that firms that adopt primarily a revenue expansion emphasis perform better and have higher return on quality than firms that emphasize either cost reduction or both revenue expansion and cost reduction together.[3]

Executives are also realizing that the link between service and profits is neither straightforward nor simple. Service quality affects many economic factors in a company, some of them leading to profits through variables not traditionally in the domain of marketing. For example, the traditional total quality management approach expresses the financial impact of service quality in lowered costs or increased productivity. These relationships involve operational issues that concern marketing only in the sense that marketing research is used to identify service improvements that customers notice and value.

More recently, other types of evidence have become available on which to examine the relationship between service and profitability. The overall goal of this chapter is to synthesize that recent evidence and to identify relationships between service and profits. This chapter is divided into six sections, paralleling the chapter's objectives. In each section we assess the evidence and identify what is currently known about the topics. The chapter is organized using a conceptual framework linking all the variables in the topics.

Service and profitability: the direct relationship

Figure 18.1 shows the underlying question at the heart of this chapter. Managers were first interested in this question in the 1980s when service quality emerged as a pivotal competitive strategy. The executives of leading service companies such as British Airways and Disney were willing to trust their intuitive sense that better service would lead to improved financial success. Without formal documentation of the financial payoff, they committed resources to improving service and were richly rewarded for their leaps of faith. In the 1990s, the strategy of using service for competitive advantage and profits was embraced by forward-thinking manufacturing and information technology companies such as IBM. However, executives in other companies withheld judgement about investing in service, waiting for solid evidence of its financial soundness.

Because tools such as return on quality analysis did not exist at the time, individual firms turned for insight to a group of early 1990s studies that explored total quality management (TQM) effects across a broad sample of manufacturing and service firms. The news was not encouraging. McKinsey and Company found that nearly two-thirds of quality programmes examined had either stalled or fallen short of delivering real improvements.[4] In two other studies, A.T. Kearney found that 80 per cent of British firms reported no significant impact as a result of TQM.[5]

In later years, evidence from more rigorous research showed the positive impact of service. One study showed the favourable financial impact of complaint recovery systems.[6] Extending the definition of financial performance to include stock returns, another study found a significant positive link between changes in customer quality perceptions and stock return while holding constant the effects of advertising expenditures and return on investment.[7]

Although some companies continued to approach the relationship at a broad level, others

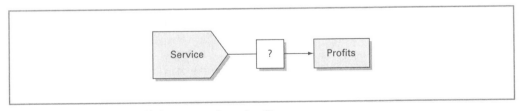

FIGURE 18.1 The direct relationship between service and profits

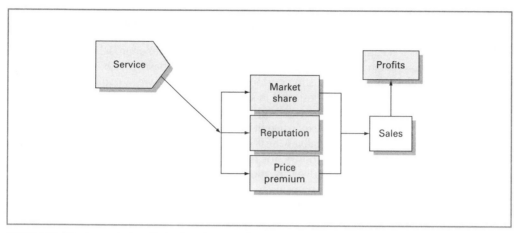

FIGURE 18.2 Offensive marketing effects of service on profits

began to focus more specifically on particular elements of the relationship. For example, executives and researchers soon recognized that service quality played a different role in getting new customers than it did in retaining existing customers.

Offensive marketing effects of service: attracting more and better customers

Service quality can help companies attract more and better customers to the business through *offensive marketing*.[8] Offensive effects (shown in Figure 18.2) involve market share, reputation and price premiums. When service is good, a company gains a positive reputation and through that reputation a higher market share and the ability to charge more than its competitors for services. These benefits were documented in a multi-year, multi-company study called PIMS (profit impact of marketing strategy). The PIMS research shows that companies offering superior service achieve higher than normal market share growth and that service quality influences profits through increased market share and premium prices as well as lowered costs and less rework.[9] The study found that businesses rated in the top fifth of competitors on relative service quality average an 8 per cent price premium over their competitors.[10]

To document the impact of service on market share, a group of researchers described their version of the path between quality and market share, claiming that satisfied customers spread positive word of mouth, which leads to the attraction of new customers and then to higher market share. They claim that advertising service excellence without sufficient quality to back up the communications will not increase market share. Further, they confirm that there are time lags in market share effects, making the relationship between quality and market share difficult to discern in the short term.[11]

Defensive marketing effects of service: customer retention

When it comes to keeping the customers a firm already has – an approach called **defensive marketing**[12] – researchers and consulting firms have in the past 15 years documented and quantified the financial impact of existing customers. In Chapter 7 we explained that customer defection, or 'customer churn', is widespread in service businesses. Customer defection is costly to companies because new customers must replace lost customers, and replacement comes at a high cost. Getting new customers is expensive; it involves advertising, promotion and sales costs as well as start-up operating expenses. New customers are often unprofitable for a period of time after acquisition. In the insurance industry, for example, the insurer does not typically recover selling costs until the third or fourth year of the relationship. Capturing customers from other companies is also an expensive proposition: a greater degree of service improvement is necessary to make a customer switch from a competitor than to retain a current customer. Selling costs for existing customers are much lower (on average 20 per cent lower) than selling to new ones.[13]

In general, the longer a customer remains with the company, the more profitable the relationship is for the organization: 'Served correctly, customers generate increasingly more profits each year they stay with a company. Across a wide range of businesses, the pattern is the same: the longer a company keeps a customer, the more money it stands to make.'[14] The money a company makes from retention comes from four sources (shown in Figure 18.3): costs, volume of purchases, price premium and word-of-mouth communication. This section provides research evidence for many of the sources.

Lower costs

Attracting a new customer is five times as costly as retaining an existing one. Consultants who have focused on these relationships assert that customer defections have a stronger effect on a company's profits than market share, scale, unit costs and many other factors usually associated with competitive advantage.[15] They also claim that, depending on the industry, companies can increase profits from 25 to 85 per cent by retaining just 5 per cent more of their customers.

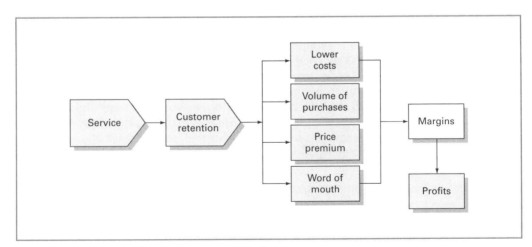

FIGURE 18.3 Defensive marketing effects of service on profits

Consider the following facts about the role of service quality in lowering costs:

- 'Our costs of not doing things right the first time were from 25 to 30 percent of our revenue' (David F. Colicchio, regional quality manager, Hewlett-Packard Company).[16]
- Profit on services purchased by a 10-year customer is on average three times greater than for a 5-year customer.[17]
- Bain and Company, a consulting organization specializing in retention research, estimates that in the life insurance business, a 5 per cent annual increase in customer retention lowers a company's costs per policy by 18 per cent.

Volume of purchases

Customers who are satisfied with a company's services are likely to increase the amount of money they spend with that company or the types of services offered. A customer satisfied with a broker's services, for example, will likely invest more money when it becomes available. Similarly, a customer satisfied with a bank's current account services is likely to open a savings account with the same bank and to use the bank's loan services as well.

Price premium

Evidence suggests that a customer who notices and values the services provided by a company will pay a price premium for those services. Most of the service quality leaders in industry command higher prices than their competitors: DHL collects more for overnight delivery than the national postal services, Hertz rental cars cost more than Budget cars, and staying at the Ritz-Carlton is a more expensive undertaking than staying at the Sofitel.

Word-of-mouth communication

In Chapter 2, we described the valuable role of word-of-mouth communications in purchasing service. Because word-of-mouth communication is considered more credible than other sources of information, the best type of promotion for a service may well come from other customers who advocate the services provided by the company. Word-of-mouth communication brings new customers to the firm, and the financial value of this form of advocacy can be calibrated by the company in terms of the promotional costs it saves as well as the streams of revenues from new customers.

Managers of service firms are only beginning to understand the topics discussed in this chapter. For each of the sections on the **service quality/profitability relationship** in this chapter, there are answers that managers and researchers most want to know.[18]

1 *What is a loyal customer?* Customer loyalty can be viewed as the way customers feel or as the way they act. A simple definition is possible with some products and services: customers are loyal as long as they continue to use a good or service. For washing machines or long-distance telephone service, customers are deemed loyal if they continue to use the machine or telephone service. Defining customer loyalty for other products and services is more problematic. What is the definition of loyalty to a restaurant: always eat there, eat there more times than at other restaurants or eat there at least once during a given period? These questions highlight the growing popularity of the concept of 'share of wallet' that company managers are very interested in. 'Share of wallet' means what percentage of the spending in a particular service category is made

on a given service provider. The other way to define loyalty is in terms of the customer's sense of belonging or commitment to the product. Some companies have been noted for their 'apostles', customers who care so much about the company that they stay in contact to provide suggestions for improvement and constantly preach to others the benefits of the company. Is this the best way to define loyalty?

2 *What is the role of service in defensive marketing?* Quality products at appropriate prices are important elements in the retention equation, but both these marketing variables can be imitated. Service plays a critical role – if not the critical role – in retaining customers. Providing consistently good service is not as easy to duplicate and therefore is likely to be the cementing force in customer relationships. Exactly how important is service in defensive marketing? How does service compare in effectiveness to other retention strategies such as price? To date no studies have incorporated all or most factors to examine their relative importance in keeping customers. Many companies actually have survey data that could answer this question but either have not analysed the data for this purpose or have not reported their findings.

3 *What levels of service provision are needed to retain customers?* How much spending on service quality is enough to retain customers? Initial investigations into this question have been argued but have not been confirmed. One consultant, for example, proposed that when satisfaction rose above a certain threshold, repurchase loyalty would climb rapidly. When satisfaction fell below a different threshold, customer loyalty would decline equally rapidly. Between these thresholds, he believed that loyalty was relatively flat. The material discussed in Chapter 3 offered a different prediction. The zone of tolerance in that chapter captured the range within which a company is meeting expectations. This framework suggests that firms operating within the zone of tolerance should continue to improve service, even to the point of reaching the desired service level. This hypothesis implies an upward-sloping (rather than flat) relationship with the zone of tolerance.

4 *What aspects of service are most important for customer retention?* The only studies that have examined specific aspects of service and their impact on customer retention have been early studies looking at customer complaint management. A decade ago such a study was appropriate because service was often equated with customer service, the after-sale function that dealt with dissatisfied customers. But today, most companies realize that service is multifaceted and want to identify the specific aspects of service provision that will lead to keeping customers.

5 *How can defection-prone customers be identified?* Companies find it difficult to create and execute strategies responsive enough to detect customer defections. Systems must be developed to isolate potential defecting customers, evaluate them and retain them if it is in the best interest of the company. One author and consultant advises that companies focus on three groups of customers who may be candidates for defection: (a) customers who close their accounts and shift business to a competitor, (b) customers who shift some of their business to another firm, and (c) customers who actually buy more but whose purchases represent a smaller share of their total expenditures. The first of these groups is easiest to identify, and the third group is the most difficult. Among the other customers who would be vulnerable are any customer with a negative service

experience, new customers and customers of companies in very competitive markets. Developing early warning systems of such customers is a pivotal requirement for companies.

Although research has come a long way in the last decade, researchers and companies must continue working on these questions for a more complete understanding of the impact of service on defensive marketing.

Customer perceptions of service and purchase intentions

In Chapter 4 we highlighted the links among customer satisfaction, service quality and increased purchases. Here we provide more research and empirical evidence supporting these relationships.

Service spotlight

Researchers at Xerox offered a compelling insight about the relationship between satisfaction and purchase intentions during the company's early years of customer satisfaction research. Initially, the company focused on satisfied customers, which they identified as those awarding either a '4' or a '5' on a five-point satisfaction scale. Careful analysis of the data showed that customers giving Xerox 5s were six times more likely to indicate that they would repurchase Xerox equipment than those giving 4s. This relationship encouraged the company to focus on increasing the 5s rather than the 4s and 5s because of the strong sales and profitability implications.[19]

Figure 18.4 shows this **service quality/customer intention relationship**.

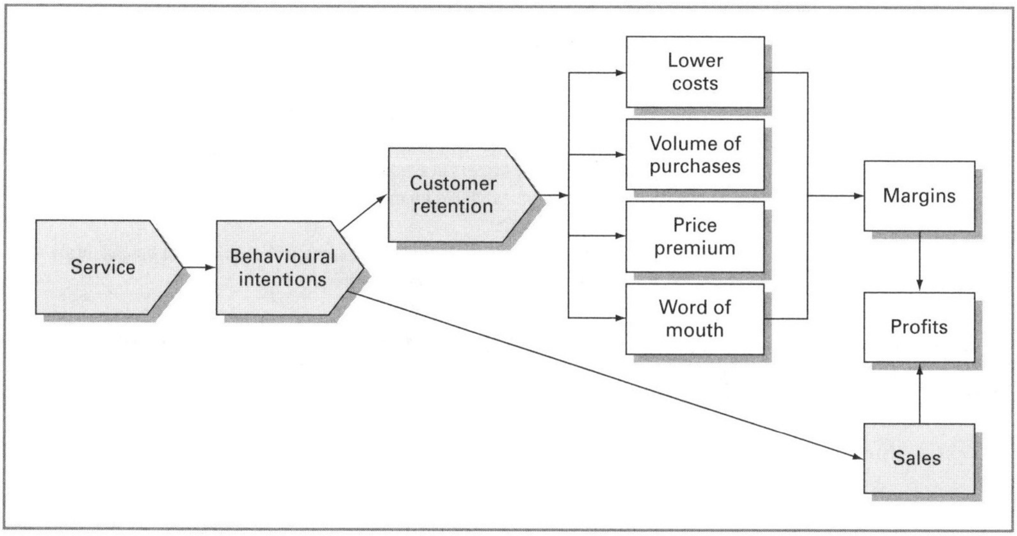

FIGURE 18.4 The effects of service

Topic	Key research questions
Service quality and profitability: the direct relationship	1. What methodologies need to be developed to allow companies to capture the effect of service quality on profit? 2. What measures are necessary to examine the relationship in a consistent, valid and reliable manner? 3. Does the relationship between service quality and profitability vary by industry, country, category of business (e.g. in services companies versus goods companies, in industrial versus packaged goods companies) or other variables? 4. What are the moderating factors of the relationship between service quality and profitability? 5. What is the optimal spending level on service in order to affect profitability?
Offensive effects of service quality	1. What is the optimal amount of spending on service quality to obtain offensive effects on reputation? 2. To obtain offensive effects, are expenditures on advertising or service quality itself more effective? 3. In what ways can companies signal high service quality to customers to obtain offensive effects?
Defensive effects of service quality	1, What is a loyal customer? 2. What is the role of service in defensive marketing? 3. How does service compare in effectiveness to other retention strategies such as price? 4, What levels of service provision are needed to retain customers? 5. How can the effects of word-of-mouth communication from retained customers be quantified? 6. What aspects of service are most important for customer retention? 7. How can defection-prone customers be identified?
Perceptions of service quality, behavioural intentions and profits	1. What is the relationship between customer purchase intentions and initial purchase behaviour in services? 2. What is the relationship between behavioural intentions and repurchase in services? 3. Does the degree of association between service quality and behaviour change at different quality levels?
Identifying the key drivers of service quality, customer retention and profits	1. What service encounters are most responsible for perceptions of service quality? 2. What are the key drivers in each service encounter? 3. Where should investments be made to affect service quality, purchase, retention and profits? 4. Are key drivers of service quality the same as key drivers of behavioural intentions, customer retention and profits?

TABLE 18.1 Service quality and the economic worth of customers: businesses still need to know more

Evidence also shows that customer satisfaction and service quality perceptions affect consumer intentions to behave in other positive ways – praising the firm, preferring the company over others, increasing volume of purchases or agreeably paying a price premium. Most of the early evidence looked only at overall benefits in terms of purchase intention rather than examining specific types of behavioural intentions. One study, using information from a Swedish customer satisfaction barometer, found that stated repurchase intention is strongly related to stated satisfaction across virtually all product categories.[20]

More recently, studies have found relationships between service quality and more specific behavioural intentions. One study involving university students found strong links between service quality and other behavioural intentions of strategic importance to a university, including behaviour such as saying positive things about the school, and planning to recommend the school to employers as a place from which to recruit.[21] Another comprehensive study examined a battery comprising 13 specific behavioural intentions likely to result from perceived service quality. The overall measure was significantly correlated with customer perceptions of service quality.[22]

Individual companies have also monitored the impact of service quality on selected behavioural intentions. Toyota found that intent to repurchase a Toyota automobile increased from a base of 37 to 45 per cent with a positive sales experience, from 37 to 79 per cent with a positive service experience, and from 37 to 91 per cent with both positive sales and service experiences.[23]

Table 18.1 shows a list of the questions that businesses still need to know more about on this topic and the others in this chapter.

The key drivers of service quality, customer retention and profits

Understanding the relationship between overall service quality and profitability is important, but it is perhaps more useful to managers to identify specific drivers of service quality that most relate to profitability (shown in Figure 18.5). Doing so will help firms understand what aspects of service quality to change to influence the relationship, and therefore where to invest resources.

Most evidence for this issue has come from examining the aspects of service (such as empathy, responsiveness and tangibles) on overall service quality, customer satisfaction and purchase intentions rather than on financial outcomes such as retention or profitability. As you have

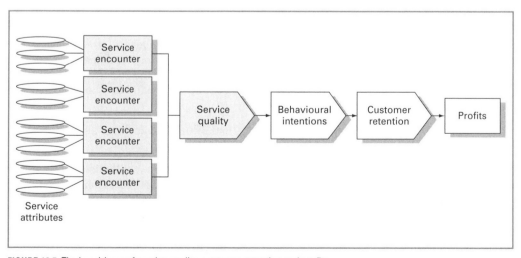

FIGURE 18.5 The key drivers of service quality, customer retention and profits

discovered in this text, service is multifaceted, consisting of a wide variety of customer-perceived dimensions including reliability, responsiveness and empathy, and resulting from innumerable company strategies such as technology and process improvement. In research exploring the relative importance of service dimensions on overall service quality or customer satisfaction, the bulk of the support confirms that reliability is most critical; but other research has demonstrated the importance of customization and other factors. Because the dimensions and attributes are delivered in many cases with totally different internal strategies, resources must be allocated where they are most needed, and study in this topic could provide direction.

Some companies and researchers have viewed the effect of specific service encounters on overall service quality or customer satisfaction and the effect of specific behaviours within service encounters.

Service spotlight

Marriott Hotels conducted extensive customer research to determine what service elements contribute most to customer loyalty. They found that four of the top five factors came into play in the first 10 minutes of the guest's stay – those that involved the early encounters of arriving, checking in and entering the hotel rooms. Other companies have found that mistakes or problems that occur in early service encounters are particularly critical, because a failure at early points results in greater risk for dissatisfaction in each ensuing encounter.

Customer equity and return on marketing[24]

Although the marketing concept has articulated a customer-centred view since the 1960s, marketing theory and practice have become incrementally customer-centred over the past 40 years. For example, marketing has only recently decreased its emphasis on short-term transactions and increased its focus on long-term customer relationships. Much of this refocus stems from the changing nature of the world's leading economies, which have undergone a century-long shift from the goods sector to the service sector.

Because service often tends to be more relationship based, this structural shift in the economy has resulted in more attention to relationships and therefore more attention to customers. This customer-centred view is starting to be reflected in the concepts and metrics that drive marketing management, including such metrics as customer value and voice of the customer. For example, the concept of brand equity, a fundamentally product-centred concept, is now being challenged by the customer-centred concept of *customer equity.*

Customer equity is the total of the discounted lifetime values summed over all the firm's customers.

In other words, customer equity is obtained by summing up the customer lifetime values of the firm's customers. In fast-moving and dynamic industries that involve customer relationships, products come and go but customers remain. Customers and customer equity may be more central to many firms than brands and brand equity, although current management practices and metrics do not yet fully reflect this shift. The shift from product-centred thinking to customer-centred thinking implies the need for an accompanying shift from product-based metrics to customer-based metrics.

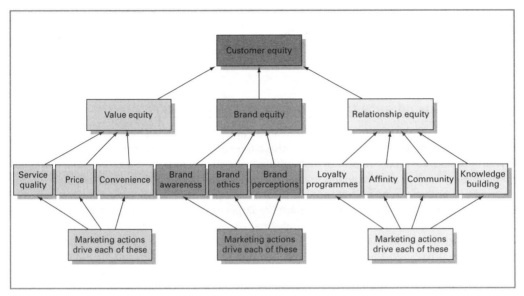

FIGURE 18.6 The customer equity model

Sources: R.T. Rust, K.N. Lemon and V.A. Zeithaml, 'Return on marketing: using customer equity to focus marketing strategy', *Journal of Marketing* 68, no. 1 (January 2004), pp. 109–27; R. Rust, V. Zeithaml and K. Lemon, *Driving Customer Equity* (New York: Free Press, 2000)

Using customer equity in a strategic framework

Consider the issues facing a typical marketing manager or marketing-oriented CEO: how do I manage my brand? How will my customers react to changes in service and service quality? Should I raise price? What is the best way to enhance the relationships with my current customers? Where should I focus my efforts? Determining customer lifetime value, or customer equity, is the first step, but the more important step is to evaluate and test ideas and strategies using lifetime value as the measuring stick. At a very basic level, strategies for building customer relationships can affect five basic factors: retention rate, referrals, increased sales, reduced direct costs and reduced marketing costs.

Rust, Zeithaml and Lemon have developed an approach based on customer equity that can help business executives answer their questions. The model that represents this approach is shown in Figure 18.6. In this context, customer equity is a new approach to marketing and corporate strategy that finally puts the customer – and, more importantly, strategies that grow the value of the customer – at the heart of the organization. The researchers identify the drivers of customer equity – value equity, brand equity and relationship equity – and explain how these drivers work, independently and together, to grow customer equity. Service strategies are prominent in both value equity and relationship equity. Within each of these drivers are specific, incisive actions ('levers') that the firm can take to enhance the firm's overall customer equity.

Why is customer equity important?

For most firms, customer equity – the total of the discounted lifetime values of all the firm's customers – is certain to be the most important determinant of the long-term value of the firm. Although customer equity will not be responsible for the entire value of the firm (consider, for example, physical assets, intellectual property, research and development competencies, etc.), the firm's current customers provide the most reliable source of future revenues and profits – and provide a focal point for marketing strategy.

Although it may seem obvious that customer equity is key to long-term success, understanding how to grow and manage customer equity is much more complex. Growing customer equity is of utmost importance, and doing it well can lead to significant competitive advantage.

Calculating return on marketing using customer equity

At the beginning of this chapter, we told you about an approach called return on quality that was developed to help companies understand where they could get the biggest impact from quality investments. A more general form of that approach is called return on marketing, which enables companies to look at all competing marketing strategy options and trade them off on the basis of projected financial return. This approach allows companies to not just examine the impact of service on financial return but also compare the impact of service with the impact of branding, price changes and all other marketing strategies. Using the customer equity model, firms can analyse the drivers that have the greatest impact, compare the drivers' performance with that of competitors' drivers, and project return on investment from improvements in the drivers. The framework enables 'what-if' evaluation of marketing return on investment, which can include such criteria as return on quality, return on advertising, return on loyalty programmes and, even, return on corporate citizenship, given a particular shift in customer perceptions. This approach enables firms to focus marketing efforts on strategic initiatives that generate the greatest return.

Company performance measurement: the balanced performance scorecard

Traditionally, organizations have measured their performance almost completely on the basis of financial indicators such as profit, sales and return on investment. This short-term approach leads companies to emphasize financials to the exclusion of other performance indicators. Today's corporate strategists recognize the limitations of evaluating corporate performance on financials alone, contending that these income-based financial figures measure yesterday's decisions rather than indicate future performance. This recognition came when many companies' strong financial records deteriorated because of unnoticed declines in operational processes, quality or customer satisfaction.[25] In the words of one observer of corporate strategy:

> Financial measures emphasize profitability of inert assets over any other mission of the company. They do not recognize the emerging leverage of the soft stuff – skilled people and employment of information – as the new keys to high performance and near-perfect customer satisfaction ... . If the only mission a measurement system conveys is financial discipline, an organization is directionless.[26]

For this reason, companies began to recognize that **balanced scorecards** – strategic measurement systems that captured other areas of performance – were needed. The developers of balanced scorecards defined them as follows:

> a set of measures that gives top managers a fast but comprehensive view of the business ... [that] complements the financial measures with operational measures of customer satisfaction, internal processes, and the organization's

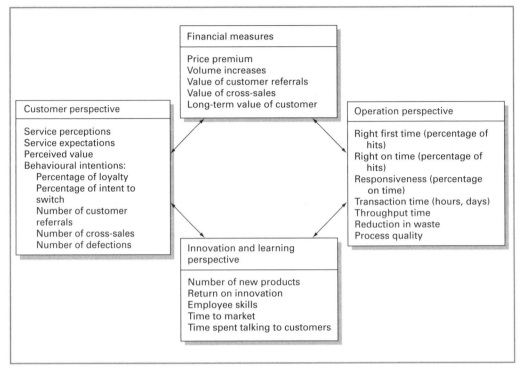

FIGURE 18.7 Sample measurements for the balanced scorecard

Sources: adapted and reprinted by permission of *Harvard Business Review*, an excerpt from J.R.S. Kaplan and D.P. Norton, 'The balanced scorecard-measures that drive performance', *Harvard Business Review* (January–February 1992). Copyright © 1992 by the Harvard Business School Publishing Corporation; all rights reserved

innovation and improvement activities – operational measures that are the drivers of future financial performance.[27] 🙴

Having a firm handle on what had been viewed as 'soft' measures became the way to help organizations identify customer problems, improve processes and achieve company objectives.

Balanced scorecards have become extremely popular. One recent report indicates that more than one-half of the largest companies worldwide use them.

As shown in Figure 18.7, the balanced scorecard captures three perspectives in addition to the financial perspective: customer, operational and learning. The balanced scorecard brings together, in a single management report, many of the previously separated elements of a company's competitive agenda and forces senior managers to consider all the important measures together. The scorecard has been facilitated by recent developments in software that allow companies to create balanced scorecards, automating and integrating measurements from all parts of the company.

Methods for measuring financial performance are the most developed and established in corporations, having been created more than 400 years ago. In contrast, efforts to measure market share, quality, innovation, human resources and customer satisfaction have only recently been created. Companies can improve their performance by developing this discipline in their measurement of all four categories.

Changes to financial measurement

One way that service leaders are changing financial measurement is to calibrate the defensive effect of retaining and losing customers. The monetary value of retaining customers can be projected through the use of average revenues over the lifetimes of customers. The number of customer defections can then be translated into lost revenue to the firm and become a critical company performance standard:

> Ultimately, defections should be a key performance measure for senior management and a fundamental component of incentive systems. Managers should know the company's defection rate, what happens to profits when the rate moves up or down and why defections occur.

Companies can also measure actual increases or decreases in revenue from retention or defection of customers by capturing the value of a loyal customer, including expected cash flows over a customer's lifetime or lifetime customer value (as described in Chapter 7). Other possible financial measures (as shown in Figure 18.7) include the value of price premiums, volume increases, customer referrals and cross-sales.

Customer perceptual measures

Customer perceptual measures are leading indicators of financial performance. As we discussed in this chapter, customers who are not happy with the company will defect and will tell others about their dissatisfaction. As we also discussed, perceptual measures reflect customer beliefs and feelings about the company and its products and services, and can predict how the customer will behave in the future. Overall forms of the measurements we discussed in Chapters 5 and 6 (shown in the customer perspective box of Figure 18.7) are measures that can be included in this category. Among the measures that are valuable to track are overall service perceptions and expectations, customer satisfaction, perceptual measures of value and behavioural intention measures such as loyalty and intent to switch. A company that notices a decline in these numbers should be concerned that the decline will translate into less profit for the company.

Operational measures

Operational measures involve the translation of customer perceptual measures into the standards or actions that must be set internally to meet customers' expectations. Although virtually all companies count or calculate operational measures in some form, the balanced scorecard requires that these measures stem from the business processes that have the greatest effect on customer satisfaction. In other words, these measures are not independent of customer perceptual measures but instead are intricately linked with them. In Chapter 9 we called these customer-linked operational measures *customer-defined standards* – operational standards determined through customer expectations and calibrated the way the customer views and expresses them.

Innovation and learning

The final area of measurement involves a company's ability to innovate, improve and learn – by launching new products, creating more value for customers and improving operating efficiencies. This measurement area is most difficult to capture quantitatively but can be accomplished using performance-to-goal percentages. For example, a company can set a goal of launching 10 new products a year, then measure what percentage of that goal it achieves in a year. If four new

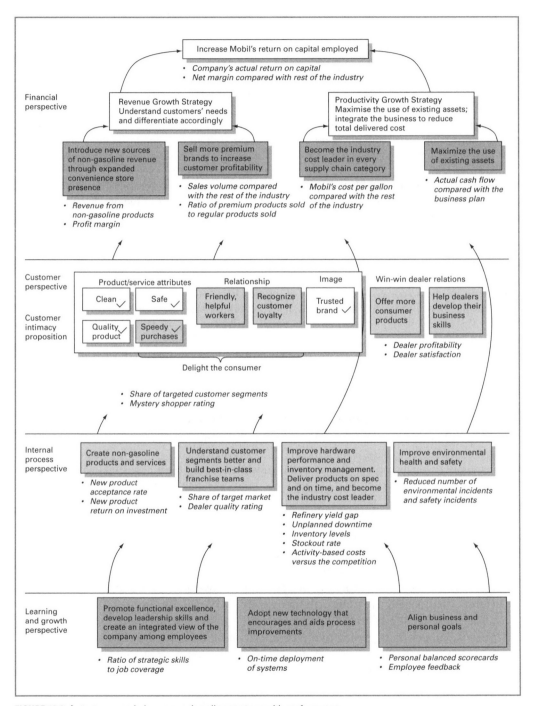

FIGURE 18.8 A strategy map helps companies align strategy with performance

Source: adapted and reprinted by permission of *Harvard Business Review*, an excerpt from 'Having trouble with your strategy? Then map it-tool kit',
Harvard Business Review (September–October 2000). Copyright © 2000 by the Harvard Business School Publishing Corporation; all rights reserved

products are launched, its percentage for the year is 40 per cent, which can then be compared with subsequent years.

Strategy maps to enhance balanced scorecards

The **strategy map** is a concept that was recently developed to help companies deploy the balanced scorecard more effectively. A strategy map provides a single-page visual representation of a firm's strategy (see Figure 18.8) that links the four perspectives of the balanced scorecard and thereby shows the cause-and-effect relationships among them.[28] Instead of merely showing the four clusters of metrics as separate categories linked by arrows, as shown in Figure 18.7, the strategy map shows how the typical 20 to 30 measures in a balanced scorecard are integrated in the creation of a single unified strategy and clearly demonstrates which variables lead, lag and feed back into other variables. The map also identifies the capabilities of the organization's intangible assets – human capital, information capital and organization capital – that are required for superior performance.

The essence of the map is that financial outcomes are possible only if targeted customers are satisfied, a complicated process achieved with a set of interrelated capabilities. The mapping process forces managers to identify cause and effect and to clarify the logic of how the company will create value and for whom.[29] As part of the process, companies must identify the customer value proposition and then describe how it will generate sales and loyalty from targeted customers. The company then must link the critical internal processes that are most important to deliver the value proposition.

Mapping helps identify any of the four categories in which management has not thought through metrics and strategies. Strategies are typically executed through a structure of strategic themes developed during the mapping.

Effective non-financial performance measurements

According to field research conducted in 60 companies and survey responses from 297 senior executives, many companies do not identify and act on the correct non-financial measures.[30] One example involves a bank that surveyed satisfaction only from customers who physically entered the branches, a policy that caused some branch managers to offer free food and drinks in order to increase their scores. According to the authors of the study, companies make four major mistakes:

1 *Not linking measures to strategy.* Companies can easily identify hundreds of non-financial measures to track, but they also need to use analysis that identifies the most important drivers of their strategy. Successful organizations use value-driver maps, tools that lay out the cause-and-effect relationships between drivers and strategic success. Figure 18.9 shows the causal model developed by a successful fast-food chain to understand the key drivers of shareholder value. The factors on the right were identified as most important in leading to the concepts on the left, and the sequence of concepts from top to bottom show the relationships among company strategies (such as selection and staffing) and intermediate results (such as employee and customer satisfaction) that result in financial results (such as sustained profitability and shareholder value). The study found that fewer than 30 per cent of the firms surveyed used this causal modelling approach.

2 *Not validating the links.* Only 21 per cent of companies in the study verify that the non-financial measures lead to financial performance. Instead, many firms decide what they

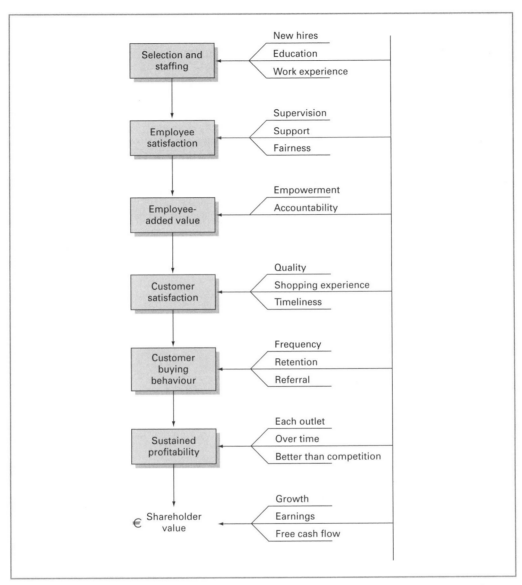

FIGURE 18.9 The measures that matter most: a causal model for a fast-food company shows the critical drivers of performance and the concepts that lead to shareholder value

Source: C.D. Ittner and D.F. Larcker, 'Coming up short on nonfinancial performance measurement', *Harvard Business Review* (November 2003), pp. 88–95

are going to measure in each category and never link the categories. Many managers believed that the relationships were self-evident instead of conducting analysis to validate the linkages. This chapter's strategy insight shows one way that companies can create this type of linkage. In general, it is critical that companies pull together all their data and examine the relationships among the categories.

3 *Not setting the right performance targets.* Companies sometimes aim too high in setting improvement targets. Targeting 100 per cent customer satisfaction might seem to be a desirable goal, but many companies expend far too many resources to gain too little improvement in satisfaction. The study's authors found that a telecommunications company aiming for 100 per cent customer satisfaction was wasting resources because customers who were 100 per cent satisfied spent no more money than those who were 80 per cent satisfied.[31]

4 *Measuring incorrectly.* Companies need to use metrics with statistical validity and reliability. Organizations cannot measure complex phenomenon with one or two simple measures, nor can they use inconsistent methodologies to measure the same concept, such as customer satisfaction. Another problem that companies may encounter is trying to use quantitative metrics to capture qualitative results for important factors such as leadership and innovation.

Creating a balanced scorecard in and of itself does not improve performance. Companies will not reap the benefits of techniques such as the balanced scorecard unless they address these four issues.

Summary

This chapter is divided into six sections, five of which assess the evidence and identify what is currently known about the relationship between service and profitability. The chapter used a conceptual framework to link all the variables in these topics: (1) the direct relationship between service and profits; (2) offensive effects of service quality; (3) defensive effects of service quality; (4) the relationship between service quality and purchase intentions; and (5) key drivers of service quality, customer retention and profits. Considerable progress has been made in the past 10 years in the investigation of service quality, profitability and the economic worth of customers, but managers are still lacking many of the answers that would help them make informed decisions about service quality investments. The chapter concluded with a discussion of the balanced scorecard approach to measuring corporate performance, which offers a strategic approach for measuring all aspects of a company's performance.

Key concepts

Balanced scorecard	466	Service quality/profitability relationship	459
Defensive marketing	458	Strategy map	470
Offensive marketing	457		
Service quality/customer intention relationship	461		

Further reading

Adams, C., Neely, A. and Kennerley, M. (2002) *Performance Prism: The Scorecard for Measuring and Managing Stakeholder Relationships.* London: FT Prentice Hall.

Fornell, C., Mithas, S., Morgeson, F. and Krishnan, M.S. (2006) 'Customer satisfaction and stock prices: high returns, low risk', *Journal of Marketing,* 70(1), 3–14.

Kaplan, R.S. and Norton, D.P. (1996) *Balanced Scorecard: Translating Strategy into Action.* Cambridge: Harvard Business School Press.

Meyer, M.W. (2003) *Rethinking Performance Measurement: Beyond the Balanced Scorecard.* Cambridge: Cambridge University Press.

Neely, A. (2002) *Business Performance Measurement: Theory and Practice.* Cambridge: Cambridge University Press.

Wilson, A.M. (2000) 'The use of performance information in the management of service delivery', *Marketing Intelligence and Planning,* 18(3), 127–34.

 ## Discussion questions

1 Why has it been difficult for executives to understand the relationship between service improvements and profitability in their companies?

2 What is the ROSQ model, and what is its significance to organizations?

3 To this day, many companies believe that service is a cost rather than a revenue producer. Why might they hold this view? How would you argue the opposite view?

4 What is the difference between offensive and defensive marketing? How does service affect each of these?

5 What are the main sources of profit in defensive marketing?

6 What are the main sources of profit in offensive marketing?

7 How will the balanced scorecard help us understand and document the information presented in this chapter? Which of the five sections that discuss different aspects of the relationship between service quality and profits can it illuminate?

 ## Exercises

1 On the Internet, use a search engine to locate three companies that make balanced scorecard software. What are the software companies' current offerings? How can the software firms help individual companies understand the concepts and relationships discussed in this chapter? Which of the three companies would you select based on the information you locate?

2 Interview a local firm and see what it knows about its key drivers of financial performance. What are the key service drivers of the firm? Does the company know whether these service drivers relate to profit?

3 Select a service industry (such as fast food) or a company (such as McDonald's) that you are familiar with, either as a customer or employee, and create a balanced scorecard. Describe the operational, customer, financial and learning measures that could be used to capture performance.

Notes

1 R.T. Rust, A.J. Zahorik and T.L. Keiningham, *Return on Quality* (Chicago, IL: Probus, 1994).

2 R.T. Rust, C. Moorman and P.R. Dickson, 'Getting return on quality: revenue expansion, cost reduction, or both?', *Journal of Marketing* 66 (October 2002), pp. 7–24.

3 Ibid.

4 J. Matthews and P. Katel, 'The cost of quality: faced with hard times, business sours on total quality management', *Newsweek*, 7 September 1992, pp. 48–9.

5 'The cracks in quality', *The Economist* 18 (April 1992), pp. 67–8.

6 R. Rust, B. Subramanian, and M. Wells, 'Making complaints a management tool', *Marketing Management* 3 (1993), pp. 40–5.

7 D.A. Aaker and R. Jacobson, 'The financial information content of perceived quality', *Journal of Marketing* 58 (May 1994), pp. 191–201.

8 C. Fornell and B. Wernerfelt, 'Defensive marketing strategy by customer complaint management: a theoretical analysis', *Journal of Marketing Research* 24 (November 1987), pp. 337–46; see also C. Fornell and B. Wernerfelt, 'A model for customer complaint management', *Marketing Science* 7 (Summer 1988), pp. 271–86.

9 B. Gale, 'Monitoring customer satisfaction and market-perceived quality', *American Marketing Association Worth Repeating Series*, no. 922CS01 (Chicago, IL: American Marketing Association, 1992).

10 Ibid.

11 R.E. Kordupleski, R.T. Rust and A.J. Zahorik, 'Why improving quality doesn't improve quality (or whatever happened to marketing?)', *California Management Review* 35 (1993), pp. 82–95.

12 Fornell and Wernerfelt, 'Defensive marketing strategy by customer complaint management', also Fornell and Wernerfelt, 'A model for customer complaint management'.

13 T.J. Peters, *Thriving on Chaos* (New York: Alfred A. Knopf, 1988).

14 F. Reichheld and E. Sasser, 'Zero defections: quality comes to services', *Harvard Business Review* (September–October 1990), p. 106.

15 Ibid., p. 105.

16 D.F. Colicchio, regional quality manager, Hewlett-Packard Company, personal communication.

17 S. Rose, 'The coming revolution in credit cards', *Journal of Retail Banking* (Summer 1990), pp. 17–19.

18 Reprinted with permission from V.A. Zeithaml, 'Service quality, profitability and the economic worth of customers', *Journal of the Academy of Marketing Science* (January 2000), © 2000 by the Academy of Marketing Science.

[19] J.L. Heskett, W.E. Sasser Jr and L.A. Schlesinger, *The Service Profit Chain* (New York: Free Press, 1997).

[20] E.W. Anderson and M. Sullivan, 'The antecedents and consequences of customer satisfaction for firms', *Marketing Science* 12 (Spring 1992), pp. 125–43.

[21] W. Boulding, R. Staelin, A. Kalra and V.A. Zeithaml, 'Conceptualizing and testing a dynamic process model of service quality', report no. 92-121, Marketing Science Institute (1992).

[22] V.A. Zeithaml, L.L. Berry and A. Parasuraman, 'The behavioral consequences of service quality', *Journal of Marketing* 60 (April 1996), pp. 31–46.

[23] J.P. McLaughlin, 'Ensuring customer satisfaction is a strategic issue, not just an operational one', paper presented at the AIC Customer Satisfaction Measurement Conference, Chicago, 6–7 December 1993.

[24] Sources: R.T. Rust, K.N. Lemon and V.A. Zeithaml, 'Return on marketing: using customer equity to focus marketing strategy', *Journal of Marketing* 68, no. 1 (January 2004), pp. 109; R. Rust, V. Zeithaml and K. Lemon, *Driving Customer Equity* (New York: Free Press, 2000).

[25] R.S. Kaplan and D.P. Norton, 'The balanced scorecard – measures that drive performance', *Harvard Business Review* (January–February 1992), pp. 71–9.

[26] Kaplan and Norton, 'The balanced scorecard'.

[27] S. Silk, 'Automating the balanced scorecard', *Management Accounting* (May 1998), pp. 38–42.

[28] R. Kaplan and D. Norton, 'Plotting success with "Strategy Maps"', *Optimize* (February 2004), pp. 61–5.

[29] R.S. Kaplan and D.P. Norton, 'How strategy maps frame an organization's objectives', *Financial Executive* 20 (2004), pp. 40–5.

[30] The material in this section comes from C.D. Ittner and D.F. Larcker, 'Coming up short on nonfinancial performance measurement', *Harvard Business Review* (November 2003), pp. 88–95.

[31] Ibid., p. 92.

Case section

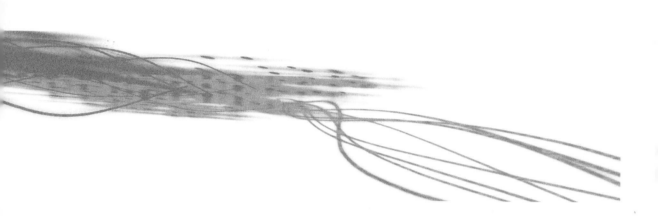

In this section there are eight cases that reflect the frameworks and theories of services marketing discussed in the previous chapters.

The cases have been chosen to reflect the service concepts discussed in the book. They have also been selected to ensure that they test understanding of these concepts and challenge students' ability to analyse company information and sythesize ideas they have learnt. Finally, we have also ensured that the case studies chosen reflect international organizations and, in particular, European companies that are relevant and familiar to students.

Case 1

TESCO – the customer relationship management champion

A master at CRM

Every three months, millions of people in the United Kingdom (UK) receive a magazine from the country's number one retailing company, Tesco. Nothing exceptional about the concept – almost all leading retailing companies across the world send out mailers/magazines to their customers. These initiatives promote the store's products, introduce promotional schemes and contain discount coupons. However, what set Tesco apart from such run-of-the-mill initiatives was the fact that it mass-customized these magazines.

Every magazine had a unique combination of articles, advertisements related to Tesco's offerings, and third-party advertisements. Tesco ensured that all its customers received magazines that contained material suited to their lifestyles. The company had worked out a mechanism for determining the advertisements and promotional coupons that would go in each of the over 150,000 variants of the magazine. This had been made possible by its world-renowned customer relationship management (CRM) strategy framework (refer Exhibit I for a brief note on CRM).

The loyalty card[3] scheme (launched in 1995) laid the foundations of a CRM framework that made Tesco post growth figures in an industry that had been stagnating for a long time. The data collected through these cards formed the basis for formulating strategies that offered customers personalized services in a cost-effective manner. Each and every one of the over 8 million transactions made every week at the company's stores was individually linked to customer-profile information. And each of these transactions had the potential to be used for modifying the company's strategies.

According to Tesco sources, the company's CRM initiative was not limited to the loyalty card scheme; it was more of a company-wide philosophy. Industry observers felt that Tesco's CRM initiatives enabled it to develop highly focused marketing strategies. Thanks to its CRM initiatives, the company became the UK's number one retailer in 1995, after having struggled at number two behind arch rival Sainsbury's for decades (refer Exhibit II for a brief note on the UK's retailing industry). In 2003, the company's market share was 26.7%, while Sainsbury's market share was just 16.8%.

Background note

The Tesco story dates back to 1919 when Jack Cohen, an ex-army man, set up a grocery business in London's East End. In 1924, Cohen purchased a shipment of tea from a company named T E Stockwell. He used the first three letters of this company's name, added the 'Co' from his name and branded the tea 'Tesco'. Reportedly, he was so enamoured of the name that he named his entire business Tesco. The first store under the Tesco name was opened in 1929 in Burnt Oak, Edgware. The company grew rapidly in the years that followed, and evolved into a general food retailing outfit. By 1930, around 100 stores were operating under the Tesco label.

Realizing that the self-service mode of running supermarkets prevalent in the US worked out much cheaper than the traditional mode and enabled companies to offer their merchandise at low prices, Cohen decided to adopt the same for Tesco stores. In 1948, the first self-service Tesco store was opened in St Albans. Over the next few years, Tesco grew to over 400 stores – many of which were purchased by Cohen from other smaller shopping store chains in the country.

In the early 1960s, the company began selling clothing, household goods and fresh food in addition to groceries. Tesco pioneered the large format stores concept in the UK with the launch of a 16,500 sq. ft. store in Leicester in 1961. By now, Tesco had become a household name in the UK and was renowned for its competitive prices. However, due to the Retail Price Maintenance (RPM) system prevalent in the country during that time (which prohibited larger retailers from pricing goods below a price agreed upon with the suppliers), companies such as Tesco were not able to compete on price with small retailing outfits.

Exhibit I - A brief note on CRM **481**

Exhibit I **A brief note on CRM**

Customer Relationship Management (CRM) deals with learning about the needs and behaviour of customers in order to develop stronger relationships with them. It involves the use of technology to enable organizations to continue attracting new and profitable customers while forming ever tighter bonds with existing ones – and optimizing on these relationships over time. With CRM, it becomes possible to launch mass-marketing activities on a one-to-one basis and treat each customer as an individual.

CRM involves the use of various tools, technologies and business procedures to attract and retain customers, prospects and business partners. These include Contact Management, Sales Force Automation (SFA), Opportunity Management, Relationship Management, Marketing Automation, Company Websites, Telesales and Telemarketing Systems. Technologies such as eCRM, iCRM, and Enterprise Relationship Management (ERM) are also tools of CRM. Essentially, any and all technologies, processes and procedures that facilitate or support the sales and marketing functions can be regarded as CRM tools.

CRM software is designed to help companies keep track of their customers and boost revenues (by increasing customer loyalty). Applications range from sales and field-service automation to call centre and customer-database management. More than its technological components, CRM is a process that helps bring together various pieces of information about customers, sales, marketing effectiveness and market trends. It helps companies provide better customer service, make call centres more efficient, cross sell products more effectively, close deals faster, simplify marketing and sales processes, find new customers and increase customer revenues. Typically, CRM software collects the following information:

* Responses to campaigns
* Sales and purchase data
* Web registration data
* Demographic data
* Shipping and fulfillment dates
* Account information
* Service and support records
* Web sales data

CRM not only helps reduce overall business costs, it helps companies provide better customer service and earn long-term customer loyalty. It allows companies to:

- Gain a better understanding of customer needs and build individual customer solutions.
- Establish a dialogue with customers (using the Internet).
- Improve marketing efforts by using readily accessible customer information.
- Link departments, giving them access to the same information (updated in real time).

Source: ICMR

Exhibit II **A brief note on UK's retailing industry**

The retailing industry is one of the UK's primary service sector industries. In 2002, its sales amounted to £234 billion. That year, there were over 322,000 retail outlets in the country (December 2002 figure) employing around 2.9 million people (11 per cent of the country's total workforce). Despite the sluggish growth since the 1990s, the industry remains one of the biggest job creators in the UK. The industry has gone through major structural changes since the mid-1980s. These include the growing importance of technology in the business, increasing influx of foreign players, overseas expansion by UK firms, and a focus on price cutting by leading chains due to intensifying competitive pressures. The top 10 players ranked according to their 2001–02 turnovers (in descending order) are listed in the following table:

Rank	COMPANY	Rank	COMPANY
1.	Tesco	6.	Dixons Gp.
2.	Sainsbury's	7.	Somerfield
3.	Asda	8.	John Lewis Prtnrshp
4.	Safeway	9.	Boots
5.	Marks & Spencer	10.	Wm Morrison Spmkt

For the 12-weeks ending 25 May 2003, Tesco was the market leader with a 26.7 per cent market share. During that period, the market share of Sainsbury's fell from 17.5 per cent to 16.8 per cent. Asda (which is owned by the world's largest retailer, the US-based Wal-Mart) was at number three with a market share of 16.3 per cent. Sainsbury's used to be the market leader till 1995, but by 1995, Tesco outstripped it and continued to grow at a scorching pace (refer to the following table for market share information).

UK RETAILING INDUSTRY – MARKET SHARES				
	1997	**1998**	**1999**	**2000**
Tesco	22.0	22.9	23.4	24.2
Sainsbury's	19.7	19.8	19.1	18.6
Asda	13.3	14.1	14.8	16.3
Safeway	10.3	10.2	10.0	10.1
Morrisons	3.9	3.9	4.5	5.1

Safeway, a leading player once, was struggling to stay afloat in 2003. The competition in the industry was on these fronts: price cuts, store modernization, product-mix expansion and premium image creation. All the stores were working towards creating an image in the minds of customers. While Tesco and Asda focused on price cuts, players such as Waitrose focused on building a high quality image for themselves. As far as price cutting was concerned, Asda was the champion (its prices were 3 per cent less than Tesco's), followed by Tesco and then Sainsbury's.

Compiled from information available on www.brc.org.co.uk and other sources.

To overcome this problem, Tesco came up with the idea of 'trading stamps'. These stamps were given to customers in return for making purchases at its stores. After the customers collected a specified number of stamps, they could exchange them in return for cash or gifts. This scheme became very popular and Tesco's popularity and sales soared substantially. While other players in the industry were busy copying this scheme, Cohen worked towards getting the RPM abolished. The RPM was abolished in 1964, following which Tesco was able to offer competitively priced merchandise to its customers. Meanwhile, it decided to continue the trading stamps scheme.

Throughout the 1960s, Tesco continued to grow through the acquisitions route. It acquired a network of 212 stores in the north of England, and during 1964–65, acquired 144 more stores. Another chain, Victor Value, came under the company's fold in 1968. In the same year, Tesco became the first retailer to formally introduce superstores to the British retailing industry with the launch of its Crawley, West Sussex store.

Though Tesco owed its success till now to its cheap prices model (referred to as the 'pile it high and sell it cheap' model by Cohen as well as industry observers), it had to rethink its pricing strategy in the 1970s. This was primarily due to the fact that customers across the UK were becoming more affluent and were no longer looking only for bargains. There was a growing need for costly, luxury merchandise.

To factor in these changes sweeping the industry, Tesco's management carried out a strategic overhaul of the company's operations. The company closed down many of its stores to concentrate on superstores. The stores that were not closed down were refurbished through better layouts (such as wider aisles) and improved atmospherics (including better lighting). The product mix was also changed and Tesco now began offering a much wider range of goods. In addition, the company renewed its focus on customer service and quality. In line with the product diversification drive, Tesco began operating petrol pumps in 1974. Since trading stamps did not fit in with its efforts to go up-market, Tesco discontinued them in 1977.

Even though Tesco went up-market, it tried to retain its image as a company offering competitive prices. In 1977, the company successfully launched a price cutting campaign named '*Checkout at Tesco*'. By the end of the 1970s, the company had emerged as one of the leading companies in the UK. In 1979, its annual turnover crossed £1 billion. In 1985, Tesco launched the '*Healthy Eating*' initiative, a path-breaking move that aimed at conveying the nutritional value of the company's merchandise to the customers. By now, Tesco had also emerged as the largest independent retailer of petrol in the UK.

The 1990s were a period of many large-scale changes at the company. For the first time in many years, Tesco began experimenting with newer store formats. Three new formats, Tesco Metro, Tesco Express and Tesco Extra Store, were launched during the 1990s. While Tesco Metro was a city centre store that served the local community of a particular region, Tesco Express was a combination of a petrol pump and a convenience store. Tesco Extra Store was a hypermarket that focused equally on food and non-food merchandise.

This decade also saw the company entering global markets. It entered France in 1994 and Hungary and Poland in 1995. In 1995, Tesco launched the Clubcard loyalty scheme. In the same year, it diversified into a new business through a joint venture (for the first time in its history) with the Royal Bank of Scotland to launch the Tesco Personal Finance (TPF) venture. TPF offered customers a wide array of personal finance services, including the Tesco Visa card, cheque deposits, car loans, life/auto/pet/home/travel insurance, loans, bonds, mortgages and pension savings programmes. Tesco classified TPF under the 'Retailing Services' division.

In 1996, the company entered the Czech Republic, and in 1998, it entered Northern Ireland and Thailand. Even in international markets, Tesco adopted the policy of offering its services to customers in innovative ways. For instance, in Thailand, its customers could buy 'tescooters' (scooters) and have them delivered to their homes.

In 1998, after the utilities business was deregulated in the UK, Tesco began offering electricity and telecommunications products and services. In 2000, Tesco established Tesco.com as a wholly-owned subsidiary functioning under the retailing services division. Besides covering all the e-commerce activities for Tesco's customers in general, Tesco.com gave special emphasis to the sale of groceries over the Internet. This service was later extended to customers in Ireland and South Korea.

In 2000, Tesco began operations in Taiwan. The following year, the company tied up with a leading supermarket chain from the US, Safeway Inc, to launch an online grocery shopping service for US customers. In the same year, Tesco entered into an agreement with leading automobile company, the US-based General Motors (GM). Under this agreement, customers could buy GM cars through Tesco.

In an innovative move, the company began offering a large number of organic food products in 2001. In addition, a host of new ranges of food products (such as 'The Food Doctor', 'Finest Dips', 'Grab and Go', 'Unwind Range', and 'Finest') were launched in the early 21st century. During this period, the company also gave a lot of importance to its non-food businesses. It carried a wide range of merchandise like toys, sports equipment, lighting, furnishing, electrical items and clothing. Many new brands in the non-food segment were successfully launched (such as Cherokee and Florence & Fred).

Continuing its thrust on global expansion, Tesco launched its first store in Malaysia in May 2002. In July 2002, it expanded its presence in Poland by acquiring a chain of hypermarkets named 'HIT'. Tesco's store network in the UK grew further in January 2003 when it acquired 870 convenience stores operating under the T&S label (the company planned to convert 450 of these stores into Tesco Express stores by 2006–07). For the accounting period ending April 2003, TPF had over 3.4 million customer accounts and earned profits of £96 million. Also, tesco.com had proven to be one of the rare, profitable dotcom ventures. In 2003, it earned a profit of £12 million.

By mid-2003, the company was operating 2291 stores in the UK, Hungary, Poland, the Czech Republic, the Slovak Republic, Thailand, South Korea, Taiwan, Malaysia and the Republic of Ireland. Employing around 296,000 people across these countries, Tesco was earning profits in at least eight of the ten countries. The group's strong financial performance was reflected in the healthy growth in revenues and net profits over the years. While revenues and net profit stood at £18.46 billion and £842 million in 1999, they were £28.61 billion and £1.36 billion in 2003 (refer Exhibit III for Tesco's key financial statistics).

CRM – the Tesco way

Tesco's efforts towards offering better services to its customers and meeting their needs can be traced back to the days when it positioned itself as a company that offered good quality products at extremely competitive prices. Even its decision to offer premium end merchandise and services in the 1970s was prompted by growing customer demand for the same (refer Table I for the company's 'core purpose' and 'values' that highlight the importance given to customer service).

Various initiatives were taken by the company over the years to improve customer service. For instance, in 1993–94, Tesco launched the '*First Class Service*' initiative. Under this initiative, the company gave customer service training to over 90,000 store staff. The programme was an innovative one in that it involved store managers in behavioural service training for the very first time. Instead of being passive participants of a training programme, employees were asked to work out the right approach for their training needs. Based on the above approach, Tesco made work teams to carry out regular training programmes focusing on customer service improvement.

In 1994, the company launched the '*One in Front*' scheme to reduce the time customers had to spend waiting at check-out counters. Under this scheme, Tesco store personnel ensured that if there was more than one person at any counter, another counter would be opened for the person second in line. This way, no customer would have to wait at the check-out counters. Of course, it was not possible for Tesco to adhere to this policy during peak traffic hours. Nevertheless, this effort to improve customer service was appreciated by customers.

The biggest customer service initiative (and the first focused CRM drive) came in the form of the loyalty card scheme that was launched in 1995. This initiative was partly inspired by the growing popularity of such schemes in other parts of the world and partly by Tesco's belief that it would be able to serve its customers in a much better (and profitable) manner by using such a scheme. Tesco knew that at any of its outlets, the top 100 customers were worth as much as the bottom 4000 (in terms of sales). While the top 5 per cent customers accounted for 20 per cent of sales, the bottom 25 per cent accounted for only 2 per cent. The company realized that by giving extra attention to the top customers (measured by the frequency of purchases and the amount spent), it stood to gain a lot.

Work in this direction began in 1994, when Tesco tied up with Dunnhumby,[4] a marketing services outfit, to develop its loyalty programme. In May 1994, Tesco began

Exhibit III **key statistics**

(in £ million)

Year Ended February	1999	2000	2001	2002	2003
Group Sales	**18456**	**20358**	**22773**	**25654**	**28613**
TURNOVER					
UK	15835	16958	18372	20052	21615
Rest of Europe	1167	1374	1756	2203	2689
Asia	156	464	860	1398	2033
Total Turnover	**17518**	**18796**	**20988**	**23653**	**26337**
UNDERLYING OPERATING PROFIT (1)					
UK	919	993	1100	1213	1297
Rest of Europe	48	51	70	90	141
Asia	(2)	(1)	4	29	71
Total Profit	**965**	**1043**	**1174**	**1332**	**1509**
Underlying Pre-Tax Profit*	881	955	1070	1221	1401
Profit Before Tax	**842**	**933**	**1054**	**1201**	**1361**
RETAIL STATISTICS					
UK					
Number of Stores	639	659	692	729	1982
Total Sales Area (000 sq.ft.)	15975	16895	17965	18822	21829
Turnover per full time employee (£)**	151138	156427	161161	165348	162457
Weekly Sales per sq.ft. (£)***	21.05	21.43	22.01	22.33	22.16
INTERNATIONAL					
Number of Stores	182	186	245	250	309
Number of Hypermarkets	22	38	68	102	152
Total Sales Area (000 sq.ft.)	5378	7144	10397	13669	18115

*   Excluding net loss on disposal of fixed assets, integration costs and goodwill amortization.

**   2003, 2002 and 2001 statistics have been calculated based on the adoption of FRS 19, 'Deferred Tax'.

*** 2003 ratios have been impacted by the acquisition of T&S Stores Plc.

Source: www.tesco.com

CORE PURPOSE

Creating value for customers, to earn their lifetime loyalty.
VALUES

1. No one tries harder for customers:
Understand customers better than anyone
Be energetic, be innovative and be first for customers
Use our strengths to deliver unbeatable value to our customers
Look after our people so they can look after our customers

2. Treat people how we like to be treated:
All retailers, there's one team – The Tesco Team
Trust and respect each other
Strive to do our very best
Give support to each other and praise more than criticize
Ask more than tell and share knowledge so that it can be used
Enjoy work, celebrate success and learn from experience

TABLE I Tesco – Core purpose & values
Source: www.tesco.com

testing of the Clubcard loyalty scheme at two of its stores for a period of six months. The scheme started off like any other loyalty card scheme. Customers became members by paying a joining fee and providing personal details such as name, address, date of birth, email, family composition, dietary requirements and product preferences.

To ensure the programme's success, it was essential that all Tesco employees understood the rationale for it as well as its importance. So, the company distributed over 140,000 educational videos about the programme to its staff at various stores. These videos explained why the initiative was being undertaken, what the company expected to gain out of it, and why it was important for employees to participate wholeheartedly in the programme.

Impressed with the programme's results over six months, the company introduced the scheme in all its stores by February 1995. The stores captured every one of the over 8 million transactions made per week at Tesco stores in a database. All the transactions were linked to individual customer profiles and generated over 50 gigabytes[5] of data every week. Dunnhumby used state-of-the-art data mining[6] techniques to manage and analyse the database. Initially, it took a few weeks to analyse the vast amount of data generated. To overcome this problem, Dunnhumby put in place new software that reduced this time to just a few days. As a result, it became possible to come up with useful and timely insights on customer behaviour in a much faster way.

The analysis of the data collected enabled Tesco to accurately pin-point the time when purchases were made, the amount the customer spent, and the kinds of products purchased. Based on the amount spent and the frequency of shopping, customers were classified into four broad categories: Premium, Standard, Potential and Uncommitted (refer Table II). Further, profiles were created for all the customers on the basis of the types of products they purchased. Customers were categorized along dimensions such as, Value, Convenience, Frozen, Healthy Eating, Fresh and Kids.

Tesco also identified over 5000 need segments based on the purchasing habits and behaviour patterns of its customers. Each of these segments could be targeted specifically with tailor-made campaigns and advertisements. The company also identified eight 'primary life stage' need segments based on the profiles of its customers.

SHOPPING FREQUENCY → EXPENDITURE ↓	Daily	Twice Weekly	Weekly	Stop Start	Now & Then	Hardly Ever
High Spend	PREMIUM		STANDARD		POTENTIAL	
Medium Spend	STANDARD		POTENTIAL		UNCOMMITTED	
Low Spend	POTENTIAL		UNCOMMITTED			
	FREQUENT		INFREQUENT		RARE	

TABLE II Tesco – classifying customers (A)

Source: www.ecrnet.org

These segments included 'single adults', 'pensioners' and 'urban professionals' among others. Another classification of customers developed from the insights generated through data mining is given in Table III.

Using the information regarding customer classification, Tesco's marketing department devised customized strategies for each category. Pricing, promotion and product related decisions were taken after considering the preferences of customers.

Category	Classification	Characteristics
UP-MARKET	Finer Foods	Foodies who are time poor, money rich and choose everyday luxury items.
MID-MARKET	Healthy	Organics shoppers, fruits and vegetables, weight watchers, etc.
	Convenience	People on the go who have not got the time or inclination for scratch cooking.
	Traditional	Traditional housecraft with time to buy and prepare ingredients.
COST CONSCIOUS	Mainstream	Family type meals, Popular brands, Kids products.
	Price Sensitive	Cost conscious customers who tend to buy cheapest on display.

TABLE III Tesco – classifying customers (B)
Source: www.ecrnet.org

Pricing	Discounts were offered on goods that were bought by highly price-conscious customers. While the company kept prices low on often-bought goods/staples, for less familiar lines, it adopted a premium pricing policy.
Merchandising	The product portfolio was devised based on customer profiles and purchasing behaviour records. Depending on the loyalty shown by customers towards a particular product, the substitutes available for the same, and the seasonality, the product ranges were modified.
Promotion	Promotions were aimed at giving special (and more) rewards to loyal customers. Few promotions were targeted at the other customers.
Customer Service	Extra attention was given to stocking those products that were bought by loyal customers.
Media Effectiveness	The effectiveness of media campaigns could be evaluated easily by noticing changes in the buying patterns of those customers whom the said campaign was targeted at.
Customer Acquisition	The launch of new ventures (such as TPF and Tesco.com) went off smoothly since Tesco targeted the 'right' kinds of customers.
Market Research	While conducting marketing research, Tesco was able to tap those customers that fit in accurately into the overall research plan.
Customer Communication	It was possible to mass-customize communication campaigns based on individual customer preferences and characteristics. Tesco began holding 'Customer Evenings' for interacting with customers, gathering more information, and gaining new customers through referrals.

TABLE IV How Tesco used the information generated by the Clubcards
Adapted from an article on www.clarityblue.com

Also, customers received communications that were tailored to their buying patterns. The data collected through the Clubcard scheme allowed Tesco to modify its strategies on various fronts such as pricing, inventory management, shopping analysis, customer acquisition, new product launches, store management, online customer behaviour and media effectiveness (refer Table IV).

Tesco began giving many special privileges, such as valet parking and personal attention from the store manager, to its high-value customers. Special cards were created for students and mothers, discounts were offered on select merchandise, and the financial services venture was included in the card scheme. The data generated was used innovatively, e.g. special attention given to expectant mothers in the form of personal shopping assistants, priority parking and various other facilities. The company also tied up with airline companies and began offering Frequent Flyer Miles[7] to customers in return for the points on their Clubcards.

Reaping the benefits

Commenting on the way the data generated was used, sources at Dunnhumby said that the data allowed Tesco to target individual customers (the rifle shot approach), instead of targeting them as a group (the carpet bombing approach). Since the customers received coupons that matched their buying patterns, over 20 per cent of Tesco's coupons were redeemed – as against the industry average of 0.5 per cent. The number of loyal customers increased manifold since the loyalty card scheme was launched (refer Figure I).

The quarterly magazine Tesco sent to its customers was customized based on the segments identified. Customers falling in different categories received magazines that were compiled specifically for them – the articles covered issues that interested them and the advertisements and discount coupons were about those products/services that they were most likely to purchase. This customization attracted third-party advertisers,

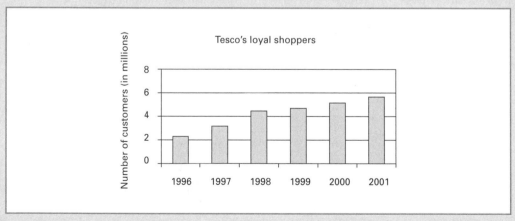

FIGURE 1 Tesco – increasing number of loyal customers

since it assured them that their products/services would be noticed by those very customers they planned to target. Naturally, Tesco recovered a large part of its investment in this exercise through revenues generated by outside advertisements.

The data collected through the cards helped the company enter the financial services business as well. The company carried out targeted research on the demographic data and zeroed in on those customers who were the most likely to opt for financial services. Due to the captive customer base and the cross-selling opportunity, the cost of acquiring customers for its financial services was 50 per cent less than what it cost a bank or financial services company.

Reportedly, the data generated by the Clubcard initiative played a major role in the way the online grocery retailing business was run. The data helped the company identify the areas in which customers were positively inclined towards online shopping. Accordingly, the areas in which online shopping was to be introduced were decided upon. Since the prospective customers were already favourably disposed, Tesco.com took off to a good start and soon emerged as one of the few profitable dotcom ventures worldwide. By 2003, the website was accessible to 95 per cent of the UK's population and generated business of £15 million per week.

By sharing the data generated with manufacturers, Tesco was able to offer better services to the customers. It gave purchasing pattern information to manufacturers, but withheld the personal information provided by customers (such as names and addresses). The manufacturers used this information to modify their own product mixes and promotional strategies. In return for this information, they gave Tesco customers subsidies and incentives in the form of discount coupons.

The Clubcards also helped Tesco compete with other retailers. For instance, if players such as Asda or Sainsbury's reduced prices on certain low-margin products to pull customers into the store so that they may be motivated to purchase high-margin products later on, Tesco was quick to reduce its own prices on such products. This way, the company ensured that the footfalls in its stores did not decline on account of competitive pressures.

When Tesco found out that around 25 per cent of its customers, who belonged to the high income bracket, were defecting to rival Marks & Spencer, it developed a totally new product range, 'Tesco Finest', to lure back these customers. This range was then promoted to affluent customers through personalized promotions. As planned, the defection of customers from this segment slowed down considerably.

Analysis of the data revealed that Tesco customers were not happy with in-store stands that displayed candy. These stands attracted children, who forced their parents to buy the candy. Similarly, many customers did not like off-shelf displays that were aimed at fuelling impulse purchases. Going against traditional retailing wisdom, Tesco decided to reduce the number of such displays, while doing away completely with the candy shelves. The company hoped that what it stood to lose in unit sales would be offset by increased customer loyalty (and thereby increased overall sales). Proving its decision right, the holiday season sales for 2002 were the best ever for Tesco, despite the removal of these impulse purchase drivers.

As a result of the above strategies, Tesco was able to increase returns even as it reduced promotions. Dunnhumby prepared a profit and loss statement for the activities of the marketing department to help assess the performance of the Clubcard initiative. Dunnhumby claimed that Tesco saved around £300 million every year through reduction in expenditure on promotions. The money saved thus was ploughed back into the business to offer more discounts to customers.

By the end of the 1990s, over 10 million households in the UK owned around 14 million Tesco Clubcards. This explained why as high as 80 per cent of the company's in-store transactions and 85 per cent of its revenues were accounted for by the cards. Thanks largely to this initiative, Tesco's turnover went up by 52 per cent between 1995 and 2000, while floor space during the same period increased by only 15 per cent.

Not only was Tesco's programme the biggest CRM programme in the UK, it was one of the most sophisticated and extensive CRM programmes in the whole world. Commenting on the reasons for Tesco's success, Clive Humby said, 'I think one is that they make sure that consumers get things that really matter to them. So the relevancy of the communication. And two, it was the first one to really use data powerfully. And, as a result, they have got a march on their competitors.'[8]

From customer service to customer delight

To sustain the growth achieved through the launch of Clubcards, Tesco decided to adopt a four-pronged approach: launch better, bigger stores on a frequent basis; offer competitive prices (e.g. offering everyday low prices in the staples business); increase the number of products offered in the Value range; and focus on remote shopping services (this included the online shopping venture). To make sure that its prices were the lowest among all retailers, Tesco employed a dedicated team of employees, called 'price checkers'. This team checked and compared Tesco's prices with those of other companies on a weekly basis. The company even helped its customers compare prices by providing the information on Tesco.com.

By late 1998, even though Tesco's CRM efforts had resulted in superior financial performance and market share, the company was still not satisfied with its customer service standards. Commenting on the need to improve on this front, Chris Reid, Customer Initiatives Manager, said, 'We have spent so much time improving the way our stores look, the range of products we sell and our service processes that we may have temporarily overlooked the impact that our people can make on customers through their behaviour. We need to redress that.'[9]

The above realization culminated in the launch of the '*Every Customer Offered Help*' (ECOH) initiative. As part of ECOH, all employees were given clear instructions about the way in which they were expected to deal with customers. Employees posted at the check-out counters, for instance, were asked to be very particular about greeting the customers, offering them help and finally, wishing them a good day. Store managers, who were responsible for making the ECOH initiative successful, participated whole-heartedly in the scheme.

In mid-2001, Tesco acquired a 53 per cent stake in Dunnhumby. Analysts said that this was a clear indication of Tesco's realization that its growth during the 1990s had occurred largely because of Dunnhumby's expertise. According to a www.1to1.com article, 'Tesco knows the customer data managed by Dunnhumby is its most valuable asset.'[10] In the same year, Dunnhumby created a separate retailing division to provide market research services to Tesco as well as its suppliers.

Tesco knew that the loyalty card initiative was just one part of the overall thrust on CRM and that customer service enhancement was needed to survive and excel in the intensely competitive British retailing market. The company therefore took a host of other initiatives to sustain its leadership position. In 2001–02, Tesco introduced Customer Champions in its stores to further the thrust given to customer service.[11] The company also successfully implemented a new scheduling scheme for store employees to increase customer satisfaction levels.

Tesco required all employees (including top level executives) to spend some time every year in the stores to help them get acquainted with the nuances of customer service. This programme not only helped ingrain customer service as a company philosophy in all employees, it also resulted in the development of many innovative ideas. Unlike Asda's customer service programme, Tesco's programme did not require employees to get 'too personal' with customers (reportedly, Asda posted employees at the doors just to greet customers).

To ensure that its CRM efforts were backed by a strong operational framework, the company paid special attention to controlling costs and streamlining its supply chain. In association with its suppliers, Tesco strove to eliminate all non-value-adding costs. It also collaborated with suppliers to develop a 'Lean Thinking' approach, which focused on smart and efficient working. The company also followed a continuous stock replenishment policy to ensure at least 99 per cent stock availability. As a result, not only were store shelves stocked adequately at all times, the chances of merchandise getting spoilt in the store backrooms was also reduced.

Commenting on Tesco's approach towards business, an April 2001 issue of *The Economist* stated, 'Irritating though it is to its detractors, Tesco's success comes from consistently good management and close attention to what customers want.'

Tesco identified long-term growth as the broad strategic goal to be achieved in the future. To do so, it focused on four aspects of its business: 'Core UK Business', 'Non-Food Business', 'Retailing Services', and 'International Business'. The 'Core UK Business' addressed the company's commitment to continue serving its UK customers in an increasingly better manner, while the 'Non-Food Business' business aimed at increasing the company's focus in new areas. In 2003, the non-food business in the UK was estimated to be worth £75 billion, of which Tesco had a 5 per cent share. Tesco believed that the market held a lot of growth potential and hence planned to focus strongly on this segment.

The success of TPF and Tesco.com prompted the company to seek other avenues for further leveraging the retailing services business. Accordingly, the company decided to launch a fixed line telephone service in the UK in September 2003, followed soon after by a mobile phone service. As far as the focus on international business was concerned, by 2003, Tesco was already earning 45 per cent of its revenues from non-UK operations. The company planned to explore the possibilities of entering new, profitable markets and expanding its global network further.

In February 2003, Tesco launched a new initiative targeted at its women customers. Named '*Me Time*', the new loyalty scheme offered ladies free sessions at leading health spas, luxury gyms and beauty saloons and discounts on designer clothes, perfumes and cosmetics. This scheme was rather innovative since it allowed Tesco customers to redeem the points accumulated through their Clubcards at a large number of third party outlets. Company official Crawford Davidson remarked, 'Up until now, our customers have used Tesco Clubcard vouchers primarily to buy more shopping for the home. However, from now on, 'Me Time' will give customers the option of spending the rewards on themselves.'

In April 2003, Tesco cut a total of £60 million off a vast range of products to continue offering competitive prices to UK customers. This was the latest addition to the price cuts that it had been carrying out since 1998. Commenting on the price cuts, Tim Mason, Tesco's Marketing Director, said, 'Many families will find some of their costs have increased recently, including their National Insurance contributions. By lowering prices we are doing our bit to help.'[12]

Not surprisingly, Tesco was the only retailing outfit that managed to get a place in the 'Top 10' of the prestigious 'The Euro BW 50' list in July 2003. The company was at number 10 in the list of the 50 top businesses in Europe compiled by *BusinessWeek*.

An invincible company? Not exactly . . .

Tesco's customer base and the frequency with which each customer visited its stores had increased significantly over the years. However, according to reports, the average purchase per visit had not gone up as much as it would have liked to see. Analysts said that this was not a very positive sign. They also said that while it was true that Tesco was the market leader by a wide margin, it was also true that Asda and Morrison were growing rapidly (refer Exhibit II).

Given the fact that the company was moving away from its core business within the UK (thrust on non-food, utility services, online travel services) and was globalizing rapidly (reportedly, it was exploring the possibilities of entering China and Japan), industry observers were rather sceptical of its ability to maintain the growth it had been posting since the late-1900s. *The Economist* stated that the UK retailing industry seemed to have become saturated and that Tesco's growth could be sustained only if it ventured overseas. However, it also cautioned that UK retailers had usually not fared well abroad and mentioned that Tesco needed to act carefully.

Tesco's growth was based largely on its loyalty card scheme. But in recent years, the very concept of loyalty cards was being criticized on various grounds. Some analysts claimed that the popularity of loyalty cards would decline in the future as all retailing companies would begin offering more or less similar schemes. Critics also commented that the name loyalty card was a misnomer since customers were primarily interested in getting the best price for the goods and services they wanted to buy.

Research conducted by Black Sun, a company specializing in loyalty solutions, revealed that though over 50 per cent of UK's adult population used loyalty cards, over 80 per cent of them said that they were bothered only about making cheaper purchases. Given the fact that many companies in the UK, such as HSBC, Egg and Barclaycard, had withdrawn their loyalty cards, industry observers were sceptical of Tesco's ability to continue reaping the benefits of the Clubcard scheme. Black Sun's Director (Business Development), David Christopherson, said, 'Most loyalty companies have a direct marketing background, which is result-driven, and focuses on the short-term. This has led to a 'points for prizes' loyalty model, which does not necessarily build the long-term foundations for a beneficial relationship with customers.'[13]

However, Tesco and Dunnhumby refused to accept the above arguments. Dunnhumby sources said that provided loyalty cards were made a part of an overall CRM strategy framework (like Tesco had done), the chances of failure would be minimal.

Commenting on the philosophy behind Tesco's CRM efforts, Edwina Dunn (Edwina) said, 'Companies should be loyal to their customers – not the other way round.'[14] Taking into consideration the company's strong performance since these efforts were undertaken, there would perhaps not be many who would disagree with Edwina.

Questions for discussion:

1 Examine the customer service efforts undertaken by Tesco prior to the loyalty card scheme's launch. Why do you think the company felt the need to launch Clubcards?

2 Analyse Tesco's Clubcard scheme in depth and comment on the various customer segmentation models the company developed after studying the data gathered.

3 How did Tesco use the information collected to modify its marketing strategies? What sort of benefits was the company able to derive as a result of such modifications?

4 What measures did Tesco adopt to support the CRM initiatives on the operational and strategic front? Is it enough for a company to implement loyalty card schemes (and CRM tools in general) in isolation? Why?

5 With Tesco moving away from its core business of grocery retailing and focusing on globalization, what do you think the future has in store for the company? What do you think the company should do to retain its growth pace and leadership status?

Additional readings & references:

1 **Tesco: Piling Up the Profits**, The Economist, April 12, 2001.

2 Breese Allan, **Tesco**, www.kamcity.com, June 09, 2000.

3 Rogers Martha, **High for Tesco and Dunnhumby**, www.1to1.com, August 06, 2001.

4 Retail Brand Value: **The Case of Tesco**, www.crm-forum.com, September 27, 2001.

5 Millar Bill, **Is Customer Loyalty in the Cards?** www.1to1.com, October 01, 2001.

6 **Marketer Masterclass**, Pharmatimes, December 2001.

7 **Loyalty Cards vs. Price Cuts: Which is More Impressive?** www.blacksun.co.uk, February 15, 2002.

8 Rowe Deborah, **Customers That Count**, www.cimcroydon.co.uk, March 21, 2002.

9 Cannon Jeff, **How a Supermarket Can be a Corner Shop**, www.crmguru.com, March 24, 2003.

10 Tso Karen, **Tesco Tests Loyalty Programs**, www.abc.net.au, June 19, 2003.

11 **The Mediocre Middle**, The Economist, June 28, 2003.

12 Lowenstein Michael, **Tesco: A Retail Customer Divisibility Champion**, www.customerloyalty.org.

13 **Tesco – The Brand Experience is Everything**, www.brandingasia.com.

14 **Tesco Clubcard and Dunnhumby**, www.clarityblue.com.

15 **Once You Get to the Top, How do You Stay There?** www.axia.com.

16 www.ecrnet.org.

17 www.brc.org.uk.

18 www.datamonitor.com.

19 www.dunnhumby.com.

20 www.tesco.com.

Notes

This case was written by A. Mukund, ICFAI Center for Management Research (ICMR). It was compiled from published sources, and is intended to be used as a basis for class discussion rather than to illustrate either effective or ineffective handling of a management situation.

To order copies, call 0091-40-2343-0462/63 or write to ICFAI Center for Management Research, Plot # 49, Nagarjuna Hills, Hyderabad 500 082, India or email icmr@icfai.org. Website: www.icmrindia.org

[1] 'How a Supermarket can be a Corner Shop', www.crmguru.com, 23 January 2003.

[2] 'How a Supermarket can be a Corner Shop', www.crmguru.com, 23 January 2003.

[3] Loyalty cards are a part of 'loyalty programmes', which fall under the domain of customer retention strategies. These cards reward customers when they make purchases from the company in the form of points that accumulate over time. These points can later on be redeemed for cash/gifts/discounts. Thus, they provide incentives to customers for remaining a particular company's customers.

[4] Dunnhumby, established in 1989 by Edwina Dunn and Clive Humby, offered marketing and employee related services to corporate clients. The company offered its services through its divisions: Dunnhumby Cinnamon (direct marketing division) and Dunnhumby Crucible (data division). Dunnhumby operated in the UK and the US, and had clients such as Virgin Mobile, Wella, Unilever, Lever Faberge and Gillette.

[5] A byte is a unit that is capable of storing a single character of data in a computer system. It is an abbreviation for 'binary term' and is equal to 8 bits. Large amounts of data are classified as kilobytes (1,024 bytes), megabytes (1,048,576 bytes), and gigabytes (1,073,741,824 bytes).

[6] Data mining refers to the process of using database applications to look for hidden patterns in a group of data and using it to predict future behaviour. This is done through specialized software that not only presents the existing data in new ways, but discovers hitherto unknown relationships among the data.

[7] Frequent Flyer Miles are customer retention programmes originally adopted by airline companies. Under this programme, customers are awarded points for each mile they flew with a particular airline. After accumulating a certain number of points, customers can 'cash' them in for air tickets, discounts and cash rewards. The concept was adopted by many industries later on as a tool for customer retention.

[8] 'Tesco Tests Loyalty Programs', www.abc.net.au, June 19, 2003.

[9] 'Once You Get to the Top, How do You Stay There?' www.axia.com.

[10] 'High for Tesco and Dunnhumby', www.1to1.com, August 06, 2001.

[11] The customer champions aimed at providing the customers with an overall better shopping experience. This move was similar to the concept of 'customer assistants' introduced by Tesco in 1996. These specially trained employees assisted customers in a friendly manner while they shopped at the company's stores.

[12] www.tesco.com.

[13] 'Loyalty Cards vs. Price Cuts: Which is More Persuasive?' www.blacksun.co.uk, February 15, 2002.

[14] 'Loyalty Cards vs. Price Cuts: Which is More Persuasive?' www.blacksun.co.uk, February 15, 2002.

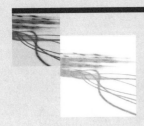

Case 2
People, service and profit at Jyske Bank

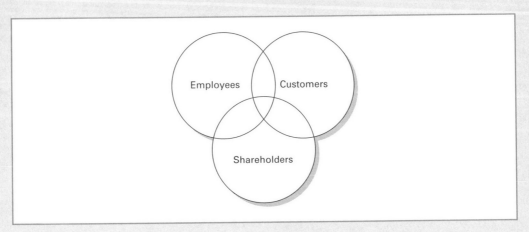

Employees Customers

Shareholders

FIGURE 1

> *The Jyske Bank Group is managed and operated as a business. At the same time, we attach great importance to treating our three groups of stakeholders – shareholders, customers and employees – with equal respect. This is illustrated by three equally big overlapping circles (Figure I) which must remain in perfect balance. If the balance shifts in favour of one or two of the groups, this will be to the long-term detriment of all the groups.*

Jyske Bank Management Philosophy

In 2003, Jyske Bank Group's primary operations consisted of Jyske Bank, which was the third largest bank in Denmark after Den Danske Bank and Nordea's Danish operations (see Exhibit 1). Jyske Bank was created in 1967 through the merger of four Danish banks having their operations in Jutland, Jyske being Danish for 'Jutlandish'. Jutland was the large portion of Denmark attached to the European mainland to the north of Germany. Until the late 1990s, Jyske Bank was characterized as a typical Danish bank: prudent, conservative, well-managed, generally unremarkable and largely undifferentiated.

Beginning in the mid-1990s, Jyske Bank embarked on a change process that led to its no longer being characterized as either unremarkable or undifferentiated. By 2003 its

Exhibit 1 Danish Banks Shareholders' Equity at January 1, 2002

Bank	Shareholders' Equity
1. DDB	57.091
2.* Jyske Bank	6.174
3. Sydbank	3.435
4. Nykredit Bank	2.708
5. Spar Nord	1.692
6. Arbejdernes Landsbank	1.518
7. Amtssparekassen Fyn	994
8. Amargerbanken	956
9. Sparbank Vest	841
10. Sparekassen, Kornjylland	816
11. Ringkøbing Landbobank	794
12. Alm. Brand Bank	749
13. Forstædernes Bank	706
14. Loskilde Bank	698
15. Lå 'n & Spar Bank	589
16. Nørresundby Bank	583
17. Sparekassen Sjælland	582
18. Sparekassen Lolland	559
19. Nordvestbank	545

*Note: Nordea is not shown as it was a Swedish bank with operations in Denmark, having acquired Unibank.

Source: Jyske Bank

unique 'flavour' of service made it a leader in customer satisfaction among Danish banks (see Exhibit 2). At the heart of these changes was the bank's determination to be, in the words of one executive, 'the most customer-oriented bank in Denmark'. The bank achieved its goal by focusing on what it called *Jyske Forskelle*, or Jyske Differences.

Denmark

At the onset of the twenty-first century Denmark had a population of approximately 5 million. A member of the European Union retaining its own currency (the Danish Kronor, DKK[1]), Denmark was the southernmost of the Scandinavian countries. Denmark had been a wealthy country for hundreds of years. This was originally due to its strategic location in the Baltic Sea (see Exhibit 3) enabling it to extract tolls from merchants who were forced to sail within cannon range of its shores. More recently, much of Denmark's wealth came from high-value-added goods such as agricultural products, pharmaceuticals, machinery, instruments and medical equipment, in addition to a highly developed service sector including shipping.

Exhibit 2 Danish Banks' Quality of Service Metrics

Part I: Analysis of Bank Image

	Total Image	Willingness to Take Risk	Management	They Are a Strategic Coach for Me	Service and Customer Treatment	Expert in Advice and Competence	Choose This Bank If We Want to Change Banks
Jyske Bank	1	1	1	1	1	1	1
Sydbank	2	2	3	2	2	2	2
Spar Nord Bank	3	4	4	3	3	5	5
Midtbank/ Handeslbank	4	6	7	4	6	4	7
Amagerbanken	5	3	5	6	4	8	6
Amtssparekassen Fyn	6	5	6	5	5	7	8
Nordea	7	7	8	8	7	6	3
Danske Bank	8	8	2	7	8	3	4
BG Bank	9	9	9	9	9	9	9

Source: Survey of 1750 small companies conducted by the Danish newspaper *Erhvervs Bladet*, 22 March 2002, p. 2

Part II: (A) Consumer Satisfaction Survey: Very Satisfied

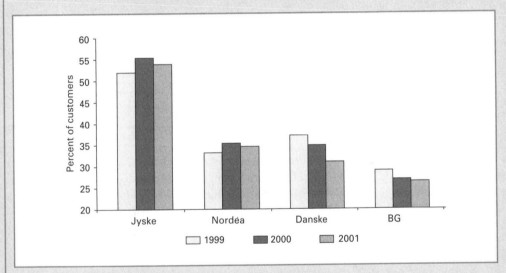

Part II: (B) Consumer Satisfaction Survey: Satisfied and Very Satisfied

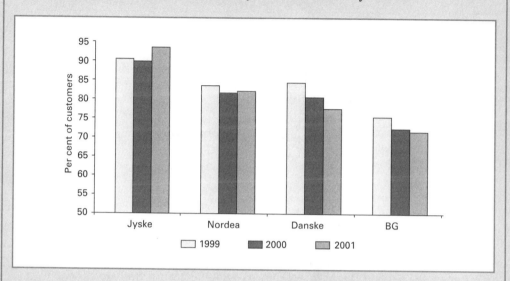

Part II: (C) Consumer Satisfaction Survey: Dissatisfied and Very Dissatisfied

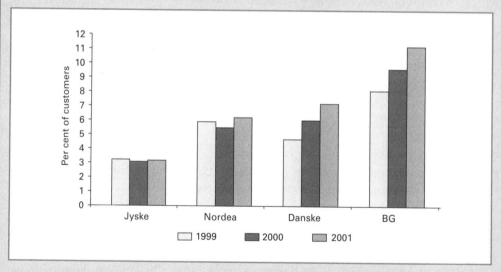

Source: AC Nielsen via Jyske Bank

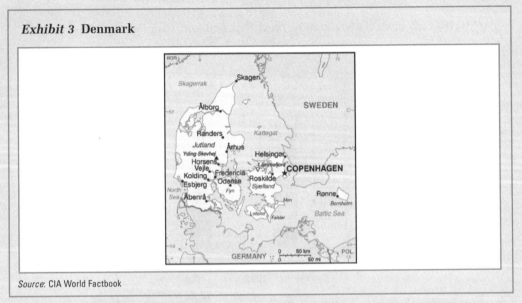

Exhibit 3 **Denmark**

Source: CIA World Factbook

Following the Second World War, Denmark adopted a social welfare system its government described as follows:

> The basic principle of the Danish welfare system, often referred to as the Scandinavian welfare model, is that all citizens have equal rights to social security. Within the Danish welfare system, a number of services are available to citizens, free of charge. ... The Danish welfare model is subsidized by the state, and as a result Denmark has one of the highest taxation levels in the world.[2]

Jutland

Jutland was physically separated from Denmark's capital, Copenhagen (see Exhibit 3 for a map). Copenhagen, with a population comprising almost one-quarter of all Danes, was located on the island of Zealand (*Sjaelland*). Jutland's isolation from the capital prior to modern transportation led to its people being characterized differently from their Zealander neighbours: Jutlanders were supposed to be honest, unpretentious, egalitarian, open and direct in their communication style (candid), commonsensical, frugal, sobre-minded and relatively unsophisticated, at least in contrast to those, as one Jutlander put it, 'slippery people from Copenhagen'.

Jyske Differences

Jyske Differences stemmed from Jyske Bank's core values. These stood as central tenets, guiding virtually all aspects of the organization's life. As one manager pointed out, the values were consistent with the bank's Jyske heritage: 'Really, when we started talking about our core values, and their Jyskeness, we just became overt about values we had

Exhibit 4 Jyske Bank's Core Values

Common sense
'With both feet placed firmly on the ground, we think before we act'

That means that we:

- consider common sense our best guide
- apply common sense when solving problems and meeting daily challenges
- allow common sense to override awkward customs and routines
- take action whenever we encounter examples of bureaucratic procedures
- observe existing rules and regulations
- accept that control measures are necessary to a certain degree
- generate satisfactory short- and long-term financial results by pursuing sound business practices
- apply common sense whenever we incur group expenses.

Open and honest
'We are open and honest in both word and action'

That means that we:

- keep each other up to date on relevant matters, and do not misuse information obtained in the course of our work
- restrict the degree of openness only by business considerations or by consideration for other stakeholders
- respect agreements entered into and do not betray the Bank's confidence
- strive towards making important decisions concerning individual employees on the basis of a constructive dialogue
- communicate openly about the mistakes we make and the problems we encounter
- accept that mistakes are made, that they are corrected, and that focus is then on learning from the process
- listen openly to new ideas and constructive criticism.

Different and unpretentious
'We think and act differently and are generally unpretentious'

That means that we:

- encourage creativity and initiative by being untraditional
- are full of initiative, and are committed and proactive
- encourage relaxed and straightforward communication – both internally and externally.

▶ **Genuine interest and equal respect**
'We demonstrate insight and respect for other people'

That means that we:

- recognize that no two people are alike
- seek lasting relations with shareholders, customers and employees
- offer qualified advice matching the financial needs and requirements of each customer
- have job security based on mutual obligations and that we pay attention to individual and personal needs
- allow the highest possible degree of personal influence on assignments, working hours, and place of work.

Efficient and persevering
'We work consistently and with determination to reach our goals'

That means that we:

- use JB 2005 (the bank's core values) as a guide in our daily work
- are not blown off course because of external circumstances – but take a bearing and plot a new course when this is deemed appropriate
- adopt an organization which promotes efficiency
- consider security important to efficiency
- are convinced that efficiency increases with the level of personal responsibility
- allow employees to assume personal responsibility for day-to-day decisions – even when the basis for decision making may not be 100 per cent perfect
- acquire the level of skills required through personal and professional development
- act on the basis of competence rather than organizational charge
- support our decisions by well-founded arguments.

long held.' Jyske Bank's core values, published for employees, customers and shareholders, were that the bank should (1) have common sense; (2) be open and honest; (3) be different and unpretentious; (4) have genuine interest and equal respect for people; and (5) be efficient and persevering. See Exhibit 4 for a more detailed description.

The core values led management to reevaluate how the bank did business with its customers. Managers determined that if the bank were to be true to its values, it would have to deliver service differently from both how it had in the past, and how other banks delivered service. Jyske Differences were thus operationalized as specific practices that distinguished Jyske Bank.

Competitive positioning

Managers looked to Jyske values and differences for the bank's competitive positioning. This process was aided by a Dutch consultant, whose market research indicated that Jyske bank's core target market of Danish families and small- to medium-sized Danish companies (earnings were 40 per cent commercial, 60 per cent retail) generally liked the idea of a bank that was Jyske. Additional research suggested that what managers described as the 'hard factors' of price, product and location had become sine qua non in the eyes of customers. In contrast, 'soft factors' relating to an individual customer's relationship with his or her service providers served as the basis for differentiation, specifically, 'being nice', 'making time for the customer', and 'caring about the customer and his family'.

Managers felt that the 'genuine interest' component of the bank's values dictated a shift from traditional product focused selling to a customer-solution approach. They characterized the new approach by contrasting the statement, 'Let me tell you about our demand-deposit account', with the question, 'What do you need?'

Although the bank's core financial products remained essentially similar to those of other Danish banks,[3] the way they were delivered changed. This required significant changes in the branches, both tangible and intangible, and how they were supported. Tools were developed to support solution-based service delivery. For example, new IT systems helped employees take customers through processes to determine their needs and find appropriate solutions. In one, the customer and her banker filled out an online investor profile to determine what style of investment products were most appropriate for her based on risk aversion, time frame and return goals, among other factors. A manager commented that, 'The tools themselves aren't proprietary. We've seen other financial services with similar programmes – it's how our people use them that makes the difference.' Another stated, 'Our tools are designed either to enhance our ability to deliver solutions, or to reduce administrative tasks and increase the amount of time our people can spend with customers – delivering solutions.'

Finally, being overtly Jyske meant that the bank would no longer be a good place for any customer meeting its demographic criteria for two reasons. First, delivering this type of service was expensive. As a result, the bank charged a slight premium and targeted only those customers who were less likely to represent a credit risk. Second, the bank would have a personality. According to one manager, 'The danger in having a personality is, someone, inevitably, won't like you'. Senior management considered this the price of being candid, and welcomed the effect it had on some customers. For example, Jyske Bank's cash/debit card had a picture of a black grouse on it, black grouses being found in Jutland's rural countryside. When a few customers complained that the bird didn't seem very business-like, or was not hip (one was 'embarrassed to pull it out at the disco') managers were happy to invite them to open accounts at competitor institutions. A manager noted: 'Actually, if no one reacts to our materials, they're not strong enough. Some people should dislike us. After all, we're only about 6 per cent of the market. I don't want everyone to like us – we're not for everyone and don't want to be.'

Tangible differences

Account teams

Delivering on the bank's competitive positioning required a number of tangible changes in its service delivery system. These began with assigning each customer a branch employee to serve as primary point of contact. Over time, managers discovered that this created problems, because customers often arrived at a branch when their service provider was busy with other customers or otherwise unavailable. Nevertheless, managers were committed to providing individualized service. According to one, 'How can we be honest in saying we care about customers as individuals if we don't get to know them as individuals? And without knowing them, we can't identify and solve their problems.' The solution was found in account teams: each customer was assigned to a small team of branch bankers. These employees worked together to know and serve their customers, sitting in close physical proximity within the branch.

Branch design

Jyske Bank planned to spend approximately DKK750 million to physically redesign its branches (most of this had been spent by 2003). Danish observers described the new branches as looking 'like an advertising agency' or 'a smart hotel'. These effects were accomplished through the use of modern, up-scale materials such as light wood, warm colours and original art. Branch redesign also included changes in the way customers interacted with their bankers, made possible by architectural and design changes. For example, customers waiting for their banker could help themselves to fresh coffee in a small part of the branch resembling a café. A customer commented on the café, 'It means more than you initially think – it makes you feel welcome, it says they're really interested in me'. Fruit juice was available for children, who could amuse themselves with toys in the play centre. Bankers' desks were now round tables, signifying equality. A team of three or four bankers sat at a single large round table, with customers making themselves comfortable between the bankers' work stations. Customers could see bankers' computer screens, reinforcing openness. Customers' ability to view the screens also facilitated the use of IT programs designed to structure interactions between account team members and customers. As equals, bankers and customers sat in the same type of chairs, and bankers no longer sat on a raised dais, the origins of which went back to feudal times when the heads of certain people were supposed to be higher than those of others. If a conversation required more discretion, specially designed meeting rooms giving the feeling of 'home' were available. Exhibit 5 contains pictures of a remodelled branch.

Details

Jyskeness was infused into the bank wherever possible, a formal policy requiring Jyske differences to be considered in all product and IT development. No detail was too small: for example, although employees' business cards had their pictures on them, as one manager put it, 'They were bad pictures, really grey. They weren't warm – the people in them looked stiff and uncaring.' To make them more Jyske, the bank hired a professional photographer who worked with each employee to 'get the genuine interest in that

Exhibit 5 **Pictures of a Remodelled Branch**

(A)

Source: Jyske Bank (A)

(B)

(C)

(D)

employee's eye to come to life'. Each picture was then tinted slightly yellow to make it resemble 'an old family photo'.

Intangible differences

Delivering the bank's new competitive positioning also required numerous intangible changes and other changes not immediately visible to the customer. Managers stated that the most important of these involved training and empowering those employees closest to the customer to serve the customer.

Training

Before a branch was remodelled, all staff took part in special training sessions. These included team-building and customer service, drawing on best practices from the 'traditional' retail sector.

Empowering the branches

Jyske Bank leadership examined its organizational structure, asking, 'Where is value created?' and 'Where should decisions be made in order to create the most value?'. The answer to both questions was 'in the branches'.

Previously, almost all lending decisions of any consequence required approval at branch, regional and headquarters levels. Specifically, a customer would approach an employee for a loan. The request would be communicated to the branch manager. The branch manager would then make out the formal application, which if the loan was for more than DKK3 million, was sent to a regional office with the branch manager's comments. The regional office would then comment on the application, and if the loan was for more than DKK15 million, send it to headquarters for approval, where additional comments were added to the application. Loans of more than DKK30 million also required approval from the head of credit for the bank as a whole. In examining this process, managers discovered that most of the debate and communication were among individuals in the middle, rather than between the employee closest to the customer (who presumably had the most information about the customer) and the ultimate decision-maker.

After reviewing the situation, the bank's leadership stated, 'If we are to be true to our value of using common sense, we shouldn't need so many people, and so many layers, reviewing loans'. First, the process was changed so that the employee receiving the request for the loan completed the formal application. This empowered that employee by giving him or her ownership of the loan, which he or she was trained in how to handle. That employee was also put in charge of pricing the loan, as long as the suggested pricing was within a set range of where the final approval authority felt it should be. Most loans received final approval from the branch manager, who was either selected in part based on his or her credit skills or given additional training in credit. A few loans required approval at the regional level because of their size. In these instances, the employee completing the application sent it directly to the regional head of credit. Ninety-eight per cent of loans were handled at the branch or regional level, where loans of up to DKK90 million were approved. The credit department at headquarters was disbanded, leaving only the bank's head of credit who reviewed loans of more than

DKK90 million. This additional review was retained for loans of this size because exposure to the customer would be so great that default could significantly affect the bank's capital.

The changes implemented were originally designed to affect internal processes. However, they also improved customers' experiences. For example, managers believed that because the employee in direct contact with the customer made the application, the quality of information in applications increased; as a result, more borrowers worthy of credit received it, and the quality of loans in the bank's portfolio improved. In addition, the time to reach a decision for the largest loans declined from a maximum of three weeks to ten days. Smaller loans able to be approved within the branch could be made almost instantly. Finally, customers' expectations regarding price and terms were more often included in the application. This helped the approving authority to see whether the loan, in a form acceptable to the bank, was likely to be accepted by the customer, saving time and effort when customers' expectations were inconsistent with the bank's requirements.

The streamlined approval process did not pose a credit risk, according to managers, because of the combination of: (1) improved branch credit skills, (2) lack of incentive to make poor loans (branch managers had no incentives immediately related to loan volume or quality), and (3) a robust internal auditing function that monitored credit quality.

At the same time that the credit process was redesigned, the bank consolidated from five regions to three, and increased spans of control so that between 35 and 45 branches reported to each business unit director, who had a staff of marketing, credit, human resources and control professionals at the regional level (many of whom had previously been at headquarters).

A senior manager commented on the roles of headquarters, the regions and the branches:

> Headquarters is where we transform our values and strategy into products, processes, and information technology. The three regions are where we make sure that what comes from headquarters is translated for the local marketplace, and where we ensure that Jyske Differences are being acted upon – that customers experience them. The 119 branches are where we serve customers and thus where value is really created. 20 per cent of what we do is development at headquarters, and 80 per cent is implementation in the field, supported by the regions. Given the small size of our branches we need the regional level to ensure that implementation is done right.

Empowerment throughout the bank

Empowerment was not limited to the branches. Throughout the bank, employees were encouraged to make decisions of all sorts if they felt comfortable doing so. In general, employees were encouraged to ask themselves, 'Does it make sense to ask for help or permission? Is there a business reason for asking? Is this something you've never done before? Is this a "big" decision (big being relative)? Is it debatable, or is it a new principle?' In general, employees were told, 'When in doubt, ask. However, if there is no doubt, go ahead'. Managers were expected to set an example.

Examples of this policy in action included working hours and vacation time. One employee noted, 'If your job makes it possible, you set your hours, you just have to agree with your colleagues, you don't need approval from your boss. You do the same with holidays'. A manager noted, 'The union[4] at headquarters didn't have a problem with this, but the union in Copenhagen worried that employees might misuse the flexibility'.

Another example involved the amount employees were able to spend on meals and entertainment while travelling or entertaining customers. Previously, there had been a set amount, DKK125, and bills consistently came to DKK125. Consistent with its value of common sense, the bank changed the policy to be (paraphrased) 'Spend what you need to spend'. This resulted in what an executive stated was a 'substantial decline in travel and entertainment expenses'. When asked, 'How do you get a system like this to work?' he replied:

> First, you tell people what's expected.
>
> Second, you check on their behaviour. If they are buying expensive wine, you ask, 'Why?' You explain what makes sense, and why. You do it in a way that tells them you honestly want to help them improve.
>
> Third, if there are continued problems, this person may not be right for the bank.
>
> The real challenge is when we hire someone from another bank. We expect them to be up to speed quickly because of their background, but they aren't used to making these kinds of decisions – they have to be taught how.

Management style

A senior manager commented:

> You can train and educate all day long, but unless your managers and employees are committed to Jyske Differences, they just won't happen. Getting them committed required a great deal of my effort.
>
> When we started this process there were times when it was hard – really hard. The branch managers didn't think strategically – they sat in their offices and focused on their day-to-day work. I wanted the branch manager to get up on a hill and look around, to get a bigger picture. To get them to change I asked them questions: what's the market? Where – and who – are your competitors? What are your strengths and weaknesses, how do they tie to Jyske Differences? Now, contrast what you need with what you have. Are the teams in your branch living up to the demands? What do you need to do to ensure that they will? There will be resistance; understand where it is coming from. One way to deal with it is to make agreements with individuals on how they will develop new skills. If there is a complete mismatch you may need new team members, but for the most part, you can coach your people through this kind of change – you can lead them.

According to another executive:

> The branch managers have to be able to motivate employees to work a little harder, and differently. The most successful give their employees a lot of latitude for decision making. They do a lot of training, 80 per cent of which is on the job. When it isn't, it's mostly role playing. There aren't any high-powered incentives to offer, but there are really good tools coming out of IT. It's more *how the branch managers do it* than *what they do*. They constantly link the tools, training and behaviours to our Jyske values. They get their employees to share the values and act on them.

A third noted:

> When I have a difficult situation I look for what I call a 'culture carrier'. I try to put that person into the middle of it, because they live our values. What I usually see is that the other employees who are on the fence about the values start to come over – they see the example and they like what they see. This leaves the few people who really don't want to be Jyske on the outside, and they tend not to last long. Most people are willing to change, but they've got to be supported in the process.

Human resources

Legal aspects of human resources, record-keeping and training were centralized at headquarters. In contrast, advice on how to deal with human issues was provided by human resource professionals located in the field (at the regional level). They delivered this advice to general managers in the field such as branch managers. The branches had to pay for this service, and they could choose to either buy the service or do without if they preferred.

Selection

An executive discussed employee selection at the bank:

> It's very important. For most of the jobs, we're not only looking for banking skills, we're looking for social abilities – service mindedness and compatibility with our Jyske values: openness, genuine interest in other people. You can smell it when you speak with someone. We don't have a systematic approach to this, although when we're hiring someone from another bank we ask why they want to work for us and listen for answers consistent with Jyske values. We can train most banking skills, but we can't train these attitudes. Maybe our biggest challenge is hiring people with them, and getting a few of our established employees to adopt them.

Some departments of the bank asked potential hires to write about themselves. A manager noted, 'We're looking to see whether they're engaged in what they do, or if they're promoting themselves'.

Training

A manager in human resources commented:

> We have told every employee that his or her development is his or her responsibility. We believe development is incredibly important. While my peers at other Danish banks are cutting staff and saving every way possible, our goal is to get employees and managers to invest in more development. But it's up to the individual to decide what to invest in. We're outsourcing a lot of development activities, but we keep anything related to Jyske values in house.

Incentives

Managers pointed out that the bank had few monetary incentives. The few in place consisted of three types: stock, one-time payments and annual raises.

> Stock incentives: if the bank's annual performance was above the average of the top ten Danish banks', a stock option grant valued at DKK8.000 was made available to all employees and managers. In addition, any employee could use up to DKK13.200 to buy company stock annually at a 20 per cent discount. If the bank's annual performance was among the top three Danish banks', the discount rose to 40 per cent.
>
> One-time payments: for truly exceptional work, employees could be awarded one-time payments. Fewer than 1 per cent of individuals at the bank received this type of payment.
>
> Raise incentives: employees and managers received annual salary increases based on their manager's evaluation of their work. The highest raise practicably possible was 10 per cent, although an employee or manager in the top 15 per cent of performers (the highest level) typically received a raise of approximately 7 per cent. Salary raises were eventually limited as total salary had to remain within the bands established for a particular position. Once an increase was granted it became a permanent part of the employee's salary.

Commitment

An employee commented on what it was like to work for Jyske Bank: 'I'm not restricted. I don't have to leave my head at home – I can take it with me to work and I'm supposed to.' Another commented:

> You're treated as a human being here. At other banks you have to be really careful what you say. Here, you can be open and honest – I can approach anyone – even the CEO.
>
> Jyske Bank is a way of life. You come in at 8.00 a.m. and you leave when you collect your pension. I pay a premium for this, I could earn more at another bank, but it's worth it for me. At some banks, bankers have prostituted themselves for higher pay, stuffing products down the throats of customers those customers may not need. We don't.

Anders Dam, Jyske Bank's CEO, stated:

> " If you can create an environment in which people aren't talking about money, but where they gain value in their relationships with their colleagues and their customers, where the bank will take care of those who work hard even if they get sick, then people will be committed to the bank. "

Metrics and financial results

Bank managers frequently referred to the importance of measuring performance, in both quantitative and qualitative ways, and at a variety of locations in the bank. Traditional financial measures were considered important, but not all-important. In addition to traditional measures, Jyske Bank implemented an information technology system to measure account profitability on a risk-adjusted basis (risk-adjusted return on capital, or RAROC). This had been a considerable effort and was just coming online in 2003.

Customer and employee measures were also considered important. Managers reported that employee satisfaction was higher at Jyske Bank than at any of its major competitors based on data collected by independent third parties. Several sources of data indicated that Jyske Bank customer satisfaction was also the highest among the bank's major competitors (see Exhibit 2). Customer satisfaction could be tracked to the regional level. Plans were in place to be able to measure and report it at the branch, and eventually the individual customer, levels.

Financial and selected operating results are presented in Exhibit 6. Jyske Bank took a conservative approach to earnings, writing off its entire investment in remodelling branches, building a new headquarters, and new information technology systems in the years in which spending occurred. This amounted to DKK302 million in 2002, DKK253 million in 2001, DKK194 million in 2000 and DKK212 million in 1999. Results for 2002 also reflected an extraordinary tax payment of DKK222 million, which was described as 'a potential liability in light of discussions with the Danish tax authorities'.[5]

Jyske Bank's statement of core values and principles included the following: 'the aim is for Jyske Bank every year to be one of the top performing Danish banks ... Jyske Bank is thus an excellent choice for shareholders who want to make a long-term investment and who do not attach great importance to decisions which generate only short-term price increases'.

Communication

Management believed that most employees liked working for the bank and appreciated Jyske Differences as they affected their jobs. Sustaining Jyske Differences required the bank to remain independent, not an easy task in the Scandinavian banking market, which had consolidated considerably during the 1990s and early twenty-first century. Executives believed that they had taken the right steps to remain independent by investing in employees, systems and infrastructure that would enable the bank to deliver superior value to its targeted customers, and thus achieve superior financial returns. This economic model was built on the bank's value chain (see Exhibit 7).

Delivering that value required considerable change. One manager stated a point that several alluded to: 'If you want employees to behave differently, you have to be sure

Exhibit 6 Jyske Bank Group Financial and Selected Operating Results

Five-year summary of financial results

Summary of profit and loss account (DKKm)	2002	2001	2000	1999	1998
Net interest income	2826	2623	2350	2078	2133
Dividend on capital holdings	64	98	69	52	34
Net fee and commission income	758	668	759	646	594
Net interest and fee income	**3648**	3389	3178	2776	2761
Revaluations	386	129	379	631	361
Other ordinary income	203	213	162	175	219
Operating expenses and depreciation	2598	2443	2142	2014	1764
Losses and provisions for bad debts	408	286	318	248	197
Revaluation of capital interests	-148	-112	-4	-44	-52
Profit/loss on ordinary activities before tax	1083	890	1255	1276	710
Tax	572	267	172	379	199
Profit/loss for the year	**511**	623	1083	897	511

Summary of balance sheet (DKKm)	2002	2001	2000	1999	1998
Advances	95302	82537	75362	49790	39762
Deposits	58963	54393	52267	49813	43816
Issued bonds	43362	36964	26902	192	623
Total assets	153169	133156	127359	92557	76938
Shareholders' funds	6658	6174	5887	5391	5108
Supplementary capital	2000	2663	2110	1395	434

Key figures	2002	2001	2000	1999	1998
Per Jyske Bank share					
Core earnings	23.17	25.39	22.07	14.68	19.89
Profit/loss on ordinary activities before tax	29.32	24.11	31.86	29.58	15.77
Net profit/loss for the year	13.84	16.77	27.51	20.83	11.22
Dividend	0.00	0.00	0.00	3.20	2.80
Price at year end	192	177	161	149	123
Book value	178	170	157	131	114
Price/book value	1.08	1.04	1.03	1.14	1.08
Price/earnings	13.8	10.5	5.9	7.2	10.9
The Jyske Bank Group					
Solvency ratio	11.3	11.4	11.0	10.5	10.4
Core capital ratio	8.2	7.9	8.0	8.2	9.5
Income on every krone of expenditure	1.36	1.33	1.51	1.56	1.36
Total provisions as % of total loans	1.8	1.9	2.0	2.7	3.0
Losses and provisions for the year as % of total loans	0.4	0.3	0.4	0.4	0.4

Source: Jyske Bank

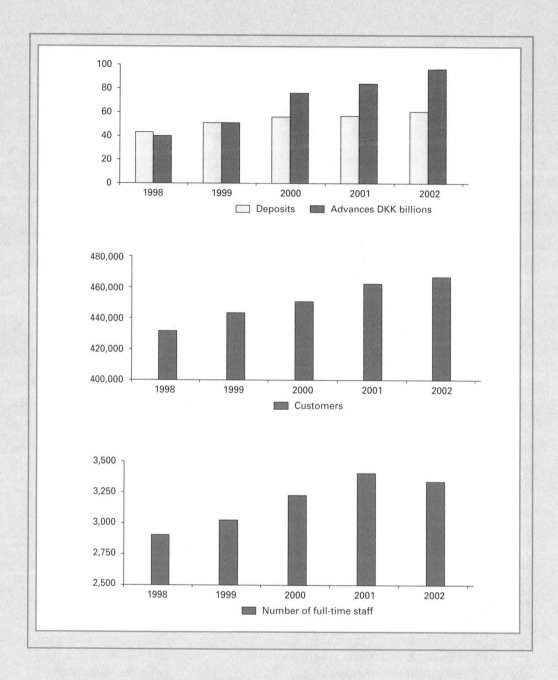

they know what that means – how they should behave going forward, and why they should change. We can't ask people to change without communicating this kind of information to them – it's not fair.'

Bank leadership believed that communication should be, in the words of an executive, 'a car wash, not a waterfall – communication must come from all directions at once, not just cascade down from above'. In that spirit, in 1997 communication

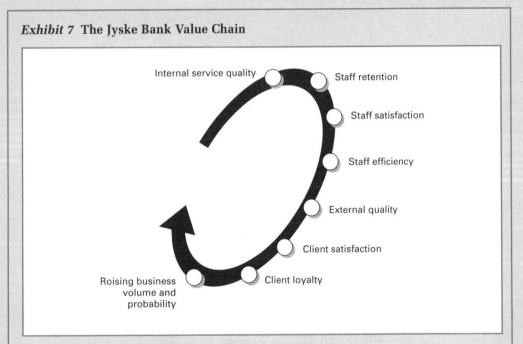

Exhibit 7 **The Jyske Bank Value Chain**

Internal service quality

Staff retention

Staff satisfaction

Staff efficiency

External quality

Client satisfaction

Client loyalty

Roising business volume and probability

Source: Jyske Bank's adaptation of Heskett, Sasser and Schlesinger's Service Profit Chain (see Heskett et al., 1997)

reinforced Jyske values and differences when the bank produced a videotape on Jyske Differences, made available to all employees. This was designed to look like a television talk show. The host was a prominent Danish television personality and the guests were Anders Dam and Danish experts on business. Each was interviewed and they discussed what Jyske Differences were, how they were being implemented, and what they meant to employees and customers, supported by video clips of employees and customers in the branches.

Communication efforts continued in 1999, executives planning a surprise for the bank's strategic meeting, to which all employees were invited every third year.

The battle at Vejle

The 1999 strategic meeting took place in Vejle, the closest city to the bank's headquarters with an auditorium large enough for the 82 per cent of the bank's 3107 employees who chose to attend. The meeting opened with a panel of senior executives, some of whom were from Jyske Bank, and others who were strangers. A grim-faced Anders Dam got up, and introduced one of the strangers as 'the CEO of a large, very large, Swedish bank'. Dam then continued, explaining that the Swedish bank had offered to buy Jyske Bank for almost twice its current stock market valuation, a premium of 2.3 times what other Danish banks had recently been acquired for. A fax was to be sent to the Copenhagen stock exchange, suspending trading in Jyske Bank shares immediately after the meeting. As he spoke, a sense of foreboding rose in the audience.

Non-Scandinavians should note that despite the currently cosy relationship between

Swedes and Danes, they fought against one another for many centuries, Southern Sweden once having been a Danish possession.

The CEO of the Swedish bank took the podium and announced (in Swedish, which is very difficult for most Danes to understand) that his Danish was very poor, so that he would 'speak Scandinavian, very slowly', after which he continued to deliver his address in Swedish.

He stated, among other things, that 'You – Jyske Bank, you are good, very good. But are you good enough? For tomorrow? For the future? For a world without borders across the continent?' After his speech Anders Dam took the podium again and asked for an 'immediate and honest response' from the employees. Over the course of several questions and responses it became clear that although the takeover was friendly, the integration would be anything but. In the words of the Swedish CEO, 'A merger has certain administrative advantages, which will require an adjustment in staffing'. Eventually, a manager got up and said, 'Do something for the environment. Put the Swedes on the ferry and send them back!' His suggestion received wild applause.

After a pause, Anders Dam returned to the podium and, now smiling, explained that it had all been a joke, which he called 'Jyske Fun'. He added that he was 'proud, proud as a peacock of your reaction to the joke', being delighted that the vast majority of the audience flatly rejected the idea of being acquired. One questioner put it bluntly, stating that (paraphrased) 'Jyske Bank couldn't live Jyske Differences, couldn't do the things for employees and customers they had been working so hard on, if it were to be acquired'. Dam finished his speech by pointing out that if Jyske Bank were to remain independent in the increasingly competitive environment Danish banks now faced, everyone would have to contribute.

Part of that contribution was an effort to diversify the bank's type of shareholders and increase their number in order to ensure that they shared its long-term perspective on financial performance. Employees encouraged customers to consider purchasing Jyske Bank Group shares. Between the 'battle at Vejle' and 2003, the number of shareholders increased from 150 000 to more than 210 000.

Managers and employees agreed that the message of the 'battle at Vejle' was heard throughout the organization and that Jyske Fun was a good idea. Subsequent examples of it included the only national advertising campaign the bank had engaged in during the past decade, which was effectively a dog beauty contest with entry requiring a visit to a local branch. When asked why advertising was so limited, an executive replied: 'Two reasons. First, we rely on word of mouth, so we don't need to advertise that much – our advertising cost as a percentage of revenue is half what banks of similar size spend. Second, we have to be absolutely sure we can consistently deliver Jyske Differences before we advertise them.'

Later in 1999, communication efforts continued when managers created a videotape illustrating Jyske Differences in an unusual way. The tape introduces Max Performa, an ex-KGB agent hired by a mysterious and beautiful senior manager of a competitor bank. Performa is assigned to find out if Jyske Differences are actually being delivered at Jyske Bank's branches. He checks off each Jyske Difference as he experiences it, pretending to be a Jutlandish farmer wanting a loan (speaking Danish with a thick Russian accent). In the course of applying for the loan he discovers that Jyske Differences are being delivered, among them that the employee opening his account has the authority necessary to meet his needs (*common sense*), that the bank will go to great lengths to show *genuine interest* in him (he and the branch manager drink an entire bottle of vodka one afternoon), and that Jyske Bank *is different* and is not for everyone: when he complains about the black grouse on his debit card he is politely told he might be happier banking with a competitor. At the end of the tape the viewer learns that the mysterious senior manager who hired Performa actually works for Jyske Bank.

Executives believed that they needed to constantly reinforce the message that remaining independent required every employee to work a little harder, and to behave in a manner consistent with Jyske Differences. To deliver that constant reinforcement, they printed the bank's values and Jyske Differences in materials that managers were asked to discuss with their employees. On one occasion, branch employees were asked to come in on a Saturday, without pay, to discuss the values and differences and their implications for day-to-day behaviour. Eighty per cent chose to come in.

In 2002, communication efforts included the bank's strategic employee meeting, called 'Return to Vejle'. The meeting, complete with live, high-energy music (a locally popular drum duo) and entertainment, celebrated the bank's accomplishments and served as a reminder of what still needed to be done.

Finally, in 2002 the bank introduced what it called a 'tool box' for communicating value chain information to and from the branches. The tool box enabled each branch to select elements on the bank's value chain (see Exhibit 7) and measure the branch's performance against goals related to that element. The tool box delivered regularly updated information including guides such as green or red lights describing the branch's performance on the selected value chain elements. An executive described the tool box as 'a way to operationalize the value chain so that everyone in the organization understands how they need to behave on a day-to-day basis in order to optimize it'.

Conclusion

The bank's leadership believed that Jyske values and differences, and the bank's value chain, provided ways to achieve the balance they wanted among their three stakeholders: employees, customers, and shareholders. Several leaders commented that with the large capital investments behind them as of 2003, net income would increase considerably in the coming years, assuming the recession of 2001 and 2002 was over. Shareholders had received a 17.8 per cent annual return on their investment for the 10 years prior to year end 2002. Anders Dam's 2002–03 goal for shareholders was to increase the bank's stock multiple approximately 40 per cent to the level of Danske Bank's, the largest and most richly priced bank in Denmark. This was achieved in July 2003.[6] While the bank's leadership was pleased with the bank's success, they were more interested in determining how the bank would remain in a position of leadership while still keeping the interests of its key stakeholders in balance.

Questions to the Jyske Bank case

1 As of the mid-1990s, what was Jyske Bank's competitive positioning, that is, what did it do for customers relative to its competitors?

2 As of 2003, what was Jyske Bank's competitive positioning?

3 What did Jyske Bank change to enable it to deliver its new competitive positioning?

4 How did Jyske Bank implement those changes?

Notes

This case was prepared under the auspices of the Scandinavian International Management Institute. It was written by Roger Hallowell. It is intended to be used as a basis for class discussion rather than to illustrate either effective or ineffective handling of an administrative situation. © 2003 SIMI, Scandinavian International Management Institute.

[1] Euro bought approximately DKK7.4 and US$1 bought approximately DKK6.3 as of 10 June 2003.

[2] See www.denmark.dk

[3] Typical core financial products included house, car and personal loans as well as cash management and investment services for individuals, as well as loans, cash management and investment services for small- to medium-sized companies. Jyske Bank did not offer credit cards.

[4] As was typical in Scandinavia, most employees and managers were members of a union.

[5] According to an executive, 'If we are right [and we eventually reverse the charge] we have an upside. If we are wrong it won't impact future results. All in all the tax issue is not related to the 2002 result and it would be more correct to judge the result before tax.'

[6] Managers attributed the increase in the bank's stock price multiple to recognition among stock analysts that investments in Jyske Differences made in the previous five years and expensed immediately were bearing fruit.

Case 3
easyCar.com

> **❝** At easyCar we aim to offer you outstanding value for money. To us
> value for money means a reliable service at a low price. We achieve this
> by simplifying the product we offer, and passing on the benefits to you
> in the form of lower prices.[1] **❞**

This quotation was the stated mission of car rental company easyCar.com. easyCar was a
member of the easyGroup family of companies founded by the flamboyant Greek
entrepreneur Stelios Haji-Ioannou, who was known to most people simply as Stelios.
Stelios founded low-cost air carrier easyJet.com in 1995 after convincing his father, a
Greek shipping billionaire, to loan him the £5 million (*Note*: in January 2003, £1 =
€1.52 = US$1.61) needed to start the business.[2] easyJet was one of the early low-cost,
no-frills air carriers in the European market. It was built on a foundation of simple
point-to-point flights booked over the Internet and of the aggressive use of yield
management policies to maximize the revenues it derived from its assets. The company
proved highly successful, and as a result, Stelios had expanded this business model to
industries with characteristics similar to the airline industry. easyCar, founded in 2000
on a £10 million investment on the part of Stelios, was one of these efforts.

easyCar's approach, built on the easyJet model, was quite different from the
approaches used by the traditional rental car companies. easyCar rented only a single
vehicle type at each location it operated, whereas most of its competitors rented a wide
variety of vehicle types. easyCar did not work with agents – more than 95 per cent of its
bookings were made through the company's website, with the remainder of bookings
being made directly through the company's phone reservation system (at a cost to the
customer of €0.95 per minute for the call). Most rental car companies worked with a
variety of intermediaries, and their own websites accounted for less than 10 per cent of
their total booking.[3] And like easyJet, easyCar managed prices in an attempt to have its
fleet rented out 100 per cent of the time and to generate the maximum revenue from its
rentals. easyCar's information system constantly evaluated projected demand and
expected utilization at each site, and the system adjusted price accordingly. Because of
its aggressive pricing, easyCar was able to achieve a fleet utilization rate in excess of 90
per cent[4] – much higher than other major rental car companies. Industry leader Avis
Europe, for example, had a fleet utilization rate of 68 per cent.[5]

easyCar had broken even in the fiscal year ending September 2002[6] on revenues of
£27 million.[7] These revenues represented a significant improvement over 2001, when
easyCar had lost £7.5 million on revenues of £18.5 million.[8] Although pleased that the
company had broken even in only its third year in operation, Stelios in January 2003
had set aggressive financial goals for easyCar for the next two years. Plans called for a
quadrupling of revenues in the next two years in preparation for a planned initial public
offering in the second half of 2004. easyCar's goal was to reach £100 million in revenue

and £10 million in profit for the year 2004. Stelios felt that the £100 million revenue goal and £10 million profit goal were necessary to obtain the desired return from an initial public offering (IPO). He thought that with this level of performance, the company might be worth about £250 million.[9] In order to achieve these financial goals, the company was pushing to open an average of two new sites a week through 2003 and 2004 to reach a total of 180 sites by the end of 2004.[10]

The rental car industry in Western Europe

The Western European rental car industry consisted of many different national markets that were only semi-integrated. Although many companies competed within this European rental car industry, a handful of companies held dominant positions, either across a number of national markets or within one or a few national markets. Industry experts saw the sector as ripe for consolidation.[11] Several international companies – notably Avis, Europcar and Hertz – had strong positions across most major European markets. Within most countries, there was also a primarily national or regional company that had a strong position in its home market and perhaps moderate market share in neighbouring markets. Sixt was the market leader in Germany, for example, whereas Atesa (in partnership with National) was the market leader in Spain. Generally these major players accounted for more than half the market. In Germany, for example, Sixt, Europcar, Avis and Hertz had a combined 60 per cent of the €2.5 billion German rental car market.[12] In Spain, the top five firms accounted for 60 per cent of the €920 million Spanish rental car market. These top firms targeted both business and vacation travellers and offered a wide range of vehicles for rent. Exhibit 1 provides basic information on these market-leading companies.

Exhibit 1 **Information on easyCar's Major European Competitors**

	easyCar	Avis Europe	Europcar	Hertz	Sixt
Number of rental outlets	46	3 100	2 650	7 000	1 250
2002 fleet size	7 000	120 000	220 000	700 000	46 700
Number of countries	5	107	118	150	50
Largest market	U.K.	France	France	U.S.A	Germany
Who owns company	EasyGroup/ Stelios Haji-Ioannou	D'Ieteren (Belgium) is majority shareholder	Volkswagen AG	Ford Motor Company	Publicly traded
European revenues	€41 million	€1.25 billion	€1.12 billion	€910 million	€600 million
Company website	www.easycar.com	www.avis-europe.com	www.europcar.com	www.hertz.com	ag.sixt.com

Source: Information in this table came from each company's website and online annual reports. European revenues are for vehicle rental in Europe and are based on market share estimates for 2001 from Avis Europes's website.

In addition to these major companies in each market, many smaller rental companies were operating in each market. Germany, for example, had more than 700 smaller companies,[13] whereas Spain had more than 1600 smaller companies. Many of these smaller companies operated at only one or a few locations and were particularly prevalent in tourist locations. A number of brokers, such as Holiday Autos, also operated in the sector. Brokerage companies did not own their own fleet of cars but managed the excess inventory of other companies and matched customers with rental companies that had excess fleet capacity.

Overall, the rental car market was composed of two broad segments: a business segment and a tourist/leisure segment. Depending on the market, the leisure segment represented somewhere between 45 per cent and 65 per cent of the overall market, and a large part of this segment was very price conscious. The business segment made up the remaining 35 per cent to 55 per cent of the market. It was less price sensitive than the tourist segment and more concerned about service quality, convenience, and flexibility.

The growth of easyCar

easyCar opened its first location in London on 20 April 2000 under the name easyRentacar. In the same week, easyCar opened locations in Glasgow and Barcelona. All three locations were popular easyJet destinations. Vehicles initially could be rented for as low as €15/day plus a one-time car preparation fee of €8. Each of these locations had a fleet consisting entirely of Mercedes A-class vehicles. It was the only vehicle that easyCar rented at the time.

easyCar had signed a deal with Mercedes, amid much fanfare, at the Geneva Motor Show earlier in the year to purchase a total of 5000 A-class vehicles. The vehicles, which came with guaranteed buy-back terms, cost easyCar's parent company a little over £6 million.[14] Many observers in the car rental industry were surprised by the choice because they were expecting easyCar to rely on less expensive models.[15] In describing the acquisition of the 5000 Mercedes vehicles, Stelios had said:

> 66 The choice of Mercedes reflects the easyGroup brand. easyRentacar will use brand new Mercedes cars in the same way that easyJet uses brand new Boeing aircraft. We do not compromise on the hardware, we just use innovation to substantially reduce costs. The car hire industry is where the airline industry was five years ago, a cartel feeding off the corporate client. easyRentacar will provide a choice for consumers who pay out of their own pockets and who will not be ripped off for travelling mid-week.[16] 99

easyCar quickly expanded to other locations, focusing first on those locations that were popular with easyJet customers, including Amsterdam, Geneva, Nice and Malaga. By July 2001, a little over a year after its initial launch, easyCar had fleets of Mercedes A-class vehicles in 14 locations in the UK, Spain, France and the Netherlands. At this point, easyCar secured £27 million from a consortium of Bank of Scotland Corporate Banking and NBGI Private Equity to further expand its operations. The package consisted of a combination of equity and loan stock.

Although easyCar added a few sites in the second half of 2001 and early 2002, volatile demand in the wake of the September 11 attacks forced easyCar to roll out new rental locations somewhat slower than originally expected.[17] Growth accelerated, however, in the spring of 2002. Between May 2002 and January 2003, easyCar opened 30 new locations, to go from 18 sites to a total of 48 sites. This acceleration in growth also coincided with a change in easyCar's policy regarding the make-up of its fleet. By May of 2002, easyCar's fleet consisted of 6000 Mercedes A-class vehicles across 18 sites. Beginning in May, however, easyCar began to stock its fleet with other types of vehicles. It still maintained its policy of offering only a single vehicle at each location, but now the vehicle the customer received depended on the location. The first new vehicle that easyCar introduced was the Vauxhall Corsa. According to Stelios,

> " Vauxhall Corsas cost easyCar £2 a day less than Mercedes A-Class so we can pass this saving on to customers. Customers themselves will decide if they want to pay a premium for a Mercedes. easyGroup companies benefit from economies of scale where relevant but we also want to create contestable markets among our suppliers so that we can keep the cost to our customers as low as possible.[18] "

By January 2003, easyCar was also using Ford Focuses (four locations), Renault Clios (three locations), Toyota Yarises (three locations), and Mercedes Smart cars (two locations) in addition to the Vauxhall Corsas (seven locations) and the Mercedes A-Class vehicles (28 locations). Plans called for a further expansion of the fleet from the 7000 vehicles that easyCar had in January to 24 000 vehicles across 180 rental sites by the end of 2004.[19]

In addition to making vehicles available at more locations, easyCar had also changed its policies for 2003 to allow rentals for as little as one hour and with as little as one hour's notice of rental. By making this change, Stelios felt that easyCar could be a serious competitor to local taxis, buses, trains and even car ownership. easyCar expected that if it made car rental simple enough and cheap enough, some people living in traffic-congested European cities who only use their car occasionally would give up the costs and inconveniences of car ownership and simply hire an easyCar when they needed a vehicle. Tapping into this broader transportation market would help the company reach its ambitious future sales goals.

Facilities

easyCar had facilities in a total of 17 cities in five European countries, as shown in Exhibit 2. It located its facilities primarily near bus and train stations in the major European cities, seeking out sites that offered lower lease costs. It generally avoided prime airport locations, because the cost for space at, or in some cases near, airports was significantly higher than most other locations. When easyCar did locate near an airport, it generally chose sites off the airport in order to reduce the cost of the lease. Airport locations also tended to require longer hours to satisfy customers arriving on late flights or departing on very early flights. easyCar kept its airport locations open 24 hours a day, whereas its other locations were generally open only from 7.00 a.m. to 11.00 p.m.

Exhibit 2 easyCar Locations in January 2003

Country	City	Number	Number near an airport
France	Nice	1	1
France	Paris	8	0
Netherlands	Amsterdam	3	1
Spain	Barcelona	2	0
Spain	Madrid	2	0
Spain	Majorca	1	1
Spain	Malagra	1	1
Switzerland	Geneva	1	1
UK	Birmingham	2	0
UK	Bromley	1	0
UK	Croydon	1	1
UK	Glasgow	2	1
UK	Kingston upon Thames	1	0
UK	Liverpool	2	1
UK	London	15	0
UK	Manchester	2	1
UK	Waterford	1	0
Total	5 countries, 17 cities	46	9

Source: easyCar.com website, January 2003

The physical facilities at all locations were kept to a minimum. In many locations, easyCar leased space in an existing parking garage. Employees worked out of a small, self-contained cubicle within the garage. The cubicle, depending on the location, might be no more than 15 m^2 and included little more than a small counter and a couple of computers at which staff processed customers as they came to pick up or return their vehicles. easyCar also leased a number of spaces within the garage for its fleet of cars. However, because easyCar's vehicles were rented 90 per cent of the time, the number of spaces required at an average site, which had a fleet of about 150 cars, was only 15 to 20 spaces.[20] To speed up the opening of new sites, easyCar had equipped a number of vans with all the needed computer and telephone equipment to run a site.[21] From an operational perspective, the company could open a new location by simply leasing 20 or so spaces in a parking garage, hiring a small staff, driving a van to the location and adding the location to the company's website. Depending on the fleet size at a location, easyCar typically had only one or two people at a time working at a site.

Vehicle pick-up and return processes

Customers arrived at a site to pick up a vehicle within a prearranged one-hour time period. Each customer selected this time slot when he or she booked the vehicle. easyCar adjusted the first day's rental price based on the pick-up time. Customers who picked their cars up earlier in the day or at popular times were charged more than were customers picking up their cars later in the day or at less busy times. Customers were required to bring a printed copy of their contract, the credit card they used to make the booking and identification. Given the low staffing levels, customers occasionally had to wait 30 minutes or more to be processed and receive their vehicles, particularly at peak times of the day. Processing a customer began with the employee accessing the customer's contract online. If the customer was new to easyCar or to the site, the basic policies and possible additional charges were briefly explained. The employee then made copies of the customer's identification and credit card and took a digital photo of the customer. The customer was charged an €80 refundable deposit, signed the contract and was on his or her way.

All vehicles were rented with more or less empty fuel tanks; the exact level was dependent on how much fuel was left in the vehicle when the previous renter returned it. Customers were provided with a small map of the immediate area around the rental site that showed the location and hours of nearby petrol stations. Customers could return vehicles with any amount of fuel in them as long as the low fuel indicator light in the vehicle was not on. Customers who returned vehicles with the low fuel indicator light on were charged a fuelling fee of €16.

Customers were also expected to return the vehicle within a prearranged one-hour time period, which they also selected at the time of booking. Although customers did not have to worry about refuelling the car before returning it, they were expected to thoroughly clean the car. This clean car policy had been implemented in May 2002 as a way to further reduce the price that customers could pay for their vehicles. Prior to this change, all customers paid a fixed preparation fee of €11 each time they rented a vehicle (up from the €8 preparation fee when the company started operations in 2000).

The new policy reduced this up-front preparation fee to €4 but required customers to either return the vehicle clean or pay an additional cleaning fee of €16. In order to avoid any misunderstanding about what it meant by a clean car, easyCar provided customers with an explicit description of what constituted a clean car, both for the interior and the exterior of the car. It had to be apparent that the exterior of the car had been washed prior to returning the vehicle. The nearby petrol stations map that customers were provided when they picked up their cars also showed nearby car washes where they could clean the car before returning it. Although easyCar had received some bad press in relation to the policy,[22] 85 per cent of customers returned their vehicles clean as a result of the policy.

When a customer returned a vehicle, an easyCar employee would check to make sure that the vehicle was clean and undamaged and that the low fuel indicator light was not on. The employee would also check the kilometres driven. The customer would then be notified of any additional charges. These charges would be subtracted from the €80 deposit and the difference refunded to the customer's credit card (or, if additional charges exceeded the €80 deposit, the customer's credit card would be charged the difference).

Pricing

easyCar clearly differentiated itself from its competitors with its low price. In addition, pricing also played a key role in easyCar's efforts to achieve high utilization of its fleet of cars. easyCar advertised prices as low as €5/day plus a per rental preparation fee of €4. Prices, however, varied by the location and dates of the rental, by when the booking was made, and by what time the car was to be picked up and returned. easyCar's systems constantly evaluated projected demand and expected utilization at each site and adjusted price accordingly. Achieving the €5/day rate usually required customers to book well in advance, and these rates were typically available only on weekdays. Weekend rates, when booked well in advance, typically started a few euros higher than the weekday rates. As a given rental date approached, however, the price typically went up significantly as easyCar approached 100 per cent fleet utilization for that day. Rates could literally triple overnight if there was sufficient booking activity. Generally, however, easyCar's price was less than half that of its major competitors. easyCar, unlike most other rental car companies, required customers to pay in full at the time of booking and, once a booking was made, the payment was non-refundable.

easyCar's base price covered only the core rental of the vehicle – the total price customers paid was in many cases much higher and depended on how the customer reserved, paid for, used and returned the vehicle. easyCar's price was based on customers booking through the company's website and paying for their rental with their easyMoney credit card. easyMoney was the easyGroup's credit and financial services company. Customers who chose to book through the company's phone reservation system were charged an additional €0.95 per minute for the call, and those who used other credit cards were charged €5 extra. All vehicles had to be paid for by a credit or debit card – cash was not accepted. The base rental price allowed customers to drive vehicles 100 kilometres per day; additional kilometres were charged at a rate of €0.12 per km. In addition, customers were expected to return their cars clean and on time. Customers who returned cars that did not meet easyCar's standards for clean were charged a €16 cleaning fee. Those who returned their cars late were immediately charged €120 and subsequently charged an additional €120 for each subsequent 24-hour period in which the car was not returned. easyCar explained the high late fee as representing the cost that they would likely incur in providing another vehicle to the next customer. Customers wishing to make any changes to their bookings were also charged a change fee of €16. Changes could be made either before the rental started or during the rental period but were limited to changing the dates, times and location of the rental and were subject to the prices and vehicle availability at the time the change was being made. If the change resulted in an overall lower price for the rental, however, no refund was provided for the difference.

Beginning in 2003, all customers were also required to purchase loss/damage insurance for an additional charge of €4 per day that eliminated the customer's liability for loss or damage to the vehicle (excluding damage to the tyres or windshield of the vehicle). Through 2002, customers were able to choose whether to purchase additional insurance from easyCar to eliminate any financial liability in the event that the rental vehicle was damaged. The cost of this insurance had been €6 per day, and approximately 60 per cent of easyCar's customers purchased this optional insurance. Those not purchasing this insurance had either assumed the liability for the first €800 in damages personally or had their own insurance through some other means (e.g. some credit card companies provide this insurance to their cardholders at no additional charge for short-term rentals paid for with the credit card).

easyCar's website attempted to make all these additional charges clear to customers at the time of their booking. The company had received a fair amount of bad press when it first opened for business, after many renters complained about having to pay undisclosed charges when they returned their cars.[23] In response, easyCar had revamped its website in an effort to make these charges more transparent to customers and to explain the logic behind many of these charges.

Promotion

easyCar's promotional efforts had through 2002 focused primarily on posters and press advertising. Posters were particularly prevalent in metro systems and bus and train stations in cities in which easyCar had operations. All this advertising focused on easyCar's low price. According to founder Stelios: 'You will never see an advert for an easy company offering an experience – it's about price. If you create expectations you can't live up to then you will ultimately suffer as a result.'[24] In 2002, easyCar spent £1.43 million on such advertising.[25]

easyCar also promoted itself by displaying its name, telephone number and website address prominently on the doors and rear window of its entire fleet of vehicles and took advantage of free publicity when the opportunity presented itself. An example of seeking out such publicity occurred when Hertz complained that easyCar's comparative advertising campaign in the Netherlands that featured the line 'The best reason to use easyCar.com can be found at hertz.nl' violated Dutch law that required comparative advertising to be exact, not general. In response, Stelios and a group of easyCar employees, dressed in orange boiler suits and with a fleet of easyCar vehicles, protested outside the Hertz Amsterdam office with signs asking 'What is Hertz frightened of?'.[26]

In an effort to help reach its goal of quadrupling sales in the next two years, easyCar had recently hired Jennifer Mowat for the new position of commercial director, which would take over responsibility for easyCar's European marketing. Ms Mowat had previously been eBay's UK country manager and had recently completed an MBA in Switzerland. Previously, Stelios and easyCar's managing director, Andrew Fitzmaurice, had handled the marketing function themselves.[27] As part of this stepped-up marketing effort, easyCar also planned to double its advertising budget for 2003, to £3 million, and to begin to advertise on television. The television advertising campaign was to feature easyCar's founder, Stelios.[28]

Legal challenges

easyCar faced several challenges to its approaches. The most significant challenge dealt with a November 2002 ruling made by the Office of Fair Trading (OFT) that easyCar had to grant customers seven days from the time they made a booking to cancel their booking and receive a full refund. The OFT was a UK governmental agency that was responsible for protecting UK consumers from unfair and/or anti-competitive business practices. The ruling against easyCar was based on the 2000 Consumer Protection Distance Selling Regulations. These regulations stipulated that companies that sell at a distance (e.g., by Internet or telephone) must provide customers with a seven-day cooling-off period during which time customers can cancel their contracts with the company and receive a full refund. The law exempted accommodation, transportation, catering and leisure service companies from this requirement. The OFT's ruling concluded that easyCar did not qualify as a transportation service company because the consumers had to drive themselves and, as such, they were not receiving a transport service, just a car.[29]

easyCar had appealed the OFT's decision to the UK High Court on the grounds that it was indeed a transportation service company and was entitled to an exemption from this requirement. easyCar was hopeful that it would eventually win this legal challenge. easyCar had argued that this ruling would destroy the company's book-early-pay-less philosophy and could lead to a tripling of prices.[30] Chairman Stelios was quoted as saying: 'It is very serious. My fear is that as soon as we put in the seven-day cooling off periods our utilization rate will fall from 90% to 65%. That's the difference between a profitable company and an unprofitable one.'[31] easyCar was also concerned that prolonged legal action on this point could interfere with its plans for a 2004 IPO.

The OFT, for its part, had also applied to the UK High Court for an injunction to make the company comply with the ruling. Other rental car companies were generally unconcerned about the ruling, because few offered big discounts for early bookings or non-refundable bookings.[32]

easyCar's new policy of posting the pictures of customers whose cars were 15 days or more overdue was also drawing legal criticism. easyCar had recently received public warnings from lawyers that this new policy might violate data protection, libel, privacy, confidentiality and human rights laws.[33] Of particular concern to some lawyers was the possibility that easyCar might post the wrong person's picture, given the large number of customers the company dealt with.[34] Such a mistake could open the company to costly libel suits. The policy of posting the pictures of overdue customers on the easyCar website, initiated in November of 2002, was designed to reduce the losses associated with customers renting a vehicle and never returning it. The costs were significant, according to Stelios: 'These cars are expensive, £15,000 each, and we have 6000 of them. At any given time we are looking for as many as several tens which are overdue. If we don't get one back, it's a write-off. We are writing off an entire car, and it's uninsurable.'[35] Stelios was also convinced of the legality of the new policy. In a letter to the editor of the *Financial Times* in which he responded to the legal concerns raised in the press, Stelios said:

> From a legal perspective, we have been entirely factual and objective and are merely reporting the details of the overdue car and the person who collected it. In addition, our policy is made very clear in our terms and conditions and the photo is taken both overtly and with the consent of the customer ... I estimate the total cost of overdue cars to be 5% of total easyCar costs, or 50p on every car rental day for all customers. In 2004, when I intend to float easyCar, this cost will amount to £5 million unless we can reduce our quantity of overdue cars.[36]

In the past, easyCar had simply provided pictures to police when a rental car was 15 days or more overdue. The company hoped that posting the picture would both discourage drivers from not returning vehicles and shame those drivers who currently had overdue cars into returning them. In fact, the first person whose photo was posted on the easyCar website did indeed return his car two days later. The vehicle was 29 days late.[37]

The future

At the end of 2002, Stelios had stepped down as the CEO of easyJet so that he could devote more of his time to the other easyGroup companies, including easyCar. He had three priorities for the new year. One was to turn around the money-losing easyInternetCafe business, which Stelios had described as 'the worst mistake of my career'.[38] The 22-store chain had lost £80 million in the last two years. A second priority was to oversee the planned launch of another new easyGroup business, easyCinema, in the spring of 2003. And the third was to oversee the rapid expansion of the easyCar chain so that it would be ready for an initial public offering in the second half of 2004.

Notes

By John J. Lawrence (University of Idaho) and Luis Solis (Instituto de Empresa).

[1] easyCar.com website.

[2] 'The big picture – an interview with Stelios', *Sunday Herald*, 16 March 2003.

[3] 'Click to fly', *The Economist*, 13 May 2004.

[4] E. Simpkins, 'Stelios isn't taking it easy', *Sunday Telegraph*, 15 December 2002.

[5] Avis Europe plc 2002 annual report, p. 10. Accessed online at http://ir.aviseurope.com/avis/reports (16 August 2004).

[6] Simpkins, 'Stelios isn't taking it easy'.

[7] 'Marketing: former eBay UK chief lands top easyCar position', *Financial Times Information Limited*, 9 January 2003.

[8] T. Burt, 'easyCar agrees deal with Vauxhall', *Financial Times*, 30 April 2002, p. 24.

[9] N. Hodgson, 'Stelios plans easyCar float', *Liverpool Echo*, 24 September 2002.

[10] Simpkins, 'Stelios isn't taking it easy'.

[11] 'Marketing Week: don't write off the car rental industry', *Financial Times Information Limited*, 26 September 2002.

[12] 'EasyCar set to shake up German car rental market', *European Intelligence Wire*, 22 February 2002.

[13] Ibid.

[14] N. Hodgson, 'Stelios plans easyCar float'.

[15] A. Felsted, 'EasyCar courts Clio for rental fleet', *Financial Times*, 11 February 2002, p. 26.

16 easyCar.com website news release, 1 March 2000.

17 T. Burt, 'EasyCar agrees deal with Vauxhall'.

18 easyCar.com website news release, 2 May 2002.

19 'Marketing Week: EasyCar appoints head of European marketing', *Financial Times Information Limited*, 9 January 2003.

20 Simpkins, 'Stelios isn't taking it easy'.

21 Ibid.

22 J. Hyde, 'Travel view: clearing up on the extras', *Observer*, 7 July 2002.

23 J. Stanton, 'The empire that's easy money', *Edinburgh Evening News*, 26 November 2002.

24 'The big picture – an interview with Stelios', *Sunday Herald*.

25 'EasyCar appoints head of European marketing', *Financial Times Information Limited*.

26 easyCar.com website news release, 22 April 2002.

27 'EasyCar appoints head of European marketing', *Financial Times Information Limited*.

28 'Campaigning: EasyGroup appoints Publicis for easyCar TV advertising brief', *Financial Times Information Limited*, 31 January 2003.

29 J. Macintosh, 'EasyCar sues OFT amid threat to planned flotation', *Financial Times*, 22 November 2002, p. 4.

30 'EasyCar appoints head of European marketing', *Financial Times Information Limited*.

31 Mackintosh, 'EasyCar sues OFT amid threat to planned flotation'.

32 Ibid.

33 B. Sherwood and A. Wendlandt, 'EasyCar may be in difficulty over naming ploy', *Financial Times*, 14 November 2002, p. 2.

34 Ibid.

35 'e-business: Internet fraudsters fail to steal Potter movie's magic and other news', *Financial Times Information Limited*, 19 November 2002.

36 S. Haji-Ioannou, 'Letters to the Editor: Costly effect of late car return', *Financial Times*, 16 November 2002, p. 10.

37 M. Hookham, 'How Stelios nets return of his cars', *Daily Post*, 14 November 2002.

38 S. Bentley, 'The worst mistake of my career, by Stelios', *Financial Times*, 24 December 2002.

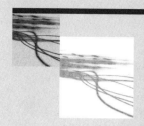

Case 4
Telecom Italia Mobile: making profits in a mature market

> Europe has always been ahead ... in terms of wireless communications and TIM has been the visionary company leading the continent. [1]
> — John MacFarlane, founder and CEO of Software.com

> Probably our most distinctive feature is our ability to be a little ahead of the market. Here, there is nothing proprietary. Everything is replicable, so the key is time to market. [2]
> — Marco De Benedetti, Chief Executive, Telecom Italia Mobile

Introduction

Telecom Italia Mobile (TIM), established in 1995, was the largest mobile operator in Italy and one of the largest in Europe. TIM had over 26 million subscribers in Italy with an additional 22 million through its international operations in Greece, Turkey and South America. In Italy, where the mobile phone market was a mature market with penetration level of over 90 per cent, TIM relied on constant innovation and aggressive marketing to attain revenue growth. In addition to voice transmissions, TIM provided its customers with various other services such as messaging, games, access to the Internet and real-time TV over mobile phones.

TIM planned to enhance its service offering, in terms of number of services and quality of service, as well as increase the number of markets in which it operated in order to sustain growth. TIM together with T-Mobile of Germany, Telefónica Móviles of Spain and Orange, which had a presence in UK and France, formed the FreeMove marketing alliance to enhance the quality of service across national boundaries and to compete effectively against Vodafone that had 130 million subscribers (Exhibit 1).

The telecom industry in Italy

Italy was amongst the top five countries in the world in terms of mobile penetration (Exhibit 2). The tremendous popularity of mobile phones in Italy stemmed from variouis reasons including outdated and expensive fixed line network, family cohesiveness, communication and style amongst the Italians.

Italy had an archaic and inadequate landline. Besides, the rate structure for wired phones in Italy was expensive and complicated. When mobile phones were introduced in Italy, the Italians, who are known for their effusive nature, embraced mobile phones enthusiastically. Mobile phones had a simple rate structure based on per second charge (Exhibit 3). The mobile operators introduced schemes whereby calls on weekends and evenings were charged at discounted rates, which further added to the popularity of mobile phones. Italians were known for being verbally expressive. These factors aided in the wider penetration of mobile phones. Parents bought mobile phones for their offspring to keep a close watch over them and their well-being. According to a survey conducted by the University of Trieste, 56 per cent of children aged between 9 and 10 owned a mobile phone in Italy.[3] In 2003, Italy had a population of 58 million and 53 million cell phones.[4] In 2004, 98 per cent of the Italians owned a cell phone.[5]

Prepaid cards were highly popular amongst the Italian mobile users, as they didn't need to bother about monthly fees, contracts and credit cards. Initially when mobile phones were launched in Italy, the handsets weren't subsidized. The style conscious Italians viewed mobile phones as a fashion statement and a status symbol. So they were willing to splurge on the latest in wireless technology. Mauro Sentinelli, managing director of TIM, stated, 'Italy has become the Hollywood of handsets. When the manufacturers have a new model they showcase it in Rome well before it appears in, for instance, London, where subsidies have discouraged consumers from splashing out on the latest handsets.'[6]

TIM was launched in 1995 to provide wireless telecommunication services. Telecom Italia had a 54.82 per cent state in TIM. It was listed on the Milan Stock Exchange in July 1995. TIM was the largest mobile telecommunications company in Italy. In 2003, the company had a 46 per cent share in Italy's mobile market. The company operated the single largest Global System for Mobile Communication[7] (GSM) network in Europe in terms of number of lines and also launched Brazil's first GSM service, which connected more than 80 cities.[8] TIM also had a presence in Greece and Turkey. TIM's distribution chain comprising company shops and authorized dealers spanned the whole of Italy. TIM had company shops called *il telefonino*, along with a network of authorized dealers, named *Centro TIM*.[9] TIM along with four other companies was given a licence to provide 3G[10] services in Italy. The other four companies were Vodafone

Omnitel, Wind Telecomunicazioni SpA, H3G and Ipse. TIM also had a license to provide 3G services in Greece. In Italy, TIM launched its 3G services in May 2004.

Its main rivals, in Italy, included Vodafone Omnitel, Wind Telecomunicazioni SpA and H3G Italy SpA. Vodafone Omnitel had the second highest number of subscribers in Italy behind TIM. The company had over 17 million customers and accounted for 35 per cent of Italy's mobile phone market; its network covered 97 per cent of Italy's territory.[11] The company was known for its high service quality. Vodafone Group, based in the UK, had a 77 per cent stake in Vodafone Omnitel and New York-based Verizon Communications owned the remaining 23 per cent. The company was one of the five that was awarded 3G licence in Italy; it launched its 3G services in May 2004. Wind Telecomunicazioni was established in 1997 as a joint venture between Deutsche Telecom, Enel and France Telecom. Deutsche Telecom sold its stake, in Wind, in 2000 and France Telecom in 2003. Wind Telecomunicazioni provided fixed line and data telecommunication services in Italy in addition to its mobile services. It was the leading ISP in Italy and its portal 'Italia On Line' was very popular. As of June 2003, the company was third in the Italian mobile market with 9.2 million customers and a 16 per cent market share. The company had a total of 30.6 million customers, which included 7.5 million fixed-line and 13.9 million Internet subscribers.[12] Wind was one of the five companies with a 3G licence in Italy and was expected to launch its 3G services in October 2004.

Hutchinson 3G was the first to provide 3G mobile services in Italy, in March 2003, under the brand name '3'. To attract customers in the Italian mobile phone market dominated by TIM, Vodafone and Wind, the company offered new video mobile phones for €99 or free to customers who spend a minimum of €40 on voice calls each month while the average cost of mobile phones in Italy was €600.[13] From January 2004, subscribers of 3 could watch the Italian show 'Big Brother 4' live on their video mobile phones. The fifth company that was given a UMTS[14] licence was Ipse, in which leading Spanish firm, Telefonica Moviles SA, had a 45.6 per cent stake. As per the conditions, Ipse had to provide 95 per cent coverage of the 30 largest cities in Italy by 30 June 2004.[15] The company failed to meet the deadline and had asked the Italian telecommunications ministry for an extension.

The Italian mobile phone market represented a saturated and price-sensitive market. Alessandro Lorenzelli, an analyst at IDC, commented, 'Operators are not really pushing business, they are all pushing consumer services.'[16] TIM concentrated on developing new wireless functions and services to increase its revenue from existing customers.

Making profits in a mature market

TIM greatly benefited from the Italians' desire to acquire the latest in mobile technology. It chose not to subsidize its handsets in Italy where mobile phones were viewed as a lifestyle product. It managed to enhance its revenue and growth by offering new and exciting services to the enthusiastic Italian mobile customers. Innovation has been the key to TIM's success in Italy. Marco De Benedetti, CEO of TIM, stated that as the services provided by one mobile phone company could be replicated by another, reducing the time taken to launch a new service in the marketplace was crucial and this was where TIM excelled. It was the first company in the world to offer prepaid cards to its customers in 1996. Mauro Sentinelli, deputy managing director of TIM, who was involved in the designing and launching of the prepaid 'TIMCard' was awarded the Outstanding Marketing Award by the GSM MoU Association. TIM was the first operator in Europe to provide real-time TV over the mobile phones to its customers.[17] TIM boosted its revenues by encouraging its customers to try out its new services.

TIM's popular 'TIM Universal Number Service' provided the subscriber with a free email box, whereby the subscriber could send and receive emails. The subscriber could also receive faxes, receive voice mail messages, surf the web and send and receive SMS (Short Messaging Service). TIM's AutoRicarica, which provided the subscribers with a bonus, in the form of an automatic recharge, for incoming traffic, was also very popular with the subscribers. It launched the '4888 Pay for Me' service, which allowed the caller to charge the cost of the call to the receiver. TIM's innovative TIM Conference Service could be used to conduct meetings where a maximum of six people could converse using a mobile or fixed line phone. The service required that a TIM GSM subscriber must initiate the conference call. TIM's services for the businesses included sending its employees automatic reminders about meetings through SMS, and setting agendas online.

SMS was very popular in Italy (Exhibit 4). On 31 December 2002, Italians sent more than 300 million SMS messages, nearly double the number from the previous year. TIM offered its subscribers a chance to receive a daily message from the Pope, in the form of an SMS, for a monthly fee of €4.50. TIM thus cashed in on the Vatican's need to spread its message and the Italians' religious fervour. De Benedetti stated, 'This shows once again that the mobile phone is part of our daily lives. In this case, it becomes a means of bringing to a wider public the messages of the sovereign pontiff.'[18] TIM in partnership with Riello SpA, a heating and air-conditioning company, developed a service, Riellonet, which enabled subscribers to remotely control the heating systems using a mobile phone. The users could activate the heater before reaching home by sending an SMS message. TIM in collaboration with a university[19] in Italy offered the students access to the university by means of a mobile phone. The service enabled the students to request information and register for exams through their mobile phone.[20]

TIM was the first in Europe to launch a special SMS service, SMS Vocali TIM, for the blind and hypo-sighted. It converted the text messages, received by subscribers to the service, into voice messages and the subscribers could record a voice message, which would be translated into a text message and then sent to the receiver. The service was free and the SMS messages were charged at the normal rates; the service was available only to TIM subscribers. To avail this service the customers needed to replace their SIM cards with the special SIM cards, which were distributed by major associations for the blind. TIM's ability to bring together innovative services and customer offerings based on its thorough knowledge of its customers' needs resulted in higher levels of customer satisfaction and loyalty. TIM was awarded the European Customer Relationship Management (CRM) Excellence Award 2001 by Gartner, a research and analysis company.

Multimedia Messaging Service (MMS) was another important non-voice source of revenue. Research showed that the average revenue per unit (ARPU) for MMS handset subscribers as compared to 2G GSM handset subscribers could be 132 per cent higher.[21] Research conducted by Nokia suggested that 70 per cent of MMS messages between individuals resulted in a voice call in response to the message received.[22] MMS enabled users to send pictures and sound in addition to text, and the users extensively used this service for entertainment. TIM was the first to launch MMS services in Italy. TIM's first MMS service was an online photo album, which allowed users to view photos on the screen of the mobile phone. The users could send a text message, which contained a link to a page in their photo album, and the receiver of the message could view the photo on his/her mobile phone by following the link. As a result of additional MMS-based services such as real-time football highlights, TIM delivered nearly two million MMS and sold about one million MMS-enabled phones in the first quarter of 2003.[23] TIM signed a distribution agreement with the Walt Disney Internet Group in 2002, wherein the services provided to TIM's subscribers included logos, ring tones, wallpapers, screensavers, games and picture messages based on characters from Walt Disney cartoons and movies. TIM stated that amongst its various Value Added Services (VAS), messaging based VAS were the most popular and a crucial requirement for successful provision of VAS was storage capability. To this end, TIM launched the i.box in which the subscribers could store photos, email and video clips. The users could invite friends to view the content of their i.box by sending their i.box address as a link in a text message.

TIM developed the i-TIM WAP service that enabled the users to surf the web using their mobile phones. The subscribers could perform e-commerce transactions or access their bank accounts on their mobile phones. In 2004, TIM announced a new service that enabled text messaging between PC and mobile phone. 'TIM Turbo-mail' enabled its subscribers to send, receive, forward and reply to SMS messages from the MS-Outlook email service. The charge for the SMS would be included in the subscribers' phone bill. Leopoldo Tranquilly, VAS (Value Added Services) Manager at TIM, commented, 'TIM Turbo Mail fits very well in TIM's service offering to the corporate segment and a request from the market for this kind of service. To be able to send, receive, forward and reply to SMS messages from MS-Outlook is a natural extension of email.'[24]

In October 2003, TIM became the first mobile operator in the world to launch a mobile TV service in collaboration with TV partners La7, MTV and CFN/CNBC Financial Network. The service was provided free to TIM subscribers till 31 December 2003.

TIM's promotional offer, valid till 31 December 2004, MAXXI TIM Messaggi enabled users to send 400 SMS messages and 100 MMS messages to all TIM mobile phones at a price of €10 for 30 days. TIM offered its customers automated daily services such as an SMS horoscope in which it embedded self-promotion content; this was believed to enhance customer loyalty. In July 2004, TIM announced that it would be the main sponsor of the 61st Venice International Film Festival, to be held in September. TIM would set up a structure, PalaTIM, which would serve as a cinema hall with a seating capacity of 17000 as part of its sponsorship. TIM's subscribers could learn about the 21 competing films and view images from the Film Festival on their mobile phones. TIM proposed to set up a stand on the grounds of the festival where the visitors would be informed about the latest in mobile telecommunications.

Expanding revenues

In 2002, the company generated sales and service revenues of €10,867 million, a growth of over 6 per cent as compared to 2001; and gross operating profit of €5,039 million, an increase of 5.9 per cent over 2001. The gross operating profit when expressed as a percentage of revenues was 46.4 per cent.[25] For the year ended 31 December 2003, TIM achieved a gross operating margin of €5,502 million, an increase of 9 per cent over the previous year, and revenues of €11,735 million. TIM had an operating margin of 32.1 per cent on sales of $14.6 billion, ahead of its rivals in Europe (Exhibit 5).[26] According to the preliminary results for the first half of 2004, TIM SpA generated revenues of €4,803 million, a growth of 6.8 per cent when compared to the first half of 2003; revenue from VAS grew by 26.1 per cent to €594 million and the gross operating profit was €2,632 million, a growth of 10.2 per cent.[27]

To sustain its growth, TIM aimed to expand the number of markets in which it was present along with its service offering. TIM had a presence in Greece through its subsidiary, Stet Hellas Telecommunications S.A. in which it had an 81.4 per cent stake. The company offered GSM services and in 2004 launched 3G services in Greece. The company provided mobile phone services in Turkey through its affiliate IS TIM, in which it had a 49 per cent stake, under the Aria trademark. The mobile market in Brazil was growing rapidly and TIM had a 15 per cent stake in the $6.4 billion market which it aimed to increase to 25 per cent by 2006.[28] At a press conference in Milan in February 2004, Marco De Benedetti announced TIM Group's preliminary financial results for the year ended 31 December 2003. He stated that the company had outperformed its own targets and that 'we would have easily achieved [top line] double-digit growth'[29] if not for currency fluctuations. TIM formed the FreeMove mobile alliance along with OrangeSA, Telefonica Moviles and T-Mobile in March 2004. The alliance had almost 170 million customers in 21 European countries and approximately 230 million worldwide.[30] The alliance aimed to provide seamless service across national borders and to simplify the cost structure. The FreeMove alliance provided its customers, who travelled abroad, with the same services they accessed in their home country. The members of the alliance agreed to jointly purchase six million handsets in 2004, which was expected to result in cost savings of 10 per cent on an average. They also signed preferred supplier agreements with Motorola and Siemens. They set a target of average annual growth of 10 per cent in the voice traffic among member countries; the alliance also aimed to double the GPRS data traffic among the members each year for the next three years by making attractive offers to the customers.[31]

3G networks enabled faster data transmission and superior voice capacity as compared to 2G networks; cheaper voice calls, photo messaging, video calls, games and streaming video clips were expected to be some of the major benefits of 3G. In 2000, five companies were given licence to provide 3G services in Italy, who paid a combined $10.2 billion for the licences. After much hype and many delays, 3G mobile phones were launched in Europe in 2003. TIM launched its 3G services in the last week of May 2004, a day before its main rival Vodafone Omnitel. TIM claimed that it had received over 450,000 orders for 3G phones from dealers before the launch of its 3G services.[32] The figure also included the order for EDGE[33] (Enhanced Data rates for Global Evolution) phones. Its brand name and scale of operation attracted more subscribers than its competitors. Unlike 3, which had spent a substantial amount on advertisement campaigns to attract customers, TIM had not launched a large-scale advertising campaign for its 3G services and was not expected to do so until Christmas 2004. TIM planned to use EDGE technology, which was substantially faster than previously available technologies although slower than 3G, to serve those areas not covered by its UMTS network.

Future outlook

TIM could exploit several future growth opportunities including 3G, the FreeMove Alliance and the rapidly growing mobile market in Brazil. H3G launched its 3G services first, spending a substantial amount of money on promoting the new services available with 3G. Although TIM launched its 3G service later, it was expected to be one of the biggest winners when 3G services became more popular in Italy because of its brand name and size. Limited models of 3G enabled phones were available but as the number of models increased and the prices of the 3G phones fell, increased demand for 3G was expected. The FreeMove alliance would help TIM to counter Vodafone's extensive presence in Europe. The alliance members would benefit from economies of scale, improved quality of service and enhanced sales potential.

In spite of TIM's impressive financial performance in 2003, analysts were concerned about the company's long-term position. Merrill Lynch, in a sector report, stated, 'We are still concerned by the risk of competition heating up in Italy, as the result of Vodafone's strong performance and the efforts of Hutchison's 3 to gain market share.'[34] The company faced stiff competition in its home market from Vodafone Omnitel and Wind Telecomunicazioni. Vodafone was known for its high quality services and had an extensive presence in Europe. H3G launched its 3G services 10 months before TIM and its promotional efforts to increase its market share in Italy might have a detrimental impact on TIM's share in the 3G market. '3' had nearly 500,000 subscribers in June 2004. The maturity of the Italian market was expected to curtail TIM's growth in the long run. TIM's presence in the international market made it vulnerable to fluctuations in foreign currency exchange rates. But the company's strong brand name and its emphasis on technologial innovation were expected to aid it in its quest to maintain its strong performance in Italy's mobile telecommunications industry.

Exhibit 1

FreeMove Alliance

Alliance Members

In 2003, four leading mobile operators, well entrenched in the five key European markets of France, Germany, Italy, Spain and the United Kingdom, formed the FreeMove Alliance. The members have an international presence. The Alliance members include:

- Orange
- Telefónica Móviles
- TIM
- T-Mobile International

The members share a unified brand, 'FreeMove', to endorse their joint offering.

Common Objectives

The four mobile operators came together with a common purpose of offering an enhanced customer experience to both business and consumer customers, across their common route.

The alliance members have the following common objectives:

- To provide customers with a seamless international presence, by providing them with superior network coverage and quality.
- To deliver attractive propositions to all different types of customers, by providing simple, competitive and transparent tariffs. To lead the industry by jointly developing an offer of innovative products, services and content.
- To exploit the alliance members' synergies and size in order to achieve cost efficiencies and to enable them to offer exclusive products including higher-end handsets that are more accessible to all.

Corporate Governance

In order to achieve their objectives, the alliance members established a cross-country organization composed of a management team and functional working groups. The alliance is a legally binding entity with a clearly defined corporate governance structure consisting of both a management board and a supervisory board. The supervisory board includes the CEOs of all four member operators:

- Sanjiv Ahuja, Orange
- Antonio Viana-Baptista, Telefónica Móviles
- Marco De Benedetti, TIM
- Rene Obermann, T-Mobile

The alliance has defined a long-term strategy to support its common objectives, with a specific set of key performance indicators and targets. The alliance has also agreed on admission criteria for broadening the alliance to other members in the future.

Source: www.freemovealliance.net

Exhibit 2

Leader economies in terms of mobile penetration, year end 2002

Mobile subscribers per 100 inhabitants, top 15 economies, 2002

Economy	Mobile subscribers per 100 inhabitants
Taiwan, China	108.45
Luxembourg	101.34
Israel	95.45
Hong Kong, China	92.98
Italy	92.65
Iceland	88.89
Sweden	88.5
Czech Republic	84.88
Finland	84.5
United Kingdom	84.49
Norway	84.33
Greece	83.86
Slovenia	83.52
Denmark	83.33
Spain	82.28

Exhibit 3

Telecom Italia Mobile (TIM) Prepaid Offer		
Zer0scatti		
Set-up Fee	TIM Mo-Su 0-24	Other nets Mo-Su 0-24
€ 0.00	€0.15	€ 0.45
Autoricarica 190		
Set-up Fee	TIM+Landline Mo-Su 0-24	Other mobile nets Mo-Su 0-24
€ 0.1549	€ 0.1177	€ 0.3470
Unica 10		
Set-up Fee	TIM+Landline Mo-Su 0-24	Other mobile nets Mo-Su 0-24
€ 0.15	€ 0.10	€ 0.40
Flash TIM 24h		
Set-up Fee	TIM+Landline Mo-Su 0-24	Other mobile nets Mo-Su 0-24
€ 0.00	€ 0.1797	€ 0.4276
Happy TIMe		
Set-up Fee	All calls Mo-Fr 8-17	All calls Mo-Fr 17-8+Wkd
€ 0.1549	€ 0.3470	€ 0.1177
Long TIM		
Set-up Fee	All calls Mo-Su 0-24	
€ 0.1549	€ 0.1549	
Unica		
Set-up Fee	All calls Mo-Su 0-24	
€ 0.15	€ 0.18	
Flash TIM		
Set-up Fee	All calls Mo-Su 0-24	
€ 0.00	€ 0.248	

Additional services and costs	
SMS sending	Unica, Zer0scatti € 0.15; Others € 15.49
MMS sending	€ 0.60

Vodafone Omnitel N.V Prepaid Offer		
Easy Day		
Set-up fee	All calls Mo-Su 0-24	
none		€ 0.25
Autoricarica Chiama		
Set-up fee	All calls Mo-Su 0-24	Autorecharge
€ 0.15	€ 0.19	every 20€ of outgoing calls in a month you gain 10€ extra recharge
Autoricarica Ricevi		
Set-up fee	All calls Mo-Su 0-24	Autorecharge
€ 0.15	€ 0.19	€ 0.25 every 10 minutes of incoming calls
Italy New		
Set-up fee	Voda+landline Mo-Su 0-24	Other mobile nets Mo-Su 0-24
€ 0.15	€ 0.10	€ 0.40

4 You New			
Set-up fee	4 Voda numbers Mo-Su 0-24	Other Voda+landline Mo-Su 0-24	Other mobile nets Mo-Su 0-24
€ 0.15	€ 0.07	€ 0.16	€ 0.40

Additional services and costs	
You & Me	1 Voda number at € 0.07 + set-up fee €0.15 (activation fee €6)
SMS sending	€ 0.15 (0.12 for old plans)
MMS sending	€ 0.50

Wind Telecomunicazioni S.p.A. Prepaid Offer	
Be Wind	
To Wind numbers Mon-Sun 0-24	Other calls Mon-Sun 0-24
€0.20	€0.35
Casa e Wind	
Wind+Landline Mon-Sun 0-24	Other mobile nets Mon-Sun 0-24
€ 0.15	€ 0.40
Autoricarica*	
Set-up fee	All calls Mon-Sun 0-24
€ 0.15	€ 0.19
Additional services and costs	

Noi2 Option	400 mins free every month to 1 Wind number with a € 2 per month fee Activation fee € 7.00
SMS sending	Be Wind: € 0.13 Other tariffs: € 0.15
MMS sending	€ 0.60

Hutchinson 3G Italia S.p.A. Prepaid Offer		
TuaMatic		
Set-up Fee for all calls	All voice calls Mo-Su 0-24	Video calls to 3 Mo-Su 0-24
€ 0.15	€ 0.15	€ 0.45
SuperTua		
Set-up Fee for all calls	All voice calls Mo-Su 0-24	Video calls to 3 Mo-Su 0-24
€ 0.15	€ 0.30 per 3 mins	€ 0.45
TuaBonus Ricaricabile			

Set-up Fee for all calls	Voice calls to 3 ITA+Landline Mo-Su 0-24	All other voice calls Mo-Su 0-24	Video calls to 3 Mo-Su 0-24
€ 0.15	€ 0.10	€ 0.25	€ 0.45

Additional services and costs	
Bonuses	TuaMatic: € 0.05/min bonus for all incoming calls except the ones from 3 ITA numbers SuperTua: € 0.10/min bonus for all incoming calls except the ones from 3 ITA numbers (60/60 bonus) TuaBonus: every 50 euros spent in a month you gain 30 euro bonus the following month
Messaging	SMS: € 0.15 MMS/VMS: € 0.55
Mobile Portal 3 navigation	€ 0.09 per 'information' page Free browsing for other pages, different prices apply for 'events' download
UMTS Internet	€ 0.60 connection fee, then € 0.004/KB

Source: www.prepaidgsm.net credit

Exhibit 4

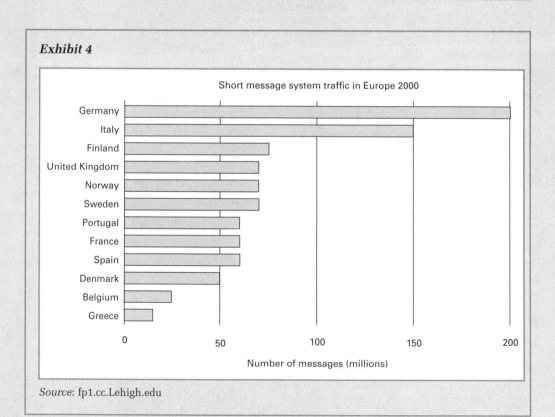

Short message system traffic in Europe 2000

Source: fp1.cc.Lehigh.edu

Exhibit 5: TIM Group: Financial Data

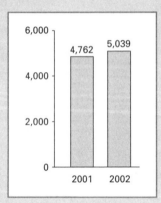

(millions of euro)	2002 (a)	2001 (b)	Change (a)-(b) amount	%
Sales and service revenues	10,867	10,250	617	6.0
Gross operating profit	5,039	4,760	279	5.9
% on Revenues	46.4%	46.4%		
Operating income	3,358	3,136	222	7.0
% on Revenues	30.9%	30.6%		
Investments				
- industrial	1,715	3,151	(1,436)	(45.6)
- difference on consolidation	196	31	165	
Employees at year end (number)	18,702	16,721	1,981	11.8

Source: www.italiatelecom.it

Mobile Phone Race 2003 operating margins	
TIM	32.1%*
VODAFONE	32.0%**
TELEFONICA MOVILES	30.2%*
ORANGE	23.8%*
* Fiscal year ended 31 Dec 2003 ** Fiscal year ended 31 Mar 2004 Data: E-Media	

Source: www.businessweek.com

Notes

This case was written by Firdaus under the direction of G Srikanth, ICFAI Business School Case Development Centre. It is intended to be used as the basis for class discussion rather than to illustrate either effective or ineffective handling of a management situation. This case was compiled from published sources.

[1] 'Software.com Provides Telecom Italia Mobile with its InterMail Platform To Bolster Wireless Messaging Services', www.mobic.com

[2] Kline, Maureen 'Telecom Italia Mobile Rings Up Profits', *Business Week*, www.businessweek.com, 5 July 2004

[3] According to a survey conducted by University of Trieste and published in June 2003, 56% of Italian children aged between 9 and 10 owned a mobile phone. Of these 68% never switched the phones off, 80% kept them on in church and 86% kept them on during lessons. The survey found that in 4 out of every 10 cases the child's parents had given the mobile to their offspring and that over 40% of the calls were made to either of the two parents. Further, 100% of the children surveyed who didn't own a mobile phone wanted a mobile phone. www.guardian.co.uk

[4] Standish, Dominic 'Telephonic Youth', *Tech Central Station*, www.techcentralstation, 9 September 2003

[5] Kline, Maureen, Telecom Italia Mobile Rings Up Profits', op. cit.

[6] Glover, Tony 'Telecom Italia Mobile Takes Edge in Italy's Mobile-Phone Race', *Knight Ridder/Tribune Business News*, 30 May 2004

[7] Global system for mobile communication (GSM) is a globally accepted standard for digital cellular communication. GSM is the name of a standardization group established in 1982 to create a common European mobile telephone standard that would formulate specifications for a pan-European mobile cellular radio system operating at 900 MHz. www.iec.org

[8] Gomez, Adriana 'IFC Invests $70 million to Support TIM Peru's Cellular Expansion in Peru', International Finance Corporation, ifcln001.worldbank.org, 12 June 2003

[9] 'Telecom Italia Mobile SpA (TIM)', www.palio.dii.unisi.it

[10] 3G systems are defined by the International Telecommunications Union initiative IMT-2000, as being capable of supporting high-speed data rates in the range of 144 Kbps to >2 Mbps, depending on the conditions and mobile speed. Analog cellular phones were first generation and digital were the second generation. www.xilinx.com. www.phonescoop.com

[11] 'Marconi Technology Lights the Way to 3G Services in Italy', www.marconi.com, 28 June 2004

[12] 'NEC's Mobile Internet Platform and I-mode Mobile Handset to Operate at Italy's WIND "I-mode" Service', www.ned.co.jp, 20 November 2003

[13] Saitto, Serena 'Hutchinson Whampoa Italy 3G Client Base Reaches 1 Million', news.morningstar.com, 15 July 2004

[14] Universal Mobile Telecommunications System (UMTS): A third generation (3G) mobile communications technology that promises data transmission speeds of up to 2 megabits per second (Mbps), although actual speeds may be significantly lower at first, due to network capacity restrictions. UMTS used WCDMA technology, and the two terms are often used interchangeably with each other. www.phonescoop.com

[15] 'Telefonica Moviles Plans Italian Licence Sale', uk.news.yahoo.com, 6 July 2004

[16] Sayer, Peter 'Sky is the limit for Italian mobile services', www.cnn.com, 1 May 2002

[17] Kline, Maureen 'Telecom Italia Mobile Rings Up Profits', op. cit.

[18] 'Pope sends text messages', www.mirabilis.ca, 14 January 2003

[19] University of Palermo

[20] Redstone, Paul 'Partnership key to success beyond voice in Italy', www.ericsson.com, 5 March 2003

[21] Ibid.

[22] 'Snap Happy', *The Economist*, www.economist.com, 25 April 2002

[23] Stefano, Cazzani 'More revenue, less competition', *Telecommunications (International Edition)*, 1 October 2003

[24] 'TIM Turbo Wireless Mail', www.3g.co.uk, 15 April 2004

[25] www.telecomitalia.it

[26] Kline, Maureen 'Telecom Italia Mobile Rings Up Profits', op. cit.

[27] 'Tim: Preliminary results for the first of 2004 approved', www.telecomitalia.it, 26 July 2004

[28] Kline, Maureen 'Telecom Italia Mobile Rings up Profits', op. cit.

[29] Wieland, Ken 'TIM boosted by GSM in Brazil and MMS at Home', www.telecommagazine.com, March 2004

[30] Kline, Maureen 'Telecom Italia Mobile Rings Up Profits', op. cit.

[31] 'Orange SA, Telefonica Moviles, TIM, and T-Mobile announce results of their collaboration and outline joint offerings', www.t-mobile.net, 29 March 2004

[32] Oates, John 'Vodafone penetrates Italian 3G market', www.theregister.co.uk, 25 May 2004

[33] Enhanced Data Rates for Global Evolution (EDGE): An upgrade for GSM/GPRS networks that triples data speeds over standard GPRS. Because it is based on existing GSM technology, EDGe is a smooth upgrade for GSM network operators. It also works within existing spectrum, making it idea for countries without dedicated 3G spectrum, such as the US. www.phonescoop.com

[34] 'TIM Ups Earnings Despite Competition', *Utility Week*, 20 February 2004

Case 5
McDonald's in UK: the competitive strategies

❝ 'McDonald's are in a little trouble but they are clever people. They know people think about their health, so now we have healthy food. We have Mighty Chicken Wings, grilled chicken on flat bread and a new McShaker Salad every month. McDonald's did not get to be number one in the world by not giving people what they want. As customers change, McDonald's changes ❞ '[1]

– *Jung Cha Park, Manager of one Franchisee of McDonald's*

Since its launch in the UK in 1974, McDonald's has developed a strong position in the fast food market of UK. The company consistently witnessed growth in profits until 2002, when, for the first time, it witnessed a drop in its profits. The company was held responsible for making people obese and unhealthy in the UK. Besides, the company also began to witness stiff competition from fast food retailers like Starbucks and Subway, which were perceived to be healthier and more sophisticated than McDonald's. To improve its image and sales, in 2003, the company introduced salads in its menu and also redesigned its stores to match with that of its competitors. While the revitalization strategy has slightly improved McDonald's sales in the UK, it is observed that McDonald's turnaround might be difficult to sustain, as its UK customers have not yet fully accepted the company's healthy image.

Fast food industry in the UK: the competitive landscape

The UK fast food and takeaway market is the largest in Europe (Exhibit I). Valued at £8.38 billion in 2004 at retail selling prices[2], the market consists of six sectors, including sandwiches, burgers, fish and chips, pizza, chicken and others.

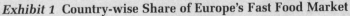

Exhibit 1 Country-wise Share of Europe's Fast Food Market

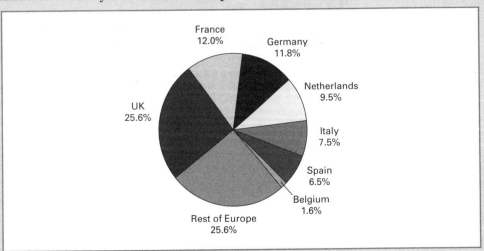

Source: 'Fast Food: Global Industry Guide', http://www.researchandmarkets.com/feats/download_
sample.asp?report_id=227366&file_name=Fast%20Food%20Global%20Guide%20-%20
Sample&file_ext=pdf

Sandwiches formed the biggest segment accounting for 36.5 per cent of all sales in 2004 (Exhibit II). Due to changing consumer tastes, shorter lunch breaks and rapid expansion of branded sandwich outlets, sales in this segment have grown at a rapid pace. Pret a Manger, Subway and Benjys are among the major players in this segment.

The second largest segment of fast food is burgers. Constituting 22.5 per cent of the fast food market in 2004, the burger segment in the UK comprises three main players, McDonald's, Burger King and Wimpy, who together account for 80 per cent of the burger market. McDonald's leads among the three. After the entry of McDonald's in the UK, the

Exhibit II Fast Food and Take-away Market in the UK by Sector

	2003		2004	
	Value (million)	Share of total fast food market	Value (million)	Share of total fast food market
Sandwiches	£2,922	36.3%	£3,056	36.5%
Burgers	£1,809	22.5%	£1,860	22.5%
Fish & chips	£924	11.5%	£939	11.2%
Pizza	£843	10.5%	£890	10.6%
Chicken	£507	6.3%	£525	6.3%
Other	£1,053	13.1%	£1,106	13.2%

Source: 'Market snapshot: Fast food and take-away', http://www.caterersearch.com/Articles/2005/05/31/
300739/ Market+snapshot+Fast+food+and+take-away.htm, May 31st 2005

burger market has grown considerably at the expense of earlier fast food segments like fish and chips. However, with negative publicity (related to obesity issues) mounting over the burger market, the pace of growth in this market has slowed down. Since 2001, the burger market has witnessed a reduction in sales and margins. The burger segment also faced competition from the other fast food segments that are perceived to be healthier as compared to burgers. Justin Ash, KFC's general manager in the UK, said, 'We are growing at a rate comparable to McDonald's. There is a huge growth in chicken because consumers consider white meat to be healthier.'[3]

Although chicken and pizza outlets gained due to a shift in consumer tastes, McDonald's maintained its position in UK. Since the launch of its first outlet at Woolwich, in 1974, the company opened 1235 outlets across the UK by 2004.

McDonald's in the UK: the competitive strategies

A key market for McDonald's, the UK accounts for 6 per cent of McDonald's total operating income.[4] In the UK, McDonald's serves burgers to 2.5 million people daily.[5] Offering the same menu of Big Macs, McNuggets, and French fries as its parent company, for years, McDonald's has enjoyed huge success in the UK. In 2001, profits peaked at McDonald's. However, since then, McDonald's faced dropping profits and stagnant sales. In 2003 McDonald's witnessed the largest drop in profits since its inception in the UK (Exhibit III). With rising concern over health and obesity, more consumers started viewing McDonald's as a fast food chain, which posed health risks for its customers. McDonald's developed an 'unhealthy' image and came under pressure with the release of the film *Super Size Me*, in which Morgan Spurlock, the maker of the film, depicted how he became obese by living only on McDonald's food for a month.

To refurbish McDonald's tarnished image, in 2003, the company adopted a revitalization strategy called 'Plan to win'. A key part of this strategy was to focus on its menu. To address obesity concerns, in March 2003, McDonald's introduced healthier

Exhibit III **McDonald's Sales and Profits Since 1994**

Year	Sales billion	Pre-tax profits million	Fall or rise in profits
2003	£ 1.09	£ 23.6	–71%
2002	£ 1.13	£ 83.8	–19%
2001	£ 1.14	£ 104.3	4%
2000	£ 1.10	£ 100.1	15%
1999	£ 1.03	£ 86.7	34%
1998	£ .927	£ 64.4	–12%
1997	£ .840	£ 73.2	12%
1996	£ .767	£ 65.1	44%
1995	£ .684	£ 45.2	37%
1994	£ .622	£ 33.1	68%

Source: Prynn Jonathan, "McDonald's profits dive", http://www.mcspotlight.org/media/press/mcds/eveningstandard280904.html

options like SaladPlus, a low-fat salad dressing to its menu. It also started providing nutritional information about its menu to its customers. Denis Hennequin, president of McDonald's Europe, said, 'Offering salads as meals in their own right responds to our customers' increasing attention to diet and lifestyle.'[6] It is felt that by conveying a message that McDonald's is 'healthier' to consumers, the company hopes to attract even those consumers who otherwise do not eat at McDonald's. Amanda Pierce, McDonald's British spokesperson, said, 'We are offering different and lighter options geared to appeal to new customers who might not otherwise have considered eating in McDonald's.'[7]

However, despite a healthier menu, McDonald's failed to improve its sales in the UK. It was opined that McDonald's shrinking sales was largely due to intense competition in UK's fast food market. Denis Hennequin said, 'If you walk down the streets of London, it's probably the most competitive marketplace from that perspective.'[8] With a number of coffee and sandwich chains saturating the UK market, McDonald's started losing its market share. It was reported that one quarter of McDonald's stores, which were 25 years old, were losing customers to sandwich and coffee outlets like Starbucks and Subway.

The declining sales at McDonald's forced the company to take a decision of closing down 25 high-rent outlets in the UK, as they were weighing down the company's overall performance and also lacked modern interiors. Denis Hennequin said, 'The UK has been in negative territory for a couple of years now. The brand 15 years ago was very trendy and modern. It is now tired.'[9] Acknowledging the fact that its restaurants looked 'tired' in contrast to its competitors, in 2003, McDonald's changed its growth strategy from opening new stores to generating more sales from the existing ones. To revive the 'hip' image of McDonald's, the company undertook a redesigning programme for its stores, under which, each store was given a new look, customized according to its surroundings. In its stores, McDonald's changed brightly coloured interiors and plastic furniture to chrome-finished interiors, sofas and modern lighting. The company also planned to include Wi-Fi centres[10] for Internet users in some of its stores. Commenting on McDonald's recognition of the increasing sophistication of its competitors, Toby Young, a restaurant critic, said, 'They're trying to catch up with the design revolution that has really transformed Britain's high streets in the past 10 to 15 years.'[11] McDonald's plans to re-image 200 of its outlets in the UK by 2011.

After the implementation of McDonald's revitalisation strategy in the UK, the company reported an increase in sales across Europe with progress particularly in the UK. The company attributed the increase in its sales momentum to its 'healthier menus'. Janice Meyer, a stock market analyst, said, 'Salads was an absolute game-changer for McDonald's. It gave the chain a halo effect. It was a fresh product. It had fresh ingredients. It was good quality and it really changed the way people thought about McDonald's and the other products it sold.'[12]

However, some critics cite that McDonald's salads are not as low in fat as they are projected to be. Ian Tokelove, a spokesman for the Food commission,[13] said, '.. .McDonald's have tried to convince us that they are making their food more healthy but their salads have been shown to have more fat than a burger when you take into account the dressing.'[14] Although salads helped improve sales at McDonald's, the company is still perceived to be responsible for increasing obesity. To counter that, in March 2005,

McDonald's launched a controversial advertising campaign carrying the slogan 'It's What I Eat and What I Do'. The campaign, which was particularly targeted at young consumers, was launched to make consumers understand that a balanced lifestyle includes exercise, apart from a healthy diet. Peter Beresfors, McDonald's UK CEO, said, 'We want them to learn at an early age that it's a balanced diet but also it's exercise.'[15]

However, analysts feel that the slogan might alienate McDonald's loyal consumers. With such risks and problems still looming over McDonald's, it is observed that McDonald's challenge is to sustain its turnaround and become one of the world's most loved brands rather than being the most hated. Still, some feel that McDonald's is a big company and can face such challenges. Commenting on McDonald's power to face challenges, Mitchell Speiser, an analyst at Lehman Brothers in New York, said, 'McDonald's is a big machine, so when there is a negative momentum, it takes time to turn it around. But on the positive side, once you get it rolling, don't ever underestimate the power of brand McDonald's.'[16]

Notes

This case was written by Priti Krishnan under the direction of Sumit Kumar Chaudhuri, ICFAI Business School Case Development Centre. It is intended to be used as the basis for class discussion rather than to illustrate either effective or ineffective handling of a management situation. This case was compiled from published sources.

[1] 'Fast food ration', http://observer.guardian.co.uk/foodmonthly/story/0,,937296,00.html, 13 April 2003

[2] 'Fast Food & Home Delivery Outlets Market Report Plus 2005', http://www.researchandmarkets.com/reports/307599/

[3] Milmo Cahal, 'KFC gains from Britain's growing takeaway culture', http://enjoyment.independent.co.uk/food_and_drink/news/article155558.ece, 28 November 2000

[4] Grant, Jeremy, 'McDonald's revamp gives platform for improvement', *Financial Times*, 22 April 2006, p. 8

[5] 'Investing in McDonald's, http://www.mcdonalds.com/corp/invest.html

[6] 'McDonald's Goes Slim-Line for Europe', http://www.dw-world.de/dw/article/0,2144,1138422,00.html, 12 March 2004

[7] 'Fast food ration', op. cit.

[8] Jamieson Alastir, 'A sofa and fries, please, at revamped McDonald's', http://news.scotsman.com/topics.drm?tid=378&id=172462006

[9] Ibid.

[10] McDonald's is providing Wi-Fi technology (a wireless networking technology) in its stores,

which enables its customers to log on to the Internet through their Wi-Fi enabled laptops. This facility allows customers to access the net as they eat at McDonald's.

[11] Choueka Elliott, 'Big Mac Fights back', http://news.bbc.co.uk/1/hi/business/4665205.stm

[12] Grant Jeremy, 'McDonald's to revamp UK outlets', http://news.ft.com/cms/s/cda2d238-934c-11da-ab7b-0000779e2340.html, 2 February 2006

[13] The Food Commission is a UK-based non-profit organisation that campaigns for the right to safe, and healthy food.

[14] Prynn Jonathan, 'McDonald's profits dive', http://www.mcspotlight.org/media/press/mcds/eveningstandard280904.html, 28 September 2004

[15] 'Big Mac Fights Back', op. cit.

[16] 'Big Mac Under Attack', http://www.mcspotlight.org/media/press/marketwk_26jun97.html, 26 June 1997

Case 6
Call Center Europe

Call Center Europe (CCE) is one of the largest outsourcing call centers in northern Europe. It specializes in representing business clients to their customers with a series of inbound and outbound calling services. As the trend for call centers is to grow into a web-enabled customer care and contact centers, CCE has to remain in readiness to face the emerging challenges and seize newer growth opportunities in the overall discipline of customer relations management (CRM). The case description below, aims to initiate a discussion regarding the growth option for the CCE.

Keywords

- Call centers
- Outsourcing
- Tele-technology
- Growth options
- Customer relationship management

Svend Hensen* looked quite happy as he finished reading an e-mail message on his laptop, noted his executive assistant. She imagined that the message probably was regarding the joint venture deal that the Call Center Europe (CCE) was working on for some time. As she looked at her boss for confirmation, Svend said that the message was from the university where he had studied and that a professor there had asked if Svend would agree to meet students in the international management program on service marketing and talk about CCE. Svend was happy that if he went, he could get away from the work for a while and enjoy the academic environment he so often missed even after fifteen years of his masters. Svend Hensen was the managing director and promoter of the CCE, which was launched seven years ago as a new service concept in Denmark and which now had grown to become one of the largest call centers in north Europe.

Since Svend had only two weeks to prepare, he began to wonder which aspects of CCE could be prepared in a short time that would also appeal to the international students. CCE was a baby he had conceived and raised it with immense care and affection, and often at great financial risk. There were moments in the seven-year old history of CCE when he felt utterly frustrated and ready to quit. It would sure be tempting to talk about it, he thought, but would the international students be as keen to listen? He was not sure of the answer. As Svend returned to his computer screen, he saw another e-mail flashing for his attention. The mail was from his marketing manager reminding him about the annual marketing meet next month and attaching a draft report on growth options for the CCE.

The report set Svend reflecting. Suddenly he felt that he might as well speak to the students on key issues facing CCE. He could always use a reaction, he thought, from the young and fresh minds in a university. Excited, Svend pressed 'reply' for his acceptance to the professor.

The Call Center Europe (CCE)

Call Center Europe (CCE) was established in 1993. Tele Danmark Group held the majority share at 80% while the remaining 20% of the capital was with Svend Hensen. By 2000, CCE had become the largest call center in Scandinavia and one of the largest in the north Europe. The business aim of the CCE was to establish and develop a telephone dialogue with the customers of its clients. The calls were both inbound (90%) and outbound (10%). The clients of CCE included 'business to business' market (or, B2B) at 10% and 'business to customers' (or B2C) at 90%. CCE operated throughout the year round the clock. The mission statement of the CCE read as follows:

> *To provide the best possible service to customers of our clients through the optimum combination of technology and human resources. Concentrating on our field of competence-customer dialogue, we give our clients the opportunity to release resources and concentrate on their main business areas. In this way, Call Center Europe helps to ensure that the amount of initiative is higher than the amount of elements in the process. Call Center Europe's existence and consequently our success depends on our ability to create success for our clients.*

CCE in recent years had grown into a multicultural call center and recruited and trained bilingual employees from many different cultures. It offered telephone services in nine languages: Danish, English, Swedish, Norwegian, Dutch, German, Spanish, Italian, and French. Depending upon the actual linguistic market, either the native or the multilinguistic agents handled the CCE assignments. However, 70% of the CCE telephone agents were German speaking. The organization had developed a process, which enabled it to implement services in any other languages for individual projects, usually within a period of one to two months. By the beginning of 2000, CCE covered the following markets and languages (Exhibit 1).

CCE had been constantly upgrading its technical ability. Among these were multitasking and multi-queuing assignments and interactive digital voice repsonse etc. The IT infrastructure of the CCE included NorTel Meridian 81/c-OS Rel.21.02. Red Hat Unix, Windows NT, Symposium Var.1.5. The net work used IPX/SPX or TCP/IP protocols on all its workstations. CCE had selected the Astea Power help for its helpdesk services. The number of employees at CCE in the beginning of 2000 stood at 250 with 200 workstations. CCE treated its employees to be its most important asset and inculcated in them qualities of service mindedness, flexibility concerning working hours and assignments, positive job attitude, independence, continuous upgrading of skills and computer proficiency. CCE claimed to deliver highly stringent service quality standards to its clients and monitored them at every stage of the assignments. Each

Exhibit 1 **Coverage of the Call Center Europe**

Country/Region	Country/Territory	Language
The Nordic countries	Denmark	Danish
	Finland	Finnish
	Norway	Norwegian
	Sweden	Swedish
Great Britain	England	English
	Scotland	English
	Ireland	English
	Wales	English
Rest of Europe	Belgium	Flanders/French
	Germany	German
	Holland	Dutch
	Austria	German
	Italy	Italian
	Spain	Spanish
	France	French
	Switzerland	French, Italian and German
	Northern Ireland	English

project was assigned a quality manager who became responsible for the qualitative follow up of everything including the CCE telephone agents. The quality monitoring and follow-up covered both the human aspects as well as the operational aspects. The quality manager carried out quality checks every three to six weeks depending upon the complexity of the assignment and covered parameters like the tone of the voice, attitude, addressing, understanding and interpretation of the customer needs and messages etc.

CCE was a flat, horizontal organizational structure that allowed 'a high degree of freedom and customer competence for the managers at all level'. The quality manager just described, was regarded as the representative of the clients in CCE since he or she managed the entire project; coached CCE agents; liaised with the client and handled all interests of the client within the CCE. Then there was a 'supervisor' responsible for the operations of the call centers. He or she allocated resources to various projects, planned workforce for a project, and liaised with quality managers, IT and finance staff. Supervisors also recruited agents and set up their profiles of various projects. CCE was proud to call itself a 'green' company in balancing natural ambience (in-house plants, sound absorption systems, and inviting colors) with the in-house environment; in recycling paper as well as in using a variety of recycled products.

CCE was a supplier of the outsourced service. A supplier of the outsourced services was one that undertook non-core projects on behalf of the principals, enabling the latter to make resources available in their own organizations to more important functions and activities and to concentrate their efforts on their own core competent products and services. As marketers moved into an unregulated environment, there was a need for higher levels of customer service in the markets. Customer service and support became competitive weapons for most of the marketers. It required a frequent customer contact.

With the emerging telecommunication and information technology, an increasing number of customers began to buy products and services non-face to face. Finally, the rules of customer focus and responsiveness demanded that organizations were always accessible to their customers. All these reasons contributed to the rapid rise in the use of telephone as customer service. Traditionally, such tasks were handled by organizations in-house by recruiting or assigning specialized personnel. However, the economic, technical, operational and human constraints dictated that companies wanting to keep the telephone dialogues open with their customers, outsourced these services to the specialized companies which delivered the same job but at a higher effectiveness and lower cost. Outsourcing became a bigger necessity when the participating organizations were small or mid-size companies. Even large companies tended to outsource the service to the specialized institutions whenever the number, frequency and timing of the telephone calls were unstable and unpredictable. It made an economic sense to outsource such tasks to the specially trained and equipped call centers. CCE was one such outsource service organization.

As an outsourcing service organization CCE accepted outsourcing of both in-coming calls (called Inbound) and outgoing calls (called outbound). Inbound services were outsourced so that its clients did not need to commit a high degree of fixed resources to receiving infrequent, irregular and variable calls. Outbound telecalls were outsourced to CCE because clients had limited resources in such areas as staff, time, space and PC capacity. Often a special expertise was needed in areas like the telephone sales, market research or other Tele-based service. CCE helped needy clients in meeting tele-needs in a more economic, effective and professional manner.

The call center industry

Call centers surfaced in early seventies when probably the airlines used them first. They quickly became pivotal to the 'connected' world where technology and telecommunications were used to communicate. Call centers were the means by which these connections worked. They could be automated or human. Call centers were essentially based on a technology of automatic call distribution, a system that routed calls to employees best trained to handle certain questions.

Since their inception, call centers enjoyed the status of one of the fastest growing segments of economy. For instance, according to the reports of Datamonitor, a research firm in the call center industry, call centers in USA numbered about 78,000 in year 1999. Call centers were steadily growing @ 6.5% annually. Experts believed that the trend was expected to continue at least until 2005. The proliferation of call centers was likely to slow down thereafter because of consolidation and new technologies that would increase the efficiency of call-center employees. Call center industry targeted mostly the business-to-customer segments although the business to business was also growing in late nineties. The industry was supported by a variety of users belonging to a number of industrial sectors. Exhibit 2 profiles the major users of the industry in the USA.

Operating a call center was a huge task as it involved not only marketing of the concept to the clients but also blending the call center technology with human resources. The industry expert believed that a multipronged treatment helped the call

Exhibit 2 Call Center Outsourcing by Industry

User class	1997 (%)	2002 (projected) (%)
Financial service	20	23
Technology/telecom	18	21
Remote shopping	19	16
Consumer goods	19	14
Utilities	03	07
Misc.	21	19
Total	100	100

Source: E Source, Inc., Boulder, Colorado (USA)

centers to survive and compete better. Exhibit 3 lists the essential steps in the direction of making a call center survive and prosper:

Call centers world over, were being transformed by the need to keep track of Internet telephony and IP (Internet Protocol) telephony. In Internet telephony typically, telephony traveled over the Internet while in the IP telephony, telephony traveled over

Exhibit 3 Strategic Considerations in Managing a Call Center

- Build a team
- Create a vision
- Be ready for change
- Uncover customer expectations
- Benchmark Your Competition
- Architect new processes
- Design an integrated infrastructure
- Prepare the staff
- Implement technologies
- Monitor and fine-tune

Source: Boelkes, Debra & Patrick O'Rourke (1998): 'Ten steps to shape your call center strategy', Telemarketing & Call Center Solutions; Norwalk; May, Vol.16, Issue 11, Pp. 88.

any network that was based on the Internet protocol such as an Intranet or the corporate LAN. Internet telephony in a call center impacted call centers since the industry was telephony-centric. Efficiencies that a traditional office enjoyed through automation were increased exponentially in a call center due to enormous calling volumes. Call centers had to increasingly integrate applications, including the Web, data warehouses, legacy systems, PBX, ACD, dialers, CTI, desktop, fax, mail and manual, mobile, and video. Call center agents had to be equipped with a power to access information that not just enabled to receive a call, but empowered them to provide exceptional service and value to the customers. They needed to build solutions for their clients that provided mission-

---

Exhibit 4 **The Survival Basics for Call Centers**

- A market and a product,
- A low-cost-base – but access to high-quality services
- A reliable and user-friendly environment,
- English as the lead language,
- Ability to serve the major "disposable" income areas,
- An infrastructure and disaster recovery services,
- A labor pool,
- A location in an area of low political and economic risk,
- High-technology
- High-marketing skills at hand.

Source: Hyslop, Maitland Hyslop (1998): 'The international call center--requirements for survival', Call Center Solutions; Norwalk; Apr; Volume: 16 Issue: 10 Page: 118-122

Exhibit 5 **Competitiveness of Call Centers: A Checklist**

- Does our call center maximize our potential to win and keep customers?
- Does our call center help us achieve the level of service our customers expect?
- Are we realizing the maximum revenue potential from each customer contact?
- Does our call center help us reduce the overall cost of sales?
- Can we support desired growth and expansion?
- Does our call center help our business contain costs?
- Are we keeping pace with our customers' needs for new and expanded services? For fast response?

Source: Saxon Jun Mimi (1998); 'Can your Call Center compete?' Call Center Solutions; Vol.16 Issue: 12 Page: 78-80

---

critical applications, superior technologies, skills, know-how and professionalism. This was the biggest threat to the traditional call centers affecting their survival and competitive effectiveness (Exhibits 4 and 5 offer the survival basics and a competitive checklist respectively for call centers).

Modern call centers were places of continuous change. The technology brought newer and more powerful versions of the Interactive Voice Response (IVR), Automatic Call distributor (ACD), Automatic Number identification (ANI), Dialed number Identification service (DNIS), Computer Telephony Integration (CTI) and Call Center Management. Software to integrate the network resources and to monitor call activity became available with the industry. But the industry suffered of a high staff turnover. It was as easy to recruit new agents for newer or expanding services. The workload frequently changed in volume, incidence and nature. Most call centers had two types of service quality targets. The first was how easily and the second was how quickly did the customer get through to an agent. How easily the customer got through was a hardware issue. But how quickly the customer's call was answered, was usually measured by the percentage of calls answered (PCA) within a specific time interval termed as service objective (SO).

Typically, in a call center, the PCA target was in the range of 80 to 90 percent and the SO was 15 to 30 seconds. Exhibit 6 lists the factors on which customer satisfaction with a call center was presently evaluated by its users. Additionally, a call center had to be wary of causes that led to the rise in the costs. Cost was critical not only to the development of call centers, but also to producing the new 'embedded systems' and the marketing tools required to ensure the continued development of the call centers (Exhibit 7).

Exhibit 6 **Criteria for Customer Satisfaction with a Call Center**

- Transactions completed on initial contact (%),
- Average speed of answer
- Abandon rate (%)
- Events reopened (%)
- Time per transaction
- Customer survey results.

Source: Boelkes Debra & Patrick O'Rourke (1998) Ibid. Pp. 88.

Exhibit 7 **The Chief Cost Culprits in a Call Center**

- Escalation of calls and complaints to upper management,
- Repeat calls from customers,
- Callbacks to customers for missing or unclear information,
- Cancellations,
- Handling product returns,
- Unnecessary service calls,
- Negative publicity from angry customers.
- CSRs take the heat for mistakes made by others (increasing turnover),
- Loss of referrals.

Source: Boelkes, Debra & Patrick O'Rourke (1998) Ibid. Pp. 88.

The service mix of CCE

Over the years, CCE had initiated, developed and improved several services to its clients. It had come to define itself as 'service agency offering customer services in outsourcing of inbound and outbound call handling for the European market'. It claimed to handle 'complex communication projects with a focus on quality competence and proactive sparring between the clients and CCE'. Exhibit 8 provides a quick list of the current CCE products and services.

Exhibit 8 **The Service Mix of CCE**

Inbound

- E-commerce support
- Handling of incoming calls
- Customer service in general
- Mail Order/Remote sales
- Help desk support
- Product and software support
- Follow up on direct marketing
- TV shopping
- TV spot response
- Financial services
- Booking services - entertainment etc.
- Booking services - Travel arrangements
- Value added service- paygate
- Customer satisfaction analyses

Outbound

- Handling of outgoing calls
- Appointment scheduling
- Private and Business Sales
- Database updating
- Follow-up on direct mails
- Business to business sales
- Market surveys and research
- Customer satisfaction analyses
- Advertising effect analysis
- Value added service- paygate

CCE general customer service aimed to offer to the clients an arrangement by which CCE handled customer service, telephone contact, and collection of market data on behalf of these clients. Mail order/remote sales offered a professional handling of orders and delivered customized full service solutions. It sought to leverage on its competence in handling mail order sales / remote including order-taking by telephone, telefax, coupons, Interactive Voice Response (IVR), and e-mail as well as credit checks and approvals. The clients were encouraged to go for a round-the-clock shopping, anywhere anytime. The service also offered customized solutions in co-operation with partners within distribution, financing, and payment procurement, if needed. The product and software support offered CCE skills and experience in communicating technological and technical solutions.

To the customers, CCE had compiled a know-how by continuous documentation, knowledge-based relation databases and helpdesk systems, which enabled it to offer assistance and communicating solutions to technical problems of customers. CCE also accepted to make a structured collection and registration of customer data in a database. It later supplied the registered data via electronic media whereby the data was integrated into the customer service and marketing activities of clients. TV-Spot-Response received and answered telephone calls in connection with TV-spots. Primarily answered by CCE telephone agents, in case of very large call volumes within a short period of time, the customers could also record their names and telephone numbers on an IVR unit. Financial services were offered by CCE in respect of money transfers, account statements, loan raising, terms and conditions, and interest rates on behalf of the client banks. Thus, the staff of the banks was not disturbed by telephone calls and yet, customers got a service both inside and outside the bank's normal opening hours. CCE undertook the job of booking and ticketing for movies, theatres, and concerts. Through an online connection to the database of the client, CCE accessed ticketing system of its clients and allowed it to inform customers on the availability of the tickets. It also avoided double bookings and offers alternative tickets. Similarly, it booked vacations and business trips for private as well as business purposes, combining different reservations such as plane tickets, hotel rooms, travels, and rental cars etc. The customer satisfaction analyses of CCE offered to conduct surveys on customers' ratings and conveyed customer feedback on products and services sold and delivered by CCE clients. The analysis was carried out in connection with the normal telephone contact. Appointment scheduling helped companies as sales representatives were better at selling than at administrating. CCE sought to assist sales representatives in scheduling their appointments and thereby save time. Through private and business sales service, CCE served the identified but small customers. This enabled its clients to concentrate their resources on large and important customers. CCE handled continuous updating of customer database offering its clients an accurate and updated line of communication to their own customers, suppliers, and partners. CCE also advised clients on how to construct and maintain their own database. CCE made follow-up calls during any direct marketing campaigns of its clients. Using its telephone skills CCE collected response on the impact of direct mail campaigns or any other ad campaign. Finally, CCE conducted market information studies using a two-way telephone communication. It also planned and carried data analyses to compare the image, products, and services of the clients vis a vis competitors and, consumer patterns, markets and outlets.

Need to re-energize CCE

Barring the early hiccups, CCE had been doing quite well. All key financial and non-financial parameters and growth pattern of CCE were reasonably strong, through Svend. However, he was not content. Svend always portrayed himself as business opportunist and entrepreneur. He therefore, would not like it if the CCE ever got too comfortable, lost out on the oportunities in the market or became a corporate dinosaur. His aim was to be in the forefront of technology of the call center industry and to use the growth avenues as they presented themselves. He noticed that call centers world over were turning more and more into an 'accessibility industry' – allowing customers and clients to access from anywhere, anytime, and in any form. He remembered hearing words of Alexander Szlam, chairman and chief executive officer, Melita International Corporation in USA in the annual industry dinner (Anonymous, 1998), that a call center of the future would be expected to:

- Address the customer's individual preferences, about best time to call or not to call – as well as about products and services,
- Communicate with the customer in the manner the customer prefers, be it via e-mail, fax, pager, telephone, the postal service or the internet,
- Convey the information the customer wants – not just what the call center manager thinks the customer ought to know.

A large part of the evolution of call centers matched the evolving telecommunication technology. Svend noted that everything in the industry was getting faster and faster even as inbound calls stayed the critical part of the industry and required better technology and infrastructure. Already major technology vendors had advanced call center a technology that connected customers to a call center via a Web site. Such innovations offered a host of new applications from medicine to catalog shopping to organizations like the CCE. Additionally, a call center in the future needed to create an unforgettable customer experience, solution and service. Call centers were fast evolving into customer care centers. The traditional call centers were no longer functioned. Svend was stunned first when he had heard Szlam term the call center industry a 'Cinderella industry'.

Concerned by the likely impact of these environmental factors pertaining to technology, higher customer expectations and newer business opportunities on CCE, Svend Hensen asked his marketing manager to prepare a note and a new growth plan, and present them to the forthcoming annual seminar of senior executives. This was the report that he had just received which of course, was the first draft.

Growth plans for CCE

The report of the marketing manager reviewed the past and the emerging roles of call center and recommended that CCE needed to chart a new growth strategy for itself to stay competitive and maintain its leadership status. The technology in the industry was so rapidly evolving that CCE needed to take both reactive and proactive steps. In order to start an internal discussion, the marketing team offered the following growth options for CCE (Exhibit 9). Many of these options were mutually inclusive, overlapping and interrelated.

Exhibit 9 **Growth Avenues for Call Center Europe**

1 Become a web-based integrated call center

2 Penetrate deeper in Europe

3 Enter E-commerce

4 Redefine CCE as a customer contact center

5 Develop into a Next-generation call/CRM center

6 Develop multi-ethnic call centers

7 Develop into virtual call centers

8 Enter E-mail business

9 Target small towns

Exhibit 10 **The Building Block of a Web-enabled Call Center**

1 A customer-profiling infrastructure that built a detailed profile of the customer's likes and dislikes, sales and service history, and his or her level of interest in various products. The profile needed to automatically updated each time the customer interacted with the call center, or with anyone else in the organization who had access to the system (e.g., sales, technical support), including the Web and other forms of contact such as e-mail and postal mail.

2 An integrated workflow mechanism with a solid, built-in case ownership models. This would ensure that every customer opportunity, customer request or customer issue was owned and managed by designated individuals according to company policies and procedures.

3 Action items, so tasks could be easily "subcontracted" to others within the organization or even outside the organization within the ownership model, such as literature fulfillment.

4 Proactive notification and escalation policies to alert managers as needed, including a management "console" for ongoing account management.

5 Enterprise-wide access and information exchange so that every individual who had contact with the customer, both inside and outside the organization, could update and share their work to expedite requests.

6 A call management system that was ready- to- use, and provided point-and-click customization for business-level changes. This would ensure rapid deployment along with easy, ongoing system maintenance.

Source: Tucci, Angela (1998); 'The "Web" creates new call center requirements ' Call Center Solutions; Norwalk; Feb; Volume: 16 Issue:8, Page: 20–27

Growth avenue 1: Become a web-based integrated call center

The marketing team noted that in the new, Web-based environment, consumers used internet to research products and services, and bought largely those products or goods that were easily understood or compared by them. The customers used the web to obtain the information they needed to make informed decisions. Consumers appreciated the way the internet gave them freedom from geography (they didn't have to visit a store or dealer) and time (they could order in the middle of the night). To many other customers, the anonymity of internet itself appealed (customers did not have to negotiate with a salesman who rather liked to close the deal than gave them full information for comparison shopping). Since a web-based customer bought without the aid of a store clerk or product representative, his or her contact with the call center was the only human interface with the company. This trend – where service and sales joined forces – presented the call center industry with an interesting set of requirements as well as opportunities.

The web-enabled call centers, so described, offered potential for organizations from nearly every business sector. When implemented properly, they opened newer channels for customer contact; achieved greater operational efficiency; and enhanced customer relationships. In order to harness the true potential of this valuable technology, the call center had to select the correct technology, employed stringent quality assurance procedures and prepared its agents to work in a new environment, the report noted.

Web-based call center was not easy to operationalize in practice as it made several new demands. First, it required the call center to integrate information as the service agents of a web-enabled call center wore several hats simultaneously. Second, the agents needed to be extremely well informed since the customer prospecting the Web might have already researched the product line and the competition quite thoroughly. The third and perhaps the most important need was that a web-based call center agents worked as the instruments to create and maintain customer loyalty. This was a key to profitability under the web-based call center technology. An integrated call center needed to build as a system and therefore needed a variety of building blocks. Exhibit 10 lists those components:

Growth avenue 2: Penetrate deeper in Europe

The call center industry in Europe was projected to grow at a much faster pace at approximately 40% annually. The European Direct Marketing Association had recently projected that by the year 2000, telemarketing of which call center was a component would account for 20 percent or $4.4 billion of Europe's $22 billion direct marketing industry. As the call center industry was people intensive, it was also a big source of employment in Europe. For instance, European call centers added more than 75,000 positions annually for the last three years. Yet, the number of persons employed in the European call centers was only 0.2 percent of the workforce in a marketplace while in USA, it was 3 percent of the workforce in a marketplace. Marketing research from Datamonitor also indicated that the number of European call center agents would grow to 600,000 by 2001.

For these reasons, the marketing team recommended that CCE moved deeper in Europe. CCE was already present in many countries of Europe but had a newer scope to penetrate further in such countries as Sweden. A recent study found three main forces that accelerated the growth of Sweden's call center industry and likewise in many other countries of Europe. These were: a high computer literacy and heavy Internet use in Europe; a trend toward establishing regional European call centers as opposed to single, pan-European centers, and the rise of an advanced economy in Europe in general. While telemarketing and market research were the leading marketing activities, many call centers too began to focus on technical support for international companies operating in the computer and information technology industries. The recommendation to go deeper in Europe was also guided by the fact that the CCE had already strong presence there and it was easier for it to locate a call center in Europe than a new company.

Notwithstanding the importance and growth potential of the call centers, it was not easy to locate a call center, especially a multicultural call center, in Europe. A call center before locating itself in the market, had to consider a number of factors (Exhibit 11). These factors varied widely within a country as well as within Europe even though Europe was getting more homogenous, politically integrated and geographically accessible union of countries. Generalizations of any kind were risky. For instance, Germany was usually generalized as being an expensive country with more restrictive laws. On the contrary, one of the German states, Saarland, had lower set up costs, including personnel and real estate for call center and flexible laws, allowing call centers greater ease of operation. Further, Germany and France represented 46 percent of the European Union's GDP. They were ranked as number 1 and 2 country respectively in Europe. Therefore, often these countries were important markets for U.S. companies entering Europe. Call centers needed to factor the importance of their largest markets into their decision on where to locate their call centers.

Exhibit 11 **Considerations in Locating a Call Center**

- Markets to be served
- Labor pool available
- Telecommunication needs
- Costs and incentives involved.
- The number of call centers already located in the vicinity.
- Support provided from the region.

Heath Terri (1998): 'Tips for choosing a Call Center site in Europe' Call Center Solutions; Norwalk; Jun., Vol.16, Issue: 12, Page: 102–107

Growth option 3: Enter E-commerce

E-commerce had of late been called the greatest business development since the industrial revolution. E-commerce helped an organization to reach hundreds of thousands of people with a targeted message at little or no cost through e-mail via the Internet. Notwithstanding the importance of direct mail, telemarketing, integrated marketing, trade show marketing, etc., none of them were as cost-effective as marketing through the Web.

The fall of telephone business was alarming as a result. For instance, according to Forrester Research Inc., a Cambridge, Mass. based market research firm in 1997, about 97 percent of all business-customer interactions took place over the phone. In 1998, that figure dropped to 60 percent. The firm predicted the number would further drop to 5 percent by 2003. The main replacements would be electronic mail and the Web. On the other hand, the rise of the web-based business was phenomenal. The e-mail interactions were 2 percent in 1997, hit 23 percent in 1999, and were expected to rise to 30 percent in 2003. Web customer interactions were growing even faster: from 1 percent in 1997 to 14 percent in 1999 and 56 percent in 2003.

The marketing team naturally recommended that CCE entered E-commerce to take advantage of the changing market. CCE stood to benefit for another reason too – the incompetence shown by most e-marketers to handle the web medium. Customers had been abused on this medium more often than not as there were frequent failures to either answer e-mail inquiries in a timely fashion or to provide a way for customers to place a call from a Web site to a call center. Recent market surveys pointed out an abysmally slow responses (or even worse, lack of responses) to customer e-mail inquiries. Nothing inspired a customer to switch vendors faster than the perception that a company did not care about its customers enough to answer their questions. It was equivalent of asking a deparment store clerk a question only to have the clerk turn around and walk away.

Apart from the web-incompetence among marketers, they also lacked the essential infrastructure such as the facility of 'call-me or talk-to-an-agent buttons'. The Frequently Asked Questions or (FAQs) lists or the Web self-help software could not answer every question of the customers. Since customers are social creatures, they always needed a human touch and the feeling that only a live call center agent could provide. Obviously, call centers were the only places equipped with the manpower, routing and customer information technologies that played such a large part in customer relationship management or CRM. Only call centers had the customer service skills to handle large volumes of direct customer interaction, whether by phone, text chat or e-mail.

The marketing team predicted that it was just a matter of short time that companies would wake up, realize their problems, and actually enhance their Web sites to encourage potential buyers to inquire about buying their products or services. It would also mean an entirely new opportunity to all centers including the CCE. Unless looking to buy some low-cost, non-sophisticated items such as napkins or socks, consumers needed a lot of information about sophisticated and expensive products such as home entertainment units, digital televisions or cutting-edge computer systems before they actually purchased the products. Among other things, the consumers often requested additional information or literature to be mailed e-mailed and eventually, when a product was purchased, since it was an online transaction, a distributor shipped the product to the consumer. Given that the core competency of many companies was not effective marketing, the assignments pertaining to distribution, CRM, processing e-mail or making the most of inbound calls to feed outbound calls, i.e., cross-selling and up-selling, would be outsourced to call centers. By turning themselves into experts in these critical functions, CCE had a privotal role to play in bridging the gap between clients and their consumers in E-commerce, the team concluded.

Growth option 4: Redefine CCE as a customer contact center

Worldwide call centers were morphing into 'customer contact' centers. They served as the central points for customers' messages from any medium, as well as companies' responses. Increasingly call centers also formed a strategic part of a business. At DaimlerChrysler AG., for instance, information gleaned from 37,000 calls from mechanics each month, fielded by 56 call-center agents, was being constantly transferred electronically to engineering, where designers reviewed it with an eye toward improving vehicles. Like DaimlerChrysler, a number of manufacturers found that information gathered by their call centers helped build better processes and products. The information also helped nurture relationships with customers and business partners. However all this to happen, a call center must reinvent itself and grow into a customer contact center or simply more enriched call centers. As the benefits of enriched call-center systems applied to companies of any size, the marketing team believed in this trend and recommended it as an option. It believed in the recommendation from another reason also – the cost vs. value tradeoffs. In the past, call centers were viewed both by the industry as well as by the clients, as a way to cut costs by using technology, rather than humans, to automatically answer routine inquiries such as questions on the status of an order. More companies now realized the value of the information offered by call centers.

In order to develop an enriched call center, the marketing team made several recommendations. For instance, it observed that CCE must invest in new technology and update traditional processes. The transition required a greater commitment to computer telephony integration, data warehousing, and data integrity and customer information management software. CCE must also empower staff with the knowledge and training needed to utilize these tools. CCE would have to do a number of actions simultaneously. For instance, CCE needed to re-train its staff holistically, to focus on trust, not just transaction; store customer information and finally allow it to create customer satisfaction. Retaining a dedicated, engaged workforce was key to the recommendation since higher agent retention meant lower costs of operating and experienced customer service.

Growth option 5: Develop into a next-generation call/CRM center

The nineties saw a huge recognition of relationship marketing as well as customer relationship management programs. As businesses focused increasingly on their customer relationships, the contact centers of the sellers including the call centers served as the primary (and sometimes only) customer forum for live interaction with buyers and often as a fundamental component of an enterprise-wide CRM strategy. According to the Oxford Group, a high-tech marketing and research firm, approximately 60 percent of contacts from customers came into the enterprise via the contact center. This fact, combined with the emerging role of customer service as a point of market differentiation and catalyst for customer loyalty, heightened the importance of call centers.

But call centers too needed to reorient their functionality in the new customer-centric business environment. They had to move beyond being as a traditional sales vehicle to a valuable tool for strengthening customer relationships through care calls, cross-selling and up-selling initiatives. Historically, call centers did not make outbound customer care calls as they were reluctant to yield revenue-generating capability to a function, labeled as overhead. Soon, call centers recognized customer care calls as a wise investment. More and more, outbound centers found a need for adding inbound and blending capabilities to meet the challenge of their expanded role within the enterprise. As a result, the line between inbound and outbound call centers began to fade. Call centers also demanded a sophisticated technology that would allow them to serve both inbound and outbound functions with equal success. This was the genesis of the Next generation Call/CRM centers.

The marketing team of CCE recommended Next generation Call/CRM centers as a potential area for future growth. In order to take advantage of the option, the team opined that CCE must adopt right technology for a web-based interactive customer contact. The new technology – away from closed, proprietary call center systems, allowed the integration of Web technologies with business applications, PBX platforms and Centrex systems, and standards-based databases. The next-generation call/CRM center would enable the CCE to lower customer contact costs and maximize agent effectiveness in providing better customer service. Next-generation call/CRM centers were expected to help to better manage customer expectations, turning CCE agents into brand-centric ambassadors. It would bring the CCE agents from the heart of CCE business to the heart of CCE brand.

The recommendation to move CCE to a next generation Call/CRM center, though vital and profitable, was not easy, the team argued. Exhibit 12 lists the essentials that CCE would have to follow in order to negotiate the transformation:

Exhibit 12 **Essentials of the Next Generation CRM/Call Centers**

In order to operationalize the concept, CCE should:

- Have the ability to support customers on their turf by effectively managing multiple customer access channels including the telephone, Web self-service, email, chat and IVR, and in the process, help build effective electronic customer relationships through the integration of these channels.

- Establish consistent quality of service guidelines across all media and provide real-time, detailed management reporting to improve productivity and monitor service levels.

- Employ open systems that support standards such as TCP/IP, and have the ability to scale upward to accommodate new applications such as voice over IP and voice recognition.

- Be able to handle application sharing through which customers can be guided online, through Web pages.

- Be sure traditional ACIIs are complemented by intelligent VoIP. email, fax, chat, and call-me-back request routers for more efficient skills-based routing and call routing based on detailed customer data.

- Use a single system to monitor customer calls, e-mail, text chat and queue times and enable agents to respond based on service level agreements and business rules.

- Use the latest technologies in agent scheduling and load-balancing to reduce wait times and keep the flow going.

- Employ interactive voice response (IVR) to route calls to the best agent for the call or allow the customers to get the information for themselves without the need for agent intervention.

- Ensure e-mail requests are answered immediately. Today, e-mail is often given last priority, with much of it not even answered

- Understand that global call centers can quickly route multinational calls or requests to the correct agent, allowing them to speak the same language as the customer.

- Have all systems integrated with their back-end databases for real-time information storage and retrieval.

- Employ expert data mining to help customers quickly find relevant information regarding their requests.

- Use immediate customer profiling (using demographics information gathered from multiple sources such as telephone, Web and fax) to provide effective cross selling and up selling.

- Be sure systems are tightly integrated with warehousing, shipping, accounting, etc., to provide customers with the latest details on their orders.

- Make a choice between training agents for specific media (e-mail agents, phone agents) or for multimedia (one agent handles e-mail, phone, etc.).
- Revamp knowledge bases and implement customer self-service solutions online before deploying online contact solutions such as Web call-through.
- Make use of voice over IP, both inbound (customer using Web call-through to contact the company) and outbound (call centers cutting costs to use Internet telephony for outbound campaigns). Provide agent training and support: Assessing the impact of the technology on staff.
- Be VPN (Virtual Private Network) capable, allowing agents to support customers from anywhere in the world.
- Increasingly become distributed, and make greater use of remote agents (home-based, for example) to decrease infrastructure costs and improve agent retention.
- Exploit the benefits of CRM to raise customer service, raise revenues and lower costs

Source: Tehrani Nadji (2000) 'Next-generation Call/CRM Centers ... a world of opportunity ... only if you do it right!' Call Center Solutions; Norwalk; Feb Vol.18, Issue: 8, Page: 4–8

Growth option 6: Develop multiethnic call centers

On the lines of USA, Europe too was getting multiethnic. The populations of several minority segments were growing faster in several countries of Europe like the Germany, France and the United Kingdom. According to the U.S. Census Bureau, Hispanic and Asian populations were projected to grow between 48 percent and 57 percent from 1996 to 2010, four times the projected growth rate for the general population. Asian sector within the multicultural market represented the most lucrative opportunities for marketers. The average AsianAmerican household had a 14-percent higher median income than the national average. The corporate world become sensitive to the rapid rise of the multiethnic market grew and began revising lists and planning print and direct mail campaigns accordingly.

Call centers had to change as a result. Consider what would happen when a Gujarati language direct mail piece with an 800-number was answered by an English-speaking agent in Leicester UK. How successful would a general outbound business-to-business telemarketing campaign be if Danish-speaking agents connected with a native Korean storeowner? However, most of these efforts to reach multiethnic groups often ended in the call centers. When trying to reach specialized markets, outsourcing made more sense to these marketers. To them dealing with customers and selling over the phone was a unique skill. It was also too much for a marketer to locate and recruit native language speaking agents for each market for calling and servicing customers. Additionally, since the vast majority of new immigrants gravitated toward urban centers, outsourcing to a foreign language call center was the only option to these marketers as they were based in areas with much less diverse populations. This was especially true for smaller but emerging markets such as Polish- and Arabic-speaking communities in Europe. It often presented marketers with a piquant situation.

Sensing a market potential of this trend as well as for better client relationship management, the marketing team proposed that CCE developed multiethnic call centers in Europe wherever possible. These new call centers had lower start-up costs as well as agents turnover and therefore both financially and operationally viable.

Growth option 7: Develop into virtual call centers

With dramatic advances in networking, more and more call centers grew into 'virtual' call centers, in which multiple sites were linked and functioned as a single contact center. A typical virtual call center was one in which several groups of agents often, but not always, in separate locations (individual call centers, remote offices, homes), were treated as a single entity for call handling, reporting, management and scheduling purposes. Another defining characteristic of the virtual call center was that the center's disperse architecture was transparent to the consumer. Virtual outbound call centers, when implemented properly, offered several important advantages, including performance improvement, enhanced reliability should a system or site become disabled, lower telecommunications costs, time zone efficiencies and access to an expanded labor pool. Virtual call centers gained more popularity in recent years. A report from the analyst group, Datamonitor, proclaimed that the virtual call center's time had come. Within the U.S., the report predicted, penetration of virtual call centres in relation to all call centers would grow at a compound annual rate of more than 40 percent through 2003.

CCE team based its recommendation on these facts of virtual call centers but cautioned that the implementation of the concept would entail a variety of new challenges: To begin with, it demanded a more sophisticated call management technology. CCE's own strength was critical in the implementation of the virtual call center environment. CCE must become more flexible, allowing for a variety of configurations, ranging from a single site to multiple sites, a single ACD/PBX to a multivendor environment or a few agents to potentially thousands. System openness was another essential, as various components and technologies needed to be integrated in the virtual call center. Effective monitoring, strong reporting and integration tools and call blending capabilities were among the other technology considerations for the virtual call center environment.

Growth option 8: Enter e-mail business

The marketing team felt that CCE could grow also by entering e-mail business, judging by the statistics on its robust growth in the market. A survey by Harris Poll found that 25% of all Americans used e-mail on a daily basis. By the year 2001, consumers would e-mail 50 million product information or service inquiries per day. In that same timeframe, according to Forrester Research, 20% to 30% of customer contacts would shift from phones, faxes and mail to Web sites. Further, accordingly to Society of Consumer Affairs Professionals in Business (SOCAP), there was a direct relationship between how a company positioned its Web site for consumer contact and the number of e-mail messages it received. In just one year's time, the 57 percent of member companies of the society that actively encouraged consumer contact through e-mail, experienced an average weekly increase in e-mail of 148 percent. Since the task was specialized and become more specialized, more and more marketers would turn to the call centers for their assistance and expertise. CCE would be in a unique place to take advantage from the trend.

Growth option 9: Target smaller towns

Finally, CCE marketing team suggested that CCE should target more aggressively the smaller towns of Europe. In the past, the vast majority of call centers located themselves in the large and metropolitan towns. Of late, smaller cities became more attractive to industries in respect of ample supplies of cheap labor, tax and land subsidies. The influx of companies to smaller towns was expected to grow faster. For call centers too, smaller towns were an economic-development bonanza. Not only did the centers, which employed several hundred people, found easy to recruit from small cities and towns, they also gave back the smaller cities a foot in the door to the new high-tech economy. It was a win-win solution for local economies and call centers, argued the marketing team. In fact, the team insisted that CCE itself was located in a smaller city of Denmark and did fairly well. CCE in smaller towns was the first step to profit from burgeoning businesses, such as distribution centers for e-commerce companies, in these towns.

The D-day

As Svend Hensen delivered his thoughts to the international students, he was highly pleased with his performance in the class. He noted with particular satisfaction that the class stayed awake (he was somewhat embarrassed since he himself had 'dozed off' during lectures several times when a student). The professor too complimented Svend for his presentation and congratulated him for making his enterprise a success. When the professor asked him out to lunch in the cafeteria, Svend was ready. He wished he were equally ready to decide which growth option(s) would suit the CCE most. He felt that the student days were better where a conceptual framework and a good lecture from a professor was all one needed to solve any marketing challenge. How he wished industry were also a class.

Notes

The case has been prepared by Mohan Lal Agrawal, Professor, Marketing, XLRI Jamshedpur (India), Professor Per Vagn Freytag, Institute of Marketing, Southern Denmark University, Sonderberg (Denmark) and Bent Thestrup, Managing Director, Call Center Europe. Inputs for the case were sourced from published literature and personal interviews. The case scenario and issues aim to facilitate a discussion in a classroom situation and do not purport in any way to judge the Call Center Europe strategy as correct or incorrect. Any correspondence in this regard may be addressed to mla@xlri.ac.in.

* Name disguised.

Case 7
Disneyland Resort Paris: Mickey goes to Europe

IMD-4-0280
21.11.2006

> *"* Globalization in the positive sense is like a mosaic of cultures where identities remain visible and where we can play freely with the interaction in between. Where people can project themselves in something that is created elsewhere but is not perceived foreign. We are contributing to something important here. We need to help Disney become global in this positive sense. It is a long journey but we now understand the magnitude of globalization and can use this learning elsewhere. *"*
>
> *Dominique Cocquet, Executive VP, Development & External Relations*

Dominique Cocquet was legendary among Disneyland Resort Paris managers for his vision. He was part of the senior management team determined to turn the vision into reality. 'We create magic,' explained Roland Kleve, director of parks & resort operations support, 'Mickey is a great boss.'

Disneyland Resort Paris opened its gates in April 1992 amidst enormous controversy as a bastion of American cultural imperialism in Europe. By 2006 it was the most visited tourist site in Europe with over 12 million annual visitors. In spite of a difficult tourist industry in the early 2000s, Disneyland Resort Paris's attendance remained stable: 60% of its visitors were repeat visitors, and guest satisfaction was extremely high. The operation had created 43,000 jobs, invested more than €5 billion and contributed to the development of a new region. 'You cannot say this is not a success!' exclaimed Cocquet.

As the leaders developed their execution plans, they wondered what principles should guide them and how to interpret Disney in multicultural Europe. Guests from different parts of Europe wanted different things from a vacation: how could they keep the classic Disney magic yet successfully appeal to European consumers? After 15 years of switching between French and American leadership, the answers were still not obvious. The leaders agreed that the 2007 celebrations of its 15th anniversary should set the scene for Disney's recognition as a well-established experience in the heart of Europe, and a long-term financial success. But what would it look like and what path would take them there?

The Walt Disney Company: a 20th century fairytale

The Walt Disney Company was founded in 1923 by Walter Elias Disney and his brother Roy, as Disney Brothers Studio. In the early years, Disney created classic cartoons such as Mickey Mouse and Donald Duck. In 1937 they bet the company and created the first – and perhaps most successful ever in the company's history – full-length animated color film: *Snow White and the Seven Dwarfs*.

The company was known early on for professional marketing as well as creativity, and continued to make animated movies. It has remained the world leader in animation ever since. Disney added live productions in 1950 with a television program called *Disneyland*. Movies and television would later prove to be long-term pillars for the Walt Disney Company. In 1995 Disney acquired ABC to become the largest entertainment company in the US, the year after the revolutionary animated film *The Lion King* had broken all box office records.

Walt, always the visionary, wanted to create a 'real' world of fantasy that families could immerse themselves in to get away from the trials of the real world and to have fun, *together*. In 1955 he bet the company for the second time and opened the first Disney theme park, Disneyland, in Anaheim, Southern California –inspired by Tivoli Gardens in Copenhagen. Disneyland was an instant success, and other parks followed. Walt Disney World opened near Orlando, Florida in 1971 and quickly became the world's largest resort area with several Disney parks and many other attractions. Tokyo Disneyland, the first Disney Park outside the US, opened in 1983. Euro Disneyland (now Disneyland Resort Paris) the first *multicultural* park, opened in 1992. Hong Kong Disneyland opened in September 2005.

By 2005, the Walt Disney Company was a large diversified organization with yearly revenues of more than US$30 billion, a film library of almost 1,000 theatrical releases and a market capitalization of almost $60 billion. Most revenues came from theme park resorts, films and the media-network business. Although the company was more than 80 years old, the strong voice of the founding father still provided guidance for decision making: *How would Walt have done it?*

The magic of stories

Disney believed in magic. And the essence of Disney magic was storytelling. The excitement of great adventures, the challenge of impossible tasks, the loneliness of being among strangers, the shame of guilt, the terror of evil, the warmth of good, the pride of accomplishment, the love of a family. All of these themes were evoked by Disney stories.

Disney told its purest stories in animated films, many of which won Academy Awards. From the classics like *Snow White*, the *Jungle Book* and *Cinderella* to more recent releases like *The Lion King, Beauty and the Beast, Finding Nemo* and *The Incredibles*,[1] millions of people around the world were drawn to the powerful stories. They related to the characters, quoted the dialogue, told the stories and sang the songs. Would the youngsters of the 21st century continue this admiration for animated characters? Disney believed so and acquired Pixar Animation Studios – their partner in many successful films – in January 2006 to ensure the creation of animated magic for many years ahead.

> " The acquisition of Pixar was a great strategic move. It will provide the storytelling we need to reach today's and tomorrow's generations, and it will also provide the foundation for building more interactive attractions. In combination with a constant revitalization of classic characters on the Disney channels, we can help ensure that experiences and emotions are shared across the different generations within families. "
>
> *Jeff Archambault, Vice President, Communications & Corporate Alliances*

At Disney resorts, the magic became real and tangible. Walt Disney, visionary founder of the company, pictured the resorts as places where families would go to live the stories – to escape from the real world's worries, highways and 'visual pollution' and become immersed in the imaginary world of magic.

> I love to stand on Main Street, just inside the front gates, and watch guests come through the gates into the park. It's amazing to see their faces light up as they come in! The kids, of course, but even the adults. They lose their self-conscious-ness, that veneer we put on to be serious in the adult world, and they remember the kid inside. You can see that happening as they walk in!
>
> Norbert Stiekema
> Vice President, Sales and Distribution

The animated films provided the link between the real world and the fantasy world: What families watched on screen in the cinemas or their homes was brought to life in the parks, as a multidimensional sharing of *emotions*. Film characters met with guests and signed autographs, many attractions immersed guests in the scenes and plots of the films and other attractions took guests into related fantasy worlds. More than 50 million visitors a year went to Disney resorts around the world to experience this magic.

This powerful experience was created by attention to detail and leaving nothing to chance. The attractions were designed by 'Imagineers' – engineers who brought together people and knowledge from hundreds of disciplines to create environments:

> " Guests enter fantasy worlds through portals. Once through a portal, everything in the world – characters, rides, shows, sidewalks, buildings, even the costumes of cleaning staff – plays a part in creating that world's experience for the guests. This is how the magic gets created. Imagineers are the only Cast Members that have a dual reporting relationship in all Disney parks: We report both to the Imagineering head office in Burbank California, and to the local management of the park. We also rotate around parks. I started off here in Paris, creating 'It's a Small World' in Fantasyland for the park opening. Then I worked in California and Tokyo before coming back here to head Imagineering. We have a strong international community of Imagineers to share ideas

and make sure we create this all-encompassing experience everywhere. **"**

Peter McGrath, Director, Creative Development & Show Quality Standards

Disneyland Resort Paris was meticulous about details in service and operations. All resort staff (Cast Members) attended Disney University[2] to learn how to provide the cheerful, friendly and flexible service to create a worry-free fantasy experience for the guests. Disneyland Resort Paris spent more than four times the French minimum legal requirement on training and education and each year they received 70,000 spontaneous job applications as an indication of being an attractive employer in the region. One of the training programs, HAT (hôte d'accueil touristique), was recognized as a professional qualification by the French Ministry of Labor and won an international Worldwide Hospitality Award in 2004.

> One afternoon I was called down to the front gates to speak to a family. When I got there, they seemed happy, so I wondered what the problem was. Then the father explained to me that his young daughter was autistic, and she had never responded to anything or communicated anything to the family. That day, at Disneyland, was the first time they had ever seen her smile. He wanted to thank me for creating something that helped them connect as a family for the first time. That's the magic we make.
>
> Roland Kleve
> Director
> Parks & Resort Operations Support

The more than 12,200 Cast Members came from more than 100 nationalities (73% were French) speaking 19 different languages and were on average 33 years old. Half of the employees had more than 5 years of tenure and 30% had more than 10 years. The total annual staff turnover was 22% which was considered very low for the industry.

Disney's attention to technical innovation, operational excellence and service provided global benchmarks for companies, especially those in the service and creative industries.

" Operations is all about making sure the guest has a seamless experience in the park. That goes from helping our shuttle bus drivers to smile and provide good, reliable, on time service taking guests between the park and their hotels, to making sure Cast Members feel comfortable in their costumes so they can focus on providing service, to ensuring that in every part of the resort we have Cast Members who speak different languages so they can help guests in their own language. It's the details that count. **"**

Roland Kleve, Director, Parks & Resort Operations Support

Euro Disneyland to Disneyland Resort Paris: magical stories in Europe

To 1992: It's a small world

When Tokyo Disneyland opened in 1983, the Disney US theme parks had known nothing but success. The park in Tokyo was deliberately designed to imitate the parks in the US and from the customer perspective little local adaptation was put in place (except covers for rain protection) so the Japanese would have 'the real thing.' Japanese culture was startlingly different from American, and Disney was aware of the risk. They hedged their investment by working with a Japanese owner who paid royalties on the revenue streams. Tokyo Disneyland soon became the most profitable Disneyland in the world. Everything that worked well in the US was positively received in Tokyo despite the obvious cultural distance.

'When you have a success it's natural that you want to replicate it,' Cocquet stated. 'We thought: why not Europe? Europeans watched Disney movies, bought Disney products and went to Walt Disney World in Florida. If it worked in Tokyo, it could work in Europe.' Because of the enormous success of Tokyo, The Walt Disney Company decided to invest significant equity this time rather than only collect royalties. Many analysts believed that the resort should have been located in Spain, which had vacation-friendly weather and was associated with leisure holidays. But The Walt Disney Company decided to build Euro Disneyland near Paris because Paris was the most visited tourist area in Europe, it offered the greatest number of visitors within driving and short-flight distance, and the French government offered incentives through infrastructure building, labor development and other vehicles.

1992–1994: Culture shock and the original sin

Amidst intense criticism from Europe's cultural elite, Euro Disney S.C.A. opened the Disneyland Park and its hotels on the planned date of April 12, 1992 with much publicity and hype. The initial public offering of 51% of the shares had been sold almost overnight. The future looked very bright, despite the continuously escalating construction costs that had climbed to more than three times the original budget, leaving Euro Disneyland with what seemed to be an eternal debt burden of $3 billion.

Unfortunately, the story did not follow the Tokyo script. The French president, François Mitterrand, did not show up for the opening event, stating that it wasn't his 'cup of tea.' Fewer guests walked through the gates than expected, especially from France. Labor relations were strained, and some early service controversies became infamous and affected the resort's reputation long after they had been resolved. For example, consistent with other Disney parks, Euro Disneyland did not serve alcohol when it first opened. This decision was ridiculed and scorned by European consumers. Soon after opening, Euro Disneyland started serving wine and beer, but the public did not forget the initial mistake. Also the long queuing for the attractions was something that needed special attention. The original planning was based on 'American queue length.' As it turned out, the same length of queue in Europe contained twice as many people as an American queue. Guests' expectations regarding line wait times were, therefore, not met.

Another major part of the Euro Disneyland project was the establishment of a number of hotels inside and just outside the Disneyland Park. The original intention was to sell the hotels quickly, then lease them back. However, the real estate value declined dramatically and it was not possible to sell them. Instead, Euro Disneyland was forced to continue payments. The decreased revenues, coupled with an investment burden that was hard to carry, put an end to the optimism and euphoria. Euro Disneyland dove into financially troubled waters in the midst of a European recession.

> It was like we bought a house in a promising neighborhood. After we moved in, prices dropped way below the mortgaged value. But we had to make the best of it, ride out the storm and try to forget about what we paid for it in the first place.
>
> *Roland Kleve, Director of Parks & Resort Operations Support*

Disney Village, located at the resort outside the Disney Parks, opened in 1992 and also struggled to find its balance between on-site resort guests and the Eastern Paris market. Disney Village was a collection of restaurants, night clubs, cinemas and a concert venue, all designed for evening entertainment. Some activities were targeted at families, while others were aimed at young adults. The first years Disney Village was open only for resort guests but it later opened to the broader public. As the Paris subway line went directly to the resort and there was no entry fee to Disney Village, it attracted a large number of local guests.

At the brink of bankruptcy, a financial re-structuring in 1994 gave some breathing space and a new major investor, Prince Alwaleed Bin Talal Abdulaziz Al Saud. Interest charges were cut, principal repayments of loans were deferred and Euro Disneyland was liberated from royalty payments (to The Walt Disney Company) for a period of 5 years.

> In the beginning there were mistakes on both sides. From our side perhaps some bloated self-assurance, power and optimism, creating investments as well as expectations that were too large. On the French side, there was some easy and non-rational anti-Americanism.
>
> *Dominique Cocquet, Executive VP of Development and External Relations*

The financial difficulties of the early years, which Euro Disney managers referred to as 'the original sin,' occupied much of the media coverage from the opening of Euro Disneyland through the end of the millennium. The high level of debt and increased focus on cost-cuttings, constrained decision-making, and the turnover of senior managers was high.

1995–2001: Becoming a landmark

From October 1994 Euro Disney began to change the public name of the resort to Disneyland Paris, partly to distance themselves from the controversial Euro currency, and partly to emphasize the Paris location. Euro Disney S.C.A., the operator of Disneyland Resort Paris, became profitable by 1997 with a positive cash flow from operating activities. Things were beginning to look and feel better in every sense. The number of guests climbed, and Disneyland Paris became the most visited tourist destination in Europe; 85% of guests were highly satisfied, and more than 70% intended to return.

The European landscape gradually became clearer. 'We had to teach Europeans what a short stay resort destination is,' Pieter Boterman, company spokesman, explained. 'There is nothing in Europe like Disneyland Paris, so there was no category in customers' minds for what we were offering.' Even in 2001, European guests did not stay as long at the resort as American guests did in Florida: In Europe most people stayed only one or two nights. European guests also did not spend as much per capita during their visits. The lower revenue per guest meant that Disneyland Paris managers became experts at providing operational excellence for less money; in fact, the resort provided other Disney theme parks an important benchmark on several important operating measures.

> Very little in our core product needs adaptation, but the way we position it and sell it is completely different in each of our key markets. This is a result of not only market conditions, competition and distribution legacy, but also the fact that Mickey or Winnie the Pooh mean different things to different people, depending on the national context. For example, Germans want tangible value for money, and it is difficult to position our product in the German market place. Try and describe emotions and a wholesome emotional family experience in a factual datasheet! Those who do come are very satisfied, but it is hard to explain it ahead of time.
>
> *Norbert Stiekema, VP of Sales and Distribution*

The most difficult challenge was learning to create universal emotional experiences:

> Picture the jungle cruise, which is a boat going down a river in a jungle. In the US the jungle guide tells you to watch out for the mighty hippopotamus, and then suddenly a hippo rises out of the river and spews water towards the group. Children love the anticipation of watching for the hippo, being just a bit afraid. Now picture the guide in Europe warning passengers about the hippo in six languages. By the time he gets to Spanish, the hippo is already out and the Italians and Dutch – whose languages we haven't got to yet – completely miss the emotion we're trying to create! At Disneyland Paris we had to learn to create emotion without verbal scripts. This was a challenge Disney hadn't ever addressed before, so we've had to start from scratch here.
>
> *Peter McGrath, Director of Creative Development and Show Quality Standards*

The cultural learning was replicated internally where American and French leadership styles were often confronted.

> Part of the cultural understanding is in the art of debate here, where people try to understand every angle of an aspect instead of just moving on when 80% is agreed upon
>
> *Wendy Crudele, VP Human Resources*

In April 2002 a second theme park opened next to the Disneyland Paris. Walt Disney Studios Park was built with an investment of more than $500 million. It was based on the theme of cinema and cartoons, and highlighted movie-making techniques and the history of films. Walking through the front gate was like walking into the studios where animated and live movies are made. Attractions ranged from interactive experiences with the technology to multimedia shows on film-making to animation-based theme rides.

> We tried to include as many European film-making elements as we could. For example, the stunt show was designed with European stunt expert Rémi Julienne, and in the historical attractions we included European directors and key players. That didn't seem to be important to the guests, but it was important to the European observers.
>
> *Peter McGrath, Director of Creative Development and Show Quality Standards*

Walt Disney Studios was established to appeal to a broader age range than the Disneyland Paris, including teenagers and young adults. It was also intended to prolong the stay of the average Disney tourist and appeal to a broader spectrum of age categories such as teenagers and young adults.

The least published success was ironically the construction of a 'real' city, Val d'Europe. This constantly growing neighboring real estate development project included a shopping center, business center, downtown with cafés and restaurants and a residential area for over 20,000 'real' people, only 10% to 15% of whom worked at Disneyland Paris. The architecture evoked images of classic Paris itself and Val d'Europe was vital to integrating Disney into France and Europe.

> Val d'Europe is the 'yin' to the Disneyland 'yang.' The imaginary village is not sustainable without the real one, or the other way around. Val d'Europe is a thriving, healthy suburban French community that brings balance to the universal magic of the Disney fantasy. The community belongs to France but has Disney as catalyst. Without the Disney values influence I would not have looked at France, my own country, in the same way. The cultural exchange has made me discover what France is heading for or what has been missing here.
>
> *Dominique Cocquet, Executive Vice President, Development & External Relations*

Val d'Europe was a profitable part of the Euro Disney portfolio, and had also been an important public relations success: It created tens of thousands of jobs and – like Disneyland Paris – contributed significantly to the French tax base. The development was done in careful balanced coordination with the public parties. Since the creation of the destination, more than €5 billion have been invested by private investors and €534 million by the public sector, that is €10 of private funds invested for every €1 of public money.

> It is a very rare and unique opportunity to have a new community built between public and private partners. The backbone of our discussions is always a healthy balance between financial interests, short term

> interests and long term interests. In a way this also works as an illustration of what it means to do business in a foreign environment and how to integrate and adapt to the culture. **"**
>
> *Dominique Cocquet, Executive Vice President, Development & External Relations*

The healthy development of Val d'Europe was perhaps reflected in the fact that it was one of the few Paris suburbs not affected by the French riots in late 2005.

2002–2004: A test of character

Starting in 2002, the leaders of Disneyland Resort Paris faced another series of challenges created by events referred to internally as 'the plagues of Moses.' Although tourism within Europe did not decrease right after the 9/11 tragedy, the consequent war in Iraq did create uncertainty and lower levels of tourism. The German economy shattered, other European economies went into decline and tourists turned to cheaper and more local travel. At the same time, the Euro increased against most other world currencies, and Disneyland Resort Paris became more expensive relative to vacations outside Europe. Tour operators in the US, northern Africa and Asia, were desperate to attract tourists and, therefore, offered vacations at loss-leading prices. As if that were not enough, Euro Disney S.C.A. had to repay €600 million in convertible bonds in late 2001. Financial statements again began to look dim.

Management turnover during this time was very high. Of the nine top management positions, eight were replaced during 2003 and 2004. Four of the eight new executives came from outside Disney. In some cases managers were brought back to Disney after a few years with other companies or at other Disney sites. It was a long-standing practice for managers to rotate between Disney sites across the world and thus act as carriers of cultural and operational practices that should remain consistent across continents.

Local input and innovation was encouraged through both formal and informal methods. For example, in 2003, management led a series of 'summer camps' during his first summer at Disneyland Paris. These were brainstorming sessions with cross-sections of Cast Members and created ideas for increasing revenue, guest satisfaction and delight and cost-cutting. Some initiatives from these sessions were grand, such as the new attraction Space Mountain: Mission 2. Others were apparently smaller but had wide impact, such as the 'Park Hopper' pass, a new class of ticket which let visitors into both Disneyland Paris and Walt Disney Studios on a single day.

Throughout the turbulent financial times, the operational excellence and spirit among employees and guests stayed high. Attendance rates held stable at Disneyland Resort Paris, while decreasing among European competitors. Satisfaction rates increased, and repeat visit rates shot up. Managers developed sophisticated knowledge about their guests in terms of spending habits, means of transportation, geographical distribution, preferred activities and competing destinations. The revenue also remained stable above €1 billion annually, of which a good half came from the Disneyland and Walt Disney Studios and almost 40% from the Disney Hotels and Disney Village. The seven medium-high standard hotels had a total capacity of 5,800 beds and since 2000 achieved occupancy rates of 80% to 89%.

Financial difficulties had plagued the resort since it opened, crippling its ability to invest and creating urgency for short-term cash flow. Disney managers had focused on survival without compromising quality. After yet another difficult couple of years, Euro Disney S.C.A. leaders sought financial restructuring and investment to allow them to enhance the resort. By the end of 2004, the package was in place. It included restructuring of debt totaling $3 billion, and an infusion of $330 million new capital from existing investors. In March 2005, shares were distributed between the Walt Disney Company (40%), Prince Alwaleed (10%) and other shareholders (50%), with the latter category including a large proportion of French banks.

The market place – 2005/2006

In its home country, Disneyland Resort Paris was part of a complex vacation and leisure market. France was the world's favorite tourist destination with over 75 million international arrivals each year. Disneyland Resort Paris was the most visited attraction, with twice as many visitors as the Eiffel Tower. France had fourteen attractions that hosted more than one million visitors annually, divided into 'cultural' and 'non-cultural' categories. The former included well-known Parisian sites such as the Louvre, Notre Dame and the Palace of Versailles, while the latter included Parc Asterix[3] and ParcFuturoscope.[4] Theme parks were the most preferred 'paid-for' attractions. 'Free' cultural attractions, including all places of historic interest, natural interest and exhibitions, had more visitors than theme parks and zoos. Visitors of theme parks and zoos tended to have average incomes, while cultural attractions often catered to the higher end of the income scale.

The European amusement park industry was much smaller than that of either the United States or East Asia. European theme parks enjoyed an increasing number of visitors, although still only a small fraction of the number in the United States. Nine parks had more than 2.5 million yearly visitors; these parks were distributed through Denmark, Holland, Germany, Spain and the United Kingdom. Unlike the so called 'thrill parks,' Disneyland Resort Paris also competed with a variety of vacation resorts such as Club Med or hotel/beach resorts.

The evolution of the 'resort concept' as a new way of vacationing was gradually establishing itself in the European public's mind. People were increasingly looking for an integrated destination where they could enjoy a wide variety of experiences according to their own choices. This trend was partially driven by socio-economic trends, such as a larger middle class with shorter but more intensive vacations. It was also partially the effect of ongoing marketing by Disneyland Resort Paris and other resorts, and people experiencing and becoming personally familiar with the resort vacation.

2005–2007: Disneyland Resort Paris comes of age

Disneyland Resort Paris had set strategic goals to return to profitability. The strategy targeted long-term traffic and increased average spending per guest through two key measures:

- a multi-year investment plan (€240 million over four years from 2005 to 2009)
- an innovative sales and marketing policy.

Four new or renewed attractions were planned for the four-year period. In 2005 the Disneyland Park star attraction, Space Mountain, was completely reprogrammed and reopened as Space Mountain: Mission 2. This was the first redesign of Space Mountain in any Disney resort. In 2006, Buzz Lightyear's Laser Blast opened, based on the Disney/Pixar movie *Toy Story 2*. This was a sophisticated, interactive ride that pitted guests in a laser shooting competition against the evil Emperor Zurg. In 2007 two new attractions would open in Walt Disney Studios Park, Crush's Coaster and Cars: Quatre Roues Rallye. Finally, in 2008 the Tower of Terror would open in Walt Disney Studios Park. This thrill ride included a long free-fall drop in the elevator of a haunted high-rise building, and was one of the most popular attractions in the other parks.

Innovation was one of Disney's core values, and experience demonstrated that new attractions had the capacity to enhance the quality and impact of the guest experience in the Parks. In addition, new attractions would bolster the Park's attractiveness and capacity. Each new attraction was designed to meet the needs of future guests and round out what was already a one-of-a-kind guest experience. Offering something new and innovative brought guests in and would make them come back.

For many years the company researched key European markets extensively to identify different categories of future guests and to determine the most effective ways to reach them. There was no such thing as 'the European consumer.' Thanks to continuous research, the company now had detailed knowledge of each of its key European markets and became one of the key experts in understanding European travelers. The challenge was how to use this information to adapt to the different market segments without losing the core of Disney magic.

The script for the future: journey to 2015

The leaders of Disneyland Resorts Paris, including the new CEO Karl Holz, were enthusiastic about the opportunities provided by the 2004 financial restructuring; however, they were also aware that investors would not wait for a financial return forever. Magic could only continue if it earned money.

Disneyland Resorts Paris had learned a lot over the years about how to compete in the European vacation market. But, just as the market signals were mixed about how the park should be positioned when it opened in 1992, the market still sent mixed messages about which road to take to reach financial success in the future. Some research suggested the resort would be more successful if managers did not worry about how true it was to the Disney formula. If Europeans really wanted a Disney experience, they went to Florida or California. Disneyland Resort Paris should, therefore, create its own brand of family experience completely adapted to the local market.

Other research suggested that Disney could never be anything but the American-style Disney, and that Disneyland Resort Paris would be better off to position itself as providing 'the real thing' in Europe. This would be a copy of the Tokyo model, which had been highly successful.

> *There is a trade-off between Disney values and cultural sensitivity. In business, as well as in private life, it is all about doing things genuinely. Be true to who you are – work on your delivery.*
>
> *Jeff Archambault, Vice President, Communications & Corporate Alliances*

The outcome of the analysis had to create a consistent and compelling experience for the guests. Management was debating, however, which principles would best guide the choice of which offerings should stay global and which offerings should be locally adapted – with what levels of adaptation?

Exhibit 1 The Walt Disney Company Timeline

- 1923: The Disney Bros. studio, founded by Walt and his brother Roy Oliver Disney, produces the *Alice in Cartoonland* series
- 1927: The Alice series ends; Walt picks up the contract to animate Oswald the Lucky Rabbit
- 1928: Walt loses of the Oswald series; first Mickey Mouse cartoon: Steamboat Willie
- 1929: First Silly Symphony: The Skeleton Dance
- 1930: First appearance of Pluto
- 1932: First three-strip Technicolor short released: Flowers and Trees; first appearance of Goofy
- 1934: First appearance of Donald Duck
- 1937: Studio produces its first feature, Snow White and the Seven Dwarfs
- 1940: Studio moves to the Burbank, California buildings where it is located to this day
- 1941: A bitter animators' strike occurs; as the USA enters World War II, the studio begins making morale-boosting propaganda films for the government
- 1944: The company is short on cash; a theatrical re-release of Dumbo generates much needed revenue and begins a reissue pattern for the animated feature films
- 1945: The studio hires its first-ever live actor for a film, James Baskett, to star as Uncle Remus in Song of the South
- 1949: The studio begins production on its first all-live action feature, Treasure Island; the popular True-Life Adventures series begins

- 1954: The studio founds Buena Vista International to distribute its feature films; beginning of the Disneyland TV program
- 1955: Opening of Disneyland in Anaheim, California
- 1961: The studio licenses the film rights to Winnie-the-Pooh, whose characters continue to be highly profitable to this day; international distribution arm Buena Vista International is established
- 1964: The company starts buying land near Orlando, Florida for Walt Disney World - then known as Disneyworld, or 'The Florida Project'
- 1965: The regular production of short subjects ceases, as theatres no longer have any demand for them
- 1966: Walt Disney dies
- 1967: Construction begins on Walt Disney World; the underlying governmental structure (Reedy Creek Improvement District) is signed into law
- 1971: Walt Disney World opens in Orlando, Florida; Roy Oliver Disney dies; Donn Tatum becomes chairman and Card Walker becomes CEO and president
- 1977: Roy Edward Disney, son of Roy and nephew of Walt, resigns from the company citing a decline in overall product quality and issues with management
- 1978: The studio licenses several minor titles to MCA Discovision for laserdisc release; only TV compilations of cartoons ever see the light of day through this deal
- 1979: Don Bluth and a number of his allies leave the animation division; the studio releases its first PG-rated film, The Black Hole
- 1980: Tom Wilhite becomes head of the film division with the intent of modernizing studio product; a home video division is created
- 1981: Plans for a cable network are announced
- 1982: EPCOT Center opens at Walt Disney World; Ron W. Miller succeeds Card Walker as CEO
- 1983: As the anthology series is canceled, The Disney Channel begins operation on US cable systems; Tom Wilhite resigns his post; Tokyo Disneyland opens in Japan
- 1984: Touchstone Pictures is created; after the studio narrowly escapes a buyout attempt by Saul Steinberg, Roy Edward Disney and his business partner, Stanley Gold, remove the Ron W. Miller as CEO and president, replacing him with Michael Eisner and Frank Wells
- 1985: The studio begins making cartoons for television; The home video release of Pinocchio is a best-seller
- 1986: The studio's first R-rated release comes from Touchstone Pictures; the

▶

anthology series is revived; the company's name is changed from Walt Disney Productions to The Walt Disney Company.

- 1989: Disney offers a deal to buy Jim Henson's Muppets and have the famed puppeteer work with Disney resources; the Disney-MGM Studios open at Walt Disney World

- 1990: Jim Henson's death sours the deal to buy his holdings; the anthology series canceled for second time

- 1992: The controversial Euro Disney opens outside Paris, France

- 1993: Disney acquires independent film distributor Miramax Films; Winnie the Pooh merchandise outsells Mickey Mouse merchandise for the first time; the policy of periodic theatrical re-issues ends with this year's re-issue of Snow White and the Seven Dwarfs but is augmented for video

- 1994: Frank Wells is killed in a helicopter crash; Jeffrey Katzenberg resigns to co-found his own studio, DreamWorks SKG

- 1995: In October, the company hires Hollywood superagent, Michael Ovitz, to be president

- 1996: The company takes on the Disney Enterprises name for non-Walt Disney branded ventures and acquires the Capital Cities/ABC group, renaming it ABC, Inc.; in December, Michael Ovitz, president of the company, leaves "by mutual consent"

- 1997: The anthology series is revived again; the home video division releases its first DVDs

- 1998: Disney's Animal Kingdom opens at Walt Disney World

- 2000: Robert Iger becomes president and COO

- 2001: Disney-owned TV channels are pulled from Time Warner Cable briefly during a dispute over carriage fees; Disney's California Adventure opens to the public; Disney begins releasing Walt Disney Treasures DVD box sets for the collector's market

- 2003: Roy Edward Disney again resigns as head of animation and from the board of directors, citing similar reasons to those that drove him off 26 years earlier; fellow director Stanley Gold resigns with him; they establish "Save Disney" (*http://www.savedisney.com*) to apply public pressure to oust Michael Eisner

- 2003: Pirates of the Caribbean: The Curse of the Black Pearl becomes the first film released under the Disney label with a PG-13 rating

- 2004:
  - The studio breaks off renegotiation talks with Pixar (their current contract expires in 2006); Disney announces it will convert its animation studio to all computer-animated production

- Announced the closure of their Florida feature-film animation department (*http://www.savedisney.com/news/se/wdfa_closure.asp*);
- Comcast makes a $66 billion unsolicited bid to buy The Walt Disney Company (Comcast withdraws its bid in April);
- Disney purchases rights to The Muppets;
- Company stockholders give Michael Eisner a 43% vote of no confidence; as a result, Eisner is removed from the role as chairman of the board (but maintains his position as CEO) and George J. Mitchell becomes chairman in his place.
- After investing $6 million into production of the documentary film *Fahrenheit 9/11* by Michael Moore, Walt Disney Pictures announced their previously mentioned intentions of not distributing the film. The director and the heads of Miramax arrange an alternate distribution arrangement and the film becomes the most successful documentary film of all time. At $100 million+, that film earns more than most of Disney's other film releases that year.

- 2005:
  - Disneyland celebrates its 50th birthday on 17 July.
  - Robert A. Iger, currently president of the company, will replace Michael Eisner as CEO on October 1.
  - Disney starts talks with Steve Jobs (Chairman of Pixar) about acquisition of Pixar Animation Studios. The $7.4 billion deal was announced in late January 2006. This made Steve Jobs the single largest Disney shareholder and Jobs also joined Disney's board of directors.

Source: Company information

Exhibit 2 Key Figures 2003–2005

KEY FIGURES

BREAKDOWN OF
ATTENDANCE BY
COUNTRY OF
ORIGIN IN 2005

FRANCE 39%
UNITED KINGDOM 20%
SPAIN 9%
NETHERLANDS 8%
BELGIUM / LUX. 7%
GERMANY 5%
ITALY 3%
OTHERS 9%

BREAKDOWN
OF REVENUES
BY ACTIVITY
IN 2005

THEME PARKS 51.1%
HOTELS AND
DISNEY VILLAGE 36.7%
OTHERS 9.6%
REAL ESTATE 2.6%

BREAKDOWN OF
VISITORS BY
TRANSPORTATION
IN 2005

CAR 53%
PLANE 17%
TRAIN 14%
COACH 6%
SUBURBAN TRAIN 10%

THEME PARKS ATTENDANCE
(IN MILLIONS OF VISITS)

	2005	2004	2003
	12.3	12.4	12.4

HOTEL OCCUPANCY
(IN %)

	2005	2004	2003
	80.7%	80.5%	85.1%

THEME PARKS AVERAGE SPENDING
PER GUEST (IN EUROS EXCLUDING VAT)

	2005	2004	2003
	44.3	42.7	40.7

AVERAGE SPENDING PER ROOM
(IN EUROS EXCLUDING VAT)

	2005	2004	2003
	179.1	186.6	185.5

IN MILLION EUROS

	2005	2004	2003 PRO-FORMA*
REVENUES	1 076.0	1 048.0	1 046.8
EBITDA**	117.1	122.9	181.6
INCOME / (LOSS) BEFORE FINANCIAL CHARGES	(26.9)	(23.9)	32.1
NET FINANCIAL CHARGES	(87.9)	(105.7)	(111.2)
LOSS BEFORE EXCEPTIONNAL ITEMS AND MINORITY INTERESTS	(114.8)	(129.6)	(79.1)
NET LOSS	(94.9)	(145.2)	(58.3)
CASH FLOW FROM OPERATING ACTIVITIES	18.4	124.6	124.7
BORROWINGS	1 943.4	2 052.8	2 448.4
SHAREHOLDERS' EQUITY AND QUASI-EQUITY	295.7	(59.9)	85.6
MINORITY INTERESTS	106.3	339.6	(41.3)

*reflects pro forma impact of consolidation of financing companies
**earnings before minority interest, income taxes, exceptional items, interest, depreciation and amortization

22 - 23

♥ PEOPLE & FIGURES

Stock Information

IDENTIFICATION SHEET OF EURO DISNEY S.C.A. SHARE ♥

NOMINAL VALUE	0,01 euro per share
NUMBER OF SHARES	3,897,649,046 shares as of 30/09/05
MARKET PLACES	Paris
	London (until 31 October 2005)
	Brussels (until 30 September 2005)
MAIN CODES	Reuters EDL.PA
	Bloomberg EDL.FP
	ISIN FR0000125874

MARKET CAPITALISATION ♥

Fiscal Year	2005	2004	2003
NUMBER OF SHARES AS OF 30 SEPTEMBER (IN MILLIONS)	3,897	1,083	1,056
MARKET CAPITALISATION AS OF 30 SEPTEMBER (IN MILLION EUROS)	507	347	634
SHARE PRICE*			
HIGH (IN EUROS)	0.19**	0.64	0.71
LOW (IN EUROS)	0.10**	0.22	0.35

*based on share price at closing
**share price adjusted for dilution impact of Equity Rights Offering in February 05

SHAREHOLDING STRUCTURE

♥ THE WALT DISNEY COMPANY*
39.8%

♥ PRINCE ALWALEED**
10.0%

♥ OTHER SHAREHOLDERS
50.2%

*Via its wholly-owned subsidiary, EDL Holding Company

**Via KINGDOM 5-KR-135 Ldt a company whose shares are held by trusts for the benefit of Prince Alwaleed and his family

EVOLUTION OF THE SHARE PRICE (BASE 100 ON OCTOBER 2004) ♥

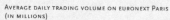

SBF 120 — EURO DISNEY S.C.A.

10-04 11-04 12-04 01-05 02-05 03-05 04-05 05-05 06-05 07-05 08-05 09-05

AVERAGE DAILY TRADING VOLUME ON EURONEXT PARIS (IN MILLIONS)

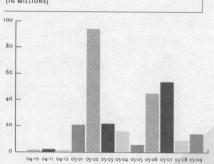

04-10 04-11 04-12 05-01 05-02 05-03 05-04 05-05 05-06 05-07 05-08 05-09

Exhibit 4 **Worldwide Park Attendance 2004[1]**

1	Magic Kingdom at Walt Disney World, Florida	15.1
2	Disneyland in Anaheim, California	13.4
3	Tokyo Disneyland, Japan	13.2
4	Disneyland Resort Paris, France [2]	12.4
5	Tokyo Disney Sea, Japan	12.2
6	Universal Studios Osaka, Japan	9.9
7	EPCOT at Walt Disney World, Florida	9.4
8	Disney-MGM Studios, Florida	8.3
9	Lotte World in Seoul (indoor), South Korea	8.0
10	Disney's Animal Kingdom, Florida	7.8

1) The world market for the 50 most visited amusement parks rose to a record level of 252.4 million visitors, an increase of 2.2% from 2003.
2) Includes visitors to both theme parks, Disneyland Paris and the Walt Disney Studios.

Europe accounted for 11 out of the top 50 parks with a total of 41 million visitors in 2004, an increase of 2.8% from 2003. Tivoli gardens (Denmark), Europa Park (Germany) and Gardaland (Italy) are the most visited after Disneyland Resort Paris. Tivoli increased its attendance nearly 30% to 4.2 million visitors, thanks in part to a new attraction "the Demon." Europa Park increased its number of attendants to 3.7 million (of which 20% were of French nationality).

Source: Amusement Business Online and le Quotidien Tourisme

***Exhibit 5* Disneyland Resort Paris: "Magic on Your Doorstep"**

Source: Company information

Exhibit 6 **Early Morning in Val d'Europe**

Source: Company information

Notes

Research Associate Karsten Jonsen prepared this case under the supervision of Professor Martha Maznevski as a basis for class discussion rather than to illustrate either effective or ineffective handling of a business situation.

Copyright © 2006 by **IMD** *– International Institute for Management Development, Lausanne, Switzerland. Not to be used or reproduced without written permission directly from* **IMD**.

[1] *Finding Nemo* and *The Incredibles* are produced by Pixar Animation Studios and distributed by The Walt Disney Company.

[2] The Disney University is located at Disneyland Resort Paris. The university offers training on-location in over 400 different training programs: from table service to animal care to water quality control to leadership development. In 2006 Disney University was awarded a quality label from the French AFNOR organization, which is highly respected in the continuing education sector.

[3] Thrills and shows in a theme park (opened in 1989) 35 km from Paris, based on the Gallic

characters of Asterix, Obelix and friends in Brittany who would never surrender to Cesar. Standard admission fee 2005 was €31.

[4] Interactive attractions and shows, primarily based on science and technology. This leisure space is situated in Poitiers, between Paris and Bordeaux (1h20 by TGV train from Paris). Standard admission fee in 2005 was €33.

Case 8
Giordano

> We are committed to provide our customers with value-for-money merchandise, professional customer service, and a comfortable shopping experience at convenient locations.
>
> *Giordano's Corporate Mission*

Giordano is a retailer of casual clothes in East Asia, South-East Asia, and the Middle East. In 1999, it operated outlets in China, Dubai, Hong Kong, Macao, Philippines, Saudi Arabia, Singapore, South Korea and Taiwan. Giordano's sales grew from HK$712 million in 1989 to HK$3,092 million in 1999 (see Exhibit 1). This case study describes the success factors that allowed Giordano to grow rapidly in some Asian countries. It looks at three imminent issues that Giordano faced in maintaining its success in existing markets and in its plan to enter new markets in Asia and beyond. The first concerns Giordano's positioning. In what ways, if at all, should Giordano change its current positioning? The second concerns the critical factors that have contributed to Giordano's success. Would these factors remain critical over the coming years? Finally, as Giordano seeks to enter new markets, the third issue, whether its competitive strengths can be transferred to other markets, needs to be examined.

Exhibit 1 Financial Highlights (in Millions of HK$)

(Consolidated)	2000*	1999	1998	1997	1996	1995	1994
Turnover	1 661.4	3 092.2	2 609.2	3 014.4	3 522.0	3 482.0	2 863.7
Turnover increase (percentage)	16.2%	18.5%	(13.4%)	(14.4%)	1.2%	21.6%	22.7%
Profit after tax and minority interests	173.3	360.0	76.1	68.0	261.2	250.2	195.3
Profit after tax and minority interests increase (percentage)	31.1%	375.0%	11.9%	(74.0%)	4.4%	28.1%	41.9%
Shareholders' fund	NA	1,250.8	1,111.1	1,068.9	1,138.3	911.7	544.5
Working capital	701.1	762.3	700.6	654.2	670.3	496.0	362.0
Total debt to equity ratio	NA	0.5	0.3	0.3	0.4	0.7	0.9
Bank borrowings to equity ratio	NA	0	0	0	0	0	0.1
Inventory turnover on sales (days)	28	28	44	48	58	55	53
Return on total assets (percentage)	NA	18.8%	5.3%	4.8%	16.5%	16.4%	18.8%
Return on average equity (percentage)	NA	30.5%	7.0%	6.2%	25.5%	34.4%	39.1%
Return on sales	NA	11.6	2.9	2.3	7.4	7.2	6.8
Earning per share (cents)	24.5	51.3	10.8	9.6	36.9	38.8	30.9
Cash dividend per share (cents)	8.5	34.5	4.5	5.0	16.0	13.5	11.0

Note: "NA" indicates data were not available at time of print; *2000 figures are for the first six months of Giordano's 2000 financial year, ended 30 June 2000. Percentages for 2000 were calculated over the figures for same period in the previous year. (Consolidated)

Company background

Giordano was founded by Jimmy Lai in 1980. To give his venture a more sophisticated image, Lai picked an Italian name for his retail chain. In 1981, Giordano started in Hong Kong selling casual clothes manufactured predominantly for the United States market by a Hong Kong–based manufacturer, the Comitex Group. Initially, it focused on wholesale trade of high-margin merchandise under the Giordano brand in Hong Kong. In 1983, it scaled back on its wholesale operation and started to set up its own retail shops in Hong Kong. It also began to expand its market by distributing Giordano merchandise in Taiwan through a joint venture. In 1985, it opened its first retail outlet in Singapore.

However, in 1987, sales were low and the business became unprofitable. Lai realized that the pricy retail chain concept was unprofitable. Under a new management team, Giordano changed its strategy. Until 1987, it sold exclusively men's casual apparel. When it realized that an increasing number of women customers were attracted to its stores, Giordano changed its positioning and started selling unisex casual apparel. It repositioned itself as a retailer of discounted casual unisex apparel with the goal of maximizing unit sales instead of margins, and sold value-for-money merchandise. Its shift in strategy was successful. Its sales almost quadrupled, from HK$712 million in 1989 to HK$3,092 million in 1999 (see Exhibit 1). A typical Giordano store is shown in Exhibit 2.

Exhibit 2 Typical Giordano Storefront

Source: Courtesy of Giordano

Management values and style

Being entrepreneurial and accepting mistakes as learning opportunities

The willingness to try new ways of doing things and learning from past errors was an integral part of Lai's management philosophy. The occasional failure represented a current limitation and indirectly pointed management to the right decision in the future. To demonstrate his commitment to this philosophy, Lai took the lead by being a role model for his employees, 'Like in a meeting, I say, look, I have made this mistake. I'm sorry for that. I hope everybody learns from this. If I can make mistakes, who the hell do you think you are that you can't make mistakes?' He also believed strongly in empowerment – if everyone is allowed to contribute and participate, mistakes can be minimized.

Treating employees as an asset

Besides the willingness to accept employees' mistakes, another factor that contributed to the success of Giordano was that it had a dedicated, trained, ever-smiling sales force. It considered front-line workers to be its customer service heroes. Charles Fung, Giordano's Chief Operations Officer and Executive Director (South-East Asia), said, 'Even the most sophisticated training programme won't guarantee the best customer service. People are the key. They make exceptional service possible. Training is merely a skeleton of a customer service programme. It's the people who deliver that give it form and meaning.'

Giordano had stringent selection procedures to make sure that only those candidates who matched the profile of what it looked for in its employees were selected. Selection continued into its training workshops. Fung called the workshops 'attitude training'. The service orientation and character of a new employee were tested in these workshops. These situations, he added, were an appropriate screening tool for 'weeding out those made of grit and mettle'.

Giordano's philosophy of quality service could be observed in its overseas outlets as well. Its Singapore operations, for example, achieved ISO9002 certification. Its obsession with providing excellent customer service was best described by Fung. 'The only way to keep abreast with stiff competition in the retail market is to know the customers' needs and serve them well. Customers pay our paychecks; they are our bosses ... Giordano considers service to be a very important element [in trying to draw customers] ... service is in the blood of every member of our staff.'

According to Fung, everyone who joined Giordano, even office employees, worked in a store for at least one week as part of his or her training. 'They must understand and appreciate every detail of the operations. How can they offer proper customer assistance – internal and external – if they don't know what goes on in operations?'

In Singapore, for instance, Giordano invested heavily in training its employees. In 1998, it spent 3.9 per cent of its overall payroll on training, with each employee receiving an average of 224 hours of training per year. It had a training room complete with one-way mirrors, video cameras and other electronic paraphernalia. A training consultant and seven full-time trainers conducted training sessions for every new sales staff member, and existing staff were required to take refresher courses. Its commitment to training and developing its staff was recognized when it was awarded the People Developer Award in 1998.

However, providing training programmes was not as important as ensuring the transfer of learning from the workshops and seminars to the store. As Fung explained, 'Training is important. Every organization is providing its employees training. However, what is more important is the transfer of learning to the store. When there is a transfer of learning, each dollar invested in training yields a high return. We try to encourage this [transfer of learning] by cultivating a culture and by providing positive reinforcement, rewarding those who practise what they learned.'

For Giordano, investment in service meant investment in people. It paid high wages to attract and keep its staff. Giordano offered what Fung claimed was 'one of the most attractive packages in an industry where employee turnover is high. We generally pay more than what the market pays'. With higher wages, there was a lower staff turnover rate. The higher wages and Giordano's emphasis on training resulted in a corps of eager-to-please sales force.

Managing its vital human resources (HR) became a challenge to Giordano when it decided to expand into global markets. To replicate its high service–quality positioning, Giordano needed to consider the HR issues involved in setting up retail outlets on unfamiliar ground. For example, the recruitment, selection and training of local employees could require modifications to its formula for success in its current markets owing to differences in the culture, education and technology of the new countries. Labour regulations could also affect HR policies such as compensation and providing welfare. Finally, expatriate policies for staff seconded to help run Giordano outside their home country and management practices needed to be considered.

Focusing Giordano's organizational structure on simplicity and speed

Giordano maintained a flat organizational structure. Fung believed that 'this gives us the intensity to react to market changes on a day-to-day basis'. It followed a relaxed management style, where management worked closely with line staff. There were no separate offices for higher and top management; rather their desks were located next to their staff's, separated only by shoulder-high panels. This closeness allowed easy communication, efficient project management and speedy decision-making, which are all critical ingredients to success amid fast-changing consumer tastes and fashion trends. Speed allowed Giordano to keep its product development cycle short. Similar demands in quickness were also expected of its suppliers.

Key competitive strengths

Giordano's home base, Hong Kong, was flooded with retailers, both big and small. To beat the dog-eat-dog competition prevalent in Asia, especially Hong Kong, Lai felt that Giordano must have a distinctive competitive advantage. Although many retail outlets in Hong Kong competed almost exclusively on price, Lai felt differently about Giordano. Noting successful Western retailers, Lai astutely observed that there were other key factors for success. He started to benchmark Giordano against best practice organizations in four key areas: (1) computerization (from The Limited), (2) a tightly controlled menu (from McDonald's), (3) frugality (from Wal-Mart), and (4) value pricing (from Marks & Spencer) (Ang, 1996).

The emphasis on service and the value-for-money concept had proven to be successful. Lai was convinced that the product was only half of what Giordano sells. Service was the other half, and Lai believed that service was the best way to make customers return to Giordano again and again. Lai said, 'We are not just a shirt retailer, we are not just an apparel retailer. We are also a service retailer because we sell feeling. Let's make the guy feel good about coming into here [our stores]' (Ang, 1996).

Service

Giordano's commitment to excellent service was reflected in the list of service-related awards it had received. It was ranked number one by the *Far Eastern Economic Review*, for being innovative in responding to customers' needs, for three consecutive years – 1994, 1995 and 1996. And when it came to winning service awards, Giordano's name kept cropping up. In Singapore, it won numerous service awards over the years. It was given the Excellent Service Award for three consecutive years: 1996, 1997 and 1998. It also received three tourism awards: 'Store of the Year' in 1991, 'Retailer of the Month' in 1993, and 'Best Shopping Experience – Retailer Outlet' in 1996. These were just some of the awards won by Giordano (see Exhibit 3).

How did Giordano achieve such recognition for its commitment to customer service? It began with the Customer Service Campaign in 1989. In that campaign, yellow badges

Exhibit 3 **Recent Giordano Company Awards**

Award	Awarding Organization	Category	Year(s)
Excellent Service Award*	Singapore Productivity and Standards Board	—	1996, 1997, 1998
American Service Excellence Award	American Express	Fashion/Apparel	1995
ISO9002**	SISIR	—	1994
People Developer Award	Singapore Productivity and Standards Board	—	1998
Ear Award	Radio Corporation of Singapore	Listeners' Choice (English Commercial)	1996
Ear Award	Radio Corporation of Singapore	Creative Merits (English Jingles)	1996
1999 HKRMA Customer Service Award	Hong Kong Retail Management Association	—	1999
The Fourth Hong Kong Awards for Services	Hong Kong Trade Development Council	Export Marketing & Customer Service	2000

Note: Awards given to the Giordano Originals Singapore.

*To be nominated for the Excellent Service Award, a company must have had, among other things, significant training and other programmes that ensured quality service. These include systems for recognizing employees and for customer feedback.

**ISO9002 refers to the guidelines from the Geneva-based International Organization for Standardization for companies that produce and install products.

bearing the words 'Giordano Means Service' were worn by every Giordano employee. This philosophy had three tenets: we welcome unlimited try-ons; we exchange – no questions asked; and we serve with a smile. The yellow badges reminded employees that they were there to deliver excellent customer service.

Since its inception, several creative, customer-focused campaigns and promotions had been launched to extend its service orientation. For instance, in Singapore, Giordano asked its customers what they thought would be the fairest price to charge for a pair of jeans and charged each customer the price that they were willing to pay. This one-month campaign was immensely successful, with some 3000 pairs of jeans sold every day during the promotion. In another service-related campaign, customers were given a free T-shirt for criticizing Giordano's service. Over 10 000 T-shirts were given away. Far from only being another brand-building campaign, Giordano responded seriously to the feedback collected. For example, the Giordano logo was removed from some of its merchandise, as some customers liked the quality but not the 'value-for-money' image of the Giordano brand.

Against advice that it would be abused, Lai also introduced a no-questions-asked and no-time-limit exchange policy, which made it one of the few retailers in Asia outside Japan with such a generous exchange policy. Giordano claimed that returns were less than 0.1 per cent of sales.

To ensure that every store and individual employee provided excellent customer service, performance evaluations were conducted frequently at the store level, as well as for individual employees. The service standard of each store was evaluated twice every month, while individual employees were evaluated once every two months. Internal competitions were designed to motivate employees and store teams to do their best in serving customers. Every month, Giordano awarded the 'Service Star' to individual employees, based on nominations provided by shoppers. In addition, every Giordano store was evaluated every month by mystery shoppers. Based on the combined results of these evaluations, the 'Best Service Shop' award was given to the top store.

Value for money

Lai explained the rationale for Giordano's 'value-for-money' policy: 'Consumers are learning a lot better about what value is. Out of ignorance, people chose the brand. But the label does not matter, so the business has become value driven, because when people recognize value, that is the only game in town. So we always ask ourselves how can we sell it cheaper, make it more convenient for the consumer to buy, and deliver faster today than yesterday. That is all value, because convenience is value for the consumer. Time is value for the customer.'

Giordano was able to consistently sell value-for-money merchandise through careful selection of suppliers, strict cost control and resisting the temptation to increase retail prices unnecessarily. For instance, to provide greater shopping convenience to customers, Giordano in Singapore located its operations in densely populated housing estates in addition to its outlets in the traditional downtown retail areas.

Inventory control

In markets with expensive retail space, retailers would try to maximize every square foot of the store for sales opportunities. Giordano was no different. Its strategy involved not having a back storeroom in each store. Instead, a central distribution centre replaced the function of a back storeroom. With information technology, Giordano was able to skilfully manage its inventory and forecast demand. When an item was sold, the barcode information, identifying size, colour, style and price was recorded by the point-of-sale cash register and transmitted to the company's main computer. At the end of each day, the information was compiled at the store level and sent to the sales department and the distribution centre. The compiled sales information became the store's order for the following day. Orders were filled during the night and were ready for delivery by early morning, ensuring that before a Giordano store opened for business, new inventory was already on the shelves.

Another advantage of its IT system was that information was disseminated to production facilities in real time. Such information allowed customers' purchase patterns to be understood, and this provided valuable input to its manufacturing operations, resulting in fewer problems and costs related to slow-moving inventory. 'If there is a slow-selling item, we will decide immediately how to sell it as quickly as possible. When the sales of an item hit a minimum momentum, we pull it out, instead of thinking of how to revitalize its [slow-selling] sales.' Giordano stores were therefore well stocked with fast-moving items, and customers were happy as they were seldom out of stock of anything.

The use of technology also afforded more efficient inventory holding. Giordano's inventory turnover on sales was reduced from 58 days in 1996 to 28 days in 1999, allowing it to thrive on lower gross margins. Savings were passed to customers, thus reinforcing its value-for-money philosophy. All in all, despite the lower margins, Giordano was still able to post healthy profits. Such efficiency became a crucial factor when periodic price wars were encountered. Giordano was able to carve out ever-greater slices of the market, because it was easy money competing against companies that were used to relying on high gross margins to make up for slow inventory turnover.

Besides the use of IT and real-time information generated from the information system, Giordano's successful inventory control was achieved through close integration of the purchasing and selling functions. As Fung elaborated, 'There are two very common scenarios that many retailers encounter: slow-selling items stuck in the warehouse and fast-selling popular items that are out of stock. Giordano tries to minimize the probability of the occurrence of these two scenarios, which requires close integration between the purchasing and selling departments.'

But more than technology and inventory control, Giordano had another competitive edge over its competitors. As Fung explained, 'In the 1980s and early 1990s, when few retailers would use IT to manage their inventory, the use of IT gave Giordano a leading edge. However, today, when many retailers are using such technology, it is no longer our real distinctive competitive strength. In a time when there is information overload, it is the organizational culture in Giordano to intelligently use the information that sets us apart from the rest.' And this was further explained by Lai: 'None of this is novel. Marks & Spencer in Britain, The Gap and Wal-Mart in America, and Seven-Eleven in Japan have used similar systems for years. Nowadays, information flows so fast that anybody can acquire or imitate ideas. What matters is how well the ideas are executed.' Indeed, with rapid development in Internet and intranet technologies, packaged solutions (e.g. MS Office, point of sale [POS] and enterprise resource planning [ERP] software) and supporting telecommunications services (e.g. broadband Internet access), acquiring integrated IT and logistics technology has become easier and more cost-effective than ever before. Hence, a competitive advantage based on technology and its implementation is likely to become smaller and more difficult to maintain in the medium- to long-term future.

Product positioning

When a business becomes successful, there would always be a temptation to expand into more products and services to meet customer needs. However, Giordano recognized the importance of limiting its expansion and focusing on one specific area. Fung said, 'Focus makes the business more manageable: positioning in the market, keeping the store simple, better inventory management. And we can get the best out of limited resources.' Simplicity and focus were reflected in the way Giordano merchandised its goods. 'You'll see no more than 100 items in a Giordano store. We have 17 core items; other retailers have 200 to 300 items. Merchandising a wide range of products causes retailers to take a longer time to react to market changes.'

Giordano's willingness to experiment with new ideas and its perseverance despite past failures could also be seen in its introduction of new product lines. Its venture into mid-priced women's fashion, Giordano Ladies', clearly illustrated this. With its line of smart blouses, dress trousers, and short skirts, the company was hoping to attract young, stylish women and benefit from the fatter profit margins enjoyed in more up-scale niches of women's clothing – about 50 to 60 per cent compared with 40 per cent for casual wear. Giordano, however, wandered into a market crowded with seasoned players. While there were no complaints about the look or quality of the line, it had to compete with more than a dozen established brands already on the racks, including Theme and Esprit. It also failed initially to differentiate its new clothing line from its mainstream product line, and even tried to sell both through the same outlets. Nevertheless, it persisted in its efforts and Giordano Ladies' made a successful comeback. In 1999, it took advantage of the financial troubles facing rivals such as Theme, as well as the post-Asian currency crisis boom in many parts of Asia, to aggressively relaunch its Giordano Ladies' line, which met with great success. By 30 June 2000, the reinforced Giordano Ladies' focused on a select segment, with 14 stores worldwide offering personalized service (e.g. staff are trained to memorize names of regular customers and recall past purchases). It also had plans to expand its five more Giordano Ladies' outlets in Hong Kong, Taiwan and the Middle East.

Giordano recently began to reposition its brand by emphasizing sensible but more stylish clothes and broadening its appeal by overhauling the stores and apparel. For instance, a large portion of its capital expenditure (totalling HK$56.9 million in the first six months of year 2000) went to renovating of its stores to enhance shop ambience. This indicated its intention to reinforce its image and to position it in line with its globalization strategy and changing consumer needs. A typical store layout is shown in Exhibits 4 and 5. Giordano's relatively mid-priced positioning worked well –

Exhibit 4 A Typical Store Layout

Source: Courtesy of Giordano.

Exhibit 5 **A Typical Store Layout**

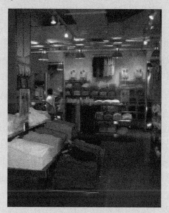

Source: Courtesy of Giordano.

inexpensive, yet contemporary looking outfits appealed to Asia's frugal customers, especially during the Asian economic crisis. However, over time, this positioning became inconsistent with the brand image that Giordano tried hard to build over the years. Says one of Giordano's top executives, 'The feeling went from "this is nice and good value" to "this is cheap". When you try to live off selling 100-Hong Kong-dollar shirts, it catches up with you' (*AsiaWeek*, 15 October 1999).

Nevertheless, while it gradually remarketed its core brand as a trendier label, Giordano continued to cater to the needs of customers who favoured its value-for-money positioning. In 1999 it launched a new product line, Bluestar Exchange, to cater to the needs of its budget-conscious customers, after successful prototyping in Hong Kong and Taiwan. The good market responses to this new line, which targeted mainly families (similar to Gap's Blue Navy), triggered plans to expand from the 14 Bluestar stores in Hong Kong and three in Taiwan, to 20 in Hong Kong, 15 in Taiwan, two in Singapore, and up to 100 in mainland China (including franchised stores).

Aggressive advertising and promotion

Fung said, 'Giordano spends a large proportion of its turnover on advertising and promotions. No retailer of our size spends as much as us.' For the past five years, Giordano in Singapore had been spending about S$1.5 million to S$2 million annually on its advertising and promotional activities. It won the Top Advertiser Award from 1991 to 1994 (see Exhibit 3). Up to 30 June 2000 total advertising and promotional expenditure for the group amounted to HK$41.5 million, or 3 per cent of the group's retail turnover. In addition to its big budget, Giordano's advertising and promotional campaigns were creative and appealing. One such campaign was the 'Round the Clock Madness Shopping' with the Singapore radio station FM93.3 on 1 May 1994. Different clothing items were discounted from 10 to 60 per cent at various times beginning at midnight. For example, jeans were offered at a 20 per cent discount from 12 a.m. to 1 a.m., whereas polo shirts and T-shirts were given a 30 per cent discount from 1 a.m. to 2 a.m. and then shorts at a 40 per cent discount from 2 a.m. to 3 a.m. To keep listeners awake and excited, the product categories that were on sale at each time slot were released only at the specified hour, so that nobody knew the next items that would be on this special sale. Listeners to the radio station were cajoled into coming to Giordano stores throughout the night (Ang, 1996). In 1996, Giordano won the Singapore Ear Award. Its English radio commercial was voted by listeners to be one of the best, with the most creative English jingle.

Another success was its 'Simply Khakis' promotion, launched in April 1999, which emphasized basic, street-culture style that 'mixed and matched' and thus fitted all occasions. In Singapore, within days of its launch, the new line sold out and had to be relaunched two weeks later. By October 1999 over a million pairs of khaki trousers and shorts had been sold. This success could be attributed partly to its clearly defined communications objectives. As Garrett Bennett, Giordano's Executive Director in charge of merchandising and operations, said, 'We want to be the key provider of the basics: khakis, jeans, and the white shirt.' Elsewhere in the region, sales were booming for Giordano, despite only moderate recovery experienced in the retail industry. Its strength in executing innovative and effective promotional strategies helped the retailer to reduce the impact of the Asian crisis on its sales and take advantage of the slight recovery seen in early 1999. Aggressive advertising and promotions also played a significant role in the successful remarketing of its core brand and relaunch or introduction of sister brands, Giordano Ladies', Giordano Junior and Bluestar Exchange.

The Asian apparel retail industry

Hit severely by the Asian crisis from 1997 to 1999, the Asian retail industry went through dramatic restructuring and consolidation. Many retailers reduced the number of shops in their chains, or closed down completely. Almost everyone in the industry implemented cost-cutting measures while at the same time cajoling reluctant customers with promotional strategies. Yet, there was a silver lining, as the more competitive firms were able to take advantage of lower rentals and the departure of weaker companies. Some firms, including Giordano, worked toward strengthening their positioning and brand image to compete better in the long run. Some retailers also explored opportunities, or accelerated their presence in markets that were less affected by the Asian crisis – mostly in markets outside Asia.

During the crisis and for the immediate future until a full recovery set in, industry analysts predicted that opportunities would continue to be driven by value. Thus, Giordano's value proposition appeared appropriate during these times. It was not surprising, then, that in spite of its problems, Giordano was ranked the fourteenth most competitive company overall in Asia by a regional business magazine (*Asia Inc.*, 6 June 1997). It even won a place on *Forbes Global*'s 1999 list of the World's 300 Best Small Companies, indicative of world-class performance, together with eight other Hong Kong companies. Giordano's performance was accredited to its management's swift cost-control strategies in the areas of rents, outsourcing, inventory control, cash management and overseas travel. The economic downturn had indeed revealed the management's flexibility and responsiveness in making decisive moves.

The retailing environment was becoming more dynamic, a change that was perhaps led by growing sophistication of tastes and rapid advancements in the media, communications and logistics environment. Giordano's response to these trends would be the key to its ability to compete in the future, especially as these trends seem to 'commoditize' its current competitive edge in IT, stock control and logistics.

Giordano's competition

Until recently, Giordano's main competitors for low-priced apparel were Hang Ten, Bossini and Baleno. However, its shift in positioning, and the squeeze of the retailing sector caused by the crisis, pushed formerly more upmarket firms such as Esprit and Theme to compete for Giordano's value-for-money segment. Exhibit 6 provides a list of their websites for more information regarding their product lines and operations.

Exhibit 6 **Websites of Giordano and Its Closest Competitors**

Firm	Website Address
Baleno	www.baleno.com.hk
Esprit	www.esprit-intl.com
The Gap	www.gap.com
Giordano	www.giordano.com.hk
Hang Ten	www.hangten.com
Theme	www.theme.com.hk

Exhibit 7 **Competitive Positioning**

Firms	Positioning	Target Market
Giordano and	Value for money	Unisex casual wear for all ages
The Gap	Mid-priced but trendy fashion	(under different brands)
Hang Ten	Value for money Sporty lifestyle	Casual wear and sports wear, teens and young adults
Bossini	Low price (comparable to Giordano)	Unisex apparel, both young and old (above 30s)
Baleno	Value for money Trendy, young age casual wear	Unisex appeal, young adults
Esprit	More upmarket than Giordano Stylish, trendy	Ladies' casual, but also other specialized lines for children
Theme	Upmarket, stylish	Ladies' smart fashion, ladies' business wear

Exhibit 8 **Competitive Financial Data for 1999: Giordano, Esprit, The Gap, Theme and Bossini (Amounts Expressed in Millions of HK$)**

	Giordano	Esprit	The Gap	Theme	Bossini
Turnover	3092	5994	90 756	319	1109
Profit after tax and minority interests	360	430	8791	(218)	18
Working capital	762	478	3470	(243.0)	182
Return on total assets (percentage)	18.8%	NA	24.6%	NA	NA
Return on average equity (percentage)	30.5%	33.1%	59.2%	NA	6.5%
Return on sales (percentage)	11.6%	7.2%	9.7%	(68.3%)	1.6%
Price/sales ratio	2.07	1.33	1.97	.82	0.23
Sales growth	18.5%	17.8%	28.5%	(69.8%)	(22.4%)
No. of employees	6237	4471	NA	NA	869
Sales per employee	495 779	1 340 599	NA	NA	1 276 254

Note: Esprit reports its earnings in Euro and The Gap in US$. All reported figures have been converted into HK$ at the following exchange rate (as of Feb. 2001): US$1 Euro$1.09 HK$7.8. *Sources*: Annual Report 1999, Giordano International; Financial Highlights 1999, Esprit International; Annual Report 1999, The Gap; Financial Report 1999, Bossini International Holdings Limited.

Exhibit 9 **Geographical Presence of Giordano and Current Competitors**

Country	Giordano	Hang Ten	Bossini	Baleno	Esprit	Theme
Asia						
HK/Macao	X	X	X	X	X	X
Singapore	X	X	X	—	X	X
South Korea	X	X	—	—	X	X
Taiwan	X	X	X	X	X	X
China	X	X	X	X	X	X
Malaysia	X	X	—	—	X	X
Indonesia	X	X	—	—	X	X
Philippines	X	X	—	—	X	X
Thailand	X	X	—	—	X	X
World						
US and Canada	—	X	X	—	X	X
Europe	—	X	X	—	X	X
Japan	X	X	—	—	X	X
Australia	X	X	—	—	X	X
Total	**750**	**NA**	**173**	**125**	**8,470**	**200**

Note: Data are as of February 2001; X indicates presence in the country/region; — indicates no presence; NA indicates data not available at time of print.

Exhibit 7 shows the relative positioning of Giordano and its competitors: The Gap, Bossini, Hang Ten, Baleno, Esprit and Theme. Financial data for Giordano, Esprit, and The Gap are shown in Exhibit 8. The geographical areas these firms operate in are shown in Exhibit 9.

United States-based Hang Ten and Italy-based Bossini were generally positioned as low-price retailers offering reasonable quality and service. The clothes emphasized versatility and simplicity. But while Hang Ten and Baleno were more popular among teenagers and young adults, Bossini had a more general appeal. Their distribution strategies were somewhat similar, but they focused on different markets. For instance, according to Fung, while Hang Ten was only strong in Taiwan, Baleno was increasingly strong in China and Taiwan. On the other hand, Bossini was very strong in Hong Kong and relatively strong in Singapore but had little presence in Taiwan and China.

Esprit is an international fashion lifestyle brand, engaged principally in the image and product design, sourcing, manufacturing, and retail and wholesale distribution of a wide range of women's, men's and children's apparel, footwear, accessories and other products under the Esprit brand name. The Esprit name was promoted as a 'lifestyle' image, and products were strategically positioned as good quality and value for money – a position that Giordano was occupying. As of 1999, Esprit had a distribution network of over 8000 stores and outlets in 40 countries in Europe, Asia, Canada, and Australia. The main markets were in Europe, which accounted for approximately 65 per cent of sales; and in Asia, which accounted for approximately 34 per cent of 2000 sales. The Esprit brand products were principally sold via directly managed retail outlets, by wholesale customers (including department stores, specialty stores, and franchisees) and by licensees for products manufactured under licence, principally through the licensees' own distribution networks.

Theme International Holdings Limited was founded in Hong Kong in 1986 by Chairman and Chief Executive Officer Kenneth Lai. He identified a niche in the local market for high-quality, fashionable ladies' business wear, although it subsequently expanded into casual wear. The Theme label and chain were in direct competition with Giordano Ladies'. From the first store in 1986 to a chain comprising over 200 outlets in Hong Kong, China, Korea, Macao, Taiwan, Singapore, Malaysia, Indonesia, the Philippines, Japan, Thailand, Canada and Holland, the phenomenal growth of Theme was built on a vertically integrated corporate structure and advanced management system. However, its ambitious expansion proved to be costly in view of the crisis, with interest soaring on high levels of debt. In 1999, the company announced a HK$106.1 million net loss for the six months up to 30 September 1998, and it closed 23 retail outlets in Hong Kong, which traded under its subsidiary The Clothing Shop. Theme International had since been acquired by High Fashion International, a Hong Kong-based fashion retailer specializing in upmarket, trendy apparel.

In general, although these firms had slightly different positioning strategies and targeted dissimilar but overlapping segments, they all competed in a number of similar areas. For example, all firms heavily emphasized advertising and sales promotion – selling fashionable clothes at attractive prices. Almost all stores were also located primarily in good ground-floor areas, drawing high-volume traffic and facilitating shopping, browsing and impulse buying. However, Giordano clearly distinguished itself from its competitors with its high-quality service and cost leadership which together provided great customer value that none of its competitors had been able to match.

In a study by *Interbrand* on top Asian marquees, Giordano was Asia's highest-ranking general apparel retailer. It was ranked number 20. The clothing names next in line were Australia's Quicksilver at number 45 and Country Road at number 47. However, Giordano as a world label was still far off. As a spokesman on consumer insights for advertising agency McCann-Erickson said, 'It is a good brand, but not a great one. Compared to other international brands, it doesn't shape opinion.'

A threat from US-based The Gap was also looming. Giordano was aware that the American retailer was invading Asia. The Gap was already in Japan. After 2005, when garment quotas are likely to be abolished, imports into the region should become more cost-effective. Hence, Giordano had to examine whether its intention to shift toward a higher position from its current value-for-money position was viable.

Giordano's growth strategy

As early as the 1980s, Giordano realized that it was difficult to achieve substantial growth and economies of scale if it operated only in Hong Kong. The key was in regional expansion. By 1999, Giordano had opened 740 stores in 23 markets, out of which Giordano directly managed 317 stores (see Exhibit 10). Until 2000, four markets dominated its retail and distribution operations – Hong Kong, Taiwan, China and Singapore (see Exhibit 11). By 2000, Giordano had 895 Giordano stores in 25 markets.

Giordano cast its sights on markets beyond Asia, driven partially by its desire for growth and partially to reduce its dependence on Asia in the wake of the 1998 economic meltdown. In Giordano's first full year of operation in Australia, sales turnover reached

---

Exhibit 10 Operational Highlights for Retail and Distribution Division (Figures as at Year-End Unless Specified)

	1999	1998	1997	1996	1995	1994	1993
Number of retail outlets • Directly managed by the Group	317	308	324	294	280	283	257
• Franchised	423	370	316	221	171	77	481
Total number of retail outlets	740	678	640	515	451	360	738
Retail floor area directly managed by the Group (sq. ft.)	301 100	358 500	313 800	295 500	286 200	282 700	209 500
Sales per square foot (HK$)	8 400	6 800	8 000	9 900	10 500	10 600	12 600
Number of employees	6 237	6 319	8 175	10 004	10 348	6 863	2 330
Comparable store sales Increase/(decrease) (percentage)	21%	(13)%	(11)%	(6)%	8%	(9)%	15%
Number of sales associates	2 026	1 681	1 929	1 958	2 069	1 928	1 502

Exhibit 11 **Regional Highlights**

	Taiwan 1999	Hong Kong 1999	China 1999	Singapore 1999	Malaysia 1999
Net sales (HK$ millions)	953.1	681.7	543.7	349.2	66.6
Sales per sq. ft. (HK$)	6 000	9 400	22 500	13 800	3 600
Comparable store sales increase (percentage)*	31%	8%	4%	48%	69%
Retail floor area (sq. ft.)	165 700	100 000	24 700	24 400	20 400
Number of sales associates	827	441	350	228	115
Number of outlets					
Σ• Directly managed	178	61	10	27	23
Σ• Franchised	0	0	243	0	11

*Note: Figures as compared to previous financial year.

HK$29 million (US$3.72 million) in December 2000. The number of retail outlets increased from four in 1999 to 14 in 2000. With the opening up of its first retail outlet in Sydney in September 2000, Giordano outlets could now be found in both Melbourne and Sydney. As part of Giordano's globalization process, it planned to open up its first shops in Germany and Japan during the first half of 2001. Currently, Giordano planned to focus its globalization efforts on new markets like Germany, Japan, Australia, Indonesia and Kuwait.

When the crisis made Giordano rethink its regional strategy, it was still determined to enter and further penetrate new Asian markets. This determination led to the successful expansion of Giordano in Mainland China, which saw the retail outlets grow from 253 stores in 1999 to 357 stores in 2000. Owing to the expanded retail network in Mainland China and improvements made to the product line, sales turnover increased by 30.9 per cent to HK$712 million (US$91.3 million) in 2000. Faced with the imminent accession of Mainland China to the World Trade Organization, Giordano's management foresees both challenges and opportunities ahead. In Indonesia, Giordano opened up seven more stores in 2000, bringing the total number of retail stores to 10. These stores covered areas in Jakarta, Surabaya and Bali. However, with the political and social instability in Indonesia, coupled with the downward pressure on the rupiah, Giordano was cautiously optimistic about further expansion and planned to proceed with caution. In Malaysia, Giordano planned to refurnish its Malaysian outlets and intensify its local promotional campaigns to consolidate its leadership position in the Malaysia market.

Giordano's success in these markets would depend on its understanding of them, and consumer tastes and preferences for fabrics, colours and advertising. In the past, Giordano relied on a consistent strategy across different countries, and elements of this successful strategy included its positioning and service strategies, information systems and logistics, and human resource policies. However, tactical implementation (e.g. promotional campaigns) was left mostly to local managers in their respective countries. A country's performance (e.g. sales, contribution, service levels and customer feedback) was monitored by regional headquarters (e.g. Singapore for South-East Asia) and the head office in Hong Kong. Weekly performance reports were made accessible to all managers. In recent years, it appeared that as the organization expanded beyond Asia, different strategies had to be developed for different regions or countries.

The future

Giordano was confronted with some important issues as it prepared itself for the new millennium. Although it had been extremely successful, as its revenue, profits and the many awards that it received clearly show, the question was how it could maintain this success in the new millennium. First, how, if at all, should Giordano reposition itself against its competitors in its existing and new markets? Would it be necessary to follow different positioning strategies for different markets (e.g. Hong Kong versus South-East Asia)?

The second issue was the sustainability of Giordano's key success factors. It clearly understood its core competencies and the pillars of its success, but it had to carefully explore how they were likely to develop over the coming years. Which of its competitive advantages would be sustainable and which ones were likely to be eroded?

A third issue was Giordano's growth strategy in Asia as well as across continents. Would Giordano's competitive strengths be transferable to other markets? Would strategic adaptations to IT strategy and marketing mix be required, or would tactical moves suffice?

Study questions

1 Describe and evaluate Giordano's product, business, and corporate strategies.

2 Describe and evaluate Giordano's current positioning strategy. Should Giordano reposition itself against its competitors in its current and new markets, and should it have different positioning strategies for different geographic markets?

3 What are Giordano's key success factors (KSF) and sources of competitive advantage?

4 Are its competitive advantages sustainable, and how would they develop in the future?

5 Could Giordano transfer its key success factors to new markets as it expanded both in Asia and the other parts of the world?

6 How do you think Giordano had/would have to adapt its marketing and operations strategies and tactics when entering and penetrating your country?

7 What general lessons can be learned from Giordano for other major clothing retailers in your country?

References

'Aiming high: Asia's 50 most competitive companies', *Asia Inc.*, 6 June 1997, pp. 34–7.

Ang, S.H. (1996), 'Giordano Holdings Limited', *Cases in Marketing Management and Strategy: An Asian-Pacific Perspective.* Quelch, J.A., Leong, S.M., Ang, S.H. and Tan, C.T. (eds), Upper Saddle River, NJ: Prentice Hall, pp. 182–90.

'An all-new dress for success', *AsiaWeek*, 15 October 1999, vol. 25, no. 41.

'And the winning store is, again . . .', *The Straits Times*, 2 December 1995.

'Asia: Giordano plans expansion', *Sing Tao Daily*, 29 June 1999.

'Asian IPO focus: analysts see little to like in HK's Veeko', *Dow Jones International News*, 12 April 1999.

Austria, C. (1994), 'The bottom line', *World Executive's Digest*, 19 December, pp. 17–20.

'Casual-wear chain prospers on cost-cutting regime', *South China Morning Post*, 15 October 1999.

'China: HK companies commended by *Forbes* for best practices', *China Business Information Network*, 12 November 1999.

Clifford, M. (1993), 'Extra large', *Far Eastern Economic Review*, 2 December, pp. 72–6.

'Company looks outside Asia', *Dow Jones International News*, 12 August 1998.

'Creditors push struggling theme fashion outlet into liquidation', *South China Morning Post*, 11 March 1999.

Esprit International, *Financial Highlights 1999*.

'Fashion free-fall', *The Asian Wall Street Journal*, 9 November 1998.

'Giordano 12-month target price raised to 16.00 HKD', *AFX (AP)*, 16 May 2000.

'Giordano's after-tax earnings soared in first half', *The Asian Wall Street Journal*, 27 July 1999.

'Giordano comes out of the cold', *Business Week*, 31 May 1999.

'Giordano details $700 million expansion', *South China Morning Post*, 4 December 1999.

'Giordano dreams up sale for insomniacs', *Business Times*, 6 May 1994.

'Giordano expects to set up ops in Europe October', *AFX (AP)*, 19 June 2000.

Giordano Holdings Limited, *Annual Report 1993*.

Giordano Holdings Limited, *Annual Report 1997*.

Giordano International Limited, *Announcement of Results*, 31 December 2000.

Giordano International Limited, *Annual Report 1998*.

Giordano International Limited, *Annual Report 1999*.

Giordano International Limited, *Interim Results 2000*.

'Giordano Intl 1998 net profit', *AFX (AP)*, 25 March 1999 (from Dow Jones Interactive).

'Giordano out of the running to buy Theme: High Fashion International emerges as favorite in race for control', *South China Morning Post*, 25 November 1999.

'Giordano predicts further growth as net profit reaches $46.3 million', *Asian Wall Street Journal*, 3 March 2000.

'Giordano scores with smart moves', *The Straits Times*, 11 September 1993.

'Giordano seeks to acquire chain stores in Australia', *AFX (AP)*, 8 February 2000.

'Giordano spreads its wings', *The Straits Times*, 13 March 1994.

'Good service has brought Giordano soaring sales', *Business Times*, 6 August 1993.

'High-end training to get more funding', *The Straits Times*, 1 October 1998.

'HK Bossini International fiscal year net profit HK$17.6 million vs. HK$45.5 million loss', *Dow Jones Business News*, 16 July 1999.

'HK Giordano gets green light to reopen in Shanghai', *Dow Jones International News*, 9 June 1999.

'Hong Kong: High Fashion to take over Theme', *Sing Tao Daily*, 26 November 1999.

'Hong Kong retailer raced to new markets, spurring Everbright loan', *The Asian Wall Street Journal*, 7 April 1998.

'Hubris catches up to Theme', *The Globe and Mail*, 7 April 1998.

'In HK: retail shares win praise amid companies' losses', *The Asian Wall Street Journal*, 25 June 1999.

'Interview', by Frances Huang, *AFX (AP)*, 16 September 1998 (from Dow Jones Interactive).

'Old loss masks Giordano growth', *South China Morning Post*, 5 March 1999.

Quinn Mills, D. and R.C. Wei (1993), 'Giordano Holdings Ltd.', *Harvard Business School*, N9-495-002.

'Service means training', *The Straits Times*, 7 October 1998.

'Simple winning formula', *Business Times*, 6 August 1993.

The Gap, *Annual Report 1999*.

'The outlook for Asian retailing', *Discount Merchandiser*, May 1999.

'Theme International unit to close 23 stores', *The Asian Wall Street Journal*, 4 August 1998.

'US news brief: Benetton Group', *The Wall Street Journal Europe*, 17 December 1998.

'What is the people developer', *The Straits Times*, 30 September 1998.

Notes

This case was prepared by Jochen Wirtz as the basis for class discussion rather than to illustrate effective or ineffective handling of an administrative situation. Jochen Wirtz is Associate Professor of Marketing with the NUS Business School, Faculty of Business Administration, National University of Singapore, 17 Law Link, Singapore 117591, tel: +65-8743656, fax: +65-7795941, Email: fbawirtz@nus.edu.sg. Http://www.nus.edu.sg. Not to be reproduced or used without written permission.

The author acknowledges the generous support in terms of time, information, and feedback on earlier drafts of this case provided by Charles Fung, Chief Operating Officer and Executive Director of Giordano (South-east Asia), and by Jill Klein, Associate Professor at INSEAD. Furthermore, the author gratefully acknowledges the input by Ang Swee Hoon, who co-authored earlier versions of this case published in the Asian Case Research Journal (2000), Volume 4, Issue 2, pp. 145–67, and in *Principles of Marketing: An Asian Casebook* (2000), Ang et al., Prentice Hall, pp. 80–87. Finally, the author also thanks Jerome S. W. Kho and Jaisey L. Y. Yip for their excellent research assistance in gathering much of the data and assisting with the write-up.

The exchange rates at the time the case was written (February 2001) were US$1 = HK$7.80 and S$1 = HK$4.49.

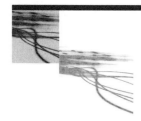

Index